GMAT
词汇精选

俞敏洪·编著

西安交通大学出版社
XI`AN JIAOTONG UNIVERSITY PRESS

图书在版编目(CIP)数据

GMAT 词汇精选 / 俞敏洪编著. —西安：西安交通
大学出版社，2013.8
ISBN 978-7-5605-5514-0

Ⅰ．①G… Ⅱ．①俞… Ⅲ．①英语—词汇—研究生—
入学考试—自学参考资料 Ⅳ．①H313

中国版本图书馆 CIP 数据核字(2013)第 185614 号

书 名	GMAT 词汇精选	
编 著	俞敏洪	
责任编辑	黄科丰	
封面设计	大愚设计	
出版发行	西安交通大学出版社	
地 址	西安市兴庆南路 10 号(邮编：710049)	
电 话	(010)62605588　62605019(发行部)	
	(029)82668315(总编室)	
读者信箱	bj62605588@163.com	
印 刷	北京海石通印刷有限公司	
字 数	370 千	
开 本	720×990　1/16	
印 张	24.5	
版 次	2014 年 8 月第 1 版　2014 年 8 月第 1 次印刷	
书 号	ISBN 978-7-5605-5514-0/H·1543	
定 价	40.00 元	

　　时间过得真快，第一次出版GMAT词汇的时候正好是1999年——世纪末的一切都充满了期待和希望。大家带着对20世纪厚重历史的记忆，以展望未来的姿态走进了21世纪。祖国以更迅猛的速度向前奔跑，新东方也在竭尽全力跟上时代的步伐。眨眼间，时光飞逝，所有外在和内在的因素正在以难以想像的力量改变着我们，随着我们一起改变的是每一个人的生活和梦想。

　　我们梦想着祖国的继续繁荣，因为个人的荣辱必然建立在国家的荣辱之中。"大国崛起"必须建立在经济复兴的基石上。孟子曾对"大国"概念及其内在逻辑关系有很好的阐述，他说"以仁假力者霸，霸必有大国"。这里的"霸"讲的并不是"霸权"，而是有影响力的国家；所谓"仁"，是指国家的价值体系、文化体系和社会制度。在当今中西方文化大融合的时代，中国已经站在了世界的最前沿，成为中西方文化汇聚最浓厚的地方。我们正在谦虚地向先进的国家学习，从而形成独特的现代的"仁"。如果这种开放心态持续几十年，中国必将成为世界上真正有实力的文化、政治和经济强国之一。

　　人才兴则一国兴。正像电影中的台词说的那样：21世纪最贵的是人才。没有人才就没有持续发展的生命力，对于一个国家是这样，对于一个企业也是这样。中国从几千年的农业文明中走出来，迅速走进了在国际平台上和强大的对手进行竞争的时代，仅仅依靠双手劳动而让一国致富的年代早已过去。我们更多地需要知识和智慧的更新，需要学习世界上最先进的理念。无数的学子也正是意识到了这一点，才不断地支付昂贵的学费，走向异国他乡去获取振兴民族、提高自己的真经。人类最重要的能力之一是用有形的财富去换取取之不尽、用之不竭的无形资产，那就是知识、智慧、能力、技能和勇气。

　　从新东方教室里走出去的学员已经从哈佛、耶鲁这样的商学院学成回国，开始了他们创业或职业的历程，国内的商学院也以更成熟的姿态培养出一批又一批商业栋梁。他们也许会成功也许会失败，但有一点我能够肯定，作为中国的核心人才团队，他们一定会越来越成熟，越来越能够推动中国社会的发展。展望未来，还有更多的人希望进入世界著名的商学院读书，我为中国层出不穷的人才高兴，更让我高兴的是他们的追求和理想。新东方唯一能做的就是更加努力地工作，为大家提供一点帮助，希望大家学习的路走得相对轻松一点。我希望这本书能够为大家的奋斗之路扫除一点词汇上的障碍。

　　如果有一天，世界上的商学院都用中文在上课，用的案例都是中国的案例，那就是我们真正成功的日子，就是我们国家强大的真正标志。

新东方教育科技集团
董事长兼总裁

　　GMAT考试其实不考词汇，之所以要编这本词汇书，主要是为了帮助大家在学习GMAT阅读和语法时扫除词汇障碍。所有书中的词汇都来自GMAT考过的试题，是很实用的词汇。但这些词汇并不代表GMAT考试中必然要出现的词汇，也并不包括GMAT的全部词汇。我们只可以这样说：背完了这本书中的词汇，就有了学习GMAT的基础，就没有必要为学习中碰到太多的单词而苦恼了。同时大家也可以比较轻松地来对待GMAT词汇，即使不能全部背出来也不用太担心，只要留下个印象，能通过上下文猜出意思就行了。获取GMAT高分的重要途径在于反复练习阅读能力、语法能力和逻辑能力，达到熟能生巧的地步。

　　不过有一点大家一定要记住：词汇量是阅读的基础。从这一点讲，词汇是不能不背的。背词汇和读文章是两种完全不同的能力，又是相互依赖的两种能力。请大家记住：最愚蠢的方法就是一边查单词一边阅读。这样做的结果是单词记不住，阅读速度也上不去。我主张背单词时绝不阅读，读文章时绝不查单词。背单词在前，读文章在后。在读文章时不管有多少单词都不能去查，要尽可能地猜出它们的意思，要注重文章的整体思路，而不是中间出现的一两个单词。

　　背单词其实很容易。我在上大学时也怕背单词，后来为了谋生才开始专研词汇记忆；一旦入了门，才发现大量的词汇是非常容易记的。最主要的方法大概有三种，首先是词根词缀分解记忆。在本书中，我对大量单词都做了词根分解，这样一来，记几个单词只需记一个单词的时间：如commod表示"方便"，因此commodity（商品），commodious（宽敞的），accommodate(提供食宿)等词都会比较容易记住。对词根、词缀不熟悉的同学可以参考我的另一本书《英语词汇速记大全——词根+词缀记忆法》。其次是千方百计联想记忆法或分解记忆。如flaunt(炫耀)，可分解为fl(=fly飞)＋aunt(姑奶奶)→飞去看姑奶奶→炫耀。这样的记忆法虽然荒谬，却十分有效。最后一点一定要记住的是：凡是背过的单词一定要反复背，这是真正有效的办法。我的词汇量就是在反复教GRE词汇时教出来的。

改革开放30多年来，中国的科学技术和管理水平有了突飞猛进的发展。然而，相对于飞速发展的中国经济，优秀管理人才的数量还远远不够。我们的国家迫切需要更多的管理人才，实现民族伟大复兴的中国梦不能缺少优秀的管理人才。众多国内高等院校都成立了工商管理学院，还有越来越多的学子希望直接到国外名校去读MBA，学习国际最先进的管理经验。新东方学校的GMAT班，从1994年至今，已经帮助了一批又一批学员成功通过GMAT考试，进入国外名校攻读MBA。有的新东方学员已经是国内知名企业家，有的学员一边苦读GMAT，一边管理着数百万甚至是数亿元的资产。这些都表明中国人的眼光看得远了，他们已经开始注视和洞察未来了。

面对这样的一群人，我不能不心潮澎湃。我所能做的就是为他们提供哪怕一点点帮助和便利，使他们在奋斗的道路上更轻松愉快一点。这本新版的GMAT词汇书，就是在这种心态下的结果。我个人的每一点进步，新东方学校的每一点成就和进步，都和广大学员对前途孜孜不倦的追求密不可分。

最后，祝广大GMAT考生顺利考入自己理想的学府。

新东方教育科技集团
董事长兼总裁

1. 增删词条

本书对上一版中较少考到的生僻词条进行了删减，增加了真题中出现的高频词1000余个，这使得选词更贴近考试，保证了目前收录的单词均为考生必备的重点词汇。

2. 更新词义

近年的GMAT真题显示，一些单词的基本释义也成为考查重点，据此，本书增加了一些常考单词的基本释义。

3. 修改英文释义

根据Webster词典，本书将上一版中偏难和过长的英文释义进行了适当的修改。对于一些词，还选用了难度稍低的同义词来解释，这不但更便于考生阅读，还能帮助考生更直观地理解词义。

4. 增加例句，主打真题

为了保证本书贴近考试的特点，尽可能地多收录一些典型的真题例句，例句难度适中，这样可以让考生更好地了解词汇在实考中的运用方法。

5. 删减生僻、较难词根

有的考生反映部分词根、词缀偏难，为了更适应考生的英语水平，本书将较生僻、较难的词根、词缀进行了删除，使所收录的词根、词缀更能体现工具性的价值。

6. 丰富附录

通过对近年GMAT阅读考题的分析，在附录中总结增加了阅读词汇的内容，以及近几年常考的数学词汇及公式。丰富、精炼的附录内容方便考生充分备考。

7. 查缺补漏

本书对上一版中欠妥的地方进行了全面修订，力求为广大考生提供最精准、可靠的学习内容。

英文释义简洁明了，帮助考生精确了解词义。

每个 Word List 标题后附二维码，方便考生下载单词及例句录音。

Word List 1

abdicate
[ˈæbdɪkeɪt]
   v. 放弃，丢弃 (to discard)
   记 词根记忆：ab(离去) + dic(说话，命令) + ate(做) → 被命令离去 → 放弃
   例 A democratic government should not *abdicate* its responsibilities as a guardian of the public interest.

abnormal
[æbˈnɔːrml]
   a. 反常的 (unusual, exceptional)
   记 词根记忆：ab(离去) + norm(标准) + al → 脱离标准的 → 反常的
   例 It is the periodic *abnormal* warming of the sea surface off Peru.
   同根词：norm(*n.* 标准，规范)；normal(*a.* 正常的，正规的)

abolish
[əˈbɑːlɪʃ]
   v. 取消，废除 (to end the observance or effect of)
   记 该词来自拉丁文 *abolere*，表示"破坏；使灭绝；阻止，妨碍"
   例 The committee *abolished* all entry requirements.
   派 abolition(*n.* 废除)；abolitionist(*n.* 废奴主义者)

absenteeism
[ˌæbsənˈtiːɪzəm]
   n. 旷工，旷课 (chronic absence, as from work or school)
   记 词根记忆：absent(缺席) + ee(人) + ism → 旷课，旷工
   例 Acorn Valley reports few instances of tardiness, *absenteeism*, or discipline problems.

absorb
[əbˈzɔːrb]
   v. 吸收 (to suck up or take up)，同化 (to take in and make part of an existent whole)
   记 词根记忆：ab(离去) + sorb(吸收) → 吸收掉 → 吸收
   例 A plant *absorbs* and stores nickel from the soil as it grows. // It is difficult to *absorb* them into a city economy.

abstract
[ˈæbstrækt]
   a. 抽象的 (difficult to understand)，*n.* 摘要 (summary)
   记 词根记忆：abs + tract(拉) → 将大意从文章中拉出 → 摘要
   例 Professor Brown's books are very *abstract* and are hard to read. // You can tell if a paper is worthwhile by reading its *abstract*.
   派 abstracted(*a.* 心不在焉的)；extract(*v.* 摘取，抽出)
   同根词：intractable(*a.* 难处理的)；contract(*n.* 合同)

absurd
[əbˈsɜːrd]
   a. 荒唐的 (ridiculously unreasonable)
   记 词根记忆：ab + surd(不合理的) → 不合理的 → 荒唐的
   例 The opponents' reasoning leads to an *absurd* conclusion.
   派 absurdity(*n.* 荒谬)

□ abdicate   □ abnormal   □ abolish   ■ absenteeism   □ absorb   □ abstract
□ absurd

大量的同根词，帮助考生更好地理解和掌握重要词根，进一步扩充词汇量。

丰富的派生词，横向扩充词汇量。

大量真题例句及难度适当的例句帮助考生记忆单词，熟悉考试难度。

apex [ˈeɪpeks]	*n.* 顶点，最高点（peak; vertex） 例 The hangar is 103 feet high at the *apex* of its roof.
apiece [əˈpiːs]	*ad.* 每个，每人，各（for each one, individually） 记 联想记忆：a + piece（片）→ 每人一片 → 每个，每人 例 Elena purchased brand X pens for $4.00 *apiece* and brand Y pens for $2.80 *apiece*.
apparatus [ˌæpəˈrætəs]	*n.* 仪器，设备（device, equipment） 例 No *apparatus* can detect neutrinos unless it is extremely massive.
apparel [əˈpærəl]	*n.* 衣服，服饰（clothing, garments） 记 联想记忆：appar（出现）+ el → 穿出来的东西 → 衣服

Man errs so long as he strives.
人只要奋斗就会犯错误。

——德国诗人、剧作家 歌德
(Johann Wolfgang Goethe, German poet and dramatist)

□ apex   □ apiece   □ apparatus   □ apparel

收录的名人名言在激励考生奋发向上的同时，还能成为 GMAT 写作中的引用素材。笔记区可供考生记录学习过程中的心得。

每页底部设有返记菜单，考生结束每页的学习后可以及时进行复习和自测，有助于巩固对单词的掌握。

目　录

序言

前言

改版说明

使用说明

音频

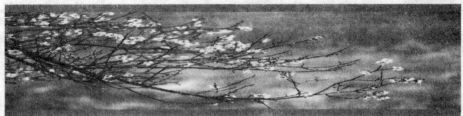

abdicate [ˈæbdɪkeɪt]	*v.* 放弃，丢弃（to discard） 记 词根记忆：ab(离去) + dic(说话，命令) + ate(做) → 被命令离去 → 放弃 例 A democratic government should not *abdicate* its responsibilities as a guardian of the public interest.
abnormal [æbˈnɔːrml]	*a.* 反常的（unusual, exceptional） 记 词根记忆：ab(离去) + norm(标准) + al → 脱离标准的 → 反常的 例 It is the periodic *abnormal* warming of the sea surface off Peru. 同根词：norm(*n.* 标准，规范); normal(*a.* 正常的，正规的)
abolish [əˈbɑːlɪʃ]	*v.* 取消，废除（to end the observance or effect of） 记 该词来自拉丁文 *abolere*，表示"破坏；使灭绝；阻止，妨碍" 例 The committee *abolished* all entry requirements. 派 abolition(*n.* 废除); abolitionist(*n.* 废奴主义者)
absenteeism [ˌæbsənˈtiːɪzəm]	*n.* 旷工，旷课（chronic absence, as from work or school） 记 词根记忆：absent(缺席) + ee(人) + ism → 旷课，旷工 例 Acorn Valley reports few instances of tardiness, *absenteeism*, or discipline problems.
absorb [əbˈzɔːrb]	*v.* 吸收（to suck up or take up）；同化（to take in and make part of an existent whole） 记 词根记忆：ab(离去) + sorb(吸收) → 吸收掉 → 吸收 例 A plant *absorbs* and stores nickel from the soil as it grows. // It is difficult to *absorb* them into a city economy.
abstract [ˈæbstrækt]	*a.* 抽象的（difficult to understand）；*n.* 摘要（summary） 记 词根记忆：abs + tract(拉) → 将大意从文章中拉出 → 摘要 例 Professor Brown's books are very *abstract* and are hard to read. // You can tell if a paper is worthwhile by reading its *abstract*. 派 abstracted(*a.* 心不在焉的); extract(*v.* 摘取，抽出) 同根词：intractable(*a.* 难处理的); contract(*n.* 合同)
absurd [əbˈsɜːrd]	*a.* 荒唐的（ridiculously unreasonable） 记 词根记忆：ab + surd(不合理的) → 不合理的 → 荒唐的 例 The opponents' reasoning leads to an *absurd* conclusion. 派 absurdity(*n.* 荒谬)

abundant
[ə'bʌndənt]

a. 大量的，丰富的；富裕的；多的(plentiful)

记 联想记忆：a(无) + bund(看作 bound 边界) + ant(…的) → 多得没边的 → 大量的

例 Japan's *abundant* rainfall and typically mild temperature have produced a lush vegetation cover.

派 abundance(*n.* 大量；充足)

---

academic
[ˌækə'demɪk]

a. 学院的；学术的(of schools, colleges)；*n.* 学者(teacher at a university, college; professional scholar)

例 Nova High School began to use interactive computer instruction in three *academic* subjects.

派 academician(*n.* 院士；学会会员)；nonacademic(*a.* 非学术的)

---

accelerate
[ək'seləreɪt]

v. 加速，促进(to hasten the progress or development of)

记 词根记忆：ac(加强) + celer(速度) + ate → 加快速度 → 促进

例 Government spending *accelerates* the pace of inflation. // The introduction of Western ideas to Korean society *accelerated* after 1977.

派 acceleration(*n.* 加速)；accelerator(*n.* 加速器)

同根词 celerity(*n.* 迅速)；decelerate(*v.* 减速)

---

access
['ækses]

n. 通路；接近(或进入)的权利(permission or liberty to enter or approach)；途径(a way or means of approaching or entering)；*v.* 进入(to get at)

记 词根记忆：ac + cess(走) → 走过去 → 接近

例 Secret passwords are often used to control *access* to computers.

派 accessible(*a.* 可进入的)；accessibility(*n.* 易接近，可到达)

同根词 procession(*n.* 行列，队伍)

---

accessible
[ək'sesəbl]

a. 易达到的(easy to approach)；易受影响的(open to the influence of)

记 来自 access(*v.* 使用；接近；*n.* 使用权)

例 No other food available to the birds on Delaware's beaches is as nutritious and *accessible* as crab eggs.

派 accessibly(*ad.* 可亲近地；可得到地)

同根词 inaccessible(*a.* 不可及的)

---

acclaim
[ə'kleɪm]

v. 欢呼；称赞(to greet with loud applause; hail)；*n.* 欢呼(praise)；称赞(applause)

记 词根记忆：ac(加强) + claim(叫喊) → 不断大叫 → 向…欢呼，为…喝彩

例 Like the Scandinavians' long refusal to recognize Edvard Grieg, the Italians' disregard for Verdi persisted for a decade after his critical *acclaim* in France and Austria.

同根词 exclaim(*v.* 呼喊，喊出来)

---

accommodate
[ə'kɑːmədeɪt]

v. 供给(某人)住宿(to provide sb. with lodgings)；使适应(to adapt)

记 联想记忆：ac + commod(方便) + ate → 给人方便 → 供给住宿

例 Boardinghouses were built to *accommodate* the Issei（第一代移居北美的日本人）. // We will be better able to *accommodate* the busy schedules of our customers.

派 accommodation(*n.* 适应；调和)；accommodationist(*n.* 妥协者)

□ abundant □ academic □ accelerate □ access □ accessible □ acclaim
□ accommodate

accompaniment [əˈkʌmpənimənt]	*n.* 伴奏(a musical part played to support a solo instrument or voice or a choir) 记 来自 accompany(*v.* 伴奏) 例 musical *accompaniment* 音乐伴奏
accomplish [əˈkɑːmplɪʃ]	*v.* 完成，做成功(to succeed in doing sth.) 记 词根记忆：ac + compl(满) + ish → 圆满 → 完成 例 One plan to *accomplish* this is to establish giant floating seaweed farms in the oceans. 派 accomplishment(*n.* 成就；完成)
accord [əˈkɔːrd]	*v.* 同意(to agree, to grant)；一致(to be consistent or in harmony)；*n.* 协议(agreement) 记 词根记忆：ac + cord(心) → 心心相印 → 一致 例 These results *accord* closely with our predictions. 派 accordance(*n.* 一致，符合) 同根词：accordion(*n.* 手风琴)
accordingly [əˈkɔːrdɪŋli]	*ad.* 因此(therefore, consequently)；相应地(correspondingly) 例 The speech was very funny. *Accordingly*, the audience laughed loudly. // Cable-television subscribers can choose which channels they wish to receive, and the fees vary *accordingly*.
accountant [əˈkaʊntənt]	*n.* 会计人员，会计师(person whose profession is to keep financial accounts) 记 词根记忆：account(账目) + ant(人) → 管理账目的人 → 会计师 例 An *accountant's* unconditional guarantee of satisfaction leads clients to believe that tax returns prepared by the *accountant* are certain to be accurate.
accounting [əˈkaʊntɪŋ]	*n.* 会计，会计学(the occupation of maintaining and auditing records and preparing financial reports for a business)；账单(work done in accounting or by accountants) 记 来自 account(*v.* 认为；解释；*n.* 账户，账目) 例 He believed that the standardized *accounting* procedures would prove to be both inexpensive and reliable indicators of economic performance.
accretion [əˈkriːʃn]	*n.* 增长(the process of growth or enlargement by a gradual build-up)；增加物(added matter or thing formed by the addition of such matter) 记 词根记忆：ac + cret(增加) + ion → 增长 例 *accretion* disks 吸积盘 // This continuous process of *accretion* and succession would be interrupted only by hurricanes or storm flushings.
accrue [əˈkruː]	*v.* 自然增长，自然产生(to come about as a natural growth, increase, or advantage) 记 词根记忆：ac + crue(增加) → 自然增长，自然产生 例 The benefits would *accrue* to the individual, while the costs would be spread among all users. 派 accrual(*n.* 获利；自然增长)

accumulate [əˈkjuːmjəleɪt]	*v.* 积累(to gather or pile up)；堆积(to amass) 记 词根记忆：ac(不断) + cumul(堆积) + ate(使) → 使不断堆积起来 → 积累 例 Recyclable trash that is allowed to *accumulate* for two weeks will attract rodents(啮齿动物). 派 accumulation(*n.* 集聚；积累)
accuracy [ˈækjərəsi]	*n.* 准确(性)，精确(性)(exactness) 记 词根记忆：ac(加强) + cur(注意) + acy(表性质) → 十分注意 → 准确 例 The *accuracy* of animals' memories is difficult to determine through direct experimentation. 派 inaccuracy(*n.* 误差，错误)
accurate [ˈækjərət]	*a.* 正确的(correct)；精确的(exact) 例 Sailors needed highly *accurate* timepieces in order to compute their longitude. 派 inaccurate(*a.* 不准确的)；accurately(*ad.* 正确地；精确地)
accustomed [əˈkʌstəmd]	*a.* (to)习惯的，适应的(adapted to existing conditions) 记 词根记忆：ac + custom(习惯，习俗) + ed → 习惯的 例 The recent immigrants have not yet become *accustomed* to American food.
acidity [əˈsɪdəti]	*n.* 酸度，酸性(the quality, state, or degree of being acid) 记 词根记忆：acid(酸) + ity(名词后缀) → 酸度 例 The quality of unrefined olive oil is not actually defined in terms of *acidity*, yet extensive tests have shown that the less free oleic acid an unrefined olive oil contains per liter, the higher its quality.
acknowledge [əkˈnɑːlɪdʒ]	*v.* 承认(to recognize as genuine or valid)；致谢(to express gratitude) 记 联想记忆：ac + knowledge(知道) → 人人都知道，不得不承认 → 承认 例 Women's oral histories *acknowledge* the influence of well-known women. 派 acknowledgement(*n.* 承认；感谢)
acoustic [əˈkuːstɪk]	*a.* 听觉的，有关声音的(having to do with hearing or sound) 例 The use of *acoustic* alarms increases the number of commercial fish caught by the fishing company's boats. 派 acoustics(*n.* 声学)
acoustical [əˈkuːstɪkl]	*a.* 声学的，听觉的(of or relating to the sense or organs of hearing, to sound, or to the science of sounds) 记 来自 acoustic(*a.* 声学的；音响的) 例 The male whistling moths of Nambung, Australia, call female moths to them by the use of *acoustical* signals. 派 acoustically(*ad.* 听觉上；声学上)

acquiesce [ˌækwiˈes]	*v.* 勉强同意，默许(to agree or consent quietly without protest; consent) 例 Where once the union had *acquiesced* to the prejudices of its English-speaking members by supporting the imposition of an alien tax on immigrant workers, after 1897 the United Mine Workers made a determined effort to enlist Italians and Slavs in its ranks. 派 acquiescence(*n.* 默许)
acquire [əˈkwaɪər]	*v.* 取得，获得(to come into possession or control of) 记 词根记忆: ac + quire(追求) → 不断追求 → 获得 例 The United States *acquired* sovereignty over New Mexico in 1848. 派 acquisition(*n.* 获得；采购)
acquisition [ˌækwɪˈzɪʃn]	*n.* 获得物(something or someone acquired or gained) 记 来自 acquire(*v.* 获得) 例 One example of social learning is the *acquisition* of preferences for novel foods. 同根词: acquisitive(*a.* 贪得的；想获得的)
acreage [ˈeɪkərɪdʒ]	*n.* 英亩数(area in acres) 记 来自 acre(*n.* 英亩) 例 Because of improvements in agricultural technology, the same amount of *acreage* produces double the number of apples.
activate [ˈæktɪveɪt]	*v.* 使活动，激活(to make sth. active) 记 词根记忆: act(行动) + ivate(使成为) → 使动起来 → 激活 例 Protein synthesis begins when the gene encoding a protein is *activated*. 派 activation(*n.* 活化，激活) 同根词: active(*a.* 积极的，主动的); activism(*n.* 行动主义，激进主义)
activism [ˈæktɪvɪzəm]	*n.* 行动主义；激进主义(a doctrine or practice that emphasizes direct vigorous action) 记 词根记忆: act(行动) + iv + ism(主义) → 行动主义 例 Her *activism* predated her husband's presidency and her projects differed from his. 同根词: active(*a.* 积极的)
activist [ˈæktɪvɪst]	*n.* 积极分子(one that is active) 记 来自 active(*a.* 积极的；主动的) 例 community *activist* 社区积极分子 同根词: activity(*n.* 活跃；活动)
acute [əˈkjuːt]	*a.* 灵敏的(sensitive)；严重的(serious) 记 词根记忆: acu(尖端) + te → 尖端的 → 灵敏的 例 The sense of smell in adult female rats is more *acute* than that in rat pups. // an *acute* parking shortage 停车位严重不足 同根词: acumen(*n.* 敏锐)

adapt [ə'dæpt]	*v.* (使)适合，适应 (to make sth. fit often by modification) 记 词根记忆：ad + apt(适当的) → 使适合 注意：adopt(*v.* 采用；收养) 例 A biocontrol agent may *adapt* in unpredictable ways, so that it can feed on or otherwise harm new hosts. 派 adaptability(*n.* 适应性); adapted(*a.* 合适的); adaptive(*a.* 适应的)
adaptation [ˌædæp'teɪʃn]	*n.* 适应 (adjustment to environmental conditions); 改编 (something that is adapted) 记 来自 adapt(*v.* 使适应) 例 The disadvantages of an *adaptation* to a particular feature of an environment often outweigh the advantages of such an *adaptation*. 同根词：adaptive(*a.* 适应的; 适合的)
adapter [ə'dæptər]	*n.* 适应者 (one that adapts); 适配器 (an attachment for adapting apparatus for uses not originally intended) 记 来自 adapt(*v.* 使适应) 例 It has established itself as a supreme *adapter* in an era when the ability to adjust to the environmental changes wrought by human beings has created a whole new class of dominant large mammals. 同根词：adaptive(*a.* 适应的)
addict	['ædɪkt] *n.* 有瘾的人 (person who is unable to stop taking drugs, alcohol, etc.) [ə'dɪkt] *v.* 使上瘾，使入迷 (to devote or surrender (oneself) to something habitually or obsessively) 记 词根记忆：ad(加强) + dict(说，要求) → 不断要求 → 使上瘾 例 drug *addict* 吸毒成瘾者 // The level of caffeine in the candy bars is enough to keep people *addicted*. 派 addictive(*a.* 使人上瘾的); addiction(*n.* 上瘾，沉溺) 同根词：dictator(*n.* 独裁者); contradict(*v.* 反驳)
addictive [ə'dɪktɪv]	*a.* 上瘾的 (causing or characterized by addiction) 记 来自 addict(*v.* 使上瘾，使着迷) 例 The phenomenon of withdrawal has always been the crucial physiological criterion for distinguishing *addictive* from nonaddictive drugs.
addition [ə'dɪʃn]	*n.* 添加，增加物 (a part added); 加法 (the act or process of adding) 记 词根记忆：add(加) + ition → 加法 例 The *addition* of another firm has a negligible impact on the intensity of competition. 派 additional(*a.* 附加的，额外的) 同根词：addable(*a.* 可增加的)
additive ['ædətɪv]	*a.* 附加的 (involving addition); *n.* 添加剂 (substance added in small amounts for a special purpose) 记 来自 add(*v.* 加) 例 Organic milk is produced without the use of chemical *additives*.

adept [əˈdept]	*a.* 精通的，内行的 (thoroughly proficient)
	记 词根记忆：ad + ept(能力) → 有能力的 → 精通的，内行的
	例 Even the most *adept* forgers cannot duplicate all of the characteristics the program analyses.
adhere [ədˈhɪr]	*v.* (to) 粘附 (to stick)；遵守，坚持 (to give support or remain faithful to)
	记 词根记忆：ad(表加强) + her(粘附) + e → 粘附
	例 *adhere* to plans 遵守计划
	派 adherent(*n.* 信徒)；adherence(*n.* 粘着；忠诚)；adhesiveness(*n.* 粘性)
	同根词：inherent(*a.* 与生俱来的)
adherence [ədˈhɪrəns]	*n.* 坚持 (the fact of behaving according to a particular rule, etc , or of following a particular set of beliefs, or a fixed way of doing sth.)；依附 (the act, action, or quality of adhering)；忠诚 (fidelity)
	记 词根记忆：adher(坚持；依附) + ence(名词后缀) → 依附；坚持
	例 It may be easier to reach agreement on a particular course of action through decision-sharing, which will in turn tend to promote *adherence* to plans.
	同根词：adherent(*n.* 追随者；*a.* 附着的)
adjacent [əˈdʒeɪsnt]	*a.* 邻近的，毗连的 (adjoining)
	记 词根记忆：ad + jacent(躺) → 躺在附近 → 邻近的
	例 Two *adjacent* faces of the solid have areas of 15 and 24 respectively.
adjust [əˈdʒʌst]	*v.* 调节，改变…以适应 (to adapt)
	记 词根记忆：ad + just(正确) → 使正确 → 调节
	例 The data have been *adjusted* to allow for differences in the ages of patients. // The Japanese government had failed to *adjust* to the needs of a changing economy.
	派 adjustment(*n.* 调节，调整)
	同根词：justify(*v.* 证明…为正当)
administer [ədˈmɪnɪstər]	*v.* 管理，执行 (to manage or supervise the execution, use, or conduct of)；用药 (dispense of apply (a remedy or drug))
	记 联想记忆：ad(做) + minis(管理) + ter → 管理
	例 *administer* tribal lands 管理部落的土地 // The nasal spray vaccine is not effective when *administered* to adults.
	派 administration(*n.* 管理；管理部门)；administrative(*a.* 管理的，行政的)
admit [ədˈmɪt]	*v.* (to) 承认 (to acknowledge)；准许…进入 (to allow entry)
	记 词根记忆：ad + mit(送) → 能送进去 → 准许…进入
	例 In a survey of job applicants, two-fifths *admitted* to being at least a little dishonest.
	派 admittance(*n.* 准入)；admission(*n.* 准许进入)

adolescent [ˌædəˈlesnt]	*n.* 青少年(young person between childhood and adulthood);*a.* 青春期的(typical of time between childhood and adulthood) 记 联想记忆:ado(看作 adult 成人) + lescent(开始或正在形成的) → 开始成为成年人的 → 青少年 例 The children of authoritative parents are likely to be responsibly independent as *adolescents*. 派 adolescence(*n.* 青春;青春期)
adoption [əˈdɑːpʃn]	*n.* 采用,采纳(accepting);收养(taking sb. into one's family, esp. as one's child or heir) 记 来自 adopt(*v.* 采用;收养) 例 *adoption* of new technologies 采用新技术 // There are far fewer children available for *adoption* than there are people who want to adopt. 派 adoptive(*a.* 采纳的;过继的)
advent [ˈædvent]	*n.* 到来,出现(coming into being or use) 记 词根记忆:ad + vent(来) → 到来 例 The *advent* of private hospital health insurance guaranteed the private hospital a regular source of income. 同根词:intervention(*n.* 干涉);convention(*n.* 大会;习俗)
adverse [ˈædvɜːrs]	*a.* 逆的(acting against or in a contrary direction);不利的(unfavorable, harmful) 记 词根记忆:ad + vers(转) + e → 对着转 → 逆的,不利的 例 The *adverse* effects of poor performance by the firm are significant for the client. 派 adversely(*ad.* 反过来,相反);adversary(*n.* 敌手,对手)
advertising [ˈædvərtaɪzɪŋ]	*n.* 广告;广告业(the business of preparing advertisements for publication or broadcast) 记 来自 advertise(*v.* 做广告) 例 A key decision required of *advertising* managers is whether a "hard-sell" or "soft-sell" strategy is appropriate for a specific target market. 同根词:advertisement(*n.* 广告;宣传)
advocacy [ˈædvəkəsi]	*n.* 拥护,支持(the act or process of advocating) 记 来自 advocate(*v.* 提倡;拥护) 例 Traditional news sources seldom report the views of political *advocacy* groups accurately.
advocate	[ˈædvəkeɪt] *v.* 提倡,支持(to support) [ˈædvəkət] *n.* 支持者,提倡者(adherent) 记 词根记忆:ad + voc(叫喊,声音) + ate → 为其摇旗呐喊 → 支持 例 The school board *advocated* purchasing new books. 派 advocacy(*n.* 拥护;鼓吹)
aerodynamic [ˌeroʊdaɪˈnæmɪk]	*a.* 空气动力学的(of a science dealing with the forces acting on solid bodies moving through air) 记 词根记忆:aero(空气) + dynamic(动力学的) → 空气动力学的

□ adolescent   □ adoption   □ advent   ■ adverse   □ advertising   □ advocacy
□ advocate   □ aerodynamic

affiliation [əˌfɪliˈeɪʃn]	*n.* 联系，联合(link or connection made by affiliating) 记 来自 affiliate(*v.* 使附属；使发生关系) 例 The information that Wulf herself provided on religious *affiliation* and gender of students is in fact accurate.
affirmative [əˈfɜːrmətɪv]	*a.* 肯定的(asserting that the fact is so)；*n.* 肯定语(a word or statement of agreement) 记 来自 affirm(*v.* 断言，肯定) 例 *Affirmative* action is good business. // More than half the customers who answered in the *affirmative* spent over $100 at the store.
afflict [əˈflɪkt]	*v.* 使痛苦，折磨(to trouble, to injure) 记 词根记忆：af(不断) + flict(打击) → 一再受到打击 → 折磨 例 A disease broke out and severely *afflicted* the campers. 派 affliction(*n.* 痛苦，烦恼) 同根词：conflict(*n.* 冲突)；infliction(*n.* 施加的痛苦)
affluent [ˈæfluənt]	*a.* 富裕的(rich) 记 联想记忆：af(不断) + flu(流) + ent → 多得不停往外流 → 富裕的 例 The Joneses are *affluent* and give money to their community. 同根词：confluence(*n.* 汇流)；superfluous(*a.* 多余的)
affordable [əˈfɔːrdəbl]	*a.* 负担得起的，便宜的(being able to buy sth.) 记 来自 afford(*v.* 买得起) 例 In countries in which new life-sustaining drugs cannot be patented, such drugs are sold at widely *affordable* prices.
aftermath [ˈæftərmæθ]	*n.* 结果，后果(consequence) 例 In the *aftermath* of the flood, people rebuilt their homes.
aggravate [ˈæɡrəveɪt]	*v.* 加重，恶化(to make worse; intensify) 记 词根记忆：ag + grav(重) + ate → 使重 → 加重，恶化 例 Doctors generally agree that such factors as cigarette smoking, eating rich foods high in fats, and alcohol consumption not only do damage by themselves but also *aggravate* genetic predispositions toward certain diseases. 派 aggravation(*n.* 加剧，恶化) 同根词：grave(*a.* 重大的；庄重的)
aggregate [ˈæɡrɪɡət]	*v.* 合计(to collect or gather into a mass or whole)；*n.* 集合体(a body of units somewhat loosely associated with one another)；*a.* 合计的，聚合的(collective) 记 词根记忆：ag + greg(团体) + ate → 成为团体 → 集合体 例 *aggregate* of consumers 消费者的集合体 // A company may be able to estimate accurately the *aggregate* number of shoes it is going to sell. 派 aggregation(*n.* 聚集；总计) 同根词：gregarious(*a.* 喜社交的)

aggression [əˈgreʃn]	*n.* 侵略，侵犯(invasion)；敌对行为(hostile, injurious, or destructive behavior) 记 联想记忆：ag + gress(走) + ion → 走到别的国家 → 侵略 例 Rhesus monkeys(猕猴)respond with *aggression* to a wider range of stimuli than any other monkeys do. 派 aggressive(*a.* 攻击性的，侵略的)；aggressiveness(*n.* 好斗)
aggressive [əˈgresɪv]	*a.* 好斗的(militant; assertive)；进取的(full of enterprise and initiative) 记 词根记忆：ag(加强) + gress(行走) + ive → 到处乱走的 → 好斗的 例 They tend to become *aggressive* when provoked. 派 aggressively(*ad.* 侵略地) 同根词：aggressor(*n.* 侵略者)
agrarian [əˈgreriən]	*a.* 土地的；农业的(relating to agricultural or rural matters) 记 词根记忆：agr(田) + arian → 土地的 例 *agrarian* revolution 农业革命
ailment [ˈeɪlmənt]	*n.* (不严重的)疾病(a bodily disorder or chronic disease) 记 词根记忆：ail(小病) + ment → (不严重的)疾病 例 An *ailment* of the nervous system can be serious.
airliner [ˈerlaɪnər]	*n.* 班机；大型客机(an airplane operated by an airline) 记 来自 airline(*n.* 航线) 例 A layer of primer on an *airliner* weighs more than a layer of the new coating by an amount large enough to make a difference to that airliner's load-bearing capacity.
ale [eɪl]	*n.* 淡色啤酒 记 联想记忆：加上 p 就变成了 pale，可以记作"喝了淡色啤酒(ale)就脸色苍白(pale)" 例 *ale* house 啤酒屋
alga [ˈælgə]	*n.* (*pl.* algae)水藻, 海藻(very simple plants found chiefly in water) 例 *Algae* grow on rocks in the lake.
alien [ˈeɪliən]	*n.* 外国人(foreigner)；*a.* 外国的(foreign)；相异的(strange) 记 发音记忆："爱恋" → 跨国恋很流行 → 外国恋人 → 外国人 例 If employers hired illegal *aliens*, they would be penalized.
alignment [əˈlaɪnmənt]	*n.* 队列(arrangement in a straight line)；结盟(political support given to one country or group by another) 记 来自 align(*v.* 使结盟) 例 The *alignment* of an automobile manufacturer with its dealers is to adopt a plan to improve automobile design.

音频

allay [əˈleɪ]	*v.* 减轻，缓和(to relieve) 记 联想记忆：al(看作 all 全都) + lay(放置) → 负担都放下了 → 减轻，缓和 例 The appointment of Forrestal as First Secretary of Defense *allayed* the suspicions of naval officers.
allege [əˈledʒ]	*v.* 断言，宣称(to assert without proof or before proving) 记 词根记忆：al(加强) + leg(指定，任命) + e → 大声任命 → 宣称 例 The company *alleged* that the employee tampered with the computer system. 派 allegation(*n.* 宣称；指控); alleged(*a.* 声称的，所谓的); allegedly(*ad.* 依其申述)
allegiance [əˈliːdʒəns]	*n.* 忠诚，拥护(loyalty, faithfulness) 记 联想记忆：al + leg(法律) + iance → 靠近法律 → 拥护 例 Most historians have underestimated the extent of women's political *allegiance* in the antebellum(战前的)period. 派 allegiant(*a.* 忠心的，忠实的)
allergic [əˈlɜːrdʒɪk]	*a.* 过敏的(of allergy); 对…讨厌的(averse or disinclined) 记 联想记忆：aller(看作 alert 警报) + gic → 皮肤出现警报 → 过敏的 例 Not all forms of sulfite are equally likely to produce the *allergic* reactions. 同根词：allergenic(*a.* 引起过敏症的)
allergy [ˈælərdʒi]	*n.* 过敏症(an unfavorable reaction to certain foods, pollens, insect bites, etc.) 记 词根记忆：all(其他) + erg(起作用，工作) + y → 起其他作用 → 过敏症 派 allergic(*a.* 过敏的)
alleviate [əˈliːvieɪt]	*v.* 减轻，缓和(to allay) 记 词根记忆：al + lev(轻) + iate → 减轻 例 The mayor claims that the fee will *alleviate* the city's traffic congestion. 同根词：levity(*n.* 轻率)
alliance [əˈlaɪəns]	*n.* 联盟(an association to further the common interests of the members); 联合(the state of being allied) 记 来自 ally(*v.* 联合，联盟) 例 The resulting cooperative *alliance* of independent agencies now comprise 32 partners spanning 37 countries.

alligator [ˈælɪɡeɪtər]	n. 短吻鳄(产于美洲的一种鳄鱼)(a reptile of the crocodile family) 例 *Alligators* prey heavily on a species of freshwater fish.
allocate [ˈæləkeɪt]	v. 分配(to distribute); 分派(to designate) 记 词根记忆：al(加强) + loc(地方) + ate(做) → 不断把东西发送到各地 → 分配 例 They seek to *allocate* capital in ways that may reduce their tax burden. 派 allocation(n. 配给, 分配)
allotment [əˈlɑːtmənt]	n. 分配(apportionment); 分配物(something that is allotted); 养家费 (money that be used to support a family) 记 来自 allot(v. 分配) 例 To meet the rapidly rising market demand for fish and seafood, suppliers are growing fish twice as fast as they grow naturally, cutting their feed *allotment* by nearly half and raising them on special diets.
allowance [əˈlaʊəns]	n. 允许(permission); 津贴, 补助费(subsidy) 记 来自 allow(v. 允许), 允许拿到的或省下的钱 → 津贴, 补助费 例 financial *allowances* 财政津贴
allude [əˈluːd]	v. (to)间接提到, 暗指(to make indirect reference) 记 词根记忆：al + lud(嬉笑) + e → 在嬉笑中说 → 间接提到 例 The author *alludes* to the well-established nature of the concept of individual rights in the Anglo-Saxon tradition. 派 allusive(a. 暗指的, 影射) 同根词：ludicrous(a. 可笑的, 滑稽的); elude(v. 躲避)
alluvial [əˈluːviəl]	a. 冲积的, 淤积的(made of sand, earth left by rivers or floods, esp. in a delta) 例 *alluvial* gold 冲积金矿
ally	[əˈlaɪ] v. (使)结盟(to unite) [ˈælaɪ] n. 同盟者, 同盟国(person, country, that joined with another in order to give help and support) 例 During World War II, Great Britain *allied* with the United States. 派 alliance(n. 结盟, 联盟)
alpha [ˈælfə]	n. 希腊语字母表的第一个字母(A, α) 记 发音记忆
alter [ˈɔːltər]	v. 改变, 变更(to change) 记 本身为词根：改变 例 The period of an organism's biological clock can be *altered* by environmental factors. 派 alteration(n. 改变, 变更); alternative(a. 二者择一的)
alternate	[ˈɔːltərnət] a. 交替的, 更迭的((of two things) happening or following one after the other regularly) [ˈɔːltərneɪt] v. 交替, 轮流(to cause to occur by turns) 记 词根记忆：alter(其他) + nate → 可以有其他的 → 交替的 例 To maintain the nutrients in the soil, corn and soybeans are often planted in a field in *alternate* years.

alternative [ɔːl'tɜːrnətɪv]	*a.* 轮流的，交替的(alternate)；两者(或两者以上)择一的(offering or expressing a choice)；*n.* 二中择一；供替代的选择(something which can be chosen instead) 记 词根记忆：alter(改变状态，其他的) + native(…的) → 其他的 → 两者择一的 例 For most commuters who use the subway system, there is no practical *alternative* public transportation available. 派 alternatively(*ad.* 非此即彼；二者择一地) 同根词：alterable(*a.* 可改变的)
altitude ['æltɪtuːd]	*n.* 高度(height above sea-level) 记 词根记忆：alt(高) + itude → 高度 例 The plane was flying at an *altitude* of 2,000 feet.
altruism ['æltruɪzəm]	*n.* 利他主义，无私(unselfish devotion to the welfare of others) 记 词根记忆：altru(其他) + ism(主义) → 利他主义 例 *Altruism* means doing good things simply because the good things are worth doing. 派 altruistic(*a.* 利他的)；altruist(*n.* 利他主义者)
aluminum [ə'luːmɪnəm]	*n.* 铝 例 Air pollution from the giant *aluminum* refinery is killing our plants.
alumna [ə'lʌmnə]	*n.* 女校友，女毕业生(a female former student of a school, college or university)
alumnus [ə'lʌmnəs]	*n.* 男校友，男毕业生(a male former student of a school, college or university) 例 He is an *alumnus* of Peking University of the class of 1986.
amalgam [ə'mælgəm]	*n.* 混合物(combination) 记 本义是"汞合金"，该词来自拉丁文 amalgama(混合)；联想记忆：am + alg + am，前后两个 am 结合 → 混合 例 *amalgam* of Chinese and Western medicines 中西药合剂 派 amalgamate(*v.* 合并，联合)；amalgamation(*n.* 混合，合并)
amass [ə'mæs]	*v.* 积聚(to gather, accumulate) 记 词根记忆：a + mass(一团) → 变成一团 → 积聚 例 While in college, John *amassed* a shelf of reference books. 派 amassment(*n.* 积蓄，聚积) 同根词：massive(*a.* 巨大的)
amateur ['æmətər]	*n.* 业余爱好者(one who practises a sport or art without receiving money for it; one who is unskilled or inexperienced in an activity) 记 词根记忆：amat(=amor 爱) + eur(人) → 爱好的人 → 业余爱好者 例 He is an *amateur* in boxing. 派 amateurish(*a.* 业余爱好的；不熟练的) 同根词：amorous(*n.* 多情的)
amber ['æmbər]	*n.* 琥珀(hard clear yellowish brown gum) 记 发音记忆："爱不" → 爱不释手的珍物 → 琥珀

ambiguity [ˌæmbɪˈgjuːəti]	*n.* 模棱两可，模糊（uncertainty） 记 词根记忆：ambi（绕着，在什么周围）+ guity → 围着什么绕来绕去 → 模棱两可 例 The *ambiguity* of the teacher's response made us realize he did not know the answer.
ambiguous [æmˈbɪgjuəs]	*a.* 意义不明的，模棱两可的（obscure） 例 The professor gave an *ambiguous* answer to Jane's question.
ambitious [æmˈbɪʃəs]	*a.* 有抱负的，雄心勃勃的（having a desire to achieve a particular goal）；宏大的（an idea or plan on a large scale and needs a lot of work to be carried out successfully） 例 Over the last ten years, overcrowding in the prisons of Barraland has essentially been eliminated as a result of an *ambitious* program of prison construction. 派 ambitiously（*ad.* 雄心勃勃地；热切地） 同根词：ambition（*n.* 野心）
ambivalent [æmˈbɪvələnt]	*a.* 有矛盾看法的（having or showing mixed feelings about a certain object, person or situation） 记 联想记忆：ambi（二）+ val（强大）+ ent → 两边都有力量，不知道怎么办 → 有矛盾看法的 例 They are *ambivalent* concerning where to go on vacation. 派 ambivalence（*n.* 矛盾心理） 同根词：valiant（*a.* 勇敢的）；valor（*n.* 勇气）
amenable [əˈmiːnəbl]	*a.*（to）顺从的（tractable）；易作出响应的（willing to be influenced or controlled）；可按照…处理的（can be dealt according to） 例 The problem of spoilage of refrigerated food is not *amenable* to any solution based on design changes.
amend [əˈmend]	*v.* 修订（to correct）；改进（to improve） 记 词根记忆：a + mend（补，修）→ 修订 注意：amends（*n.* 赔偿，补偿） 例 A theory is proposed, considered, and then *amended*.
amenity [əˈmenəti]	*n.* 舒适（the quality of being pleasant or agreeable）；方便设施（something that conduces to comfort, convenience, or enjoyment） 记 联想记忆：a + men（人）+ ity → 为人民服务 → 方便设施 例 Private hospitals provided services and *amenities* that distinguished between paying and non-paying patients.
amino acid [ˌmiːnəʊ ˈæsɪd]	*n.* 氨基酸，胺酸 例 Cancer can be caused by excessively rapid degradation of certain *amino acids* in the cytoplasm（细胞质）of cells.
amphitheater [ˈæmfɪθiːətər]	*n.* 竞技场（a very large auditorium） 记 分拆记忆：amphi（两个）+ theater（剧场）→ 有两个剧场那么大的场地 → 竞技场 例 Flavian *Amphitheater* 弗拉维亚竞技场 同根词：theatre（*n.* 电影院；剧场）

ample [ˈæmpl]	*a.* 丰富的，充足的(sufficient and adequate) 记 词根记忆：ampl(大，多) + e → 充足的 注意：amble(*v.* 漫步) 例 The *ample* availability of land makes security of land tenure unimportant.
amplifier [ˈæmplɪfaɪər]	*n.* [电子]放大器，扩大器；扩音器(one that amplifies) 记 来自amplify(*v.* 放大，扩大) 例 Although they are more temperamental and far more expensive than transistor-driven *amplifiers*, many audiophiles and audio professionals prefer the warmer, richer tones produced by vacuum-tube-driven *amplifiers*. 同根词：amplification(*n.* 放大；扩增)
amplify [ˈæmplɪfaɪ]	*v.* 增强(声音等)(to increase)；详述(to expand, as a statement, by the use of detail or illustration or by closer analysis) 记 词根记忆：ampl(大) + ify(使…) → 放大 → 增强 例 Can you *amplify* the sound so we can hear it better? // Could you *amplify* your answer a bit?
amplitude [ˈæmplɪtuːd]	*n.* 广度(the extent or range of a quality, property, process, or phenomenon)；振幅(the extent of a vibratory movement) 记 词根记忆：ampl(大) + itude → 广度 例 the sound's *amplitude* 声域
anaerobic [ˌænəˈroʊbɪk]	*a.* 厌氧的(occurring, or existing in the absence of oxygen) 记 词根记忆：an(不，无) + aero(空气) + bic → 不要空气的 → 厌氧的 例 *anaerobic* metabolism 无氧代谢
analog(ue) [ˈænəlɔːg]	*n.* 类似物(something that is similar to something else) 记 词根记忆：ana(并列) + log → 类似 → 类似物 例 *analog* recording 模拟录音 派 analogous(*a.* 类似的)
analogy [əˈnælədʒi]	*n.* 类推；类比(comparison based on resemblance) 记 词根记忆：ana(并列) + log(说话) + y → 放在一起说 → 类比 例 The teacher made an *analogy* between the lens of a camera and the lens of an eye. 同根词：prologue(*n.* 序言)；epilogue(*n.* 后记)
analytic(al) [ˌænəˈlɪtɪk(l)]	*a.* 分析(法)的(of or relating to analysis or analytics) 例 *analytical* writing 分析性写作
anatomical [ˌænəˈtɑːmɪkl]	*a.* 解剖学的(of or relating to anatomy) 记 来自anatomy(*n.* 解剖学) 例 New genetic evidence—together with recent studies of elephants' skeletons, tusks, and other *anatomical* features—provide compelling support for classifying Africa's forest elephants.

anatomy [əˈnætəmi]	*n.* 解剖 (dissection)；解剖学 (scientific study of the structure of animal bodies) 词根记忆：ana(向上) + tomy(切，割) → 解剖 例 The *anatomy* of pterosaurs'(翼龙)wings suggests that they did not evolve into the class of birds. 派 anatomic(*a.* 解剖学的)；anatomist(*n.* 解剖学家，剖析者)
ancestor [ˈænsestər]	*n.* 祖先 (forefather) 词根记忆：an(在前面) + cest(行走) + or → 在前面走的人 → 祖先 例 Mr. Macdonald's *ancestors* came from Scotland. 同根词：ancestral(*a.* 原始的；祖传的)
ancestry [ˈænsestri]	*n.* 祖先 (ancestors)；世系，血统 (line of descent, lineage) 例 It excluded American-born citizens of Japanese *ancestry* from landownership. // shared *ancestry* and culture 共有的血统和文化
anecdotal [ˌænɪkˈdoʊtl]	*a.* 轶事的 (of short, interesting stories about a real person or event) 来自 anecdote(*n.* 轶事) 注意：antidote(*n.* 解毒药) 例 There is no written or *anecdotal* record that Leonardo da Vinci ever painted over major areas of his *Mona Lisa*.
anemia [əˈniːmiə]	*n.* 贫血 (ischemia)；贫血症 (a condition in which the blood is deficient in red blood cells, in hemoglobin, or in total volume) 词根记忆：an(无) + (a)em(血) + ia → 没血 → 贫血 例 People who inherit the sickle cell *anemia* gene from only one parent seem to be resistant to malaria. 同根词：anemic(*a.* 患贫血症的，贫血的)
anesthesia [ˌænəsˈθiːʒə]	(=美 anaesthesia) *n.* 麻醉 (loss of sensation) 词根记忆：an(无) + esthe(感觉) + sia → 无感觉 → 麻醉 例 Surgical patients operated on at night need less *anesthesia*. 同根词：anesthetic(*a.* 麻醉的；*n.* 麻醉剂)；aesthetics(*n.* 美学)
animate [ˈænɪmeɪt]	*n.* 有生命的 (alive)；*v.* 使有生气 (to give spirit and support to)；绘制(动画片) (to make or design in such a way as to create lifelike movement) 联想记忆：anim(生命) + ate → 使图画有生命 → 绘制(动画片) 例 *animated* cartoon 动画
animosity [ˌænɪˈmɑːsəti]	*n.* 憎恶，仇恨 (enmity) 联想记忆：anim(生命) + osity → 用整个生命去恨 → 憎恶，仇恨 例 Much *animosity* existed between the two opponents.
announce [əˈnaʊns]	*v.* 宣布，发表 (to proclaim)；通报…的到来 (to give notice of the arrival) 词根记忆：an + nounce(讲话，说出) → 说出来 → 宣布 例 The OPEC had long been expected to *announce* a reduction in output to bolster sagging oil prices. 派 announcement(*n.* 公告；发表) 同根词：renounce(*v.* 宣布放弃)

□ anatomy　　□ ancestor　　□ ancestry　　□ anecdotal　　□ anemia　　□ anesthesia
□ animate　　□ animosity　　□ announce

announcement [əˈnaʊnsmənt]	*n.* 宣告（the act of announcing or of being announced）；公告，通告（a public notification or declaration） 记 来自 announce（*v.* 宣布；述说） 例 The following appeared in an *announcement* issued by the publisher of *The Mercury*, a weekly newspaper. 同根词：denouncement（*n.* 公开谴责，抨击）
anole [əˈnəʊlɪ]	*n.* 变色龙（产于美洲的蜥蜴类）（a kind of lizard with the ability to change color） 例 *anole* lizard species 变色蜥蜴种群
anomaly [əˈnɑːməlɪ]	*n.* 异常，反常（deviation from the common rule） 记 联想记忆：a(不) + nomal（看作 normal 正常的）+ y → 不正常 → 反常 例 The test results contained *anomalies* that the scientists could not explain. 派 anomalous（*a.* 异常的，不规则的）
anonymous [əˈnɑːnɪməs]	*a.* 匿名的（unnamed） 记 词根记忆：an(无) + onym（名称）+ ous → 无名称的 → 匿名的 例 An *anonymous* donor gave a million dollars to the charity. 同根词：synonym（*n.* 同义词）
answerable [ˈænsərəbl]	*a.* (to)应负责的（responsible） 记 来自 answer（*v.* 回答，尽责） 例 I am *answerable* to the company for the use of this equipment.
antagonism [ænˈtæɡənɪzəm]	*n.* 对抗，敌对（opposition, hostility） 记 词根记忆：ant(反) + agon（打斗，比赛）+ ism → 对着打 → 对抗 例 Randolph helped to weaken organized labor's *antagonism* toward Black workers. 同根词：antagonise（*v.* 使反抗，使敌对）；antagonize（*v.* 对抗）；antagonist（*n.* 敌手，对手）
antedate [ˌæntiˈdeɪt]	*v.* 早于，先于（to be earlier than） 记 词根记忆：ante（前面）+ date（日期）→ 早于，先于 例 This old carriage *antedates* the invention of the car.
anterior [ænˈtɪrɪər]	*a.* 先前的（more forward）；前面的（toward the front） 记 词根记忆：ante（前面）+ rior → 以前的 → 先前的 例 The *anterior* side of the turtle's shell is lighter in color.
anthropologist [ˌænθrəˈpɑːlədʒɪst]	*n.* 人类学家（expert in the study of mankind） 记 来自 anthropology（*n.* 人类学） 例 *Anthropologists* once thought that the ancestors of modern humans began to walk upright because it freed their hands to use stone tools.
antibiotic [ˌæntibaɪˈɑːtɪk]	*n.* 抗生素（a substance that is produced by a microorganism and is able to inhibit or kill another micro-organism） 记 词根记忆：anti(反) + bio（生命）+ tic → 抗生素 例 Healthy lungs produce a natural *antibiotic* that protects them from infection.

antibiotics [ˌæntibaɪ'ɑːtɪks]	*n.* 抗生素（a substance produced by or a semisynthetic substance derived from a microorganism and able in dilute solution to inhibit or kill another microorganism） 记 词根记忆：anti（对抗的）+ biotic（生物的）+ s → 抗生素 例 Many lung infections can be treated by applying synthetic *antibiotics* to the airway surfaces. 同根词：biotype（*n.* 生物型）
antibody ['æntibɑːdi]	*n.* 抗体（身体中的抗病物质）（substance formed in the blood in response to harmful bacteria and then attacks and destroys） 记 词根记忆：anti（对抗的）+ body（体）→ 抗体 例 specific *antibody* 特种抗体 同根词：antigen（*n.* 抗原）
anticipate [æn'tɪsɪpeɪt]	*v.* 预见，预期（to foresee） 记 词根记忆：anti（前）+ cip（落下）+ ate → 提前落下 → 预见 例 A company that does not correctly *anticipate* the expectations of its customers is certain to fail. 派 anticipation（*n.* 预料）；unanticipated（*a.* 未曾料到的） 同根词：incipient（*a.* 开始的）
antifreeze ['æntifriːz]	*n.* 抗冻剂（a substance added to a liquid to lower its freezing point） 记 词根记忆：anti（对抗的）+ freeze（冷冻）→ 抗冻剂 例 Brand X *antifreeze* is sold by gallons.
antiquated ['æntɪkweɪtɪd]	*a.* 过时的（outmoded） 记 联想记忆：antiqu（看作 antique 古董）+ ated → 古董的 → 过时的 例 an *antiquated* theory 过时的理论
antique [æn'tiːk]	*a.* 古时的，古老的（ancient）；*n.* 古董（an object that is old and valuable） 记 词根记忆：anti（前）+ que → 以前的 → 古时的 例 Grandma's house is filled with *antique* furniture. // Be careful with that bowl; it's an *antique*.
antiquity [æn'tɪkwəti]	*n.* 古代（ancient times）；古物（relics or monuments of ancient times） 例 Rome under Augustus and fifth-century Athens provide the most obvious examples in *antiquity*.
antitrust [ˌænti'trʌst]	*a.* 反托拉斯的，反垄断的（opposing or intended to regulate business monopolies, such as trusts on cartels） 记 词根记忆：anti（反对）+ trust（联合企业，托拉斯）→ 反托拉斯的 例 *antitrust* laws 反垄断法
aperiodic [ˌepɪrɪ'ɑdɪk]	*a.* 不定期的，非周期性的（of irregular occurrence） 记 词根记忆：a（不）+ period（周期）+ ic → 不定期的，非周期性的 例 The work of mathematician Roger Penrose in the early 1970s, on the geometry of what are called *aperiodic* tiles, turned out to describe the architecture of a previously unknown class of crystals. 同根词：periodic（*a.* 周期的；定期的）

apex ['eɪpeks]	*n.* 顶点，最高点（peak; vertex） 例 The hangar is 103 feet high at the *apex* of its roof.
apiece [ə'piːs]	*ad.* 每个，每人，各（for each one, individually） 记 联想记忆：a + piece（片）→ 每人一片 → 每个，每人 例 Elena purchased brand X pens for $4.00 *apiece* and brand Y pens for $2.80 *apiece*.
apparatus [ˌæpə'rætəs]	*n.* 仪器，设备（device, equipment） 例 No *apparatus* can detect neutrinos unless it is extremely massive.
apparel [ə'pærəl]	*n.* 衣服，服饰（clothing, garments） 记 联想记忆：appar（出现）+ el → 穿出来的东西 → 衣服

Man errs so long as he strives.

人只要奋斗就会犯错误。

——德国诗人、剧作家 歌德

（Johann Wolfgang Goethe, German poet and dramatist）

Word List 3

音频

apparent [əˈpærənt]	*a.* 显然的，明显的(evident)；表面上的(seeming) 记 联想记忆：ap + parent(父母) → 父母对儿女的爱显而易见 → 明显的 例 There were some *apparent* exceptions to the general correlation observed between adenosine-receptor binding and stimulation.
appeal [əˈpiːl]	*n.* 呼吁(earnest plea)；吸引力(attraction)；*v.* 吸引；上诉(accuse) 记 词根记忆：ap + peal(=pull 拉) → 拉过去 → 吸引 例 The state legislature need not heed(留意)the *appeals* of the protesting students. // The case of sex discrimination has been *appealed* from a lower court.
appendicitis [əˌpendəˈsaɪtɪs]	*n.* 阑尾炎，盲肠炎(inflammation of the vermiform appendix) 例 Patients with symptoms strongly suggesting *appendicitis* almost always have their appendix removed.
appetite [ˈæpɪtaɪt]	*n.* 食欲(desire to eat)；欲望(any of the instinctive desires) 记 来自拉丁语 appetere，ap + peter(寻找，尝试) + e → 寻找、尝试是因为欲望 例 stimulate/inhibit the *appetite* 刺激/抑制食欲 派 appetizing(*a.*美味可口的,促进食欲的)
appliance [əˈplaɪəns]	*n.* 用具，用品(implement) 记 来自 apply(*v.* 运用，使用) 例 The original retail price of an *appliance* was 60 percent more than its wholesale cost.
applicable [əˈplɪkəbl]	*a.* (to)适用的，适宜的(appropriate, fitting) 记 联想记忆：appli(看作 apply 运用) + cable(…的) → 能运用的 → 适用的 例 The findings are *applicable* to other industrial areas. 派 applicability(*n.* 适用性)
appoint [əˈpɔɪnt]	*v.* 任命，指派(to name officially) 记 词根记忆：ap(加强) + point(指向，指出) → 指定某人做某事 → 任命 例 Most were already known to the chairs of the board to which they were *appointed*. 派 appointment(*n.* 指定)

apportion [ə'pɔːrʃn]	*v.* （按比例或计划）分配 to divide and share out according to a plan） 记 词根记忆：ap（=ad 做）+ portion（一部分，一份）→ 分配 例 The city council *apportions* all the tax money to the different departments.
apprentice [ə'prentɪs]	*n.* 学徒；初学者（a young person who works for an employer for a fixed period of time in order to learn） 例 *Some Tame Gazelle* was Barbara Pym's first novel, but it does not read like an *apprentice* work. 派 apprenticeship（*n.* 学徒的身份）
apprenticeship [ə'prentɪʃɪp]	*n.* 学徒期；学徒身份（the position of apprentice） 记 词根记忆：ap + prentice（徒弟）+ ship → 学徒身份 例 The average length of *apprenticeship* for carpenters has declined significantly since 1930. 同根词：apprentice（*n.* 学徒；*v.* 当学徒）
approbation [ˌæprə'beɪʃn]	*n.* 赞成，同意（sanction） 记 词根记忆：ap（表加强）+ prob（=prove 证实）+ ation → 证实是好的 → 赞成 例 qualified *approbation* 有条件的赞成
appropriate [ə'proʊpriət]	*a.* 适当的，相称的（fitting, suitable） 记 词根记忆：ap + propri（适当的）+ ate → 适当的 例 The tropical wildlands that are still relatively intact do not provide *appropriate* habitats for reproduction.
appropriation [əˌproʊpri'eɪʃn]	*n.* 拨款（money set aside by formal action for a specific use） 例 *appropriations* for the military services 军备拨款
approval [ə'pruːvl]	*n.* 批准；认可；赞成（an act or instance of approving） 记 来自 approve（*v.* 批准；认可；赞成） 例 Such *approval* is denied if the commander judges that the evidence on which the provisional arrest is based is insufficient. 同根词：disapprove（*v.* 不赞成）
approve [ə'pruːv]	*v.* 赞成（to accept as satisfactory）；批准，认可（to ratify） 记 词根记忆：ap（一再）+ prove（证实）→ 一再证实是好的 → 赞成 例 The board has *approved* an annual salary of over one million dollars for our company's chief executive officer. 派 disapprove（*v.* 不同意）；approval（*n.* 赞成；批准）
approximate	[ə'prɑːksɪmeɪt] *v.* 接近（to bring near） [ə'prɑːksɪmət] *a.* 近似的，大概的（nearly correct or exact） 记 词根记忆：ap + proxim（接近）+ ate → 接近的 → 近似的 例 In 1982 the *approximate* average cost of operating a subcompact car for 10,000 miles was $3,400. 派 approximation（*n.* 近似值）；approximately（*ad.* 近似地，大约）

□ apportion   □ apprentice   □ apprenticeship   □ approbation   □ appropriate   □ appropriation
□ approval   □ approve   □ approximate

21

aquarium [əˈkweriəm]	*n.* 水族馆；养鱼池（artificial pond where live fish and other water creatures are kept） 记 词根记忆：aqua(水) + rium → 水族馆 例 Feeding hours at the *aquarium* are popular with the children.
aquatic [əˈkwætɪk]	*a.* 水的，与水有关的（relating to water） 记 词根记忆：aqua(水) + tic → 水的 例 *aquatic* animals 水生动物 同根词：aqueous(*a.* 水的；似水的)
arable [ˈærəbl]	*a.* 可耕的（suitable for plowing） 记 词根记忆：ar(耕种) + able → 可耕的 例 *arable* lands 耕地
arbitrary [ˈɑːrbətreri]	*a.* 任意的，主观的（depending on individual discretion） 记 词根记忆：arbit(判断) + rary → 自作判断的 → 主观的 例 Taxes were irregular in timing and *arbitrary* in amount. // This intuition is not *arbitrary* or irrational, but is based on years of painstaking practice. 同根词：arbitrator(*n.* 仲裁人)；arbitration(*n.* 仲裁，公断)
arboreal [ɑːrˈbɔːriəl]	*a.* 树木的（of or like a tree）；栖息在树上的（inhabiting or frequenting trees） 记 词根记忆：arbor(树) + eal → 树木的 例 Their cardiovascular system is not as complicated as that of *arboreal* snakes.
arch [ɑːrtʃ]	*n.* 拱形；拱门（a typically curved structural member spanning an opening and serving as a support）；*a.* 调皮的，淘气的（playful in a deliberate way） 例 an *arch* smile
archaeological [ˌɑːrkiəˈlɑːdʒɪkl]	*a.* 考古学的（the scientific study of material remains of past human life and activities） 记 来自 archaeology(*n.* 考古学) 例 They tend to reflect *archaeological* evidence that has become outdated. 同根词：archaeologist(*n.* 考古学家)
archaeologist [ˌɑːrkiˈɑːlədʒɪst]	*n.* 考古学家（scientists that study material remains of past human life and activities） 记 词根记忆：archae(古) + olog(y)(学科) + ist(表人) → 考古学家 例 *Archaeologists* deal with priceless objects every day. 同根词：archaeology(*n.* 考古学)
archaeology [ˌɑːrkiˈɑːlədʒi]	*n.* 考古学（study of ancient civilizations by scientific analysis of physical remains found in the ground） 记 词根记忆：archae(古) + ology(学科) → 考古学 例 A technique called proton-induced x-ray emission, is finding uses in medicine, *archaeology* and criminology. 派 archaeologist(*n.* 考古学家)；archaeological(*a.* 考古学的)

archenemy [ˌɑːtʃˈenəmɪ]	*n.* 天敌；主要敌人（a principal enemy） 记 词根记忆：arch（主要的）+ enemy（敌人）→ 天敌；主要敌人 例 The wolf remains the *archenemy* of cattle and sheep.
architect [ˈɑːrkɪtekt]	*n.* 建筑师，设计师（person who designs buildings） 记 联想记忆：archi（看作 archy 统治）+ tect（遮蔽）→ 统治建造人类蔽身之 所的人 → 建筑师 例 A prolific *architect* worked from the turn of the century until the late 1950's. 派 architecture（*n.* 建筑学）；architectural（*a.* 建筑的）
ardent [ˈɑːrdnt]	*a.* 热心的，热烈的（eager） 记 词根记忆：ard（热）+ ent → 热心的，热烈的 例 The president is an *ardent* supporter of civil affairs. 派 ardency（*n.* 热心，热烈） 同根词：arduous（*a.* 费力的）；ardor（*n.* 热心）
arid [ˈærɪd]	*a.* 干旱的（very dry）；荒芜的（lacking in interest and life） 例 These kinds of plants are normally found in *arid* regions. 派 semiarid（*a.* 半干旱的）
aristocracy [ˌærɪˈstɑːkrəsi]	*n.* 贵族政府，贵族统治（government by people of the highest social class） 记 词根记忆：aristo（最好的）+ cracy（统治）→ 最好的统治 → 贵族政府 同根词：aristocratic（*a.* 贵族的，贵族统治的）
arithmetic [əˈrɪθmətɪk]	*n.* 算术（calculations using numbers） 例 An *arithmetic* sequence is a sequence in which each term after the first is equal to the sum of the preceding term and a constant.
array [əˈreɪ]	*v.* 排列（to set or place in order）；*n.* 大批（large number） 例 The project calls for placing an *array* of light sensors at a depth of five kilometers under the ocean surface. // *arrayed* in parallel lines 平行排列
arrest [əˈrest]	*v.* 依法逮捕，拘留（to seize）；阻止，抑制（to stop or check） 记 联想记忆：ar（加强）+ rest（休息）→ 强制休息 → 拘留 例 Did the police have reasonable grounds to *arrest* him? 派 arrester（*n.* 避雷器；逮捕者）
artery [ˈɑːrtəri]	*n.* [医] 动脉 记 词根记忆：arter（管道）+ y →（体内的）管道 → 动脉 注意：vein（*n.* 静脉） 例 Studies indicate that refraining from eating certain foods could help reverse blockage of coronary *arteries*. 派 arterial（*a.* 动脉的）
arthritis [ɑːrˈθraɪtɪs]	*n.* 关节炎（inflammation of a joint or joints of the body） 记 词根记忆：arthr（连结；关节）+ itis（炎症）→ 关节炎 同根词：arthropod（*n.* 节肢动物）

articulate	[ɑːrˈtikjuleɪt] *v.* 清楚地表达(to give clear and effective utterance to) [ɑːrˈtɪkjələt] *a.* 善于表达的(expressing oneself clearly and effectively) 记 联想记忆:articul(关节) + ate → 关节之间相连,(说话)上下相连 → 清楚地表达 例 The manager takes action without being able to *articulate* reasons for that particular action. // Please practice your speech until you are more *articulate*. 派 articulation(*n.* 发音;连接;关节)
artifact [ˈɑːrtɪfækt]	*n.* 手工艺器物;文物(thing made by man, esp. of archaeological interest) 记 词根记忆:arti(技巧) + fact(做) → 技巧做成的 → 手工艺器物 例 The museum can store and exhibit its more than 12,000 *artifacts*.
artificial [ˌɑːrtɪˈfɪʃl]	*a.* 人工的,人造的(man-made) 记 词根记忆:arti(=skill 技术) + fic(面) + ial(…的) → 在表面使用技术的 → 人造的 例 People who use the *artificial* sweetener aspartame are better off consuming sugar. 派 artificially(*ad.* 人工地)
artisan [ˈɑːrtəzn]	*n.* 手工业工人,手艺人(craftsperson) 记 词根记忆:arti(技巧) + san(人) → 有技巧的人 → 手艺人 例 In ancient Thailand, much of the local *artisans*' creative energy was expended for the creation of Buddha images.
ascending [əˈsendɪŋ]	*a.* 上升的(moving or going upward) 记 词根记忆:a + scend(爬) + ing → 向上爬的 → 上升的 例 *ascending* order 升序
ascribe [əˈskraɪb]	*v.* (to)归于,归因于(to credit) 记 词根记忆:a(向) + scribe(写) → 写在什么上面 → 归于 例 Productivity should be *ascribed* to categories of workers, not to individuals.
aspect [ˈæspekt]	*n.* (问题等的)方面(a particular status or phase in which sth. appears or may be regarded);面貌,外表(appearance) 记 词根记忆:a+spect(看) → 看向的地方 → (问题等的)方面 例 It explains why one *aspect* of anole lizard species' habitat use has been difficult to account for. 同根词:expect(*n./v.* 期待);inspect(*v.* 检查)
aspen [ˈæspən]	*n.* 白杨(a type of poplar tree, with leaves that move even when there is very little wind);*a.* 类似白杨的 记 联想记忆:as + pen(笔) → 像笔一样直的树木 → 白杨 例 The leaves of the *aspen* tree that leaned past the window flickered in the breeze.
aspersion [əˈspɜːrʒn]	*n.* 诽谤,中伤(slander) 记 词根记忆:a + spers(散开) + ion → 散布坏东西 → 诽谤 例 I resent your casting *aspersions* on my brother and his ability!

□ articulate   □ artifact   □ artificial   □ artisan   □ ascending   □ ascribe
□ aspect   □ aspen   □ aspersion

aspiration [ˌæspəˈreɪʃn]	*n.* 志向，抱负（ambition） 记 来自 aspire（*v.* 渴望，抱负） 例 Employers assumed that women's "real" *aspirations* were for marriage and family life. 同根词：respire（*v.* 呼吸）
assemble [əˈsembl]	*v.* 集合（to gather）；装配（to fit together the parts of） 记 词根记忆：as（加强）+ semble（类似）→ 物以类聚 → 集合 例 A group of store managers must *assemble* 280 displays（显示器）for an upcoming sale. 派 assembler（*n.* 装配工）；assembly（*n.* 组装，装配）；disassembly（*n.* 分解，拆卸）
assembler [əˈsemblər]	*n.* 汇编程序（a computer program that automatically converts instructions written in assembly language into machine language）；装配工（one that assembles） 记 来自 assemble（*v.* 集合；聚集） 例 The average number of hours it takes a Borodian television *assembler* to assemble a television has not decreased significantly during the past three years. 同根词：assembly（*n.* 装配；集会）
assert [əˈsɜːrt]	*v.* 断言（to affirm）；声称（to declare） 记 词根记忆：as + sert（插入）→ 强行插入观点 → 断言 例 One argument against my contention *asserts* that, by nature, textbooks are culturally biased. 派 self-assertion（*n.* 自作主张；专断）
assertion [əˈsɜːrʃn]	*n.* 宣布（declaration）；断言，主张（affirmation） 记 来自 assert（*v.* 声明；坚持） 例 Such an *assertion* ignores critical differences between seventeenth-century England and New England.
assess [əˈses]	*v.* 估计（to determine the importance, size, or value of）；评价（to evaluate） 例 Differences among the habitats of Lepidoptera species make it difficult to *assess* the effects of weather on them. 派 assessment（*n.* 确定，评定）
asset [ˈæset]	*n.* 资产，财产（resource） 例 intangible *assets* 无形资产 // physical *assets* 有形资产 // fixed *assets* 固定资产
assign [əˈsaɪn]	*v.*（to 指派（to appoint as a task）；分配；归于（to ascribe） 记 词根记忆：as + sign（签名，做记号）→ 记下某人做某事 → 指派 例 The most effective way for managers to *assign* work is to divide complex tasks into their simpler component parts. // the role *assigned* by society // Under Mr. Harel's system, each business must *assign* a value to each job. 派 assignment（*n.* 任务；分配）

03

assist [əˈsɪst]	n. 帮助(an act of assistance)；v. 参加，出席(to be present as a spectator)；帮助，促进(to give support or aid) 记 联想记忆：as + sist(站立) → 站在你这边 → 帮助 例 They were rarely allowed to *assist* master tailors in the production of men's clothing. 派 assistance(n. 援助，帮助)
associate	[əˈsəʊʃiət] a. 联合的(joined)；n. 合伙人(partner；colleague) [əˈsəʊʃieɪt] v. 将人或事物联系起来(to join people or things together) 记 联想记忆：as(加强) + soci(看作 social 社会的，交际的) + ate(做) → 进行社交(的人) → 合伙人 例 Most customers *associate* shopping carts with low-quality discount stores. 派 association(n. 协会，联盟；联合) 同根词：dissociate(v. 分离；使分裂)
association [əˌsəʊʃiˈeɪʃn]	n. 协会，联盟(an organization of persons having a common interest)；联想(something linked in memory or imagination with a thing or person) 记 来自 associate(v. 结交；联合) 例 They made a transition from old patterns of an *association* to new ones. 派 associational(a. 联想的；协会的) 同根词：dissociation(n. 分解；分离)
assume [əˈsuːm]	v. 假定，假设(to suppose)；担任…的职位(to undertake the duties of) 记 词根记忆：as + sume(拿，取) → 担任 例 It is widely *assumed* that a museum is helped financially when a generous patron donates a potential exhibit. 派 assumption(n. 假定，假设)
assumption [əˈsʌmpʃn]	n. 假定，设想(an assuming that something is true)；担任(a taking to or upon oneself) 记 来自 assume(v. 假定，设想) 例 This claim contradicts the basic *assumption* of organization theory. 同根词：presume(v. 假定)
asteroid [ˈæstərɔɪd]	n. 小行星(a small planet) 记 词根记忆：aster(星星) + oid(像…一样) → 小行星 例 Scientists calculated that the *asteroid*, traveling at 46,000 miles an hour, is on an elliptical path. 派 asteroidal(a. 星状的)
asthma [ˈæzmə]	n. 哮喘(chronic chest illness causing difficulty in breathing) 例 *Asthma*, a bronchial condition, is a much less common aliment than hay fever.

astronomical
[ˌæstrəˈnɑːmɪkl]

a. 庞大的(enormously or inconceivably large or great);天文学的(of astronomy)

记 词根记忆:astro(星星).+ nomical → 星星的,星体的 → 天文学的

例 It seems likely that a number of *astronomical* phenomena, such as the formation of planetary nebulas, may be caused by the interaction where two stars orbit each other at close range.

同根词:astronaut(*n.* 宇航员)

astronomy
[əˈstrɑːnəmi]

n. 天文学(scientific study of the sun, moon, stars, planets, etc.)

记 词根记忆:astro(星,天体)+ nomy(学科)→ 天文学

派 astronomical(*a.* 天文学的)

同根词:astronaut(*n.* 宇航员);astrophysics(*n.* 天体物理学)

atmosphere
[ˈætməsfɪr]

n. 大气(the whole mass of air surrounding the earth);气氛(a surrounding influence or environment)

记 词根记忆:atmo(大气)+sphere(球体)→ 围绕地球的空气 → 大气

例 Scientists are discussing ways to remove excess carbon dioxide from the *atmosphere* by increasing the amount that is absorbed by plant life.

派 atmospheric(*a.* 大气的,大气层的)

attain
[əˈteɪn]

v. 达到,完成(to achieve);获得(to gain)

记 词根记忆:at + tain(拿住)→ 稳稳拿住 → 获得

例 Many European breeds of cattle *attain* average milk production levels exceeding 2,700 liters.

派 attainment(*n.* 成就;到达)

attempt
[əˈtempt]

n. 企图,尝试(the act or an instance of attempting);*v.* 试图,尝试(to make an effort to do, accomplish, solve)

记 词根记忆:at(加强)+ tempt(尝试)→ 尝试,试图

例 Firms will begin to cross national borders in an *attempt* to gain a competitive advantage.

同根词:temptation(*n.* 引诱;诱惑物)

attendance
[əˈtendəns]

n. 出席,到场(the act or fact of attending);出席人数(the persons or number of persons attending)

记 来自attend(*v.* 出席;照料)

例 Total *attendance* at Moviemania's movie theaters was more than 20 percent higher last year than the year before.

同根词:attendant(*n.* 服务员;*a.* 伴随的)

attendee
[ˌætenˈdiː]

n. 出席者,在场者(a person who is present on a given occasion or at a given place)

记 来自attend(*v.* 参加,出席)

例 *attendee* party 与会者晚会

同根词:attendant(*n.* 服务员;*a.* 伴随的)

attorney
[əˈtɜːrni]

n. 律师(lawyer)

记 词根记忆:at + torn(转)+ ey → 扭转乾坤的人 → 律师

例 white-collar professionals such as *attorneys*

同根词:tornado(*n.* 龙卷风)

attraction [əˈtrækʃn]	*n.* 吸引，吸引力(the act, process, or power of attracting) 记 来自 attract(*v.* 吸引) 例 It is the recognizable increase in sales that is their main *attraction* to management. 同根词: distraction(*n.* 注意力分散)
attributable [əˈtrɪbjətəbl]	*a.* 可归于的(capable of being attributed) 记 来自 attribute(*n.* 属性，特质; *v.* 归属) 例 Such improvements would be *attributable* primarily to companies' facing global competitive pressure. 同根词: distribute(*v.* 分配; 散布)
attribute	[ˈætrɪbjuːt] *n.* 属性，品质(quality) [əˈtrɪbjuːt] *v.* 把…归于(to ascribe) 记 词根记忆: at + tribute(给，献) → 给予，献给 → 归于 例 In part, this stress can be *attributed* to the overlords' failure to adjust to a rapidly expanding economy. 派 attributable(*a.* 可归于…的)
attrition [əˈtrɪʃn]	*n.* 磨损(the act of wearing or grinding down by friction); 人员耗损(a reduction in numbers usually as a result of resignation, retirement, or death) 记 词根记忆: at + trit(磨擦) + ion → 磨损 例 The labor agreement permits staff reductions through *attrition*. 同根词: contrition(*n.* 悔恨)
auction [ˈɔːkʃn]	*n.* 拍卖(a sale of property to the highest bidder) 记 词根记忆: auct(=aug 提高) + ion → 提高价格 → 拍卖 例 This was the second highest price ever paid for a painting at *auction*. 同根词: augment(*v./n.* 增大)
audiophile [ˈɔːdioʊfaɪl]	*n.* 唱片爱好者; 爱玩高级音响的人(a person who is enthusiastic about high-fidelity sound reproduction) 记 词根记忆: audio(声音的) + phile(爱好) → 爱玩声音 → 唱片爱好者 例 Many *audiophiles* and audio professionals think the warmer, richer tones produced by vacuum-tube-driven amplifiers make them preferable.
audit [ˈɔːdɪt]	*n.* 审计(a formal examination of an organization's or individual's accounts or financial situation) 记 词根记忆: aud(听) + it → 听…报告 → 审计 例 Recent *audits* revealed that Banque Card has erred in calculating the interest it charges its clients. 同根词: auditor(*n.* 审计员); auditorium(*n.* 观众席; 礼堂)

□ attraction   □ attributable   □ attribute   □ attrition   □ auction   □ audiophile
□ audit

auditorium [ˌɔːdɪˈtɔːriəm]	*n.* 礼堂(a room, hall, or building used for public gatherings)；观众席(the part of a public building where an audience sits) 记 分拆记忆：auditor(听者) + ium(地点) → 听者的地点 → 礼堂 例 Reno praised Lee in her address to the packed *auditorium* of civil rights lawyers.
aura [ˈɔːrə]	*n.* (人或物发出的)气味，香味(distinctive atmosphere caused by a person or thing) 例 Continued sales depend directly on the maintenance of an *aura* of exclusivity of the premium coffee.

Ordinary people merely think how they shall spend their time; a man of talent tries to use it.

普通人只想到如何度过时间，有才能的人设法利用时间。

——德国哲学家 叔本华(Arthur Schopenhauer, German philosopher)

Word List 4

音频

aurora [ɔːˈrɔːrə]	*n.* 极光(bands of coloured light seen in the sky at night near the North Pole and caused by electrical radiation) 记 注意: aurore(*a.* 朝霞色的) 例 Displays of the *aurora* borealis(北极光)can heat the atmosphere over the arctic.
austere [ɔːˈstɪr]	*a.* 严格的, 节制的(strict or severe in discipline) 记 词根记忆: au + ster(冷) + e → 冷面孔 → 严格的 例 The *austere* professor never smiled. // The *austere* budgets have caused the slowdown in the growth in state spending. 派 austerity(*n.* 严格; 国家开支上的紧缩)
authentic [ɔːˈθentɪk]	*a.* 真正的(genuine; real); 法律证实的(legally attested) 记 词根记忆: authent(=author 作家) + ic → 自己就是作家 → 真正的 例 Although many art patrons can readily differentiate a good debenture from an undesirable one, they are much less expert in distinguishing good paintings and poor ones, or *authentic* art and fakes. 派 authentically(*ad.* 真正地; 确实地)
authenticate [ɔːˈθentɪkeɪt]	*v.* 证明…是真的(to confirm) 记 来自 authentic(*a.* 真的; 真正的) 例 We *authenticate* the coins we sell through a nationally recognized firm. 派 authentication(*n.* 证明, 鉴定)
authoritative [əˈθɔːrəteɪtɪv]	*a.* 权威的, 官方的(having or proceeding from authority); 专断的(dictatorial) 记 来自 authority(*n.* 权威) 例 *Authoritative* parents are more likely than permissive parents to have children who as adolescents are self-confident, high in self-esteem, and responsibly independent. 派 authoritatively(*ad.* 权威地; 命令式地)
authority [əˈθɔːrəti]	*n.* 权力(power); [*pl.*]当局, 权威(person or group having the power) 记 词根记忆: author(权力) + ity → 权力 例 The best strategy for managing a business, or any enterprise, is to give them as much *authority* as possible. 同根词: authoritarian(*a.* 独裁的); authoritative(*a.* 有权威的, 命令的)

authorize [ˈɔːθəraɪz]	v. 授权(to grant authority or power to); 批准, 认可(to ratify) 记 词根记忆: author(权力) + ize → 把权力下放 → 授权; 批准 例 *authorize* a loan 批准贷款 派 authorized(a. 经授权的)
autobiography [ˌɔːtəbaɪˈɑːgrəfi]	n. 自传(story of a person's life written by that person) 记 词根记忆: auto(自己) + bio(生命) + graphy(写) → 写自己的一生 → 自传 例 Current feminist theory, has encouraged scholars of women's history to view the use of women's oral narratives as the methodology, next to the use of women's written *autobiography*.
automate [ˈɔːtəmeɪt]	v. (使)自动化(to convert to largely automatic operation) 记 词根记忆: auto(自己) + mat(动) + e → 自己动 → 自动化 例 Many corporations that have failed to *automate* have seen their profits decline. 派 automatic(a. 自动的; 机械的); automation(n. 自动化)
automatic [ˌɔːtəˈmætɪk]	a. 自动的(having a self-acting or self-regulating mechanism); 无意识的(largely or wholly involuntary) 记 词根记忆: auto(自己) + mat(动) + ic(…的) → 自动的 例 Airline executives are convinced that, just as one-third of bank customers still prefer human tellers to *automatic* teller machines, many travelers will still use travel agents. 派 automatically(ad. 自动地; 机械地) 同根词: autonomy(n. 自治; 自治权)
automation [ˌɔːtəˈmeɪʃn]	n. 自动装置(mechanism that imitates actions of humans) 记 词根记忆: auto(自己) + mat(动) + ion → 自动 → 自动装置 例 Many workers who lose their jobs to *automation* will need government assistance to survive. 同根词: autoalarm(n.自动报警器)
automobile [ˈɔːtəməbiːl]	n. 汽车(a usually four-wheeled automotive vehicle) 记 词根记忆: auto(自己) + mobile(可移动的) → 可以自己移动的 → 汽车 例 The *automobile* industry dominated the American economy in the 1920's. 同根词: automatic(a. 自动的)
autonomy [ɔːˈtɑːnəmi]	n. 自治(self-government with respect to local or internal affairs); 自主(权)(the right of self-government) 记 词根记忆: auto(自己) + nomy(名字) → 给命运写上自己的名字 → 自主 例 women's *autonomy* 派 autonomous(a. 自主的; 自治的)
availability [əˌveɪləˈbɪləti]	n. 可用性(quality or state of being available) 记 来自 available(a. 可用的) 例 The ample *availability* of land makes security of land tenure unimportant.

□ authorize   □ autobiography   □ automate   □ automatic   □ automation   □ automobile
□ autonomy   □ availability

avalanche [ˈævəlæntʃ]	*n.* 雪崩(a large mass of snow, ice, earth, rock, or other material in swift motion down a mountainside or over a precipice); *v.* 雪崩(to descend in an avalanche) 例 Over the same period, however, the number of visitors to ski resorts who were caught in *avalanches* decreased, even though there was no reduction in the annual number of *avalanches* in the Sordellian Mountains.
aversion [əˈvɜːrʒn]	*n.* 厌恶, 反感(antipathy) 记 联想记忆: a + vers(转) + ion → 转开 → 厌恶 例 Their *aversion* to government paperwork made them reluctant to pursue many government contracts. 同根词: adverse(*a.* 不利的)
avian [ˈeɪviən]	*n.* 鸟; *ε.* 鸟类的(of, relating to, or derived from birds) 记 词根记忆: avi(鸟) + an → 鸟; 鸟类的 例 These results confirmed that *avian* species can develop preferences for palatable food through social learning. 同根词: aviator(*n.* 飞行员)
aviation [ˌeɪviˈeɪʃn]	*n.* 航空(术)(the operation of heavier-than-air aircraft); 飞机制造业(airplane manufacture) 记 词根记忆: avi(鸟) + ation(表名词) → 像鸟一样飞 → 航空 例 *Aviation* fuel is projected to decline in price over the next several years. 同根词: aviary(*n.* 鸟舍, 鸟笼)
aviator [ˈeɪvieɪtər]	*n.* 飞行家, 飞行员(the pilot of an aircraft) 记 来自 aviate(*v.* 飞行) 例 All trainees in a certain *aviator* training program must take both a written test and a flight test. 同根词: aviation(*n.* 航空)
avidly [ˈævɪdli]	*ad.* 渴望地, 热心地(eagerly) 例 The more rare something becomes, the more *avidly* it is sought by collectors.
avoid [əˈvɔɪd]	*v.* 避开, 躲避(to keep oneself away from) 例 Having learned of an upcoming environmental ban on a certain chemical, a company designs its new plant to employ processes that *avoid* use of that chemical. 派 avoidance(*n.* 逃避; 空缺) 同根词: devoid(*a.* 缺乏的)
backwater [ˈbækwɔːtər]	*n.* 回水(water backed up in its course); 死水(a body of water that is out of the main current of a larger body) 例 The Emerald River annually overflowed its banks, creating *backwaters*.

□ avalanche □ aversion □ avian □ aviation □ aviator □ avidly
□ avoid □ backwater

bacterium [bæk'tɪriəm]	*n.* [*pl.* bacteria] 细菌(simplest and smallest forms of plant life, microscopic organisms that are often a cause of disease) 记 联想记忆：bac(看作 back 背后) + ter + ium → 总是偷偷(背后)让人得病的东西 → 细菌 例 Scientists hypothesize that in high salt environments the antibiotic becomes ineffective at killing harmful *bacteria*. 派 bacterial(*a.* 细菌的；由细菌引起的)
balcony ['bælkəni]	*n.* 阳台(veranda)；包厢，楼座(loge) 记 发音记忆："包给你" → 把整个包厢都"包给你" 例 This theater has 100 *balcony* seats.
ballistic [bə'lɪstɪk]	*a.* 弹道的，发射的(of things that are shot or fired through the air, eg. bullets, missles, etc.) 记 联想记忆：ball(子弹) + istic → 发射子弹的 → 弹道的 例 *ballistic* missiles 弹道导弹
bankruptcy ['bæŋkrʌptsi]	*n.* 破产，倒闭(the quality or state of being bankrupt) 记 词根记忆：bank(银行) + rupt(断) + cy → 银行都关门了 → 破产 例 The automobile company was brought back from the verge of *bankruptcy*. 同根词：corruption(*n.* 腐败)
bar [bɑːr]	*v.* (from) 禁止，阻止(to prevent, forbid)；*n.* 棒；酒吧(a place where drinks are served) 例 The purpose of the legislation is to *bar* companies from financing their own unions. // candy *bar* 棒棒糖
barb [bɑːrb]	*n.* 倒钩(a sharp projection extending backward)；伤人的话(a biting or pointedly critical remark or comment)；*v.* 装倒钩于(to furnish with a barb) 例 The honeybee's stinger is heavily *barbed* and stays where it is inserted.
bark [bɑːrk]	*n.* 树皮(无复数)(tough outer covering of tree trunks and branches) 记 注意：bark 还有一些动词意思是"狗吠；咆哮；剥树皮"
barracks ['bærəks]	*n.* 兵营(large buildings for soldiers to live in) 例 Nightingale was the first to notice the poor living conditions in British military *barracks* in peacetime.
barrel ['bærəl]	*n.* 桶(cask)；*v.* 把…装桶(to put or pack sth. in a barrel) 记 联想记忆：bar(栅栏，障碍) + rel → 横木围住的桶 例 World consumption of oil is currently 26 billion *barrels* a year.
barren ['bærən]	*a.* 贫瘠的(not productive)；(of) 没有的，缺乏的(devoid, lacking) 记 词根记忆：bar(栅栏，障碍) + ren → 阻碍发展 → 没有的，缺乏的 例 No doubt castle and cathedral building was not totally *barren* of profit.
barrier ['bæriər]	*n.* 栅栏(fence)；障碍，壁垒(obstacle) 记 词根记忆：bar(栅栏，障碍) + rier → 栅栏，障碍 例 trade *barriers* 贸易壁垒

04

batch [bætʃ]	*n.* 一批 (a quantity (as of persons or things) considered as a group); *v.* 分批处理 (to bring together or process as a batch) 记 联想记忆：bat(蝙蝠) + ch → 蝙蝠都是成群生活 → 一批 例 Some *batches* of polio vaccine used around 1960 were contaminated with SV40, a virus that in monkeys causes various cancers. 派 batcher(*n.* 混凝土材料计量器)
battalion [bəˈtæliən]	*n.* 军营，军队 (army) 记 词根记忆：bat(战斗) + talion → 用于战斗的 → 军队 例 The army policies kept most Black units working in labor *battalions*. 同根词：battle(*n.* 战争)
bead [biːd]	*n.* 小珠子 (a small piece of material pierced for threading on a string or wire); (水、血、汗的)小滴 (drop of liquid) 例 The *beads* are DNA segments wrapped around the histones.
beam [biːm]	*v.* 堆满笑容 (to smile with joy); *n.* (光线等的)束，柱 (ray or stream of light or other radiation) 记 联想记忆：be + am → 做我自己，成为国家的栋梁 → 柱 例 In each 30-second period, the *beam* sweeps through 3.690°.
bearer [ˈberər]	*n.* 搬运工 (porter); 生育者 (one who breeds) 记 来自bear(*v.* 负荷；运载) 例 child *bearer* 孕妇
beckon [ˈbekən]	*v.* 召唤 (to summon); 吸引，引诱 (to attract) 例 Employers showed surprisingly little interest in changing that perception, even when higher profits *beckoned*.
beehive [ˈbiːhaɪv]	*n.* 蜂窝，蜂箱 (a hive for bees) 记 分拆记忆：bee(蜜蜂) + hive(蜂房，蜂箱) → 蜂窝，蜂箱 例 A *beehive's* honeycomb cannot have some sections that contain toxic honey and other sections that contain nontoxic honey.
behavioral [bɪˈheɪvjərəl]	*a.* 行为的 (of or relating to behavior) 记 来自behavior(*n.* 行为举止) 例 Geneticists consider the gene to be a *behavioral* gene. 派 behaviourism(*n.* 行为主义)
bellows [ˈbeloʊz]	*n.* 风箱 (apparatus for driving air into or through sth.) 记 和bellow(*v.* 吼叫)一起记
benchmark [ˈbentʃmɑːrk]	*n.* 基准 (something that serves as a standard by which others may be measured or judged); *v.* 标准测试 (to study, as a competitor's product or business practices, in order to improve the performance of one's own company) 记 联想记忆：bench(法官席，引申为法律) + mark(记号) → 将法律作为我们的基准 例 The technique to judge the performance of a company by comparing it with other companies is called "*benchmarking*".

benefactor [ˈbenɪfæktər]	*n.* 行善者，捐助者(one that confers a benefit) 记 词根记忆：bene(好) + fact(做) + or → 做好事的人 → 行善者 例 Since private institutions had also lost *benefactors*, they began to charge patients. 同根词：benevolent(*a.* 慈善的)
beneficiary [ˌbeni ˈfɪʃieri]	*n.* 受益人，受惠者(one that benefits from sth.) 记 来自 benefit(*n.* 利益) 例 Moreover, part of this remaining third is received by workers who are shareholders, pension *beneficiaries*, and the like. 同根词：beneficial(*a.* 受益的，有利的)
benefit [ˈbenɪfɪt]	*n.* 利益，好处(sth. that promotes well-being)；救济金(financial help in time of sickness, old age, or unemployment)；*v.* 有益于，对…有益(to be useful or profitable to) 记 词根记忆：bene(好) + fit → 利益；有助于 例 There are no types of vegetation on Tufe Island that are known to *benefit* from dry conditions. 派 beneficial(*a.* 有益的；有利的)
benevolence [bə ˈnevələns]	*n.* 仁慈；善行(an act of kindness) 记 词根记忆：bene(好) + vol(意志) + ence → 好的意志 → 仁慈 例 The cult of female domesticity developed independently of the concept of female *benevolence*. 同根词：benevolent(*a.* 善心的)
bestow [bɪ ˈstou]	*v.* 放置(to put in a particular place)；授予(to give) 记 词根记忆：be + stow (装载，收藏) → 收藏起来 → 放置 例 The committee *bestowed* an engraved plaque on the contest winner.
betrayal [bɪ ˈtreɪəl]	*n.* 背叛(defection) 记 来自 betray(*v.* 背叛) 例 In broadcast debates, critics dismissed the program as a *betrayal* of national identity.
better-off [ˈbetər ˈɔːf]	*a.* 境况较好或较富裕(be happier or richer) 例 Many of them are no *better-off* financially than they were before the increase in production.
beverage [ˈbevərɪdʒ]	*n.* 饮料(any type of drink except water) 记 词根记忆：bever(喝) + age → 喝的东西 → 饮料 例 food and *beverages* 食品和饮料
bias [ˈbaɪəs]	*n.* 偏见(prejudice)；偏心(preference)；*v.* 使有偏见(to give a settled and often prejudiced outlook to) 记 词根记忆：bi(两) + as → 两者只取其一 → 偏见 例 A political *bias* was evident in the newspaper article. 派 biased(*a.* 结果有偏倚的)

bicker [ˈbɪkər]	*v.*争吵，争论 (to quarrel) 记 联想记忆：bick(看作 brick 砖头) + er → 互相扔砖头 → 争吵 例 The services *bickered* unceasingly over their respective roles and missions.
bid [bɪd]	*n.*出价，投标 (an offer of a price)；投标的价格 (the price offered) 例 They revise their procedure for making *bids* for federal contracts and subcontracts. // They lost the contract because their *bid* was too high. 派 bidder(*n.* 投标人)
bifurcation [ˌbaɪfərˈkeɪʃn]	*n.*分歧 (difference) 例 The Geminid data between 1970 and 1979 show just such a *bifurcation*.
bilateral [ˌbaɪˈlætərəl]	*a.*双边的 (affecting two nations or parties) 记 词根记忆：bi(两) + later(边的) + al → 双边的 例 The *bilateral* talks between Russia and the U.S. produced an important agreement.
billing [ˈbɪlɪŋ]	*n.*营业额 (total amount of business within a given period)；广告 (advertising) 例 *billing* cycle 结账周期
bind [baɪnd]	*v.*捆绑 (to tie or to fasten)；结合 (to combine or be taken up especially by chemical action)；约束 (to restrain as if with bonds) 记 发音记忆："绑的" → 绑着的东西是受约束的 → 约束 例 Western women were free from the constraints *binding* their eastern sisters.
biodegradable [ˌbaɪoʊdɪˈgreɪdəbl]	*a.*可由生物降解的 (can be made to rot by bacteria) 记 词根记忆：bio(生物) + degradable(能降解的) → 可由生物降解的 例 Since most paper is entirely *biodegradable*, paper goods are environmentally preferable.
bioengineer [ˌbaɪoʊˌendʒɪˈnɪr]	*v.*生物工程制成 (to modify or produce by bioengineering)；*n.*生物工程师 记 词根记忆：bio(生物) + engineer(工程师) → 生物工程师 例 Plantings of cotton *bioengineered* to produce its own insecticide against bollworms, a major cause of crop failure, sustained little bollworm damage until this year.
biography [baɪˈɑːgrəfi]	*n.*传记 (a usually written history of a person's life) 记 词根记忆：bio(生命) + graph(写) + y → 记录生命 → 传记 例 There was a *biography* of each musician in the concert program. 派 autobiography(*n.* 自传)
biomedical [ˌbaɪoʊˈmedɪkl]	*a.*生物医学的 (of, relating to, or involving biological, medical, and physical science) 记 词根记忆：bio(生物) + medical(医学的) → 生物医学的 例 Junior *biomedical* researchers have long assumed that their hirings and promotions depend significantly on the amount of their published work.

biophysicist [ˌbaɪoʊ ˈfɪzɪsɪst]	*n.* 生物物理学家（a person who is specialized in biophysics） 记 词根记忆：bio（生物）+ physicist（物理学家）→ 生物物理学家 例 There is a striking similarity that *biophysicists* have discovered between algae and cows.
biosphere [ˈbaɪousfɪr]	*n.* 生物圈（the part of the world in which life can exist） 记 词根记忆：bio（生物）+ sphere（球，圈）→ 生物圈 例 This ecosystem is one of the fascinating paradoxes of the *biosphere*. 同根词：atmosphere（*n.* 大气层）；hemisphere（*n.* 半球）
bisect [baɪ ˈsekt]	*v.* 平分（to divide into two equal parts） 记 词根记忆：bi（两）+ sect（切，割）→ 分成两份 → 平分 例 The partition *bisected* the room into two smaller rooms. 派 bisector（*n.* 平分线）
bizarre [bɪ ˈzɑːr]	*a.* 奇异的，古怪的（very strange, eccentric） 记 联想记忆：集市上（bazaar）有各种古怪的（bizarre）东西 例 A *bizarre* series of events preceded the murder.
blackout [ˈblækaʊt]	*n.* 无线电通讯中断，信号消失（a usually temporary loss of a radio signal） 记 来自词组 black out（熄灯；停电） 例 Electric currents can cause *blackouts* in some areas.
bland [blænd]	*a.* （指人）温和的（characterized by a moderate quality）；乏味的（dull） 记 注意：blend（*n.* 混合物） 例 Michael was listening to a *bland* doctor.
blast [blæst]	*n.* 爆炸（an explosion） 记 和 gust（*n.* 阵风，一阵狂风）一起记 例 nuclear *blast* 核爆炸
bloc [blɑːk]	*n.* 集团，组织（a temporary combination of parties） 例 trading *blocs* 贸易组织
block [blɑːk]	*v.* 阻碍（hinder）；堵塞（obstruct）；*n.* 街区（street） 例 No country should *block* any of its markets to foreign trade. // We know all the neighbors on our *block*. 派 blockade（*n./v.* 封锁）；blockage（*n.* 封锁，妨碍）
blot [blɑːt]	*n.* 墨迹，污迹（spot）；*v.* 模糊，遮暗（to make obscure） 例 It sends up a global pall of dust that *blots* out the Sun. 派 blotter（*n.* 吸墨纸）
bluegrass [ˈbluːɡræs]	*n.* 蓝草音乐（from the Blue Grass Boys, performing group）；莓系属的牧草，早熟禾属植物（any of several grasses of which some have bluish-green culms） 记 联想记忆：blue（蓝色）+ grass（草）→ 有蓝色草的地方的音乐风格 → 蓝草音乐 例 Bluegrass musician Bill Monroe's repertory, views on musical collaboration, and vocal style were influential on generations of *bluegrass* artists.

bluntly [ˈblʌntli]	*ad.* 坦率地，率直地(directly) 记 来自 blunt(*a.* 坦诚的，直率的) 例 Many *bluntly* admitted that they thought *Jane Eyre* was a masterpiece.
boarder [ˈbɔːrdər]	*n.* 寄膳者；寄宿生(one that is provided with regular meals and lodging) 记 来自 board(*n.* 膳食；*v.* 寄宿) 例 Foul play was suspected but never confirmed in the death of the *boarder* in 1985.
boardinghouse [ˈbɔːrdɪŋˌhaʊs]	*n.* 寄宿公寓(house providing meals and accomodation) 例 *Boardinghouses* were built to accommodate the Issei.

A man is not old as long as he is seeking something. A man is not old until regrets take the place of dreams.

只要一个人还有所追求，他就没有老。直到后悔取代了梦想，一个人才算老。

——美国演员 巴里穆尔(J. Barrymore, American actor)

音频

bold [boʊld]	*a.* 勇敢的，大胆的（showing a fearless daring spirit） 記 联想记忆：b + old（年长）→ 年长的人通常比较胆大→勇敢的，大胆的 例 In 1928 he took the *bold* step of threatening a strike against Pullman. 派 boldface(*n.* 黑体字)
bolster [ˈboʊlstər]	*v.* 支持（to support），鼓励（to give a boost to） 例 The proposed legislation failed to *bolster* workplace safety regulations.
bolt [boʊlt]	*n.* 螺栓（metal pin with a head at one end, and a thread），雷电（a lightning stroke, thunderbolt） 記 联想记忆：大胆（bold）不怕雷电（bolt）劈 例 a lightning *bolt* 闪电，霹雳 // All of the fasteners, such as *bolts* and screws have for several years been supplied by Brindon Bolt Barn.
bombard [bɑːmˈbɑːrd]	*v.* 炮轰，射击（to attack especially with artillery or bombers），*n.* 射石炮（a late medieval cannon used to hurl large stones） 記 词根记忆：bomb（轰炸）+ ard → 炮轰 例 A team of scientists has recently provided evidence of Earth being *bombarded* daily with as many as 40,000 small comets, which vaporize in the upper atmosphere and fall to Earth as rain. 派 bombardment(*n.* 轰炸，炮击)
bona fide [ˌboʊnə ˈfaɪd]	*a.* 可信的（authentic），真诚的，真实的（genuine） 例 the *bona fide* bills 正当票据
bond [bɑːnd]	*n.* 结合（a uniting force or tie a link），债券（certificate issued by a government or a company acknowledging that money has been lent to it and will be paid back with interest），*v.* （使）结合（to cause to adhere firmly） 記 发音记忆："绑得" → 绑在一起 → 结合 例 Customer loyalty programs are attempts to *bond* customers to a company and its products and services. 派 bonded(*a.* 束缚的，结合的)；bondage(*n.* 束缚)
bonus [ˈboʊnəs]	*n.* 奖金，红利（dividend） 記 联想记忆：bon（好的）+ us（我们）→ 发奖金啦，我们都说好！→ 奖金 例 A union contract specifies a 6 percent salary increase plus a $450 *bonus* for each employee.

boom
[buːm]
v. 迅速发展(to grow rapidly in economy); 兴旺(flourish); n. 繁荣(vigorous growth)
例 Enrollment figures *boom* during these periods. // The current economic *boom* ends and consumers can no longer buy major luxury items.

boomerang
[ˈbuːməræŋ]
n. 回飞棒(a bent or angular throwing club designed to return near the thrower); 自食其果的言行(an act or utterance that backfires on its originator)
例 *boomerang* effects 回旋效果

boost
[buːst]
v./n. 推，举(to lift); 促进(to promote); 吹捧(to praise)
例 The jet engine could help *boost* cargoes into space at significantly low costs. // Citizens want the government to take action to *boost* the economy.

booth
[buːθ]
n. (隔开的)小房间(a small enclosure that isolates its occupant)
记 和 tooth(n. 牙齿)一起记
例 voting *booth* 投票站

boreal
[ˈbɔrɪəl]
a. 北方的(of, relating to, or located in northern regions)
例 *Boreal* owls range over larger areas in regions where food of the sort eaten by small animals is sparse than in regions where such food is abundant.

bounce
[baʊns]
v. (使)弹起，(使)反弹(to rebound); n. (球)弹起(a sudden leap or bound)
记 联想记忆：又跳(bound)又弹(bounce)
例 The basketball *bounced* off the backboard and missed the basket. // After the third *bounce* the ball was caught.

bound
[baʊnd]
v. 包围，限制(to constitute the boundary or limit of); a. (to)必定的(sure, certain); (up with)密切关联的(closely connected)
例 The triangular flower bed is *bounded* by three driveways. // Retail sales in Aroca City are *bound* to increase substantially. // My fate was *bound* up with hers.
派 boundary(n. 边界)

bounty
[ˈbaʊnti]
n. 奖金，赏金(reward)
记 词根记忆：bount(=bon 好) + y → 表现好 → 奖金，赏金
例 By the 1930's, *bounty* hunters had exterminated most of the gray wolves in the United States.
派 bountiful(a. 丰裕的，充足的)

bourgeois
[ˌbʊrˈʒwaː]
n. 资本家(burgher); 中产阶级的人(a middle-class person)
例 "*Bourgeois*" feminism, so called by its more radical opponents, emphasized "individualist" feminist goals such as access to education, career opportunities, and legal equality.
派 bourgeoisify(v. 使中产阶级化；使资产阶级化)

bower ['bauər]	*n.* 凉亭；树荫（a shady, leafy shelter in a garden or wood） 例 Young male bowerbirds are inept at bowerbuilding and apparently spend years watching their elders before becoming accomplished in the local *bower* style. 派 bowery(*a.* 有亭子的；有树荫的)
boycott ['bɔɪkɑːt]	*v./n.* 联合抵制（usu. of a group of people, refuse to deal or trade with a person or a country） 记 联想记忆：boy + cott（音似：cut 剃）→ 男孩子们剃头以示抗议 → 抵制 例 The union leaders are considering as their principal new tactic a consumer *boycott* against Gasco gas stations.
brace [breɪs]	*n.* 支柱，支撑（something that connects or fastens）；*v.* 准备（to prepare） 例 In spring St. John's residents are less likely to be sitting at outdoor cafes than to be *bracing* themselves against arctic chills.
brass [bræs]	*n.* 黄铜（bright yellow metal made by mixing copper and zinc） 例 Many clothes incorporate thick metal parts such as decorative *brass* studs(纽扣)or buttons. 派 brazen(*a.* 厚颜无耻的)
brew [bruː]	*v.* 酿造（to make by mixing, boiling and fermenting malt, hops and water）；冲泡(茶、咖啡等)（to prepare by infusion in hot water） 记 联想记忆：喝下自酿（brew）的苦酒，他紧皱起眉头（brow） 例 To boost sales, other small breweries should *brew* low-calorie beers as well. // Jane *brews* her tea in a special way. 派 brewery(*n.* 酿酒厂)
bring about [brɪŋ ə'baut]	使发生，导致（to cause sth. to happen） 例 Those lymphocytes(淋巴细胞)can *bring about* the death of the foreign-tissue cells.
brochure [brou'ʃur]	*n.* 小册子；说明书（booklet or pamphlet containing imformation about sth. or advertising sth. ） 记 发音记忆："不用求" → 有了小册子，就不用求别人了
broker ['broukər]	*n.* 经纪人（the person who buys and sells things for others; middleman） 例 Our stock *broker* helped us choose our investments.
brokerage ['broukəridʒ]	*n.* 经纪业，中间人业务（the business or establishment of a broker）；佣金，回扣（a broker's fee or commission） 记 来自 broker(*n.* 中间人，经纪人) 例 *brokerage* firms 经纪商
bronze [brɑːnz]	*n.* 青铜（alloy of copper and tin） 例 These ceremonial drinking vessels were made of *bronze*.
brutal ['bruːtl]	*a.* 残忍的（cruel） 例 *brutal* criminal 凶残的罪犯
bucket ['bʌkɪt]	*n.* 桶（a typically cylindrical vessel for catching, holding, or carrying liquids or solids）；一桶的量（bucketful）；*v.* 颠簸前进（to drive hurriedly or roughly） 例 a *bucket* of… 一桶的量

bucolic [bjuːˈkɑːlɪk]	*a.* 乡村的 (of country life or the countryside); 田园风味的 (idyllic) 记 词根记忆: buc(牛) + olic(养…的) → 养牛的 → 乡村的 例 Dirt roads may evoke the *bucolic* simplicity of another century.
budget [ˈbʌdʒɪt]	*n.* 预算 (a systematic plan for the expenditure of a usually fixed resource, such as money or time, during a given period) 记 联想记忆: bud(蓓蕾, 发芽) + get(得到) → 得到了发芽 → 初步计算出来了 → 预算 例 *budget* deficit 预算赤字
budworm [ˈbʌdwɜːrm]	*n.* 蚜虫 (a moth larva that feeds on the buds of plants) 记 分拆记忆: bud(芽) + worm(虫) → 蚜虫 例 The drop in the population of the spruce *budworm* is expected to be only temporary.
buffalo [ˈbʌfəloʊ]	*n.* 水牛; 北美野牛 (any of several wild bovids) 记 联想记忆: buff(软牛皮) + alo → 经常泡在水里的牛皮会软 → 水牛 例 These researchers have overlooked the economic impact of rural development projects that improve people's daily lives at the village level—such as the cooperative raising of water *buffalo*.
buffer [ˈbʌfər]	*n.* 缓冲物 (a means or device used as a cushion against the shock of fluctuations in business or financial activity) 记 来自 buff(*v.* 缓冲, 减震) 例 *buffer* stock 调节性库存储备 // *buffer* funds 缓冲基金
bulge [bʌldʒ]	*v.* 膨胀 (to swell); 凸出 (to bend outward) 例 Our stomachs *bulged* after we ate too much.
bulk [bʌlk]	*n.* 主体, 绝大部分 (main or greater part) 记 联想记忆: 公牛(bull)总是大批(bulk)地行动 例 The *bulk* of the health-care dollar is spent on the illnesses of some significance.
buoyant [ˈbuːjənt]	*a.* 有浮力的 (showing buoyancy); 快乐的 (cheerful) 例 The relative low density of the hottest rock makes that material *buoyant*. 派 buoyantly(*ad.* 心情愉悦地; 有浮力地); buoyancy(*n.* 浮力; 轻快)
burden [ˈbɜːrdn]	*n.* 负担 (load, duty, obligation); *v.* 加重压于 (to oppress) 例 tax *burden* 税负
bureau [ˈbjʊroʊ]	*n.* (政府机构的)局, 部, 处 (a specialized administrative unit) 记 法语词, 意为"办公室" 派 bureaucracy(*n.* 官僚主义; 政府机构)
burglarize [ˈbɜːrɡləˌraɪz]	*v.* 破门盗窃 (to enter a building in order to steal) 记 词根记忆: burglar(夜盗) + ize → 进行夜盗 → 破门盗窃 例 It is against the law to *burglarize* people's homes. 同根词: burglary(*n.* 入室行窃)
burrow [ˈbɜːroʊ]	*n.* 洞穴 (a hole in the ground made by an animal, such as a rabbit, for shelter and habitation); *v.* 挖洞 (make sth. by digging) 例 These rats stay in *burrows* during the hot part of the day.

□ bucolic □ budget □ budworm □ buffalo □ buffer □ bulge
□ bulk □ buoyant □ burden □ bureau □ burglarize □ burrow

butterfly [ˈbʌtərflaɪ]	*n.* 蝴蝶(an insect with large colourful wings and a thin body); 追求享乐的人(a person chiefly occupied with the pursuit of pleasure) 記 联想记忆: butter(黄油) + fly(飞) → 颜色像黄油一样会飞的东西 → 蝴蝶 例 The blue *butterfly's* survival was indirectly dependent on sustaining a rabbit population of a particular size.
buttress [ˈbʌtrəs]	*n.* 扶壁(a projecting structure of masonry or wood for supporting or giving stability to a wall or building); *v.* 支持(support) 例 This pragmatic approach is *buttressed* by Arizona and California.
bygone [ˈbaɪɡɔːn]	*n.* 过去的事(past things); *a.* 以前的(past); 过时的(outmoded) 例 All things antique have grown a market for *bygone* styles of furniture and fixtures.
bylaw [ˈbaɪˌlɔ]	*n.* 地方法规(a local ordinance); 规章制度(rule) 例 The proposal to amend the *bylaws* of an organization was circulated to its members.
cabin [ˈkæbɪn]	*n.* (船、机)舱(small room or compartment on a ship or an aircraft) 記 联想记忆: cab(出租车) + in(在里面) → 出租车一般小的屋子 → 船舱
cabinet [ˈkæbɪnət]	*n.* 贮藏橱,陈列柜(piece of furniture with drawers or shelves for storing or displaying things)
caffeine [kæˈfiːn]	*n.* 咖啡因(stimulant drug found in tea leaves and coffee beans) 例 The candy company adds *caffeine* to the chocolate candy bars.
calamitous [kəˈlæmɪtəs]	*a.* 灾难的,悲惨的(being, causing, or accompanied by calamity) 記 来自 calamity(*n.* 灾难) 例 Growing evidence that coastal erosion occurs continuously, not just in *calamitous* bursts such as hurricanes, has led scientists and planners to urge a stringent new approach to limiting development along the nation's shoreline.
calcium [ˈkælsiəm]	*n.* 钙(a silver-white divalent metallic element of the alkaline-earth group occurring only in combination) 記 词根记忆: calc(石头) + ium → 像石头一样硬 → 钙 例 A new study finds that the more hostility people show in their behavior and attitudes, the more likely they are to have *calcium* deposits in the arteries of their hearts.
calculate [ˈkælkjuleɪt]	*v.* 计算(to count); 估计(to figure out); 推测(to judge to be true or probable) 記 词根记忆: calcul(计算) + ate(做) → 计算;推测 例 The unemployment rates that James *calculates* appear to be modest. // Canadian scientists have *calculated* that one human being should be struck every nine years by a meteorite. 派 calculated(*a.* 有计划的;适合的)

05

calculus
['kælkjələs]

n. 结石 (a concretion usually of mineral salts around organic material found especially in hollow organs or ducts); 微积分学 (the mathematical methods comprising differential and integral calculus)

记 词根记忆：calcul(计算) + us → 微积分学

例 Newton developed mathematical concepts and techniques that are fundamental to modern *calculus*.

calefaction
[ˌkælɪ'fækʃən]

n. 加热 (heating up); 变暖作用

记 词根记忆：cale(热) + fact(做) + ion → 加热

calendar
['kælɪndər]

n. 日历 (a page or series of pages showing the days, weeks and months of a particular year, especially one that you hang on a wall); 历法；日程表 (a record of what you have to do each day)

记 联想记忆：cal(看作 call 叫) + end(结束) + ar → 一年到头对日子的叫法 → 日历

例 The North American Indians developed advanced full-year *calendars* based on systematic astronomical observation.

calf
[kæf]

n. 牛犊，幼崽 (the young of the domestic cow)

记 联想记忆：小牛(calf)是半(half)大的牛

caller
['kɔːlər]

n. 访客 (a person who goes to a house or a building); 打电话者；召集员 (one that calls)

记 来自 call(v. 呼叫；拜访)

例 They thus automatically inform the operator of the location and phone number of the *caller*.

同根词：callable(a. 随时可偿还的；请求即付的)

calligraphic
[ˌkælɪ'græfɪk]

a. 书法的，书写的 (of beautiful handwriting)

记 来自 calligraphy(n. 书法)

例 a miniature *calligraphic* composition 微型书法作品

camcorder
['kæmkɔːrdər]

n. 摄录像机 (a small portable combined camera and VCR)

记 和 recorder(n. 录音机)一起记

例 The electronics company has unveiled what it claims to be the world's smallest network digital *camcorder*.

campaign
[kæm'peɪn]

n. 战役 (series of military operations); 系列活动 (a connected series of operations designed to bring about a particular result)

记 联想记忆：打起战役(campaign)或搞起运动来都需露营(camp)

例 sales *campaign* 销售大战 // election *campaign* 竞选活动

campsite
['kæmpsaɪt]

n. 营地 (site of a camp)

记 联想记忆：camp(露营) + site(地点) → 露营的地点 → 营地

例 Another *campsite* was found in New Mexico with remains dated at 16,000 years old.

canary
[kə'neri]

n. 金丝雀 (a small yellow bird with a beautiful song, often kept in a cage as a pet); 女歌星 (female singer)

记 联想记忆：can(能够) + ary → 有能耐，能歌善舞的人 → 女歌星

例 I cleaned the bird cage and the *canary* disappeared.

candidate
[ˈkændɪdeɪt]

n. 候选人 (a person who applies for a job or is nominated for election); 投考者 (a person taking an examination)

记 联想记忆：can(能) + did(做) + ate → 能做的人 → 候选人；投考者

例 To win the election, a *candidate* needed to receive more than 50 percent of the votes.

派 candidacy(*n.* 候选资格)

cannon
[ˈkænən]

n. 加农炮，大炮 (a large heavy gun usually mounted on a carriage)

记 发音记忆

例 An ancient *cannon* sat in the middle of the town square.

canopy
[ˈkænəpi]

n. 顶棚 (hanging cover forming a shelter above a throne or bed, etc.); 树冠层 (the uppermost spreading branchy layer of a forest)

例 tree *canopy* 树冠

canyon
[ˈkænjən]

n. 峡谷 (a long, narrow valley between cliffs)

例 Those who have visited the Grand *Canyon* have typically seen layers of sediment in the gaping *canyon*.

capacity
[kəˈpæsəti]

n. 最大容量 (ability to hold or contain sth.); 最大生产量 (power to produce sth.); 能力 (aptitude, ability)

记 词根记忆：cap(拿，容纳) + acity → 最大容量

例 memory *capacity* 内存容量 // operate at full *capacity* 满负荷运转

派 incapacity(*n.* 无能力)

capitalize
[ˈkæpɪtəlaɪz]

v. 资本化 (to convert sth. into capital); 获利 (to profit); 利用 (to use sth. to one's own advantage)

记 来自 capital(*n.* 资本)

例 Seeking to *capitalize* on the books' success, they plan to produce a movie sequel based on the books.

派 capitalism(*n.* 资本主义)；capitalization(*n.* 资本化)

capsule
[ˈkæpsjuːl]

n. 胶囊 (small soluble case containing a dose of medicine and swallowed with it)

记 联想记忆：cap(帽子) + sule(看作 seal 密封) → 封在帽状物中 → 胶囊

例 Painkillers come in tablets and *capsules*. // The nematodes can lie dormant for several years in their cysts, which are protective *capsules*.

captivate
[ˈkæptɪveɪt]

v. 迷住，迷惑，吸引 (to attract)

记 词根记忆：capt(抓住) + ivate → 抓住 → 迷住

例 Most economists in the United States seem *captivated* by the spell of the free market.

captive
[ˈkæptɪv]

n. 俘虏 (one held as a prisoner)

记 词根记忆：capt(抓) + ive(…的) → 被俘虏的 → 俘虏

例 The captor also benefited financially by having his *captive* raise the ransom himself.

同根词：captivity(*n.* 监禁，束缚)；captor(*n.* 捕捉者，逮捕者)

□ candidate　　□ cannon　　□ canopy　　□ canyon　　□ capacity　　□ capitalize
□ capsule　　□ captivate　　□ captive

capture ['kæptʃər]	*v.* 捕捉(to catch); 占领(to gain control of); 吸引,赢得(to gain or win especially through effort) 记 词根记忆: capt(抓住) + ure → 捕捉; 占领 例 Pterosaurs had to fly in order to *capture* prey. // The company employed a new strategy to *capture* foreign markets. // The major party is likely to *capture* much more than half of the votes.
carbohydrate [,kɑːrbou'haɪdreɪt]	*n.* 碳水化合物, 糖类(organic compound, such as sugar and starch, containing carbon, hydrogen and oxygen) 记 词根记忆: carbo(碳) + hydr(水) + ate → 碳水化合物 例 In cold-water habitats, certain invertebrates and fish convert starches into complex *carbohydrates*.
carbonate ['kɑːrbənət]	*n.* 碳酸盐(a salt or ester of carbonic acid) 记 来自 carbon(*n.* 碳) 例 These sediments are composed of calcium *carbonate* shells of marine organisms. 同根词: carbonize(*v.* 碳化)
carcass ['kɑːrkəs]	*n.* 尸体(corpse); (屠宰后)畜体(the dressed body of a meat animal); (大的)身躯(the living, material, or physical body) 记 联想记忆: car(汽车) + cass(看作 cast 投掷) → 发生车祸,汽车被甩到一边,留下尸体 →(动物的)尸体 例 In Pleistocene carnivore species, older individuals consumed *carcasses* as thoroughly as younger individuals did.
carcinogen [kɑːr'sɪnədʒən]	*n.* 致癌物(substance that produces cancer) 记 词根记忆: carcino(ma)(癌) + gen(产生) → 产生癌 → 致癌物 例 The tests indicated that the chemical was a *carcinogen* in laboratory rats.
carcinogenic [,kɑːrsɪnə'dʒenɪk]	*a.* 致癌的; 致癌物的(causing a cancer) 记 来自 carcinogen(*n.* 致癌物质) 例 The two insect-repelling chemicals in the secretions of the millipedes are *carcinogenic* for humans but do not appear to be *carcinogenic* for capuchins.
cardiac ['kɑːrdiæk]	*a.* 心脏的; 心脏病的(relating to the heart or heart disease) 记 词根记忆: cardi(心脏的) + ac → 心脏的; 心脏病的 例 a *cardiac* surgeon 心脏外科医生
cardiopulmonary [,kɑrdɪo'pʌlməneri]	*a.* 心肺的; 与心肺有关的(of or relating to the heart and lungs) 记 词根记忆: cardio(有氧的) + pulmonary(肺部的) → 肺部的有氧活动 → 心肺的 例 To be successful, *cardiopulmonary* resuscitation should begin within one to four minutes after a cardiac arrest.

Word List 6

音频

cardiovascular [ˌkɑːrdiou ˈvæskjələr]	*a.* 心血管的 记 词根记忆：cardio(心脏的) + vascul(血管) + ar → 心血管的 例 *cardiovascular* response 心血管反应
cargo [ˈkɑːrɡou]	*n.* 货物(freight) 记 联想记忆：装在汽车(car)上运走(go)的物品 → 货物 例 *cargo* planes 货机
caribou [ˈkærɪbuː]	*n.* 北美驯鹿(reindeer) 例 *Caribou* are wary animals with excellent hearing.
carnivore [ˈkɑːrnɪvɔːr]	*n.* 肉食动物(flesh-eating animal) 记 词根记忆：carni(肉) + vore(吃) → 肉食动物 例 The older an individual *carnivore* is, the more likely it is to have a large number of tooth fractures. 派 carnivorous(*a.* 肉食动物的)
carpenter [ˈkɑːrpəntər]	*n.* 木匠(worker who builds or repairs wooden structures) 记 发音记忆："卡朋特"，美国六七十年代风靡一时的乐队 例 The materials available to *carpenters* working before 1930 were not significantly different in quality from the materials available to *carpenters* working after 1930. 同根词：carpentry(*n.* 木器；木工手艺)
carpentry [ˈkɑːrpəntri]	*n.* 木器；木工手艺；[木]木工业(the art or trade of a carpenter) 例 I have visited hotels throughout the country and have noticed that in those built before 1930 the quality of the original *carpentry* work is generally superior to that in hotels built afterward. 同根词：carpenter(*n.* 木匠)
carpet [ˈkɑːrpɪt]	*n.* 地毯(a heavy often tufted fabric used as a floor covering)；*v.* 铺地毯(to furnish with a carpet) 例 The *carpet* of the Cormond Hotel's lobby is not the most durable carpet that Duratex manufactures.
carpeting [ˈkɑːrpɪtɪŋ]	*n.* 毛毯，地毯(a heavy often tufted fabric used as a floor covering) 记 来自 carpet(*n.* 地毯；*v.* 铺地毯) 例 The carpet that is being used to replace *carpeting* near the other lobby entrances is not Duratex carpet.

cartel
[kɑːrˈtel]
n. 卡特尔(为协调生产、价格和商品市场而组成的独立的商业组织联合体)(group of business firms which combine to control production and marketing and to avoid competing with one another)
例 Formal price-fixing by *cartels* and informal price-fixing by agreements covering the members of an industry are commonplace.

cascade
[kæˈskeɪd]
n. 小瀑布(a steep usually small fall of water)
记 词根记忆: cas(落下) + cade(落下) → 一再落下 → 小瀑布
例 When a neutrino interacts with a particle in an atom of seawater, the result is a *cascade* of electrically charged particles.
同根词: casual(*a.* 偶然的)

caseload
[ˈkeɪsloʊd]
n. 办案量(the number of cases handled usually in a particular period)
例 There isn't sufficient funding to process the increased *caseload* of arrests and convictions that new officers usually generate.

cashew
[ˈkæʃuː]
n. 腰果(the nuts of a tropical American tree); 腰果树(a tropical American tree)
例 If the tariff were lifted and unprocessed *cashews* were sold at world market prices, more farmers could profit by growing cashews.

caste
[kæst]
n. 社会等级制度(hereditary social class system); 社会团体(any exclusive social class)
记 发音记忆: "卡死他" → 在一个等级上卡死他, 不让他上来 → 社会等级制度
例 a rigid *caste* system 严格的社会等级制度 // The black smiths belong to a special *caste*.

casualty
[ˈkæʒuəlti]
n. 伤亡(人)(person who is killed or injured in war or in an accident); [*pl.*] 伤亡人数(total of the killed and injured persons)
记 联想记忆: casual(随便的) + ty → 因为随随便便造成的 → 伤亡
例 They resulted in extremely high overall *casualty* rates in Black combat units.

cataclysm
[ˈkætəklɪzəm]
n. 大灾难(catastrophe); (社会政治的)大变动(a momentous and violent event)
例 A little under a million years ago, the briny waters of the Baltic Sea began flooding into the cold North Atlantic: geologists are still debating whether the flood was gradual or created by a *cataclysm*.
派 cataclysmic(*a.* 大变动的; 洪水的)
同根词: catastrophe(*n.* 大灾难)

cataclysmic
[ˌkætəˈklɪzmɪk]
a. 大变动的(of a sudden violent change or a disaster)
记 来自 cataclysm(*n.* 巨变; 灾难)
例 Elements heavier than helium would remain there if it were not for the *cataclysmic* supernova explosions.

catalog(ue)
[ˈkætələɡ]
n. 商品目录(complete list of items); *v.* 为…编目录(to make a catalog of)
例 Kim purchased some items from a *catalog* for $8 each. // Such artifacts are already *catalogued* in museum collections.

catalyst
[ˈkætəlɪst]

n. 催化剂 (a substance that enables a chemical reaction to proceed at a usually faster rate); 促使事物发展的因素 (a person or a thing that causes a change)

记 词根记忆：cata(下面) + lyst(=lysis 溶解) → 促进溶解 → 催化剂

例 The new taxes imposed by the government were a *catalyst* for revolution.

同根词：analyst(*n.* 分析家)

---

catalytic
[ˌkætəˈlɪtɪk]

a. 催化的，起催化作用的 (causing, involving, or relating to catalysis)

例 Many people who own cars made before 1993 have had *catalytic* converters installed in their cars.

派 catalytically(*ad.* 催化地)

---

catastrophe
[kəˈtæstrəfi]

n. 灾难，灾祸 (disaster)

记 词根记忆：cata(下面) + strophe(转) → 天转地覆 → 灾难

例 The perceived threat of nuclear *catastrophe* decreases the willingness of people to postpone consumption.

派 catastrophic(*a.* 灾难性的；巨大的)

同根词：apostrophe(*n.* 省略符号)

---

categorical
[ˌkætəˈgɔːrɪkl]

a. 无条件的，绝对的 (absolute); 分类的 (of a category)

记 来自 category(*n.* 种类；范畴)

例 The boss gave a *categorical* no for an answer.

---

category
[ˈkætəgɔːri]

n. 类别，种类 (any of several fundamental and distinct classes)

例 There are several *categories* of surgical procedures that are often performed unnecessarily.

派 categorical(*a.* 类的)

---

cater
[ˈkeɪtər]

v. 满足(需要) (to supply what is required or desired)

例 Will the restaurant *cater* to our special requests?

---

caterpillar
[ˈkætərpɪlər]

n. 毛虫 (larva of a butterfly or moth)

记 该词本意是 hairy cat(长毛的猫)，其中 pillar 意为 hair

例 Once ingested by a *caterpillar*, the crystals dissolve, releasing the virus to infect the insect's cells.

---

cathedral
[kəˈθiːdrəl]

n. 大教堂 (main church of a district under the care of a bishop); *a.* 大教堂的 (of a cathedral)

记 词根记忆：cathedra(拉丁文：主教座位) + l → 设有主教座位的地方 → 大教堂

例 No doubt castle and *cathedral* building was not totally barren of profit.

Catholic
[ˈkæθlɪk]

a. 罗马天主教的 (Roman Catholic)

例 Roman *Catholic* church 罗马天主教堂

---

causative
[ˈkɔːzətɪv]

a. 成为原因的 (effective or operating as a cause)

记 来自 cause(*n.* 原因)

例 Sources of financing must be a more important *causative* factor in the success of a start-up company.

cease

[siːs]

v./n. 终止，停止(to stop)

记 联想记忆：c + ease(安逸，安心) → 生于忧患，死于安乐 → 终止，停止

例 The government *ceased* to regulate major industries.

celestial

[sə'lestʃl]

a. 天体的，天空的(of or relating to the sky)

记 词根记忆：celest(天空) + ial → 天空的

例 *celestial* body 天体

同根词：celeste(n. 天蓝色)

cellular

['seljələr]

a. 细胞的(of or consisting of cells)；蜂窝状的(full of cells, shaped like a beehire)

记 词根记忆：cell(细胞) + ular → 细胞的

例 *cellular* structure 蜂窝状结构

派 intracellular(a. 细胞内的)；multicellular(a. 多细胞的)；subcellular(a. 亚细胞的)；unicellular(a. 单细胞的)

censure

['senʃər]

n. 指责，谴责(a judgment involving condemnation)；v. 指责，谴责(to find fault with and criticize as blameworthy)

例 Although recent *censure* of corporate boards of directors as "passive" and "supine" may be excessive, those who criticize board performance have plenty of substantive ammunition.

派 censurable(a. 该责备的；可非难的)

census

['sensəs]

n. 人口调查，人口普查(a usually complete enumeration of a population)

记 词根记忆：cens(审查，判断) + us → 官方评价 → 人口普查

例 The *census* information was inadequate and did not reflect certain economic changes in the United States.

centrality

[sen'træləti]

n. 中心性(the quality or state of being central)；向心性(tendency to remain in or at the center)

记 词根记忆：centr(中心) + ality → 中心性

例 the *centrality* in the United States economy 美国经济的集中性

ceramic

[sə'ræmɪk]

a. 陶的，制陶的(of or relating to pottery)

记 来自 ceram(n. 陶土)

例 Samples from a *ceramic* vase found at a tomb in Sicily(西西里)prove that the vase was manufactured in Greece.

cereal

['sɪriəl]

n. 谷类(grain)；谷类食品(food made of grain)

记 联想记忆：ce + real(真正的) → 真正的好东西 → 谷类食品

例 Many breakfast *cereals* are fortified with vitamin supplements.

certificate

[sər'tɪfɪkət]

n. 证券(a document evidencing ownership or debt)；证明书(official written or printed statement used as proof of certain facts)

记 词根记忆：cert(确定) + i + fic(做) + ate → 用来确定的东西 → 证明书

例 savings *certificates* 储蓄券

certify

['sɜːrtɪfaɪ]

v. 保证(to assure)；证明(to attest as being true)

记 词根记忆：cert(确定) + ify(使 …) → 使确定 → 证明

例 The physician must *certify* the need for hospitalization, and determine what procedures will be performed.

派 certification(n. 证明)

certitude
[ˈsɜːrtɪtuːd]

n. 确定无疑（certainty）

记 词根记忆：cert(确定) + itude(状态) → 确定无疑

例 They can no longer be used with *certitude* to explain many major economic developments.

cessation
[seˈseɪʃn]

n. 停止（stop）

记 词根记忆：cess(停止) + ation → 停止

例 The *cessation* of armed conflict was a relief to the people of the nation.

chaise
[ʃeɪz]

n. 两轮(或四轮)轻便马车（a two or four-wheeled carriage drawn by one horse）

记 联想记忆：chase(追赶)加上 i 就成了轻便马车(chaise)，我(I)坐上马车(chaise)好追赶

例 the *chaise* lounge 躺椅

chalice
[ˈtʃælɪs]

n. 杯（a drinking cup）；圣餐杯（large cup from which consecrated wine is drunk at Eucharist）

记 拉丁语为 calix，英语中也有 calix，和 chalice 同词根同词义

例 The recently discovered *chalice* was probably buried to keep from being stolen by invaders.

chamber
[ˈtʃeɪmbər]

n. 室，房间（room, esp. a bedroom）；*a.* 【音】室内的（of or for a small group of instruments: chamber concert）

例 Researchers detected a weak electrical signal emanating from the nesting *chamber* of an ant colony. // *chamber* music 室内音乐

character
[ˈkærəktər]

n. 性格（disposition）；特征（quality）；字符（letter, sign or mark）

记 联想记忆：char + acter(看作 actor 演员) → 演员刻画人物性格惟妙惟肖

派 characteristic(*a.* 特有的)；characterize(*v.* 表现…的特色)

characterization
[ˌkærəktəraɪˈzeɪʃn]

n. 描述（the act of characterizing）

例 I object to your *characterization* of our X-387 jets as dangerous.

charity
[ˈtʃærəti]

n. 慈善（mercy）；慈善团体（organization for helping the needy）

例 The Internal Revenue Service provided a tangible incentive for businesses to contribute their products to *charity*.

chart
[tʃɑːrt]

n. 图表（graph）；*v.* 记录，记载（to chronicle）

例 An exploration of that theme will *chart* accurately the development of civilizations.

charter
[ˈtʃɑːrtər]

n. 宪章（a written instrument or contract executed in due form）；租赁（hiring a ship, an aircraft or a vehicle）；*v.* 租（to hire or rent）；给予特权（to grant certain rights and privileges to）

例 *charter* cost 租金 // If the 25 members of a club *chartered* the plane and shared the cost equally, what was the cost per member?

派 chartered(*a.* 受特许的)

chatter
[ˈtʃætər]

v. 喋喋不休地说（to talk idly, incessantly, or fast）；颤动（to vibrate rapidly）

记 来自 chat(*v.* 聊天；*n.* 闲谈)

例 The bird leads another animal, such as a honey-badger or a human, to a bees' nest with their *chattering* when they fly ahead.

同根词：chattily(*ad.* 饶舌地；爱讲闲话地)

□ certitude   □ cessation   □ chaise   □ chalice   □ chamber   □ character
□ characterization   □ charity   □ chart   □ charter   □ chatter

chatty
[ˈtʃæti]
a. 喜欢唠叨的 (talkative)；话题轻松的 (in the style of light informal talk)
例 My *chatty* neighbor likes to gossip.

chauvinism
[ˈʃouvɪnɪzəm]
n. 沙文主义；盲目爱国主义 (excessive or blind patriotism)
记 来自一法国人名: Chauvin, 因其过分的爱国主义和对拿破仑的忠诚而闻名

chip
[tʃɪp]
n. 芯片 (microchip)；碎片 (thin piece)
例 Computer memory *chips* have become thinner and the *chips'* circuits more complex.

cholesterol
[kəˈlestərɔːl]
n. 胆固醇 (a steroid alcohol that is present in animal cells and body fluids)
记 词根记忆: chole(胆, 胆汁) + sterol(固醇) → 胆固醇
例 Garnet pays for both testing of its employees' *cholesterol* levels and treatment of high cholesterol.

chord
[kɔːrd]
n. 【几何】弦 (straight line that joins two points on the circumference of a circle or the ends of an arc)
记 和 cord(*n.* 索, 弦)一起记
例 P is the midpoint of *chord* AB.

chore
[tʃɔːr]
n. 家庭杂务 (the regular or daily light work of a household)；令人厌烦的工作 (a difficult or disagreeable task)
记 联想记忆: 家庭杂务(chore)总是令人很烦(bore)
例 Women were by nature patient in carrying out repetitive *chores*.

choreographer
[ˌkɔːriˈɑːgrəfər]
n. 舞蹈指导 (director, for ballet and dancing on the stage)
记 词根记忆: choreo(舞蹈) + graph(写) + er(人) → 书写舞蹈的人 → 舞蹈指导
例 Her innovative masterworks made her the most honored of American *choreographers*.

chronic(al)
[ˈkrɑːnɪk(l)]
a. 长期的, 慢性的 (marked by long duration or frequent recurrence)
记 词根记忆: chron(时间) + ic → 耗时间的 → 长期的
例 *chronic* diseases 慢性病
派 chronically(*ad.* 长期地, 慢性地)
同根词: chronometer(*n.* 计时器); anachronism(*n.* 年代错误)

chronicle
[ˈkrɑːnɪkl]
n. 编年史 (record of historical events in the order in which they happened);
v. 记录, 记载 (to record)
记 词根记忆: chron(时间) + icle → 按照时间顺序编写 → 编年史
例 the early *chronicles* of America // *chronicle* a development
同根词: chronological(*a.* 按年代顺序排列的); chronology(*n.* 年代学; 年表)

chronology
[krəˈnɑːlədʒi]
n. 年表; 年代学 (the science that deals with measuring time by regular divisions and that assigns to events their proper dates)
记 词根记忆: chrono(时间) + logy(一门学科) → 年代学
例 A *chronology* of the development of different methods for mapping Native American lands describes the content of the passage.
同根词: chronicle(*v.* 记录; *n.* 编年史)

circuit [ˈsɜːrkɪt]	*n.* 电路 (complete path along which an electric current flows); 环道 (a usually circular line encompassing an area) 记 词根记忆：circ(圆，环) + uit → 电路是环形的 → 环道 例 *circuit* board 电路板 派 circuitry(*n.* 电路，线路)
circular [ˈsɜːrkjələr]	*a.* 圆形的；环绕的 (round) 记 词根记忆：circ(圆，环) + ular → 圆形的；环绕的 例 An artist wishes to paint a *circular* region on a square poster.
circulate [ˈsɜːrkjəleɪt]	*v.* 散布，传播 (to cause to become widespread) 记 词根记忆：circ(圆) + ul + ate(做) → 绕圈走 → 散布，传播 例 The proposal to amend the bylaws of an organization was *circulated* to its members for comment. 派 circulation(*n.* 循环；传播)
circulation [ˌsɜːrkjəˈleɪʃn]	*n.* 循环，流通 (the process of going round continuously); 发行额 (the average number of copies of a publication sold over a given period) 记 来自 circulate(*v.* 循环，流通；散布) 例 The *circulation* of the poetry was confined to young Quaker women. 同根词：circus(*n.* 圆形广场；马戏团)
circulatory [ˈsɜːrkjələtɔːri]	*a.* 循环的 (of or relating to circulation or the circulatory system) 记 来自 circular(*a.* 圆形的；循环的) 例 A peculiar feature of the embryonic mammalian *circulatory* system is that in the area of the heart the cells adhere to one another, beating in unison and adopting specialized orientations exclusive of one another. 同根词：circulative(*a.* 循环性的；促进循环的)
circumference [sərˈkʌmfərəns]	*n.* 圆周；圆周长 (the perimeter of a circle) 记 词根记忆：circum(环绕) + fer(带来) + ence → 带来一圈 → 圆周长 例 There are cogs around the *circumference* of a wheel. 同根词：circumspect(*a.* 仔细的); circumstance(*n.* 环境); circumstantial (*a.* 不重要的)
circumspect [ˈsɜːrkəmspekt]	*a.* 谨慎的 (cautious) 记 词根记忆：circum(环绕) + spect(看) → 绕着看 → 谨慎的 例 The investor was *circumspect* when making predictions about the economy.
circumstance [ˈsɜːrkəmstæns]	*n.* 环境；事件 (a condition, fact, or event) 记 词根记忆：circum(周围) + stance(站) → 周围的存在 → 环境 例 The first is a *circumstance* for which the astronomer seeks to provide an explanation. 同根词：circumfluence(*n.* 环流)
circumvent [ˌsɜːrkəmˈvent]	*v.* 环绕 (to make a circuit around); 回避，规避 (to manage to get around) 记 词根记忆：circum(环绕) + vent(来) → 绕着圈儿来规避 → 规避 例 Immigrants could *circumvent* such exclusionary laws by leasing or purchasing land in their American-born children's names. 派 circumvention(*n.* 规避)

□ circuit   □ circular   □ circulate   □ circulation   □ circulatory   □ circumference
□ circumspect   □ circumstance   □ circumvent

citywide [ˈsɪtɪˌwaɪd]	*a.* 全市的，全市性的（including or involving all parts of a city） 记 分拆记忆：city(城市) + wide(广泛的) → 全市的 例 Yet the fact is that not only were more jobs created than were eliminated, but the average pay for these new jobs has been higher than the average pay for jobs *citywide* every year since Delmont took office.
civic [ˈsɪvɪk]	*a.* 城市的（municipal）；公民的；平民的（of citizens or citizenship） 例 *civic* symbols 城市象征 // *civic* virtues 公民道德 // *civic* education 平民教育
civilization [ˌsɪvələˈzeɪʃn]	*n.* 文明，文化（a relatively high level of cultural and technological development） 记 来自 civilize(*v.* 使文明；使开化) 例 Confused by the many strata and substrata of ancient *civilizations* overlying one another, Schliemann temporarily halted his excavations of the fabled city of Ilium, the ancient Troy.
claim [kleɪm]	*n.* 声称（assertion）；*v.* 声称（to assert），认领（to take as the rightful owner），索取（to ask for especially as a right） 记 本身为词根：叫喊 例 Many of the economists *claim* that the government's plan has been successful. // She persuaded Charles VII of France to *claim* his throne.
clan [klæn]	*n.* 部落，氏族（group of families descended from a common ancestor） 记 和 tribe(*n.* 部落；类)一起记 例 matrilineal *clans* 母系氏族
clandestine [klænˈdestɪn]	*a.* 秘密的，暗中从事的（secret） 记 联想记忆：clan(部落) + destine(命中注定) → "部落"和"命定"都有一些"秘密"色彩 → 秘密的，暗中从事的 例 The demand for the *clandestine* product would be substantially reduced.
clarify [ˈklærəfaɪ]	*v.* 澄清（to make clear, to free of confusion） 记 词根记忆：clar(清楚) + ify(使…) → 澄清 例 The explanation *clarified* the details of the plan.
clarity [ˈklærəti]	*n.* 清楚，明晰（the quality or state of being clear） 例 Many writers of modern English have acquired careless habits that damage the *clarity* of their prose.
classify [ˈklæsɪfaɪ]	*v.* 分类（to arrange in classes），归类（to assign to a category） 记 词根记忆：class(种类) + ify(使…) → 分类 例 The pterosaurs(翼龙)should be *classified* as birds, not reptiles. 派 classification(*n.* 分类法)；classified(*a.* 分类的)

□ citywide □ civic □ civilization □ claim □ clan □ clandestine
□ clarify □ clarity □ classify

Word List 7

音频

clergy [ˈklɜːrdʒi]	*n.* 牧师；神职人员(priests or ministers) 例 Separation of church and state barred Protestant *clergy* from the role that priests assumed in Brazil. 派 clerical(*a.* 牧师的；办事员的)
client [ˈklaɪənt]	*n.* 委托人(a person who engages the professional advice or services of another)；顾客(customer) 例 The firm is having difficulty retaining its *clients* of long standing. 派 clientele(*n.* 诉讼委托人，客户)
cliff [klɪf]	*n.* 悬崖，峭壁(steep, high face of rock, esp. at the edge of the sea) 记 联想记忆：cli(看作 climb 爬) + ff(像两个钩子) → 用钩子在悬崖峭壁上爬 → 悬崖，峭壁 例 They launched themselves by jumping from *cliffs*, and dropping from trees.
clinging [ˈklɪŋɪŋ]	*a.* 黏着的(sticky) 记 来自 cling(*v.* 粘紧，附着) 例 The workers removed the *clinging* vine from the brick wall.
clockwise [ˈklɑːkwaɪz]	*a./ad.* 顺时针方向的(地)(in the same direction as the rotating hands of a clock) 记 词根记忆：clock + wise(以…方向) → 以钟走的方向 → 顺时针方向的 例 a *clockwise* direction 顺时针方向
clog [klɑːg]	*v.* 妨碍(to obstruct)；阻塞(to block up) 记 联想记忆：圆木(log)一般很重，搁在 c 后自然是妨碍(clog)了 例 The recent surge in the number of airplane flights has *clogged* the nation's air-traffic control system.
clot [klɑːt]	*n.* 凝块(a thickened lump formed within a liquid)；*v.* 使凝结成块(to thicken into a clot) 例 According to a study published in *The New England Journal of Medicine*, aspirin prevents blood *clots* just as well as a commonly used and more expensive blood-thinning drug does. 派 cloture(*n.* 讨论终结)

clump [klʌmp]	*n.* 丛，簇(a group of things clustered together)；*v.* 使密集(to form sth. in a group) 记 和 lump(*n.* 块，团)一起记 例 The brim of the hat was decorated with a *clump* of silk flowers.
cluster ['klʌstər]	*n.* (任何的)群，堆，团(number of people, animals or things grouped closely together)；*v.* 使聚集在一起(to surround sb./sth. closely) 记 词根记忆：clust(=clot 凝成块) + er → 凝块 → 团 例 *clusters* of houses 房屋建筑群 // *clustered* suburban houses 密集的郊区房屋
coalition [ˌkoʊə'lɪʃn]	*n.* 结合，联合(union) 例 A coalition of lawyers defended the workers in court.
coaster ['koʊstər]	*n.* 杯垫(a small mat that is put underneath a glass or cup to protect the surface of a table)；(供娱乐用的)滑坡铁路 记 来自 coast(*n.* 海岸) 例 roller *coaster* 过山车
cocaine [koʊ'keɪn]	*n.* 可卡因(drug used as a local anaesthetic by doctors, and as a stimulant by drug addicts) 记 词根记忆：coca(古柯) + ine → 可卡因 例 Thus enforcement efforts have ironically resulted in an observed increase in the illegal use of *cocaine*.
code [koʊd]	*n.* 法规(a body of law)；准则(a system of principles or rules) 例 the Education *Code* 教育法 // *code* of ethics 道德准则
codify ['kɑːdɪfaɪ]	*v.* 整理(法律)(to classify)；系统化(to systematize) 记 来自 code(*n.* 法规) 例 Jim Crow laws did not go as far in *codifying* traditional practice as they might have.
cognitive ['kɑːgnətɪv]	*a.* 认知的(of, characterized by, involving, or relating to cognition) 记 词根记忆：cogn(知道) + itive → 知道的 → 认知的 例 *cognitive* ability 认知能力
coherent [koʊ'hɪrənt]	*a.* 连贯的(consistent)；清楚的(having clarity or intellig bility)；附着的，黏在一起的(sticking together) 记 词根记忆：co(一起) + her(黏着，黏附) + ent → 附着的 例 The bacteria indeed form a large *coherent* group. 派 cohesive(*a.* 黏着的)；coherence(*n.* 一致)
coinage ['kɔɪnɪdʒ]	*n.* 货币，货币制度(system of coins in use) 记 词根记忆：coin(币) + age(行为，结果) → 货币 例 Debasement of the *coinage* had compensated for the loss.
coincide [ˌkoʊɪn'saɪd]	*v.* 巧合(to concur)；一致，符合(to correspond) 记 词根记忆：co(共同) + in + cide(切) → 共同切分 → 一致，符合 例 The discovery of leavened bread(膨松面包)roughly *coincided* with the introduction of a wheat variety. 派 coincidence(*n.* 巧合之事)；coincident(*a.* 巧合的)；coincidental(*a.* 一致的)

□ clump □ cluster □ coalition □ coaster □ cocaine □ code
□ codify □ cognitive □ coherent □ coinage □ coincide

collaborate [kə'læbəreɪt]	v. 协作(to work together); 勾结, 通敌(to cooperate treasonably as with an enemy occupation force in one's county) 记 词根记忆: col(一起) + labor(工作) + ate → 一起工作 → 协作 例 The prisoners *collaborated* to plan the escape. 派 collaboration(n. 合作; 勾结)
collapse [kə'læps]	v./n. 崩溃(to break down completely); 失败(to fail completely) 记 词根记忆: col(一起) + lapse(滑, 落) → 全部滑落 → 崩溃 例 The local sugar beet(糖用甜菜)industry *collapsed* in 1902. 同根词: elapse(v. 时间流逝); lapse(v./n. 失误); relapse(v. 旧病复发)
collateral [kə'lætərəl]	n. 抵押品, 担保(property pledged by a borrower to protect the interests of the lender) 记 词根记忆: col + later(边) + al → 需要一边提供支持的 → 担保 例 I have no *collateral*, so the bank probably won't give me a loan. 同根词: bilateral(a. 双边的); equilateral(a. 等边的)
collective [kə'lektɪv]	a. 集体的(relating to a group or society as a whole) 例 Using our *collective* resources, we made a bid for the property. 派 collectively(ad. 全体地, 共同地)
collide [kə'laɪd]	v. 碰撞; 抵触(to clash) 例 Two planes *collided* in midair. 派 collision(n. 碰撞; 冲突)
collinear [kə'lɪnɪr]	a. 在同一直线上的(passing through or lying on the same straight line) 记 词根记忆: col(一起) + linear(直线的) → 在同一直线上的 例 Three or more points P1, P2, P3..., are said to be *collinear* if they lie on a single straight line L.
colonize ['kɑːlənaɪz]	v. 建立殖民地, 拓殖(to establish a colony in an area) 记 来自colony(n. 殖民地) 例 An ancestral species might have adapted to exploit a particular ecological niche on one island and then traveled over water to *colonize* other islands. 派 colonization(n. 殖民; 殖民化)
coloration [ˌkʌlə'reɪʃn]	n. 着色法, 染色法(the method of dying); 颜色, 色泽(color) 记 来自color(n. 颜色) 例 Studies of several animal species have shown that when choosing mates, females prefer males with brighter carotenoid-based *coloration*.
colossal [kə'lɑːsl]	a. 巨大的, 庞大的(enormous) 例 Buying computers for an entire company is a *colossal* expense.
combat ['kɑːmbæt]	n. 战斗(war, conflict); v. 与…作战; 同…斗争(to struggle against); a. 战斗的 记 词根记忆: com + bat(打, 战斗) → 战斗 例 To *combat* this problem we must establish a board to censor certain movies. // the *combat* mortality rates 战斗死亡率 派 combatant(n. 参战者, 战士); combative(a. 斗志旺盛的) 同根词: baton(n. 警棍); acrobat(n. 杂技演员)

07

combine [kəm'baɪn]	*v.* 联合，结合(to join) 记 词根记忆：com(共同) + bi(两个) + ne → 使两个在一起 → 结合 例 Mexican American leaders *combined* ethnic with contemporary civic symbols. 派 combined(*a.* 组合的); combination(*n.* 组合，化合)
combustion [kəm'bʌstʃən]	*n.* 燃烧(burning, catching fire) 记 词根记忆：com + bust(燃烧) + ion → 燃烧 例 The quick *combustion* of the dry forest was caused by the lack of rain.
comedian [kə'miːdiən]	*n.* 喜剧演员(an actor who plays comic roles) 记 来自 comedy(*n.* 喜剧) 例 The evening schedule was crowded with *comedians* and variety shows.
comet ['kɑːmət]	*n.* 彗星 记 联想记忆：come(来) + t → 很多年才来一次的星星 → 彗星 例 They are ejected by the *comet*.
commend [kə'mend]	*v.* 推荐(to recommend); 表扬(to praise) 记 词根记忆：com(共同) + mend(命令；委托) → 大家都委托他 → 推荐 例 The employees were *commended* with a bonus.
commensurate [kə'menʃərət]	*a.* (with) 相称的；相当的(corresponding in size, extent, amount, or degree) 记 词根记忆：com(共同) + mensur(测量) + ate → 测量相同 → 相当的 例 Your salary is *commensurate* with your experience level.
comment ['kɑːment]	*n.* 评论，意见(a statement of fact or opinion, especially a remark that expresses a personal reaction or attitude); *v.* 发表评论(to make a comment on) 记 词根记忆：com(共同) + ment(思考) → 一起思考 → 评论 例 Managers will save time by simply choosing *comments* from a preexisting list. 派 commentator(*n.* 评论员，解说员)
commerce ['kɑːmɜːrs]	*n.* 贸易，商业(the exchange or buying and selling of commodities on a large scale involving transportation from place to place) 记 词根记忆：com(加强) + merce(贸易) → 贸易，商业 例 *Commerce*—its profit-making, its self-interestedness, its individualism—became the enemy of these classical ideals. 派 commercial(*a.* 商业的; *n.* 商业广告)
commercial [kə'mɜːrʃl]	*a.* 商业的(occupied with or engaged in commerce or work intended for commerce); *n.* 商业广告(an advertisement broadcast on radio or television) 记 来自 commerce(*n.* 贸易；商业) 例 The classical conception of virtuous leadership was being undermined by *commercial* forces that had been gathering since at least the beginning of the eighteenth century. 派 commercially(*ad.* 商业上)

□ combine □ combustion □ comedian □ comet □ commend □ commensurate
□ comment □ commerce □ commercial

commission
[kəˈmɪʃn]

n. 委员会 (a group of persons directed to perform some duty); 佣金 (fee); *v.* 委托 (to place an order for)

记 词根记忆: com + miss(委派) + ion → 委托

例 the International Trade *Commission* 国际贸易委员会 // Jean's *commission* was 5 percent of the total amount of her sales. // This study was *commissioned* by the Department of Agriculture.

同根词: mission(*n.* 使命); remission(*n.* 缓解; 免除)

commit
[kəˈmɪt]

v. 做; 犯(to carry into action deliberately); 交付(to pledge or assign to some particular use); (使)受约束, 致力于(to obligate, bind)

记 词根记忆: com + mit(送) → 送给 → 调配…供使用

例 *commit* a crime 犯罪 // They must *commit* some of their own resources to the choice. // Each partner will remain *committed* to the relationship.

派 commitment(*n.* 许诺); committed(*a.* 忠于…的, 坚定的)

commitment
[kəˈmɪtmənt]

n. 承诺, 许诺(an agreement or pledge to do sth. in the future)

记 词根记忆: commit(使…承担义务) + ment → 承诺, 许诺

例 Our actions demonstrate not a bias in favor of liberal views but rather a *commitment* to a balanced presentation of diverse opinions.

同根词: commission(*n.* 委员会)

commodity
[kəˈmɑːdəti]

n. 商品(an economic good)

记 词根记忆: com + mod(方式, 范围) + ity → 各种各样的东西 → 商品

例 The ability to deal with people is as purchasable a *commodity* as sugar or coffee.

commoner
[ˈkɑːmənər]

n. 平民(a person without noble rank of title)

记 来自 common(*a.* 普通的)

例 The Forbidden City in Beijing was a site which a *commoner* or foreigner could not enter without any permission.

commonplace
[ˈkɑːmənpleɪs]

a. 平凡的, 普通的(plain and ordinary); *n.* 平庸的东西, 陈词滥调(something that is ordinary or common)

记 联想记忆: common(通常的) + place(地方) → 平庸之处 → 平凡的, 普通的

例 By the mid-1850's the inclusion of women in the rituals of party politics had become *commonplace*. // *commonplace* book 摘录簿

communal
[kəˈmjuːnl]

a. 全体共用的, 共享的(characterized by collective ownership and use of property)

记 词根记忆: com + mun(公共) + al → 公共的 → 共享的

例 The editors shared a set of *communal* computers for their work.

communist
[ˈkɑːmjənɪst]

n. 共产党员, 共产主义者(an adherent or advocate of communism); *a.* 共产主义的(of or relating to communism)

记 词根记忆: commun(=commune 公社) + ist(人) → 在公社工作的人 → 共产党员

例 Although all the proceedings of the *Communist* party conference held in Moscow were not carried live, Soviet audiences have seen a great deal of coverage.

同根词: communal(*a.* 公共的)

07

community
[kə'mjuːnəti]

n. 团体；共同体(a unified body of individuals)

记 词根记忆：com(共同) + mun(公共) + ity → 共同体

例 Some *communities* in Florida are populated almost exclusively by retired people. // coral reef *communities* 珊瑚礁群落 // business *community* 企业界

commute
[kə'mjuːt]

v. 坐公交车往返于两地(to travel back and forth regularly)；变换(to convert)；交换(to exchange)

记 词根记忆：com(共同) + mut(改变) + e → 坐车换车 → 坐公交车往返于两地

例 Children *commute* to school rather than living on campus.

派 commuter(*n.* 经常往返者)

同根词：mutation(*n.* 突变)；immutable(*a.* 不可变的)

compact
['kɑːmpækt]

a. 紧密的(condensed)；*n.* 契约(an agreement or covenant)

记 词根记忆：com(共同) + pact(打包，压紧) → 一起压紧 → 紧密的；pact 本身是一个单词，意为"契约"

例 *compact* disc 光盘 // a matrimonial *compact* 婚约

派 compactor(*n.* 压土机)；subcompact(*n.* 微型汽车)

companionate
[kəm'pænjənɪt]

a. 伙伴的；和睦的(harmoniously)

记 来自 company(*n.* 陪伴)

例 a *companionate* family 和睦的家庭

comparable
['kɑːmpərəbl]

a. 可比较的；比得上的(capable of or suitable for comparison)

记 来自 compare(*v.* 比较，相比)

例 Other towns and cities nearby have yet to embark on any *comparable* plans to attract new citizens.

派 comparability(*n.* 相似性；可比性)

同根词：comparative(*a.* 比较的)

comparison
[kəm'pærɪsn]

n. 比较，对照(an examination of two or more items to establish similarities and dissimilarities)；比喻(the representing of one thing or person as similar to or like another)

记 来自 compare(*v.* 比较)

例 In *comparison* to public rest areas, private parking lots near highways tend to be time-consuming for drivers to reach.

同根词：comparative(*a.* 比较的)

compassion
[kəm'pæʃn]

n. 同情，怜悯(pity)

记 词根记忆：com + pass(感情) + ion → 共同的感情 → 同情

例 The nurse had *compassion* for the sick patient.

派 compassionate(*a.* 富于同情心的)

compatible [kəmˈpætəbl]	*a.* 协调的(capable of existing together in harmony); 兼容的(designed to work with another device or system without modification) 记 词根记忆：com(一起) + pat(=path 感情) + ible → 有共同感受的 → 协调的 例 Price-fixing and the operation of the free market are not *compatible*. // Equipment used in the electronic network for transferring funds will be *compatible* with equipment used in other such networks. 派 compatibility(*n.* 和谐共处)
compel [kəmˈpel]	*v.* (to) 强迫(to force) 记 词根记忆：com + pel(驱使) → 驱使去做 → 强迫 例 This *compelled* the prisoner to establish a value without much distortion. 派 compelling(*a.* 必须接受的，强迫的) 同根词：repel(*v.* 打退); expel(*v.* 驱逐；开除)
compelling [kəmˈpelɪŋ]	*a.* 引起兴趣的(keenly interesting; captivating) 记 联想记忆：compel(强迫) + ling → 事物太优秀迫使人们引起兴趣和注意 → 引起兴趣的 例 Women therefore have more *compelling* common interest with men of their own economic class than with women outside it.
compensate [ˈkɑːmpenseɪt]	*v.* 补偿(to equalize); 偿还(to repay); 付报酬(to pay) 记 词根记忆：com + pens(花费) + ate → 花费都还回来 → 补偿 例 A small business is able to cut back sharply on spending and thereby *compensate* for a loss of revenue. 派 compensation(*n.* 补偿); compensative(*a.* 偿还的，补充的) 同根词：expense(*n.* 支出); dispense(*v.* 分发，分配)
compensation [ˌkɑːmpenˈseɪʃn]	*n.* 补偿(the act of compensating); 赔偿金(payment to unemployed or injured workers or their dependents); 报酬(payment) 记 来自 compensate(*v.* 补偿) 例 Most corporate boards' *compensation* committees focus primarily on peer-group comparisons. 同根词：expenditure(*n.* 消耗，花费)
compensatorily [kəmˈpensətɔːrili]	*ad.* 补偿性地 例 An authority can call things to a halt, and begin things again from *compensatorily* staggered "starting lines".
competence [ˈkɑːmpɪtəns]	*n.* 能力(the state or quality of being well qualified) 记 词根记忆：com + pet(力争) + ence → 能够力争的 → 能力 例 The most important quality in an employee is not specific knowledge or technical *competence*. 派 competent(*a.* 能干的); competency(*n.* 能力，资格)

07

competitive
[kəmˈpetətɪv]

a. 有竞争性的；比赛的（relating to, characterized by, or based on competition）

记 来自compete（*v.* 竞争；比赛；对抗）

例 At high density levels, however, *competitive* effects outweigh legitimation effects, discouraging foundings.

派 competitively（*ad.* 有竞争力地；好竞争地）

同根词：competent（*a.* 有能力的）

---

compile
[kəmˈpaɪl]

v. 编辑，编撰（to collect and edit into a volume）

记 词根记忆：com（一起）+ pile（堆）→ 堆积在一起加工 → 编辑

例 Lists of hospitals have been *compiled* showing which hospitals have patient death rates exceeding the national average.

---

complacency
[kəmˈpleɪsnsi]

n. 自满，自得（self-satisfaction especially when accompanied by unawareness of actual dangers or deficiencies）

记 联想记忆：com（共同，所有）+ place（地方）+ ncy → 对自己各个地方都满意 → 自满，自得

例 They may truly have to struggle against *complacency* arising from their current success.

---

complainant
[kəmˈpleɪnənt]

n. 控诉者（one who complains）；原告（plaintiff）

记 来自complain（*v.* 控诉）

例 The organization acted unfairly toward the *complainant* in its investigation.

---

complaint
[kəmˈpleɪnt]

n. 抱怨，诉苦（expression of grief, pain, or dissatisfaction）；疾病（a bodily ailment or disease）

记 来自complain（*v.* 抱怨）

例 On average, 9 out of every 1,000 passengers who traveled on Avia Airlines last year filed a *complaint* about our baggage-handling procedures.

---

complement

[ˈkɑːmplɪment] *v.* 补充（to reinforce）

[ˈkɑːmplɪmənt] *n.* 补足物（something that fills up, completes, or makes perfect）；【生】（血清中的）补体

记 词根记忆：com（加强）+ ple（装满，填满）+ ment → 补充

注意：compliment（*v.* 恭维）

例 John's work *complements* Larson's theory. // All of the cells in a particular plant start out with the same *complement* of genes.

派 complementary（*a.* 补充的）；complemented（*a.* 有补助物的）

---

complex
[kəmˈpleks]

a. 复杂的（complicated）

记 词根记忆：com（一起）+ plex（重叠，多）→ 重叠在一起的 → 复杂的

例 The most effective leaders are those who can solve *complex* problems by finding simple, immediate solutions.

派 complexity（*n.* 复杂；复杂的事物）

complication [ˌkɑːmplɪˈkeɪʃn]	*n.* 并发症(a secondary disease or condition developing in the course of a primary disease or condition);复杂,复杂化(complexity) 记 来自 complicate(*v.* 使复杂化) 例 They have been used primarily by older adults, who are at risk for *complications* from influenza.
comply [kəmˈplaɪ]	*v.* (with)遵循(to conform, submit, or adapt as required) 记 词根记忆:com(一起) + ply(用) → 大家一起都要用的 → 遵循 例 A good citizen *complies* with the laws of the country. 派 compliance(*n.* 依从,顺从)
component [kəmˈpoʊnənt]	*n.* 成分(ingredient);要素(element) 记 词根记忆:com(一起) + pon(放置) + ent → 放置在一起的东西 → 成分 例 The most effective way for managers to assign work is to divide complex tasks into their simpler *component* parts.
compose [kəmˈpoʊz]	*v.* (of)组成(to form by putting together);使安定(to calm) 记 词根记忆:com(一起) + pose(放) → 放到一起 → 组成 例 The stars in the Milky Way galaxy are *composed* of several different types of gas. 派 composer(*n.* 作家,设计者);composition(*n.* 组成,合 成物;作文)
composition [ˌkɑːmpəˈzɪʃn]	*n.* 作文;作曲;构成(the manner in which sth. is composed) 记 来自 compose(*v.* 组成,构成;作曲) 例 Geochemist John Gurney showed that garnets with this *composition* were formed only in the diamond-stability field. 同根词:composite(*n.* 复合材料;*a.* 复合的)
compound [ˈkɑːmpaʊnd]	*n.* 混合物,化合物(something formed by a union of elements or parts);*a.* 混合的(composed of or resulting from union of separate elements, ingredients, or parts) 记 词根记忆:com(一起) + pound(放) → 混合物 例 Water is a chemical *compound* of oxygen and hydrogen.
comprehend [ˌkɑːmprɪˈhend]	*v.* 理解,领会(to understand);包含(to include) 记 词根记忆:com(一起) + prehend(抓住) → 一起抓住 → 领会 例 They assume that commercial institutions cannot *comprehend* the special needs of minority enterprises. 同根词:prehensile(*a.* 适于抓住的);comprehensible(*a.* 容易了解的)
comprehension [ˌkɑːmprɪˈhenʃn]	*n.* 理解(the act or action of grasping with the intellect);包含(the act or process of comprising) 记 词根记忆:com(加强) + prehens(抓) + ion → 全部抓住 → 理解 例 Each of the reading *comprehension* questions is based on the content of a passage. 同根词:apprehend(*v.* 理解;逮捕)
compress [kəmˈpres]	*v.* 压缩,浓缩(to press or squeeze together) 记 词根记忆:com(共同) + press(压) → 全部压 → 压缩 例 A transmitter *compresses* the digital signal as it is sent. 派 compression(*n.* 压缩)

comprise [kəmˈpraɪz]	*v.* 包含(to include)；组成(to make up, compose) 记 词根记忆：com(共同) + pris(握取) + e → 被握在一起 → 包含；组成 例 In the country, women *comprise* 45 percent of the labor force.
compromise [ˈkɑːmprəmaɪz]	*v.* 妥协(to settle by concessions)；*n.* 折衷(settlement of differences by consent reached by mutual concessions) 记 词根记忆：com(共同) + promise(保证) → 相互保证 → 妥协 例 The legislation that came out of Congress was a *compromise* measure.

You have to believe in yourself. That's the secret of success.

人必须相信自己，这是成功的秘诀。

——美国演员 卓别林(Charles Chaplin, American actor)

Word List 8

compulsory [kəmˈpʌlsəri]	*a.* 强制性的(mandatory)；义务的(required) 记 词根记忆：com(一起) + puls(推，冲) + ory → 一起推 → 强制性的 例 *compulsory* military conscription 强制征兵 // *compulsory* education 义务教育 同根词：repulse(*v.* 反击)；repulsive(*a.* 排斥的)；compulsive(*a.* 强制的)
computation [ˌkɑːmpjuˈteɪʃn]	*n.* 计算，估计(calculation) 记 词根记忆：com + put(思考，估计) + ation → 计算，估计 例 The decorator did a few *computations* to determine how much wallpaper was needed.
compute [kəmˈpjuːt]	*v.* 计算(to determine or calculate by means of a computer)；估算(to determine especially by mathematical means)；推断(to reckon) 记 computer(*n.* 电脑)的动词形式 例 This tax, which was assessed on villages, was *computed* by the central government using the annual census figures. 派 computation(*n.* 估计；计算)
conceal [kənˈsiːl]	*v.* 隐瞒；隐藏(to hide) 记 词根记忆：con(一起) + ceal(隐藏) → 隐瞒；隐藏 例 Slips of the tongue do not necessarily reveal *concealed* beliefs or intentions.
concede [kənˈsiːd]	*v.* 让步(to yield)；(不情愿地)承认(to acknowledge grudgingly or hesitantly) 记 词根记忆：con + cede(割让) → 让出去 → 让步 例 The lawyer *conceded* that his argument was not logical.
conceive [kənˈsiːv]	*v.* 怀孕(to become pregnant)；构思，设想(to think) 例 The ancients *conceived* the world as flat. 派 conceivably(*ad.* 令人信服的)；preconceived(*a.* 预想的) 同根词：perceive(*v.* 知觉)；receive(*v.* 收到)
concentrate [ˈkɑːnsntreɪt]	*v.* 聚集，浓缩(to bring into one main body) 记 词根记忆：con(加强) + centr(中心) + ate → 聚集在一个中心 → 聚集 例 We should discontinue the deluxe air filter and *concentrate* all our advertising efforts on the economy filter. 派 concentration(*n.* 集中；浓度) 同根词：central(*a.* 中心的)

concentration [ˌkɑːnsn'treɪʃn]	*n.* 专心，专注 (the act or process of concentrating)；集中 (a concentrated mass or thing)；浓度 (the amount of a component in a given area or volume) 记 来自 concentrate (*v.* 集中；全神贯注；*n.* 浓缩) 例 The salt *concentration* soon returns to normal. 同根词：concentric (*a.* 同心的；集中的)
conceptual [kən'septʃuəl]	*a.* 观念的，概念的 (of, relating to, or consisting of concepts) 记 来自 concept (*n.* 观念，概念) 例 *conceptual* model 概念模型
concern [kən'sɜːrn]	*v.* 涉及，关系到 (to relate to)；使担心 (to be a care, trouble, or distress to)；*n.* 关心 (matter for consideration) 例 Clearly, the customer's main *concern* is the convenience afforded by one-stop shopping. 派 concerned (*a.* 有关的；关心的)
concerning [kən'sɜːrnɪŋ]	*prep.* 关于 (regarding)；就…而言 (relating to) 记 来自 concern (*v.* 涉及，关系到) 例 More evidence *concerning* women became available to historical researchers.
concert ['kɑːnsərt]	*n.* 一致 (agreement in design or plan)；音乐会 (a public performance of music) 记 词根记忆：con (共同) + cert (确实的事) → 共同确定的事 → 一致 例 He is working in *concert* with his colleagues. // *concert* tour 巡回音乐会
concession [kən'seʃn]	*n.* 让步 (the act of conceding) 记 词根记忆：con + cess (行走，前进) + ion → 向后走 → 让步 例 It is important to continuously test the market and use the results to secure *concessions* from existing suppliers. 同根词：secession (*n.* 脱离；分离)
conclude [kən'kluːd]	*v.* 推断，做结论 (to reach as a logically necessary end by reasoning) 记 词根记忆：con + clud (关闭) + e → 关闭，闭幕 → 做结论 例 Many analysts *conclude* that evidence of a recovering automotive market remains slight. 派 conclusion (*n.* 结论，结局) 同根词：preclude (*v.* 预防；杜绝)
concrete ['kɑːŋkriːt]	*a.* 具体的，有形的 (actual, definite)；*n.* 混凝土 (a hard strong building material made by mixing cement with sand, gravel etc. and water) 记 联想记忆：混凝土 (concrete) 当然是具体的，有形的 (concrete) 例 a *concrete* instance 一个具体的例子
concurrent [kən'kɜːrənt]	*a.* 同时发生的 (simultaneous) 记 词根记忆：con + current (发生的) → 同时发生的 例 A *concurrent* sharp decline in the populations of seals and sea lions was certainly caused by a pollution-related disease.

condemn [kən'dem]	v. 声讨，谴责(to criticize) 记 词根记忆：con + demn(=damn 伤害)→ 共同伤害 → 谴责 例 The principal *condemned* smoking by students at school. 派 condemnation(n. 谴责，定罪) 同根词：damnify(v. 损害); indemnify(v. 赔偿，补偿)
condense [kən'dens]	v. 使冷凝，浓缩(to make denser); 缩短(to contract) 记 词根记忆：con(一起) + dense(变浓厚)→ 浓缩 例 Warmed by the Sun, ocean water evaporates, rises high into the atmosphere, and *condenses* in tiny droplets on minute particles of dust to form clouds. 派 condensation(n. 浓缩)
condescending [ˌkɑːndɪ'sendɪŋ]	a. 俯就的，屈尊的(patronizing); 有优越感的(displaying a superior attitude) 记 来自 condescend(v. 屈尊) 例 The professor had a *condescending* attitude toward uneducated people. 同根词：descend(v. 下降); ascend(v. 上升)
condition [kən'dɪʃn]	n. 条件(a restricting or modifying factor); 情况(situation); 环境(environment) 例 Several senior officials spoke to the press on *condition* that they not be named in the story.
condominium [ˌkɑːndə'mɪniəm]	n. 共管(joint sovereignty by two or more nations); 公寓公私共有方式(individual ownership of a unit in a multiunit structure or on land owned in common) 记 词根记忆：con(共同) + dom(统治) + inium → 共同统治 → 共管 例 *condominium* corporation 共管物业立案法团 // *condominium* apartment 共管式公寓(所属房产为私有，庭园等共用场地为共有)
conduct	[kən'dʌkt] v. 实施，指导(to direct or take part in the operation or management of); 传导(to convey in a channel) ['kɑːndʌkt] n. 行为 记 词根记忆：con(加强) + duct(引导)→ 指导 例 *conduct* a survey 进行调查 // Unions *conducted* wage negotiations for employees. // *conduct* heat 导热 // informality in dress and *conduct* 非正式的穿着和行为
confederation [kənˌfedə'reɪʃn]	n. 同盟，联盟(alliance, league) 记 词根记忆：con + feder(联盟) + ation(状态)→ 联盟 例 The disease eliminated half the population of the Huron and Iroquois *confederations*.
confer [kən'fɜːr]	v. 讨论(to consult); 授予(to give) 记 词根记忆：con(共同) + fer(带来，拿来)→ 共同带来观点 → 讨论 例 The system of patent granting *confers* temporary monopolies for the exploitation of new technologies.

08

confess [kənˈfes]	*v.* (to) 承认，供认 (to acknowledge) 记 词根记忆：con(全部) + fess(说) → 全部说出 → 承认，供认 例 The driver would not *confess* to being the cause of the accident. 派 confession(*n.* 自白，招供)
confidential [ˌkɑːnfɪˈdenʃl]	*a.* 秘密的 (secret) 记 联想记忆：confident(相信) + ial → 亲信才知道 → 秘密的 例 The police taped her *confidential* conversations with her client . 派 confidentiality(*n.* 机密)
configuration [kənˌfɪɡjəˈreɪʃn]	*n.* 构造；外形 (shape)；【天】(行星等的)相对位置 记 词根记忆：con + figur(e)(形状) + ation → 全部形状 → 外形 例 There is a new kind of star: one with a flat, "two-dimensional" *configuration*. 同根词 figurative(*a.* 比喻的)；figurehead(*n.* 傀儡，领袖)
confine [kənˈfaɪn]	*v.* 限制，禁闭 (to hold within a location)；*n.* [*pl.*]界限 (scope) 记 词根记忆：con(加强) + fine(限制) → 限制，禁闭 例 Judge Bonham denied a motion to allow members of the jury to go home at the end of each day, and instead *confined* them to a hotel. 派 confined(*a.* 狭窄的，受限制的)；confinement(*n.* 限制，监禁)
confirm [kənˈfɜːrm]	*v.* 证实，使有效 (to validate)；确定 (to strengthen) 记 词根记忆：con(加强) + firm(坚定) → 十分坚定 → 确定 例 It cannot be tested and *confirmed* until further research on volcanic activity is done. 派 confirmation(*n.* 证实)；confirmed(*a.* 惯常的)
conflict [ˈkɑːnflɪkt]	*n.* 斗争，冲突，抵触 (a clash between ideas；opposition) 记 词根记忆：con(共同) + flict(打击) → 共同打 → 斗争，冲突 例 The *conflict* between the guilds was not purely economic.
conform [kənˈfɔːrm]	*v.* (to)遵照 (to be obedient or compliant)；符合 (to act in accordance with) 记 词根记忆：con(共同) + form(形状，形式) → 共同的形式 → 符合 例 *conform* to conventional practices 墨守成规 派 conformism(*n.* 因循守旧)
confront [kənˈfrʌnt]	*v.* 面对 (to encounter)；面对挑战 (to face especially in challenge) 记 联想记忆：con + front(前面) → 冲到前面面对挑战 → 面对挑战 例 They found themselves *confronted* with generous criticism.
Confucian [kənˈfjuːʃən]	*a./n.* 孔子的；儒家的；儒家学者 (of or relating to the Chinese philosopher Confucius or his teachings or followers) 记 发音记忆："孔夫子" 例 *Confucian* civilization 儒家文明 派 Confucianism(*n.* 儒教，孔教)
congenial [kənˈdʒiːniəl]	*a.* 舒适的 (pleasant) 记 联想记忆：con + gen(产生) + ial → 产生好感的 → 舒适的 注意：congenital(*a.* 天生的，先天的) 例 The country provided a *congenial* environment where women could aspire to their own goals.

□ confess   □ confidential   □ configuration   □ confine   □ confirm   □ conflict
□ conform   □ confront   □ Confucian   □ congenial

congested [kən'dʒestɪd]	*a.* 拥挤不堪的，充塞的 (clogged) 记 来自 congest(*v.* 充满，拥塞) 例 The only bridge over the channel is *congested* and trucks typically spend hours in traffic. 派 congestion(*n.* 充血；拥挤)
congestion [kən'dʒestʃən]	*n.* 拥挤，堵塞 (the state of being crowded and full of traffic)；充血 (the state of part of the body being blocked with blood or mucus) 记 来自 congest(*v.* 充塞，拥挤) 例 During the average workday, private vehicles owned and operated by people living within the city account for twenty percent of the city's traffic *congestion.* 同根词：indigestion(*n.* 消化不良)
conglomerate [kən'glɑːmərət]	*n.* 企业集团 (a widely diversified corporation) 记 联想记忆：con + glomer(聚集) + ate → 集成物 → 企业集团 例 The publishing company is owned by a large media *conglomerate.* // *conglomerate* company 综合公司 同根词：agglomerate(*v.* 使凝聚)
congregation [ˌkɑːŋɡrɪ'ɡeɪʃn]	*n.* (某地区的) 全体教徒 (the members of a specific religious group who regularly worship at a church) 记 词根记忆：con + greg(群体) + ation → 共同信仰的群体 → 全体教徒 例 South Korea has witnessed the world's most dramatic growth of Christian *congregations.* 同根词：aggregate(*v.* 聚集)
congress ['kɑːŋɡrəs]	*n.* 议会，国会；代表大会 (a formal meeting of delegates for discussion and usually action on some questions) 记 词根记忆：con(共同) + gress(行走) → 走到一起开议会 → 议会，国会 例 Some members of *Congress* disagree with the president's position. 派 congressional(*a.* 会议的)
congressional [kən'ɡreʃənl]	*a.* 国会的，议会的 (of or relating to congress) 记 来自 congress (*n.* 国会，会议) 例 The Lone Wolf decision had a greater long-term impact than did the *congressional* action of 1871. 派 congressionally(*ad.* 国会地，议会地)
conjunction [kən'dʒʌŋkʃn]	*n.* 结合，联合 (occurrence together in time or space)；连接词 (words that join together sentences, clauses, phrases, or words) 记 词根记忆：con(加强) + junct(连接，联合) + ion → 联合 例 They are often implemented in *conjunction* with a company's efforts to reconfigure its work processes. 同根词：juncture(*n.* 接合，连接)

08

connotation [ˌkɑːnəˈteɪʃn]	*n.* 言外之意，内涵（idea or notion suggested in addition to its explicit meaning or denotation） 记 词根记忆：con(共同) + not(注意) + ation → 共同注意的内容 → 内涵 例 This has enriched the strategic *connotation* of bilateral relations from another perspective.
conscience [ˈkɑːnʃəns]	*n.* 良心，是非感（a person's awareness of right and wrong with regard to his own thoughts and actions） 记 词根记忆：con(加强) + sci(知道) + ence → 知道好坏是非 → 良心，是非感 例 Those kinds of people are apparently incapable of feeling compassion or the pangs of *conscience*. 派 conscientious(*a.* 尽责的); consciousness(*n.* 知觉；个人 思想)
conscription [kənˈskrɪpʃn]	*n.* 征兵，征募（compulsory enrollment of persons especially for military service） 记 来自 conscript(*v.* 征兵，征募) 例 military *conscription* 征兵
consecutive [kənˈsekjətɪv]	*a.* 连续的，连贯的（following one after another in order） 记 词根记忆：con + secut(跟随) + ive → 一个跟着一个的 → 连续的，连贯的 例 The total time allotted to the average cluster of *consecutive* television commercials is decreasing. 派 consecutively(*ad.* 连续地)
consensus [kənˈsensəs]	*n.* 意见一致（agreement in opinion） 记 词根记忆：con(共同) + sens(感觉) + us → 感觉相同 → 意见一致 例 There is no *consensus* among researchers regarding what qualifies a substance as a pheromone.
consent [kənˈsent]	*v.* 同意，答应（to agree） 记 词根记忆：con(共同) + sent(感觉) → 有共同的感觉 → 同意 例 The modernization was implemented without the *consent* of the employees directly affected by it. 派 consensus(*n.* 共识)
consequence [ˈkɑːnsəkwens]	*n.* 结果(result)；重要(性)(importance)；推论(inference) 记 词根记忆：con + sequ(跟随) + ence → 跟随其后 → 结果 例 Unemployment does not have the same dire *consequences* today as it did in the 1930's. 派 consequently(*ad.* 因而)
conservatism [kənˈsɜːrvətɪzəm]	*n.* 保守主义（disposition in politics to preserve what is established）；守旧性（the tendency to prefer an existing or traditional situation to change） 记 词根记忆：con(加强) + serv(保持) + atism(主义) → 都保持下来的主义 → 保守主义 例 The technological *conservatism* of bicycle manufacturers is a reflection of the kinds of demand they are trying to meet. 同根词：preserve(*v.* 保存；保持)

□ connotation   □ conscience   □ conscription   □ consecutive   □ consensus   □ consent
□ consequence   □ conservatism

conservative [kənˈsɜːrvətɪv]	*a.* 保守的(traditional); *n.* 保守派(a political party professing the principles of conservatism) 记 来自 conserve(*v.* 保存; 保守) 例 Recent polls indicate that many people in the United States hold a combination of *conservative* and liberal political views. 派 conservatively(*ad.* 保存地; 保守地) 同根词: preservative(*n.* 防腐剂; *a.* 防腐的)
conservatively [kənˈsɜːrvətɪvli]	*ad.* 保守地 例 Newscasters, who read the news on TV, are considered to be more convincing, honest, and competent when they are dressed *conservatively*.
conserve [kənˈsɜːrv]	*v.* 保存(to preserve); 节约(to avoid wasteful or destructive use of) 记 词根记忆: con(全部) + serve(服务, 保持) → 保存 例 Camels do rely on a special mechanism to *conserve* internal water. // It is unrealistic to expect individual nations to make, independently, the sacrifices necessary to *conserve* energy. 派 conservatism(*n.* 保守主义); conservative(*a.* 保守的; *n.* 保守派)
considerable [kənˈsɪdərəbl]	*a.* 相当多的(great in amount or size); 值得考虑的(worth consideration) 记 来自 consider(*v.* 考虑) 例 The conversion of methane to electricity would occur at a *considerable* distance from the landfills. 派 considerably(*ad.* 非常地; 相当地) 同根词: considerate(*a.* 体贴的; 考虑周到的)
consideration [kənˌsɪdəˈreɪʃn]	*n.* 考虑(continuous and careful thought); 报酬(payment) 记 来自 consider(*v.* 考虑) 例 The first is a generalization about the likely effect of a policy under *consideration* in the argument; the second points out a group of exceptional cases to which that generalization does not apply.
consistency [kənˈsɪstənsi]	*n.* 一致性(agreement or harmony of parts); 连接(condition of adhering together) 记 来自 consist(*v.* 一致) 例 A company's two divisions performed with remarkable *consistency* over the past three years. 派 inconsistency(*n.* 矛盾); consistent(*a.* 一致的, 相符的)
consistent [kənˈsɪstənt]	*a.* 始终如一的, 一致的(marked by harmony, regularity, or steady continuity); 坚持的 记 注意与constant(*a.* 不变的; 经常的)区分 例 The symptoms that he began showing five days before his death are *consistent* with lead poisoning, not arsenic poisoning. 派 consistently(*ad.* 一贯地; 一致地)

consolidate
[kənˈsɑːlɪdeɪt]

v. 巩固(to make stable and firmly established); (使)坚强(to strengthen); 合并(to merge; unite; join)

记 词根记忆: con(加强) + solid(结实) + ate → 巩固

例 Even though OLEX could *consolidate* all its refining at the Tasberg plant, doing so at the Grenville plant would not be feasible.

派 consolidation(*n.* 巩固; 合并)

同根词: solidly(*ad.* 坚固地)

consortium
[kənˈsɔːrtiəm]

n. [*pl.*consortia]协会(an association); 联营, 集团(an association or a combination, as of businesses, financial institutions, or investors, for the purpose of engaging in a joint venture); 财团(financial group)

记 词根记忆: con(共同) + sort(类型) + ium → 联合, 合伙 → 协会

例 Many satellites are built by international *consortia*.

conspire
[kənˈspaɪər]

v. 阴谋, 共谋(to plot)

例 The bank tellers *conspired* to rob the bank.

派 conspirator(*n.* 阴谋者, 谋叛者); conspiracy(*n.* 阴谋)

constant
[ˈkɑːnstənt]

a. 稳定的, 不变的(invariable); *n.* 常数, 恒量(a number that is assumed not to change value in a given mathematical discussion)

记 词根记忆: con(始终) + stant(站, 立) → 始终站立 → 不变的

例 The cost would remain *constant* even if such treatments were instituted on a large scale. // In this equation, the *constant* equals the speed of light.

派 constancy(*n.* 恒久不变)

constellation
[ˌkɑːnstəˈleɪʃn]

n. 星座, 星群(named group of stars)

记 词根记忆: con(共同) + stell(星星) + ation → 在一起的一簇星星 → 星座, 星群

例 The cooling-flow theory gained support when Fabian observed a cluster of galaxies in the *constellation* Perseus.

同根词: stellar(*a.* 星的, 恒星的)

constituent
[kənˈstɪtjuənt]

n. 成分, 要素(component; element); 选民(a member of a constituency)

例 The amino acid is one of the sweetener's principal *constituents*.

派 constituency(*n.* 选民; 支持者)

constitute
[ˈkɑːnstətuːt]

v. 组成, 建立(to set up, establish); 制定(to enact)

记 词根记忆: con + stitute(建立, 放) → 建立, 组成

例 What *constitutes* an American Indian reservation is a question of practice, not of legal definition.

派 constitution(*n.* 宪法; 构造)

constraint
[kənˈstreɪnt]

n. 约束, 抑制(restraint, limitation)

记 词根记忆: con(共同) + straint(拉紧) → 拉紧到一起 → 约束

例 Western women were free from the *constraints* binding their eastern sisters.

□ consolidate □ consortium □ conspire □ constant □ constellation □ constituent
□ constitute □ constraint

constrict
[kənˈstrɪkt]

v. 收缩；使狭窄 (to make narrow or draw together)

例 When the seal dives below the surface of the water and stops breathing, arteries become *constricted*.

派 constriction (*n.* 压缩，收缩); constrictive (*a.* 压缩性的)

construct
[kənˈstrʌkt]

v. 建筑，建造 (to build)；构成 (to make or form by combining or arranging parts or elements)

记 词根记忆：con (加强) + struct (建造) → 建造

例 Male bowerbirds *construct* elaborately decorated nests, or bowers.

派 construction (*n.* 建设；建筑物；结构)

同根词：restructure (*v.* 调整；重建)

construction
[kənˈstrʌkʃn]

n. 建筑，建筑物 (the process, art, or manner of constructing sth.)；结构，句法关系 (syntactical arrangement)

记 词根记忆：con (共同) + struct (建造) + ion → 共同建立 → 建筑

例 The *construction* of the cable car terminal at Machu Picchu will require the use of potentially damaging heavy machinery at the site.

同根词：destruction (*n.* 破坏，毁灭)

constructivism
[kənˈstrʌktɪvɪzm]

n. 结构主义，构成派 (an art movement concerned with formal organization of planes and expression of volume in terms of modern industrial materials)

记 词根记忆：con (共同) + struct (建造) + iv + ism (主义) → 结构主义

例 The modernization gave credence to the view of advocates of social *constructivism*.

同根词：construction (*n.* 建筑)

constructivist
[kənˈstrʌktɪvɪst]

n. 构成主义者 (an artist of the school of constructivism)

记 来自 construct (*v.* 构造，建造)

例 Clark refutes the extremes of the *constructivists* by both theoretical and empirical arguments.

同根词：constructivism (*n.* 构成主义；构成派)

consult
[kənˈsʌlt]

v. 咨询 (to ask the advice or opinion of)；(with) 商议 (to confer)

记 联想记忆：不顾侮辱 (insult)，不耻请教 (consult)

例 The employees' job functions required them to *consult* at least once a day with employees from other companies.

派 consultant (*n.* 顾问，咨询者); consulting (*a.* 咨询的)

consultant
[kənˈsʌltənt]

n. 顾问 (one who gives professional advice or services)；咨询者 (one who consults another)

记 来自 consult (*v.* 咨询)

例 For some reason the new *consultant* treats his clients like idiots.

派 consultancy (*n.* 咨询工作)

同根词：consultive (*a.* 咨询的)

consumption
[kənˈsʌmpʃn]

n. 消耗 (量)，消费 (量) (the utilization of economic goods)

例 The annual number of fish caught for human *consumption* has not increased.

08

□ constrict   □ construct   □ construction   □ constructivism □ constructivist □ consult
□ consultant   □ consumption

contaminate [kən'tæmɪneɪt]	*v.* 污染 (to pollute); 感染 (to corrupt or infect by contact) 记 词根记忆: con + tamin(接触) + ate → 接触脏东西 → 污染 例 Dental researchers discovered that toothbrushes can be *contaminated* with bacteria. 派 contaminant (*n.* 污染物)
contamination [kən,tæmɪ'neɪʃn]	*n.* 污染, 玷污; 污染物 (a state of being contaminated) 记 来自 contaminate (*v.* 污染) 例 Extensive use of chemicals in numerous future full-scale solar ponds would lead to *contamination* of the Dead Sea, which now enjoys a lucrative tourist trade. 同根词: contaminative (*a.* 污损的)
contemplate ['kɑːntəmpleɪt]	*v.* 沉思 (to ponder); 打算, 预期 (to view as probable or as an intention) 记 联想记忆: con + templ(看作 temple 庙) + ate → 在庙里打坐沉思 → 打算 例 After the date all actions *contemplated* in the treaty are to be complete.

Trouble is only opportunity in work clothes.
困难只是穿上工作服的机遇。

──美国实业家 凯泽(H.J. Kaiser, American businessman)

音频

Word List 9

contemporary [kən'tempəreri]	*a.* 当代的(modern)；同时代的(happening, existing, living, or coming into being during the same period of time)；*n.* 同代人(a person who lives or lived at the same time as another) 记 词根记忆：con(一起) + tempor(时间) + ary → 同时代的；同代人 例 *contemporary* society 当今社会 // Samuel Johnson was Pope's *contemporary*.
contemptuous [kən'temptʃuəs]	*a.* 轻蔑的，傲慢的(disdainful) 记 词根记忆：con + tempt(轻视，引诱) + uous → 轻蔑的，傲慢的 例 The author's attitude toward public hospitals can best be described as *contemptuous* and prejudiced.
contend [kən'tend]	*v.* (with)与困难做斗争，应付(to strive against difficulties)；主张(to maintain, assert) 例 Those industries had to *contend* with the fact that other countries banned imports from the country. // Advocates of loyalty programs *contend* that such programs are beneficial. 派 contention(*n.* 竞争；论点)；contentious(*a.* 有异议的)；contestant(*n.* 竞争者)
contiguous [kən'tɪgjuəs]	*a.* 接近的，接壤的(adjoining) 记 词根记忆：con(共同) + tig(接触) + uous → 相互接触 → 接壤的 例 Minnesota is the only one of the *contiguous* forty-eight states that still has a sizable wolf population.
contingent [kən'tɪndʒənt]	*a.* 偶然发生的(occurrent)；(on)有条件的(dependent on or conditioned by something else)；*n.* 分遣队(detachment) 例 Eligibility to buy shares was *contingent* on employees' agreeing to increased work loads. // Their government has a large *contingent* of armed guards patrolling its borders.
contraband ['kɑːntrəbænd]	*n.* 走私(illegal or prohibited traffic in goods)；走私货(goods or merchandise whose importation, exportation, or possession is forbidden) 记 词根记忆：contra(相反) + band(束缚) → 违反禁令得到的东西 → 走私货 例 It will become the largest *contraband* problem faced by the United States Customs Service.

contract	[ˈkɑ:ntrækt] *n.* 合同，契约 a binding agreement between two or more persons or parties) [kənˈtrækt] *v.* 感染 to become affected with)；收缩 to draw together) 记 词根记忆：con(共同) + tract(拉) + ion → 将双方拉到一起 → 合同 例 a labor *contract* 劳动合同 // Children who *contract* measles develop an immunity to the virus. 派 contractor(*n.* 承包人)；contractual(*a.* 合同的)；contraction(*n.* 感染)
contraction [kənˈtrækʃn]	*n.* 收缩 the action or process of contracting) 例 Spasmodic(一阵阵的)winking is caused by the involuntary *contraction* of an eyelid muscle.
contractor [kənˈtræktər]	*n.* 承包人；立契约者 one that contracts or is party to a contract) 记 来自 contract(*v.* 订约) 例 The *contractor* and the engineer agree on the cause of the bridge failure, but both blame the other. 同根词：distract(*v.* 转移；分心)
contradict [ˌkɑ:ntrəˈdɪkt]	*v.* 否定 to deny)；反驳 to assert the contrary of) 记 词根记忆：contra(反) + dict(说话，断言) → 反着说 → 反驳 例 They tend to *contradict* earlier findings about such unemployment. // There is much evidence to *contradict* this hypothesis. 派 contradiction(*n.* 反驳；矛盾)；contradictory(*a.* 对抗的；反驳的) 同根词：dictator(*n.* 独裁者)；benediction(*n.* 祝福)
contradiction [ˌkɑ:ntrəˈdɪkʃn]	*n.* 矛盾 a statement or phrase whose parts contradict each other)；反驳 (act or an instance of contradicting) 记 来自 contradict(*v.* 反驳；否认) 例 It indicates why a *contradiction* described in the previous paragraph has been overlooked by historians.
contrast	[ˈkɑ:ntræst] *n.* 对比；差别 the difference or degree of difference between things having similar or comparable natures) [kənˈtræst] *v.* 对比；使与对照 to compare or appraise in respect to differences) 例 In *contrast*, in the year prior to the tax increase, sales had fallen one percent. 派 contrastive(*a.* 对比的)
contribute [kənˈtrɪbjuːt]	*v.* 贡献 to play a significant part in bringing about an end or result)；投稿 (to submit articles to a publication)；捐献 to give or supply in common with others) 记 词根记忆：con(全部) + tribute(给予) → 全部给予 → 捐献 例 Automobiles become less fuel efficient and therefore *contribute* more to air pollution as they age. 派 contribution(*n.* 贡献；捐献；投稿) 同根词：attribute(*v.* 归属；把…归于)

contributor
[kənˈtrɪbjətər]

n. 贡献者，捐助者one that contributes a sum of money）；投稿者a writer who submits his articles to a publication）

记 来自 contribute（*v.* 捐献）

例 Sulfur dioxide, a major *contributor* to acid rain, is an especially serious pollutant because it diminishes the respiratory system's ability to deal with all other pollutants.

派 contributory（*a.* 捐献的；贡献的）

同根词：tribute（*n.* 赠品）

---

control
[kənˈtroʊl]

v. 控制，管理to rule）；*n.* （实验的）对照，参照物an individual or group used as a standard of comparison in a control experiment）

记 control 作为"参照物"的意思时是专业术语

例 It served as a *control* for the experiment.

---

controversial
[ˌkɑːntrəˈvɜːrʃl]

a. 引起或可能引起争论的causing controversy）

记 词根记忆：contro（相反）+ vers（转）+ ial → 反着转 → 引起争论的

例 The relationship between corpulence and disease remains *controversial*.

派 controversially（*ad.* 颇有争议地）

同根词：controvert（*v.* 争论；辩论）

---

controversy
[ˈkɑːntrəvɜːrsi]

n. 争论，辩论dispute）

记 词根记忆：contro（相反）+ vers（转）+ y → 意见相反 → 争论，辩论

例 There are some possible approaches to resolving this long-standing *controversy*.

派 controversial（*a.* 争议的，争论的）

---

convection
[kənˈvekʃn]

n. 对流the circulatory motion that occurs in a fluid at a nonuniform temperature owing to the variation of its density and the action of gravity）

例 Theoretically, this *convection* would carry the continental plates（板块）along as though they were on a conveyor belt.

---

convenience
[kənˈviːniəns]

n. 便利fitness or suitability for performing an action or fulfilling a requirement）

记 联想记忆：con（共同）+ ven（来）+ i + ence → 共同行动来维护便民设施 → 便利

例 People buying pancake syrup at *convenience* stores, unlike those buying it at supermarkets, generally buy it only a few times.

同根词：convene（*v.* 召集）

---

conventional
[kənˈvenʃənl]

a. 因循守旧的according with a mode of artistic representation that simplifies or provides symbols or substitutes for natural forms）；传统的of traditional design）

记 来自 convention（*n.* 习俗，惯例）

例 *Conventional* wisdom has it that large deficits in the United States budget cause interest rates to rise.

派 conventionally（*ad.* 按照惯例地）

同根词：convene（*v.* 召集）

conversion [kən'vɜːrʒn]	*n.* 转换; 折合(the exchange of one type of security or currency for another); 财产转移(the changing of real property to personal property or vice versa) 记 词根记忆: con + vers(转) + ion → 转换 例 Those farmers started the *conversion* of their intangible worth into cash terms. // *conversion* to cooperative ownership 转移合作所有权
convert [kən'vɜːrt]	*v.* (into)(使)转化, (使)改变(to transform); 换算(to transform) 记 词根记忆: con + vert(转) → 转换 例 The equipment is used to *convert* solar energy into electricity.
convey [kən'veɪ]	*v.* 运载, 运送(to bear from one place to another); 表达(to impart or communicate) 记 词根记忆: con(共同) + vey(道路) → 通过道路一起走 → 运载, 运送 例 Human beings can see the spatial relations among objects by processing information *conveyed* by light. // The author intended to *convey* a negative attitude toward the role of race in determining status. 派 conveyor(*n.* 运送者; 运送设备)
conviction [kən'vɪkʃn]	*n.* 判罪(the act or process of convicting of a crime); 坚信(strong belief) 记 来自convict(*v.* 定罪), con + vict(征服) → 征服罪犯 → 判罪; 尤其注意conviction"坚信"一意 例 Many migrants came to America out of religious or political *conviction*. // The Revolutionary generation asserted its *conviction* that the welfare of the Republic rested upon an educated citizenry. 同根词: victory(*n.* 胜利); invincible(*a.* 无敌的)
convince [kən'vɪns]	*v.* (使)某人确信(to bring to belief); 说服(to persuade) 记 词根记忆: con(全部) + vince(征服, 克服) → 彻底征服对方 → 说服 例 People will follow medical advice when they are *convinced* that it is effective. // The mayor's publicity campaign has *convinced* many people to leave their cars at home and ride the bus to work. 派 convinced(*a.* 确信的); convincingly(*ad.* 信服地, 有说服力地)
convoluted ['kɑːnvəluːtɪd]	*a.* 错综复杂的(twisted and tangled) 记 词根记忆: con(共同) + volut(滚) + ed → 缠绕在一起的 → 错综复杂的 例 The message was so *convoluted* that Bill couldn't understand it. 派 convolve(*v.* 卷, 缠绕); convolution(*n.* 回旋, 卷绕)
cooperate [koʊ'ɑːpəreɪt]	*v.* 合作(to associate with another or others for mutual benefit); 配合(to act or work with another or others) 记 词根记忆: co(共同) + oper(工作) + ate → 一起工作 → 合作 例 Employees who are frequently absent are the least likely to *cooperate* with or to join a corporate fitness program. 派 cooperation(*n.* 合作) 同根词: operable(*a.* 可操作的; 可动手术的)

□ conversion   □ convert   □ convey   □ conviction   □ convince   □ convoluted
78   □ cooperate

coordinate [kou'ɔːrdɪnət]	[kou'ɔːrdɪnət] *n.* 坐标(any of a set of numbers used in specifying the location of a point on a line, on a surface, or in space) [kou'ɔːrdɪneɪt] *v.* 协调(harmonize) 例 x-*coordinate* X(坐标)轴 // The firms *coordinated* such activities by using available means of communication and transport. 派 coordination(*n.* 协调,调和)
copper ['kɑːpər]	*n.* 铜(chemical element, a common reddish-brown metal); *a.* 铜(制)的 记 联想记忆:cop(警察)+ per → 警察制服上的铜扣 例 copper mining *company* 铜矿开采企业
coral ['kɔːrəl]	*n.* 珊瑚;珊瑚虫 记 联想记忆:cor(看作 core 核心)+ al → 大海的核心之处有珊瑚 → 珊瑚 例 *coral* reef 珊瑚礁
cord [kɔːrd]	*n.* 绳,索(rope);【解】索状组织(an anatomical structure resembling a cord) 记 本身为词根:心 例 vocal *cord* 声带 // spinal *cord* 脊髓 同根词:record(*v.* 录制);accord(*v.* 一致;符合)
cork [kɔːrk]	*n.* 软木塞(a cork stopper for a bottle or jug);软木制品(the elastic tough outer tissue of the cork oak that is used especially for stoppers and insulation) 例 *Cork* prices, however, are expected to rise dramatically in the near future.
coronary ['kɔːrəneri]	*a.* 冠状动脉的(of the arteries supplying blood to the heart) 记 词根记忆:corona(冠状物)+ ry → 冠状动脉的 例 *coronary* arteries 冠状动脉
corporate ['kɔːrpərət]	*a.* 团体的(incorporated);法人的,公司的(of or relating to a corporation) 记 词根记忆:corpor(体)+ ate → 团体的;公司的 例 The accomplished women are potential candidates for *corporate* boards. 派 corporation(*n.* 公司);incorporate(*a.* 合并的;*v.* 合并)
corporation [ˌkɔːrpə'reɪʃn]	*n.* 公司(company);法人(a body formed and authorized by law to act as a single person) 记 词根记忆:corpor(团体)+ ation → 公司是由一个大团体构成的 → 公司 例 The number of women holding top executive positions in a *corporation* is compared to the number of women available for promotion to those positions. 同根词:corporate(*a.* 法人的;共同的)
corps [kɔːrz]	*n.* 军团(an organized subdivision of the military establishment) 记 词根记忆:corp(体)+ s → 一个整体 → 军团 例 the Army *Corps* of Engineers 工程兵

corral
[kə'ræl]

n. 畜栏 a pen or enclosure for confining livestock) ; *v.* 关进畜栏 to enclose in a corral)

记 词根记忆：corr(=curr 跑) + al → (不让)动物跑掉 → 关进畜栏

注意：coral(*n.* 珊瑚)

例 They leave cattle alone while they feed themselves, then *corral* them, and drive them to market when they grow up.

correlate
['kɔːrəleɪt]

v. (with) 和…相关 to bear mutual relations)

记 词根记忆：cor(共同) + relate(相关) → 和…相关

例 Demographic changes in the workforce did not *correlate* with variations in the total number of temporary workers.

派 correlation(*n.* 相互关系)

correspond
[ˌkɔːrə'spɑːnd]

v. (with) 相一致 to be in conformity or agreement) ; 通信 to communicate with a person by exchange of letters) ; (to) 相应 to be equivalent or parallel)

记 词根记忆：cor(共同) + respond(作出反应) → 作出相同的反应 → 相一致

例 The labor force should be restructured so that it *corresponds* to the range of job vacancies.

派 corresponding(*a.* 相应的); correspondence(*n.* 相应；信函)

corresponding
[ˌkɔːrə'spɑːndɪŋ]

a. 相当的 comparing closely) ; 一致的 being in conformity or agreement) ; 通信的 communicating with a person by exchange of letters)

记 来自 correspond(*v.* 符合；一致)

例 The rings *corresponding* to the overlapping years could not be complacent rings.

同根词：correspondingly(*ad.* 相应地)

corroborate
[kə'rɑːbəreɪt]

v. 证实 to support with evidence or authority)

记 词根记忆：cor + robor(力量 strength) + ate → 加强力量来证实 → 证实

例 These data *corroborate* the hypothesis of the experiment.

派 corroborator(*n.* 确证者)

同根词：corroborant(*a.* 确证的；补身的); roborant(*n.* 强壮剂)

corrosion
[kə'roʊʒn]

n. 腐蚀(状态), 侵蚀 the action, process, or effect of corroding)

记 来自 corrode(*v.* 侵蚀)

例 It can cause blackouts in some areas and *corrosion* in north-south pipelines.

派 corrosive(*a.* 腐蚀性的)

corrosive
[kə'roʊsɪv]

a. 腐蚀性的, 蚀坏的 tending or having the power to corrode)

记 来自 corrode(*v.* 侵蚀；损害)

例 The cable car will replace the tour buses whose large wheels and *corrosive* exhaust at present do significant damage to the site.

corruption
[kə'rʌpʃn]

n. 腐化, 堕落 depravity)

记 来自 corrupt(*v.* 腐化，使堕落)

例 The socialization was a way of resisting what they perceived as the relentless *corruption* of human values by the marketplace. // The *corruption* of public officials makes the government look bad.

cortex [ˈkɔːrteks]	*n.* (内部器官的)皮质 (the outer layer of an internal organ or body structure, as of the kidney or adrenal gland) 记 该词也有"(植物的)皮层，树皮"之意。 注意：bark(*n.* 树皮) 例 adrenal *cortex* 肾上腺皮质
cosmetic [kɑːzˈmetɪk]	*n.* 化妆品 (makeup) 记 联想记忆：cos(看作 cost 花费) + metic → 化妆品花费很高 例 *Cosmetics* are being tested on sentient animals.
cosmic [ˈkɑːzmɪk]	*a.* 宇宙的 (of or relating to the cosmos) 记 词根记忆：cosm(宇宙) + ic → 宇宙的 例 *cosmic* explosion 宇宙大爆炸 同根词：cosmopolis(*n.* 国际都市)；cosmos(*n.* 宇宙)
council [ˈkaʊnsl]	*n.* 理事会，委员会 (an assembly or meeting for consultation, advice, or discussion) 例 the National Security *Council* 国家安全委员会
counteract [ˌkaʊntərˈækt]	*v.* 消除，抵消 (to make ineffective or neutralize the ill effects of) 记 词根记忆：counter(反) + act(动作) → 做相反的动作 → 消除，抵消 例 To help *counteract* our declining market share, we should increase the productivity of our professional staff members.
counterattack [ˈkaʊntərəˌtæk]	*n.* 反攻，反击 (beat back) 记 分拆记忆：counter(相反的) + attack(攻击) → 反击 例 The Environmental Protection Agency's proposal to place restrictions on both diesel fuel and diesel engines has sparked a *counterattack* by the oil industry.
counterevidence [ˈkaʊntərˌevɪdəns]	*n.* 反证 (contrary or opposite evidence) 记 分拆记忆：counter(反的) + evidence(证据) → 反证 例 A viewpoint is introduced, *counterevidence* is presented, and a new perspective is suggested.
counterfeit [ˈkaʊntərfɪt]	*n.* 赝品 (forgery)；*v.* 伪造(货币等)，仿造 (to imitate) 记 词根记忆：counter(反) + feit(=fact 做) → 反着做 → 伪造 例 Piracy and *Counterfeiting* Amendments Act 反盗版和假币的修正案 // *Counterfeiting* artifacts will become more commonplace now.
countermeasure [ˈkaʊntərmeʒər]	*n.* 对策，对抗手段 (an action or device designed to negate or offset another) 例 The *countermeasure* seems not effectual at all.
counterpart [ˈkaʊntərpɑːrt]	*n.* 相应的人(或物) (one having the same function or characteristics as another) 例 Like their male *counterparts*, women scientists are above average in terms of intelligence and creativity.

counterproductive
[ˌkaʊntərprəˈdʌktɪv]

a. 事与愿违的(having the opposite effect to that intended)

记 分拆记忆: counter(反的) + productive(有成效的) → 与想象有相反效果的 → 事与愿违的

例 A given government policy can be *counterproductive* when that policy has already unofficially been implemented.

countervail
[ˈkaʊntərveɪl]

v. 补偿(to compensative); 对抗, 抵消(to counteract)

例 There were no *countervailing* social programs for those failing in the labor market.

coupon
[ˈkuːpɑːn]

n. 赠券; 优待券(a ticket or form authorizing purchases of rationed commodities)

例 discount *coupons* 折扣券

courier
[ˈkʊriər]

n. 送急件的人(messenger)

记 词根记忆: cour(跑) + ier → 跑着的人 → 送急件的人

例 Much of the material could be delivered much faster by special package *couriers*.

courtesy
[ˈkɜːrtəsi]

n. 礼貌, 谦恭(courteous behavior)

记 联想记忆: court(法庭) + esy(看作 easy 从容的) → 在法庭上既要从容不迫又要谦恭有礼 → 谦恭

例 *Courtesy* is rapidly disappearing from everyday interactions, and as a result, we are all the poorer for it.

cowhide
[ˈkaʊhaɪd]

n. 牛皮(leather made from the skin of a cow); 牛皮鞭(strip of this leather used as whip)

记 分拆记忆: cow(牛) + hide(兽皮, 痛打) → 牛皮, 牛皮鞭

例 *Cowhide* is an inexpensive leather.

crack
[kræk]

n. 强效纯可卡因(a potent form of cocaine); *v.* 裂开, 断裂(to break, split, or snap apart)

例 The use of *crack* and cocaine is growing rapidly among workers. // In most earthquakes the Earth's crust *cracks* like porcelain

cramped
[kræmpt]

a. 狭窄的(confined, restricted); 狭促的(restrained)

记 词根记忆: cramp(铁箍, 夹子) + ed → 箍得很紧的 → 狭窄的

例 No more people could fit into the *cramped* elevator. // The *cramped* kennel was filled with too many dogs.

cranium
[ˈkreɪniəm]

n. 头颅(braincase); 头盖(skull)

例 What scientists know about dinosaur brains comes from studies of the *cranium*, the bony house of the brain located in the back of the skull.

crass
[kræs]

a. 粗劣的(gross); 愚钝的(stupid)

例 Protecting children from the *crass* business world became enormously important.

crate
[kreɪt]

n. 篮, 篓(an open box of wooden slats or a usually wooden protective case or framework for shipping)

记 联想记忆: 编篮子(crate)也是一种创造(create)

creative [kri'eɪtɪv]	*a.* 创造性的 (marked by the ability or power to create) 记 来自 create (*v.* 创作；创造) 例 Scientists typically do their most *creative* work before the age of forty. 派 creatively (*ad.* 创造性地；有创造力地)；creativity (*n.* 创造力) 同根词：recreate (*v.* 再创造；娱乐，消遣)
creativity [ˌkriːeɪ'tɪvəti]	*n.* 创造力，创作力 (the ability to create) 记 词根记忆：cre (生长) + tivity → 生长出新东西 → 创造力 例 Like their male counterparts, women scientists are above average in terms of intelligence and *creativity*.
credence ['kriːdns]	*n.* 信任 (belief) 记 词根记忆：cred (相信) + ence → 相信 → 信任 例 Students are less likely to give *credence* to history textbooks than to mathematics textbooks. 同根词：credibility (*n.* 可信，可靠)；accredit (*v.* 信任，授权于)
credit ['kredɪt]	*n.* 信用，信任 (trust)；*v.* 把…归给 (to ascribe)；把…记入贷方 (to enter upon the credit side of an account) 记 词根记忆：cred (相信) + it → 相信 例 Agricultural technology is *credited* with having made our lives better. // Interest was *credited* on the last day of each month. 派 discredit (*v.* 怀疑)
creditworthiness ['kredɪtwɜːrðinəs]	*n.* 有资格接受信用贷款 (financially sound enough to justify the extension of credit) 例 Members of society have varying degrees of purchasing power and *creditworthiness*.
crest [krest]	*n.* 顶部 (peak) 例 the *crests* of waves 浪尖
criminology [ˌkrɪmɪ'nɑːlədʒi]	*n.* 犯罪学 (the scientific study of crime as a social phenomenon, of criminals, and of penal treatment) 记 词根记忆：crimin (犯罪) + ology (学科) → 犯罪学 例 The police detective took courses in *criminology*.
cripple ['krɪpl]	*n.* 瘸子 (a lame or partly disabled person or animal)；*v.* 使…成残废 (to deprive of the use of a limb and especially a leg) 记 和 creep (*v.* 爬行) 一起记 例 His right hand and arm were *crippled* by a sniper's bullet during the First World War. 派 crippling (*a.* 极有害的)
criteria [kraɪ'tɪriə]	*n.* 标准 (measure of value) 记 词根记忆：crit (评断) + eria → 判断的手段 → 标准 例 They invoke four principal *criteria* for determining climatic conditions existing in the past.

09

criterion
[kraɪˈtɪriən]

n. 评判的标准，尺度（standard by which sth. is judged）

记 词根记忆：crit（判断）+ er（看作 err 错误）+ ion → 评判的标准

注意：复数形式 criteria

例 Using a *criterion* based on an object's color, astronomers recently identified 23 galaxies so distant from Earth that their light has taken 85 percent of the age of the universe to reach us.

critic
[ˈkrɪtɪk]

n. 评论家，批评家（one who engages often professionally in the analysis, evaluation, or appreciation of works, of art or artistic performances）

记 词根记忆：crit（评断）+ ic → 做评断的人 → 评论家

例 The *critics* are correct on this point.

派 critical（*a.* 批评的；关键的）；criticism（*n.* 评判，批评）；criticize（*v.* 批评；评论）

The supreme happiness of life is the conviction that we are loved.

生活中最大的幸福是坚信有人爱我们。

——法国小说家 雨果（Victor Hugo, French novelist）

critical [ˈkrɪtɪkl]	*a.* 挑毛病的（looking for faults）；关键的；危急的（of or at a crisis） 记 来自 critic(*n.* 评论家，批评家；爱挑剔的人） 例 Proponents of IT argued that it takes both time and a *critical* mass of investment for IT to yield benefits. 派 critically(*ad.* 危急地；批评性地） 同根词：hypercritical(*a.* 吹毛求疵的）
criticism [ˈkrɪtɪsɪzəm]	*n.* 批评（the act of criticizing usually unfavorably）；评论（a critical observation or remark） 记 来自 critic(*n.* 批评家；评论家） 例 The old government was more tolerant of *criticism* by the press than the new one is. 同根词：critical(*a.* 批评的；批判的）
critique [krɪˈtiːk]	*n.* 评论(文)（a critical estimate or discussion）；*v.* 批判性地讨论（to examine critically） 记 词根记忆：crit(评断) + ique → 评论 例 It is a *critique* of a particular women's studies program. // The purpose of the passage is to explain and *critique* the methods used by early statisticians.
crossbred [ˈkrɒsbred]	*a.* 杂种的（hybrid） 例 The *crossbred* cows can produce, on average, 2,700 liters per year.
crucial [ˈkruːʃl]	*a.* 决定性的（decisive）；至关紧要的（significant） 记 词根记忆：cruc(十字) + ial → 十字关头的 → 决定性的 例 It will be *crucial* that land managers know what statistical measures actually mean.
crude [kruːd]	*a.* 天然的（natural）；粗糙的，拙劣的（marked by the primitive, gross, or by uncultivated simplicity or vulgarity） 例 *crude* oil 原油 // The sanitary conditions were uniformly *crude* throughout the country.

crusade [kruːˈseɪd]	*n.* 十字军东征，宗教战争 (any of the military expeditions undertaken by Christian powers in the 11th, 12th, and 13th centuries to win the Holy Land from the Muslims) 记 词根记忆：crus(十字) + ade → 原指十字军东征 → 宗教战争 例 Louis VII did spend great sums on an unsuccessful *crusade*. 同根词：cruciform(*n.* 十字形); crusader(*n.* 十字军战士)
crush [krʌʃ]	*n.* 粉碎；压榨 (an act of crushing); 迷恋 (an intense and usually passing infatuation); *v.* 挤压 (to squeeze or force by pressure so as to alter or destroy structure); 压碎 (to squeeze together into a mass) 记 联想记忆：碰撞(crash)后被碾碎(crush) 例 Both partially biodegradable and non-biodegradable plastic beverage containers can be *crushed* completely flat by refuse compactors.
crust [krʌst]	*n.* 外壳 (the hardened exterior or surface); 地壳 (the outer part of the Earth) 例 In most earthquakes the Earth's *crust* cracks like porcelain. 派 crustal(*a.* 地壳的)
crustal [krʌstl]	*a.* 壳的；地壳的 (of or relating to or characteristic of the crust of the Earth) 记 来自 crust(*n.* 外壳) 例 Deep events occur in places other than where *crustal* plates meet. 同根词：crusty(*a.* 有壳的)
cryptic [ˈkrɪptɪk]	*a.* 神秘的 (secret); 含义模糊的 (obscure) 记 词根记忆：crypt(秘密，隐藏) + ic → 秘密的 → 神秘的 例 Can you explain this *cryptic* message I got from my boss?
crystallize [ˈkrɪstəlaɪz]	*v.* 结晶 (to cause to form crystals or assume crystalline form); 具体化 (to cause to take a definite form) 记 来自 crystal(*n.* 水晶; *a.* 水晶的) 例 Moisture exhaled by tourists had raised the humidity within them to such levels that salt from the stone was *crystallizing*. 派 crystallization(*n.* 结晶化；具体化) 同根词：crystal(*n.* 水晶; *a.* 水晶的)
cube [kjuːb]	*n.* 立方体 (the regular solid with six equal square sides) 记 和 tube(*n.* 管，显像管)一起记 例 The surface area of the *cube* is 600 square inches. 派 cubic(al)(*a.* 立方的，立方体的)
cue [kjuː]	*n.* 暗示，信号 (hint) 记 联想记忆：有线索(clue)可以暗示(cue) 例 visual *cues* 视觉信号
cuisine [kwɪˈziːn]	*n.* 烹饪，烹调法 (style of cooking) 记 发音记忆："口味新" → 烹饪出新口味 → 烹饪，烹调法 例 The famous cook introduced the preparation of traditional *cuisine*.

culminate [ˈkʌlmɪneɪt]	*v.* 达到顶点(to reach the highest point, degree, or stage of development in) 记 词根记忆：culmin(顶点，高峰) + ate → 达到顶点 例 This is the painting that *culminated* the artist's long career.
culpability [ˌkʌlpəˈbɪləti]	*n.* 有罪，有过失(blameworthiness) 记 来自culpable(*a.* 有罪的)，culp(罪行) + able(有…的) → 有罪的 例 They think the damage awards should be based on the degree of *culpability* of the party causing the death. 同根词：culprit(*n.* 犯人)；exculpate(*v.* 无罪释放)
cult [kʌlt]	*n.* 崇拜(worship) 例 Recent excavations suggest that the ancient people of the Italian peninsula merged the *cult* of Damia.
cultivate [ˈkʌltɪveɪt]	*v.* 种植(to grow from seeds)；向…讨好(to seek to develop familiarity with) 记 词根记忆：cult(种植；培养) + ivate(表动作) → 种植 例 Poor women working in urban areas actively seek to *cultivate* long-term employer-employee relations. 派 cultivation(*n.* 培养；耕种) 同根词：culture(*n.* 文化)；floriculture(*n.* 花卉栽培)
cultivated [ˈkʌltɪveɪtɪd]	*a.* 耕种的；栽植的；有修养的(educated) 例 *cultivated* land 耕地 // The distinguished gentleman married a *cultivated* woman. 派 cultivation(*n.* 耕作；栽培；教养)
cultivation [ˌkʌltɪˈveɪʃn]	*n.* 教化(refinement)；耕种(the act or art of cultivating or tilling) 记 来自cultivate(*v.* 培养；陶冶) 例 Not all of the acreage in Teruvia *currently* planted with rice is well suited to the cultivation of rice. 同根词：cultivator(*n.* 耕者)
cumbersome [ˈkʌmbərsəm]	*a.* 累赘的(burdensome)；麻烦的(troublesome) 记 词根记忆：cumber(妨碍) + some → 妨碍的 → 麻烦的 例 Insulin must still be administered by the *cumbersome* procedure of injection under the skin.
cupidity [kjuːˈpɪdəti]	*n.* 贪婪，贪心(greed) 记 Cupid(丘比特)是罗马神话中的爱神，爱神引起人们对爱情的"贪婪"。 注意：covet(*v.* 贪求) 例 The woman gazed at the silverware and jewels with *cupidity*.
curb [kɜːrb]	*n.* 路边(an edging built along a street to form part of a gutter)；*v.* 控制(to control, to check) 例 The containers will be placed at the *curb* twice a week for trash collection. // They propose a way to *curb* illegal digging while benefiting the archaeological profession.

10

curiosity [ˌkjuri'ɑːsəti]	*n.* 好奇，好奇心(desire to know)；珍品，古董(antique) 记 词根记忆：curio(古董) + sity → 对罕见的古董充满了好奇心 → 好奇；古董 例 In 1905 Béla Bartók and Zoltán Kodály began their pioneering work in ethnomusicology, traveling the back roads of Hungary armed only with an Edison phonograph and insatiable *curiosity*. 同根词：curious(*a.* 好奇的)
currency ['kɜːrənsi]	*n.* 流通(circulation)；货币(something as coins treasury notes, and banknotes that is in circulation as a medium of exchange) 例 Predictions of slower economic growth sometimes trigger declines in *currency* value. // *currency* exchange rates 外汇汇率
curriculum [kə'rɪkjələm]	*n.* 全部课程(the courses offered by an educational institution) 例 Mathematics and history are required courses in the high school *curriculum*.
cursorial [kər'sɔːriəl]	*a.* 适于行走的，善于奔跑的(adapted to or involving running) 例 Two opposing scenarios, the "arboreal" hypothesis and the "*cursorial*" hypothesis, have traditionally been put forward concerning the origins of bird flight.
curtail [kɜːr'teɪl]	*v.* 缩减(to shorten) 记 把 cur 看作 cut，tail 是尾巴之意，整个词可以理解为把尾巴削了，即"截短，缩短"之意 例 If we are to reduce the risk of an oil spill without *curtailing* our use of oil, we must invest more in offshore operations.
customize ['kʌstəmaɪz]	*v.* 定制，定做(to make or alter according to the buyer's or owner's wishes) 例 *customized* computer software 定制的计算机软件
customs ['kʌstəmz]	*n.* 关税(duties, tolls, or imposts imposed by the sovereign law of a country on imports or exports)；海关(the agency, establishment, or procedure for collecting such customs) 例 *customs* agent 报关代理人
cutback ['kʌtbæk]	*n.* 减少，削减(reduction) 记 来自词组 cut back(减少，削减) 例 Soaring rates of liability insurance have risen to force *cutbacks* in the operations of everything.
cyclic ['sɪklɪk]	*a.* 循环的(of, relating to, or being a cycle) 例 *cyclic* system 循环系统
cylinder ['sɪlɪndər]	*n.* 圆柱体(solid or hollow curved body with circular ends and straight sides) 例 Two oil cans are right circular *cylinders*.
cylindrical [sə'lɪndrɪkl]	*a.* 圆柱体的；圆筒形的(relating to or having the form or properties of a cylinder) 记 来自 cylinder(*n.* 圆柱体，圆筒) 例 A right *cylindrical* container with a radius of 2 meters and a height of 1 meter is filled to capacity with oil.

cynical [ˈsɪnɪkl]	*a.* 愤世嫉俗的 (distrustful) 记 来自古希腊哲学流派"cynicism(犬儒主义)"; cyn 原意为"犬" 例 The tone of the passage is persuasive and *cynical*. 派 cynicism(*n.* 愤世嫉俗，犬儒主义)
dealership [ˈdiːlərʃɪp]	*n.* 代理商，经销商 (an authorized sales agency) 记 分拆记忆: dealer(经销商) + ship → 经销商 例 an automobile *dealership* 汽车经销商
debase [dɪˈbeɪs]	*v.* 降低 (to lower in status, esteem, quality or character); 降低(硬币)的成色 (to reduce the intrinsic value by increasing the base-metal content) 记 词根记忆: de + base(低) → 低下去 → 降低 例 The coinage had been sharply *debased*. 派 debasement(*n.* 成色降低) 同根词: basement(*n.* 地下室); basis(*n.* 基础)
debate [dɪˈbeɪt]	*n./v.* 辩论，讨论 (discuss) 记 词根记忆: de(加强) + bate(打，击) → 互相打击 → 辩论 例 The *debate* was about the social values. 同根词: rebate(*n.* 回扣); abate(*v.* 减轻)
debilitate [dɪˈbɪlɪteɪt]	*v.* 使衰弱 (to make weak or feeble, weaken) 例 Secretions of these millipedes have been shown to contain two chemicals that are potent mosquito repellents, and mosquitoes carry parasites that *debilitate* the capuchins. 派 debilitation(*n.* 衰弱; 乏力)
debris [dəˈbriː]	*n.* 碎片，残骸 (the remains of something broken down) 记 法语词，注意该词的发音比较特别，末尾的"s"不发音 例 The excavation revealed a pattern of *debris* and collapsed buildings.
debunk [ˌdiːˈbʌŋk]	*v.* 揭穿真相；暴露 (to expose the falseness of) 例 The new data *debunked* the theory.
decade [ˈdekeɪd]	*n.* 十年，十年期 (a period of 10 years) 记 词根记忆: deca(十) + de → 十年，十年期 例 Over the past *decade* the technology of microelectronics has evolved rapidly.
decay [dɪˈkeɪ]	*v./n.* 腐朽 (to rot); 衰退 (to decline from a prosperous condition) 例 Wood *decays* rapidly in the humid climate. // radioactive *decay* 放射性衰变
decimal [ˈdesɪml]	*n.* 小数 (fraction expressed in tenths, hundredths, etc.); *a.* 小数的; 十进制的 (based on or reckoned in tens or tenths) 记 词根记忆: decim(十分之一) + al → 将数分成十分之一 → 小数 例 Any *decimal* that has only a finite number of nonzero digits is a terminating decimal.
decimate [ˈdesɪmeɪt]	*v.* 使(数量)急剧减少 (to reduce drastically especially in number) 例 Cholera(霍乱)*decimated* the population.

decipher [dɪˈsaɪfər]	*v.* 破译(to decode) 记 词根记忆：de(去掉) + cipher(密码) → 破译 例 The environmental signal can be *deciphered* by modern physical or chemical means. 派 decipherable(*a.* 可破译的); decipherment(*n.* 破译；译文)
declension [dɪˈklenʃn]	*n.* 衰退(deterioration) 记 词根记忆：de + clen(倾斜) + sion → 向下倾斜 → 衰退 例 After gradual *declension* down to about 39 hours in 1970, the workweek in the United States has steadily increased.
decorate [ˈdekəreɪt]	*v.* 装饰，点缀(to adorn) 记 词根记忆：decor(装饰) + ate → 装饰，点缀 例 Male bowerbirds(澳洲产的一种鸟)construct elaborately *decorated* nests. 派 decoration(*n.* 装饰，奖章); decorative(*a.* 装饰性的); decorator(*n.* 装饰者)
decoration [ˌdekəˈreɪʃn]	*n.* 装饰，装潢(the act or process of decorating)；装饰品(sth. that adorns, enriches, or beautifies)；奖章(a badge of honor) 记 来自 decorate(*v.* 装饰) 例 Much of the local artisans' creative energy was expended on the creation of Buddha images and on construction and *decoration* of the temples.
decorous [ˈdekərəs]	*a.* 符合礼节的(correct) 例 A reserved and *decorous* style had been a more highly valued literary ideal.
dedicated [ˈdedɪkeɪtɪd]	*a.* 专注的(given over to a particular purpose)；献身的(devoted) 记 来自 dedicate(*v.* 献身，致力) 例 Except for the most idealistic and *dedicated*, there were no incentives to seek change.
deduce [dɪˈduːs]	*v.* 推断，演绎(to infer) 记 词根记忆：de(往下) + duce(引导) → 往下引导 → 推断，演绎 例 Relative land ice volume for a given period can be *deduced* from the ratio of two oxygen isotopes.
deduct [dɪˈdʌkt]	*v.* 扣除(to subtract)；演绎(to infer) 记 词根记忆：de + duct(引导) → 往下引导 → 演绎 例 The waitress *deducted* the cost of the cold coffee from our bill. // *deductive* reasoning 演绎推理 派 deduction(*n.* 扣除；演绎); deductive(*a.* 演绎的)
deduction [dɪˈdʌkʃn]	*n.* 扣除，减除(an act of taking away)；推论(the deriving of a conclusion by reasoning) 记 来自 deduct(*v.* 扣除；推断，演绎) 例 As a result, these companies have shifted health care costs to employees in the form of wage *deductions* or high deductibles. 同根词：conduct(*v.* 引导；管理); induct(*v.* 引导；传授)

□ decipher　　□ declension　　□ decorate　　□ decoration　　□ decorous　　□ dedicated
□ deduce　　□ deduct　　□ deduction

deem
[di:m]

v.认为 (to consider); 相信 (to believe)

记 联想记忆: 别以为事情表面似乎 (seem) 是这样, 就认为 (deem) 八九不离十了

例 Native Americans recognized that events that they thought significant were often *deemed* unimportant by their interviewers.

---

default
[dɪ'fɔ:lt]

v.违约 (to fail to fulfill a contract, agreement, or duty); 拖欠 (to fail to meet a financial obligation)

记 联想记忆: de + fault(错误) → 错下去 → 拖欠

例 Bank failures are caused when big borrowers *default* on loan repayments.

---

defendant
[dɪ'fendənt]

n.被告 (a person required to make answer in a legal action or suit); *a.* 为自己辩护的 (being on the defensive)

记 词根记忆: defend(保护) + ant → 保护自己 → 被告

注意: plaintiff(n. 原告)

例 a criminal *defendant* 被告犯罪嫌疑人

---

deferential
[ˌdefə'rənʃl]

a.恭顺的 (respectful, humble)

记 defer(遵从, 听从) → deference(遵从; 尊敬) → deferential; 注意这儿的 defer 不是"拖延"的意思

例 Bill is always *deferential* to his parents.

---

defiant
[dɪ'faɪənt]

a.蔑视的 (bold)

记 来自defy(v. 藐视)

例 The hardliners are angrily *defiant* of the government's refusal and threaten to take action.

---

deficiency
[dɪ'fɪʃnsi]

n.缺陷 (absence of sth. essential; incompleteness); 不足 (shortage)

记 词根记忆: de + fic(做) + iency → 没做好 → 缺陷

例 Persons who suffer from a *deficiency* of the blood enzyme G6PD discover that eating fava beans triggers hemolytic anemia.

同根词: deficient(a. 不足的; 有缺陷的)

---

deficit
['defɪsɪt]

n.赤字 (an excess of expenditure over revenue)

例 A shrinking trade *deficit* actually added 1.57% to GDP this quarter.

派 deficiency(n. 缺乏, 不足)

---

definition
[ˌdefɪ'nɪʃn]

n.定义 (a statement expressing the essential nature of sth.)

记 来自definite(a. 一定的; 确切的)

例 A more precise *definition* of the term "small firm" is crucial to making a conclusive analysis about small firms' roles.

同根词: definitive(a. 确定的; 权威性的; n. 限定词)

---

definitive
[dɪ'fɪnətɪv]

a.确定的 (conclusive); 权威性的 (authoritative)

记 词根记忆: de(加强) + fin(结束) + itive(…的) → 最终拍板的 → 权威性的

例 While raising important questions, Eisenstein's essays do not provide *definitive* answers.

10

deflect [dɪˈflekt]	*v.* (使)偏斜，(使)转向(to turn aside, deviate) 🔲 联想记忆：de(离开) + flect(弯曲) → 弯到旁边 → 偏斜 📖 With no electric charge, a neutrino can cross the entire universe without being absorbed or even *deflected*.
deform [dɪˈfɔːrm]	*v.* 使变形(to alter the shape by stress) 🔲 词根记忆：de(表否定) + form(形状) → 使不再是原来的形状 → 使变形 📖 The stress is severe enough to *deform* it like putty. 📛 deformation(*n.* 变形)
defrost [ˌdiːˈfrɔːst]	*v.* 除霜(to free from ice)；解冻(to release from a frozen state)· 🔲 词根记忆：de(去掉) + frost(霜) → 去除霜 → 除霜；解冻 📖 No attempt was made to *defrost* the back window.
degradation [ˌdeɡrəˈdeɪʃn]	*n.* 退化；降级(decline to a low, destitute, or demoralized state)；堕落(moral or intellectual decadence) 🔲 来自degrade(*v.* 贬低；降级；退化) 📖 Indeed, most analysts believe that some kind of environmental *degradation* underlies the demise of many extinct salmon populations.
degrade [dɪˈɡreɪd]	*n.* 降低…的身份(to demote)；(使)降解(to decompose)；(使)退化(to decompose) 🔲 词根记忆：de(去掉) + grade(级别) → 去掉级别 → 降低…的身份 📖 They argued that the technique had *degraded* works of art.
dehydrate [diːˈhaɪdreɪt]	*v.* (使)脱水(to remove water from; to lose water) 🔲 词根记忆：de(去掉) + hydr(水) + ated → 去水的 → 脱水 📖 Retail prices of *dehydrated* potatoes have declined. 📛 dehydration(*n.* 脱水)
deleterious [ˌdeləˈtɪriəs]	*a.* (对身心)有害的(injurious) 🔲 联想记忆：delete(删除) + rious → 对身心有害的定要删除 → 有害的 📖 Efforts to control the spruce budworm have had *deleterious* effects on the red-osier dogwood.
deliberate [dɪˈlɪbərət]	*a.* 深思熟虑的(characterized by or resulting from careful and thorough consideration)；蓄意的(voluntary) 🔲 词根记忆：de + liber(自由) + ate → 按自由意志的 → 蓄意的 📖 The *deliberate* selective breeding produced modern domesticated sheep. // The *deliberate* and even brutal aggression integral to some forms of competitive athletics increase the likelihood of imitative violence. 同根词：liberality(*n.* 自由，慷慨)；liberty(*n.* 自由)
delicacy [ˈdelɪkəsi]	*n.* 美味，佳肴(sth. pleasing to eat that is considered rare or luxurious)；精妙(the quality or state of being luxurious) 🔲 来自delicate(*a.* 精美的；可口的) 📖 A special Japanese green tea called genmai-cha contains brown rice and is considered as a *delicacy* fit for a gourmet by most Japanese, though it is virtually unavailable outside Yokohama.

delicate [ˈdelɪkət]	*a.* 微妙的(subtle); 精致的(pleasing to the senses); 脆弱的(fragile) 记 词根记忆: de + lic(引诱) + ate → 一再引诱人的 → 精致的 例 The new variety of wheat had a more *delicate* flavor. // Tom was a *delicate* child who is often ill.
delineate [dɪˈlɪnieɪt]	*v.* 描画(to indicate or represent by drawn or painted lines); 描绘轮廓(to mark the outline of) 记 联想记忆: de + line(线条) + ate → 用线条画 → 描画 例 An argument is *delineated*, followed by a counterargument.
delinquent [dɪˈlɪŋkwənt]	*n.* 行为不良的人(a delinquent person); *a.* 拖欠的(being overdue in payment); 违法的(offending by neglect or violation of duty or of law) 记 词根记忆: de + linqu(离开) + ent → 离开自己的岗位 → 失职 → 违法的 例 The bank holds $3 billion in loans that are seriously *delinquent*. // *delinquent* behavior 违法行为 派 delinquency(*n.* 逾期债款)
deliver [dɪˈlɪvər]	*v.* 交付(to take and hand over to or leave for another); 递送(to send); 实现(to come through with) 记 词根记忆: de(离开) + live(举起) + r → 举起然后拿走 → 递送 例 In Borania many people who want to quit smoking wear nicotine skin patches, which *deliver* small doses of nicotine through the skin. 派 delivery(*n.* 交付; 递送)

11

And gladly would learn, and gladly teach.
勤于学习的人才能乐于施教。

——英国诗人 乔叟(Chaucer, British poet)

Word List 11

音频

delta	*n.*(河流的)三角洲(the alluvial deposit at the mouth of a river)
['deltə]	记 本身是希腊语的第四个字母"Δ",也指形状像 Δ 的河流的三角洲
	例 The Hyksos(希克索斯王) invaded the Nile *Delta* of Egypt and ruled it from 1650 B.C.
deluxe	*a.*豪华的(notably luxurious, elegant, or expensive)
[də'lʌks]	记 词根记忆:de + luxe(光) → 闪闪发光的 → 豪华的
	例 Our company started manufacturing and marketing a *deluxe* air filter six months ago.
delve	*v.*钻研,深入探索(to make a careful search for information)
[delv]	记 联想记忆:整天埋在书架(shelves)里钻研(delve)
	例 The investigator *delved* into the matter of Tom's sudden wealth.
demobilization	*n.*遣散(军人)(discharging from military service);复员
[diˌmoubələ'zeiʃn]	记 来自 demobilize(*v.* 复员),de + mobilize(动员) → 动员回家 → 复员
	例 The bill was passed to help the nation's *demobilization* effort.
	同根词:mobility(*n.* 能动性)
democracy	*n.*民主,民主主义;民主政治(government by the people)
[di'mɑːkrəsi]	记 词根记忆:demo(人民) + cracy(统治) → 人民统治 → 民主
	例 Many scholars have theorized that economic development, particularly industrialization and urbanization, contributes to the growth of participatory *democracy*.
	同根词:demography(*n.* 人口统计学)
democrat	*n.*民主主义者(an adherent of democracy);[D~ 美国民主党人
['deməkræt]	记 词根记忆:demo(人民) + crat → 民主主义者
	例 A certain state legislature consists of 124 members each of whom is either a *Democrat* or a Republican.
	派 democratic(*a.* 民主的;民主主义的); democratically(*ad.* 民主地;民主主义地)
demographer	*n.*人口统计学家(expert in demography)
[di'mɑːgrəfər]	记 词根记忆:demo(人民) + graph(写) + er → 人口统计学家
	例 *Demographers* are doing research for an international economics newsletter claim.
	派 demographic(*a.* 人口统计的)

demographic [ˌdeməˈgræfɪk]	*a.* 人口统计学的（of demography or demographics） 词根记忆：demo(人民，人口) + graph(写，画) + ic → 描写人口状况的 → 人口统计学的 例 The researchers dismissed *demographic* bias because older individuals were not overrepresented in the fossil samples. 同根词：democracy(*n.* 民主)
demonstrably [dɪˈmɑːnstrəbli]	*ad.* 可证实地，显然地（apparently, evidently） 来自 demonstrable(*a.* 可论证的，可证实的) 例 That *demonstrably* slowed the economic growth of medieval France.
demonstrate [ˈdemənstreɪt]	*v.* 证明（to prove by reasoning or evidence）；显示（to show clearly）；示威游行（或集会）（to make a demonstration, to participate in a public display of opinion） 词根记忆：de(加强) + monstr(表示) + ate(做) → 加强表示 → 证明 例 Her work aims to *demonstrate* that wage work enabled women to become aware of themselves as a distinct social group. // The citizens *demonstrated* against the new taxes. 派 demonstrator(*n.* 示威者；论证者)
denote [dɪˈnoʊt]	*v.* 表示，意味着（indicate） 词根记忆：de(下面) + note(做记号) → 在下面做记号 → 表示 例 In astronomy the term "red shift" *denotes* the extent to which light from a distant galaxy has been shifted toward red.
denounce [dɪˈnaʊns]	*v.* 公然抨击（to accuse publicly）；告发（to tell the police, the authorities, etc. about sb's illegal political activities） 词根记忆：de + nounce(讲，说) → 打小报告 → 告发 例 They *denounce* big government, saying government is doing too much and has become too powerful. 派 denouncement(*n.* 告发；痛骂) 同根词：announce(*v.* 宣布)；renounce(*v.* 宣布放弃)
dense [dens]	*a.* 密集的（crowded closely together, compact）；浓厚的（not easily seen through (of liquids or vapour)） 和 tense(*a.* 紧张的)一起记 例 Over time the distribution of dust in a meteor stream(流星群)will usually become *denser* at the outside edges of the stream than at the center. 派 densely(*ad.* 密度大地，浓厚地)；density(*n.* 浓度，密度)
density [ˈdensəti]	*n.* 浓度，密度（the quality or state of being dense） 来自 dense(*a.* 稠密的；浓厚的) 例 There are changes in the population *density* of both Meadowbrook and Parkdale over the past four years. 同根词：condense(*v.* 使浓缩)

11

denunciatory
[dɪˈnʌnsɪəˌtɔri]

a. 谴责的(condemning publicly)

记 来自 denunciate(*v.* 谴责)

例 The author's attitude toward the affair can best be described as scornful and *denunciatory*.

同根词：denunciation(*n.* 谴责)

depart
[dɪˈpɑːrt]

v. 背离，违反(to vary, as from a regular course)；出发(to leave)

记 词根记忆：de(离开) + part(分开) → 离开

例 Textbooks written in the middle part of the 19th century *departed* radically in tone and style from earlier textbooks. // Did the train *depart* for Chicago?

派 departure(*n.* 变更；开始)

departure
[dɪˈpɑːrtʃər]

n. 离开(the act or an instance of departing)；出发(setting out)

记 来自 depart(*v.* 离开；出发)

例 The labor activists' position represented a *departure* from the voluntarist view held until 1935 by leaders of the American Federation of labor, a leading affiliation of labor unions.

同根词：departed(*a.* 去世的)

dependence
[dɪˈpendəns]

n. 依赖，依靠(the quality or state of being dependent)

记 来自 depend(*v.* 依靠，依赖)

例 While several studies have found a significant correspondence between the density *dependence* model and actual patterns of foundings, other studies have found patterns not consistent with the model.

同根词：dependent(*a.* 依靠的；从属的)

depict
[dɪˈpɪkt]

v. 刻画，描述(to describe)

记 词根记忆：de(起强调作用) + pict(画) → 刻画，描述

例 A careful review of how school textbooks *depict* Native Americans is certainly warranted.

派 depiction(*n.* 描写，叙述)

depiction
[dɪˈpɪkʃn]

n. 描写(description)；叙述(a graphic or vivid verbal description)

记 来自 depict(*v.* 描述)

例 The failing of the book lies not in a lack of attention to scientific detail but in the *depiction* of scenes of life and death in the marine world with emotional overtones that reduce the credibility of the work.

同根词：pictorial(*a.* 绘画的)

deplete
[dɪˈpliːt]

v. 倒空，耗尽(to drain, to exhaust)

记 词根记忆：de(去除) + plete(满) → 使不满 → 倒空

例 A series of costly wars had *depleted* the national treasury.

派 depletion(*n.* 损耗)

depletion
[dɪˈpliːʃn]

n. 消耗，损耗(the act of decreasing sth. markedly)

记 来自 deplete(*v.* 耗尽，倒空)

例 Unlike cod and haddock, there are no legal size limits on catching monkfish, which contributes to its *depletion* by being overfished.

同根词：complete(*v.* 完成；*a.* 完整的)

---

96 denunciatory □ depart □ departure □ dependence □ depict □ depiction
□ deplete □ depletion

deposit [dɪˈpɑːzɪt]	v. 储蓄(to put in a bank); 放置(to place); n. 存款(money deposited in a bank); 押金(money given as a pledge or down payment); 沉积物(something laid down) 记 词根记忆: de(起强调作用) + posit(放) → 把财物妥善保管 → 储蓄 例 Most of the gold *deposits* discovered during the original gold rushes were exposed at the Earth's surface. // Ms. Fox *deposited* $10,000 in a new account at the annual interest rate of 12 percent. 派 depositor(n. 存款人); depository(n. 存放处)
deprecate [ˈdeprəkeɪt]	v. 反对(to disapprove); 藐视(to belittle) 记 词根记忆: de(去除) + prec(=preci 价值) + ate → 去掉价值 → 藐视 例 They *deprecate* the numerous Native American cultures.
depreciation [dɪˌpriːʃiˈeɪʃn]	n. 贬值(falling in value) 记 来自 depreciate(v. 贬值) 例 Because of rapid technological change, computers have a fast *depreciation*. 同根词: appreciate(v. 赏识)
depress [dɪˈpres]	v. 使沮丧(to sadden); 削弱(to lessen the activity or strength); 使萧条(to decrease the market value or marketability) 记 词根记忆: de(往下) + press(压) → 往下压 → 削弱 例 Adenosine(腺苷)normally *depresses* neuron firing in many areas of the brain. // Putting such large amounts of stock on the market would only *depress* its value. 派 depressed(a. 沮丧的, 消沉的); depression(n. 抑郁; 萧条); depressive(a. 令人沮丧的; 抑郁的)
depression [dɪˈpreʃn]	n. 消沉(dejection); 萧条(期) 记 来自 depress(v. 消沉, 沮丧) 例 Only one percent of Americans born before 1905 suffer major *depression* by the age of seventy-five. // the Great *Depression* 大萧条 派 depressive(a. 郁闷的)
deprivation [ˌdeprɪˈveɪʃn]	n. 剥夺(the act or an instance of depriving); 缺乏(the state of being deprived) 记 来自 deprive(v. 剥夺) 例 Sleep-*deprivation* is not used to treat depression. // oxygen *deprivation* 缺氧 同根词: privacy(n. 独处, 私下); privation(n. 贫乏)
deregulation [ˌdiːˌregjuˈleɪʃn]	n. 违反规定, 撤销管制规定(the act or process of removing restrictions and regulations) 记 来自 deregulate(v. 解除对…的管制) 例 Since the *deregulation* of airlines, delays at the nation's increasingly busy airports have increased by 25 percent. 同根词: regulation(n. 规则; 校准)

11

derivative
[dɪˈrɪvətɪv]

*a.*派生的（derived）; 无创意的（not original）; *n.*转成物

记 来自 derive（*v.* 源自）

例 The Madagascar periwinkle has a *derivative* which has proved useful in decreasing mortality among young leukemia patients.

同根词: derivation（*n.* 引出; 来历; 词源）

derive
[dɪˈraɪv]

v.（from 得到, 得自（to take, receive, or obtain especially from a specified source）; 推论出（to infer, to deduce）

记 词根记忆: de + rive（=river 河流）→ 支流 → 得到

例 Most geologists believe that crude oil is *derived* from organisms buried under ancient seas. // The set of objective criteria is *derived* from these analyses.

派 derivative（*a.* 引出的）

descend
[dɪˈsend]

*v.*下降（to come or go down）; 遗传（to derive）

记 词根记忆: de + scend（爬）→ 往下爬 → 下降; 遗传

例 A plane *descended* 2,000 feet from an altitude of 10,000 feet.

派 descendant（*n.* 子孙, 后裔）

description
[dɪˈskrɪpʃn]

*n.*描写, 描述（an act of describing）

记 词根记忆: de + script（写）+ ion → 描写, 描述

例 vivid *description* 生动的描述

desegregation
[ˌdiːˌsegrɪˈgeɪʃn]

*n.*取消种族隔离（the action or an instance of desegregating）

记 来自 desegregate（*v.* 取消种族隔离）, de（解除）+ segregate（隔离）→ 解除隔离 → 取消种族隔离

例 School *desegregation* has worked well in Buffalo and New York.

deserve
[dɪˈzɜːrv]

*v.*应受, 值得（to be worthy of）

记 联想记忆: de + serve（服务）→ 充分享受服务 → 应受, 值得

例 American Indian poems have not yet attracted the scholarly attention they *deserve*.

designate
[ˈdezɪɡneɪt]

*v.*指派（to appoint）; 指明, 指定（to specify）

记 词根记忆: de（起强调作用）+ sign（标出）+ ate → 标出来 → 指明, 指定

例 Each prisoner was made to *designate* the amount of ransom（赎金）to be paid for his return.

派 designated（*a.* 指定的, 指派的）

desire
[dɪˈzaɪər]

*v.*渴望（to long or hope for）; 要求（to request）; *n.*愿望（longing）

例 The politician *desired* power and would stop at nothing to get it. // Seeing or hearing an advertisement for a product tends to increase people's *desire* for that product.

派 desirable（*a.* 值得要的; 令人满意的）

despise
[dɪˈspaɪz]

*v.*轻视, 轻蔑（to look down on）

记 词根记忆: de（不）+ spise（=spic 看）→ 不值得看 → 轻视

例 Mary *despised* her rude neighbors.

detach
[dɪˈtætʃ]

*v.*分开, 分离（to separate）

记 词根记忆: de（去掉）+ tach（接触）→ 去掉接触 → 分开

例 He had to *detach* himself from social activities in order to concentrate on his studies.

同根词: attachment（*n.* 附件; 依恋）

detached [dɪ'tætʃt]	*a.* 不含个人偏见的(free from prejudice or self interest) 例 The tone of the passage can best be described as *detached*.
detection [dɪ'tekʃn]	*n.* 察觉；发现(the act or process of detecting; discovery) 记 来自 detect(*v.* 察觉；发现)，de(去除) + tect(遮盖) → 去掉遮盖 → 发现 例 Virtually everything astronomers know about objects outside the solar system is based on the *detection* of photons.
deter [dɪ'tɜːr]	*v.* 威慑(to overawe)；阻止(to discourage, or prevent from acting) 记 词根记忆：de(起强调作用) + ter(=terr 吓唬) → 威慑 例 The legislature enacts severe laws to *deter* motorists from picking fruit off the trees. 派 deterrence(*n.* 妨碍物)；deterrent(*n.* 威慑)
deteriorate [dɪ'tɪriəreɪt]	*v.* （使）恶化(to impair, to degenerate) 记 来自 deterior(拉丁文：糟糕的) 例 Compared with conditions before the war, sanitary conditions had *deteriorated*. 派 deterioration(*n.* 变坏；退化)
deterioration [dɪ,tɪriə'reɪʃn]	*n.* 恶化；退化；堕落(the action or process of deteriorating) 记 来自 deteriorate(*v.* 恶化；变坏) 例 To reverse the *deterioration* of the postal service, the government should raise the price of postage stamps. 同根词：deteriorator(*n.* 堕落者)
determination [dɪ,tɜːrmɪ'neɪʃn]	*n.* 决心；果断(the quality that makes you continue trying to do sth. even when this is difficult) 记 来自 determine(*v.* 决定) 例 It reinforced the religious elite's *determination* to resist cultural change. 同根词：interminable(*a.* 无穷无尽的)
determinism [dɪ'tɜːrmɪnɪzəm]	*n.* 决定论(a theory or doctrine that acts of the will, occurrences in nature, or social or psychological phenomena are causally determined by preceding events or natural laws) 记 来自 determine(*v.* 决定) 例 Jon Clark's study is a solid contribution to a debate that encompasses two lively issues in the history and sociology of technology: technological *determinism* and social constructivism. 同根词：determinist(*n.* 决定论者)
detrimental [,detrɪ'mentl]	*a.* 损害的，造成伤害的(causing detriment, harmful) 记 来自 detriment (*n.* 伤害)，de(变坏) + trim(修剪) + ent → 剪坏了 → 伤害 例 The *detrimental* effects were attributed to an amino acid that is one of the sweetener's principal constituents. 派 detrimentally(*ad.* 有害地；不利地)

11

□ detached   □ detection   □ deter   □ deteriorate   □ deterioration   □ determination
□ determinism   □ detrimental

devastate
['devəsteɪt]

v. 毁坏(to bring to ruin by violent action)

记 联想记忆:de(去除) + vast(大量) + ate → 大量去除 → 毁坏;vast 本身为词根:广阔的、大量的

例 Agriculture experts announced that the disease has *devastated* some of the corn crops.

派 devastating(a. 毁灭性的)

deviate
['di:vieɪt]

v. 越轨, 脱离(to diverge; to digress)

记 词根记忆:de(离开) + vi(路) + ate → 离开道路 → 脱离

例 Why firms adhere to or *deviate* from their strategic plans is poorly understood. However, theory and limited research suggest that the process through which such plans emerge may play a part.

派 deviation(n. 偏差;误差)

deviation
[,di:vi'eɪʃn]

n. 背离(noticeable or marked departure from accepted norms of behavior)

记 来自 deviate(v. 脱离,偏轨)

例 The Chinese used a gravity meter to correct for local *deviations* in sea level.

同根词:deviant(n. 不正常者;变异物;a. 不正常的;离经叛道的)

devise
[dɪ'vaɪz]

v. 想出(to think out); 设计, 发明(to invent)

例 Several procedures were *devised* to reduce transaction costs.

devoid
[dɪ'vɔɪd]

a. (of)空的, 缺乏的(absent)

记 词根记忆:de + void(空) → 空的, 缺乏的

例 The space between the galaxies is *devoid* of matter.

dexterity
[dek'sterəti]

n. 纯熟, 灵巧(skill and ease in using the hands)

记 词根记忆:dexter(右) + ity → 用右手做事 → 纯熟

例 Manual *dexterity* and mental alertness are lower in the late night than they are during the day.

diagnose
[,daɪəg'noʊs]

v. 诊断(to recognize a disease by signs and symptoms)

记 词根记忆:dia(穿过) + gnose(知道) → 古时通过望、闻、问、切诊断病情,透过表面看实质 → 诊断

例 Angiograms(血管造影片)can be used to *diagnose* conditions other than blockages in arteries.

派 diagnosis(n. 诊断); diagnostic(a. 诊断的;判断的)

diagnostic
[,daɪəg'nɑ:stɪk]

a. 诊断的, 判断的(of, relating to, or used in diagnosis); n. 诊断程序(the art or practice of diagnosis)

记 来自 diagnose(v. 诊断)

例 Researchers have questioned the use of costly and experimental *diagnostic* tests to identify food allergies.

diagonal
[daɪ'ægənl]

n. 对角线(a straight line than joins two opposite sides of sth. at an angle)

记 词根记忆:dia(穿过) + gon(角) + al → 穿过两个角的线 → 对角线

例 The size of a television screen is given as the length of the screen's *diagonal*.

dialect ['daɪəlekt]	*n.* 方言，语调(a regional variety of language distinguished by features of vocabulary, grammar, and pronunciation from other regional varieties and constituting together with them a single language) 例 Cajuns speak a *dialect* brought to southern Louisiana by the four thousand Acadians who migrated there in 1755.
diameter [daɪ'æmɪtər]	*n.* 直径(a straight line segment passing through the center of a figure, especially of a circle or sphere, and terminating at the periphery) 记 词根记忆：dia(通过) + meter(量) → 穿过它来测量直径 → 直径 注意：circumference(*n.* 圆周长) 例 The *diameter* of the bicycle wheel was 0.5 meters.
diaper ['daɪpər]	*n.* 尿布 记 联想记忆：di(分开) + aper(看作 paper 纸) → 能把水分隔开的纸 → 尿布 例 disposable *diapers* 一次性尿布
dichotomy [daɪ'kɑːtəmi]	*n.* 一分为二(a division into two especially mutually exclusive or contradictory groups) 记 词根记忆：dicho(二份) + tom(切、割) + y → 切成二份 → 一分为二 例 the good bad *dichotomy* 好与坏的二分法 派 dichotomous(*a.* 二分的；分叉的)
dictate ['dɪkteɪt]	*v.* 规定，支配(to impose, or specify authoritatively) 记 词根记忆：dict(说) + ate → 规定 例 Capitalists who owned enough stock to dominate the board of directors always *dictate* company policy.
diesel ['diːzl]	*n.* 内燃机，柴油机(a diesel engine) 记 由德国的发明家 Diesel(狄赛尔)而来 例 *diesel* fuel 柴油
dietary ['daɪəteri]	*a.* 饮食的(of or relating to a diet or to the rules of a diet) 记 来自 diet(*n.* 饮食) 例 When maize was introduced into southern Europe, it quickly became a *dietary* staple.
differentiate [ˌdɪfə'renʃieɪt]	*v.* 区别(to mark or show a difference in)；【生】分化(to undergo a progressive, developmental change to a more specialized form or function) 记 来自 different(*a.* 不同的) 例 Improved customer service is the best way for us to *differentiate* ourselves from competitors. // The hormones will cause plant cells to *differentiate* to perform different functions.
differentiation [ˌdɪfəˌrenʃi'eɪʃn]	*n.* 变异(the act or process of differentiating)；分化；区别(a discrimination between things as different and distinct) 记 来自 differentiate(*v.* 区分) 例 While studying the genetic makeup of corn, Barbara McClintock discovered a new class of mutant genes, a discovery that led to greater understanding of cell *differentiation*. 同根词：differentially(*ad.* 区别地)

11

digest [daɪ'dʒest; dɪ'dʒest]	[daɪ'dʒest; dɪ'dʒest] *v.* 消化(to convert (food) into absorbable form); 吸收(to absorb; to take into the mind or memory) ['daɪdʒest] *n.* 摘要(a summation or condensation of a body of information) 记 词根记忆：di(向下) + gest(运) → 将食物向下运 → 消化 例 If proteins are taken orally, they are *digested* and cannot reach their target cells. 派 digestion(*n.* 消化力)；digestive(*a.* 消化的)
digit ['dɪdʒɪt]	*n.* 数字(number)；【数】十位数 例 the tens *digit* 派 digitize(*v.* 将…数字化)；digital(*a.* 数字的)
digitize ['dɪdʒɪtaɪz]	*v.* 数字化(to convert (as data or an image) to digital form) 记 词根记忆：digit(数字) + ize → 数字化 例 The sound emissions were *digitized* and analyzed on computers. 同根词：digital(*a.* 数字的；手指的)
dilemma [dɪ'lemə]	*n.* 困境，左右为难(a problem involving a difficult choice) 记 发音记忆："地雷嘛" → 被陷雷区，进退两难 → 困境 例 The company solved its globalization *dilemma* effectively by forging alliances with the best foreign partners.
dilute [daɪ'luːt]	*v.* 冲淡，稀释(to make thinner or more liquid by admixture) 例 Those concentrated cleaning products must be *diluted* before using them. 派 dilution(*n.* 稀释，渗水)
dimension [daɪ'menʃn]	*n.* 尺度(size)；维(a measurement of space)；方面(aspect) 记 词根记忆：di + mens(测量) + ion → 有关测量的 → 尺度 例 The inside *dimensions* of a rectangular wooden box were 6 inches by 8 inches by 10 inches. // Earnings and income data overstated the *dimensions* of hardship. 派 dimensional(*a.* 空间的)
diminish [dɪ'mɪnɪʃ]	*v.* 减少，削弱(to reduce) 记 词根记忆：dimin(小) + ish → 使变小 → 减小，削弱 例 Sulfur dioxide can *diminish* the respiratory system's ability to deal with all other pollutants.
diminution [ˌdɪmɪ'nuːʃn]	*n.* 减少，缩减(a case or the state of diminishing or being diminished) 记 词根记忆：di + minu(变小，减少) + tion → 减少 例 It prevented the Hopis from experiencing a *diminution* in population.
dinosaur ['daɪnəsɔːr]	*n.* 恐龙 记 词根记忆：dino(恐怖的) + saur(蜥蜴) → 恐龙

□ digest　　□ digit　　□ digitize　　□ dilemma　　□ dilute　　□ dimension
□ diminish　　□ diminution　　□ dinosaur

dioxide [daɪˈɑːksaɪd]	*n.* 二氧化物（an oxide（as carbon dioxide）containing two atoms of oxygen in the molecule） 记 词根记忆：di（二）+ oxide（氧化物）→ 二氧化物 例 carbon *dioxide* 二氧化碳
diploma [dɪˈploumə]	*n.* 文凭（a document bearing record of graduation from or of a degree conferred by an educational institution） 例 high school *diploma* 高中毕业证

The man who has made up his mind to win will never say "impossible".
凡是决心取得胜利的人是从来不说"不可能的"。

——法国皇帝 拿破仑（Bonaparte Napoleon, French emperor）

11

Word List 12

音频

diplomatic [ˌdɪpləˈmætɪk]	*a.* 外交的 (of, relating to, or concerned with diplomacy or diplomats) 记 联想记忆：diploma (文凭) + tic → 外交工作需要高文凭 → 外交的 例 *diplomatic* relation 外交关系
dire [ˈdaɪər]	*a.* 可怕的 (exciting horror)；悲惨的 (dismal) 例 *dire* consequences 可怕的后果
disability [ˌdɪsəˈbɪləti]	*n.* 无能 (the condition of being disabled)；无资格 (lack of legal qualification to do sth.) 记 词根记忆：dis (不) + ability (能力) → 没有能力 → 无能 例 A common *disability* in test pilots is hearing impairment, a consequence of sitting too close to large jet engines for long periods of time.
disaster [dɪˈzæstər]	*n.* 灾难；彻底的失败 (a sudden or great failure) 记 联想记忆：dis (离开) + aster (星星) → 星星偏离轨道 → 灾难 例 natural *disaster* 自然灾害 // In fact, privatization has rescued individual industries but the economy as a whole is headed for *disaster*. 派 disastrous (*a.* 损失惨重的；灾难性的)
discard [dɪsˈkɑːrd]	*v.* 扔掉，丢弃 (to get rid of or cast) 记 词根记忆：dis (消失掉) + card (心) → 从心里消失掉 → 扔掉，丢弃 例 Those researchers won't *discard* their theories about the effects of microwave radiation on organisms.
discern [dɪˈsɜːrn]	*v.* (费劲) 识别，辨认 (to detect with senses other than vision) 记 词根记忆：dis (分离) + cern (分开，辨别) → 识别 例 Human beings can *discern* spatial relations through their sense of hearing. 派 discernible (*a.* 可辨别的) 同根词：concern (*v.* 关注)
discharge [dɪsˈtʃɑːrdʒ; ˈdɪstʃɑːrdʒ]	*v./n.* 排放 (to emit)；释放 (to release from confinement, custody or care)；解雇 (to dismiss) 记 词根记忆：dis (离开) + charge (装，委托) → 不装载 → 释放 例 Federal regulations requiring a drop in industrial *discharges* of lead went into effect in 1975. // The physician knew when the patient may be *discharged*.

□ diplomatic　　□ dire　　□ disability　　□ disaster　　□ discard　　□ discern
□ discharge

disciple [dɪ'saɪpl]	n. 门徒, 弟子 (follower) 例 This famous musician founded no school and left behind only a handful of *disciples*.
discipline ['dɪsəplɪn]	v. 训练, 调教 (to teach, to train); n. 纪律; 学科 (a field of study) 记 联想记忆: dis + cip(拿) + line(线) → 拿一条线来训练 → 训练 例 The sergeant *disciplined* the recruits. // academic *discipline* 学科
disclosure [dɪs'kloʊʒər]	n. 披露, 揭发 (the act or an instance of disclosing) 记 来自disclose(v. 公开, 揭露) 例 Among those making the required financial *disclosure* this year is a prominent local businessman, Arnold Bergeron. 同根词: close(v. 关; 结束; a. 亲近的)
discord ['dɪskɔːrd]	n. 不和, 纷争 (strife, conflict) 记 词根记忆: dis(不) + cord(一致) → 不和, 纷争 例 international *discord* 国际争端
discount	[dɪs'kaʊnt] v. 忽视 (to disregard); 打折 (to sell or offer for sale at a reduced price) ['dɪskaʊnt] n. 折扣 (a reduction from the full or standard amount of a price or debt) 记 词根记忆: dis(不) + count(计算) → 不计算在内 → 折扣 例 Many scholars *discount* the role of public policy when explaining employers' maternity leave policies. // *discount* stores 折扣店
discrepancy [dɪs'krepənsi]	n. 差异 (difference); 矛盾 (the quality or state of being discrepant) 记 词根记忆: dis(分开) + crep(破裂) + ancy → 裂开 → 差异; 矛盾 例 There was a *discrepancy* in the two reports of the accident.
discrete [dɪ'skriːt]	a. 个别的 (individually distinct); 不连续的 (noncontinuous) 记 注意: discreet(a. 小心的, 谨慎的) 例 The American classical virtue stressed civic duty and made the whole community greater than its *discrete* parts. // Digital recordings reduce the original sound to a series of *discrete* numbers.
discretion [dɪ'skreʃn]	n. 谨慎 (the quality of being discreet); 审慎 (prudence) 例 Ten years ago physicians were allowed more *discretion*.
discretionary [dɪ'skreʃəneri]	a. 自由决定的 (exercised at one's own discretion); 可随意使用的 (available for use as needed or desired) 记 来自discretion(n. 自行处理) 例 *discretionary* powers 自主行事的权力 // You may be eligible for a *discretionary* grant for your university course.
discriminate [dɪ'skrɪmɪneɪt]	v. (against) 歧视 (to look down upon sb./sth.); 辨别 (to distinguish) 记 词根记忆: dis + crimin(罪行) + ate → 一种罪行 → 歧视 例 It's totally wrong to *discriminate* against women. // We must learn to *discriminate* right from wrong. 派 discrimination(n. 歧视); discriminatory(a. 歧视的, 不公平的)

12

□ disciple □ discipline □ disclosure □ discord □ discount □ discrepancy
□ discrete □ discretion □ discretionary □ discriminate

105

disdainful

[dɪsˈdeɪnfl]

*a.*轻蔑的，鄙视的（scornful and contemptuous）

记 来自 disdain（*v./n.* 鄙视，蔑视）

例 He's *disdainful* of anyone who is from America.

---

disenchanted

[ˌdɪsɪnˈtʃæntɪd]

*a.*不再着迷的，不抱有幻想的（disappointed, dissatisfied）

记 来自 disenchant（*v.* 使清醒）

例 Little Tom quickly became *disenchanted* with his new toy.

---

disenfranchise

[ˌdɪsɪnˈfræntʃaɪz]

*v.*剥夺…的公民权（to deprive of a franchise）

记 词根记忆：disenfranchise=disfranchise，dis（剥夺）+ franchise（选举权）→ 剥夺选取权 → 剥夺…的公民权

例 White supremacists devised new methods to *disenfranchise* Negroes.

---

disinclined

[ˌdɪsɪnˈklaɪnd]

*a.*不愿的（reluctant）

记 词根记忆：dis（不）+ inclined（愿意的）→ 不愿的

例 Many people are *disinclined* to recognize that their analytical skills are weak.

派 disinclination（*n.* 不愿意）

---

disintegration

[dɪsˌɪntɪˈgreɪʃn]

*n.*分解（separation into component parts）；瓦解（total destruction）

记 来自 disintegrate（*v.* 瓦解；分裂）

例 A comet's spectacular *disintegration* occurred in full view of ground and space-based telescopes last year.

同根词：integrate（*v.* 使完整；*a.* 整合的）

---

dislocation

[ˌdɪsloʊˈkeɪʃn]

*n.*混乱，紊乱（the state of being dislocated）

记 来自 dislocate（*v.* 混乱）

例 The Issei（第一代移居北美的日本人）suffered a massive *dislocation* caused by unemployment.

---

dislodge

[dɪsˈlɑːdʒ]

*v.*逐出（to drive from a position of hiding, defense, or advantage）；去除（to get rid of）

记 联想记忆：dis（分开）+ lodge（小屋）→ 逐出小屋 → 逐出

例 Tidal currents themselves do not *dislodge* barnacles from the shells of horseshoe crabs. // These drugs have the ability to *dislodge* caffeine from receptors in the brain.

---

dismal

[ˈdɪzməl]

*a.*凄凉的（bleak）；暗淡的（gloomy）

记 词根记忆：dis（不）+ mal（高兴）→ 不高兴 → 凄凉的

注意：decimal（*n.* 小数；*a.* 小数的）

例 a *dismal* failure 惨败

---

dismantle

[dɪsˈmæntl]

*v.*拆除（to strip of furniture and equipment）；废除，取消（to put an end in a gradual systematic way）

记 词根记忆：dis（去掉）+ mantle（覆盖）→ 去掉覆盖 → 拆除

例 The European Community has *dismantled* impediments to the free flow of goods among member states.

---

dismay

[dɪsˈmeɪ]

v./n.（使）沮丧（to cause to lose courage or resolution）

记 联想记忆：dis（不）+ may（可能）→ 因为不可能做到，所以沮丧 → 沮丧

例 The news *dismayed* Anne. // John showed considerable *dismay* at his child's bad behavior.

□ disdainful □ disenchanted □ disenfranchise □ disinclined □ disintegration □ dislocation
□ dislodge □ dismal □ dismantle □ dismay

dismiss [dɪsˈmɪs]	*v.* 解散(to permit or cause to leave); 解雇(to remove from position or service) 记 词根记忆: dis(消失掉) + miss(送, 放出) → 放掉 → 解散 例 No state law forbids an employer to reject a job applicant or *dismiss* an employee based on the results of a lie detector test. 派 dismission(*n.* 解散; 免职)
disorient [dɪsˈɔːrient]	*v.* 使迷惑(to confuse); 使分不清方向或目标(to cause to lose the sense of time, place, or identity) 记 词根记忆: dis(无) + orient(方向) → 没有方向 → 使分不清方向或目标 例 The sound emitted temporarily *disorients* the porpoises and frightens them away. 派 disoriented(*a.* 迷惑的; 分不清方向的) 同根词: orientate(*v.* 定向; 向东)
disparaging [dɪˈspærɪdʒɪŋ]	*a.* 贬低的, 轻蔑的(belittling, unkind) 记 来自disparage(*v.* 蔑视, 贬低), dis(不) + par(平等) + age → 不平等看人 → 贬低的 例 His tone was *disparaging*. 同根词: parity(*n.* 平等)
disparate [ˈdɪspərət]	*a.* (种类)全异的(entirely dissimilar); 迥然不同的(unequal, distinct) 记 词根记忆: dis(不) + par(平等) + ate → 不等的 → 迥然不同的 例 *disparate* species 异类物种 // Economists pointed out the similarities between two seemingly *disparate* trading alliances.
dispel [dɪˈspel]	*v.* 驱散(to drive away); 消除(to rid one's mind of) 记 词根记忆: dis(分开) + pel(推) → 推开 → 驱散 例 A warm sun quickly *dispelled* the morning fog. // *dispel* all doubts 消除一切疑虑
dispense [dɪˈspens]	*v.* 分配, 分发(to distribute) 记 词根记忆: dis(分开) + pense(花费) → 分开花费 → 分配, 分发 例 The drug is *dispensed* to doctors from a central authority. 派 indispensable(*a.* 不可少的)
disperse [dɪˈspɜːrs]	*v.* 分散, 散布(to scatter) 例 Maize pollen is *dispersed* by the wind.
displace [dɪsˈpleɪs]	*v.* 免职(to remove from an office, status, or job); 转移(to remove from the usual or proper place); 取代(to move physically out of position) 记 词根记忆: dis(消失掉) + place(放置) → 放走 → 转移 例 A few days after the iron compounds were released, ocean currents *displaced* the iron-rich water from the surface. 派 displacement(*n.* 取代; 免职)
dispose [dɪˈspoʊz]	*v.* (of)处置(to settle a matter finally); 安排(to arrange) 记 词根记忆: dis + pose(布置) → 处置; 安排 例 One common way to *dispose* of this outdated merchandise is to sell it to a liquidator(清算人). 派 disposal(*n.* 处理; 安排); disposable(*a.* 可处理的; 可任意使用的)

disproportionate [ˌdɪsprəˈpɔːrʃənət]	*a.* 不成比例的(being out of proportion) 例 The tycoon left his children *disproportionate* amounts of money.
dispute [dɪˈspjuːt]	*v.* 争论(to argue about; debate); *n.* 争辩(verbal controversy) 记 联想记忆：dis(不) + pute(思考) → 想法不同 → 争论 例 It is not a matter of widespread scientific *dispute*. 派 disputation(*n.* 争论；辩论)
disrupt [dɪsˈrʌpt]	*v.* 扰乱(to throw into disorder); (使)中断，(使)瓦解(to break apart) 记 词根记忆：dis(分开) + rupt(断) → 断开 → 中断 例 Closing the refinery would mean the lives of more than 10,000 people would be seriously *disrupted*. 派 disruption(*n.* 破坏；瓦解)
disseminate [dɪˈsemɪneɪt]	*v.* 传播，散布(to spread abroad as though sowing seeds) 记 词根记忆：dis(分开) + semin(种子) + ate → 散布种子 → 传播 例 *disseminate* rumors 散布谣言 派 dissemination(*n.* 传播，散布)
dissent [dɪˈsent]	*v./n.* 不同意(to differ in opinion) 记 词根记忆：dis(不) + sent(感觉) → 没有同感 → 不同意 例 Of the ten members, only one *dissented*. // There is rarely any *dissent* among the club members.
dissimilar [dɪˈsɪmɪlər]	*a.* 不同的，不相似的(unlike) 记 词根记忆：dis(不) + similar(相似的) → 不相似的 例 Some fraternal twins resemble each other greatly and others look quite *dissimilar*. 派 dissimilarly(*ad.* 不同地) 同根词：similar(*a.* 相似的；*n.* 类似物)
dissipate [ˈdɪsɪpeɪt]	*v.* (使)消散，(使)消失(to break up and scatter or vanish) 记 词根记忆：dis(分开) + sip(吸) + ate → 吸走 → 消失 例 The warm air from the stove rapidly *dissipated* in such a cold room.
dissociate [dɪˈsoʊʃieɪt]	*v.* 分离，分开(to separate from association or union with another) 记 词根记忆：dis(不) + soci(同伴，引申为社会) + ate → 不要同伴 → 分离 例 Max *dissociated* himself from the radical group.
distill [dɪˈstɪl]	*v.* 蒸馏(to let fall, exude, or precipitate in drops or in a wet mist); 提取(to extract the essence of) 记 词根记忆：di(分离) + still(滴) → 分离出来的水滴 → 蒸馏 注意：distillate(*n.* 馏出液，精华)；instill(*v.* 滴注，灌输) 例 This alcohol is *distilled* from cereal grain. // They left it to the textbook writers to *distill* the essence of those values for school children. 派 distillation(*n.* 蒸馏)
distinct [dɪˈstɪŋkt]	*a.* 不同的，有差别的(different) 记 词根记忆：di(分开) + stinct(=sting 刺) → 用刺促使分开 → 不同的 例 There are several *distinct* strains of malaria. 派 distinctly(*ad.* 不同地)；distinction(*n.* 区别)；distinctiveness(*n.* 特殊性)

□ disproportionate □ dispute □ disrupt □ disseminate □ dissent □ dissimilar
□ dissipate □ dissociate □ distill □ distinct

distinctive
[dɪˈstɪŋktɪv]

a. 出众的，有特色的(that distinguishes sth. by making it different from others)

记 词根记忆：distinct(明显的) + ive → 出众的，有特色的

例 The binding of different kinds of information is not a *distinctive* feature of episodic memory.

派 distinctively(*ad.* 特殊地；区别地)

distinguish
[dɪˈstɪŋgwɪʃ]

v. 区别，辨清(to perceive a difference in)；(使)杰出(to give prominence or distinction to)

记 词根记忆：di(分开) + sting(刺) + uish → 将刺挑出来 → 区别

例 Researchers successfully trained an anteater to *distinguish* between two troughs of water. // Tom *distinguished* himself in chemistry.

派 distinguished(*a.* 杰出的)；distinguishing(*a.* 有区别的)

distort
[dɪˈstɔːrt]

v. 弄歪(to twist out of a natural, normal, or original shape of condition)；歪曲(to deform)

记 词根记忆：dis + tort(扭曲) → 弄歪，歪曲

例 My research suggests that textbooks sometimes *distort* history to suit a particular cultural value system.

派 distorted(*a.* 扭曲的)；distortion(*n.* 扭曲，曲解)

distribute
[dɪˈstrɪbjuːt]

v. 分配，分发(to divide among several or many)

记 词根记忆：dis + tribute(给) → 给予 → 分配

例 The courts in theory are available to all but in fact are unequally *distributed* between rich and poor.

派 distribution(*n.* 分配)；distributive(*a.* 分配的)；distributor(*n.* 发行人)

distribution
[ˌdɪstrɪˈbjuːʃn]

n. 分布；分配(the act or process of distributing)

记 来自 distribute(*v.* 分配；散布)

例 They were not an effective means of solving the problem of different resource *distribution*.

同根词：tribute(*n.* 礼物；颂词)

distributor
[dɪˈstrɪbjətər]

n. 经销商(one that markets a commodity)；分配器；分配者(one that distributes)

记 来自 distribute(*v.* 分配；散布)

例 During the 1980's in Jurania, profits of wholesale *distributors* of poultry products increased at a greater rate than did profits of wholesale distributors of fish.

同根词：attribute(*v.* 归因于)

district
[ˈdɪstrɪkt]

n. 地区(a territorial division)；行政区(a territorial division as for administrative or electoral purposes)

例 commercial *district* 商业区 // civil *district* 民政区域

disturb
[dɪˈstɜːrb]

v. 打乱，扰乱(interrupt)

记 词根记忆：dis(分开) + turb(搅乱) → 搅开了 → 打乱

例 They felt guilty about *disturbing* the traditional division of labor within the family.

派 disturbance(*n.* 打扰；骚乱)；disturbing(*a.* 令人不安的)

12

□ distinctive   □ distinguish   □ distort   □ distribute   □ distribution   □ distributor
□ district   □ disturb

diverge [daɪˈvɜːrdʒ]	*v.* (from) 偏离 (to move or extend in different directions from a common point)；离题 (to turn aside from a course) 记 词根记忆：di + verge(转向) → 转开 → 偏离 例 Their path *diverge* at the fork in the road. 派 divergent(*a.* 有分歧的)；divergence(*n.* 分歧)
diverse [daɪˈvɜːrs]	*a.* 不同的，多种多样的 (varied, different) 例 Jane made a pretty bouquet of *diverse* flowers. 派 diversify(*v.* 使多样化)；diversity(*n.* 差异，多样性) 同根词：adversity(*n.* 苦难)；versatile(*a.* 多才多艺的)
diversification [daɪˌvɜːrsɪfɪˈkeɪʃn]	*n.* 多样化，变化 (the state of being diversifying) 记 来自 diversify(*v.* 使多样化) 例 George Washington Carver dedicated his life to strengthening the economy of the South through soil improvement and crop *diversification*.
diversify [daɪˈvɜːrsɪfaɪ]	*v.* 使多样化 (give variety to) 记 词根记忆：di(分开) + vers(转) + ify → 转开 → 不同 → 使多样化 例 It should therefore *diversify* its commercial enterprises. 派 diversification(*n.* 多样化) 同根词：inverse(*a.* 翻转的)
diversion [daɪˈvɜːrʒn]	*n.* 转移 (the act or an instance of diverting from a course, activity, or use)；消遣 (sth. that diverts or amuses) 记 词根记忆：di(分开) + vers(转) + ion → 分开转 → 转移 例 Some American Indian tribes have established water rights through the courts based on their traditional *diversion* and use of certain waters prior to the United States' acquisition of sovereignty. 同根词：diverse(*a.* 不同的)
divest [daɪˈvest]	*v.* (of) (使)摆脱 (to free)；剥夺 (to deprive especially of property, authority, or title) 记 词根记忆：di(去掉) + vest(穿衣) → 脱去衣服，摆脱束缚 → 剥夺 例 The workers *divested* themselves of stock in the company. // The murderer was *divested* of political right for life. 派 divestment(*n.* 剥夺，摆脱) 同根词：vested(*a.* 穿着衣服的)；vestment(*n.* 外衣；法衣)
dividend [ˈdɪvɪdend]	*n.* (股份的)红利 (bonus)；效益 (a resultant return or reward)；被除数 (a number to be divided) 记 词根记忆：divid(=divis 分) + end → 分享的利润 → 红利 例 Mr. Jackson's 1980 *dividends* on his shares totaled $150. 同根词：divisor(*n.* 除数，约数)
divisible [dɪˈvɪzəbl]	*a.* 可分割的；可整除的 (capable of being divided) 记 词根记忆：divis(分) + ible → 可分开的 → 可整除的 例 This positive integer is *divisible* by both 5 and 7.

division [dɪˈvɪʒn]	*n.* 部门；分裂(繁殖)(plant propagation by dividing parts)；区分(something that divides, separates, or marks off) 记 词根记忆：divis(分) + ion → 区分 例 Our company has just reduced its workforce by laying off fifteen percent of its employees in all *divisions*. // This determined the egg cell's potential for *division*. // *division* of labor in the family 家庭中的劳动分工
divisive [dɪˈvaɪsɪv]	*a.* 分裂的，不和的(creating disunity or dissension) 例 The issue is a very *divisive* one about which many people have strong opinions. 派 divisiveness(*n.* 不和)
divulge [daɪˈvʌldʒ]	*v.* 泄漏(秘密等)(to disclose) 记 词根记忆：di + vulge(普通) → 使…普通 → 泄漏(秘密等) 例 The stockbroker refuses to *divulge* the source of her information on the possible future increase in a stock's value. 同根词：vulgar(*a.* 粗俗的，普通的)
doctorate [ˈdɑːktərət]	*n.* 博士学位(the degree, title, or rank of a doctor) 例 A total of 774 *doctorates* in mathematics were granted to United States citizens in the 1972-1973 school year.
doctrine [ˈdɑːktrɪn]	*n.* 教义(dogma)；学说(a set of beliefs) 记 词根记忆：doct(教) + rine → 教义 例 the *doctrine* of evolution 进化论
documentation [ˌdɑːkjumenˈteɪʃn]	*n.* 证明文件(an instance of furnishing or authenticating with documents)；史实(conformity to historical or objective facts) 例 Mary Leakey contributed to archaeology through her discovery of the earliest direct evidence of hominid activity and through her painstaking *documentation* of East African cave paintings. 同根词：doctrine(*n.* 学说，教义)
dogma [ˈdɔːɡmə]	*n.* 教条(something held as an established opinion) 例 Church *dogma* 宗教信条
domain [doʊˈmeɪn]	*n.* 领地，领土(complete and absolute ownership of land) 记 词根记忆：dom(控制) + ain → 牢牢控制的地方 → 领地 例 The *domains* of samurai overlords were becoming smaller and poorer as government revenues decreased.
domestic [dəˈmestɪk]	*a.* 本国的(of, relating to, or originating within a country and especially one's own country)；家(庭)的(of or relating to the household or the family)；驯养的(domesticated) 记 词根记忆：dom(家) + estic(…的) → 家庭的 例 The demand for crude oil has grown in both *domestic* and foreign markets. // *domestic* responsibilities 家庭负担 // *domestic* hens 家鸡 派 domesticity(*n.* 家庭生活)

12

domesticate [dəˈmestɪkeɪt]	*v.* 驯养，教化(to tame) 例 Local people *domesticated* elephants to perform various essential tasks. 派 domestication(*n.* 驯养，教化)
domestication [dəˌmestɪˈkeɪʃn]	*n.* 驯养，教化(the process to adapt an animal or plant to life in intimate association with and to the advantage of humans) 记 来自 domestic(*a.* 国内的；家庭的；驯养的) 例 After 7,000 years of *domestication* in Eurasia, reindeer have developed a tendency to circle in tight groups, while caribou tend to spread far and wide.
domesticity [ˌdoʊmeˈstɪsəti]	*n.* 家庭生活(domestic activities or life)；专心于家务(the quality or state of being domestic or domesticated) 记 来自 domestic(*a.* 家庭的；国内的；一心只管家务的) 例 The cult of female *domesticity* developed independently of the concept of female benevolence.
dominate [ˈdɑːmɪneɪt]	*v.* 支配(to rule, to control)；在…占首要地位(to have a commanding or preeminent place or position in) 记 词根记忆：domin(=dom 控制) + ate → 支配 例 Two divergent definitions have *dominated* sociologists' discussions of the nature of ethnicity. 派 dominant(*a.* 占优势的，支配的)；dominance(*n.* 优势，统治)
donate [ˈdoʊneɪt]	*v.* 捐赠，赠送(to give) 记 词根记忆：don(给予) + ate → 给出去 → 捐赠，赠送 例 Manufacturers should *donate* excess inventory to charity rather than dump it. 派 donation(*n.* 捐赠品，捐款)；donor(*n.* 捐赠人)
dormant [ˈdɔːrmənt]	*a.* 【生】休眠的(latent) 记 词根记忆：dorm(睡眠) + ant → 休眠的 例 Potato cyst nematodes(马铃薯包囊线虫)can lie *dormant* for several years in their cysts(包囊). 同根词：dormitory(*n.* 宿舍)

音 频

dosage ['dousɪdʒ]	*n.* 剂量(the giving of a dose) 记 来自 dose(*v.* 给药；给…服药) 例 a *dosage* of a prescribed drug 一剂处方药 同根词：dosimetry(*n.* 剂量学)
dose [dous]	*n.* (药的)剂量(measured quantity of medicine)；一服(an amount of something likened to a prescription) 例 The medicine costs less per *dose* than that one. 派 dosage(*n.* 剂，剂量)
dough [dou]	*n.* 生面团(a mixture that consists essentially of flour or meal and a liquid and is stiff enough to knead or roll) 记 联想记忆：硬硬的(tough)的生面团(dough) 例 bread *dough* 生面团
downplay [ˌdaʊnˈpleɪ]	*v.* 贬低，不予重视(to de-emphasize) 例 The individualist feminist tradition *downplays* the importance of gender roles.
downstream [ˌdaʊnˈstriːm]	*ad.* 顺流而下，朝下游方向(in the direction of or towards the mouth of a stream) 记 词根记忆：down(向下的) + stream(溪，流) → 顺流而下 例 The leaf fell off the tree and floated *downstream*.
drab [dræb]	*a.* 土褐色的(of a dull light brown) 记 和 grab(*v.* 夺取)一起记
draft [dræft]	*n.* 草稿，草案(preliminary written version of sth.)；汇票(written order to a bank to pay money to sb.) 例 When Elizabeth Cady Stanton *drafted* the Declaration of Sentiments that was adopted at the Seneca Falls Women's Rights Convention in 1848, she included in it a call for female enfranchisement.
drainage ['dreɪnɪdʒ]	*n.* 排水(the act or method of drawing off)；排水系统(a system of drains)；污水(sth. drained off) 记 词根记忆：drain(排水) + age(名词后缀) → 排水 例 Changes in land use and *drainage* patterns around the lake mean that the lake's waters are increasingly likely to be affected by agricultural runoff.

dramatize [ˈdræmətaɪz]	*v.* (使)戏剧化(to present or represent in a dramatic manner) 记 词根记忆：drama(戏剧) + tize → 戏剧化 例 The television movie *dramatized* the historical event.
drastic [ˈdræstɪk]	*a.* 激烈的，剧烈的(severe) 例 Desertification(沙漠化)is not always the result of *drastic* climate changes alone. 派 drastically(*ad.* 激烈地；彻底地)
drift [drɪft]	*v.* 漂流，漂移(to cause to be driven in a current)；(价格等)缓慢变动(to vary or deviate from a set course or adjustment) 记 联想记忆：在大峡谷(rift)漂流(drift) 例 We watched the leaves *drift* downstream. // Consumers recognize that the quality of products sold under invariant brand names can *drift* over time.
drilling [ˈdrɪlɪŋ]	*n.* 钻孔(an action to make a hole with a drill)；训练，演练(exercise, training) 记 来自 drill(*v.* 训练；钻孔) 例 Jackson likened the questions about *drilling* risk to those about the link between smoking and lung cancer.
drizzle [ˈdrɪzl]	*n.* 细雨(a fine misty rain)；细流(streamlet) 例 a *drizzle* from the faucet 水龙头里流出的一股小水流
droplet [ˈdrɑːplət]	*n.* 小滴，微滴(a tiny drop) 记 联想记忆：drop(滴) + let(允许) → 允许滴下来的 → 小滴 例 Warmed by the Sun, ocean water evaporates, rises high into the atmosphere, and condenses in tiny *droplets* on minute particles of dust to form clouds.
dropout [ˈdrɑːpaʊt]	*n.* <美>中途退学(的学生)(one who drops out of school) 记 来自词组 drop out(中途退学) 例 The school *dropout* rate declined immediately after the adoption of interactive computer instruction.
drought [draʊt]	*n.* 干旱，旱灾(a period of dryness especially when prolonged) 记 联想记忆：dr(看作 dry) + ought(应该) → 应该干 → 干旱
dubious [ˈduːbɪəs]	*a.* 可疑的(doubtful)；不确定的(giving rise to uncertainty) 记 词根记忆：du(二) + bious → 有两种想法 → 不确定的 例 The manager decided not to hire the *dubious* applicant. // The result is still *dubious*.
ductile [ˈdʌktaɪl]	*a.* 易变形的(easily led or influenced)；可塑的(plastic) 记 词根记忆：duct(引导) + ile → 可引导的 → 可塑的 例 The descending rock is less *ductile* and much more liable to fracture.

dump [dʌmp]	*v.* 倾倒 (to release or throw down in a large mass); 倾销 (to sell in quantity at a very low price; specifically to sell abroad at less than the market price at home); *n.* 堆存处 (a place where materials are stored) 记 发音记忆: "当铺" → 到当铺去倾销 例 Residents were not allowed to *dump* their trash in the parklands. // Many companies charge that foreign companies dumped their products at less than fair value. 派 dumping(*n.* 倾销)
dumpster ['dʌmpstər]	*n.* 垃圾桶 (used for a large trash receptacle) 例 Residents deposit recyclable trash in municipal *dumpsters* located in the parking lot.
duplicate ['duːplɪkət]	['duːplɪkət] *a.* 复制的 (being the same as another); *n.* 复制品 (an additional copy of something already in a collection) ['duːplɪkeɪt] *v.* 复制 (to make a copy of); 重复 (to do again often needlessly) 记 词根记忆: du + plic(重叠) + ate → 使重叠 → 复制 例 Cyprus (塞浦路斯) would become the primary source of marketable *duplicate* artifacts. // The secretary *duplicated* the documents for her boss. 派 duplication(*n.* 副本; 复制)
duplication [ˌduːplɪ'keɪʃn]	*n.* 复制 (the act or process of duplicating); 副本 (counterpart) 例 This priority might often lead them to be less vigilant in streamlining their services—eliminating *duplication* between departments, for instance.
durability [ˌdʊrə'bɪləti]	*n.* 经久, 耐久性 (existing for a long time without significant deterioration) 记 词根记忆: dur(持续) + ability(能力) → 持续的能力 → 耐久性 例 Nylons have the virtue of *durability*.
duration [du'reɪʃn]	*n.* 持续, 持久 (continuance in time) 记 词根记忆: dur(持续) + ation(表状态) → 持续, 持久 例 The brightening of such a star is observed to be of shorter *duration* than the brightening of neighboring stars. 同根词: endurance(*n.* 忍耐力; 持久)
dwarf [dwɔːrf]	*n.* 矮子 (a person of unusually small stature); *v.* (使)变矮小 (to cause to appear smaller or to seem inferior) 记 联想记忆: 战争(war)使战败国在战胜国面前相形见绌(dwarf) 例 white *dwarf* star 白矮星 // The giant oak *dwarfed* the seedling.
dwelling ['dwelɪŋ]	*n.* 住处, 寓所 (residence) 记 来自 dwell(*v.* 居住) 例 For protection from the summer sun, the Mojave lived in open-sided, flat-topped *dwellings*.

13

dwindle
['dwɪndl]

v. 变小 (to diminish, to shrink, to decrease)

记 联想记忆: d + wind(风) + le → 随风而去越来越小 → 变小

注意: 不要和 swindle(*v.* 欺骗, 诈骗)相混

例 Contrary to financial analysts' predictions last year that the market for home computers would *dwindle*, the personal computer industry continued to show strong growth in the first quarter of this year.

dye
[daɪ]

n. 染料 (a substance used to color materials); *v.* 给…染色 (to color, especially by soaking in a coloring solution)

例 *Dyes* can be made from plants or from chemicals. // Each of the eggs in the bowl is *dyed* red, green, or blue.

dynamic
[daɪ'næmɪk]

n. 动力 (an underlying cause of change or growth); [常 *pl.*] 动态 (a pattern or process of change, growth, or activity)

记 词根记忆: dynam(力量) + ic → 有力量的 → 动力; 动态

例 market *dynamics* 市场活力 // population *dynamics* 人口动态

同根词: dynamo(发电机); dynamite(炸药)

ease
[iːz]

v. 缓和 (to alleviate); *n.* 不费力 (effortlessness)

例 The drugs *eased* my pain. // She picked up her second gold medal with ridiculous *ease*.

派 easing(*n.* 放松)

echolocation
[ˌekoʊloʊ'keɪʃn]

n. 回声定位法 (physiological process for locating distant or invisible objects by sound waves reflected back to the emitter from the objects)

记 分拆记忆: echo(回声) + location(位置) → 回声定位法

例 Dolphins use *echolocation* to locate distant prey.

eclipse
[ɪ'klɪps]

n. (日、月)食 (the partial or complete obscuring relative to a designated observer, of one celestial body by another); (声誉、地位等的)消失, 衰落 (falling into obscurity)

记 联想记忆: ec + lip(嘴唇) + se → 日月变得像弯弯的唇 → 日食, 月食

例 solar *eclipse* 日食 // The role of the U.S. Navy was threatened with permanent *eclipse*.

ecology
[i'kɑːlədʒi]

n. 生态学, 环境适应学 (a branch of science concerned with the inter-relationship of organisms and their environments)

记 词根记忆: eco(环境, 生态) + logy(学科) → 生态学

economy
[ɪ'kɑːnəmi]

n. 经济 (the system of production, distribution and consumption); 节约 (thrifty and efficient use of material resources); *a.* 经济的 (designed to save money)

记 发音记忆: "依靠农民" → 中国是农业大国, 经济发展离不开农民 → 经济的

例 Manufacturing constitutes a relatively small proportion of the *economy*.

派 economic(*a.* 经济的)

ecosystem
['iːkoʊsɪstəm]

n. 生态系统 (the complex of a community of organisms and its environment functioning as an ecological unit)

记 词根记忆: eco(环境, 生态) + system(体系) → 生态系统

例 Coral reefs are one of the most fragile marine *ecosystems* on earth.

□ dwindle   □ dye   □ dynamic   ■ ease   □ echolocation   □ eclipse
□ ecology   □ economy   □ ecosystem

edge [edʒ]	*n.* 优势(advantage); 边(缘)(border) 例 These changes will enhance our bank's image and give us the *edge* over our competitors. // the *edge* of the galaxy
edible ['edəbl]	*n.* 食品(things be able to eat); *a.* 可食用的(fit to be eaten) 记 词根记忆: ed(吃) + ible(可…的) → 可食用的 例 Higher-than-normal levels of manganese, strontium, and vanadium probably indicate a less nutritious diet heavily dependent on *edible* plants. 派 edibility(*n.* 可食性) 同根词: inedible(*a.* 不能吃的)
editorial [ˌedɪ'tɔːriəl]	*n.* 社论(a newspaper or magazine article that gives the opinions of the editors or publishers); *a.* 编辑的; 社论的(of or relating to an editor or editing) 记 来自 editor(*n.* 编辑; 社论撰稿人) 例 The first provides evidence in support of a recommendation that the *editorial* supports. 派 editorially(*ad.* 以编辑身份地; 以社论形式) 同根词: editorship(*n.* 编辑; 校订)
educator ['edʒukeɪtər]	*n.* 教育家(one skilled in teaching) 记 来自 educate(*v.* 教育, 培养) 例 She was an *educator* and a builder of institutions and organizations. 同根词: education(*n.* 教育)
effect [ɪ'fekt]	*v.* 生效(to put into operation); 引起(to cause to come into being); *n.* 效应(influence); 结果(accomplishment) 记 词根记忆: ef(出) + fect(做) → 做出效果 → 生效 例 People's enthusiasm for the product *effected* an increase in sales. // Too much stress can have an adverse *effect* on one's health.
efficacy ['efɪkəsi]	*n.* 功效, 效力(the capacity or power to produce an effect) 例 Patients' ages may affect a treatment's *efficacy*. 同根词: efficient(*a.* 有效率的)
efficiency [ɪ'fɪʃnsi]	*n.* 效率, 功效(the quality or degree of being efficient) 记 来自 efficient(*a.* 有效率的) 例 production *efficiency* 生产效率 派 inefficiency(*n.* 无效率; 无能)
efficient [ɪ'fɪʃnt]	*a.* 有效率的(being or involving the immediate agent in producing an effect); 有能力的(competent) 记 联想记忆: ef(姨夫) + fici(做事) + ent(形容词后缀) → 姨夫做事很有效率 → 有效率的 例 Automobiles become less fuel *efficient* and therefore contribute more to air pollution as they age. 派 efficiently(*ad.* 有效地; 高效地) 同根词: efficacy(*n.* 功效, 效力)

13

effigy ['efɪdʒi]	*n.* 雕像，肖像（an image or representation especially of a person） 记 词根记忆：ef(出) + fig(塑造) + y → 塑造出外形 → 雕像 例 The objects found in the excavated temple were small terracotta(赤土陶器的) *effigies*. 同根词：figment(*n.* 虚构的事); figure(*n.* 形体)
effluent ['efluənt]	*n.* 支流（an outflowing branch of a main stream or lake）; 废水（waste liquid） 记 词根记忆：ef(出) + flu(流) + ent → 流出来的 → 支流 例 The factory generates the largest quantities of *effluents*.
egalitarianism [iˌgælɪ'teriənɪzəm]	*n.* 平等主义（a belief in human equality especially with respect to social, political, and economic rights and privileges） 记 来自 egalitarian(*a.* 平等主义的) 例 racial *egalitarianism* 种族平等主义
egoistic [ˌegoʊ'ɪstɪk]	*a.* 自我主义的，利己主义的（believing that individual self-interest is the actual motive of all conscious action） 记 词根记忆：ego(我) + istic → 以我为中心的 → 自我主义的 例 The youth tend to translate the individualistic and humanistic goals of democracy into *egoistic* and materialistic ones.
eject [i'dʒekt]	*v.* 喷射；驱逐（to throw out） 记 词根记忆：e(出) + ject(扔) → 被扔出来 → 喷射 例 A meteor stream is composed of dust particles that have been *ejected* from a parent comet. 派 ejection(*n.* 喷出，喷射)
elaborate	[ɪ'læbərət] *a.* 精心制作的（planned or carried out with great care） [ɪ'læbəreɪt] *v.* 详述，详细制定（to work out in detail） 记 联想记忆：e(出) + labor(工作) + ate → 辛苦劳动做出来 → 精心制作 例 The first paragraph introduces a general thesis that is *elaborated* on in detail elsewhere in the passage. 派 elaborately(*ad.* 苦心经营地，精巧地)
elective [ɪ'lektɪv]	*n.* 选修课（an elective course or subject）; *a.* 选修的（optional） 记 词根记忆：e(出) + lect(选择) + ive → 选择出 → 选修课 例 Home economics is only an *elective*, and few students choose to take it. // *elective* course 选修课
electorate [ɪ'lektərət]	*n.* 全体选民（a body of people entitled to vote） 记 词根记忆：elector(选举人) + ate → 全体选民 例 The *electorate* voted the corrupt politician out of office.
electricity [ɪˌlek'trɪsəti]	*n.* 电力（electric current or power）; 电学（a science that deals with the phenomena and laws of electricity）; 强烈的紧张情绪（keen contagious excitement） 记 来自 electric(*a.* 电的；发电的；*n.* 电) 例 Most household appliances use *electricity* only when in use. 同根词：electrical(*a.* 有关电的)

electro [ɪˈlektroʊ]	*n.* 电镀物品，电版 例 *electro*-acupuncture 电针疗法
electromagnetic [ˌɪlektroʊmægˈnetɪk]	*a.* 电磁的(of, relating to, or produced by electromagnetism) 记 分拆记忆：electro(=electric 电的) + magnetic(有磁性的) → 电磁的 例 Sunspots, vortices of gas associated with strong *electromagnetic* activity, are visible as dark spots on the surface of the Sun. 同根词：electromagnet(*n.* 电磁体)
electron [ɪˈlektrɑːn]	*n.* 电子(a very small piece of matter that moves round the NUCLEUS (= central part) of an atom and that by its movement causes an electric current in metal) 记 词根记忆：electr(电) + on → 电子 例 an *electron* microscope 电子显微镜 派 electronic(*a.* 电子的); electronics(*n.* 电子学)
element [ˈelɪmənt]	*n.* 元素，要素(component) 例 They identified the most important *element* in their jobs as customer service. 派 elementary(*a.* 初步的，基本的)
elevate [ˈelɪveɪt]	*v.* 抬起(to lift); 使升高(to raise) 记 词根记忆：e(出) + lev(举，升) + ate → 抬起; 使升高 例 The island lake is sufficiently *elevated* that water from Lake Superior does not reach it. 派 elevated(*a.* 抬高的) 同根词：lever(*n.* 杠杆)
elevation [ˌelɪˈveɪʃn]	*n.* 高地(an elevated place); 海拔(the height to which sth. is elevated); 正面图(a geometrical drawing that depicts one vertical plane of an object or structure) 记 来自 elevate(*v.* 提升; 举起) 例 They sighted each pole, reading off measurements that were then used to calculate the change in *elevation* over each increment. 同根词：elevator(*n.* 电梯)
elicit [iˈlɪsɪt]	*v.* 引出，引起(to draw forth or bring out) 记 词根记忆：e(出来) + licit(诱导) → 引出 例 We gave the rats a meal that we knew would *elicit* insulin secretion.
eligible [ˈelɪdʒəbl]	*a.* 合格的，符合条件的(qualified, entitled) 记 词根记忆：e(出来) + lig(=lect 选择) + ible → 能被选择出来的 → 合格的 例 In most places fifteen year olds are not *eligible* for driver's licenses. 派 eligibility(*n.* 适任，合格) 同根词：intelligent(*a.* 聪明的); negligent(*a.* 疏忽的)

13

eliminate [ɪˈlɪmɪneɪt]	*v.* 排除，消除(to remove, to eradicate) 记 联想记忆：e + limin(门槛) + ate → 扔出门槛 → 消除，排除 例 Corporations should try to *eliminate* the many ranks and salary grades that classify employees. 派 elimination(*n.* 排除，消除)
elite [eɪˈliːt]	*n.* 精英(the best of a class)；*a.* 卓越的，精锐的(prominent) 记 联想记忆：e + lite(=lig 选择) → 选出来的都是精英 → 精英 例 They hated political privilege and wanted freedom from an *elite* dominated state. 派 elitist(*n.* 优秀人才，杰出者)
elliptical [ɪˈlɪptɪkl]	*a.* 椭圆形的(oval) 记 联想记忆：el + lip(嘴唇) + tical → 嘴唇看来像椭圆 → 椭圆形的 例 Scientists calculated that the asteroid is on an *elliptical* path that orbits the Sun once a year.
elongate [ˈiːlɔːŋɡeɪt]	*v.* 延长，伸长(to lengthen, to extend) 记 词根记忆：e(出) + long(长) + ate → 长出去 → 伸长 例 The elephant *elongated* its trunk to reach the peanut. 派 elongation(*n.* 伸长) 同根词：longevity(*n.* 长寿)；longitude(*n.* 经度)
eloquent [ˈeləkwənt]	*a.* 雄辩的(marked by forceful and fluent expression) 记 词根记忆：e(出) + loqu(说) + ent → 滔滔不绝地说出来 → 雄辩的 例 He is the most *eloquent* spokesman of our government.
elude [iˈluːd]	*v.* 逃避(追捕等)(to escape) 记 联想记忆：e(出) + lude(玩) → 玩出花样 → 逃避 例 The robber's immediate goal was to *elude* capture.
emancipation [ɪˌmænsɪˈpeɪʃn]	*n.* 解放，释放(the act or process of emancipating) 记 联想记忆：e(出) + man(手) + cip(抓住) + ation → 把被抓的手放出来 → 解放，释放 例 They hoped to reassure merchants that despite the *emancipation* of the slaves, planters would produce crops and pay debts.
embalm [ɪmˈbɑːm]	*v.* 保存；铭记(to preserve)；以香油(或药料)涂尸防腐(to protect from decay) 记 词根记忆：em + balm(香油，香膏) → 把香油涂在…上 → 以香油涂尸防腐 例 Egyptians are credited for having pioneered *embalming* methods as long ago as 2650 B.C.
embargo [ɪmˈbɑːrɡoʊ]	*n.* 禁运(令)(an order of a government prohibiting the departure of commercial ships from its ports) 记 词根记忆：em(拿) + bar(阻挡) + go → 阻拦，不让拿 → 禁运 例 trade *embargo* 贸易禁运
embark [ɪmˈbɑːrk]	*v.* 着手，开始做(to make a start) 例 Our company *embarked* on the major construction project of the government building.

embarrass [ɪmˈbærəs]	*v.* （使）尴尬（to place in doubt, perplexity, or difficulties） 记 联想记忆：em + barr（看作 bar 酒吧）+ ass（蠢驴）→ 在酒吧喝醉了表现得像一头驴 → 尴尬 例 The author's statements were made in order to *embarrass* the officials responsible for the drug-control program.
embarrassed [ɪmˈbærəst]	*a.* 尴尬的；窘迫的（uncomfortable because of shame or difficulties） 记 来自 embarrass（*v.* 使困窘） 例 In his later years he was *embarrassed* by what he considered as the excessive sentiment in the poems in his first two collections. 同根词：embarrassment（*n.* 窘迫；难堪）
embed [ɪmˈbed]	*v.* 嵌入（to enclose closely in） 记 联想记忆：em（进入…中）+ bed（床）→ 把…嵌入床中 → 嵌入 例 a crown *embedded* with jewels
embellish [ɪmˈbelɪʃ]	*v.* 装饰（to decorate）；润色（to add ornamental or fictitious details to） 记 词根记忆：em + bell（美）+ ish → 使…美 → 装饰 例 We *embellished* our room with a new rug, lamp, and picture. // Just tell the truth and don't *embellish* the story by any means. 派 embellishment（*n.* 装饰）
embrace [ɪmˈbreɪs]	*v.* 拥抱（to hug）；信奉；接受（to take up readily） 记 词根记忆：em（进入…中）+ brace（胳膊）→ 搂进胳膊里 → 拥抱 例 Many Irish American people *embrace* St. Patrick's Day. // The new democratic value system was not immediately *embraced* by society as a whole.

13

Victory won't come to me unless I go to it.
胜利是不会向我走来的，我必须自己走向胜利。

——美国女诗人 穆尔（M. Moore, American poetess）

embryo [ˈembriʊʊ]	*n.* 胚胎(an organism in its early stages of development, especially before it has reached a distinctively recognizable form) 记 词根记忆：em + bryo(变大) → (种子等)变大 → 胚胎 例 By studying the fruit fly, scientists begin to unravel the secrets of how *embryos* develop. 派 embryology(*n.* 胚胎学)；embryonic(*a.* 胚胎的；开始的)
embryonic [ˌembriˈɑːnɪk]	*a.* 胚胎的；萌芽期的(incipient；rudimentary) 记 来自 embryo(*n.* 胚胎) 例 *embryonic* stem cells 胚胎干细胞 同根词：embryology(*n.* 胚胎学)
emerge [iˈmɜːrdʒ]	*v.* 浮现(to rise from)；(事实等)暴露(to become manifest) 记 词根记忆：e(出) + merge(浸没) → 从浸没之中出来 → 浮现 例 The new school of political history *emerged* in the 1960's and 1970's. 派 emergence(*n.* 浮现，出现) 同根词：emersion(*n.* 浮出)；immerge(*v.* 浸入)；submerge(*v.* 淹没)
emergence [iˈmɜːrdʒəns]	*n.* 出现，浮现(the act or an instance of emerging)；露头(any of various superficial outgrowths of plant tissue) 记 来自 emerge(*v.* 浮现；暴露) 例 There is widespread belief that the *emergence* of giant industries has been accompanied by an equivalent surge in industrial research. 同根词：emergent(*a.* 紧急的)；emergency(*n.* 紧急情况)
emergency [iˈmɜːrdʒənsi]	*n.* 紧急情况，紧急事件(an urgent need for assistance or relief) 记 联想记忆：紧急情况(emergency)出现(emerge) 例 an *emergency* exit 紧急出口
emigrate [ˈemɪɡreɪt]	*v.* 移居他国(to leave one's place of residence or country to live elsewhere) 记 词根记忆：e(出) + migrate(移动) → 移出本国 → 移居他国 例 Less successful after she *emigrated* to New York than she had been in her native Germany, photographer Lotte Jacobi nevertheless earned a small group of discerning admirers. 派 emigration(*n.* 移民出境) 同根词：immigrate(*v.* 移入)

eminent [ˈemɪnənt]	*a.* 杰出的(prominent); 突出的(projecting) 记 词根记忆: e(出) + min(突出) + ent → 突出的; 杰出的 例 She established her reputation as an *eminent* social reformer. // *eminent* peaks 巍峨的山峰 同根词: preeminent(*a.* 杰出的)
emission [iˈmɪʃn]	*n.* (光、热等的)散发(an act or instance of emitting) 记 词根记忆: e(出) + miss(放出) + ion → 放出 → (光、热等)的散发 例 Automobile *emissions* are the largest source of air pollution.
emit [iˈmɪt]	*v.* 放射(光、热、味等)(to send out; to eject) 记 词根记忆: e(出) + mit(放出) → 放射 例 Elephants *emit* low-frequency sounds that may be used as a secret language to communicate with other members of the herd. 派 emission(*n.* 发射)
emphasis [ˈemfəsɪs]	*n.* 重点; 强调(importance given in sth.) 例 The first six Presidents placed great *emphasis* on individualism and civil rights. 同根词: emphasize(*v.* 着重, 强调)
emphasize [ˈemfəsaɪz]	*v.* 着重, 强调(to place emphasis on) 记 联想记忆: em + phas(看作 phrase 用短语表达) + ize → 用短语表达是 为了强调 → 强调 例 The committees must develop incentive compensation policies to *emphasize* long-term performance. 派 emphasis(*n.* 重点, 强调)
empirical [ɪmˈpɪrɪkl]	*a.* 经验主义的, 经验的(originating in or based on observation or experience) 记 联想记忆: empiri(看作 empire 帝国) + cal → 参照帝国以前的经验 → 经验的 例 These models are constructed primarily from *empirical* observations.
emulate [ˈemjuleɪt]	*v.* 效仿(to imitate); 努力赶上或超越(to strive to equal or excel) 记 词根记忆: emul(竞争) + ate → 一种竞争的姿态 → 努力赶上或超越 例 Mexican Americans should *emulate* the strategies of Native American political leaders. // I tried to *emulate* Mary's skill at playing the piano. 派 emulous(*a.* 好胜的)
enact [ɪˈnækt]	*v.* 制定或通过(法令)(to make or pass (a decree)) 记 词根记忆: en(使) + act(行动) → 使(法律)行动 → 制定或通过(法令) 例 Several towns in Vorland *enacted* restaurant smoking restrictions five years ago. 同根词: interact(*v.* 相互作用, 互相影响); transact(*v.* 处理; 执行)
enamel [ɪˈnæml]	*n.* 牙釉质(a hard calcareous substance that forms a thin layer capping the teeth); 搪瓷(a usually opaque vitreous composition applied by fusion to the surface of metal, glass, or pottery); *v.* 彩饰(to beautify with a colorful surface) 例 Applying a new method for analyzing the chemistry of tooth *enamel*, scientists have examined molars of prehuman ancestors and determined that their diets were more varied than had been supposed.

14

□ eminent   □ emission   □ emit   □ emphasis   □ emphasize   □ empirical
□ emulate   □ enact   □ enamel

encephalitis [enˌsefəˈlaɪtəs]	*n.* [医] 脑炎 (inflammation of the brain)
enclose [ɪnˈkloʊz]	*v.* 围绕, 包围 (to surround) 例 The *enclosed* seas are an important feature of the earth's surface.
encode [ɪnˈkoʊd]	*v.* 译码, 编码 (to convert, usu. a message, into code) 记 词根记忆: en + code(电码, 密码)→ 译码 例 In a certain coding scheme, each word is *encoded* by replacing each letter in the word with another letter.
encompass [ɪnˈkʌmpəs]	*v.* 包含 (to include); 围绕 (to surround, to encircle) 记 词根记忆: en + compass(罗盘; 范围)→ 进入范围 → 包含 例 The themes in her poetry are universal, *encompassing* much of the human condition.
encounter [ɪnˈkaʊntər]	*v.* 偶然碰到, 遭遇 (to come upon or experience unexpectedly); *n.* 意外相见 (a chance meeting) 记 词根记忆: en + counter(相反的)→ 从两个相反方面来 → 偶然碰到 例 Most meteor streams that the earth *encounters* are more than 2,000 years old.
encroach [ɪnˈkroʊtʃ]	*v.* 侵犯, 侵害 (to enter into the possessions or rights of another) 例 The lawyer argues that a state law prohibiting smoking in public places unfairly *encroaches* on the rights of smokers. 派 encroachment(*n.* 侵犯) 同根词: crochet(*v.* 用钩针编织)
encyclopedia [ɪnˌsaɪkləˈpiːdiə]	*n.* 百科全书 (a work that contains information on all branches of knowledge or treats comprehensively a particular branch of knowledge usually in articles arranged alphabetically often by subject) 记 词根记忆: en + cyclo(环, 圆) + ped(儿童) + ia → 教给儿童全面知识的书 → 百科全书 例 A salesman sells 12 identical sets of *encyclopedias* and makes $1,800 in commissions. 派 encyclopedic(*a.* 如百科辞典的, 百科全书式的) 同根词: pediatrics(*n.* 儿科)
endanger [ɪnˈdeɪndʒər]	*v.* 危及, 危害 (to bring into danger or peril) 记 词根记忆: en + danger(危险)→ 危及 例 The use of pesticides may be *endangering* certain plant species dependent on insects for pollination.
endeavor [ɪnˈdevər]	*n.* 努力 (serious and determined effort); 事业 (enterprise) 记 词根记忆: en + deavor(责任)→ 责任重大的事情 → 事业 例 They were frequently joint *endeavors* by members of two or three different ethnic groups. // Cattle raising is less lucrative than other *endeavors*.

□ encephalitis □ enclose □ encode □ encompass □ encounter □ encroach
□ encyclopedia □ endanger □ endeavor

endemic [en'demɪk]	*a.* 地方性的（restricted or peculiar to a locality or region）；*n.* 地方病 例 *endemic* disease 地方病 同根词：epidemic（*a.* 流行性的）；pandemic（*a.* 广泛的）
endorphin [en'dɔːrfɪn]	*n.* 【生化】内啡肽（主要存在大脑中，可缓解痛感并影响情绪）（any of a group of endogenous peptides found especially in the brain that bind chiefly to opiate receptors and produce some pharmacological effects like those of opiates） 例 The presence of *endorphins* may help to explain differences in response to pain signals.
endorse [ɪn'dɔːrs]	*v.* 背书（to sign one's name as payee on the back of a check in order to obtain the cash or credit represented on the face）；支持，赞同（to approve） 记 词根记忆：en + dorse(背) → 在背面写字 → 背书，商业上的背书一般表示认可，引申为支持 例 The bank teller reminded me to *endorse* the check I was cashing. // I do not *endorse* your choice of friends. 派 endorsement（*n.* 背书，认可）
endothermic [ˌendoʊ'θɜːrmɪk]	*a.* 【动】温血的，恒温的（warm-blooded） 记 词根记忆：endo(到…里面) + therm(热) + ic → 从里面散发热的 → 温血的，恒温的 例 *endothermic* species 温血物种
enforce [ɪn'fɔːrs]	*v.* 实施，执行（to carry out effectively） 记 词根记忆：en(使…) + force(力量) → 使力量体现 → 实施，执行 例 The extant workplace safety regulations were stringently *enforced*. 派 enforcement（*n.* 执行，强制）；unenforceable（*a.* 无法执行的）
enfranchisement [ɪn'fræntʃaɪzmənt]	*n.* 解放，释放（setting free） 记 来自 franchise（*v.* 解放；给予权利） 例 female *enfranchisement* 妇女解放 同根词：enfranchise（*v.* 给予选举权；解放）
engage [ɪn'geɪdʒ]	*v.* (in)从事于，忙于（to begin and carry on an enterprise or activity）；使订婚（to promise to marry） 例 Canadians now increasingly *engage* in "out-shopping", which is shopping across the national border.
engender [ɪn'dʒendər]	*v.* 产生（to bring into existence）；引起（to produce） 记 词根记忆：en + gender(=gen 产生) → 产生 例 Managers can use intuition to bypass in-depth analysis and move rapidly to *engender* a plausible solution.
engulf [ɪn'gʌlf]	*v.* 吞噬（to flow over and enclose） 记 联想记忆：en + gulf(海湾) → 被海湾的巨浪吞噬 → 吞噬 例 The water levels of the oceans would rise 250 feet and *engulf* most of the world's great cities.

14

125

enhance [ɪnˈhæns]	*v.* 提高，增加（to heighten, to increase） 记 词根记忆：en + hance（高）→ 提高 例 This strategy might enable the automaker to *enhance* its profitability. 派 enhancement（*n.* 提高，增加）
enhanced [ɪnˈhænst]	*a.* 加强的；增大的（increased or intensified in value or beauty or quality） 记 来自 enhance（*v.* 提高；加强） 例 Tom produced an *enhanced* podcast that tells the story and analyses the copyright picture. 同根词：enhancive（*a.* 加强的；增加的）
enlightened [ɪnˈlaɪtnd]	*a.* 开明的，进步的（free from ignorance and prejudice） 记 来自 enlighten（*v.* 启发，启蒙） 例 The author responded to questions from her *enlightened* readers. // *enlightened* gentry 开明绅士
enlist [ɪnˈlɪst]	*v.* 服兵役（to enter the armed forces）；征募（to engage（a person）for duty in the armed forces）；谋取（支持、赞助等）（to secure the support and aid of） 记 词根记忆：en + list（名单）→ 进入（战士的）名单 → 服兵役 例 Our company is *enlisting* computer dealers now. // No educator had thought to *enlist* the help of village schoolmasters in introducing new teaching techniques.
enormous [ɪˈnɔːrməs]	*a.* 巨大的，极大的（huge, gigantic） 记 词根记忆：e（出）+ norm（规范）+ ous（…的）→ 超出规范的 → 巨大的 例 The children needed *enormous* amounts of security and affection. 派 enormously（*ad.* 非常地，巨大地）
enrich [ɪnˈrɪtʃ]	*v.*（使）富裕（to make rich or richer）；（使）丰富（to make rich or richer especially） 记 词根记忆：en + rich（富足）→（使）富裕 例 Many Americans believed that increasing commercial activity would *enrich* the nation. // Reading *enriches* the mind. 开卷有益。 派 enriched（*a.* 富含…的；强化的）
enroll [ɪnˈroʊl]	*v.* 入学，招收（to enter or register in a roll, list, or record）；加入（to register or enter in a list, catalog, or roll） 记 联想记忆：en（进入）+ roll（名单）→ 上了名单 → 入学；加入 例 Of the female students *enrolled* at the school, 40 percent are members of the drama club. // The number of people *enrolled* in health maintenance organizations increased by 15 percent. 派 enrollment（*n.* 注册，入学）
ensemble [ɑːnˈsɑːmbl]	*n.* 合唱团（的全体演员）（a group of supporting players, singers, or dancers） 记 联想记忆：en + semble（相同）→ 唱相同的（歌）→ 合唱 注意：resemble（*v.* 像，类似） 例 Tom was the leader of a musical *ensemble*.

enshrine [ɪnˈʃraɪn]	*v.* 奉为神圣 (to preserve or cherish as sacred) 记 词根记忆：en (进入) + shrine (圣地) → 进入圣地 → 奉为神圣 例 Much of the local artisans' creative energy was expended on the creation of Buddha images and on construction and decoration of the temples in which they were *enshrined*. 派 enshrinement (*n.* 置于神龛中；铭记；珍藏)
entail [ɪnˈteɪl]	*v.* 伴随；(使) 承担 (to impose, involve, or imply as a necessary accompaniment or result) 例 The practical application of the new law will not *entail* indiscriminate budget cuts. // Offshore oil-drilling operations *entail* an unavoidable risk of an oil spill.
enterprise [ˈentərpraɪz]	*n.* 事业 (a project or undertaking that is especially difficult, complicated, or risky)；企业 (a unit of economic organization or activity) 记 联想记忆：enter (进入) + prise (把握) → 能够最先进入市场，把握先机 → 企业 例 scientific *enterprise* 科学事业 // minority *enterprise* 少数民族企业
entertainment [ˌentərˈteɪnmənt]	*n.* 娱乐 (the act of entertaining) 例 Popular *entertainment* is overly influenced by commercial interests.
enthusiastically [ɪnˌθuːziˈæstɪkli]	*ad.* 热情地，热烈地 (filled with enthusiasm) 例 Porters, more than other Pullman employees, *enthusiastically* supported this union.
entice [ɪnˈtaɪs]	*v.* 诱惑，引诱 (to tempt, to lure) 例 To *entice* customers away from competitors, the company began offering discounts on home appliances.
entitle [ɪnˈtaɪtl]	*v.* 命名 (to give a title to)；(使) 有权 (拥有或做某事) (to furnish with a right or claim to something) 记 词根记忆：en (使…) + title (题目，标题) → 使有标题 → 命名 例 A petition *entitled* "Petition for Statewide Smoking Restriction" is being circulated to voters. // Any customer who made a purchase of ten or more gallons of gasoline was *entitled* to a free car wash.
entity [ˈentəti]	*n.* 实体 (being, existence)；统一体 (an organization such as a business or governmental unit that has an identity separate from those of its members) 例 Government does not exist as an independent *entity* defining policy.
entrant [ˈentrənt]	*n.* 进入者 (one that enters)；新成员 (fresh blood) 记 词根记忆：entr (=enter 进入) + ant → 进入者 例 The number of new *entrants* into the labor market declined in the past year.
entrapment [ɪnˈtræpmənt]	*n.* 诱捕的行动 (或过程) (the action of luring) 记 来自 entrap (*v.* 诱捕) 例 Federal agents used *entrapment* to catch the senator committing a crime.

14

entrepreneur
[ˌɑːntrəprəˈnɜːr]
n.企业家；承包人（one who organizes manages, and assumes the risks of a business or enterprise）
记 来自 enterprise(n. 企业)
例 This program enabled many minority *entrepreneurs* to form new businesses.
派 entrepreneurship(n. 企业家的身份等); entrepreneurial(a. 创业的，企业的)

entrepreneurship
[ˌɑːntrəprəˈnɜːrʃɪp]
n.企业家精神（spirit of entrepreneuer）
记 分拆记忆：entrepreneur(企业家) + ship → 企业家精神
例 *Entrepreneurship* and small business administration is now the fastest-growing major in business schools.

entry
[ˈentri]
n.进入（the act of entering）；入口（entrance）；登记（the act of making a record）
例 *entry* tickets 入场券 // Is there a back *entry* into the house?

enumerate
[ɪˈnuːməreɪt]
v.列举，枚举（to count, to list）
记 词根记忆：e(出) + numer(数字) + ate → 列出数字 → 列举，枚举
例 The errors are too many to *enumerate*.
派 enumeration(n. 列举，枚举)

envelop
[ɪnˈveləp]
v.笼罩，包住（to enclose or enfold completely with or as if with a covering）
例 Swirling snow *enveloped* the hikers.
派 envelope(n. 包层)

envelope
[ˈenvəloʊp]
n.信封（a flat usually paper container）；【天】包层（coma）
记 词根记忆：en + velope(包) → 包层
例 stellar *envelope* 恒星包层

envision
[ɪnˈvɪʒn]
v.想像（think）
记 联想记忆：en + vis(看) + ion → 用心去看 → 想像
例 The automaker *envisions* that customers initially attracted by the discounts may become loyal customers.

enzyme
[ˈenzaɪm]
n.酵素，酶（organic chemical substance that is formed in living cells and assists chemical changes（e.g. in digestion）without being changed itself）
记 词根记忆：en + zyme(酶) → 酵素，酶
例 The amino acid sequences of various *enzymes* tend to be typically prokaryotic(原核的)or eukaryotic(真核的).
同根词：zymurgy(n. 酿造学); zymic(a. 酶的，酵母的)

epic
[ˈepɪk]
n.史诗；叙事诗（a long narrative poem in elevated style recounting the deeds of a legendary or historical hero）
例 It is still not widely known that American Indians have *epics*.

epicenter
[ˈepɪsentər]
n.震中（the part of the earth's surface directly above the focus of an earthquake）
记 发音记忆：epi(挨劈) + center(中心) → 土地挨劈的中心 → 震中
例 The *epicenter* is in the crust, whereas the focus is in the mantle.

epidemic [ˌepɪ'demɪk]	*a.* 传染的（catching）；流行性的（spreading quickly among many people in the same place for a time）；*n.* 流行病（disease spreading rapidly and extensively by infection） 记 词根记忆：epi(向) + dem(人) + ic → 在人之间传染的 → 传染的；流行性的 例 *epidemic* disease 流行性疾病 // The Black Plague was an *epidemic* in the Middle Ages.
episode ['epɪsoʊd]	*n.* 一段情节（a usually brief unit of action in a dramatic or literary work）；(一个)事件（an incident or event that is part of a progression or a larger sequence） 例 Major *episodes* of extinction can result from widespread environmental disturbances.
episodic [ˌepɪ'sɑːdɪk]	*a.* 偶然发生的；分散性的（occurring irregularly） 记 来自 episode(*n.* 片断) 例 The binding of different kinds of information is not a distinctive feature of *episodic* memory.
epochal ['epəkl]	*a.* 划时代的（of or relating to an epoch）；有重大意义的（uniquely or highly significant） 记 词根记忆：epoch(时代) + al → 划时代的 例 The Supreme Court had issued its ruling in this *epochal* desegregation case.
equalize ['iːkwəlaɪz]	*v.* (使)平衡，相等（to make equal） 例 Bob *equalized* the amount of soup in the bowls he was filling.
equilibrium [ˌiːkwɪ'lɪbriəm]	*n.* 平衡（a state of balance or equality between opposing forces） 记 词根记忆：equi(平等) + libr(平衡) + ium → 平衡 例 By persuading people to eat what had previously been horse feed, market *equilibrium* was restored. 同根词：equilibrate(*v.* 使平衡)
equip [ɪ'kwɪp]	*v.* (with) 装备，配备（to furnish） 例 This hotel was *equipped* with cable television. 派 equipment(*n.* 装备，配备)
equity ['ekwəti]	*n.* 公平，公正（justice） 记 词根记忆：equi(相等) + ty → 两边都相等 → 公平，公正 例 They should consider promoting pay *equity* between temporary and permanent workers. 派 equitable(*a.* 公平的，公正的)
equivalent [ɪ'kwɪvələnt]	*a.* 相同的，相当的（equal, same）；*n.* 等价物（something that is essentially equal to another） 记 词根记忆：equi(相等) + val(力量) + ent → 力量相等的 → 相同的 例 The myth that labor rates and labor costs are *equivalent* is supported by business journalists.

14

era [ˈerə]	*n.* 纪元，年代（period in history starting from a particular time or event）；时代（period） 例 For the first time in the modern *era*, non-Hispanic Whites are officially a minority in California.
eradicate [ɪˈrædɪkeɪt]	*v.* 根除，消灭（to exterminate） 记 词根记忆：e(出) + radic(根) + ate → 连根拔出 → 根除 例 The anopheles mosquito(疟蚊)has been *eradicated* in many parts of the world.
eradication [ɪˌrædɪˈkeɪʃn]	*n.* 消灭，根除（the complete destruction of every trace of sth.） 记 来自 eradicate(*v.* 根除，消灭) 例 The success of the program to eradicate smallpox has stimulated experts to pursue what they had not previously considered possible—better control, if not *eradication*, of the other infections such as measles and yaws.
erase [ɪˈreɪs]	*v.* 擦掉，抹去（to rub or scrape out）；消除（to remove from existence or memory as if by erasing） 记 词根记忆：e + rase(擦) → 擦掉 例 Please *erase* the blackboard. // The considerable progress made by Black people was *erased* by the new law.
ergonomic [ˌɜːrɡəˈnɑːmɪk]	*a.* 人类环境改造学的；人类工程学的（of or relating to ergonomics） 例 Designers of everything from cars to computer monitors have adopted a cornerless style of smooth surfaces and curves that is more *ergonomic*.
erode [ɪˈroʊd]	*v.* 侵蚀（to wear away by the action of water or wind）；削弱，损害（to cause to diminish, deteriorate, or disappear） 记 词根记忆：e + rode(咬) → 咬掉 → 侵蚀 例 A constant stream of water *eroded* the rock mountain. 派 erosion(*n.* 侵蚀，腐蚀)
errand [ˈerənd]	*n.* 差使(事)(如送信，买东西等)（a short trip taken to attend to some business often for others） 记 词根记忆：err(漫游) + and → 跑来跑去 → 差使 例 Some family vehicles are used primarily for making short local trips, such as to do *errands*.

erratic [ɪˈrætɪk]	*a.* 反复无常的；古怪的(irregular; uneven)
	例 The solar day cycle makes this behavior somewhat more *erratic*.
eruption [ɪˈrʌpʃn]	*n.* 爆发，喷发(an act, process, or instance of erupting)
	记 来自 erupt(*v.* 爆发，喷出)
	例 An unusually severe winter occurred in Europe after the continent was blanketed by a blue haze resulting from the *eruption* of the Laki Volcano in the European republic of Iceland in the summer of 1984.
	同根词：interruption(*n.* 中断；干扰)
escalate [ˈeskəleɪt]	*v.* (使)迅速增加(to increase in extent, volume or number)
	例 An assassination attempt *escalated* the tension between the two countries.
eschew [ɪsˈtʃuː]	*v.* 避开(to escape, to shun)
	例 Bill *eschewed* the rude behavior of his older brother.
essence [ˈesns]	*n.* 本质；精华(the most significant element, quality or aspect of a thing or person)
	记 词根记忆：ess(存在) + ence → 存在的根本 → 本质
	例 Native Americans recognized that the *essence* of their life could not be communicated in English.
	派 essential(*a.* 本质的；重要的)
estate [ɪˈsteɪt]	*n.* 财产，地产(possessions, property)；遗产(heritage)
	例 real *estate* 房地产// The man who died left an *estate* valued at $111,000.
esteem [ɪˈstiːm]	*v./n.* 尊重，尊敬(to regard highly)
	例 What we obtain too cheap we *esteem* too lightly.
estimate [ˈestɪmeɪt; ˈestɪmət]	*v./n.* 估计，评价(to appraise)
	例 The population of India will probably have what is *estimated* as 1.6 billion people by 2050.
	派 estimation(*n.* 估计，评价)
et al [ˌet ˈæl]	(拉丁文 et alibi 的缩写)以及其他人，等人(and others)
	例 Snyder *et al* suggest that this is not a major stumbling block to their hypothesis.

etched ['etʃid]	*a.* (金属)被(酸)蚀刻的(being cut into the surface by the action of acid) 例 The *etched* lines on computer memory chips have become infinite and thinner.
eternal [ɪ'tɜːrnl]	*a.* 永久的,永恒的(existing forever) 例 Some astronomers hold that the universe was *eternal* and infinitely steady-state.
ethanol ['eθənɔːl]	*n.* 乙醇,酒精(a colorless volatile flammable liquid that is the intoxicating agent in liquors and is also used as a solvent and in fuel) 例 Many countries that are large consumers of sugarcane increased their production of sugarcane-based *ethanol*.
ethic ['eθɪk]	*n.* 道德标准,行为准则(a theory or system of moral values) 例 Some academicians believe that business *ethics* should be integrated into every business course. 派 ethical(*a.* 与伦理有关的)
ethnic ['eθnɪk]	*a.* 种族的,民族的(of a national, racial or tribal group that has a common cultural tradition) 记 词根记忆:ethn(种族) + ic → 种族的,民族的 例 Such self-help networks encourage and support *ethnic* minority entrepreneurs. 派 ethical(*a.* 种族的); ethnicity(*n.* 种族划分) 同根词:ethnocentric(*a.* 种族中心主义的); ethnological(*a.* 人种学的)
ethnographic [ˌeθnə'ɡræfɪk]	*a.* 人种学的,人种论的(the study and systematic recording of human cultures) 记 来自 ethnography(*n.* 人种学,人种论) 例 *ethnographic* information 人种学信息 同根词:ethnologist(*n.* 人种学者;人类文化学者); ethnocentrism(*n.* 民族优越感)
ethnomusicology [ˌeθnəʊmjuːzɪ'kɒlədʒɪ]	*n.* 人种音乐学(the study of music in a sociocultural context) 记 词根记忆:ethno(=ethnic 人种的) + music(音乐) + ology(学科) → 人种音乐学 例 In 1905, Béla Bartók and Zoltán Kodály began their pioneering work in *ethnomusicology*, and they were armed only with an Edison phonograph and insatiable curiosity. 派 ethnomusicological(*a.* 人种音乐学的)
euphoria [juː'fɔːrɪə]	*n.* 精神欢快;兴奋(a feeling of well-being or elation) 记 词根记忆:eu(好) + phor(带来) + ia → 带来好的情绪 → 兴奋 例 I cannot describe the *euphoria* I felt when my daughter was born. // For a small percentage of depressed patients, missing a night's sleep induces a temporary sense of *euphoria*.
eusocial [juː'səʊʃəl]	*a.* (昆虫)完全群居的(living in a cooperative group) 记 词根记忆:eu(好) + social(社会的) → 喜欢融入社会的 → 完全群居的 例 *eusocial* insects 群居类昆虫

evacuation [ɪˌvækjuˈeɪʃn]	*n.* 撤离，疏散(the act or process of evacuating) 记 来自 evacuate(*v.* 撤离，疏散)，e + vacu(空) + ate → 撤空了 → 撤离 例 The *evacuation* was done in a calm and orderly manner. 同根词: vacant(*a.* 空的); vacuum(*n.* 真空)
evade [ɪˈveɪd]	*v.* 躲开(to slip away); 逃避(to escape or avoid by cleverness or deceit) 记 词根记忆: e + vade(走) → 走出去 → 躲开 例 *evade* an attack 躲避攻击 // *evade* taxes 逃税 派 evader(*n.* 逃避者); evasion(*n.* 躲避; 逃避)
evaluate [ɪˈvæljueɪt]	*v.* 评价; 估计(to determine or fix the value of) 记 词根记忆: e(出) + valu(=val 价值) + ate → 给出价值 → 评价 例 There are two independent variables that companies should use to *evaluate* the feasibility of subjecting suppliers of indirect purchases to competitive scrutiny. 派 evaluation(*n.* 评价; 估计) 同根词: valuable(*a.* 有价值的)
evaporate [ɪˈvæpəreɪt]	*v.* (使)蒸发(to convert into vapor); 消失(to diminish quickly) 记 词根记忆: e(出) + vapor(水汽) + ate(使…) → 出水汽 → 蒸发 例 Warmed by the Sun, ocean water *evaporates* and rises high into the atmosphere. 派 evaporative(*a.* 蒸发的); evaporation(*n.* 蒸发)
eventual [ɪˈventʃuəl]	*a.* 最后的，最终的(final) 记 来自 event(*n.* 结果) 例 Homesteading policies required residency on the land itself in order to obtain *eventual* ownership.
evident [ˈevɪdənt]	*a.* 明显的，清楚的(obvious) 记 词根记忆: e + vid(看见) + ent → 能够看得见的 → 明显的 例 The results of the company's cost cutting measures are *evident* in its profits. 派 evidently(*ad.* 明显地，显然)
evil [ˈiːvl]	*n.* 邪恶(the fact of suffering, misfortune, and wrongdoing); 坏事，恶行(something that brings sorrow, distress, or calamity) 记 联想记忆: live → evil 位置颠倒 → 生活过得颠倒就容易产生邪恶 → 邪恶 例 Good coexists with *evil* in this world.
evolve [iˈvɑːlv]	*v.* (使)进化(to undergo evolutionary change); (使)逐渐形成(to develop) 记 词根记忆: e(出) + volve(卷，转) → 转化出来 → (使)进化 例 This ancestral species might have *evolved* at a time when the islands were connected. 派 evolution(*n.* 进化，进展)
exacerbate [ɪɡˈzæsərbeɪt]	*v.* 加重，恶化(to make more violent, bitter, or severe) 记 词根记忆: ex + acerb(酸) + ate → 变酸了 → 恶化 例 The accident *exacerbated* the slow flow of traffic. 同根词: acerbic(*a.* 酸苦的); acerbate(*v.* 激怒)

15

exaggerate [ɪgˈzædʒəreɪt]	v. 夸张，夸大(to enlarge beyond bounds or the truth) 记 词根记忆：ex(出) + agger(堆积) + ate → 越堆越高 → 夸张 例 In many ways, our social statistics *exaggerate* the degree of hardship.
excavate [ˈekskəveɪt]	v. 挖掘，掘出(to dig out) 记 词根记忆：ex(出) + cav(洞) + ate → 挖出一个洞 → 挖掘 例 Documents on wooden tablets are *excavated* at the site of the old Roman fort. 派 excavation(n. 挖掘，发掘)
excavation [ˌekskəˈveɪʃn]	n. 挖掘(the action or process of excavating) 记 词根记忆：ex(出) + cav(洞) + ation → 从洞里挖出来 → 挖掘 例 *Excavation* of the ancient city of Kourion on the island of Cyprus revealed a pattern of debris. 同根词：excavate(v. 挖掘)
exceedingly [ɪkˈsiːdɪŋli]	ad. 极端地，非常(extremely) 记 来自 exceeding(a. 非常的，极度的) 例 Advertisements in the mass media have been an *exceedingly* large part of the expenditures of tobacco companies.
exceptional [ɪkˈsepʃənl]	a. 例外的，罕见的(rare)；杰出的(superior) 记 来自 exception(n. 除外，例外) 例 *exceptional* competence 杰出的能力
excerpt [ˈeksɜːrpt]	n. (from)摘录，选录(extract) 例 The following is an *excerpt* from a memo written by the head of a governmental department. 同根词：excerption(n. 选录，精华录)
excessive [ɪkˈsesɪv]	a. 过分的，极度的，过多的(extravagant, extreme) 记 词根记忆：ex(出) + cess(走) + ive → 走出了界限，走过了 → 过分的 例 *Excessive* synthesis of one protein can create severe protein imbalances.
exclude [ɪkˈskluːd]	v. 排斥，排除(to bar from participation, or inclusion) 记 词根记忆：ex(出) + clude(关闭) → 关出去 → 排斥 例 The Supreme Court ruled that Blacks could not be *excluded* from jury service. 派 exclusion(n. 排斥，排除)；exclusionary(a. 排除的)；exclusive(a. 排外的，唯一的) 同根词：occlude(v. 堵塞)；preclude(v. 预防；排除)
excluder [ɪkˈskluːdər]	n. 排除器 记 来自 exclude(v. 排除) 例 Their compliance with laws requiring that turtle-*excluder* devices be on shrimp nets protects adult sea turtles. 同根词：include(v. 包括)

exclusion [ɪkˈskluːʒn]	*n.* 排除；驱逐(the act or an instance of excluding or the state of being excluded) 记 来自 exclude(*v.* 排除；排斥) 例 Most historians distort reality by focusing on national concerns to the *exclusion* of local concerns. 同根词：inclusion(*n.* 包含)
exclusively [ɪkˈskluːsɪvli]	*ad.* 专有地，排他地(excluding others from participation) 记 来自 exclusive(*a.* 排外的，唯一的) 例 Caterpillars of monarch butterflies(黑脉金斑蝶)feed *exclusively* on milkweed leaves.
excrete [ɪkˈskriːt]	*v.* 分泌，排泄((of an animal or a plant) to pass out (waste matter, sweat, etc.) from the system) 记 词根记忆：ex(出) + crete(生长) → 身体生出 → 分泌，排泄 例 Desert rats' kidneys can *excrete* a urine having twice as high a salt content as sea water. // *excrete* body wastes 排泄体内的废物
excursion [ɪkˈskɜːrʒn]	*n.* 远足，短途旅行(trip, expedition) 记 词根记忆：ex(出) + curs(跑) + ion → 跑出去 → 远足 例 Our family took a two-week *excursion* to France. 同根词：incursion(*n.* 闯入)
execute [ˈeksɪkjuːt]	*v.* 执行(to carry out fully)；制成(to make or produce) 记 词根记忆：ex + ecu(=secu 跟随) + te → 跟随下去 → 执行 例 The workers have been trained to *execute* one operation efficiently. // None of the contemporary paintings are *execute*d as skillfully as the older paintings. 派 execution(*n.* 实行，执行)；executive(*a.* 行政的；*n.* 行政领导，经理) 同根词：executioner(*n.* 刽子手)
executive [ɪgˈzekjətɪv]	*n.* 执行者(one that exercises administrative or managerial control)；*a.* 行政的；经营管理的(of or relating to the execution of the laws and the conduct of public and national affairs) 记 Chief Executive Officer(首席执行官)，缩写 CEO 例 The following appeared as part of a plan proposed by an *executive* of the Easy Credit Company to the president. 同根词：executant(*n.* 执行者；演奏者)；executable(*a.* 可执行的；可实行的)
exemplary [ɪgˈzempləri]	*a.* 榜样的，模范的(serving as a pattern) 例 Jet engines have achieved *exemplary* performance and safety records.
exemplify [ɪgˈzemplɪfaɪ]	*v.* 是(或成为)…的典型(或榜样)，例示(to be an instance of or serve as an example) 例 Your diligence *exemplifies* the characteristics of a good employee.

15

exempt [ɪɡˈzempt]	*v.* 免除，豁免(to excuse, release)；*a.* (from)被免除的(free or released from some liability or requirement to which others are subject) 记 联想记忆：ex(出) + empt(拿) → 拿出去 → 免除 例 The legislation *exempts* all small businesses from paying any minimum wage. // Citizens who fail to earn federally taxable income are *exempt* from the state sales tax in this country. 同根词：preempt(*v.* 先取，占先)
exert [ɪɡˈzɜːrt]	*v.* 发挥、运用(力量等)(to put (oneself) into action or to tiring effort)；施加(to employ, to wield) 记 词根记忆：ex(出) + ert(能量) → 使出能量 → 发挥，运用 例 This theory asserts that climatic factors *exert* the same regulatory effect on populations. 同根词：inert(*a.* 惰性的，不活跃的)
exhale [eksˈheɪl]	*v.* 呼出，呼气(to breathe out) 记 词根记忆：ex(出) + hale(气) → 呼出，呼气 例 Every time a human being or other mammal *exhales*, there is some carbon dioxide released into the air. 派 exhalation(*n.* 蒸发；呼气) 同根词：inhale(*v.* 吸入，呼入)
exhaust [ɪɡˈzɔːst]	*v.* 用尽(to use up)；*n.* (机器排出的)废气(the fumes or gases released) 记 词根记忆：ex(出) + haust(抽水) → 抽干 → 用尽 例 Oil reserves of the country are *exhausted*. // automobile *exhaust* 汽车尾气 派 exhaustion(*n.* 彻底；耗尽)
exhaustive [ɪɡˈzɔːstɪv]	*a.* 详尽的，无遗漏的(complete, thorough) 例 an *exhaustive* analysis 详尽的分析
exile [ˈeksaɪl]	*v./n.* 放逐，流放(to banish or expel) 记 词根记忆：ex(出) + ile → 赶出 → 放逐 例 The country *exiled* some 160,000 criminals to an iso lated island.
exodus [ˈeksədəs]	*n.* (大批的)离开，移居(a mass departure, emigration) 记 词根记忆：ex(出) + (h)odus(路) → 都到路上去 → (大批)的离去，移民 例 Numerous investigations documented an *exodus* from rural southern areas to southern cities.
exonerate [ɪɡˈzɑːnəreɪt]	*v.* 证明…无罪(to exculpate)；(使)免受指控(to clear from accusation or blame) 记 词根记忆：ex(出) + oner(负担) + ate → 走出负担 → 证明…无罪 例 Alfred was imprisoned for twelve years before he was *exonerated*. 派 exoneration(*n.* 证明无罪)
exotic [ɪɡˈzɑːtɪk]	*a.* 外来的(introduced from another country)；异乎寻常的(strikingly, excitingly, or mysteriously different or unusual) 记 词根记忆：exo(外面) + tic → 外面来的 → 外来的 例 an *exotic* word 外来词 // *exotic* situations 异常状况

expatriate

[ˌeksˈpeɪtriət]

v. 移居国外(to leave one's native country to live elsewhere); n. 移居国外的人(one who removed to a foreign country)

记 联想记忆: ex(出) + patri(父亲) + ate → 离开自己的父亲 → 移居国外

例 The *expatriate* made her new home in France.

同根词: patriotism(n. 爱国主义); patricide(n. 杀父)

expedient

[ɪkˈspiːdiənt]

n. 权宜之计(makeshift); 对策(something that is a means to an affair)

记 联想记忆: ex(出) + ped(脚) + ient → 将脚抽出 → 抽身而退 → 对策

例 a temporary *expedient* 权宜之计

同根词: centipede(n. 蜈蚣)

expedition

[ˌekspəˈdɪʃn]

n. 远征队, 探险队(the group of persons making a journey or excursion undertaken for a specific purpose)

例 scientific archeological *expeditions* 科学考古队

expenditure

[ɪkˈspendɪtʃər]

n. 消耗(the act or process of expending); 花费(sth. expended); 支出(disbursement)

记 来自 expend(v. 花费, 消耗)

例 For several years, per capita *expenditure* on prescription drugs in Voronia rose by fifteen percent or more annually.

同根词: expensive(a. 昂贵的)

15

experience

[ɪkˈspɪriəns]

n. 经历(sth. personally encountered or undergone); 经验(the knowledge and skill gained through doing sth for a period of time); v. 经历(to have experience of); 经验(to learn by experience)

例 Women's oral histories depict *experience* from the point of view of women.

派 experienced(a. 老练的; 富有经验的)

同根词: experiment(n. 实验; v. 尝试)

expertise

[ˌekspɜːrˈtiːz]

n. 专门知识(或技能等), 专长(the skill of an expert)

记 来自 expert(n. 专家)

例 The hospital administrators lack the *expertise* to question medical decisions.

expire

[ɪkˈspaɪər]

v. 期满, 终止(to come to an end); 断气(to breathe one's last breath); 呼气(to emit the breath)

记 词根记忆: ex(出) + pire(=spire 呼吸) → 出了呼吸 → 断气

例 My labor agreement with the company is due to *expire* next January. // Bill *expired* in his sleep after a long illness.

explicit

[ɪkˈsplɪsɪt]

a. 清楚的(clear); 明确的(specific; clearly stated)

记 联想记忆: ex(出) + plic(重叠) + it → 重叠在一起的意义出来了 → 清楚的

例 The companionate family is a family in which members were united by *explicit* bonds of love rather than duty.

explode

[ɪkˈsploʊd]

v. (使某物)爆炸, 炸开(to cause to burst noisily)

记 词根记忆: ex(出) + plode(爆裂) → 爆炸, 炸开

例 Gases released from airplanes following accidents often *explode* soon after being released.

exploit
[ɪkˈsplɔɪt]

v. 开发, 利用(to utilize)

记 词根记忆: ex(出) + ploit(利用) → 开发, 利用

例 Most lands suitable for farming have already been *exploited*.

派 exploitation(*n.* 开发)

同根词: sexploit(*v.* 对…进行性利用)

exploration
[ˌekspləˈreɪʃn]

n. 探索, 探测(the act or an instance of exploring)

记 来自explore(*v.* 探索, 探测)

例 A newly developed jumbo rocket, which is expected to carry the United States into its next phase of space *exploration*, will be able to deliver a heavier load of instruments into orbit than the space·shuttle can, and at a lower cost.

同根词: deplore(*v.* 悲叹)

explore
[ɪkˈsplɔːr]

v. 探索, 探究(to investigate, study, or analyze)

记 词根记忆: ex(出) + plore(大喊) → 把隐藏的大喊出来 → 探索

例 Managers of the factory were *exploring* ways of reducing the production costs.

派 explorer(*n.* 探险家, 探索者); exploration(*n.* 探险, 勘探); unexplored(*a.* 未调查过的)

explosion
[ɪkˈsploʊʒn]

n. 爆炸, 爆发(a large-scale, rapid, or spectacular expansion or bursting out or forth)

记 来自explode(*v.* 爆炸, 炸开)

例 As a result of a supernova *explosion*, every human being on Earth was bombarded on February 23, 1987.

同根词: explosive(*a.* 爆炸的; *n.* 炸药)

export
[ɪkˈspɔːrt; ˈekspɔːrt]

v./n. 出口(物), 输出(品)(to carry or send a commodity to another country)

记 词根记忆: ex(出) + port(运) → 运出去(的东西) → 出口(物)

例 In 1980, the United States *exported* twice as much of its national output of goods as they had in 1970. // The value of our country's *exports* was lower last year than it was the year before.

expound
[ɪkˈspaʊnd]

v. 解释(to explain); 阐述(to clarify)

记 词根记忆: ex(出) + pound(=pon 放) → 把(道理)放出来 → 解释

例 The priest *expounded* his religion. // School textbooks are required to *expound* democratic principles.

派 expounder(*n.* 解释者)

expulsion
[ɪkˈspʌlʃn]

n. 驱逐; 开除(the act of expelling)

记 词根记忆: ex(出) + puls(推) + ion → 推出去 → 驱逐

例 The *expulsion* of the dictator was accomplished by the army. // We soon heard of the *expulsion* of the military adviser.

□ exploit   □ exploration   □ explore   □ explosion   □ export   □ expound
□ expulsion

exquisite [ɪk'skwɪzɪt]	*a.* 精致的(elaborately made; delicate); 近乎完美的(consummate; perfected) 记 词根记忆：ex(出) + quisit(要求，寻求) + e → 按要求做出的 → 精致的 例 To compare the lightning-fast genius of playwright Tom Stoppard with the pedestrian efforts of some of his contemporaries is to compare the *exquisite* bouquet of a fine wine with that of ordinary grape juice. 派 exquisitely(*ad.* 精致地；精巧地)
extend [ɪk'stend]	*v.* 延展，延长(to spread or stretch forth) 记 词根记忆：ex(出) + tend(伸展) → 伸出去 → 延展 例 The installments(分期付款)will *extend* over a period of exactly 3 years. 派 extension(*n.* 延伸；提供); extended(*a.* 延长的)
extensive [ɪk'stensɪv]	*a.* 大量的；多方面的，广泛的(having wide or considerable extent) 记 来自 extend(*v.* 延伸；推广) 例 His *extensive* experience in other parts of Asia helped him to overcome cultural barriers. 派 extensively(*ad.* 广阔地) 同根词: extent(*n.* 程度；范围)
exterminate [ɪk'stɜːrmɪneɪt]	*v.* 消除，消灭(to get rid of completely, usually by killing off) 记 词根记忆：ex(出) + termin(界限) + ate → 超出生存的界限 → 消除 例 By the 1930's, bounty hunters had *exterminated* most of the gray wolves in the United States.
external [ɪk'stɜːrnl]	*a.* 外面的，表面的(outside) 记 词根记忆：ex(外) + ternal → 外面的，表面的 例 external *environment* 外部环境
extinct [ɪk'stɪŋkt]	*a.* 灭绝的(no longer existing); (火山等)熄灭的(no longer active) 记 词根记忆：ex + tinct(促使) → 使…失去 → 灭绝的 例 Unless tiger hunting decreases, tigers will soon be *extinct* in the wild. 派 extinction(*n.* 消失，废止) 同根词: distinction(*n.* 差别); instinct(*n.* 本能，天性); extinguish(*v.* 熄灭，消灭)
extinction [ɪk'stɪŋkʃn]	*n.* 消灭，废除(the process of eliminating or reducing a conditioned response by not reinforcing it) 记 来自 extinct(*v.* 使熄灭) 例 The *extinction* of the salmon populations that spawn in polluted streams is accelerated. 同根词: extinctive(*a.* 使消灭的)
extinguish [ɪk'stɪŋgwɪʃ]	*v.* 消灭(to bring to an end); 熄灭(to cause to cease burning) 记 联想记忆：ex(出去) + ting(=sting 刺) + uish → 去掉刺 → 熄灭 例 Arabs and Bulgarians at times threatened to take Constantinople and *extinguish* the empire altogether. // Most individuals have no formal training in how to *extinguish* fires.

15

Word List 16

extract [ɪk'strækt]	*v.* 提取，榨取(to withdraw, usu. a juice, by physical or chemical process) 记 词根记忆：ex(出) + tract(拉) → 拉出 → 提取，榨取 例 A special process *extracts* the ink from the recycled newspapers. 派 extracted(*a.* 萃取的)
extraction [ɪk'strækʃn]	*n.* 取出，抽出(the act or process of extracting sth.)；抽出物(sth. extracted) 记 来自 extract (*v.* 提取，榨取) 例 mineral *extraction* 矿物提炼 同根词：protract(*v.* 延长)
extracurricular [ˌekstrəkə'rɪkjələr]	*a.* 课外的(not falling within the scope of a regular curriculum) 记 词根记忆：extra(额外的) + curricular(课程的) → 课外的 例 *extracurricular* activities 课外活动
extraneous [ɪk'streɪniəs]	*a.* 无关的(having no relevance)；外来的(extrinsic) 记 词根记忆：extran(外面) + eous → 外来的 例 The digitized signal has been processed by a computer to remove the *extraneous* sound(杂音). // *extraneous* force 外力
extraordinary [ɪk'strɔːrdəneri]	*a.* 非凡的，特别的(going beyond what is usual, regular, or customary)；离奇的(exceptional to a very marked extent) 记 词根记忆：extra(以外的) + ordinary(平常的) → 平常之外的 → 非凡的 例 Never before in the history of music have musical superstars been able to command such *extraordinary* fees of the kind they do today. 派 extraordinarily(*ad.* 格外地；非凡地)
extrapolation [ɪk'stræpəleɪt]	*n.* 推断，推知(inference) 记 词根记忆：extra(外面) + pol(放) + ation → 放出想法 → 推断，推知 例 He estimates his income tax bill by *extrapolation* from figures submitted in previous years. 同根词：interpolate(*v.* 插入；窜改)
extraterrestrial [ˌekstrətə'restriəl]	*a.* 地球外的(originating, existing, or occurring outside the earth or its atmosphere) 记 词根记忆：extra(外面) + terr(陆地) + estrial → 陆地外面的 → 地球外的 例 The government pledged a $100 million investment in the search for *extraterrestrial* intelligence.

□ extract　　□ extraction　　□ extracurricular　□ extraneous　　□ extraordinary　□ extrapolation
□ extraterrestrial

extreme [ɪkˈstriːm]	*n.* 极端(的事物)(something situated at or marking one end or the other of a range); *a.* 极度的，极端的(excessive) 例 Clark refutes the *extremes* of the constructivists by both theoretical and empirical arguments. // Over half the population of Bahlton lives in *extreme* poverty.
fabric [ˈfæbrɪk]	*n.* 织物(cloth); 构造(structure) 记 词根记忆：fabr(制作) + ic → 制作出来的东西 → 构造；织物 例 My shirt is made of cotton *fabric*. // American Indian poetry is always fully woven into the *fabric* of ordinary life. 派 fabrication(*n.* 捏造的东西)
facial [ˈfeɪʃl]	*a.* 面孔的；面部的(of or relating to the face) 记 词根记忆：fac(面) + ial → 面孔的 例 *facial* expressions 面部表情
facilitate [fəˈsɪlɪteɪt]	*v.* (使)容易，促进(to make easier, help bring about) 例 The function of capital markets is to *facilitate* an exchange of funds among all participants. 派 facility(*n.* 容易；设备)
facility [fəˈsɪləti]	*n.* 设施，设备(sth. that makes an action, operation, or course of conduct easier); 容易，灵巧(ease in performance) 记 词根记忆：fac(做) + ility(性质，状态) → 经常做的结果 → 灵巧 例 Wind farms require more land per unit of electricity generated than any other type of electrical-generation *facility*. 同根词：facilitate(*v.* 促进；帮助)
faction [ˈfækʃn]	*n.* 派系，派别(a party or group) 例 the radical *faction* 激进派
factor [ˈfæktər]	*n.* 因素(ingredient);【数】因子(any of the numbers or symbols in mathematics that when multiplied together form a product) 记 词根记忆：fac(做) + tor → 做，发挥作用的 → 因素 例 Output is a major *factor* in GDP. 派 factorization(*n.* 因数分解)
faculty [ˈfæklti]	*n.* 全体教员(all the lecturers, etc. in an educational institution); (大学的)系(department or group of related departments in a university, etc.); 才能(ability) 记 词根记忆：fac(做) + ult + y → 做事的本领 → 才能 例 Jane is a member of the *faculty* at the local university. // The village schoolmaster encourages children to use their *faculties* of observation as much as possible.
faith [feɪθ]	*n.* 信任(trust); 信仰(belief) 例 Even during the war, I kept *faith* in the government.
fallow [ˈfæloʊ]	*a.* 休耕的(plowed but left unseeded during a growing season) 记 联想记忆：休耕(fallow)的时候和伙伴(fellow)一起玩 例 The farmers leave a few fields *fallow* every year.

falsify [ˈfɔːlsɪfaɪ]	v. 篡改(to alter a record, etc. fraudulently); 说谎(to tell falsehoods; to lie) 记 词根记忆：fals(假) + ify → 造假 → 篡改 例 In 1978 a national study found that not only had many contractors licensed by a self-policing private guild failed to pass qualifying exams, but they had also *falsified* their references. 派 falsification(n. 伪造；歪曲)
fatal [ˈfeɪtl]	a. 致命的(causing death) 记 词根记忆：fat(=fate 命运) + al → 要命的 → 致命的 例 During the 1630's smallpox, the disease was most *fatal* to the Native American people.
fatality [fəˈtæləti]	n. 死亡(事故)(death resulting from a disaster) 记 词根记忆：fat(=fate 命运) + ality → 夺命 → 死亡(事故) 例 The rate of automobile *fatalities* in our country is very high.
fault [fɔːlt]	n. 过错(mistake);【地】断层(a fracture in the crust of a planet) 记 fault 本身为词根：错误 例 Henyey found that temperatures in drill holes near the *fault* were not as elevated as had been suspected.
feasible [ˈfiːzəbl]	a. 可做的，可实行的(capable of being done or carried out) 记 词根记忆：feas(=fac 做) + ible → 能做的 → 可实行的 例 Mass marketing remains the only economically *feasible* mode. 派 feasibility(n. 可行性)
fecundity [fiˈkʌndətɪ]	n. 多产(prolific);繁殖力(fertility, productiveness) 记 来自 fecund(a. 肥沃的) 例 A plant's *fecundity* decreases as the number of flowers produced by the plant decreases.
federal [ˈfedərəl]	a. 联邦(制)的，联邦政府的(of a system of government in which several states unite, usu. for foreign policy etc., but retain considerable control over their own internal affairs) 记 词根记忆：feder(联盟) + al → 联邦(制)的 例 Few manufacturers have taken advantage of the changes in the *federal* tax laws. 派 federate(a. 同盟的); federation(n. 同盟，联邦)
feign [feɪn]	v. 假装，伪装(to make a false show of, to pretend) 例 The hognose snake puts on an impressive bluff, hissing and rearing back, broadens the flesh behind its head the way a cobra does, *feigning* repeated strikes, but, having no dangerous fangs and no venom.
feminist [ˈfemənɪst]	n. 女权主义者(a person who supports that women should have the same rights and opportunities as men) 记 词根记忆：femin(女人) + ist → 女权主义者 例 western *feminist* theory 西方女权说 同根词：feminine(a. 女性的)

□ falsify   □ fatal   □ fatality   □ fault   □ feasible   □ fecundity
□ federal   □ feign   □ feminist

ferrous
[ˈferəs]
a. 含铁的(containing iron)
记 词根记忆：ferr(铁) + ous → 含铁的

fertility
[fərˈtɪləti]
n. 繁殖力(the birthrate of a population)；丰产(the quality or state of being fertile)
记 词根记忆：fer(带，生) + tility → 带来新生命 → 繁殖力
例 *fertility* rates 人口出生率 // Venus is a goddess of *fertility* and harvest.
同根词：fertilizer(*n.* 肥料)；fertilization(*n.* 受孕，受精)

fertilized
[ˈfɜːrtəlaɪzd]
a. 已受精的(being made fertile)
记 来自 fertilize(*v.* 使受精)
例 *fertilized* eggs 受精卵

fertilizer
[ˈfɜːrtəlaɪzər]
n. 肥料，化肥(natural or artificial substance added to soil to make it more productive)
记 来自 fertilize(*v.* 使肥沃)
例 Research has shown that Tanco could reprocess the by-product of potassium chloride use to yield a crop *fertilizer*, leaving a relatively small volume of waste for disposal.

fervent
[ˈfɜːrvənt]
a. 强烈的，热烈的(passionate, zealous)
记 词根记忆：ferv(热) + ent → 热情的 → 热烈的
注意：ferment(*v.* 发酵)
例 The church members listened to their minister's *fervent* prayers.
派 fervently(*ad.* 热烈地)

fetal
[ˈfiːtl]
a. 胎儿的(of fetus)
记 词根记忆：fet(胎儿) + al → 胎儿的
注意：fatal(*a.* 致命的)
例 Using a Doppler ultrasound device, *fetal* heartbeats can be detected.
同根词：fetology(*n.* 胎儿学)；feticide(*n.* 堕胎)

fetch
[fetʃ]
v. 售得(to be sold for)
例 Individual bulls and cows received awards, *fetched* unprecedented prices, and excited enormous interest.

feudal
[ˈfjuːdl]
a. 封建制度的(of or according to the system during the Middle Ages in Europe, under which people receive land and protection from the landowner and work and fight for him in return)
记 来自 feud(*n.* 封地)
例 *feudal* landholders 封建地主
派 feudalism(*n.* 封建主义，封建制度)

fiber
[ˈfaɪbər]
n. 纤维(a thread or a structure or an object resembling a thread)
例 *fiber*-optic cable 光纤电缆

fibrosis
[faɪˈbrousɪs]
n. 纤维化(a condition marked by increase of interstitial fibrous tissue)
记 来自 fibre(*n.* 纤维)
例 When lung tissue from people with cystic *fibrosis* is maintained in a solution with a normal salt concentration, the tissue can resist bacteria.
派 fibrotic(*a.* 纤维化的)
同根词：fibroid(*a.* 纤维性的；纤维状的)

16

fickle

['fɪkl]

a. 易变的，不坚定的（unstable, unreliable）

记 词根记忆：fic(做) + kle → 做得不坚决 → 不坚定的

例 a fickle *fortune* 多变的命运

fierce

[fɪrs]

a. 残酷的（cruel）；凶猛的（violent）

记 和 force(v. 强制，强迫) 一起记

例 *fierce* competition 残酷的竞争 // *fierce* struggle 激烈的挣扎

派 fiercely(ad. 猛烈地；很)

figurine

[ˌfɪgjə'riːn]

n. 小塑像，小雕像（a small sculptured or molded figure; statuette）

记 来自 figure(n. 雕像)

例 Twenty-one ceramic dog *figurines* were discovered during the excavation of a 1,000-year-old Hohokam village in Tempe.

同根词：transfigure(v. 使变形；使改观)

filament

['fɪləmənt]

n. 灯丝（thin wire in a light bulb that glows when electricity passed through）；纤维（fiber）

记 词根记忆：fila(丝) + ment → 灯丝

例 The underground *filaments* of chanterelles(鸡油菌)provide nutrients and water for their hosts.

file

[faɪl]

n. 文件（paper, document）；档案（record）；v. 提出申请（to place among official records as prescribed by law）

例 Employees should not have full access to their own personnel *files*. // *file* patents 申请专利权

filibuster

['fɪlɪbʌstər]

n. 阻挠议案通过；妨碍议事（the use of extreme dilatory tactics in an attempt to delay or prevent action especially in a legislative assembly）

记 联想记忆：fili + buster(破坏者) → 破坏者阻挠别人发展 → 阴挠议案通过

例 There were not enough votes to stop the senator's *filibuster*.

filter

['fɪltər]

n. 滤纸（a porous article（as of paper）through which a gas or liquid is passed to separate out matter in suspension）；v. 过滤（to remove by means of a filter）

记 发音记忆："非要它" → 香烟的过滤嘴是非要它不可的 → 过滤

例 *Filter* out all the dirt before using the water.

financier

[ˌfɪnən'sɪr]

n. 金融家（a person skilled in large scale financial transactions）；v. 对…提供资金（to conduct financial operations, often in an unethical manner）

记 来自 finance(n. 财政，金融)

例 It is argued that *financiers* will expect the deficit to cause inflation and will raise interest rates.

同根词：financial(a. 金融的，财政的)

finite

['faɪnaɪt]

a. 有限的（limited）；【数】有穷的

记 词根记忆：fin(范围) + ite → 有范围的 → 有限的

例 The number of possible radio stations in an area is *finite*.

派 infinite(a. 无穷的；n. 无限)；infinitely(ad. 无限地)

fiscal [ˈfɪskl]	*a.* 国库的，财政的（of or relating to taxation, public revenues, or public debt） 记 词根记忆：fisc(国库) + al → 国库的，财政的 例 A project scheduled to be carried out over a single *fiscal* year has a budget of $12,600. 同根词：confiscate(*v.* 充公，没收)
fivefold [ˈfaɪvfoʊld]	*a./ad.* 五倍的(地)（being five times as great or as many） 例 He repaid the loan *fivefold*.
fixture [ˈfɪkstʃər]	*n.* [常 *pl.*]（房屋等的）装置，配置（something that is fixed or attached in a building as a permanent appendage or as a structural part） 例 I installed a new light *fixture* above the kitchen sink.
fjord [ˈfjɔːrd]	*n.* 峡湾(尤指挪威海岸边的)（bay, gulf） 记 和 lord(*n.* 地主)一起记
flat [flæt]	*a.* 平滑的（having a smooth, even, level surface）；（收费）统一的（having a single price for a variety of goods or services）；固定的（fixed）；*n.* 公寓（an apartment on one floor） 例 Those plastic beverage containers can be crushed completely *flat* by refuse compactors. // Property taxes are typically set at a *flat* rate per $1,000 of officially assessed value. 派 flatly(*ad.* 水平地，平平地)
flatten [ˈflætn]	*v.* 变平（to become or make sth. flat）；彻底打败某人（to defeat sb. completely） 记 来自 flat(*n.* 平面；*a.* 平坦的) 例 Jazz singer Billie Holiday used her voice in the same way that other musicians use their instruments, in that she ranged freely over the beat, *flattening* out the melodic contours of tunes. 同根词：flatness(*n.* 平坦；单调)
flaunt [flɔːnt]	*v.* 炫耀，夸耀（to display or obtrude oneself to public notice） 例 Designers have adopted a cornerless style of smooth surfaces and curves that is more ergonomic, conforming to the shape of the body rather than *flaunting* shape for its own sake.
flavor [ˈfleɪvər]	*n.* 风味（the blend of taste and smell sensations）；香料（spice） 例 The bread had a more delicate *flavor* because it was not toasted. // *flavor* additives 香料添加剂
fledgling [ˈfledʒlɪŋ]	*n.* 雏鸟（nestling）；*a.* 新兴的（inexperienced, new） 记 和 fledge(*v.* 长羽毛)、fledged(*a.* 羽毛长成的，成熟的)一起记 例 *fledgling* sea eagles 雏海鹰 // *fledgling* industries 新兴产业
flexible [ˈfleksəbl]	*a.* 易弯曲的，灵活的（elastic） 记 词根记忆：flex(弯曲) + ible → 易弯曲的，灵活的 例 Time management needs to be *flexible* so that employees can respond to unexpected problems.

16

flip [flɪp]	*v.* 轻弹(to flick); 按(开关)(to press a button or switch); 蹦跳 *a.* 无礼的(rude); 冒失的; 轻率的(flippant) 记 联想记忆: f(看作 fly 飞) + lip(嘴唇) → 飞吻轻抛 → 无礼的 例 *flip* over 翻页 派 flippant(*a.* 轻率的; 没礼貌的)
flippant ['flɪpənt]	*a.* 无礼的(impolite); 轻率的(rude; casually disrespectful) 例 If your *flippant* attitude doesn't improve, you're going to be fired.
flock [flɑːk]	*n.* (鸟、兽等)一群(a group of animals, e.g. birds or sheep etc.) 记 和 block(*v.* 妨碍)一起记 例 a *flock* of large birds 一群大鸟
flourish ['flɜːrɪʃ]	*v.* 繁荣(to thrive, to prosper); 活跃(to be in a period of highest productivity, excellence, or influence) 记 词根记忆: flour(=flor 花) + ish → 花一样开放 → 繁荣 例 People are friendly, the environment is safe, and the arts are *flourishing*. // This bacterium can *flourish* on the dried grain.
fluctuate ['flʌktʃueɪt]	*v.* (使)涨落, (使)变化(to swing) 记 词根记忆: fluct(=flu 流动) + uate → 波动 → 变化 例 A minority shareholder buys and sells stocks as prices *fluctuate* over short periods of time.
fluctuation [ˌflʌktʃuˈeɪʃn]	*n.* 波动(swing) 记 来自 fluctuate(*v.* 波动) 例 Such *fluctuations* in population are known as population cycles.
fluid ['fluːɪd]	*n.* 流体(liquid); *a.* 流体的, 流动的(able to flow freely, as gases and liquids do) 记 词根记忆: flu(流动) + id → 流体; 流动的 例 These rats stay in burrows to avoid loss of *fluid* through panting or sweating. 派 fluidounce(*n.* 液量盎司)
fluorescent [ˌflɔːˈresnt]	*a.* 荧光的(of, having or showing fluorescence) 记 词根记忆: fluor(荧光) + escent(发生…的) → 荧光的 例 Continuous indoor *fluorescent* light benefits the health of hamsters with inherited heart disease. 同根词: fluorometry(*n.* 荧光计)
focus ['foʊkəs]	*v.* (使)聚焦, (使)集中(to concentrate); *n.* 震源, 震中(the place of origin of an earthquake) 例 The key to success is to *focus* on the specific task at hand and not to worry about results. // the earthquake *focus* 震源
fodder ['fɑːdər]	*n.* 草料(something fed to domestic animals) 记 联想记忆: fodd(看作 food 食物) + er → 动物的食物 → 草料 例 Mongolia's terrain is suitable for grazing native herds but not for growing the *fodder*.

☐ flip ☐ flippant ☐ flock ☐ flourish ☐ fluctuate ☐ fluctuation
☐ fluid ☐ fluorescent ☐ focus ☐ fodder

folklore [ˈfoʊklɔːr]	*n.* 民俗文化(traditional customs, tales, sayings, dances, or art forms preserved among a people); 民俗学(a branch of knowledge that deals with folklore) 记 分拆记忆：folk(乡民) + lore(传说，学问) → 民俗学 例 Many of our fairy tales come from English *folklore*.
folkway [ˈfoʊkweɪ]	*n.* 民风，社会习俗(a mode of thinking, feeling, or acting common to a given group of people) 记 联想记忆：folk(民族，人们) + way(方式) → 人们生活的方式 → 民风 例 The inhabitants of the Lofotens have evolved *folkways* and a life-style that bring warmth to their harsh environment.
follicle [ˈfɑːlɪkl]	*n.* 【解】(体内的)小囊(a vesicle in the mammalian ovary that contains a developing egg surrounded by a covering of cells) 例 the ovarian *follicle* cells 卵巢囊细胞
forage [ˈfɔːrɪdʒ]	*n.* 饲料，粮草(fodder); *v.* (for)搜寻，翻寻(search) 记 联想记忆：for(为了) + age(年龄) → 为了年龄成长需要的粮草 → 粮草 例 *forage* crop 饲料作物 // When elephants *forage* for food, they typically travel in herds. 派 forager(*n.* 抢劫者)
forager [ˈfɔːrɪdʒər]	*n.* 抢劫者(someone who hunts for food and provisions); 强征队员(someone who secures by foraging) 记 来自forage(*v.* 搜寻) 例 A flaw in this strategy is that *forager* societies are extremely varied.
foraging [ˈfɔːrɪdʒɪŋ]	*n.* 觅食(the act of searching for food and provisions) 记 来自forage(*n.* 饲料; *v.* 搜寻) 例 They cannot be replenished through *foraging*.
forecast [ˈfɔːrkæst]	*v./n.* 预测，预报(to foretell) 记 词根记忆：fore(预先) + cast(计算) → 预先计算出 → 预测，预报 例 Weather *forecasts* are more detailed today than they were 36 years ago. // People could not *forecast* the weather with real precision. 派 forecaster(*n.* 预报员)
foreclosure [fɔːrˈkloʊʒər]	*n.* 取消抵押品赎回权(a legal proceeding that bars or extinguishes a mortgagor's right of redeeming a mortgaged estate) 记 词根记忆：fore(预先) + closure(关闭) → 预先关闭了 → 取消抵押品赎回权 例 *Foreclosures* on these types of loans could double over the next three years. 同根词：disclosure(*n.* 公开；揭发)
foresee [fɔːrˈsiː]	*v.* 预见(to see or know beforehand) 记 词根记忆：fore(预先) + see(看见) → 预先看见 → 预见 例 How comparable worth will affect the hierarchy of wages is difficult to *foresee*.

16

foreseeable [fɔːˈsiːəbl]	*adj.* 可预知的(being such as may be reasonably anticipated); 能预测的 记 词根记忆：fore(预先) + see(看见) + able(有能力的) → 有能力预先看见的 → 可预知的 例 Teruvia's total rice acreage will not be expanded in the *foreseeable* future, nor will rice yields per acre increase appreciably.
foreshadow [fɔːrˈʃædoʊ]	*v.* 成为先兆，预示(to represent, indicate, or typify beforehand) 记 词根记忆：fore(预先) + shadow(影子) → 影子先来 → 预示 例 Given this failure, Duverger's study *foreshadowed* the enduring limitations of the behavioralist approach to the multinational study of women's political participation.

The tragedy of life is not so much what men suffer, but what they miss.
生活的悲剧不在于人们受到多少苦，而在于人们错过了什么。
——英国散文家、历史学家 卡莱尔(Thomas Carlyle, British essayist and historian)

Word List 17

音频

foresight [ˈfɔːrsaɪt]	*n.* 远见，深谋远虑(prescience) 记 词根记忆：fore(预先) + sight(眼光) → 有预见的眼光 → 远见 例 The treasurer had the *foresight* to sell the company stocks right before the market crashed.
forestall [fɔːrˈstɔːl]	*v.* 预防，阻止(to prevent) 记 词根记忆：fore(预先) + stall(停止) → 预先停止 → 预防 例 Treatment for hypertension *forestalls* certain medical expenses by preventing strokes and heart disease.
forfeit [ˈfɔːrfət]	*n.* 罚金(penalty); *v.* 丧失(to abandon, give up) 记 联想记忆：for(因为) + feit(看作 fect"做") → 因为做了错事所以被罚 → 丧失 例 Increasing commercial activity would cause some people to *forfeit* their liberty and virtue.
forge [fɔːrdʒ]	*v.* 锻造(to form metal etc. by heating and hammering); 达成, 使形成(to form or bring into being, especially by an expenditure of effort); *n.* 铁匠铺 记 联想记忆：forge 和 forget 就差一个字母，忘了(forget)铁(t)就开始锻造(forge) 例 The blacksmith *forged* horseshoes from iron. // *forged* in battle 派 forger(*n.* 伪造者); forgery(*n.* 伪造; 赝品)
format [ˈfɔːrmæt]	*n.* 格式, 版式(the shape, size, and general makeup of something printed); *v.* (使)格式化(to prepare, usu. as a computer disk, for storing data in a particular format) 记 词根记忆：form(形式) + at → 固定的形式 → 格式, 版式 例 Mannis Corporation has stored its archival(关于档案的)records in a computerized *format*.
formation [fɔːrˈmeɪʃn]	*n.* 组织, 形成(thing that is formed); (军队)编队(an arrangement of a group of persons in some prescribed manner or for a particular purpose) 记 词根记忆：form(形式) + at + ion → 固定的形式 → 形成 例 It misrepresented how horizontal displacements cause the *formation* of mountain chains. 同根词：formula(*n.* 公式; 信条)

formidable
[ˈfɔːrmɪdəbl]

a. 可怕的(causing fear, dread, or apprehension)；困难的(having qualities that discourage approach or attack)

记 联想记忆：for + mid(中间) + able → 处在中间，左右为难 → 困难的

例 In the speaking contest Randolph faced *formidable* obstacles.

formula
[ˈfɔːrmjələ]

n. 公式(a statement, especially an equation, of a fact, rule, principle, or other logical relation)

记 词根记忆：form(形成，形状) + ula → 结构式 → 公式

例 In the *formula*, integers(整数)"p"and"t"are positive constants.

派 formulaic(*a.* 公式的)

forthcoming
[ˌfɔːrθˈkʌmɪŋ]

a. 将来的(approaching)；现成的，随要随到的(being about to appear or to be produced or made available)

例 Bill and Anne eagerly awaited their *forthcoming* wedding. // No answer was *forthcoming*.

fortify
[ˈfɔːrtɪfaɪ]

v. 增强营养(to impart physical strength or endurance to)

记 词根记忆：fort(强大) + ify → 使强大 → 增强营养

例 Many breakfast cereals are *fortified* with vitamin supplements.

同根词：fortitude(*n.* 刚毅)

fossil
[ˈfɑːsl]

n. 化石(a remnant, impression, or trace of an organism of past geologic ages that has been preserved in the earth's crust)

记 词根记忆：foss(石头) + il → 变成了石头 → 化石

例 *fossil* bones 骨骼化石

派 fossilize(*v.* 使成化石，使陈腐)

fossilize
[ˈfɑːsəlaɪz]

v. (使)成为化石(to cause sth. to become a fossil)；(使)过时(to make sth. out of date)

记 来自 fossil(*n.* 化石)

例 The four-million-year-old *fossilized* skeleton known as Lucy is so small compared with many other skeletons.

派 fossilization(*n.* 石化，僵化)

同根词：fossiliferous(*a.* 含有化石的)

foster
[ˈfɔːstər]

v. 养育，培养(to nurture)；加强，促进(to promote the growth or development of)

记 注意：bolster(*v.* 支持)

例 The regional developments will *foster* integration in the two largest and richest markets of the world.

fraction
[ˈfrækʃn]

n. 片段(fragment)；小部分(portion)；分数(an expression that indicates the quotient of two quantities)

记 词根记忆：fract(破开) + ion → 片段

例 Parking charges here are $0.75 for the first hour and $0.50 for each additional hour or *fraction* of an hour.

fracture
[ˈfræktʃər]

n. 骨折(the breaking of bone)；折断(breaking)

记 词根记忆：fract(破开) + ure → 破开 → 折断

例 The healing of ankle *fractures* is always checked by means of a follow-up x-ray.

□ formidable   □ formula   □ forthcoming   □ fortify   □ fossil   □ fossilize
□ foster   □ fraction   □ fracture

fragile ['frædʒl]	a. 脆的，易碎的(easily broken)；脆弱的(delicate) 记 词根记忆：frag(=fract 破开) + ile(易…的) → 易碎的 例 Coral reefs(珊瑚礁)are one of the most *fragile*, biologically complex, and diverse marine ecosystems on earth. 同根词：fragment(*n.* 碎片)
fragment ['frægmənt]	*n.* 碎片(a broken piece)；部分(a part) 记 词根记忆：frag(破碎) + ment → 碎片 例 The bone *fragments* were joined together to form the complete skeleton of the animal.
frame [freɪm]	*n.* 框架(border of wood, metal, etc. in which a picture, door, pane of glass, etc. is enclosed or set)；*v.* 诬陷(to contrive the evidence against (an innocent person) so that a verdict of guilty is assured) 例 picture *frame* 相框 // time *frame* 时限 // *Framed* by traitorous colleagues, Alfred was imprisoned for twelve years. 同根词：framework(*n.* 框架，构架)
framework ['freɪmwɜːrk]	*n.* 框架(a basic conceptional structure) 例 Relational feminism provides the best theoretical *framework* for contemporary feminist politics.
franchise ['fræntʃaɪz]	*n.* 特权(a special privilege granted to an individual or group)；经销权(a team and its operating organization having such membership) 例 We should not approve the business loan application of the local group that wants to open a *franchise* outlet for the Kool Kone chain of ice cream parlors. 同根词：enfranchise(*v.* 给予选举权)
fraternal [frə'tɜːrnl]	a. 兄弟的(of, relating to, or involving brothers) 记 词根记忆：fratern(兄弟) + al → 兄弟的 例 *fraternal* twins 异卵双生
frequency ['friːkwənsi]	*n.* 频率(rate of occurrence or repetition of sth.) 记 来自 frequent(a. 频繁的) 例 Southern Airways has a far worse safety record than Air Dacentaria over the past few years, in terms of both the *frequency* of accidents and the severity of accidents.
friction ['frɪkʃn]	*n.* 摩擦(the rubbing of one body against another) 例 Under normal conditions, rocks composed of clay produce far less *friction* than other rocks do. 派 frictional(a. 摩擦的)；frictionless(a. 无摩擦的)
frontier ['frʌn'tɪr]	*n.* 国境(a border between two countries)；边缘地带(a region that forms the margin of settled or developed territory) 记 来自 front(*n.* 前方) 例 the North American *frontier* 北美边境

17

□ fragile   □ fragment   □ frame   □ framework   □ franchise   □ fraternal
□ frequency   □ friction   □ frontier

frugal [ˈfruːgl]	*a.* 节约的，节俭的(sparing, thrifty, economical) 记 发音记忆："腐乳过日" → 吃腐乳过日子 → 节约的 例 Personal savings have been accumulated, often through *frugal* living habits. 派 frugality(*n.* 节约，节俭)
frustrate [ˈfrʌstreɪt]	*v.* 挫败(to defeat)；(使)沮丧(to induce feelings of discouragement in) 例 The difficult exam *frustrated* the entire class. 派 frustration(*n.* 沮丧，挫折)
fuel [ˈfjuːəl]	*n.* 燃料(a material used to produce heat or power by burning)；*v.* 给…加燃料(to provide with fuel)；刺激(to stimulate)；推动(to support) 记 联想记忆：加满(full)燃料(fuel) 例 The use of coal as a *fuel* has declined from the level it was at in the previous twenty years. // The growth of the restaurant industry was *fueled* by recent social changes. 派 refuel(*v.* 加油，加燃料)
function [ˈfʌŋkʃn]	*v.* 运行(to operate)；起作用(to serve)；*n.* 职责(duty)；作用；功能(effect) 记 发音记忆："放颗心" → 公务员的职责就是让人民放心 → 职责 例 The old watch can't *function* properly. // A major *function* of self-help networks is financial support. 派 functional(*a.* 起作用的；实用的)；functioning(*n.* 运转，操作)
fundraise [ˈfʌndˌreɪz]	*n.* 募捐(raising money) 记 分拆记忆：fund(资金) + raise(筹集) → 筹集资金 → 募捐 例 The Arnmore Laboratories and Arnmore Research Facilities were founded by Leo and Fontove Arnmore in 1989 after ten years of *fundraising*.
fungi [ˈfʌŋgaɪ]	*n.* (fungus 的复数)真菌(any of various of types of plants without leaves, flowers or green colouring-matter growing on other plants or decaying matter)；突然发生并迅速发展的东西(something taking place suddenly and developing quickly) 记 发音记忆："房盖" → 真菌的形状像房盖 例 The study shows that the death of those plants is due to insects and *fungi*.
fungus [ˈfʌŋgəs]	*n.* 真菌，霉菌；菌类 记 联想记忆：fun(有趣) + g + us(我们) → 我们第一次看到有趣的真菌 → 真菌 例 Beneath the soil of the Malheur National Forest in eastern Oregon, a *fungus* that has been slowly weaving its way through the roots of trees for centuries has become the largest single living organism known to biologists.
funnel [ˈfʌnl]	*n.* 漏斗(a utensil that is usually a hollow cone with a tube extending from the smaller end and that is designed to catch and direct a downward flow)；*v.* 汇集，集中(to move to a focal point) 记 注意：tunnel(*n.* 隧道) 例 Mary *funneled* all her efforts into her studies.

□ frugal □ frustrate □ fuel □ function □ fundraise □ fungi
□ fungus □ funnel

furnace [ˈfɜːrnɪs]	*n.* 熔炉(an enclosed structure in which heat is produced (as for heating a house or for reducing ore)) 例 This *furnace* is used to melt the iron that will be made into steel. // blast *furnace* 鼓风机
fuse [fjuːz]	*v.* 熔化, 熔融(to reduce to a liquid or plastic state by heat); 融合(to combine, to become blended or joined) 例 Wynton and Branford Marsalis, brothers who have *fused* the complex rhythms of contemporary jazz with the rollicking musical legacy of their hometown, are fitting symbols of the New Orleans jazz revival. 派 fusion(*n.* 融合; 熔化)
fusion [ˈfjuːʒn]	*n.* 融合(a union by or as if by melting); 聚变(union of atomic nuclear) 记 来自 fuse(*v.* 融合; 熔化) 例 Stars like the Sun can continue to shine steadily for billions of years because its light and heat are produced by nuclear *fusion*. 同根词: fusible(*a.* 易熔的; 可熔的)
futile [ˈfjuːtl]	*a.* 无益的(worthless); 无用的(useless) 记 联想记忆: fut(=fus 流出, 倒出) + ile(能…的) → 能倒出去的 → 无用的 例 The mayor's *futile* gestures to the angry citizens only angered them further. 同根词: refute(*v.* 反驳, 驳倒)
gadgeteering [gædʒɪˈtɪərɪŋ]	*n.* 精妙的机器发明(设计) 例 high-technology *gadgeteering* 高科技发明
galactic [gəˈlæktɪk]	*a.* 银河的(of or relating to a galaxy and especially the Milky Way galaxy) 例 *galactic* luminosity 银河光度 同根词: galaxy(*n.* 银河; 星系)
galaxy [ˈgæləksi]	*n.* 银河, 星系 记 联想记忆: gala(乳) + xy → 银河像乳汁 例 the Milky Way *galaxy* 银河系 派 protogalaxy(*n.* 原星系); galactic(*a.* 银河的; 乳汁的)
garment [ˈgɑːrmənt]	*n.* (一件)衣服, 外衣(an article of clothing) 例 David's *garments* were torn in the accident.
gauge [geɪdʒ]	*n.* 标准规格(a measurement (as of linear dimension) according to some standard or system); 量具(an instrument for a means of measuring or testing); *v.* 测量(to measure); 判断(to judge) 例 the same *gauge* 相同的规格 // *gauge* manufacturer 量具制造商 // It was difficult to *gauge* how people would respond.
gear [gɪr]	*n.* 齿轮(a toothed wheel); 设备, 工具(a mechanism that performs a specific function in a complete machine); *v.* 使…准备好(to make ready for effective operation) 记 联想记忆: g + ear(耳朵) → 耳朵是身体上的设备 → 设备 例 Very few children wear any kind of protective *gear*, such as helmets, while sledding.

17

generalization [ˌdʒenrələˈzeɪʃn]	*n.* 概括；普遍化（the act or process of generalizing） 记 来自 generalize（*v.* 概括，使…一般化） 例 The first is a *generalization* that the argument seeks to establish. 同根词：generally（*ad.* 通常；普遍地）
generate [ˈdʒenəreɪt]	*v.* 生成，产生（to bring into existence）；引起（to be the cause of） 记 词根记忆：gener（产生）+ ate → 产生，生成 例 Superior service can *generate* a competitive advantage for a company. // friction-*generated* heat 摩擦产生的热量 同根词：generation（*n.* 一代人；产生）；morphogenetic（*a.* 形态发生的）
generational [ˌdʒenəˈreɪʃənl]	*a.* 一代的；生育的（of or relating to a generation） 记 词根记忆：generation（一代）+ al（…的）→ 一代的 例 The argument that the dominant form of family structure today is not the nuclear family but a modified extended family is based on a number of facts: the existence of three-*generational* families, the amount of vertical and horizontal communication between family subunits, and the extent to which family members offer assistance to one another. 同根词：generative（*a.* 生殖的；生产的）
generic [dʒəˈnerɪk]	*a.* 种类的（relating to or having the rank of a biological genus）；类属的（relating to or characteristic of a whole group or class） 记 来自 genus（*n.* 种类）；注意不要和 genetic（*a.* 遗传的；起源的）相混 例 In addition to imposing a price freeze, the government encouraged doctors to prescribe *generic* versions of common drugs instead of the more expensive brand-name versions. 派 generically（*ad.* 一般地；类属地）
genetic [dʒəˈnetɪk]	*a.* 基因的，遗传的（of, relating to, or controlled by genes） 记 来自 gene（*n.* 基因） 例 *genetic* code 遗传密码 派 genetics（*n.* 遗传学）；genetically（*ad.* 由基因决定地）
genial [ˈdʒiːniəl]	*a.* 亲切的（gracious）；和蔼的（friendly） 记 联想记忆：gen（产生）+ ial → 产生好感的 → 亲切的 注意：genital（*a.* 生殖的） 例 a *genial* character 和蔼的性格
gentry [ˈdʒentri]	*n.* 贵族，绅士，上等人（people of gentle birth, good breeding, or high social position） 记 联想记忆：gen（产生）+ try → 出生于高贵门第 → 贵族 例 The political and social privileges enjoyed by the landed *gentry* would have been destroyed.
genuine [ˈdʒenjuɪn]	*a.* 真正的（real, actual） 记 词根记忆：genu（=gen 产生）+ ine → 产生，来源清楚 → 真正的 例 *genuine* leather 真皮

☐ generalization ☐ generate ☐ generational ☐ generic ☐ genetic ☐ genial
☐ gentry ☐ genuine

geographic [ˌdʒiːə'ɡræfɪk]	*a.* 地理的；地理学的(of or relating to geography) 记 来自 geography(*n.* 地理) 例 The North Pacific populations of seals and sea lions cover a wider *geographic* area than does the population of sea otters. 同根词：geographer(*n.* 地理学者)
geological [ˌdʒiːə'lɑːdʒɪkl]	*a.* 地质的(of, relating to, or based on geology) 记 来自 geology(*n.* 地质学) 例 The ways in which a particular *geological* phenomenon is exceptional are detailed and classified. 派 geologically(*ad.* 从地质学角度) 同根词：geologist(*n.* 地质学家)
geologist [dʒi'ɑːlədʒɪst]	*n.* 地质学家(a person who deals with the history of the earth and its life) 记 词根记忆：geo(地，地球) + log(记录) + ist(专家) → 记录地球的专家→ 地质学家 例 Henry's findings provided support for an assumption long held by *geologists*. 同根词：geography(*n.* 地理学)；geocentric(*a.* 以地球为中心的)
geometric [ˌdʒiːə'metrɪk]	*a.* 几何的(of, relating to, or according to the methods or principles of geometry)；成几何级数增长的(increasing in a geometric progression) 记 来自 geometry(*n.* 几何学)
geophysical [ˌdʒiːoʊ'fɪzɪkl]	*a.* 地球物理学的(a branch of earth science dealing with the physical processes and phenomena occurring especially in the earth and in its vicinity) 同根词：geophysicist(*n.* 地球物理学家)
gimmick ['ɡɪmɪk]	*n.* 伎俩，噱头(a trick used to attract business or attention) 例 marketing *gimmick* 营销手段
glacier ['ɡleɪʃər]	*n.* 冰河，冰川(a large body of ice moving slowly down a slope or valley or spreading outward on a land surface) 记 词根记忆：glac(冰) + ier → 冰河，冰川 例 The most favorable locations for the growth of *glaciers* would be the cool, moist middle latitudes.
gland [ɡlænd]	*n.* 【解】腺(a cell, a group of cells, or an organ that produces a secretion for use elsewhere in the body or in a body cavity or for elimination from the body) 例 adrenal *gland* 肾上腺
glean [gliːn]	*v.* 收集，采集(to gather bit by bit) 记 和 clean(*a.* 干净的)一起记 例 These maps incorporating some information were *gleaned* directly from Native Americans.
gloomy ['ɡluːmi]	*a.* 悲观的(lacking in promise or hopefulness) 例 The use of Antarctic krill as a food is an innovation whose future is *gloomy*.

17

□ geographic   □ geological   □ geologist   □ geometric   □ geophysical   □ gimmick
□ glacier   □ gland   □ glean   □ gloomy

glucose [ˈgluːkoʊs]	*n.* 葡萄糖(the sweet colorless soluble dextrorotatory form that occurs widely in nature and is the usual form in which carbohydrate is assimilated by animals) 例 *glucose* solution 葡萄糖溶液
gorilla [gəˈrɪlə]	*n.* 大猩猩(a very large typically black-colored anthropoid ape) 例 The number of mountain *gorillas* is declining in this area.
gourmet [ˈgʊrmeɪ]	*n.* 美食家(epicure) 记 联想记忆：这些美食(gourmet)够(g)我们(our)米西(met) 例 *gourmet* food 鲜美食品
gradient [ˈgreɪdiənt]	*n.* 梯度(the rate at which a physical quantity, such as temperature or pressure, changes relative to change in a given variable, especially distance)；【生】生理梯度(a graded difference in physiological activity along an axis) 记 词根记忆：gradi(=grad 步，级) + ent → 梯度 例 thermal *gradient* 热梯度
granite [ˈgrænɪt]	*n.* 花岗岩 记 联想记忆：gran(=grain 颗粒) + ite → 颗粒状石头 → 花岗岩 例 Geologists' pre-1965 assumptions concerning heat generated in the fault were based on calculations about common varieties of rocks, such as limestone and *granite*. 派 granitic(*a.* 花岗石的)
grant [grænt]	*v.* 同意，认可(to accord)；允许(to permit as a right privilege, or favor)；提供，授予(to bestow formally)；*n.* 补助(something granted) 记 联想记忆：授予(grant)显赫的(grand)贵族爵位 例 The country does not *grant* patents on life-sustaining drugs. // They are not *granted* governmental subsidies to assist in underwriting the cost of economic development. // *grants* for higher education 高等教育补助
graph [græf]	*n.* 图表，坐标图(diagram) 记 本身为词根：书写，画图 例 The dots on the *graph* indicate the weights and fuel efficiency ratings for 20 cars. 派 graphic(*a.* 图表的)；graphics(*n.* 绘图，制图法) 同根词：photograph(*n.* 照片)；telegraph(*n.* 电报)
graphite [ˈgræfaɪt]	*n.* 石墨(a soft black lustrous form of carbon) 记 词根记忆：graph(写；图) + ite → 用来写字、画画的东西 → 石墨 例 Under high pressure and intense heat, *graphite* changes into diamond.
gravel [ˈgrævl]	*n.* 碎石，砂砾(a loose mixture of pebbles and rock fragments) 记 联想记忆：和 gavel(*n.* 小木槌)一起记；grav(重) + el → 重的东西 → 碎石 例 Opening with tributes to jazz-age divas like Bessie Smith and closing with Koko Taylor's electrified *gravel*-and-thunder songs, the program will trace the blues' vigorous matriarchal line over more than 50 years.

156
□ glucose   □ gorilla   □ gourmet   □ gradient   □ granite   □ grant
□ graph   □ graphite   □ gravel

gravitational [ˌɡrævɪˈteɪʃənl]	*a.* 重力的，万有引力的(of or relating to gravity) 记 来自 gravitation(*n.* 重力，万有引力) 例 The *gravitational* potential of compact stars(致密星)does not vary from star to star.
gregarious [ɡrɪˈɡeriəs]	*a.* 群居的(sociable) 记 词根记忆：greg(群体) + arious → 群体的 → 群居的 例 These *gregarious* creatures live in stable groups. 同根词：egregious(*a.* 异乎寻常的，极坏的)
grill [ɡrɪl]	*n.* 烤架(a cooking utensil of parallel bars on which food is exposed to heat) 记 联想记忆：gr + ill(生病) → 生病了就不想吃烧烤 → 烤架 例 barbecue *grills* 烤肉架
grind [ɡraɪnd]	*v.* 磨(碎)(to reduce to powder or small fragments by friction)；伴随摩擦而移动(to move with difficulty or friction) 记 联想记忆：将一块大(grand)石头磨碎(grind) 例 *grind* one's teeth 咬牙切齿 // The two *giant* rock plates generate heat through friction as they grind past each other.
groove [ɡruːv]	*n.* 凹线(a long, narrow furrow)；(刻出的)线条；习惯(habitual way) 记 注意不要和 grove(*n.* 树丛)相混 例 Clovis points are spear points of longitudinal *grooves* chipped onto their faces.
grove [ɡrouv]	*n.* 树丛，小果园(a planting of fruit or nut trees) 例 The yield per tree for the 18 trees in the eastern half of the *grove* was 55 kilograms last year.
guarantee [ˌɡærənˈtiː]	*v./n.* 保证，担保(to undertake to do or secure) 记 联想记忆：guar(看作 guard 保卫) + antee → 保证 例 Brand names are taken by consumers as a *guarantee* of getting a quality product.
gut [ɡʌt]	*n.* [*pl.*]内脏(internal organs of the abdomen)；肠子(intestine) 例 The Virginia white-tailed deer was a source of meat, and its sinews and *guts* for bindings and glue.

17

Word List 18

音频

gymnast ['dʒɪmnæst]	*n.* 体操运动员(a person trained in gymnastics) 📝 词根记忆：gym(健身) + nast → 体操运动员 📖 Young female ballet dancers and *gymnasts* sometimes fail to maintain good eating habits because they desire to be as thin as possible. 同根词：gymnastic(*a.* 体操的；体育的)
gyroscope ['dʒaɪrəskoʊp]	*n.* 陀螺，回转仪 📝 词根记忆：gyro(旋转) + scope(观察，镜) → 回转仪
habitat ['hæbɪtæt]	*n.* 栖息地(the place or environment where a plant or animal naturally or normally lives and grows) 📝 词根记忆：habit(住) + at → 住的地方 → 栖息地 📖 Species of plants that thrive in a saline *habitat* require salt to flourish. 📑 habitant(*n.* 居民，居住者)；habitation(*n.* 住处；聚居地)
hail [heɪl]	*n.* 冰雹；*v.* 向…欢呼(to acclaim) 📝 联想记忆：hai(音似：嗨) + l → 招呼 → 向…欢呼 📖 Economists in the United States have *hailed* the change as a return to the free market.
halo ['heɪloʊ]	*n.* 光环(a circle of light appearing to surround the Sun or Moon)；*v.* 围以光环(to form into or surround with a halo) 📖 There is a strict *halo* of seriousness around science in Egypt.
halt [hɔːlt]	*n.* 停止，休息(stop)；*v.* 使停止(to bring to a stop) 📖 Targland plans to *halt* this population decline by blocking the current access routes into the desert and announcing new regulations to allow access only on foot.
hamper ['hæmpər]	*v.* 阻碍(to impede, to curb)；牵制(to restrain) 📖 The productivity of our factory is not *hampered* by insufficient resources.
handicap ['hændikæp]	*n.* 障碍(holdback)；残废(disability)；*v.* (使)不利(to put at a disadvantage) 📝 联想记忆：handi(手) + cap(帽子) → 手上套了一个帽子，就形成了障碍 → 障碍 📖 *handicap* of interpersonal relationships 人际关系障碍 📑 handicapped(*a.* 有生理缺陷的)

handlebar ['hændlbɑːr]	*n.* 手把 a straight or bent bar with a handle at each end) 记 分拆记忆: handle(柄，把手) + bar(条，棒) → 手把 例 New York City ordinance of 1897 regulated the use of bicycles, required cyclists to keep feet on pedals and hands on *handlebars* at all times, and granted pedestrians right-of-way.
harbor ['hɑːrbər]	*n.* 海港，避难所 a place of security and comfort)；*v.* 庇护 to give shelter or refuge to) 例 *Harbor* seals are small compared with other phocids species such as grey seals, all of which are known to fast for the entire lactation period. 派 harborage(*n.* 停泊处；避难所)
hardcover ['hɑːrdkʌvər]	*n.* 精装版本；*a.* 精装的 having rigid boards on the sides covered in cloth or paper) 记 分拆记忆: hard(硬的) + cover(包装) → 硬包装版 → 精装版本 例 *hardcover* album of paintings 精装画册
harden ['hɑːrdn]	*v.* (使)变硬，变坚固 to make hard or harder) 记 词根记忆: hard(坚硬的) + en(使) → 使变硬 例 *harden* the arteries 使动脉硬化 同根词: hardy(*a.* 坚硬的；坚强的); hardness(*n.* 硬度；坚硬)
hardy ['hɑːrdi]	*a.* (植物)抵抗力强的 able to endure cold or difficult conditions) 记 词根记忆: hard(硬，强) + y → 抵抗力强的 例 These *hardy* plants will live through winter.
harmonize ['hɑːrmənaɪz]	*v.* (with) (使)和谐，(使)协调 to bring into accord) 记 词根记忆: harmon(一致) + ize(使…) → (使)一致 → 和谐 例 The colors do not *harmonize* with each other. 派 harmony(*n.* 相符；和谐)
harness ['hɑːrnɪs]	*n.* 马具 military equipment for a horse)；*v.* 利用 to utilize) 记 联想记忆: har(看作 hard 结实的) + ness → 马具通常都很结实 → 马具 例 A group of astrophysicists has proposed a means of detecting cosmic neutrinos by *harnessing* the mass of the ocean.
harsh [hɑːrʃ]	*a.* 严酷的(difficult and unpleasant to live in)；严厉的(stern)；粗糙的(rough)；刺耳的(sharp) 记 联想记忆: har(看作 hard 坚硬的) + sh → 态度强硬的 → 严厉的 例 Winters in the prairie voles' habitat are often *harsh*, with temperatures that drop well below freezing.
hatch [hætʃ]	*v.* (out) 孵出，孵化 to brood) 例 Houseflies that *hatch* in summer live only about three weeks.
haunt [hɔːnt]	*v.* 常去，常到(某地)(to visit often)；*v.* 萦绕于(to recur constantly and spontaneously to sb.) 记 联想记忆: 姑妈(aunt)常来拜访(haunt)，使人苦恼 例 The cafe was *haunted* by students after school.
haven ['heɪvn]	*n.* 港口；安息所，避难所 shelter, refuge) 记 联想记忆: 比天堂(heaven)少一个字母(e)，是活着时的港口(haven) 例 investment *haven* 投资的安全港

18

havoc [ˈhævək]	*n.* 大破坏，浩劫（destruction, ruin） 记 联想记忆：hav(有) + oc(看作 occur 发生) → 有事发生 → 浩劫 例 wreak *havoc* 带来灾难
hazard [ˈhæzərd]	*n.* 危险，冒险（risk）；*v.* 尝试着做（或提出）（to venture） 记 发音记忆："骇人的" → 危险 例 Smoking would constitute a fire *hazard*. // Jarold Ramsey *hazards* a summary. 派 hazardous(*a.* 危险的)
hazardous [ˈhæzərdəs]	*a.* 危险的，冒险的（risky） 记 来自 hazard(*n.* 危险；冒险) 例 When the program began in 1994, the division's *hazardous* waste output was 90 pounds per production worker. 派 hazardously(*ad.* 危险地)
haze [heɪz]	*n.* 霾，薄雾（atmospheric moisture, dust, smoke, and vapor that diminishes visibility） 例 The continent was blanketed by a blue *haze* resulting from the eruption of the Laki Volcano.
headquarters [ˈhedkwɔːrtərz]	*n.* 总部，指挥部（a center of operations or administration） 例 Six corporations have located their *headquarters* here.
hedge [hedʒ]	*v.* (about with) 围困；限制（to obstruct with or as if with a barrier） 记 联想记忆：边缘(edge)被 h 围住了，围困(hedge) 例 Manumission for persons of mixed race was *hedged* about with difficulties in the 19th century.
hedgehog [ˈhedʒhɔːg]	*n.*【动】猬；<美>豪猪（any of several spiny animals, such as the porcupine, that are similar to the hedgehog） 记 分拆记忆：hedge(树篱) + hog(猪) → 豪猪
heed [hiːd]	*v.* 注意，留心（to give consideration or attention to） 记 联想记忆：需要(need)的东西格外关心、注意、留心(heed) 例 The state legislature needs to *heed* the appeals of the protesting students.
heist [haɪst]	*n.* 抢劫（armed robbery）；*v.* 抢劫，强夺（to commit armed robbery on） 记 联想记忆：电影《偷天盗影》的英文是 *Heist* 例 The time it took to produce The Big *Heist* was considerably shorter than the time it took to produce Thieves.
helicopter [ˈhelɪkɑːptər]	*n.* 直升飞机（an aircraft that derives its lift from blades that rotate about an approximately vertical central axis） 记 词根记忆：helico(螺旋) + pter → 带螺旋翼的飞机 → 直升飞机 例 A medical *helicopter* crashed last week.
helium [ˈhiːliəm]	*n.* 氦（a very light gas that does not burn, often used to fill balloons and to freeze food） 记 氦的化学符号是 He 例 The government will not incur any costs in closing its facilities for stockpiling *helium*.

□ havoc　　□ hazard　　□ hazardous　　□ haze　　□ headquarters　□ hedge
□ hedgehog　□ heed　　□ heist　　□ helicopter　　□ helium

hemoglobin [ˌhiːməˈɡloubɪn]	*n.* 【生化】血红蛋白，血色素(the red substance in blood, which combines with oxygen and carries it around the body) 派 nonhemoglobin(*n.* 非血色素)
herbicide [ˈɜːrbɪsaɪd]	*n.* 除草剂(weedkiller) 记 词根记忆：herb(草) + i + cide(杀) → 除草剂 例 The residue of the *herbicide* in the soil a year after application is not enough to control most weeds effectively.
herbivore [ˈɜːrbɪvɔːr]	*n.* 【动】食草动物(an animal that feeds chiefly on plants) 记 词根记忆：herb(草) + i + vore(吃) → 食草动物 例 The growth of coral reef communities tends to destabilize underwater *herbivore* populations. 同根词：carnivore(*n.* 食肉动物)
herd [hɜːrd]	*n.* 兽群(a number of wild animals of one species that remain together as a group)；牧群(a group of cattle or other domestic animals of a single kind kept together for a specific purpose)；*v.* 放牧(to tend sheep or cattle) 记 联想记忆：her(她的) + d → 成为她的小羊，与她一起放牧 → 放牧 例 When elephants forage for food, they typically travel in *herds*. // The dogs will require training to learn to *herd* the geese.
hereditary [həˈredɪteri]	*a.* 世袭的(having title or possession through inheritance)；遗传的(transmitted or capable of being transmitted genetically from parents to offspring) 记 词根记忆：heredit(留给后人) + ary → 世袭的 例 *hereditary* officeholding 世袭职位 // *hereditary* factors 遗传因素 派 heredity(*n.* 遗传)；heritage(*n.* 遗产)
heretical [həˈretɪkl]	*a.* 异端的，异教的(of heresy or heretics) 记 词根记忆：here(异) + tical → 异端的，异教的 例 The belief was considered as *heretical*. 同根词：heresy(*n.* 异端；异教)；heretic(*n.* 异教徒)
heritage [ˈherɪtɪdʒ]	*n.* 遗产(property that descends to an heir)；传统(tradition) 记 词根记忆：her(继承人) + it + age(物) → 继承下来的东西 → 遗产 例 Moreover, ancient artifacts are part of our global cultural *heritage*, which should be available for all to appreciate. 同根词：heritable(*a.* 可继承的)
hexagonal [heksˈæɡənl]	*a.* 六角形的(containing a hexagon or shaped like one)；六边形的(having six sides) 记 词根记忆：hexa(六) + gon(角) + al(…的) → 六角形的 例 The *hexagonal* face of the block shown in the figure above has sides of equal length and angles of equal measure. 同根词：pentagonal(*a.* 五角形的；五边形的)

18

hide [haɪd]	*v.* 隐藏(to put out of sight)；隐瞒(to keep secret)；*n.* 兽皮(the skin of an animal, especially the thick tough skin or pelt of a large animal) 例 The Virginia white-tailed deer was a source of meat and its *hide* was used for clothing. 派 cowhide(*n.* 牛皮)
hierarchical [ˌhaɪə'rɑːrkɪkl]	*a.* 分层的；等级的(of, relating to, or arranged in a hierarchy) 记 来自 hierarchy(*n.* 等级，层次) 例 *Hierarchical* management structures are the most efficient management structures possible in a modern context. 派 hierarchically(*ad.* 分等级地) 同根词：anarchy(*n.* 无政府状态)
hierarchy ['haɪərɑːrki]	*n.* 等级制度，层次(a graded or ranked series) 记 词根记忆：hier(神圣) + archy(统治) → 神圣僧侣统治 → 等级制度 例 Organizations should be structured in a clear *hierarchy*. 派 hierarchical(*a.* 分等级的)；hierarchically(*ad.* 分等级地)
hieroglyphic [ˌhaɪərə'glɪfɪk]	*n.* 象形文字 例 The figure of the jaguar is prominent among the *hieroglyphics* inscribed on a monument.
highlight ['haɪlaɪt]	*v.* (使)突出(to emphasize)；集中注意力于(to center attention on) 例 To convey a scene's rhythm effectively, a moviemaker must *highlight* many different aspects of the action taking place.
hike [haɪk]	*n.* 徒步旅行(a long walk or march) 记 联想记忆：穿着耐克(Nike)鞋徒步旅行(hike) 例 Harry started a 6-mile *hike* with a full 10-cup canteen of water. 派 hiker(*n.* 徒步旅行者)
hinder ['hɪndər]	*v.* 阻止(to be or get in the way of)；妨碍(to hamper) 记 词根记忆：hind(后面) + er → 落在后面 → 阻止 例 Personality development is *hindered* if a person is not permitted to be independent.
hint [hɪnt]	*n.* 线索(a slight indication or intimation)；[常 *pl.*]建议(suggestion) 记 联想记忆：打(hit)在门(n)上有一些细微的线索(hint) 例 Einstein's unfinished study offers tantalizing *hints* rather than an exhaustive analysis.
hinterland ['hɪntərlænd]	*n.* 内地(a region lying inland from a coast)；穷乡僻壤(a region remote from urban areas) 记 词根记忆：hinter(=hinder 后面的) + land(土地) → 内地 例 The colonies were a half-civilized *hinterland* of the European culture system.
Hispanic [hɪ'spænɪk]	*a.* 西班牙的，说西班牙语的(of or relating to Spain or Spanish-speaking Latin America) 例 *Hispanic* Americans 美籍西班牙人

historical [hɪ'stɔːrɪkl]	*a.* 历史的，史学的（of, relating to, or having the character of history）；基于历史的（based on history） 记 来自 history（*n.* 历史） 例 The lack of complete *historical* records from the mid-to-late 1800's has made it difficult to trace some inventions to their Black originators. 派 historically（*ad.* 历史地） 同根词：historian（*n.* 历史学家）
hitherto [ˌhɪðər'tuː]	*ad.* 迄今，到目前为止（till now） 记 词根记忆：hither（到…为止）+ to → 迄今，到目前为止 例 a *hitherto* unknown species of moth 至今仍不清楚种类的蛾子
hoary ['hɔːri]	*a.* 古老的（ancient） 例 *hoary* stereotypes 老套
homeostasis [ˌhoʊmiə'steɪsɪs]	*n.* 体内平衡（the ability or tendency of an organism or a cell to maintain internal equilibrium by adjusting its physiological processes） 记 词根记忆：homeo（相同）+ sta（站）+ sis → 处于相同的水平 → 体内平衡 例 *Homeostasis* has long interested biologists.
homestead ['hoʊmsted]	*n.* 宅地；家园（the home and adjoining land occupied by a family） 记 词根记忆：home（家园）+ stead（用处）→ 被用作家园的地方 → 宅地 例 He looked around, not just up the road but toward the *homestead* and edge of the woods.
homing ['hoʊmɪŋ]	*a.* （动物）有回家本能的（having the instinct or trained to fly home from a great distance） 例 *homing* pigeons 信鸽
hominid ['hɑːmɪnɪd]	*n./a.* 原始人类（的）；灵长目动物（的）（a primate of the family Hominidae, of which Homo sapiens is the only extant species） 记 词根记忆：homi（人）+ nid → 像人的动物 → 灵长目动物 例 There is evidence that early *hominids* used fire as many as 500 thousand years ago.
homogeneity [ˌhɑːmədʒə'niːəti]	*n.* 同种，同质（same kind or nature） 记 词根记忆：homo（同类）+ gene（基因）+ ity（表性质）→ 具有同种基因 → 同种，同质 例 The rise of multinational corporations is leading to global *homogeneity*. 同根词：homogeneous（*a.* 同类的；同质的）；homogeneously（*ad.* 同种类地；均匀地）
hone [hoʊn]	*v.* 用磨刀石磨（to sharpen on a fine-grained whetstone）；磨练（to make more acute, intense, or effective） 记 注意：horn（*n.* 号角） 例 Their organizational skills were *honed* by the combat.
hoof [huːf]	*n.* 蹄（a hoofed foot especially of a horse）；*v.* 用蹄踢（to kick, to trample）；步行（to walk） 例 He was *hoofed* and injured by his horse. 派 hoofer（*n.* 踢踏舞舞蹈家；徒步旅行者）

18

hormone [ˈhɔːrmoʊn]	*n.* 荷尔蒙 (a substance, usually a peptide or steroid produced by one tissue and conveyed by the bloodstream to another to effect physiological activity, such as growth or metabolism); 激素 (any of various similar substances found in plants and insects that regulate development) 记 发音记忆 例 These *hormones* have specific effects on target organs all over the body.
horseshoe [ˈhɔːrʃʃuː]	*n.* 马蹄铁 (a usually U-shaped band of iron fitted and nailed to the rim of a horse's hoof to protect it); ∪ 形物 (sth. shaped like a horseshoe) 记 分拆记忆:horse(马) + shoe(鞋;蹄铁) → 马蹄铁 例 In order to withstand tidal currents, juvenile *horseshoe* crabs frequently burrow in the sand.
horticultural [ˌhɔːrtɪˈkʌltʃərəl]	*a.* 园艺的;园艺学的 (the science and art of growing fruits, vegetables, flowers, or ornamental plants) 记 来自 horticulture(*n.* 园艺) 例 a *horticultural* experiment 园艺试验
hospitable [hɑːˈspɪtəbl]	*a.* 热情友好的 (given to generous and cordial reception of guests); (气候,环境)宜人的 (offering a pleasant or sustaining environment) 记 词根记忆:hospit(主人和客人) + able → 主客皆相宜 → 宜人的 例 Human beings rely primarily on the first to provide a *hospitable* thermal microclimate for themselves.
hostility [hɑːˈstɪləti]	*n.* 敌对,不友好 (conflict, opposition, or resistance in thought or principle); 憎恨 (enmity) 例 It was expected that workers under forty would show *hostility* to the plan. 同根词:hostile(*a.* 敌对的)
household [ˈhaʊshoʊld]	*n.* 家庭 (family); *a.* 普通的 (common, ordinary); 家庭的 (domestic) 记 分拆记忆:house(家庭) + hold(拥有) → 家庭拥有的 → 家庭的 例 Rural *households* have more purchasing power than urban households do at the same income level. // *household* electric appliances 家电 派 householder(*n.* 住户;户主)
hover [ˈhʌvər]	*v.* (鸟等)盘旋 (to hang fluttering in the air or on the wing); 徘徊 (to move to and fro near a place) 记 联想记忆:爱人(lover)在自己身边徘徊(hover) 例 The unemployment rates of the United States *hovered* around 15 percent during the period of 1870 -1920.
howl [haʊl]	*v./n.* (狼、狗等)嗥叫 (to utter or emit a long, mournful plaintive sound); (风等)呼啸 (similar noise made by a strong wind) 例 The winds that *howl* across the Great Plains blew away valuable topsoil.

hue [hjuː]	*n.* 颜色，色彩(color) 记 和 cue(*v.* 暗示，提示)一起记 例 rosy *hues* 玫瑰色
hum [hʌm]	*v.* 哼，发出嗡嗡声(to emit a continuous low droning sound like that of the speech sound when prolonged) 例 When locusts are placed with others of the species, they become excited, change color, vibrate and even *hum*.
humane [hjuːˈmeɪn]	*a.* 仁慈的(marked by sympathy or consideration for humans or animals) 记 词根记忆：human(人) + e → 讲人道的 → 仁慈的 例 In some textbooks white settlers are pictured as more *humane*, skillful, and wiser than Native Americans. 派 humanitarian(*n.* 人道主义者；*a.* 博爱的)；humanity(*n.* 人性)
humble [ˈhʌmbl]	*a.* 谦逊的(not arrogant)；地位(或身份)低下的(low in rank, quality, or station; unpretentious or lowly) 记 联想记忆：hum(地) + ble → 接近地的 → 低下的 例 the *humblest* samurai 身份卑微的武士
humid [ˈhjuːmɪd]	*a.* 潮湿的，湿润的(wet) 记 联想记忆：hum(地) + id → 接近地的 → 潮湿的，湿润的 例 Wood decays rapidly in the *humid* climate. 派 humidity(*n.* 潮湿，湿度)
humidity [hjuːˈmɪdəti]	*n.* 湿度，湿气(moistness, dampness) 记 来自 humid(*a.* 潮湿的；湿润的) 例 Museums that house Renaissance oil paintings typically store them in environments that are carefully kept within narrow margins of temperature and *humidity* to inhibit any deterioration. 同根词：humidify(*v.* 使潮湿)
hurricane [ˈhɜːrəkən]	*n.* 飓风 记 联想记忆：hurri(看作 hurry 匆忙) + cane → 来去很匆忙的风 → 飓风 例 The *hurricane* is approaching the Atlantic coast.
husk [hʌsk]	*n.* 外皮(an outer layer)；*v.* 削皮(to strip the husk from) 例 That discovery roughly coincided with the introduction of a wheat variety that was preferable to previous varieties because its edible kernel could be removed from the *husk* without first toasting the grain. 派 husky(*a.* 声音嘶哑的；有壳的)
hybrid [ˈhaɪbrɪd]	*a.* 杂交的，杂种的(cross-bred) 例 the wheat-rye *hybrid* triticale 小麦和黑麦的杂交麦，黑小麦
hydrogen [ˈhaɪdrədʒən]	*n.* 氢 记 词根记忆：hydro(水) + gen(产生) → 能合成产生水的 → 氢 注意：oxygen(*n.* 氧) 例 *hydrogen* bomb 氢弹

hydroponic

[ˌhaɪdrə'pɑːnɪk]

a. 溶液培养的，无土栽培的（the growing of plants in nutrient solutions without soil）

记 词根记忆：hydro（水）+ pon（放）+ ic → 放置在水中让其生长的 → 溶液培养的

例 a *hydroponic* spinach 无土栽培的菠菜

派 hydroponically（ad. 溶液培养地）

You never know what you can do till you try.

除非你亲自尝试一下，否则你永远不知道你能够做什么。

——英国小说家 马里亚特（Frederick Marryat, British novelist）

Word List 19

音频

hypertension [ˌhaɪpərˈtenʃn]	*n.* 高血压（abnormally high blood pressure and especially arterial blood pressure）；过度紧张（the systemic condition accompanying high blood pressure） 记 词根记忆：hyper（亢奋的）+ tension（紧张）→ 过度紧张 例 Treatment for *hypertension* forestalls certain medical expenses by preventing strokes and heart disease.
hypnotize [ˈhɪpnətaɪz]	*v.* 对…施催眠术（to put into a state of hypnosis） 记 注意：hypothesize（*v.* 假设） 例 When *hypnotized* subjects are asked whether they can hear the hypnotist, they reply, "No." 派 hypnotist（*n.* 施行催眠术的人）
hypothesis [haɪˈpɑːθəsɪs]	*n.* 假设，假说（an unproved theory） 记 联想记忆：hypo（在…下面）+ thesis（论点）→ 论点下面是空的 → 假说 例 This *hypothesis* makes intuitive sense, but certain aspects are troubling. 同根词：thesis（*n.* 论文；论点）
hypothesize [haɪˈpɑːθəsaɪz]	*v.* 假定，假设（to make a hypothesis） 例 Archaeologists（考古学家）have *hypothesized* that the destruction was due to a major earthquake. 派 hypothesis（*n.* 假设，假说） 同根词：hypothetical（*a.* 假设的）
iconography [ˌaɪkəˈnɑːgrəfi]	*n.* 肖像（portrait）；图像（pictorial illustration of a subject） 记 词根记忆：icon（肖像）+ o + graphy（画法）→ 肖像
identical [aɪˈdentɪkl]	*a.* 同一的；相同的（same） 记 词根记忆：ident（相同）+ ical → 同一的；相同的 例 Using new tissue-culture and cloning techniques, millions of *identical* copies of a plant can be produced.
identifiable [aɪˌdentɪˈfaɪəbl]	*a.* 可辨认的（acknowledgeable） 记 来自 identify（*v.* 识别；确定） 例 There are clearly *identifiable* thinking skills that students can be taught to recognize and apply appropriately. 派 identifiably（*ad.* 可辨认地）

identification [aɪˌdentɪfɪˈkeɪʃn]	*n.* 鉴定，识别（an act of identifying）；认同（psychological orientation of the self in regard to sth. with a resulting feeling of close emotional association） 🔑 来自 identify（*v.* 确定；认同） 📖 Such an *identification* depends primarily on the species' relationship to the dominant species.
identify [aɪˈdentɪfaɪ]	*v.* 识别，鉴别（to recognize） 🔑 词根记忆：ident(相同) + ify → 使对上号 → 识别 📖 Interviewers can accurately *identify* applicants whose personalities are unsuited to the requirements of the job. 📑 identifiable(*a.* 可辨认的，可识别的)；identification(*n.* 认明，鉴定)
identity [aɪˈdentəti]	*n.* 身份，特征（sameness of essential or generic character in different instances）；同一(性)(oneness) 📖 national *identity* 民族一致性 // Biometric access-control systems work by degrees of similarity, not by *identity*.
ideographic [ˌɪdɪəˈɡræfɪk]	*a.* 表意文字(符号)的（of or relating to ideogram） 🔑 词根记忆：ideo(=idea 思想，意义) + graph(写) + ic → 把意义记录下来的 → 表意文字的 📖 Chinese consists of tens of thousands of *ideographic* characters.
ideology [ˌaɪdiˈɑːlədʒi]	*n.* 思想体系，意识形态（a set of doctrines or beliefs that form the basis of a political, economic, or other system） 🔑 词根记忆：ideo(思想) + logy → 思想体系 📑 ideological(*a.* 思想体系的)
idiosyncrasy [ˌɪdɪəˈsɪŋkrəsi]	*n.* 癖好，特性（eccentricity） 🔑 词根记忆：idio(个人的，独特的) + syn(共同) + crasy(混合) → 混合了个人特性的行为 → 癖好 📖 *idiosyncrasies* of behavior 行为特性 📑 idiosyncratic(*a.* 特殊的，异质的) 同根词：idiom(*n.* 习语)；idiopathy(*n.* 特发病)
idle [ˈaɪdl]	*a.* 闲置的（not turned to normal use）；无用的（vain）；懒散的（lazy） 📖 In this country, growers of certain crops were paid to leave a portion of their land *idle*. // What you have said is an *idle* boast. 📑 idleness(*n.* 闲散，懒惰)
ignite [ɪɡˈnaɪt]	*v.* 点燃（to kindle）；着火（to catch fire） 🔑 词根记忆：ign(点燃) + ite → 点燃，着火 📖 Forest fires were *ignited* by a meteorite impact. 📑 ignition(*n.* 点火，着火)
illegal [ɪˈliːɡl]	*a.* 违法的，非法的（unlawful, illicit） 🔑 词根记忆：il(不) + legal(合法的) → 不合法的 → 违法的 📖 *illegal* drugs 违禁药物 📑 illegally(*ad.* 非法地，违法地)
illicit [ɪˈlɪsɪt]	*a.* 违法的，不正当的（unlawful） 🔑 词根记忆：il(不) + licit(合法的) → 不合法的 → 违法的 📖 *illicit* trade 非法贸易

illiterate [ɪ'lɪtərət]	*n.* 文盲 (having little or no education; ignorant) 🔢 词根记忆: il(不) + literate(识字的) → 不识字的 → 文盲 📝 People between 18 and 24 are more likely to be technologically *illiterate* than somewhat older adults. 📎 illiteracy(*n.* 文盲; 无学识)
illuminate [ɪ'lu:mɪneɪt]	*v.* 照明 (to light); 说明 (to make clear) 🔢 词根记忆: il(加强) + lumin(明亮) + ate → 照明 📝 Could you please *illuminate* your theory with a little more explanation? 同根词: luminous(*a.* 发光的; 明亮的)
illustrate ['ɪləstreɪt]	*v.* 举例说明 (to demonstrate) 🔢 词根记忆: il(加强) + lustr(清晰) + ate → 为使…更清晰 → 举例说明 📝 A specific example is presented to *illustrate* the main elements of the argument. 📎 illustration(*n.* 说明; 插图)
illustration [ˌɪlə'streɪʃn]	*n.* 说明 (the action of illustrating); 例证; 图解 (sth. that serves to illustrate) 🔢 来自 illustrate(*v.* 举例; 阐明) 📝 In her book *illustrations*, which she carefully coordinated with her narratives, Beatrix Potter capitalized on her keen observation and love of the natural world.
imbalance [ɪm'bæləns]	*n.* 不平衡 (a lack of balance or state of disequilibrium); 不安定 (a lack of stability) 🔢 词根记忆: im(不) + balance(平衡) → 不平衡 📝 It is not likely that the competitive *imbalance* that now exists between Japan and all major industrial nations will be redressed during the foreseeable future. 📎 imbalanced(*a.* 不平衡的; 比例失调的)
imitate ['ɪmɪteɪt]	*v.* 模仿 (to mimic); 仿造 (to reproduce) 🔢 词根记忆: im(使成…) + it + ate → 使成…样子 → 模仿, 仿造 📝 Anne *imitated* the famous artist's style in her own paintings. 📎 imitation(*n.* 模仿; 仿制品); imitative(*a.* 模仿的)
imitative ['ɪmɪteɪtɪv]	*a.* 模仿的 (inclined to imitate); 仿制的 (imitating sth. superior) 🔢 来自 imitate(*v.* 模仿; 仿造) 📝 He's an *imitative* artist, who does very little original stuff. 同根词: imitator(*n.* 模仿者)
immigration [ˌɪmɪ'greɪʃn]	*n.* 外来移民; 移居 (to come into a country of which one is not a native for permanent residence) 🔢 来自 immigrate(*v.* 移入, 移居) 📝 This *immigration* has continued and even increased. 同根词: emigrate(*v.* 移居国外)

19

□ illiterate □ illuminate □ illustrate □ illustration □ imbalance □ imitate
□ imitative □ immigration

immobilize [ɪ'mͻʊbəlaɪz]	*v.* 使固定，使不动（to make immobile）；使停止流通（to withhold（money or capital）from circulation） 记 词根记忆：im(不) + mobil(运动的) + ize(使…) → 使不动 例 Putting a collar on a rhinoceros involves *immobilizing* the animal by shooting it with a tranquilizer dart.
immune [ɪ'mjuːn]	*a.* 免疫的（having resistance to a disease） 例 *immune* system 免疫系统 派 immunity(*n.* 免疫力，免疫性)；immunology(*n.* 免疫学)
impact ['ɪmpækt]	*n.* 碰撞（strike）；影响（a significant or major effect） 记 词根记忆：im(加以…) + pact(压) → 加以压力 → 碰撞 例 It is believed that the extinction of the dinosaurs was caused by the asteroid *impact* on earth. // Researchers analyzed the negative economic *impact* of downsizing on firms.
impartial [ɪm'pɑːrʃl]	*a.* (in, to)不偏不倚的，公正的（fair） 记 词根记忆：im(不) + partial(偏见的) → 没有偏见的 → 公正的 例 *impartial* criticism 公正的批评 派 impartially(*ad.* 公平地)
impeachment [ɪm'piːtʃmənt]	*n.* 弹劾，控告（the act or process of impeaching） 记 来自 impeach(*v.* 弹劾，控告) 例 Not until Barbara Jordan's participation in the hearings on the *impeachment* of President Richard Nixon in 1974 was she made a nationally recognized figure.
impede [ɪm'piːd]	*v.* 妨碍，阻碍（to hinder） 记 词根记忆：im(进入) + pede(脚) → 插足 → 妨碍 例 The reluctance to abandon this hypothesis *impeded* new research. 派 impediment(*n.* 防碍，阻碍物) 同根词：centipede(*n.* 蜈蚣)
imperative [ɪm'perətɪv]	*a.* 必要的（absolutely necessary）；紧急的（urgent）；命令的（mandatory） 记 词根记忆：imper(命令) + ative → 命令的；紧急的 例 Reform of the tort system is *imperative* for bringing malpractice insurance premiums under control. 派 imperatively(*ad.* 命令式地)
implausible [ɪm'plͻːzəbl]	*a.* 难以置信的（unbelievable） 记 词根记忆：im(不) + plausible(可信的) → 不可信的 → 难以置信的 例 It is *implausible* that the butler killed the cook, because he was in London then.
implement	['ɪmplɪment] *v.* 实施，贯彻（to carry out, accomplish） ['ɪmplɪmənt] *n.* [常 *pl.*]工具（tool, appliance） 记 词根记忆：im + ple(满) + ment → (使)圆满 → 贯彻 例 Our company *implemented* "shift-work equations" to reduce sickness and fatigue among shift workers. // stone *implements* 石制工具 派 implementation(*n.* 执行)

□ immobilize　□ immune　□ impact　■ impartial　□ impeachment　□ impede
□ imperative　□ implausible　□ implement

implementation [ˌɪmplɪmenˈteɪʃn]	*n.* 实现(accomplishment); 履行(the act of implementing) 记 来自implement(*v.* 实施; 实现) 例 The procedures for congressional approval and *implementation* of federal Indian policy were made more precise. 同根词: complement(*v.* 补足; *n.* 补足物)
implication [ˌɪmplɪˈkeɪʃn]	*n.* 含义(significance); [常 *pl.*]推断, 结论(conclude, deduce) 记 来自implicate(*v.* 暗示) 例 Some analysts believe that wage-work had other *implications* for women's identities and consciousness.
implicit [ɪmˈplɪsɪt]	*a.* 含蓄的(hinted, indirect); 潜在的(potential) 记 联想记忆: im(进入) + plic(重叠) + it → (意义)叠在里面 → 含蓄的 例 *implicit* conclusions 含蓄的结论 // an *implicit* contradiction 潜在的矛盾 同根词: explicit(*a.* 直率的, 清楚)
imply [ɪmˈplaɪ]	*v.* 暗示, 暗指(to hint) 记 联想记忆: im(进入) + ply(重叠) → 重叠表达 → 暗示, 暗指 例 The look of guilt on John's face *implied* that he committed the crime.
impose [ɪmˈpəʊz]	*v.* (on/upon)征(税等)(to levy); 处以(罚款、监禁等); 强制实行; 强加于(to establish or bring about as if by force) 记 词根记忆: im(使…) + pose(放) → 强行放置 → 强加于 例 The government decided to *impose* a restaurant meal tax. // *impose* penalties 施以惩罚 // The national speed limit of 55 miles per hour was *imposed* in 1974. 派 imposing(*a.* 使人难忘的, 壮丽的); imposition(*n.* 征税; 强加) 同根词: dispose(*v.* 布置, 处理)
imposition [ˌɪmpəˈzɪʃn]	*n.* 征收(sth. imposed); 强加(the act of imposing) 记 词根记忆: im(使…) + pos(放置) + ition → 强行放置 → 强加 例 The *imposition* of quotas limiting imported steel will not help the big American steel mills. 同根词: imposture(*n.* 欺诈; 冒牌)
impoverished [ɪmˈpɑːvərɪʃt]	*a.* 穷困的(poor) 记 来自impoverish(*v.* 使贫穷) 例 Both private and public hospitals provided mainly food and shelter for the *impoverished* sick.
impulse [ˈɪmpʌls]	*n.* 冲动(a sudden spontaneous inclination); 脉冲(a surge of electrical power in one direction) 记 词根记忆: im(使…) + puls(推) + e → 推动 → 冲动 例 electrical *impulse* 电脉冲 // *impulses* to kill 杀人冲动 同根词: repulse(*v.* 打退; 厌恶)
in lieu of [ˌɪnˈluːəv]	代替(instead of) 例 They used an inked thumbprint *in lieu of* signature.

19

inability [ˌɪnə'bɪləti]	*n.* 无才能，无能力(lack of ability (especially mental ability) to do sth.) 词根记忆：in(无) + ability(能力) → 无能力 例 A major impediment to wide acceptance of electric vehicles even on the part of people who use their cars almost exclusively for commuting is the *inability* to use electric vehicles for occasional extended trips. 同根词：ability(*n.* 才能；能力)
inaccessible [ˌɪnæk'sesəbl]	*a.* 难达到的，难接近的，难见到的(not accessible) 例 The plant generally grows in largely *inaccessible* places. 派 inaccessibly(*ad.* 难接近地)
inaccurate [ɪn'ækjərət]	*a.* 错误的(wrong)；不准确的(not accurate) 词根记忆：in(非) + accurate(精确的) → 非精确的 → 错误的 例 The methods used to determine the gold content of Frobisher's samples must have been *inaccurate*. 派 inaccurately(*ad.* 不准确地；不精确地)；inaccuracy(*n.* 错误)
inadequate [ɪn'ædɪkwət]	*a.* 不充分的(insufficient) 词根记忆：in(不) + adequate(充足的) → 不充分的 例 Only states with seriously *inadequate* road systems need to spend large amounts of money on road improvements. 派 inadequately(*ad.* 不适当地；不够好地)
inalienable [ɪn'eɪliənəbl]	*a.* (指权利等)不可让与的，不可剥夺的(that cannot be transferred to another or others) 例 the *inalienable* rights of the individual 个人不可剥夺的权利 同根词：alienate(*v.* 疏远；转让)
incandescent [ˌɪnkæn'desnt]	*a.* 白炽的(strikingly bright, radiant, or clear)；遇热发光的(white, glowing, or luminous with intense heat) 词根记忆：in(使…) + cand(白；发光) + escent(开始出现…的) → 遇热发光的 例 It may be sad to think that we no longer have domestic sources of steel flatware, rebar, and *incandescent* bulbs.
incentive [ɪn'sentɪv]	*n.* 刺激(stimulant)；动机(motive) 例 The system of patent-granting was originally established as an *incentive* to the pursuit of risky new ideas.
incinerate [ɪn'sɪnəreɪt]	*v.* 焚化(to burn to ashes；cremate)；毁弃 词根记忆：in(使) + ciner(灰) + ate → 使成灰 → 焚化 例 Last year all refuse collected by Shelbyville city services was *incinerated*. 派 incineration(*n.* 焚化，烧成灰)
incineration [ɪnˌsɪnə'reɪʃn]	*n.* 焚烧(setting on fire) 来自 incinerate(*v.* 焚化，火葬) 例 *incineration* of solid wastes 焚烧固体垃圾 派 incinerator(*n.* 焚化炉)

incipient [ɪnˈsɪpiənt]	*a.* 初期的，刚出现的(beginning to exist or appear) 例 Its ability to climb trees was likely hindered by the presence of *incipient* feathers on its forelimbs. 派 incipiently(*ad.* 起初地；早期地)
incline	[ˈɪnklaɪn] *n.* 斜坡(an inclined plane) [ɪnˈklaɪn] *v.* 使倾斜(to lean, tend, or become drawn toward an opinion or course of conduct) 记 词根记忆：in + cline(倾斜) → 斜坡 例 In pursuing a moving insect, the beetles usually respond immediately to changes in the insect's direction, and pause equally frequently whether the chase is up or down an *incline*. 派 inclination(*n.* 倾向；爱好) 同根词：inclinometer(*n.* 倾角罗盘)
inclusion [ɪnˈkluːʒn]	*n.* 包含(the state of being included)；内含物(sth. that is included) 记 来自include(*v.* 包含，包括) 例 They believed that the Whigs' *inclusion* of women in party politics had led to the Whigs' success in many elections. 同根词：exclusion(*n.* 排除；排斥)
incompatible [ˌɪnkəmˈpætəbl]	*a.* 不能和谐共存的(not able to exist in harmony or agreement) 记 词根记忆：in(不) + compatible(和谐的) → 不能和谐共存的 例 The cult of female domesticity was *incompatible* with women's participation in social activism. 派 incompatibly(*ad.* 矛盾地；不相容地)
inconclusive [ˌɪnkənˈkluːsɪv]	*a.* 非决定性的，无结果的(leading to no conclusion or definite result) 记 词根记忆：in(不) + con(加强) + clus(关闭，停止) + ive(…的) → 不能强行停止的 → 非决定性的，无结果的 例 An *inconclusive* polygraph test result is sometimes unfairly held against the examinee. 派 inconclusively(*ad.* 非决定性地) 同根词：exclusive(*a.* 独有的；排外的)
inconsistent [ˌɪnkənˈsɪstənt]	*a.* 不一致的，矛盾的(not compatible) 记 词根记忆：in(不) + consistent(一致的) → 不一致的，矛盾的 例 Two hypotheses are *inconsistent* with each other. 派 inconsistency(*n.* 不一致，矛盾)
incorporate [ɪnˈkɔːrpəreɪt]	*v.* 合并，并入(to combine) 记 词根记忆：in(进入) + corpor(体) + ate → 成为一体 → 合并 例 In the 1960's the Mexican American community began to *incorporate* the customs of other ethnic groups. 派 incorporation(*n.* 合并)
increment [ˈɪŋkrəmənt]	*n.* 增量；增加(increase) 记 词根记忆：in(进入) + cre(增加) + ment → 增加 例 The athlete added weights to the barbells in five-pound *increments*. 同根词：accretion(*n.* 自然增大)

19

□ incipient   □ incline   □ inclusion   □ incompatible   □ inconclusive   □ inconsistent
□ incorporate   □ increment

incubate [ˈɪŋkjubeɪt]	*v.* 孵化(to sit on (eggs) so as to hatch by the warmth of the body);酝酿 记 词根记忆:in(里面) + cub(睡) + ate → 睡在里面 → 孵化 例 In contrast to some fish, whose eggs require months to *incubate*, the Rio Grande silvery minnow produces eggs that hatch in about 24 hours, yielding larvae that can swim in just three to four days. 派 incubation(*n.* 孵化;潜伏期) 同根词:cubicle(*n.* 小卧室)
incur [ɪnˈkɜːr]	*v.* 招致(to beget);遭受,遭遇(to become subject to) 记 词根记忆:in(进入) + cur(跑;发生) → 使发生 → 招致;遭受 例 Companies that seek legal protection from import competition may *incur* legal costs.
incursion [ɪnˈkɜːrʒn]	*n.* 侵犯,入侵(raid) 例 In the 1860's the Byzantine Empire began to recover from Arab *incursions*.
indenture [ɪnˈdentʃər]	*n.* 契约(a contract binding one person to work for another for a given period of time);*v.* 以契约约束(to bind by or as if by indenture) 记 词根记忆:in + dent(牙齿) + ure(状态) → 原指古代师徒间分割成锯齿状的契约 → 以契约约束 例 *indentured* servants 契约工
independence [ˌɪndɪˈpendəns]	*n.* 独立性,自立性;自主(the quality or state of being independent) 记 词根记忆:in(不) + depend(依靠) + ence → 不依靠别人 → 独立性 例 The relative *independence* of Ghanaian women prior to colonialism was unique in Africa.
independent [ˌɪndɪˈpendənt]	*a.* 独立的,单独的(not dependent);*n.* 独立自主者(one that is independent);无党派者(one that is not bound by or definitively committed to a political party) 记 词根记忆:in(不) + depend(依靠) + ent → 不依靠的 → 独立的 例 Outsourcing is the practice of obtaining from an *independent* supplier a product or service that a company has previously provided for itself. 派 independently(*ad.* 独立地;自立地) 同根词:append(*v.* 悬挂;附上)
index [ˈɪndeks]	*n.* 索引(reference);指数(a number, such as a ratio derived from a series of observations and used as an indicator) 例 price *index* 物价指数
indicate [ˈɪndɪkeɪt]	*v.* 显示,表明(to show);指出(to point) 记 词根记忆:in + dic(说) + ate(做) → 说出 → 显示,指出 例 Previous studies have *indicated* that eating chocolate increases the likelihood of getting heart disease. 派 indication(*n.* 表示;暗示);indicator(*n.* 指示器;指示装置)

indication [ˌɪndɪˈkeɪʃn]	*n.* 指示；迹象(sth. that serves to indicate) 记 来自 indicate(*v.* 显示，表明) 例 The presence of telomerase in bone marrow is no *indication* of bone marrow cancer. 同根词: predicate(*n.* 谓语；*v.* 断言)
indicative [ɪnˈdɪkətɪv]	*a.* (of)标示的，象征的(serving to indicate) 记 词根记忆: in + dic(说) + ative → 指示性的 → 标示的 例 Blond hair is often *indicative* of European ancestry.
indicator [ˈɪndɪkeɪtər]	*n.* 暗示(one that indicates)；指示器(an instrument for automatically making a diagram that indicates the pressure in and volume of the working fluid of an engine throughout the cycle) 记 来自 indicate(*v.* 表明；显示) 例 Degrees of market turbulence are the primary *indicator* of small firms' roles.
indifference [ɪnˈdɪfrəns]	*n.* 冷漠，不关心(the state or quality of being indifferent) 例 He treated me with *indifference*.
indigenous [ɪnˈdɪdʒənəs]	*a.* 土产的，本地的(native) 记 来自 indigene(*n.* 土著) 例 *indigenous* population of America 美洲的土著居民
indigent [ˈɪndɪdʒənt]	*a.* 贫穷的(impoverished) 记 联想记忆: in(不) + dig(挖) + ent → 挖不出东西的 → 贫穷的 例 The *indigent* family lived under a bridge.
indirect [ˌɪndəˈrekt]	*a.* 间接的；迂回的(not direct) 记 词根记忆: in(不) + direct(直接的) → 不直接的 → 间接的 例 Biocontrol agents are likely to have *indirect* as well as direct adverse effects on nontarget species. 派 indirectly(*ad.* 间接地)
indiscriminate [ˌɪndɪˈskrɪmɪnət]	*a.* 不加区别的(not marked by careful distinction)；不受限制的(unrestrained) 记 词根记忆: in(不) + discriminate(区别) → 不加区别的 例 Bill is quite *indiscriminate* in his choice of clothing. 派 indiscriminately(*ad.* 不分皂白地，不加选择地)
indispensable [ˌɪndɪˈspensəbl]	*a.* 必不可少的(absolutely necessary) 记 词根记忆: in(不) + dispensable(可有可无的) → 不是可有可无的 → 必不可少的 例 Satellites are *indispensable* in the identification of weather patterns.

19

Word List 20

indistinct [ˌɪndɪˈstɪŋkt]	*a.* 模糊的，朦胧的(not distinct)；难以清楚辨认的(not clearly recognizable or understandable) 记 词根记忆：in(不) + distinct(清楚的) → 不清楚的 → 模糊的 例 Although the lines of competition are clearly defined in industries that are more established, they are blurred and *indistinct* in the Internet industry, as competing companies one day may be partners the next. 派 indistinction(*n.* 无差别；不清楚)
indistinguishable [ˌɪndɪˈstɪŋɡwɪʃəbl]	*a.* 难区分的，不能分辨的(not distinguishable) 记 词根记忆：in(不) + distinguish(区分) + able(能) → 不能分辨的 例 The patients who underwent coronary bypass surgery but did not benefit from it were medically *indistinguishable*. 派 indistinguishably(*ad.* 不能识别地；无差别地) 同根词：distinguished(*a.* 著名的；高贵的)
individual [ˌɪndɪˈvɪdʒuəl]	*a.* 单独的，个人的(single; separate)；*n.* 个人，个体(single human being) 记 词根记忆：in + divid(分割) + ual → 分割开的 → 单独的 例 Some *individual* firms in developing countries have raised their productivity but kept their wages low. 派 individually(*ad.* 个别地，单独地)；individualist(*n.* 利己主义者；个人主义者) 同根词：division(*n.* 分割；部门)
individualism [ˌɪndɪˈvɪdʒuəlɪzəm]	*n.* 利己主义，个人主义(a doctrine that the interests of the individual are or ought to be ethically paramount) 例 Influenced by Western *individualism*, these historians define a peculiar form of personhood: an innately bounded unit, autonomous and standing apart from both nature and society.
induce [ɪnˈduːs]	*v.* 引诱(to allure, to tempt)；促使，引起(to cause) 记 词根记忆：in + duce(引导) → 引导 → 引诱 例 Charging households a fee for each pound of trash will *induce* residents to reduce the amount of trash they create. 派 inducement(*n.* 劝诱；动机)；inducing(*a.* 产生诱导作用的)

indulge
[ɪnˈdʌldʒ]

v. (in) 享受(to take unrestrained pleasure in); 沉湎于(to immerse); 放纵(to give free rein to)

记 发音记忆：一打就急 → 放纵

例 When the current economic boom ends, consumers will still want to *indulge* in small luxuries. // Today's low gasoline prices make consumers willing to *indulge* their preference for larger cars.

派 indulgence(*n.* 放纵，任性); indulgent(*a.* 放纵的)

---

industrialization
[ɪnˌdʌstriələˈzeɪʃn]

n. 工业化(the development of industry on an extensive scale)

记 来自 industrialize(*v.* 使工业化)

例 It is based on an underestimation of the time that married women spent on housework prior to the *industrialization* of the household.

同根词：industrious(*a.* 勤勉的)

---

industrialize
[ɪnˈdʌstriəlaɪz]

v. 工业化(to make industrial)

记 来自 industry(*n.* 产业；工业)

例 The expected rise in the price of oil could be a serious impact to *industrialized* nations and could severely diminish the possibility to have an economy free of inflation.

派 industrialization(*n.* 工业化)

同根词：industrial(*a.* 工业化的)

---

ineffective
[ˌɪnɪˈfektɪv]

a. 无效的(not producing an intended effect)

记 词根记忆：in(不) + effective(有效的) → 无效的

例 Biocontrol agents may be *ineffective* in destroying targeted species.

派 ineffectively(*ad.* 无效地)

同根词：effective(*a.* 有效的)

---

inefficient
[ˌɪnɪˈfɪʃnt]

a. 效率低的(not efficient); 无能的，不称职的(incapable, incompetent)

记 词根记忆：in(不) + efficient(有效率的；有能力的) → 效率低的

例 They are *inefficient* in their locomotion.

派 inefficiently(*ad.* 无效率地；缺乏能力地)

同根词：efficient(*a.* 有效率的)

---

inequality
[ˌɪnɪˈkwɑːləti]

n. 不平等，不平均(the quality of being unequal or uneven); 不同(the condition of being variable)

记 词根记忆：in(不) + equality(平等) → 不平等

例 A government supports research that analyzes the connection between wage *inequality* and poverty among single-parent families headed by women.

---

inertia
[ɪˈnɜːrʃə]

n. 惰性(resistance or disinclination to motion, action or change); 惯性(a property of matter by which it remains at rest or in uniform motion in the same straight line unless acted upon by some external force)

记 来自 inert(*a.* 惰性的), in(不) + ert(动) → 静止的 → 惰性的

例 This might help you overcome *inertia*.

20

inescapable [ˌɪnɪˈskeɪpəbl]	*a.* 不可避免的；逃脱不了的（incapable of being avoided, ignored, or denied） 记 词根记忆：in(不) + escap(逃避) + able(…的) → 不可避免的 例 Since there are very few signed works of hers, the conclusion seems *inescapable* that part of Rodin's enormous production of that period was conceived and executed by Claudet.
inevitable [ɪnˈevɪtəbl]	*a.* 不可避免的（incapable of being avoided） 记 词根记忆：in(不) + evitable(可以避免的) → 不可避免的 例 Death is the *inevitable* thing of life. 派 inevitably(*ad.* 不可避免地)
inextricably [ˌɪnɪkˈstrɪkəbli]	*ad.* 无法分开地（incapable of being disentangled） 记 来自 inextricable, extricable(能逃脱的), inextricable(逃脱不掉的，解不开的) + ly → 无法分开地 例 Theory is *inextricably* tied to action.
infancy [ˈɪnfənsi]	*n.* 婴儿期（early childhood）；初期（a beginning or early period of existence） 记 来自 infant(*n.* 婴儿) 例 Infection had occurred during *infancy*. // The modeling of accretion disks is still in its *infancy*.
infect [ɪnˈfekt]	*v.* 感染（to contaminate）；使恶化（to corrupt） 例 Animals *infected* with the virus take more than a year to develop symptoms. // Business relations are *infected* through and through with the disease of short-sighted motives. 派 infected(*a.* 被感染的); infection(*n.* 传染，感染); infectious(*a.* 传染的)
infectious [ɪnˈfekʃəs]	*a.* 传染性的，易传染的（capable of causing infection, communicable by infection） 记 来自 infect(*v.* 感染，传染) 例 Typhus cannot be transmitted by ingesting bread or beer contaminated with the *infectious* agents of this disease. 同根词：infective(*a.* 有传染性的)
infer [ɪnˈfɜːr]	*v.* 推论，推断（to derive as a conclusion from facts or premises） 例 Biologists can *infer* how species are related evolutionarily by comparing DNA sequences. 派 inferential(*a.* 推论性的); inference(*n.* 推论，结论)
inferior [ɪnˈfɪriər]	*a.* (to)次的，较差的（of less importance, value, or merit） 记 联想记忆：infer(推断) + ior → 推断的东西是次要的，事实才是依据 → 次的 例 My strength is *inferior* to that of a younger man.
infest [ɪnˈfest]	*v.* 大批滋生，蔓延（to spread over in a troublesome manner） 记 词根记忆：in(进入) + fest(匆忙) → (繁殖)得很快 → 大批滋生 例 The newly developed pesticide is effective against the insects that have *infested* cotton crops. 派 infestation(*n.* 群袭，横行) 同根词：festive(*a.* 欢庆的); festinate(*a.* 仓促的)

infirmary [ɪnˈfɜːrməri]	*n.* 医院，医务室（a place where the infirm or sick are lodged for care and treatment） 记 词根记忆：in(不) + firm(结实的) + ary → 柔弱的人常去的地方 → 医院
inflammation [ˌɪnfləˈmeɪʃn]	*n.* 发炎（the act of inflaming）；炎症（the state of being inflamed） 记 联想记忆：in(使…) + flam(火焰) + m + ation(名词后缀) → 发炎像火烧似的疼痛 → 发炎 例 Asthma, a bronchial condition, is a much less common ailment than hay fever, an allergic *inflammation* of the nasal passages.
inflammatory [ɪnˈflæmətɔːri]	*a.* 煽动性的（tending to excite anger or disorder）；发炎的（characterized or caused by inflammation） 记 词根记忆：in(进入) + flam(火) + matory → 起火的 → 发炎的 例 The language used in newspaper headlines is *inflammatory*. // an *inflammatory* condition of the tonsils 扁桃腺发炎
inflate [ɪnˈfleɪt]	*v.* 充气（to fill with air or gas so as to make it swell）；抬高（物价）（to increase abnormally）；（通货）膨胀 记 词根记忆：in(进入) + flate(气) → 让气进去 → 充气 例 *inflate* the tires 给轮胎充气 // *inflate* prices 抬高价格 派 inflation(*n.* 膨胀；通货膨胀) 同根词：deflate(*v.* 放气)
inflation [ɪnˈfleɪʃn]	*n.* 膨胀（an act of inflating）；通货膨胀（a continuing rise in the general price level） 记 来自 inflate(*v.* 膨胀) 例 It fits the rational expectations theory of *inflation* but not the inertia theory of *inflation*.
inflationary [ɪnˈfleɪʃəneri]	*a.* 通货膨胀的（of, characterized by, or productive of inflation） 记 来自 inflate(*v.* 膨胀) 例 Many economists predict that the next recession will be caused by Federal Reserve action taken to prevent an *inflationary* upsurge. 同根词：inflatable(*a.* 膨胀的；得意的)
inflict [ɪnˈflɪkt]	*v.* 使…遭受（to cause something unpleasant to be endured） 记 词根记忆：in(使) + flict(打击) → 打击 → 使…遭受 例 The environmental damage already *inflicted* on the North Sea is reversible. 同根词：affliction(*n.* 苦难，折磨)；conflict(*n.* 冲突)
influenza [ˌɪnfluˈenzə]	*n.* 流行性感冒（an acute highly contagious virus disease that is caused by any of three orthomyxo viruses） 记 记住它的简写形式 flu 例 Until now, only injectable vaccines against *influenza* have been available. 同根词：influence(*n.* 影响力)

20

influx [ˈɪnflʌks]	*n.* 流入，汇集（a coming in） 记 词根记忆：in（向内）+ flux（流）→ 流入 例 Since World War II there has been a tremendous *influx* of federal money into private medical schools.
infrared [ˌɪnfrəˈred]	*a.* 红外线的，红外区的（situated outside the visible spectrum at its red end used of radiation having a wavelength between about 700 nanometers and 1 millimeter） 记 词根记忆：infra（在下）+ red → 光谱上在红光下面的光线 → 红外线的 例 *infrared* photography 红外线照相 // *infrared* radiation 红外辐射
infrastructure [ˈɪnfrəstrʌktʃər]	*n.* 基础设施，公共建设（the system of public works of a country, state, or region）；下部构造（the underlying foundation or basic framework） 记 词根记忆：infra（在下）+ struct（建筑）+ ure → 建筑下面的结构 → 基础设施 例 Public products, in addition to *infrastructure*, include supply systems.
infringement [ɪnˈfrɪndʒmənt]	*n.* 侵犯（an encroachment or trespass on a right or privilege）；违反（violation） 记 来自 infringe（*v.* 侵犯，违反） 例 Firms' attempts to derive more patents from existing research and development expenditures may have contributed to a decline in *infringement* suites.
infringer [ɪnˈfrɪndʒər]	*n.* 侵犯人（one that goes against, as of rules or laws） 记 来自 infringe（*v.* 侵犯） 例 Federal prosecutors were unlikely to pursue criminal copyright *infringers*, and offenders were subject to relatively small penalties. 同根词：infringement（*n.* 侵犯；违反）
infuse [ɪnˈfjuːz]	*v.* (with) 灌输（to cause to be permeated with something） 记 词根记忆：in（进入）+ fuse（流）→ 流进去 → 灌输 例 Since most textbook writers were New Englanders, the texts were *infused* with Puritan outlooks（清教徒观点）. 派 infusion（*n.* 灌输）
ingenious [ɪnˈdʒiːniəs]	*a.* 聪明的（bright, smart）；创新的（inventive） 记 联想记忆：in（内在）+ gen（产生）+ ious → 由内产生的 → 聪明的 注意：ingenuous（*a.* 坦率的，天真的） 例 Your *ingenious* ideas have saved the company millions of dollars.
ingenuity [ˌɪndʒəˈnuːəti]	*n.* 巧思（imaginative and clever design or construction）；独创性（inventiveness） 记 联想记忆：in + gen（产生）+ uity → 能产生很多点子 → 巧思 例 They surprised us with their *ingenuity*.
ingest [ɪnˈdʒest]	*v.* 咽下，吸收（to take in） 记 词根记忆：in（进入）+ gest（运，载）→ 运入 → 吸收 例 Newborn mice do not normally *ingest* any substance other than their mother's milk. 派 ingestion（*n.* 吸收，摄取） 同根词：congestion（*n.* 拥挤）；digest（*v.* 消化）

□ influx □ infrared □ infrastructure □ infringement □ infringer □ infuse
□ ingenious □ ingenuity □ ingest

ingrained [ɪnˈɡreɪnd]	*a.* 根深蒂固的(deep-seated) 词根记忆：in(进入) + grain(木头的纹理) + ed → 进入纹理之内 → 根深蒂固的 例 a deeply *ingrained* belief 一个根深蒂固的信仰
ingredient [ɪnˈɡriːdiənt]	*n.* 成分，要素(element)；(烹调的)配料(something that enters into a compound or is a component part of any combination or mixture) 词根记忆：ingr(=integr 完整，进入) + edi(吃) + ent → 放入食物内的东西 → 配料 例 Most people agreed that the principal *ingredient* of a civic education was literacy. // A chef purposely excludes the special *ingredient* from the recipe of his delicious dessert.
inhabit [ɪnˈhæbɪt]	*v.* 居住于，栖居于(to live in, dwell) 词根记忆：in(进入) + habit(居住) → 住在里面 → 居住于 例 The waters the creatures *inhabit* contain few nutrient resources. 派 inhabitant(*n.* 居民；栖息的动物); uninhabited(*a* 无人居住的)
inhalation [ˌɪnhəˈleɪʃn]	*n.* 吸入(the act or an instance of inhaling) 来自 inhale(*v.* 吸入) 例 Smoke hoods can prevent their users from *inhalation* of toxic gases. 同根词：exhale(*v.* 呼气); halitus(*n.* 气息；蒸气)
inherent [ɪnˈherənt]	*a.* 固有的，内在的(intrinsic) 词根记忆：in(内在) + her(继承) + ent → 天生继承下来的 → 固有的 注意：coherent(*a.* 粘在一起，一致的) 例 *inherent* contradictions 内在矛盾 派 inherently(*ad.* 天性地，固有地)
inherit [ɪnˈherɪt]	*v.* 遗传(to pass down)；继承(to receive from a parent or ancestor by genetic transmission) 词根记忆：in + her(继承) + it → 继承 例 *inherited* illnesses 遗传病 派 inheritance(*n.* 遗传；遗产); inherited(*a.* 遗传的)
inhibit [ɪnˈhɪbɪt]	*v.* 阻止(to prohibit)；抑制(to restrain) 词根记忆：in(不) + hibit(拿住) → 不让拿住 → 阻止，抑制 例 Some substances in the tranquilizer(镇定剂)will *inhibit* fertility. 派 inhibitory(*a.* 抑制的); inhibitor(*n.* 抑制剂) 同根词：exhibit(*v.* 展览); prohibit(*v.* 阻止)
initial [ɪˈnɪʃl]	*a.* 最初的，初始的(first) 词根记忆：init(开始) + ial → 开始的 → 最初的，初始的 例 *Initial* increases in bird deaths had been noticed by agricultural workers. 派 initially(*ad.* 开始，最初)

20

initiate [ɪˈnɪʃieɪt]	*v.*开始，发起（to begin） 记 词根记忆：init(开始) + iate → 开始，发起 例 Lark Manufacturing Company *initiated* a voluntary program for machine operators. 派 initiation(*n.* 开始，发起); initiative(*n.* 主动的行动，倡议)
injection [ɪnˈdʒekʃn]	*n.*注射（an act or instance of injecting）；注射剂（sth. as a medication that is injected） 记 词根记忆：in(里) + ject(投掷) + ion → 向里投 → 注射 例 Parents are reluctant to subject children to the pain of *injections*. 同根词：injector(*n.* 注射器)
inland	[ˈɪnlænd] *n.*内陆（the interior part of a country）；*a.*内陆的（of or relating to the interior of a country） [ɪnˈlænd] *ad.*在内地（into or toward the interior） 记 词根记忆：in(里面) + land(陆地) → 在里面的陆地 → 内陆 例 Surveyors marched *inland* from the coast for thousands of miles. 同根词：outland(*n.* 边境地区；*a.* 外国的)
inlet [ˈɪnlet]	*n.*<口>进水（an opening for intake） 例 *inlet* pipe 进水管
inmate [ˈɪnmeɪt]	*n.*居民，同住者（any of a group occupying a single place of residence） 记 词根记忆：in(里面) + mate(结伴) → 结伴在里面住的人 → 同住者 例 Taking high school level courses in prison has less effect on an *inmate's* subsequent behavior than taking college-level courses does. 同根词：matey(*n.* 伙伴；*a.* 友好的)
innate [ɪˈneɪt]	*a.*天生的，固有的（inborn, instinctive） 记 词根记忆：in(内生) + nate(出生) → 出生时带来的 → 天生的 例 an *innate* defect 固有的缺点 派 innately(*n.* 天赋地，天生就有地) 同根词：natality(*n.* 出生率)
innovation [ˌɪnəˈveɪʃn]	*n.*创新，革新（the introduction of sth. new） 记 来自 innovate(*v.* 革新，创新) 例 They differed markedly in their approach to the business aspects of *innovation*. 派 innovational(*a.* 革新的；富有革新精神的) 同根词：innovator(*n.* 改革者；创新者)
innovative [ˈɪnəveɪtɪv]	*a.*革新的（introducing or using new ideas or techniques） 记 词根记忆：in(进入) + nov(新) + ative(与…有关的) → 进入新时代的 → 革新的 例 Many customers will abandon their loyalty to older firms as more *innovative* firms enter the market. 派 innovativeness(*n.* 创新性，创新精神) 同根词：novelty(*n.* 新奇)

inoculate [ɪˈnɑːkjuleɪt]	*v.* 接种；给…预防注射 (to introduce a serum, a vaccine, or an antigenic substance into, especially to produce or boost immunity to a specific disease) 记 词根记忆：in(不) + ocul(萌芽) + ate → 不让萌芽成长 → 给…预防注射 例 The local people have been *inoculated* against measles. 派 inoculation(*n.* 接种，接木)
inquisitive [ɪnˈkwɪzətɪv]	*a.* 好奇的 (curious) 记 词根记忆：in + quisit(询问) + ive → 不断询问的 → 好奇的 例 The tone of the passage is *inquisitive*. 同根词：prerequisite(*n.* 先决条件)；inquisition(*n.* 调查)
inscribe [ɪnˈskraɪb]	*v.* 刻 (to engrave)；【数】使(图形)内接(切) (to draw within another figure so that every vertex of the enclosed figure touches the outer figure) 记 词根记忆：in + scribe(写，刻) → 刻 例 Bill gave Susan a ring *inscribed* with the words "To my best girl". 派 inscription(*n.* 铭刻；题字)
inscription [ɪnˈskrɪpʃn]	*n.* 题词 (the dedication of a book or work of art)；铭文 (sth. that is inscribed) 记 来自 inscript(*v.* 碑铭；题字) 例 Stone *inscriptions* in a form of the Greek alphabet that was definitely used in Cyprus after A.D. 365 were found in Kourion. 同根词：description(*n.* 描绘)
insecticide [ɪnˈsektɪsaɪd]	*n.* 杀虫剂 (a chemical substance used to kill insects) 记 词根记忆：insect(昆虫) + i + cide(杀) → 杀昆虫的东西 → 杀虫剂 例 a powerful *insecticide* 一种强效杀虫剂 同根词：pesticide(*n.* 杀虫剂)
insert [ɪnˈsɜːrt]	*v.* 插入 (to put or thrust in) 记 词根记忆：in(进入) + sert(插，放) → 插进去 → 插入 例 Please *insert* your credit card into the slot. 同根词：exsert(*v.* 突出，伸出)；assert(*v.* 断言)
insight [ˈɪnsaɪt]	*n.* 洞察力，见识 (penetration, discernment) 记 联想记忆：in + sight(眼光) → 眼光深入 → 洞察力 例 Life stories provide incidental information as well as significant *insights* into a way of life.
insignificant [ˌɪnsɪɡˈnɪfɪkənt]	*a.* 无价值的，无意义的，无用的 (lacking meaning or importance, unimportant) 记 词根记忆：in(无) + signifi(意味着) + cant → 无意义的 例 The scrapping of automobiles causes *insignificant* amounts of air pollution. 派 insignificantly(*ad.* 无关紧要地) 同根词：significant(*a.* 有意义的)
insofar as [ˌɪnsəˈfɑːr əz]	到…程度；在…范围内 (to the degree or extent that) 例 This is the truth *insofar as* I know it.

20

insomnia [ɪnˈsɑːmniə]	*n.* 失眠(chronic inability to fall asleep or remain asleep for an adequate length of time) 记 词根记忆：in(不) + somn(睡眠) + ia(病) → 不能入睡的病 → 失眠 例 Any combination of overwork and stress inevitably leads to *insomnia*. 同根词：somniferous(*a.* 催眠的)；somnolent(*a.* 想睡的)
inspection [ɪnˈspekʃn]	*n.* 检查(examination)；视察 例 safety *inspections* 安全检查
inspector [ɪnˈspektər]	*n.* 检查员(a person employed to inspect sth.)；巡视员(a police officer who is in charge of usually several precincts and ranks below a superintendent or deputy superintendent) 记 来自 inspect(*v.* 检查；观察) 例 No matter how patiently they explain their reasons for confiscating certain items, customs *inspectors* are often treated by travelers as if they were wanton poachers rather than government employees. 同根词：spectator(*n.* 观众)
inspiration [ˌɪnspəˈreɪʃn]	*n.* 启示，灵感(thought or emotion inspired by sth.) 记 联想记忆：in(进入) + spir(呼吸) + ation → 吸入(灵气) → 灵感 例 a sudden *inspiration* 灵机一动 同根词：expiration(*n.* 呼气；届满)
install [ɪnˈstɔːl]	*v.* 安装，安置(to set up for use or service) 例 Some residents in the community have *installed* a solar-energy system on the roof of their houses. 派 installation(*n.* 安装，安置)；installment(*n.* 分期付款)
installation [ˌɪnstəˈleɪʃn]	*n.* 安装(the act of installing)；装置(sth. that is installed for use) 记 词根记忆：install(安装) + ation → 安装 例 Since the *installation* of the alarms, the average number of porpoises caught in the company's nets has dropped from eight to one per month. 同根词：installment(*n.* 分期付款；安装)
instantaneous [ˌɪnstənˈteɪniəs]	*a.* 即时的(immediate, at once) 记 词根记忆：instant(马上的，立即的) + aneous → 即时的 例 The explosion caused *instantaneous* destruction. 派 instantaneously(*ad.* 即时地，瞬间地)
instill [ɪnˈstɪl]	*v.* 逐渐灌输(to impart gradually, implant) 记 词根记忆：in(进入) + still(水滴) → 像水滴一样进入 → 逐渐灌输 例 Courtesy must be *instilled* in childhood.
institute [ˈɪnstɪtuːt]	*v.* 制定，创立(社团、规章)(to set up; establish)；*n.* 学院，协会(an association organized to promote art or science or education) 记 词根记忆：in + stitut(建立) + e → 创立 例 Gandania cannot afford to *institute* the proposed laws. 派 institution(*n.* 制度；建立) 同根词：constitute(*v.* 组成，构建)

institution [ˌɪnstɪ'tuːʃn]	*n.* (教育、慈善等)社会公共机构(an established organization or foundation, especially one dedicated to education, public service, or culture); 制度, 习俗(a significant practice, relationship, or organization in a society or culture) 例 The financial *institutions* owe their success to their unique formal organization. 派 institutionalize(*v.* 制度化, 习俗化)
instruct [ɪn'strʌkt]	*v.* 指示(to command); 教育, 指导(to teach, to direct) 记 词根记忆: in + struct(建造) → 指示人如何建造 → 指示 例 How many years of education were sufficient to *instruct* young citizens in civic virtue? 派 instruction(*n.* 命令; 教导)
instrument ['ɪnstrəmənt]	*n.* 仪器(device); 手段(means); 工具(tool implement) 例 optical *instrument* 光学仪器 // financial *instrument* 金融手段 派 instrumental(*a.* 起作用的)
insulate ['ɪnsəleɪt]	*v.* (from, against)使绝缘(尤指热量、电流等)(to prevent the passage of heat, electricity, or sound into or out of, especially by surrounding with a nonconducting material) 记 词根记忆: insul(岛) + ate → 成为岛一样 → 绝缘 例 How do they manage to *insulate* against loss of body heat in such a cold condition?
insulin ['ɪnsəlɪn]	*n.* 胰岛素 例 Diabetes(糖尿病)can result from an *insulin* deficiency.

20

Activity is the only road to knowledge.
行动是通往知识的唯一道路。
——英国剧作家 肖伯纳(George Bernard Shaw, British dramatist)

Word List 21

音 频

insuperable [ɪnˈsuːpərəbl]	*a.* 难以克服的（incapable of being overcome or solved） 记 词根记忆：in(不) + super(超越) + able → 不可超越的 → 难以克服的 例 *insuperable* obstacles 无法克服的障碍 同根词：supernatural(*a.* 超自然的)
intact [ɪnˈtækt]	*a.* 完整的，未动过的（not damaged, whole） 记 词根记忆：in(不) + tact(接触) → 未接触过 → 未动过的 例 Less than 50 percent of a certain tropical country's wildlands remain *intact*. 同根词：contact(*v.* 接触)；tactile(*a.* 接触的)
intake [ˈɪnteɪk]	*n.* 摄取，摄入（a taking in） 例 People are not as concerned as they were a decade ago about regulating their *intake* of red meat.
intangible [ɪnˈtændʒəbl]	*a.* 无形的，难以确定的（not capable of being identified or realized） 记 词根记忆：in(不) + tangible(可触摸的) → 不可触摸的 → 无形的 例 *intangible* and physical assets 无形资产和有形资产
integer [ˈɪntɪdʒər]	*n.* 整数（any of the natural numbers, the negatives of these numbers, or zero） 派 integral(*a.* 整体的)
integrate [ˈɪntɪɡreɪt]	*v.* 一体化，成整体（to unify） 记 词根记忆：integr(完整) + ate → 完整化 → 成整体 例 Some academicians deem that business ethics should be *integrated* into every business course. 派 integration(*n.* 结合，综合)；integrant(*a.* 不可分割的) 同根词：integrity(*n.* 完整；正直)
integrated [ˈɪntɪɡreɪtɪd]	*a.* 综合的；完整的（united） 例 *integrated* international market 综合国际市场
integration [ˌɪntɪˈɡreɪʃn]	*n.* 集成；综合（the act or process or an instance of integrating） 记 来自integrate(*v.* 使完整，使成整体) 例 School *integration* plans that involve busing between suburban and central-city areas have contributed, according to a recent study, significant increases in housing integration, which, in turn, reduces any future need for busing.

□ insuperable □ intact □ intake □ intangible □ integer □ integrate
□ integrated □ integration

intelligence [ɪnˈtelɪdʒəns]	*n.* 智力(the ability to learn, understand and think in a logical way about things); 情报(information concerning an enemy or possible enemy or an area) 记 来自 intelligent(*a.* 智能的；聪明的) 例 Women scientists are above average in terms of *intelligence* and creativity. 同根词: intellectual(*a.* 智力的；*n.* 知识分子)
intense [ɪnˈtens]	*a.* 强烈的，剧烈的(existing in an extreme degree) 记 词根记忆: in + tense(紧张) → 紧张的 → 强烈的 例 *intense* pain 剧烈的疼痛 派 intensely(*ad.* 集中地；猛烈地；热情地); intensive(*a.* 加强的；集约的); intensity(*n.* 强烈；强度)
intensify [ɪnˈtensɪfaɪ]	*v.* 加强，增强(to strengthen) 例 The lens *intensified* the sun's rays and made them hot enough to start a fire.
intensity [ɪnˈtensəti]	*n.* 强度(the magnitude of a quantity); 紧张(the quality or state of being intense) 记 来自 intense(*a.* 强烈的) 例 Wadati saw a similar pattern when he analyzed data on the *intensity* of shaking. 同根词: intensive(*a.* 加强的；集中的)
intensive [ɪnˈtensɪv]	*a.* 加强的(tending to strengthen or increase); 集中的(highly concentrated) 记 词根记忆: in(不) + tens(伸展) + ive → 不能再拉伸了的 → 集中的 例 Any decrease in the need for police patrols in the late evening would not mean that there could be more *intensive* patrolling in the afternoon. 派 intensively(*ad.* 强烈地；集中地) 同根词: extensive(*a.* 广泛的；广阔的)
intent [ɪnˈtent]	*n.* 意图，目的(purpose); *a.* (on)专心的(concentrated); 急切的(directed with eager attention) 例 She had demanded dignity and independence without any revolutionary *intent*. // Both sides are *intent* on creating difficulties for the other. 派 intention(*n.* 意图，目的); intentional(*a.* 存心的，故意的)
interact [ˌɪntərˈækt]	*v.* (with)相互作用(to act upon one another); 相互配合(to act together or cooperatively) 记 词根记忆: inter(在…之间) + act(行动) → 互动 → 相互作用 例 Those substances will *interact* with genes. // They can choose whether to play computer games alone or to *interact* with other people. 派 interaction(*n.* 相互作用，相互影响); interactive(*a.* 交互式的)

21

interaction [ˌɪntər'ækʃn]	*n.* 相互作用；互动(mutual or reciprocal action or influence) 记 词根记忆：inter(相互) + act(行动) + ion → 互动 → 相互作用 例 The propagation of rare wildflowers often depends on the plants' *interaction* with other organisms in their environment. 同根词：interactive(*a.* 相互作用的)
intercept [ˌɪntər'sept]	*v.* 拦截，截取(to stop, seize, or interrupt in progress) 记 词根记忆：inter(在…之间) + cept(拿) → 从中间拿拦截 例 I tried to hand a note to Mary, but the teacher *intercepted* it. 派 interception(*n.* 拦截，截取)
interdependence [ˌɪntərdɪ'pendəns]	*n.* 互相依赖(depending on each other) 例 Species *interdependence* in nature confers many benefits on the species involved. 派 interdependency(*n.* 相互依赖)
interest rate ['ɪntrɪst reɪt]	利率 例 Commercial institutions cannot charge unreasonably high *interest rates*.
interfere [ˌɪntər'fɪr]	*v.* 干涉，妨碍(to intervene) 记 词根记忆：inter(在…之间) + fer(带来) + e → 来到中间 → 干涉 例 The church should not *interfere* in political affairs. 派 interference(*n.* 干涉；妨碍)
interior [ɪn'tɪriər]	*n./a.* 内部(的)(inner) 记 词根记忆：inter(在…之间) + ior → 在其间 → 内部 例 *interior* angle 内角
interloper ['ɪntərloupər]	*n.* 闯入者(intruder; one who interferes) 记 来自 interlope(*v.* 闯入；干涉) 例 A watchdog group recently uncovered a trick that enables an *interloper* to rig an E-mail message so that this person will be privy to any comments.
interlude ['ɪntərluːd]	*n.* 插入的时期或事件(an interval) 例 My grandmother moved to America during the *interlude* between the two World Wars.
intermediary [ˌɪntər'miːdieri]	*n.* 中间人，媒介物(mediator) 记 词根记忆：inter(在…之间) + medi(中间) + ary → 中间人 例 market *intermediary* 市场媒介 同根词：intermediate(*a.* 中间的，中等程度的)
intermediate [ˌɪntər'miːdiət]	*a.* 中间的，居中的(lying or occurring between two extremes or in a middle position or state) 记 词根记忆：inter(在…之间) + medi(中间) + ate → 中间的 例 They form an *intermediate* social level between the individual and larger "secondary" institutions.

interpolation [ɪnˌtɜːrpə'leɪʃn]	*n.* 插入(cutting in); 【数】内推法 记 来自 interpolate(*v.* 插入，窜改), inter(在中间) + pol(=polish 修饰) + ate → 在中间修饰 → 插入 例 extrapolation and *interpolation* 外推法和内推法
interpretation [ɪnˌtɜːrprɪ'teɪʃn]	*n.* 解释，说明(the act or the result of interpreting); 翻译(a particular adaptation or version of a work, method, or style) 记 来自 interpret(*v.* 解释，说明) 例 The two points of view can be readily harmonized into a coherent *interpretation*. 同根词: misinterpret(*v.* 误解)
intersect [ˌɪntər'sekt]	*v.* 相交(to cross) 记 词根记忆: inter + sect(切，割) → 从中间切 → 相交 例 Clark Street and North Avenue *intersect* near the park. 同根词: dissect(*v.* 解剖); section(*n.* 部分)
intersection ['ɪntər'sekʃn]	*n.* 交叉点(a place or area where two or more things intersect); 【数】交集 (the set of elements common to two or more sets) 记 词根记忆: inter(在…中间) + sect(切割) + ion → 在路面中间切割 → 十字路口 → 交叉点 例 Two runners leave at the same time from the *intersection* of two country roads.
interservice [ˌɪntə'sɜːvɪs]	*a.* 【军】各军种间的(existing between or relating to two or more of the armed services) 例 Passage of the bill did not bring an end to the bitter *interservice* disputes.
intersperse [ˌɪntər'spɜːrs]	*v.* 散布(to place something at intervals in or among) 记 词根记忆: inter(在…之间) + sperse(散布) → 散布 例 The author *interspersed* useful charts throughout the book. 同根词: disperse(*v.* 驱散); asperse(*v.* 诽谤)
interstate ['ɪntərsteɪt]	*a.* 洲际的(of, connecting, or existing between two or more states); *n.* 美洲际公路(any of a system of expressways connecting most major United States cities) 记 分拆记忆: inter(在…之内) + state(洲) → 洲际的 例 Not one of the potential investors is expected to make an offer to buy First *Interstate* Bank until a merger agreement is signed.
interstellar [ˌɪntər'stelər]	*a.* 星际的(located, taking place, or traveling among the stars especially of the Milky Way galaxy) 记 词根记忆: inter(在…之间) + stell(星) + ar → 星际的 例 the *interstellar* gas 星际气体
interval ['ɪntərvl]	*n.* 间隔，间距(the amount of time between two specified instants, events, or states) 记 词根记忆: inter(在…之间) + val → 间距 例 the time *interval* 时间间隔

21

intervention [ˌɪntərˈvenʃn]	*n.* 干涉, 介入(interposition) 例 Government *intervention* cannot affect the rate of inflation to any significant degree.
intestinal [ɪnˈtestɪnl]	*a.* 肠的(of, relating to, or constituting the intestine) 记 来自 intestine(*n.* 肠) 例 *intestinal* disease 肠道疾病
intimate [ˈɪntɪmət]	[ˈɪntɪmət] *n.* 密友(confidant); *a.* 极为熟知的(very familiar) [ˈɪntɪmeɪt] *v.* 暗示(to hint) 记 词根记忆: in(不) + tim(害怕) + ate → 不害怕的 → 极为熟知的 例 The indigenous people have *intimate* knowledge of the ecology of the land where they live.
intricate [ˈɪntrɪkət]	*a.* 复杂的(complex) 记 词根记忆: in + tric(琐碎, 复杂) + ate → 复杂的 例 As corporations begin to function globally, they develop an *intricate* web of marketing relationships. 同根词: extricate(*v.* 解救)
intrigue [ɪnˈtriːg]	*n.* 阴谋(secret scheme); *v.* 引起兴趣(to arouse the interest or curiosity of) 记 词根记忆: in(使) + trigue(引出, 引发) → 引起兴趣 例 The fossil remains of the pterosaurs(翼龙) have *intrigued* paleontologists(古生物学者)for more than two centuries. 派 intriguing(*a.* 引起极大兴趣的)
intrinsic [ɪnˈtrɪnsɪk]	*a.* 固有的, 内在的(essential and inherent) 例 *intrinsic* value 内在的价值
introductory [ˌɪntrəˈdʌktəri]	*a.* 引导的(of, relating to, or being a first step that sets sth. going or in proper perspective); 介绍的(serving as an introduction or preface) 记 来自 introduce(*v.* 介绍) 例 Teachers of *introductory* courses in Asian American studies have been facing a dilemma nonexistent a few decades ago. 同根词: introduction(*n.* 介绍)
intuition [ˌɪntuˈɪʃn]	*n.* 直觉(quick and ready insight); 由直觉获知的信息 记 词根记忆: intuit(由直觉知道) + ion → 直觉 例 Some practicing managers rely heavily on *intuition*. 派 intuitive(*a.* 直觉的)
intuitive [ɪnˈtuːɪtɪv]	*a.* 直觉的(of intuition) 记 来自 intuit(*v.* 凭直觉知道) 例 Managers cannot justify their *intuitive* decisions. 派 intuitively(*ad.* 直观地; 直觉地) 同根词: intuition(*n.* 直觉)
invade [ɪnˈveɪd]	*v.* 侵略, 侵袭(to enter for conquest or plunder) 记 词根记忆: in(进入) + vad(走) + e → 未经允许走进来 → 侵略 例 The girl's organs were *invaded* by parasites. 派 invader(*n.* 侵略者, 侵入的人或物); invasion(*n.* 入侵, 侵略)

invariant [ɪnˈveriənt]	*a.* 不变的(unchanging) 例 Consumers recognize that the quality of products sold under *invariant* brand names can drift over time.
inventory [ˈɪnvəntɔːri]	*n.* 存货(stock) 例 In an effort to reduce their *inventories*, Italian vintners(葡萄酒商)have to cut prices.
invertebrate [ɪnˈvɜːrtɪbrət]	*n.* 无脊椎动物(an animal, such as an insect or a mollusk, that lacks a backbone or spinal column) 记 词根记忆: in(无) + vertebrate(脊椎的) → 无脊椎的 → 无脊椎动物 例 In cold-water habitats, certain *invertebrates* can convert starches into complex carbohydrates.
inverted [ɪnˈvɜːrtɪd]	*a.* 反向的, 倒转的(reversed) 例 When a pterosaur(翼龙)walked or remained stationary, its wing could only turn upward in an extended *inverted* V-shape. 同根词: inversely(*ad.* 相反地, 倒转地)
investigate [ɪnˈvestɪɡeɪt]	*v.* 调查(to examine in order to obtain the truth) 记 联想记忆: invest(投资) + igate → 投资前的必要步骤 → 调查 例 Such studies have neglected to *investigate* firms that attempt to serve only a narrow target market. 派 investigation(*n.* 调查, 调查研究) 同根词: investment(*n.* 投资)
invoke [ɪnˈvoʊk]	*v.* 行使(法权等), 实行(to implement) 记 词根记忆: in(进入) + voke(喊, 唤) → 唤起 → 实行 注意: revoke(*v.* 废除) 例 *invoke* the veto in the dispute 在辩论中行使否决权
involvement [ɪnˈvɑːlvmənt]	*n.* 参与(participation); 牵扯, 卷入(be involved in sth.) 记 来自involve(*v.* 卷入, 连累) 例 Greater land rights and greater *involvement* in trade made women in precolonial Ghana less dependent on men than were European women at that time.
irate [aɪˈreɪt]	*a.* 生气的, 愤怒的(very angry) 记 词根记忆: ir(生气, 发怒) + ate → 生气的, 愤怒的 例 *irate* consumers 愤怒的消费者
iridescence [ˌɪrɪˈdesns]	*n.* 彩虹色(colors of rainbow) 记 词根记忆: irid(=iris 虹光) + escence → 彩虹色 例 Scientists have recently discovered that the ultrathin, layered construction of a butterfly's wings—the same construction that makes some butterflies shimmer via the phenomenon of *iridescence*—also enables the insect to control how much heat energy is absorbed by its wings and how much is reflected away.

21

ironic [aɪˈrɑːnɪk]	*a.* 说反话的，讽刺的(sarcastic) 记 来自 irony(*n.* 反话) 例 an *ironic* smile 冷笑 派 ironically(*ad.* 说反话地，讽刺地)
irradiate [ɪˈreɪdieɪt]	*v.* 照射(to cast rays of light upon)；使明亮，生辉(to shine；to light up) 记 词根记忆：ir(使) + radiate(发热，生光) → 使发光 → 使明亮 例 However, this fact is either beside the point, since much *irradiated* food is eaten raw, or else misleading. 派 irradiation(*n.* 照射；发光) 同根词：radiation(*n.* 辐射；发光)
irradiation [ɪˌreɪdiˈeɪʃn]	*n.* 放射，照射(the act of exposing to radiation or the condition of being so exposed) 记 词根记忆：ir + radi(光线，辐射) + ation → 辐射开去 → 放射，照射 例 microwave *irradiations* 微波照射
irreconcilable [ɪˈrekənsaɪləbl]	*a.* 矛盾的，不能协调的(impossible to reconcile) 记 词根记忆：ir(不) + reconcilable(可调和的) → 不能协调的 例 The goals of the two approaches began to seem increasingly *irreconcilable*.
irregularity [ɪˌregjəˈlærəti]	*n.* 不规则；无规律；不整齐(the quality or state of being irregular) 记 词根记忆：ir(不) + regular(规则的) + ity(名词) → 不规则 例 According to one expert, the cause of genetic *irregularities* in many breeds of dog is not so much that dogs are being bred for looks or to meet other narrow criteria as that the breeds have relatively few founding members.
irreversible [ˌɪrɪˈvɜːrsəbl]	*a.* 不可改变的(impossible to reverse) 记 词根记忆：ir(不) + reversible(可改变的) → 不可改变的 例 Continued use of fossil fuels will cause an *irreversible* shift in earth's climatic pattern. 派 irreversibility(*n.* 不可改变性)；irreversibly(*ad.* 不可改变地)
irrigation [ˌɪrɪˈɡeɪʃn]	*n.* 灌溉(the watering of land by artificial means to foster plant growth) 记 来自 irrigate(*v.* 灌溉) 例 Because of new government restrictions on the use of Davison River water for *irrigation*, per acre yields for winter wheat, though not for spring wheat, would be much lower than average.
irritant [ˈɪrɪtənt]	*n.* 刺激物(stimulus) 记 词根记忆：ir + rit(刺激) + ant → 刺激物 例 chemical *irritant* 化学刺激物
irritating [ˈɪrɪteɪtɪŋ]	*a.* 刺激的(irritative)；使人愤怒的，气人的(annoying) 记 来自 irritate(*v.* 刺激，使恼怒) 例 Unlike cigarette tobacco, which yields an acid smoke, pipe tobacco, cured by age-old methods, yields an alkaline smoke too *irritating* to be drawn into the lungs. 同根词：irritative(*a.* 刺激的)

□ ironic   □ irradiate   □ irradiation   □ irreconcilable   □ irregularity   □ irreversible
□ irrigation   □ irritant   □ irritating

islet [ˈaɪlət]	*n.* 小岛（a small island） 例 Even tiny *islets* can be the basis for claims to the fisheries and oil fields of large sea areas under provisions of the new maritime code.
isolate [ˈaɪsəleɪt]	*v.* 使孤立（to set apart from others）；隔离（to segregate）；*a.* 孤立的（being alone） 记 词根记忆：i + sol(单独) + ate → 使单独 → 孤立 例 Domestic work tended to *isolate* women from one another. 派 isolated(*a.* 隔离的；孤立的)；isolation(*n.* 隔离；孤立)
isotope [ˈaɪsətoʊp]	*n.* 同位素(两个或更多具有相同原子序数却具有不同的质量数的原子中的一个)（one of two or more atoms having the same atomic number but different mass numbers） 记 词根记忆：iso(等，同) + tope → 同位素 例 heavy *isotope* 重同位素 派 isotopic(*a.* 同位素的)
jeopardize [ˈdʒepərdaɪz]	*v.* 危及，危害（to expose to danger or risk） 记 词根记忆：jeopard(危险) + ize → 使处于危险中 → 危及，危害 例 If too little attention is given to basic research today, future technological advancement will be *jeopardized*. 派 jeopardy(*n.* 危险，危害)
judicial [dʒuˈdɪʃl]	*a.* 司法的（of, relating to, or proper to courts of law or to the administration of justice）；公正的（just） 记 词根记忆：judic(评判，法律) + ial → 司法的；公正的 例 *judicial* rules 司法规定
jumbo [ˈdʒʌmboʊ]	*a.* 巨大的（unusually large） 记 联想记忆：本是一头大象的名字，代指"体大而笨拙的人"，作形容词用时意为"巨大的" 例 The development of a new *jumbo* rocket is expected to carry the U.S. into its next phase of space exploration.
jurisdiction [ˌdʒʊrɪsˈdɪkʃn]	*n.* 管辖权（authority or control）；管辖区域（the limits within which authority may be exercised） 记 词根记忆：juris(=jury 法律) + dict(命令) + ion → 按照法律享有命令权 → 管辖权 例 These islands are under U.S. *jurisdiction*. // One state adds a 7 percent sales tax to the price of most products purchased within its *jurisdiction*.
juror [ˈdʒʊrər]	*n.* 陪审团成员（a member of a jury） 记 词根记忆：jur(评判，法律) + or → 按照法律评判的人 → 陪审团成员 例 Civil trials often involve great complexities that are beyond the capacities of *jurors* to understand.

21

justify [ˈdʒʌstɪfaɪ]	*v.* 证明…正当或有理(to prove or show to be just, right, or reasonable) 记 词根记忆：just(正义) + ify(使…) → 证明…正当(或有理) 例 Companies are never *justified* in employing young children, even if the child's family would benefit from the income. 派 justification(*n.* 正当理由；辩护)；justifiably(*ad.* 有理由地)；unjustified(*a.* 未被证明正确的)
juvenile [ˈdʒuːvənl]	*a.* 青少年的(youthful) 记 词根记忆：juven(年青) + ile → 青少年的 例 *Juvenile* delinquency is a serious social problem. 同根词：rejuvenate(*v.* 返老还童)
juxtapose [ˌdʒʌkstəˈpouz]	*v.* 并放，并列(to place side by side) 记 词根记忆：juxta(接近) + pose(放) → 挨着放 → 并放，并列 例 The central idea is restated and *juxtaposed* with evidence that might appear to contradict it.
kernel [ˈkɜːrnl]	*n.* 果仁(the inner part of a nut or seed)；核心(most important part) 记 词根记忆：kern(=corn 种子) + el → 核心 例 Heating a wheat *kernel* destroys its gluten, a protein that must be present in order for yeast to leaven bread dough.
kidney [ˈkɪdni]	*n.* 肾脏 例 Desert rats' *kidneys* can excrete a urine having twice as high a salt content as sea water.
kin [kɪn]	*n.* <集合词>家属，亲戚(relatives) 例 Self-help and the help of *kin* got most workers through jobless spells. 派 kinship(*n.* 亲属关系)
kinetic [kɪˈnetɪk]	*a.* 运动的(of, relating to, or produced by motion) 记 词根记忆：kinet(动) + ic → 运动的 例 *kinetic* energy 动能 同根词：kinescope(*n.* 显像管)；kinematics(*n.* 运动学)

Word List 22

lactation [læk'teɪʃn]	*n.* 哺乳,哺乳期(the period following birth during which milk is secreted) 记 来自 lactate(*v.* 哺乳,喂奶) 例 They depleted less than a third of their stored body fat during *lactation*. 同根词: lactogenic(*a.* 催乳的)
lactic ['læktɪk]	*a.* 乳的(of or relating to milk) 记 词根记忆: lact(乳) + ic → 乳的 例 *lactic* acid 乳酸 同根词: lactate(*v.* 哺乳); lactogenic(*a.* 催乳的)
lag [læg]	*v.* 落后(to stay or fall behind) 记 联想记忆: leg(腿)中间的零件 e 换 a 了 → 腿坏了 → 落后 例 Changes in retail prices always *lag* behind changes in wholesale prices.
lame duck ['leɪm dʌk]	*n.* 任期将满而未能重新当选的官员(或议员等)(one whose position or term of office will soon end) 记 联想记忆: lame(跛足的) + duck(鸭子;人) → 残疾人 → 残废了,要离职了 → 任期将满而未能重新当选的官员 例 a *lame duck* president 即将离职的总统
lamellar [lə'melər]	*a.* 薄膜的(having the form of a thin plate);薄层状的(composed of or arranged in lamellae) 记 来自 lamella(*n.* 薄层) 例 Those who suspect they were warm-blooded point out that dinosaur bone is generally fibro-*lamellar* in nature.
landfill ['lændfɪl]	*n.* 垃圾堆(laystall);垃圾填埋法(a system of trash and garbage disposal in which the waste is buried between layers of earth to build up low-lying land) 记 联想记忆: land(地) + fill(满) → 堆得满地的地方 → 垃圾堆 例 An incinerator(焚化炉)could offer economic advantages over the typical old-fashioned type of *landfill*.
landlocked ['lændlɑːkt]	*a.* 为陆地所包围的(enclosed or nearly enclosed by land)

landownership

[ˈlændˌəʊnərʃip]

n. 土地所有权(a state or quality of landowner)

记 词根记忆：land(土地) + owner(拥有者) + ship(…的身份，性质) → 拥有土地的性质 → 土地所有权

例 Another view claims that Algonquian family hunting territories predate contact with Europeans and are forms of private *landownership* by individuals and families.

landscape

[ˈlændskeɪp]

n. (陆上)风景(scenery)

记 分拆记忆：land(陆地) + scape(景色) → (陆上)风景

例 Anne sat on a hill and gazed at the *landscape* around her.

lane

[leɪn]

n. 行车道(a strip of roadway for a single line of vehicles)

记 联想记忆：小路(lane)可作为一条行车道(line)

例 The driver changed *lanes* in order to pass a slow car.

lapse

[læps]

n. (时间的)流逝(pass)

记 词根记忆：laps(滑) + e → 滑走 → 流逝

例 time *lapse* 时滞，时延

同根词：collapse(*n./v.* 倒塌，崩溃); elapse(*v.* 时间流逝)

larva

[ˈlɑːrvə]

n. [*pl.* larvae]幼虫(the newly hatched, wingless often wormlike form of many insects before metam orphosis)

latch

[lætʃ]

n. 门锁(any of various devices in which mating mechanical parts engage to fasten but usually not to lock something)

记 和 catch(*v.* 抓)一起记

例 door *latch* 门锁

lateral

[ˈlætərəl]

a. 侧生的，侧(面)的(of or relating to the side)

记 词根记忆：later(边) + al → 侧面的，侧生的

例 Auxin(植物激素)causes the plant to form *lateral* roots.

派 bilateral(*a.* 双边的); quadrilateral(*a.* 四条边的)

latitude

[ˈlætɪtuːd]

n. 纬度(angular distance north or south from the earth's equator measured through 90 degrees); 自由(freedom of action or choice)

记 词根记忆：lati(阔) + tude → 地球的阔度 → 纬度

例 I have the *latitude* at work to set my own hours.

同根词：latifoliate(*a.* 阔叶的)

launch

[lɔːntʃ]

v. 发起(to initiate); 推出(产品)(to introduce to the market); 发射(to send off)

记 和 lunch(*n.* 中餐)一起记

例 *launch* campaign 发起运动 // *launch* new products and services 推出新产品及服务

laurel

[ˈlɔːrəl]

n. 月桂树(bay tree); 荣誉(fame, honor)

例 Victors in the ancient Greek Olympic Games received cash prizes in addition to their *laurel* wreaths(花冠).

laxity

[ˈlæksəti]

n. 疏忽，不严格(the quality or state of being lax)

记 词根记忆：lax(松) + ity → 松弛 → 不严格

例 The students took advantage of the teacher's *laxity* in grading.

leach [liːtʃ]	*v.* (into)过滤(to filtrate) 记 和 beach(*n.* 海滩)一起记 例 Workers *leached* minerals from the soil.
lease [liːs]	*n.* 租约，租期(a rental contract)；*v.* 出租，租赁(to rent) 例 the provisions of the *lease* 租借条款 // The government prefers *leasing* facilities to owning them.
leaven ['levn]	*v.* 发酵(to ferment) 记 联想记忆：leave(离开) + n → 离开旧的状态 → 发酵 例 *leavened* bread 发酵面包 派 unleavened(*a.* 未经发酵的)
leery ['lɪəri]	*a.* (of)怀疑的，不相信的(suspicious) 记 联想记忆：leer(斜眼看，睨视) + y → 斜眼看 → 怀疑的 例 Mom told me to be *leery* of strangers.
legislation [ˌledʒɪsˈleɪʃn]	*n.* 立法(the action of legislating)；法律(the enactments of a legislator or a legislative body) 记 来自 legislate(*v.* 制定法律)，leg(法律) + islate → 制定法律 例 Corporate boards themselves could act to make such *legislation* unnecessary. 同根词：legislative(*n.* 立法权；*a.* 立法的)
legislature ['ledʒɪsleɪtʃər]	*n.* 立法机关，立法团体(body of people with the power to make and change laws) 记 词根记忆：leg(法律) + is + lature → 立法机关，立法团体 例 The *legislature's* move to raise salaries has done nothing to improve the situation. 同根词：legislate(*v.* 立法)
legitimate [lɪˈdʒɪtɪmət]	*a.* 合法的(lawful)；正当的(justified) 例 *legitimate* defence 正当防卫 派 legitimize [*v.* (使)合法]；legitimacy(*n.* 合法性)
legitimation [lɪˌdʒɪtəˈmeɪʃne]	*n.* 合法化(the state of legitimating)；承认为嫡出(the state of a legitimate child before the law by legal means) 记 来自 legitimate(*v.* 使合法) 例 *Legitimation* occurs as a new type of firm moves from being viewed as unfamiliar to being viewed as a natural way to organize. 同根词：legitimately(*ad.* 合理地；正当地)
leopard ['lepərd]	*n.* 豹，美洲豹(panther) 例 There are fewer than 100 Arabian *leopards* left in the wild due to poaching and increased cultivation in their native habitats.
lessen ['lesn]	*v.* 减轻，减少(to decrease) 记 词根记忆：less(更少) + en → 使更少 → 减轻，减少 例 These programs can increase workers' productivity and *lessen* insurance costs for employees' health care.

22

□ leach □ lease □ leaven □ leery □ legislatior □ legislature
□ legitimate □ legitimation □ leopard □ lessen

197

lethal ['li:θl]	*a.* 致命的（fatal）；极其有害的（devastating） 记 词根记忆：leth（死，僵）+ al → 致死的 → 致命的 例 Carnivorous mammals can endure what would be *lethal* levels of body heat. // Milk, improperly handled, is a *lethal* carrier of bacteria. 派 lethality（*n.* 致死性） 同根词：lethargy（*n.* 昏睡）
letup ['letʌp]	*n.* 停顿（pause） 记 来自词组 let up（中止） 例 There was no *letup* in the heavy rainfall all day.
levy ['levi]	*v./n.* 征税（to tax） 记 词根记忆：lev（升起）+ y → 把税收上来 → 征税 例 A 5% tax was *levied* on all imported goods.
liable ['laɪəbl]	*a.* (to) 易于…的（prone） 例 This material is less ductile and *liable* to fracture. 派 liability（*n.* 债务；责任）
liberalize ['lɪbrəlaɪz]	*v.* 使自由化（to make liberal or more liberal）；宽大；自由化（to become liberal or more liberal） 记 词根记忆：liberal（自由的）+ ize（动词后缀，使…）→ 使自由化 例 *liberalize* world trade 世界贸易自由化 派 liberalization（*n.* 自由化）
limestone ['laɪmstoʊn]	*n.* 石灰石（a common sedimentary rock consisting mostly of calcium carbonate, $CaCO_3$, used as a building stone and in the manufacture of lime, carbon dioxide, and cement） 记 分拆记忆：lime（石灰）+ stone（石头）→ 石灰石
linear ['lɪniər]	*a.* 线的，直线的（of, relating to, or resembling a line; straight） 记 来自 line（*n.* 直线） 例 *linear* system 线性系统
linkage ['lɪŋkɪdʒ]	*n.* 连接；结合（the manner or style of being united） 记 来自 link（*n.* 环节；联合） 例 Furthermore, empirical evidence demonstrates clear *linkages* between human resource practices based in the behavioral sciences and various aspects of a firm's financial success. 同根词：linker（*n.* 链接器）
lipoprotein ['lɪpəproʊtiːn]	*n.* 脂蛋白（一种复合蛋白质，至少一种成分为油脂） 记 词根记忆：lipo（脂）+ protein（蛋白质）→ 脂蛋白
liquidation [ˌlɪkwɪ'deɪʃn]	*n.* (企业的)清算（closing down a business and dividing up the proceeds to pay its debts） 记 来自 liquidate（*v.* 清算），liquid（清澈的）+ ate → 弄清澈 → 清算 例 *liquidation* sale 清仓廉价销售 同根词：liquidator（*n.* 清算人）

listlessness [ˈlɪstləsnəs]	*n.* 倦怠，无精打采(characterized by lack of interest, energy, or spirit) 记 联想记忆：list(名单) + less(无) + ness → 榜上无名 → 无精打采 例 Most victims of infectious mononucleosis can recover after a few weeks of *listlessness*.
literacy [ˈlɪtərəsi]	*n.* 识字(the ability to read and write)；有文化(having knowledge and competency) 记 词根记忆：liter(文字) + acy → 识字，有文化 例 The level of *literacy* in New England communities was very high. 同根词：literate(*a.* 有文化的)；literary(*a.* 文学的，文人的)
literally [ˈlɪtərəli]	*ad.* 照字面意思地(in a literal sense or manner) 记 来自literal(*a.* 文字的) 例 Some researchers claim that by the time students are in high school, they know they cannot take textbooks *literally*.
litigant [ˈlɪtɪɡənt]	*n.* 诉讼人(one engaged in a lawsuit) 记 词根记忆：litig(打官司) + ant → 打官司的人 → 诉讼人 同根词：litigation(*n.* 诉讼，起诉)
litter [ˈlɪtər]	*n.* 垃圾(trash, wastepaper, or garbage lying scattered about)；*v.* 乱丢(to strew litter) 记 联想记忆：把little 的"l"乱丢，错放成"r" → 乱丢 例 These problems, coupled with the increase in trash and *litter* in nearby Oak City park, demonstrate that Oak City did not use good judgment in allowing the construction of the mall in the first place.
liver [ˈlɪvər]	*n.* 肝脏(an organ in invertebrates that is similar to the vertebrate liver) 记 联想记忆：没有肝(liver)，人便无法生存(live)
lizard [ˈlɪzərd]	*n.* 蜥蜴(any of numerous reptiles of the suborder Sauria or Lacertilia, characteristically having a scaly elongated body, movable eyelids, four legs, and a tapering tail) 记 联想记忆：巫师(wizard)像蜥蜴(lizard)一样恶毒
loaf [loʊf]	*n.* [*pl.* loaves]块(a shaped mass of bread) 例 The bakery sells rye bread in 16-ounce *loaves* and 24-ounce *loaves*.
lobby [ˈlɑːbi]	*n.* 大厅，休息室(hall)；*v.* 向(议员等)进行游说(to try to influence the thinking of legislators or other public officials for or against a specific cause) 例 The parents *lobbied* the city council members for school reform. 派 lobbyist(*n.* 游说立法者的人，说客)
lobe [loʊb]	*n.* (脑，肺，肝等的)叶(a subdivision of a bodily organ or part bounded by fissures, connective tissue, or other structural boundaries)
lobster [ˈlɑːbstər]	*n.* 龙虾(any of several crustaceans, such as the spiny lobster, that are related to the lobsters) 记 发音记忆："老不死的" → 老不死的龙虾

22

localize [ˈloʊkəlaɪz]	*v.* 使地方化(to make local)；局部化(to accumulate in or be restricted to a specific or limited area) 记 来自 local(*a.* 当地的) 例 Gall's hypothesis that different mental functions are *localized* in different parts of the brain is widely accepted today. 派 localization(*n.* 局限；地方化) 同根词: localism(*n.* 地方主义)
loch [lɑːk]	*n.* 湖(lake)；狭长的海湾(a bay or arm of the sea especially when nearly landlocked) 记 和 lake(*n.* 湖)一起记 例 Inhabitants of the area around Lake Champlain claim sightings of a long and narrow "sea monster" similar to the one reputed to live in *Loch* Ness, which, like Lake Champlain, is an inland lake connected to the ocean by a river.
locomotion [ˌloʊkəˈmoʊʃn]	*n.* 运动(力)，移位(the act or power of moving from place to place) 记 词根记忆: loco(地方) + mot(移动) + ion → 从一地方移到另一地方 → 移位 例 Alcohol can impair your *locomotion*.
locomotive [ˌloʊkəˈmoʊtɪv]	*n.* 机车，火车头(a self-propelled vehicle that runs on rails and is used for moving railroad cars)；*a.* 火车头的；运动的(of or relating to travel) 记 词根记忆: loco(地方) + mot(移动) + ive(的) → 移动地方的 → 运动的 例 Unlike the steam *locomotive*, which required an hour or two of firing up before it could move under its own power, the diesel *locomotive* could summon nearly full power from a cold engine almost instantly. 同根词: motivate(*v.* 刺激；使有动机)
lodge [lɑːdʒ]	*n.* 房子，住处(inhabitancy, dwelling) 例 After a day of skiing, we returned to the *lodge* for dinner.
logotype [ˈlɔːgotaɪp]	*n.* 标志(an identifying symbol) 例 company *logotypes* 公司标志
longevity [lɔːnˈdʒevəti]	*n.* 长寿(a long life) 记 词根记忆: long(长) + ev(时间) + ity → 活得时间长 → 长寿 例 Good environmental factors tend to favor *longevity*.
longitudinal [ˌlɑːndʒəˈtuːdnl]	*a.* 长度的；纵向的(placed or running lengthwise)；经线的(of or relating to length or longitude) 记 来自 longitude(*n.* 经线) 例 Even though Clovis points, spear points with *longitudinal* grooves chipped onto their faces, have been found all over North America, they are named for the New Mexico site where they were first discovered in 1932. 派 longitudinally(*ad.* 长度上；经向) 同根词: longitude(*n.* 经线)

□ localize   □ loch   □ locomotion   □ locomotive   □ lodge   □ logotype
□ longevity   □ longitudinal

loom [lu:m]	v. 隐现 (to come into sight in enlarged or distorted and indistinct form); n. 织布机 (a frame or machine for interlacing at right angles two or more sets of threads or yarns to form a cloth) 例 Dark clouds *loomed* on the horizon.
loosen ['lu:sn]	v. 变松，松开 (to become less firmed or fixed) 记 来自 loose (*a.* 松的) 例 *loosen* up 放松肌肉；松弛
lore [lɔ:r]	n. 知识 (knowledge); 学问 (something that is learned) 记 和 lure (*v.* 诱惑) 一起记 例 The ample evidence is derived from the *lore* of traditional folk medicine.
lounge [laʊndʒ]	n. 长沙发 (a long couch) 例 a chaise *lounge* 躺椅
lucrative ['lu:krətɪv]	*a.* 赚钱的 (profitable); 有利可图的 (profitable) 记 词根记忆: lucr (=lucre 钱财) + ative → 赚钱的 例 The small business is able to pay off its debt when it is awarded a *lucrative* government contract.
lumber ['lʌmbər]	n. 木材 (wood, timber) 记 和 number (*n.* 数字) 一起记 例 *lumber* manufacture 木材加工
luminosity [ˌlu:mɪ'nɑ:səti]	n. 光度，发光度 (the quality or state of being luminous) 记 词根记忆: lumin (光) + osity → 发光度 例 Why can astronomers use galactic *luminosity* to estimate baryonic mass? 同根词: illuminate (*v.* 照亮; 使明白)
luminous ['lu:mɪnəs]	*a.* 发光的，明亮的 (of or relating to light or to luminous flux); 清楚的 (clear) 记 词根记忆: lumin (光) + ous → 发光的 例 Baryons—subatomic particles that are generally protons or neutrons—are the source of stellar, and therefore galactic, luminosity, and so their numbers can be estimated based on how *luminous* galaxies are. 派 luminousness (*n.* 透光率) 同根词: illuminate (*v.* 照亮; 阐明)
lump [lʌmp]	n. 块，肿块 (bump); *v.* (together) 将…归并到一起 (to group indiscriminately) 例 Please don't *lump* all teenagers together. 派 lumpy (*a.* 结成块的; 矮胖而笨拙的)
lunar ['lu:nər]	*a.* 月球的，有关月球的 (of, involving, caused by, or affecting the moon) 记 词根记忆: lun (月亮) + ar → 月亮的 → 月球的 例 *lunar* geology 月球学，月质学
lure [lʊr]	v. 吸引，诱惑 (to tempt) 记 联想记忆: 纯 (pure) 属诱惑 (lure) 例 I *lured* the rabbit into the trap with a carrot.

22

lymph [lɪmf]	*n.* 淋巴(腺) 记 发音记忆："淋" → 淋巴 例 *lymph* system 淋巴系统 派 lymphocyte(*n.* 淋巴细胞)
lysis [ˈlaɪsɪs]	*n.* (细胞的)分解(a process of disintegration or dissolution, usu. of cells)
magmatic [ˈmæɡmətɪk]	*a.* 岩浆的(of or relating to magma) 记 来自 magma(*n.* 岩浆)
magnesium [mæɡˈniːziəm]	*n.* 【化】镁 记 联想记忆：magn(大) + esium → 镁光灯亮度很大 → 镁
magnet [ˈmæɡnət]	*n.* 磁铁，磁体(an object that is surrounded by a magnetic field and that has the property, either natural or induced, of attracting iron or steel) 记 联想记忆：magn(大) + et(互联网) → 互联网有很大的吸引力 → 磁铁，磁体 例 *magnet* schools 磁力学校(以办学特色吸引学生就读的学校，为学生提供其感兴趣的特殊专长学科学习的机会)
magnitude [ˈmæɡnɪtuːd]	*n.* 重要性(importance)；长度(length)；震级(the intensity of an earthquake represented by a number) 记 词根记忆：magn(大) + itude(状态) → 重大 → 重要性 例 The president deals with problems of great *magnitude*.
mainstream [ˈmeɪnstriːm]	*n.* 主流；主要倾向(a prevailing current or direction of activity or influence) 记 词根记忆：main(主要的) + stream(流) → 主流，主要倾向 例 *mainstream* political parties 主流政党
maintenance [ˈmeɪntənəns]	*n.* 维护，维修(the upkeep of property or equipment)；保持(the act of maintaining) 记 联想记忆：main(手) + ten(拿住) + ance → 用手拿住 → 维护，保养 例 The modernization had an impact that went significantly beyond *maintenance* routines.

音频

malaria [məˈleriə]	n. 疟疾 (swamp fever); 瘴气 记 词根记忆: mal(坏) + aria(空气) → 不好的空气 → 瘴气 派 malarial(a. 疟疾的, 瘴气的)
malarial [məˈleriəl]	a. 患疟疾的 (affected by malaria); 毒气的 (miasmal) 记 来自 malaria(n. 疟疾) 例 The use of mosquito nets over children's beds can significantly reduce the incidence of *malarial* infection for children in areas where malaria is common.
maldistribution [ˌmældɪstrɪˈbjuːʃən]	n. (财、物等)分配不当 (bad or faulty distribution) 例 income *maldistribution* 收入分配不公
malfunction [ˌmælˈfʌŋkʃn]	v. 失灵, 发生故障 (to function imperfectly or badly); n. 故障 记 词根记忆: mal(坏) + function(功能) → 功能不好 → 故障 例 The satellite fell from orbit because of *malfunctions*.
malice [ˈmælɪs]	n. 恶意, 怨恨 (desire to do mischief; spite) 记 词根记忆: mal(坏的) + ice(表性质) → 心眼坏 → 恶意 例 Crises in international diplomacy do not always result from *malice*; for nations, like individuals, can find themselves locked into difficult positions, unable to back down. 派 malicious(a. 恶意的; 恶毒的)
malleable [ˈmæliəbl]	a. 易改变的 (capable of being altered or controlled by outside forces); 可塑的 (having a capacity for adaptive change) 记 词根记忆: malle(=mallet 锤子) + able → 可锤打的 → 易改变的 例 Labor rates appear to be a company's most *malleable* financial variable. 同根词: malleate(v. 锻, 锤薄); mallet(n. 木锤)
malpractice [ˌmælˈpræktɪs]	n. 治疗失当 (an improper practice) 记 词根记忆: mal(坏) + practice(实行) → 实行得不好 → 治疗失当 例 A patient accusing a doctor of *malpractice* will find it difficult to prove damage.
mammalian [mæˈmeɪliən]	a. 哺乳动物的 (mamiferous) 记 词根记忆: mamma(乳房) + lian → 哺乳动物的 例 *mammalian* species 哺乳类 同根词: mammilla(n. 乳头); mammalogy(n. 哺乳动物学)

managerial
[ˌmænəˈdʒɪriəl]

a. 管理的（of management）

记 来自 manage（*v.* 管理）

例 It has deflected researchers' attention from a critical factor affecting *managerial* decision-making.

同根词：manageable（*a.* 易管理的；易办的）

mandate
[ˈmændeɪt]

n. 命令，指令（an authoritative order or command），*v.* 授权（to give sb the authority to do sth.），责令（to order sb to behave, do sth. or vote in a particular way）

记 词根记忆：mand(命令) + ate → 命令

例 Neighboring countries with laws that *mandate* the minimum wage an employer must pay an employee have higher unemployment rates than Ledland currently has.

派 mandator（*n.* 命令者，委托者）

同根词：command（*v.* 指挥；命令）

mandatory
[ˈmændətɔːri]

a. 强制的，命令的（obligatory）

记 来自 mandate（*n.* 命令，指令）

例 A reply to this letter is *mandatory*.

maneuver
[məˈnuːvə]

n./v. 操纵，管理（an action taken to gain a tactical end）

记 词根记忆：man(手) + euvre → 用手来做 → 操纵

例 The driver's skillful *maneuver* saved the passengers' lives.

manic
[ˈmænɪk]

a. 狂躁的（relating to, affected by, or resembling mania），*n.* 狂躁者

记 联想记忆：man(男人) + ic → 男人气的 → 狂躁的

例 *manic*-depressive 躁狂抑郁病的(患者)

manipulate
[məˈnɪpjuleɪt]

v. 操纵，操作（to manage or utilize skilfully）

记 词根记忆：mani(手) + pul(=pull 拉) + ate → 用手拉 → 操作

例 What techniques have industrialists used to *manipulate* a free market?

派 manipulation（*n.* 处理，操纵）

mannerism
[ˈmænərɪzəm]

n. 特殊习惯，怪癖（a distinctive behavioral trait）

记 词根记忆：manner(风格，方式) + ism(表风格、特征) → 个人独有的言行 → 怪癖

例 One of John's *mannerisms* is raising his eyebrows.

mantle
[ˈmæntl]

n. 覆盖物（cover）；地幔（位于地壳和地核之间的地层）（the layer of the earth between the crust and the core）

记 联想记忆：man(手) + tle → 一手遮天 → 覆盖物

例 *mantle* rock 风化层(地表上因未固结而松散的风化层)

manual
[ˈmænjuəl]

a. 手工的（of, relating to, or involving the hands）

记 词根记忆：manu(手) + al(…的) → 手工的

例 Arthritis limits *manual* dexterity.

manufacture
[ˌmænjuˈfæktʃər]

v. 生产（to produce）

记 词根记忆：manu(手) + facture(制作) → 用手做 → 生产

例 Companies should determine well in advance of the selling season how many units of a new product to *manufacture*.

派 manufacturer（*n.* 制造商，厂商）

manufacturing

[ˌmænjuˈfæktʃərɪŋ]

n. 制造，制造业（the act of making sth.（a product）from raw materials）

a. 制造业的（of or related to machinery）

记 来自 manufacture（v. 生产）

例 Last year a record number of new *manufacturing* jobs were created.

manumission

[ˌmænjəˈmɪʃən]

n. 解放（formal emancipation from slavery）

例 *Manumission* for persons of mixed race was easier in Brazil than in other countries.

manuscript

[ˈmænjuskrɪpt]

n. 原稿，手稿（written by hand or typed）

记 词根记忆：manu（手）+ script（写）→ 手写 → 手稿

例 Each photocopy of a *manuscript* costs 4 cents.

margin

[ˈmɑːrdʒən]

n. 差额（balance）；页边的空白（the blank space bordering the written or printed area on a page）；边缘（edge）；利润（profit）

例 by a narrow *margin* 比分相差不大 // Tom's family lived on the *margin* of subsistence. // profit *margin* 利润；利润率

派 marginal（a. 边缘的；很少的）

marital

[ˈmærɪtl]

a. 婚姻的；夫妻的（of or relating to marriage）

记 词根记忆：marit（=marriage 婚姻）+ al → 婚姻的

例 The counselor specialized in *marital* problems.

同根词：maritage（n. 嫁妆）

maritime

[ˈmærɪtaɪm]

a. 海的；海事的（of or relating to navigation or commerce on the sea）

记 词根记忆：mari（海）+ time → 海的

例 Even tiny islets can be the basis for claims to the fisheries and oil fields of large sea areas under provisions of the new *maritime* code.

同根词：marine（a. 航运的；海产的）

marketplace

[ˈmɑːrkɪtpleɪs]

n. 市场（market）；市集（an open square or place in a town where markets or public sales are held）

记 词根记忆：market（市场）+ place（地方）→ 市场存在的地方 → 市集

例 Neither a rising standard of living nor balanced trade, by itself, establishes a country's ability to compete in the international *marketplace*.

marrow

[ˈmæroʊ]

n. 骨髓，精华（the best or essential part, core）

记 和 narrow（a. 狭窄的）一起记

例 bone *marrow* 骨髓

marshy

[ˈmɑːʃɪ]

a. 沼泽的，生于沼泽的（of, resembling, or characterized by a marsh or marshes）

记 来自 marsh（n. 沼泽）

例 *marshy* vegetation 沼泽植物

martial

[ˈmɑːrʃl]

a. 军事的（military）

记 联想记忆：Martial 为罗马战神

例 *martial* exercises 军事演习

masculine

[ˈmæskjəlɪn]

a. 男性的（male）；男子气概的（manful）

记 词根记忆：mascul（男子气的）+ ine → 男子气概的

例 Do you think aggression is a *masculine* trait?

派 masculinity（n. 男性）

23

mass [mæs]	*v.* 使集合（to assemble in a mass）；*n.* 大量（a large quantity）；【物】质量（the measure of the quantity of matter that a body or an object contains. The mass of the body is not dependent on gravity and therefore is different from but proportional to its weight）；大量（a large quantity, amount, or number） 记 mass 还有"群众"之意 注意：amass（*v.* 收集） 例 *mass* transit 大量客运
mass-transit [mæs 'trænzɪt]	*n.* 公共交通（public traffic） 例 The system would require major repairs to many highways, and *mass-transit* improvements.
materialistic [məˌtɪriə'lɪstɪk]	*a.* 唯物主义的（materialism） 记 来自 material（*a.* 物质的） 例 The youth translated the individualistic and humanistic goals of democracy into egoistic and *materialistic* ones. 派 materialist（*n.* 唯物主义者）
maternal [mə'tɜːrnl]	*a.* 母亲的；母方的；母系的（relating to or characteristic of a mother or motherhood or motherly） 记 词根记忆：mater（母亲）+ nal → 母亲的；母系的 例 *maternal* behaviour 母性行为 同根词：maternity（*n.* 母性，母道）
maternity [mə'tɜːrnəti]	*n.* 母性（the quality or state of being a mother）；妇产科医院（a hospital facility designed for the care of pregnant women）；*a.* 产妇的 记 词根记忆：mater（母亲）+ nity → 母性 例 Employers did create *maternity*-leave programs in the 1970's and 1980's. 同根词：maternal（*a.* 母性的）
matriarch ['meɪtriɑːrk]	*n.* 女统治者，女负责人（a woman who rules or dominates a family, group, or state）；女家长（a mother who is head and ruler of her family and descendants） 记 联想记忆：matri（母亲）+ arch（拱形的）→ 母亲像拱形桥似的囊括全局 → 女统治者；女家长 例 In her home, Aho, a Kiowa *matriarch*, held festivals that featured the preparation of great quantities of ceremonial food, the wearing of many layers of colorful clothing adorned with silver, and the recounting of traditional tribal jokes and stories.
matrix ['meɪtrɪks]	*n.* 模型（model）；母体（a situation or surrounding substance within which something else originates, develops or is contained） 记 词根记忆：matri（母亲）+ x → 母体 例 An experiment was done in which human subjects recognize a pattern within a *matrix* of abstract designs.

maturation [ˌmætʃuˈreɪʃn]	*n.* 成熟（the process of becoming mature） 例 sexual *maturation* 性成熟
mature [məˈtʃʊr]	*v./a.* 成熟（的）（to ripen） 记 联想记忆：自然（nature）中的 n 更换成 m 就是成熟的（mature） 例 Cotton plants *mature* quickly.
maturity [məˈtʃʊrəti]	*n.* 成熟（the quality or state of being mature） 记 来自 mature（*a.* 成熟的） 例 If the group faces excessive hunting, individuals that reach reproductive *maturity* earlier will come to predominate. 同根词：maturation（*n.* 成熟；化脓）
maxim [ˈmæksɪm]	*n.* 格言（a succinct formulation of a fundamental principle, general truth, or rule of conduct） 记 联想记忆：max（伟大）+ im → 最伟大的建议 → 格言 例 "A penny saved is a penny earned" is an old *maxim*. 同根词：maximal（*a.* 最大的）；maximum（*n.* 最大量）
maximize [ˈmæksɪmaɪz]	*v.* 最大化（to increase to a maximum） 记 来自 max（*n.* 最大值） 例 Therefore, to increase repeat sales and *maximize* profits, we should discontinue the deluxe light bulb. 派 maximization（*n.* 极大化，最大化） 同根词：maximum（*n.* 最大量；*a.* 最高的）
measles [ˈmiːzlz]	*n.* （单复数同）麻疹（an acute, contagious viral disease usually occurring in childhood and characterized by eruption of red spots on the skin, fever, and catarrhal symptoms）
mechanical [məˈkænɪkl]	*a.* 机械的（of or relating to machinery or tools）；呆板的（done without thinking, like a machine） 记 来自 mechanic（*a.* 手工的） 例 Most geologists and many historians today believe that Wegener's theory was rejected because of its lack of an adequate *mechanical* basis. 派 mechanically（*ad.* 机械地；呆板地） 同根词：mechanism（*n.* 机制；技巧）
mechanism [ˈmekənɪzəm]	*n.* 机械装置（a piece of machinery）；机制（a process, technique, or system for achieving a result） 记 词根记忆：mechan（机械）+ ism → 机械装置 例 The new vaccine uses the same *mechanism* to ward off influenza as injectable vaccines do.
mechanization [ˌmekənəˈzeɪʃn]	*n.* 机械化，机动化（to make mechanical） 记 来自 mechanize（*v.* 使机械化） 例 The *mechanization* of farming in the village of Long Bow doubled the corn yield while the previous year's costs were cut in half. 同根词：mechanical（*a.* 机械的；力学的）

median [ˈmiːdiən]	*a.* 中间的 (relating to, located in, or extending toward the middle); *n.* (三角形) 中线 (a line that joins a vertex of a triangle to the midpoint of the opposite side); 中数 (把观测值按大小次序排列后，排在中间位置的数值) (the middle value in a distribution, above and below which lie an equal number of values) 记 词根记忆：medi(中间) + an → 中间的；中数
mediate [ˈmiːdieɪt]	*v.* 调解 (to reconcile differences); 作为媒介引起 (to effect by action as an intermediary); *a.* 居中的 (occupying a middle position) 记 词根记忆：medi(中间) + ate → 在中间起作用 → 作为媒介引起；调解 注意：meditate(*v.* 沉思) 例 One immunological(免疫的) reaction is *mediated* through the lymphocytes(淋巴细胞). 派 mediation(*n.* 调停); mediator(*n.* 调解人；介质)
medication [ˌmedɪˈkeɪʃn]	*n.* 药物疗法 (the act or process of treating with medicine); 药物，药剂 (medicament) 记 词根记忆：medic(医疗，治疗) + ation → 药物 例 Physicians have the final say as to whether to prescribe a *medication* for a patient.
medieval [ˌmediˈiːvl]	*a.* 中世纪的，中古的 (relating or belonging to the Middle Ages) 记 词根记忆：medi(中间) + ev(时代) + al → 中世纪的，中古的 例 In *medieval* society, breaking one's word had serious consequences.
medium [ˈmiːdiəm]	*a.* 中等的 (intermediate in quantity, quality position, size, or degree); *n.* [*pl.* media] 媒体 (an agency by which something is accomplished, conveyed, or transferred) 记 词根记忆：medi(中间) + um → 中间的 → 中等的 例 small and *medium*-sized businesses // The news *medium* focuses people's attention most strongly on local crimes.
megacity [ˈmegəsɪti]	*n.* 大城市 (metropolis) 记 词根记忆：mega(巨大的) + city(城市) → 大城市 例 The population of *Megacity*, a sprawling metropolis in Remsland, has grown at a fairly steady rate for over a century.
megalithic [ˌmegəˈlɪθɪk]	*a.* 巨石制的 (being made of megalith) 记 来自 megalith(*n.* 巨石) 例 The *megalithic* monument is nearly 2,000 years old.
melancholy [ˈmelənkɑːli]	*a.* 忧郁的 (sad, unhappy) 记 联想记忆：melan(黑色) + chol(=bile 胆汁) + y → 胆汁发黑 → 忧郁的 例 The twentieth century is regarded as an age of fretfulness and *melancholy* skepticism.
meld [meld]	*v.* (使)混合，(使)合并 (to blend, mix) 例 Often billed as "The Genius", American pianist, singer, composer, and bandleader Ray Charles is credited with the early development of soul music, a genre based on a *melding* of gospel, rhythm and blues, and jazz.

208
□ median   □ mediate   □ medication   □ medieval   □ medium   □ megacity
□ megalithic   □ melancholy   □ meld

membrane ['membreɪn]	*n.* 薄膜, 细胞膜 (cell membrane) 例 In pterosaurs(翼龙), a greatly elongated fourth finger of each forelimb supported a winglike *membrane*.
memoir ['memwɑːr]	*n.* [常 *pl.*] 回忆录 (a written remembrance) 记 词根记忆: memo(记忆) + ir → 回忆录 例 The former president wrote his *memoirs* shortly before he died.
memorandum [ˌmemə'rændəm]	*n.* 备忘录 (a written reminder); 便笺 (an informal written note of a transaction or proposed instrument) 记 来自 memo(*n.* 备忘录) 例 The following appeared as part of a company *memorandum*. 同根词: memorial(*n.* 纪念碑); commemorate(*v.* 纪念)
merchandise ['mɜːrtʃəndaɪz]	*v.* 买卖, 销售 (to sell sth. using advertising, etc.); 经商; *n.* 商品 (commodities) 记 来自 merchant(*n.* 商人) 例 Most *merchandise* orders placed in response to advertisements in Systems last year were placed by Systems subscribers over age thirty-five. 派 merchandiser(*n.* 商人) 同根词: mercantile(*n.* 商品; *a.* 商业的)
merchant ['mɜːrtʃənt]	*n.* 商人 (businessman) 记 词根记忆: merc(贸易, 商业) + h + ant → 商人 例 A *merchant* discounted the sale price of a coat and the sale price of a sweater. 同根词: merchandise(*n.* 商品, 货物)
merge [mɜːrdʒ]	*v.* 合并 (to become combined into one); 使合并 (to cause to combine, unite, or coalesce); 吞没 (to plunge or engulf in sth.) 记 词根记忆: merg(沉没) + e → 吞没 例 The two oil companies agreed to *merge* their refining and marketing operations in the Midwest and the West, forming a new company that would control nearly fifteen percent of the nation's gasoline sales. 派 mergence(*n.* 合并)
merger ['mɜːrdʒər]	*n.* (企业等的)合并 (absorption by a corporation of one or more others); 并购 (the act or process of merging) 记 来自 merge(*v.* 合并; 融合) 例 Not one of the potential investors is expected to make an offer to buy First Interstate Bank until a *merger* agreement is signed that includes a provision for penalties if the deal were not to be concluded.
metabolic [ˌmetə'bɑːlɪk]	*a.* 新陈代谢的 (of, relating to, or resulting from metabolism) 记 来自 metaboly(*n.* 新陈代谢) 例 Plants with the highest *metabolic* efficiency in a given habitat tend to exclude other plants. 同根词: metabolism(*n.* 新陈代谢, 代谢作用); metabolize [*v.* (使)产生代谢变化]

23

metabolism [mə'tæbəlɪzəm]	*n.*新陈代谢 记 来自 metabolize(*v.* 使新陈代谢) 例 Some scientists contend that many species of dinosaur had a *metabolism* more like a warm-blooded mammal's than a cold-blooded reptile's.
metabolize [mə'tæbəlaɪz]	*v.*使新陈代谢(to subject to metabolism) 例 In virtually all types of tissue in every animal species, dioxin induces the production of enzymes that are the organism's attempt to *metabolize*, or render harmless, chemical irritants. 同根词: metabolism(*n.* 新陈代谢)
metallic [mə'tælɪk]	*a.*金属的(of, relating to, or being a metal) 记 来自 metal(*n.* 金属) 例 Plate movements are the surface expressions of motions in the mantle—the thick shell of rock that lies between Earth's crust and its *metallic* core. 同根词: metalize(*v.* 使金属化)
metamorphic [ˌmetə'mɔːrfɪk]	*a.*变质的; 变性的(of or relating to metamorphosis) 例 According to the passage, the widely held view of Archean-age gold-quartz vein systems is that such systems were formed from *metamorphic* fluids. 同根词: metamorphosis(*n.* 变形; 变质)
metaphor ['metəfər]	*n.*隐喻, 暗喻(a figure of speech in which a word or phrase that ordinarily designates one thing is used to designate another, thus making an implicit comparison) 记 词根记忆: meta(变化) + phor(带有) → 以变化的方式表达 → 隐喻 例 The candidate's speech contained many *metaphors* and little substance.
meteor ['miːtiər]	*n.*【天】流星(a bright trail or streak that appears in the sky when a meteoroid is heated to incandescence by friction with the earth's atmosphere) 例 the *meteor* shower 流星雨 派 meteorite(*n.* 陨星)
meteorite ['miːtiəraɪt]	*n.*陨星, 流星(a meteor that reaches the surface of the earth without being completely vaporized) 记 来自 meteor(*n.* 流星) 例 Some fullerenes have been found on the remains of a small *meteorite* that collided with a spacecraft. 同根词: meteoric(*a.* 大气的; 流星的)
meteorological [ˌmiːtiərə'lɑːdʒɪkl]	*a.*气象学的; 气象的(aerography) 记 来自 meteorology(*n.* 气象学; 气象状态) 例 Mathematical models of the *meteorological* aftermath of such catastrophic events are beginning to be constructed. 同根词: meteorologist(*n.* 气象学家)

methane [ˈmeθeɪn]	*n.* 甲烷，沼气(firedamp) 例 Natural gas is composed mostly of *methane*.
metric [ˈmetrɪk]	*a.* 公制的(made, measured, etc. according to the metric system) 记 词根记忆：metr(计量，测量) + ic(…的) → 公制的 例 Trucking transportation rates are 30 dollars per *metric* ton per kilometer.
microbe [ˈmaɪkroʊb]	*n.* 微生物(animalcule)；病菌(germ) 记 词根记忆：micro(小) + be(=bio 生命) → 小的生命 → 微生物
microcomputer [ˈmaɪkroʊkəmpjuːtər]	*n.* 微型计算机(a small computer usually equipped with a microprocessor) 记 词根记忆：micro(微型的) + computer(计算机) → 微型计算机 例 It can hardly be said that it is the fault of educators who have not anticipated the impact of *microcomputer* technology.
microorganism [ˌmaɪkroʊ ˈɔrgənˌɪzəm]	*n.* 微生物(an organism of microscopic or submicroscopic size, especially a bacterium or protozoan) 记 词根记忆：micro(小) + organism(生物) → 微生物 例 pathogenic *microorganisms* 病原微生物
microscopic [ˌmaɪkrə ˈskɑːpɪk]	*a.* 极小的(very small) 记 词根记忆：micro(小) + scop(观察) + ic → 小得无法观察 → 极小的 例 My bloodstream was infected with *microscopic* bacteria.
migraine [ˈmaɪgreɪn]	*n.* 周期性偏头痛(a condition marked by recurrent severe headache often with nausea and vomiting) 记 联想记忆：migr(移动) + aine → 头部疼痛移到一侧 → 周期性偏头痛 例 *Migraine* is the most debilitating common form of headache.

23

If you shed tears when you miss the sun, you also miss the stars.
如果你因错过太阳而流泪，那么你也将错过群星。
——印度诗人 泰戈尔(Ranbindranath Tagore, Indian poet)

Word List 24

音频

migrate [ˈmaɪgreɪt]	*v.* 移居（to move from one country, place, or locality to another） 记 词根记忆：migr（移动）+ ate → 移居 例 The three species most closely related to crookbeaks do not *migrate* at all. 派 migration（*n.* 迁移） 同根词：immigrate（*v.* 移入）
mileage [ˈmaɪlɪdʒ]	*n.* 英里数；（耗油 1 加仑所行驶的）英里里程（total length, extent, or distance measured or expressed in miles） 记 来自 mile（*n.* 英里） 例 This brand of gasoline will improve your *mileage*.
milieu [miːˈljɜː]	*n.* 环境（an environment or a setting） 记 联想记忆；mi(d)（中间）+ lieu（地方）→ 在一个地方之中就是在一个环境里 → 环境 例 Reactionist writers took the view that frontier women were lonely, displaced persons in a hostile *milieu*.
militancy [ˈmɪlɪtənsi]	*n.* 战斗(性)；战斗精神（the quality or state of being militant） 记 词根记忆：milit（战斗）+ ancy（表性质）→ 战斗 例 political *militancy* 政治交战状态 同根词：militarily（*ad.* 以武力地）；militarism（*n.* 军国主义）；military（*a.* 军事的）
millennium [mɪˈleniəm]	*n.* [*pl.* millennia] 一千年（a span of one thousand years） 记 词根记忆：mill（千）+ ennium（年）→ 一千年 例 *millennium* baby 千禧婴儿 同根词：biennium（*n.* 二年期间）
millipede [ˈmɪlɪpiːd]	*n.* 千足虫（a small creature with a long thin body divided into many sections, each with two pairs of legs） 记 词根记忆：milli（千）+ ped（脚）+ e → 千足虫 例 Capuchin monkeys often rub their bodies with a certain type of *millipede*. 同根词：centipede（*n.* 蜈蚣，百足虫）

mimic [ˈmɪmɪk]	*v.* 模仿，效仿(to copy, to imitate) 例 Advertising firms will continue to use imitators to *mimic* the physical mannerisms of famous singers.
mineralize [ˈmɪnrəlaɪz]	*v.* 使矿物化(to transform (a metal) into an ore) 记 词根记忆：mine(矿) + ralize → 使矿物化 例 None of these high-technology methods are of any value if the sites to which they are applied have never *mineralized*. 派 mineralization(*n.* 矿化；矿化作用) 同根词：mineral(*a.* 矿物的； *n.* 矿物)
miniature [ˈmɪnətʃər]	*a.* 微型的，小型的(small)； *n.* 缩小的模型(a copy or model that represents or reproduces something in a greatly reduced size) 记 词根记忆：mini(小) + ature → 小型的，微型的 例 This model car is a *miniature* of a real one. 同根词：minikin(*n.* 小东西)；minimal(*a.* 最小的)
minimum [ˈmɪnɪməm]	*n.* 最小值(the least of a set of numbers)； *a.* 最低的(the lowest) 记 词根记忆：mini(小) + mum → 最小值 例 *minimum* wage 最低工资
minivan [ˈmɪnivæn]	*n.* 小型货车(a small passenger van) 记 词根记忆：mini(小) + van(厢式货车) → 小型货车 例 *Minivans* carry as many as seven passengers, allow passengers to get in and out more easily, and have a smoother ride.
minority [maɪˈnɔːrəti]	*n.* 少数民族，少数(the smaller in number of two groups constituting a whole) 记 来自 minor(*a.* 较小的) 例 *Minority* graduates are nearly four times as likely as other graduates to plan on practicing in socioeconomically deprived areas.
mint [mɪnt]	*v.* 铸造(to make out of metal) 例 The government *mints* coins from silver, nickel, copper and zinc.
minus [ˈmaɪnəs]	*prep.* 减去(reduced by)； *a.* 减的；负的(negative) 记 词根记忆：min(小) + us → 减小 → 减法 注意：plus(*v.* 加)；multiply(*v.* 乘)；divide(*v.* 除) 例 Seven *minus* four is three.
minute [maɪˈnjuːt]	*a.* 微小的，极小的(very small) 记 词根记忆：minu(小) + te → 微小的，极小的 例 Oceans' water warmed by the Sun rises high into the atmosphere and condenses in tiny droplets on *minute* particles of dust.
miraculous [mɪˈrækjələs]	*a.* 不可思议的，奇迹的(of the nature of a miracle) 记 词根记忆：mirac(奇迹) + ul + ous(…的) → 奇迹的 例 For many people, household labor remains demanding although they could afford household appliances their grandparents would find *miraculous*. 派 miraculously(*ad.* 奇迹般地)

24

miscarriage
['mɪskærɪdʒ]

n. 流产(spontaneous expulsion of a human fetus before it is viable and especially between the 12th and 28th weeks of gestation); 失败; 误送 (corrupt or incompetent management)

例 The herbicide Oryzalin was still being produced in 1979, three years after the wives of workers producing the chemical in Rensselaer, New York, were found either to have had *miscarriages* or to have borne children with heart defects; none of the pregnancies was normal.

mishap
['mɪshæp]

n. 不幸, 坏运气(bad luck, an unfortunate accident)

记 词根记忆: mis(坏) + hap(运气) → 运气不好 → 不幸, 坏运气

例 The journey went off without *mishap*.

misinterpret
[ˌmɪsɪn'tɜːrprɪt]

v. 误解(to understand wrongly)

记 词根记忆: mis(错误) + interpret(解释) → 误解

例 They have *misinterpreted* descriptions of women's involvement in party politics.

misrepresent
[ˌmɪsˌreprɪ'zent]

v. 歪曲, 不如实地叙述(或说明)(to distort)

记 词根记忆: mis(错误) + represent(表示) → 表示错误 → 歪曲

例 The constructivists gain acceptance by *misrepresenting* technological determinism.

missile
['mɪsl]

n. 导弹 (esp. an explosive weapon directed at a target by remote control or automatically)

记 词根记忆: miss(发送) + ile(物体) → 发送出去的物体 → 导弹

例 nuclear-*missile* defense system 核子导弹防御系统

同根词: dismiss(*v.* 开除, 解散); emissary(*n.* 使者, 间谍)

mitigate
['mɪtɪɡeɪt]

v. 减轻(to relieve)

记 词根记忆: miti(小, 轻) + gate(=ag 做) → 减轻

例 Improved social welfare protection has unquestionably *mitigated* the consequences of joblessness.

派 mitigation(*n.* 缓解, 减轻)

modem
['moʊdəm]

n. 调制解调器(a device that converts data from one form into another, as from one form usable in data processing to another form usable in telephonic transmission)

例 Computers are becoming faster, more powerful, and more reliable, and so are *modems*.

moderate

['mɑːdəreɪt] *v.* 减轻; 节制(to lessen the intensity or extremeness of)

['mɑːdərət] *a.* 温和的(temperate); 适度的(having average or less than average quality)

记 联想记忆: mod(方式) + erate → 有方式的, 不过分的 → 适度的

例 In Patton City, days are categorized as having heavy rainfall, *moderate* rainfall, light rainfall, or no rainfall.

派 moderately(*ad.* 适度地; 中庸地; 有节制地)

modest [ˈmɑːdɪst]	*a.* 适度的(temperate)；朴实的(earthy)；谦逊的(neither bold nor self-assertive) 记 联想记忆：mode(方式；时尚) + (e)st(表最高级) → 最时尚的也许也是最"朴实的" → 朴实的 例 The owners of the Good Earth Café, an old vegetarian restaurant, are still making a *modest* living.
modification [ˌmɑːdɪfɪˈkeɪʃn]	*n.* 修正，修改(the making of a limited change in sth.) 记 来自modify(v. 修改) 例 Many prehistoric microbes evolved without significant *modification* of their sheaths.
modify [ˈmɑːdɪfaɪ]	*v.* 修改，更改(to make minor changes in) 记 词根记忆：mod(方式) + ify → 使改变方式 → 修改 例 The government plans to *modify* the income-tax. 派 modification(n. 修改，改变) 同根词：mode(n. 方式，样式)
moisture [ˈmɔɪstʃər]	*n.* 水分，湿度(liquid diffused or condensed in relatively small quantity) 记 来自moist(n. 潮湿) 例 Corn that does not receive adequate *moisture* during its critical pollination stage will not produce a bountiful harvest. 派 moisturize(v. 增加水分；变潮湿) 同根词：moistener(n. 润湿器)
mold [mould]	*n.* 模子(a frame or model around or on which something is formed or shaped)；*v.* 塑造(to give shape to)；对…产生影响(to determine or influence) 例 The wax conforms perfectly to the *mold*. // Customized computer software can be *molded* to fit the way a company does business. // His character was *molded* by his early childhood experiences.
mole [moul]	*n.* 鼹鼠 记 联想记忆：鼹鼠(mole)会打洞(hole) 例 *mole* rat 鼹鼠
molecule [ˈmɑːlɪkjuːl]	*n.* 分子(the smallest particle of a substance that retains all the properties of the substance and is composed of one or more atoms) 记 词根记忆：mol(摩尔，克分子) + ecule → 分子 例 Studies of plants have now identified a new class of regulatory *molecules*. 派 molecular(a. 分子的)
molten [ˈmoultən]	*a.* 熔融的，熔化的(melted, made into liquid) 记 曾是古语中 melt 的过去分词，现用作形容词 例 *Molten* lava flowed down the mountain from the volcano.

monarch [ˈmɑːnərk]	*n.* 君主（one who reigns over a state or territory usually for life and by hereditary right） 记 词根记忆：mon(单个) + arch(统治者) → 个人统治 → 君主 例 Many *monarchs* were tyrannical. // *monarch* butterfly 黑脉金斑蝶
monitor [ˈmɑːnɪtər]	*v.* 监控（to watch, keep track of, or check for a special purpose）; *n.* 班长（a student appointed to assist a teacher） 例 Small transmitters are now used to *monitor* heart patients' exercise, as well as athletes exercising.
mononucleosis [ˌmɑːnouˌnuːkliˈousɪs]	*n.* 单核细胞增多症（an abnormal increase of mononuclear white blood cells in the blood） 例 Most victims of infectious *mononucleosis* recover after a few weeks of listlessness.
monopolistic [məˌnɑːpəˈlɪstɪk]	*a.* 垄断的；独占性的（of or related to monopolizing）; 专利的（having exclusive control over a commercial activity by possession or legal grant） 记 词根记忆：mono(单一) + polistic(政治的) → 单一的政治 → 垄断的 例 Despite these findings, we are urged to support *monopolistic* power on the grounds that such power creates an environment supportive of innovation.
monopoly [məˈnɑːpəli]	*n.* 垄断（exclusive possession or control）; 专利权（patent） 记 词根记忆：mono(单个) + poly(运用) → 仅让单个用垄断 例 In the United States, the Postal Service has a *monopoly* on first-class mail. 同根词：employ(*v.* 雇用); deploy(*v.* 调度，部署)
monsoon [ˌmɑːnˈsuːn]	*n.* 季风（a periodic wind）; 雨季（rainy season） 例 The rains in most parts of Sri Lanka are concentrated in the *monsoon* months, June to September.
monumental [ˌmɑːnjuˈmentl]	*a.* 极大的（massive, impressively large）; 纪念碑的（built as a monument） 记 来自 monument(*n.* 纪念碑) 例 A prolific architect who worked from the turn of the century until the late 1950's, Julia Morgan designed nearly 800 buildings in California, perhaps most notably William Randolph Hearst's *monumental* estate at San Simeon.
mooring [ˈmʊrɪŋ]	*n.* 停泊处（a place where something as a craft can be moored） 记 来自 moor(*v.* 使停泊) 例 Those *moorings* were destroyed by the hurricane.
moral [ˈmɔːrəl]	*a.* 道德的（conforming to a standard of right behavior）; 精神上的（perceptual or psychological） 记 联想记忆：m + oral(口头的) → 很多人口头称颂的 → 道德的 例 They feared that their party was losing its strong *moral* foundation. 派 morally(*ad.* 道德上)

morale [məˈræl]	*n.* 士气（the mental and emotional condition of an individual or group） 记 和 moral（*a.* 道德的）一起记 例 The physical work environment affects employees' productivity and *morale*.
morphine [ˈmɔːrfiːn]	*n.* 吗啡（a bitter, crystalline alkaloid, extracted from opium, the soluble salts of which are used in medicine as an analgesic, a light anesthetic, or a sedative） 记 发音记忆
mortality [mɔːrˈtæləti]	*n.* 死亡率（death rate） 记 词根记忆：mort（死）+ ality → 死亡率 例 The reduction in the food supply will increase *mortality*.
mortar [ˈmɔːrtər]	*n.* 灰泥（a plastic building material that hardens and is used in masonry or plastering）；*v.* 用灰泥涂抹（to plaster or make fast with mortar） 例 The most extensively used method has been to form the mud or clay into bricks, and, after some preliminary air drying or sun drying, to lay them in the wall in mud *mortar*.
mortgage [ˈmɔːrgɪdʒ]	*n.* 抵押贷款（a loan of money which you get from a bank in order to buy a house or other property）；*v.* 抵押（use house or land as a guarantee in order to borrow money） 记 词根记忆：mort（死亡）+ gage（抵押品）→ 用抵押品使债务死亡 → 抵押 例 Interest rates for home *mortgages* are expected to rise sharply.
mosaics [mouˈzeɪɪks]	*n.* 马赛克（a surface decoration made by inlaying small pieces of variously colored material to form pictures or patterns）；嵌合体（an organism or one of its parts composed of cells of more than one genotype） 记 发音记忆：mo（马）+ saic（赛克）+ s → 马赛克 例 There is no single region to which all the species depicted in the Sepphoris *mosaics* are native.
mosque [mɑːsk]	*n.* 清真寺（a Moslem house of worship） 记 发音记忆：和"莫斯科"发音颇像 例 The Turkish sultan established a *mosque* in the building and used the Acropolis as a fortress.
mosquito [məˈskiːtou]	*n.* 蚊子 记 发音记忆："貌似黑头" → 像鼻子上的黑头 → 蚊子 例 I left the picnic early because there were too many *mosquitoes*.
moth [mɔːθ]	*n.* 蛾；蛀虫（typically crepuscular or nocturnal insect having a stout body and feathery or hairlike antennae） 记 发音记忆："莫死" → 不畏死 → 飞蛾（moth）扑火哪畏死 例 Each species of *moth* has an optimal body temperature for effective flight. 派 mothy（*a.* 多蛾的；虫蛀的）
motion [ˈmouʃn]	*n.* 运动（movement）；提议（尤指会议提案）（proposal） 记 词根记忆：mot（动）+ ion → 运动 例 Those objects are in *motion*. // Judge Bonham denied a *motion*.

motivate [ˈmoʊtɪveɪt]	v. 激发，刺激(to provide with a motive) 记 词根记忆：mot(动) + iv + ate(使…) → 激发 例 In order to *motivate* our advertising agency to perform better, we should start basing the amount that we pay it on how much total profit we make each year. 派 motivation(n. 动机；积极性) 同根词：promote(v. 推动，促进)
mound [maʊnd]	n. 土丘，土墩(a small hill) 记 和 ground(n. 地面)一起记：mound on the ground 例 Archaeologists are excavating in a middle and a lower layer of a large *mound*.
mount [maʊnt]	v. 增加，增长(to rise, ascend) 记 本身为词根：升，上 例 The national debt continued to *mount* throughout the decade. 派 mounting(n. 衬垫)
mow [moʊ]	v. 割(草等)(to cut grass or grain from) 记 联想记忆：割(mow)草喂牛(cow) 例 Raymond took several days to *mow* the lawn. 派 mower(n. 割草工人，割草机)
multicellular [ˌmʌltɪˈseljʊlər]	a. 多细胞的(having or consisting of many cells) 记 词根记忆：multi(多) + cellular(细胞的) → 多细胞的 例 *multicellular* plants and animals
multiple [ˈmʌltɪpl]	n. 倍数(the product of a quantity by an integer) 派 multiply(v. 乘); multiplication(n. 乘法；增加)
multinational [ˌmʌltɪˈnæʃnəl]	a. 跨国公司的；多国的(of or relating to more than two nationalities); n. 跨国公司 记 词根记忆：multi(多) + nation(国) + al → 多国的 例 They are used more frequently by *multinational* corporations than by companies with strictly domestic operations. 同根词：multilateral(a. 多边的)
multiple [ˈmʌltɪpl]	a. 多样的，多重的(various; including more than one) 记 词根记忆：multi(多) + ple → 多样的，多重的 例 Both Ryan's model of class and the traditional model consider *multiple* factors, including wealth, marital status, and enfranchisement, in determining women's status. 派 multiply(ad. 多样地; v. 乘)
multiply [ˈmʌltɪplaɪ]	v. 乘(to perform multiplication on)；增加(to increase) 记 词根记忆：multi(多) + ply(表动词) → 变多 → 增加 例 When 6 is *multiplied* by 8, the result is 48. // Since 1970 the number of Blacks elected to federal offices in the United States has *multiplied* nearly four times. 派 multiplication(n. 乘法；增加)

□ motivate □ mound □ mount □ mow □ multicellular □ multiple
□ multinational □ multiple □ multiply

multitude [ˈmʌltɪtuːd]	*n.* 大量，众多 (a great number) 词根记忆：multi(多) + tude → 多的状态 → 大量 例 The concert was attended by *multitudes* of music lovers.
municipal [mjuːˈnɪsɪpl]	*a.* 市的 (civic)；市政的 (of or relating to the internal affairs of a major political unit) 词根记忆：muni(官方职责) + cipal → 市政的 例 Paper of all kinds is the biggest single component of *municipal* trash. // *municipal* government 市政府 派 municipality(*n.* 市，市政当局)
municipality [mjuːˌnɪsɪˈpæləti]	*n.* 市；市政当局 (the governing body of an urban political unit) 来自 municipal(*a.* 市政的) 例 In order to avoid the serious health threats associated with many landfills, our *municipality* should build a plant for burning trash. 同根词：municipally(*ad.* 市政上)
mural [ˈmjʊrəl]	*n.* 壁画 (a very large image, such as a painting or an enlarged photograph, applied directly to a wall or ceiling) 词根记忆：mur(墙) + al → 墙上的画 → 壁画 例 Margaret has traveled to photograph the art of Ndebele women, whose *murals* are brilliantly colored. 同根词：demur(*v.* 反对)；immure(*v.* 监禁)
mutation [mjuːˈteɪʃn]	*n.* 突变，变异 (a significant and basic change) 词根记忆：mut(变) + ation → 突变，变异 例 Genetic *mutations* in bacteria and viruses can lead to epidemics. 同根词：immutable(*a.* 不可变的)
mutual [ˈmjuːtʃuəl]	*a.* 相互的 (directed and received in equal amount)；共同的 (possessed in common) 词根记忆：mut(变) + ual → 改变是相互作用的结果 → 相互的；共同的 例 *mutual* fund 共有基金(一种投资公司形式)
mystic [ˈmɪstɪk]	*a.* 神秘的 (mysterious; strange)；神秘主义的 (of or relating to mysticism)；*n.* 神秘主义者 (one who practices or believes in mysticism or a given form of mysticism) 词根记忆：myst(神秘) + ic → 神秘的；神秘主义的 例 The *mystic* writing on the wall could not be understood by anyone. // This most bland and circumspect of men was a *mystic* in both public and private life.
mythic [ˈmɪθɪk]	*a.* 虚构的 (fancied)；神话(般)的 (of or relating to the myth) 词根记忆：myth(神话) + ic → 神话(般)的 例 The downsizing's *mythic* properties give the company added prestige in the business community.

24

mythology [mɪˈθɑːlədʒi]	*n.* 神话(a body of myths concerning an individual event, or institution)；神话学(the field of scholarship dealing with the systematic collection and study of myths) 记 词根记忆：myth(神话) + ology(学) → 神话；神话学 例 The classical scholar specialized in Greek *mythology*. 派 mythological(*a.* 神话学的)
narrative [ˈnærətɪv]	*a.* 叙述的，讲故事的(of, or in the form of story-telling)；导航 记 来自 narrate(*v.* 叙述) 例 *narrative* device 叙事手法 同根词：narration(*n.* 叙述，讲述)
naturalize [ˈnætʃrəlaɪz]	*v.* 使(外国人)入籍(to admit to citizenship) 例 Each newly *naturalized* citizen was issued a social security number.
navigation [ˌnævɪˈgeɪʃn]	*n.* 航行，航海(the act or practice of navigating)；导航 记 词根记忆：nav(船) + ig + ation(行为；状态) → 开船 → 航海 例 For some birds the sense of smell appears to play a role in *navigation*. 同根词：naval(*a.* 船的；海军的)
navy [ˈneɪvi]	*n.* 海军(a nation's ships of war and of logistic support) 记 词根记忆：nav(船) + y → 驾驶舰船保卫祖国 → 海军 例 Most of the opposition to the bill came from the *Navy* and its numerous civilian spokesmen. 同根词：naval(*a.* 海军的)；navigate(*v.* 航行)；navigation(*n.* 航行)
nebula [ˈnebjələ]	*n.* 星云(any of numerous clouds of gas or dust in interstellar space) 例 galactic *nebula* 银河星云
necessitate [nəˈsesɪteɪt]	*v.* 需要(to need, to require)；(使)成为必要(to make necessary) 记 词根记忆：necessit(需要) + ate → 需要；(使)成为必要 例 The reduction in government revenues will *necessitate* cuts in other government programs. 派 necessity(*n.* 必需品；必要性)
needy [ˈniːdi]	*a.* 贫穷的(poverty-stricken) 记 联想记忆：need(需要) + y(…的) → 什么都需要的 → 贫穷的 例 The church distributes food and clothing to *needy* people.
negative [ˈnegətɪv]	*a.* 否定的(marked by denial)；消极的(passive)；负的(minus) 记 词根记忆：neg(否定) + ative(…的) → 否定的 注意：positive(*a.* 肯定的) 例 *negative* evaluation 否定性的评价 // *negative* impact 消极的影响 // *negative* number 负数

□ mythology   □ narrative   □ naturalize   □ navigation   □ navy   □ nebula
□ necessitate   □ needy   □ negative

negligence [ˈneglɪdʒəns]	*n.* 疏忽，粗心大意（carelessness） 记 来自 negligent(*a.* 忽略的；疏忽的) 例 If the insurance company is able to prove excessive loss due to owner's *negligence*, it may decline to pay the money. 派 negligible(*a.* 可忽略不计的)
negligible [ˈneglɪdʒəbl]	*a.* 可忽略不计的（so small or unimportant or of so little consequence as to warrant little or no attention）；微不足道的（trifling） 例 Inflation in the intervening period has been *negligible*, and the increase has been duly received by all eligible Runagians. 同根词：neglect(*v.* 疏忽；忽视)
negotiate [nɪˈgoʊʃieɪt]	*v.* (with) 谈判；(通过谈判或协商)达成协议（to arrange or settle by discussion and mutual agreement） 记 联想记忆：ne + got(获得) + iate → 谈判是为了获得一致意见 → 谈判 例 It is against the police department's policy to *negotiate* with kidnappers. // They gathered workers for particular jobs and then *negotiated* a contract between workers and employers. 派 negotiation(*n.* 谈判，协商)
negotiation [nɪ͵goʊʃiˈeɪʃn]	*n.* 谈判；协商（the action or process of negotiating or being negotiated） 记 来自 negotiate(*v.* 商议，谈判) 例 The methods of *negotiation* are available to the purchasing company. 同根词：negotiable(*a.* 可协商的)
nematode [ˈnɪmətoʊd]	*n.* 线虫类（any of a phylum, Nematoda or Nemata of elongated cylindrical worms parasitic in animals or plants or free-living in soil or water） 例 The *nematodes* can lie dormant for several years in their cysts(包囊).
neural [ˈnʊrəl]	*a.* 神经(系统)的（of, relating to, or affecting a nerve or the nervous system） 记 词根记忆：neur(神经) + al → 神经的 例 This drug will damage *neural* connections in rats. 派 neurotransmitter(*n.* 【生】神经传递素)

neuron
['nʊrɑːn]

n. 神经元，神经细胞 (a grayish or reddish granular cell with specialized processes that is the fundamental functional unit of nervous tissue)

记 词根记忆：neur(神经) + on(物) → 神经元

例 Neurotransmitters are chemicals that carry nerve impulses from one *neuron* to the next.

派 neuronal(*a.* 神经元的)

neutral
['njuːtrəl]

a. 中立的 (not engaged on either side)

记 词根记忆：neutr(中) + al → 中间的；中立的

例 Switzerland remained *neutral* during World War II.

派 neutrality(*n.* 中性；中立)

neutron
['njuːtrɑːn]

n. 中子

记 词根记忆：neutr(中) + on(物) → 中子

例 *neutron* star 中子星(假想天体，主要是由高密度中子组成，具有强大的吸力)

同根词：neutrino(*n.* 中微子)

newlywed
['njuːlɪwed]

n. 新婚的人 (a person recently married)

记 分拆记忆：newly(新近地) + wed(结婚) → 新婚的人

例 The *newlywed* couple from Louisiana planned to begin their family in Hawaii.

nexus
['neksəs]

n. 关系，连结 (connection, link)

记 词根记忆：nex(=nect 联系) + us → 关系

例 cash *nexus* 金钱关系

niche
[niːʃ]

n. 壁龛 (a recess in a wall, as for holding a statue or an urn)；【生】生态龛 (a habitat supplying the factors necessary for the existence of an organism or species)；特定市场 (a specialized market)

记 发音记忆："你吃" → 这块市场等你来吃 → 特定市场

例 ecological *niche* 生态龛 // market *niche* 市场利基(经济学名词，指具有特定顾客且不受重视的小市场领域)

nihilism
['naɪɪlɪzəm]

n. 虚无主义 (a viewpoint that traditional values and beliefs are unfounded and that existence is senseless and useless)

记 词根记忆：nihil(虚无) + ism → 虚无主义

例 The pessimistic idea "everything has been tried and nothing works" sometimes borders on *nihilism*.

nitrogen
['naɪtrədʒən]

n. 氮 (a colorless tasteless odorless element that as a diatomic gas is relatively inert)

记 词根记忆：nitro(含氮的) + gen(产生) → 氮

例 The release of the iron compounds did not increase the supply of *nitrogen* compounds in the area.

派 nitrogenous(*a.* 氮的；含氮的)

nocturnal
[nɑːk'tɜːrnl]

a. 夜晚的，夜间活动的 (active at night)

记 词根记忆：noct(夜) + urnal → 夜晚的

例 Bats are the chief consumers of *nocturnal* insects.

□ neuron　　□ neutral　　□ neutron　　□ newlywed　　□ nexus　　□ niche
□ nihilism　　□ nitrogen　　□ nocturnal

nomad [ˈnoʊmæd]	*n.* 流浪者 (wanderer); 游牧部落的人 (a member of a group of people who have no fixed home and move according to the seasons from place to place in search of food water, and grazing land) 例 The *nomads* viewed themselves as victims of a natural disaster. 派 nomadic(*a.* 游牧的)
nomadic [noʊˈmædɪk]	*a.* 游牧的 (of nomad) 记 来自 nomad(*n.* 游牧民, 流浪者) 例 Until recently, the Inuit people led a *nomadic* existence, sheltering in igloos, the ice-block domes that are peculiar to north-central Canada, and in structures made of stones, bones, driftwood and skins.
nominate [ˈnɑːmɪneɪt]	*v.* 提名 (to designate, name) 记 词根记忆: nomin(名称) + ate → 提名 例 The board *nominated* Mary for the sales award for the third year in a row. 派 nomination(*n.* 提名, 任命); nominee(*n.* 被提名的候选人)
nonbiodegradable [ˌnɒnˌbaɪəʊdɪˈɡreɪdəbl]	*a.* 不能生物降解的 记 词根记忆: non(不) + bio(生物) + degradable(可降解) → 不能生物降解的 例 Plastic containers account for the primary part of *nonbiodegradable* waste.
noncommercial [ˌnɑːnkəˈmɜːrʃl]	*a.* 非商业的 (not occupied with or engaged in commerce or work intended for commerce) 记 词根记忆: non(不) + commercial(商业的) → 非商业的 例 The average *noncommercial*-vehicle driver is involved in less long-distance driving than is the average commercial-vehicle driver.
noncommittal [ˌnɑːnkəˈmɪtl]	*a.* 不负责的 (not revealing what one feels or thinks); 不明朗的 (giving no clear indication of attitude or feeling) 记 词根记忆: non(不) + commit(负责) + tal → 不负责的 例 The *noncommittal* candidate refused to debate the issues.
nonessential [ˌnɑnɪˈsenʃl]	*a.* 不重要的 (unimportant); 非必需的 (not essential) 记 词根记忆: non(不) + essential(重要的, 必要的) → 不重要的; 非必需的 例 Only expenditures for *nonessential* services were actually reduced.
nonstarter [ˌnɑnˈstɑːrtər]	*n.* 毫无成功希望的人 (someone that is not productive or effective) 例 Those *nonstarters* were considered the ones who wanted stability.
note [noʊt]	*n.* 记录 (record); 音符 (melody); *v.* 注意 (to notice); 指出 (to indicate) 例 My boss *noted* my reluctance to work on Saturdays. // This musical scale has 13 *notes*. // This report *noted* that the closer one came to town, the more the city air would become increasingly acidic. 派 noted(*a.* 著名的)
notify [ˈnoʊtɪfaɪ]	*v.* 通知, 报告 (to inform) 记 词根记忆: not(标识) + ify(使…) → 使…知道 → 通知, 报告 例 Each country was to *notify* the six other countries when it had completed its action. 派 notification(*n.* 通知, 告示)

25

notorious
[nou'tɔ:riəs]

a. 声名狼藉的（widely and unfavorably known）

记 词根记忆：not(知道) + orious(多的) → 人所共知的 → 声名狼藉的

例 Napoleon was *notorious* for refusing to share power with any of his political associates.

novel
['nɑ:vl]

n. (长篇)小说（an invented prose narrative that is usually long and complex and deals especially with human experience through a usually connected sequence of events）；*a.* 新颖的（new）；新奇的（original new）

记 词根记忆：nov(新) + el → 新颖的

例 *novel* behaviour 怪异的行为 // The early buyers of a *novel* product are always people who are quick to acquire novelties.

派 novelty(*n.* 新奇性)

同根词：innovate(*v.* 革新)

novice
['nɑ:vɪs]

n. 新手（beginner）

记 词根记忆：nov(新) + ice(人) → 新手

例 I helped my boss train the *novices*.

noxious
['nɑ:kʃəs]

a. 有毒的，有害的（harmful, poisonous）

记 词根记忆：nox(毒) + ious → 有毒的

例 A shed behind the factory is filled with *noxious* chemicals.

nuclear
['nu:kliər]

a. 核心的（center）；核子的，原子能的（atomic）

记 词根记忆：nucle(核的) + ar → 核心的；核子的

例 *nuclear* family 核心家庭 // *nuclear* weapon 核武器

nucleon
['nu:klɪɑn]

n. 核子（a proton or neutron especially in the atomic nucleus）

记 词根记忆：nucle(核的) + on(物) → 核子

例 Great mass is synonymous with huge numbers of *nucleons*.

派 nucleic(*a.* 核的，核子的)

nucleotide
['nu:klɪətaɪd]

n. 核苷酸（any of various compounds consisting of a nucleoside combined with a phosphate group and forming the basic constituent of DNA and RNA）

例 *nucleotide* sequence 核苷酸序列

nucleus
['nu:kliəs]

n. [pl. nuclei]核，核心（a central or essential part around which other parts are gathered or grouped; a core）

例 cell *nuclei* 细胞核

nuisance
['nu:sns]

n. 讨厌的人；麻烦事（one that is annoying, unpleasant, or obnoxious）

记 联想记忆：讨厌的人(nuisance)说什么都是废话(nonsense)

例 This method allows for effective control of *nuisance* algae while leaving solar ponds as one of the cleanest technologies providing energy for human use.

numerator
['nu:məreɪtər]

n. 【数】分子（the part of a fraction that is above the line and signifies the number to be divided by the denominator）

记 联想记忆：numer(数) + ator → 变化了产生新的数 → 分子

注意：denominator(*n.* 分母)

例 What is the sum of the *numerator* and denominator of the original fraction?

nutrient ['nuːtriənt]	*n.* 营养物，滋养物质（substance serving as or providing nourishment） 记 词根记忆：nutri(滋养) + ent(表物) → 滋养物质 例 To maintain the *nutrients* in the soil, corn and soybeans are often planted in a field in alternate years. 同根词：nutritious(*a.* 有营养的；滋养的)
nutrition [nuˈtrɪʃn]	*n.* 营养（the act or process of nourishing or being nourished） 记 词根记忆：nutri(营养) + tion → 营养 例 A balanced diet is important in *nutrition*. 派 nutritional(*a.* 营养的，滋养的) 同根词：nutritious(*a.* 富含营养的)；nutrient(*n.* 营养品；*a.*滋养的)
nutritious [nuˈtrɪʃəs]	*a.* 有营养成分的，营养的（nourishing） 记 来自 nutrition(*n.* 营养) 例 The milk of mammals would be less *nutritious* if it did not contain cannabinoids. 派 nutritiousness(*n.* 有营养成分) 同根词：nutrient(*n.* 营养物，*a.* 营养的)
oats [outs]	*n.* 燕麦（a crop or plot of the oat）；燕麦片(oatmeal) 记 发音记忆："饿吃" → 饿了吃燕麦 注意：oatmeal(*n.* 燕麦粥) 例 A breakfast cereal contains *oats*, raisins and nuts.
obese [ouˈbiːs]	*a.* 肥胖的（having excessive body fat） 记 发音记忆："藕必是" → 藕必是圆圆的 → 肥胖的 例 Many people become *obese* more due to the fact that their bodies burn calories too slowly than overeating. 派 obesity(*n.* 肥胖)
objection [əbˈdʒekʃn]	*n.* 厌恶，反对（dislike or disapproval） 记 词根记忆：ob(倒逆) + ject(投掷) + ion → 反着投 → 反对 例 This *objection* was reasonable when only early theropod clavicles had been discovered. 同根词：objective(*n.* 目的；*a.* 客观的)
objective [əbˈdʒektɪv]	*a.* 客观的（external）；*n.* 目标，目的（aim, goal） 记 和 object(*n.* 目标)一起记 例 *objective* criteria 客观标准 // political *objective* 政治目标 派 objectivity(*n.* 客观性)
oblique [əˈbliːk]	*a.* 斜的，倾斜的（inclined） 记 词根记忆：ob(躺) + lique(离开) → 躺着都能滑开 → 斜的 例 an *oblique* angle 斜角（包括锐角和钝角）
obscure [əbˈskjʊr]	*a.* 模糊的（faint, undefined）；*v.* 使…不明显（to make dim） 记 联想记忆：ob(离开) + scure(跑) → 越跑越远渐渐地就看不清楚了 → 使…不明显 例 Clark believes the possibility has been *obscured* by the recent sociological fashion.

25

observation
[ˌɑːbzər'veɪʃn]

n. 观测 (an act of recognizing and noting a fact or occurrence); 遵守 (an act or instance of observing a custom, rule, or law); 观察报告 (a record or description so obtained)

记 来自 observe(*v.* 观察；遵守)

例 The first is an *observation* that the editorial disputes.

派 observational(*a.* 观测的)

同根词：deserve(*v.* 应受，应得)

observatory
[əb'zɜːrvətɔːri]

n. 天文台 (a building, a place, or an institution designed and equipped for making observations of astronomical, meteorological, or other natural phenomena)

记 来自 observe(*v.* 观察)

例 Astronomers at the Palomar *Observatory* have discovered a distant supernova explosion.

obsess
[əb'ses]

v. (使)困扰，(使)着迷 (to haunt or excessively preoccupy the mind of)

记 词根记忆：ob + sess(=sit 坐) → 坐着不走 → (使)困扰，(使)着迷

例 The fear of death *obsessed* her throughout her old age.

派 obsession(*n.* 迷住；萦绕)

obsolescence
[ˌɑːbsə'lesns]

n. 荒废；过时 (the condition of being nearly obsolete)

记 来自 obsolete(*a.* 废弃的)

例 technical *obsolescence* 技术过时

obstacle
['ɑːbstəkl]

n. 障碍 (something that impedes progress or achievement)

记 词根记忆：ob(反) + st(=stand 站) + acle(东西) → 反着站的东西 → 障碍

例 In the speaking contest, Randolph faced formidable *obstacles*.

occupation
[ˌɑːkju'peɪʃn]

n. 工作，职业 (a job; employment); 占领 (the act or process of taking possession of a place or area)

记 来自 occupy(*v.* 占领；使用)

例 There is no *occupation* for which the risk of developing an animal-induced allergy is higher than 30 percent.

派 occupational(*a.* 职业的；占领的)

同根词：preoccupation(*n.* 全神贯注，入神)

occupational
[ˌɑːkju'peɪʃənl]

a. 职业的 (of the activity in which one engages); 占领的 (taking possession of a place or area)

记 来自 occupation(*n.* 职业，占领)

例 Unlike men of science, women of science have had to work against the grain of *occupational* stereotyping to enter a "man's world".

同根词：preoccupation(*n.* 全神贯注；当务之急)

occurrence
[ə'kɜːrəns]

n. 发生 (the action or instance of occurring); 事件 (sth. that occurs)

记 词根记忆：oc(加强) + curr(发生) + ence → 发生

例 It provides an explanation for the *occurrence* of a situation described in the first paragraph.

同根词：concur(*v.* 同时发生)

□ observation □ observatory □ obsess □ obsolescence □ obstacle □ occupation
□ occupational □ occurrence

odd [ɑːd]	*a.* 奇怪的(peculiar)；奇数的(impar)；*n.* [*pl.*]可能性(possibility)；不平等(imparity) 记 联想记忆：奇奇(odd)相加(add)为偶 例 I avoided the *odd* person who was talking to himself. // The *odds* are 10 to 1 against your winning. // against *odds* 尽管有极大的困难 // at *odds* 争执，不一致 派 oddity(*n.* 奇特的人或物；古怪的性质)
odometer [oʊˈdɑːmɪtər]	*n.* (汽车)里程表(an instrument for measuring the distance traveled as by a vehicle) 记 词根记忆：odo(旅行) + meter(测量) → 测量旅行的东西 → 里程表 例 I couldn't determine how far I'd driven because my car's *odometer* is broken.
odor [ˈoʊdər]	*n.* 气味(smell) 记 词根记忆：od(闻) + or → 气味 例 The *odor* of freshly baked apple pie came from the kitchen.
offender [əˈfendər]	*n.* 冒犯者；违法者(one that transgresses the moral or divine law) 记 来自offend(*v.* 冒犯；违反) 例 habitual *offender* 惯犯 同根词：offensive(*a.* 攻击的；冒犯的)
off-season [ˈɔfˌsizən]	*n.* 淡季(slack)；*a.* 淡季的(being in a period of slack) 例 The football players became more aggressive during the season and remained so during the *off-season*.
offset [ɔfˈset]	*v.* 抵销(to countervail)；补偿(to compensate for) 记 来自词组：set off(抵销) 注意：onset(*n.* 袭击；突然开始) 例 Great risks must be *offset* by the chance of great rewards. // Henry has to *offset* his small salary by living economically.
offshoot [ˈɔːfʃuːt]	*n.* 分支(a branch, descendant, or member) 例 They originated as *offshoots* of church-related groups.
offspring [ˈɔːfsprɪŋ]	*n.* (动物的)崽；后代(descendant) 记 联想记忆：off(出来) + spring(春天) → 春天出来的 → (动物的)崽 例 Monogamous parents should cooperate to care for their *offspring*.
olfactory [ɑːlˈfæktəri]	*a.* 嗅觉的(of, relating to, or contributing to the sense of smell) 记 词根记忆：ol(=smell 味) + fact(做) + ory → 做出味道来 → 闻到 → 嗅觉的 例 The poisonous gas damaged my *olfactory* nerves.
omen [ˈoʊmən]	*n.* 征兆，预兆(a phenomenon supposed to portend good or evil; a prophetic sign) 例 Black rain clouds are an *omen* of heavy rainstorms.
omission [əʊˈmɪʃn]	*n.* 遗漏(something neglected or left undone) 记 词根记忆：omi(t)(省略，遗漏) + ssion → 遗漏 例 The *omission* of your article from the journal was accidental.

25

ongoing [ˈɑːngouɪŋ]	*a.* 进行中的，不间断的（continuing） 例 They highlight her *ongoing* efforts to reform sanitary conditions after the war.
onset [ˈɑːnset]	*n.* 发作，（突然）开始（beginning, start） 记 分拆记忆：on + set（放）→ 放在…上 → 发作，开始 例 I knew my sneezing was the *onset* of a major cold. // at the very *onset* 刚一开始
opaque [ouˈpeɪk]	*a.* 不透明的（not transparent）；难懂的（obscure） 记 词根记忆：opa（不透明）+ que → 不透明的 例 The room was dark because all of the windows were *opaque*. // I couldn't understand my professor's *opaque* lecture.
operagoer [ˈɑːprəˌgouər]	*n.* 经常看歌剧的人（a person who frequently goes to operas） 记 分拆记忆：opera（歌剧）+ goer（常去的人）→ 经常看歌剧的人 例 Just as reading Samuel Pepys's diary gives a student a sense of the seventeenth century—of its texture and psyche—so listening to Jane Freed's guileless child narrator takes the *operagoer* inside turn-of-the-century Vienna.
optical [ˈɑːptɪkl]	*a.* 眼的，视觉的（visual）；光学的（of or relating to optics） 记 词根记忆：optic（眼的）+ al → 眼的，视觉的 例 *optical* illusion // an *optical* instrument 光学仪器
optimal [ˈɑːptɪməl]	*a.* 最佳的（best）；*n.* 最大限度（top） 记 词根记忆：optim（最好）+ al → 最佳的 例 This is the *optimal* time for harvesting apples.
optimism [ˈɑːptɪmɪzəm]	*n.* 乐观，乐观主义（a tendency to expect the best possible outcome or dwell on the most hopeful aspects of a situation） 记 词根记忆：optim（最好）+ ism → 认为自己是最好的 → 乐观，乐观主义 注意：pessimism（*n.* 悲观，悲观主义） 例 Increasing commercial activity would create a mood of *optimism* about national prosperity. 派 optimistic（*a.* 乐观主义的）；optimistically（*ad.* 乐观地）
optimum [ˈɑːptɪməm]	*a.* 最好的，最有利的（most favorable or advantageous） 记 词根记忆：optim（最好）+ um → 最好的 例 I raised my exotic plants under *optimum* conditions.
optometrist [ɑːpˈtɑːmətrɪst]	*n.* 验光师（a specialist licensed to practice optometry） 记 来自 optometry（*n.* 验光） 例 The *optometrist* charges $150 per pair for soft contact lenses.
orator [ˈɔːrətər]	*n.* 演说者（one who delivers an oration）；演讲者；雄辩家（one distinguished for skill and power as a public speaker） 记 联想记忆：oral（口头的），用特"t"换掉"l"，后面加上"or"，就成了"特"别能说的"人" → 演说者 例 In the late nineteenth century Annie Besant was widely regarded as one of the greatest living public *orators*, second only to Gladstone in a culture where oratory was the dominant public medium.

□ ongoing □ onset □ opaque □ operagoer □ optical □ optimal
□ optimism □ optimum □ optometrist □ orator

ordinance [ˈɔːrdɪnəns]	*n.* 地方法令（a local rule） 记 词根记忆：ordin（命令）+ ance → 地方法令 注意：ordnance（*n.* 大炮） 例 In our country, all cities and most towns have anti-smoking *ordinances*.
ore [ɔːr]	*n.* 矿，矿砂，矿石（a naturally occurring mineral containing a valuable constituent for which it is mined and worked） 记 联想记忆：矿石（ore）多一个 m 就是更多（more） 注意：roe（*n.* 鱼卵） 例 iron *ore* 铁矿
organization [ˌɔːrɡənəˈzeɪʃn]	*n.* 组织（the act or process of organizing or of being organized）；机构，团体（an administrative and functional structure） 记 来自 organize（*v.* 组织；成立） 例 Clark makes the point that the characteristics of a technology have a decisive influence on job skills and work *organization*. 同根词：disorganize（*v.* 扰乱；瓦解）
orientation [ˌɔːriənˈteɪʃn]	*n.* 方向，取向，目标（the act or process of orienting or of being oriented） 记 来自 orient（*v.* 使确定方向；*n.* 东方） 例 It has diverted attention from the need for *orientation* of nonsupervisory employees to organizational values. 同根词：oriental（*a.* 东方的；*n.* 东方人）

A novel is a mirror walking along a main road.
一部小说犹如一面在大街上走的镜子。
——法国作家 司汤达（Stendhal, French writer）

25

Word List 26

oriented [ˈɔːrientɪd]	*a.* 导向的(intellectually, emotionally, or functionally directed) 例 issue-*oriented* 以议题为导向的 派 disoriented(*a.* 迷失方向的)
originality [əˌrɪdʒəˈnæləti]	*n.* 创意，独创性(the quality of being original) 记 来自original(*a.* 新颖的，有创意的) 例 *Originality* is not the only valuable attribute that a work of art can possess.
originate [əˈrɪdʒɪneɪt]	*v.* 出现(to appear)；开始(to initiate, begin) 记 来自origin(*n.* 起源，产生) 例 United States automakers will *originate* net production processes before Japanese automakers do. 派 originator(*n.* 创始者)；originality(*n.* 创造性)
originator [əˈrɪdʒɪneɪtər]	*n.* 发起人(one that creates new things) 记 来自originate(*v.* 起源) 例 The lack of complete historical records from the mid-to-late 1800's has made it difficult to trace some inventions to their Black *originators*.
ornamentation [ˌɔːrnəmenˈteɪʃn]	*n.* 装饰物；装饰(decoration) 例 The bowers of one species of bowerbird(园丁鸟)lack the towers and *ornamentation*.
orthodox [ˈɔːrθədɑːks]	*a.* 正统的，通常的(traditional and usual) 记 词根记忆：ortho(正) + dox(观点) → 正统观点的 → 正统的 例 This *orthodox* view of the universe is now being challenged by those astronomers. 同根词：heterodox(*a.* 异端邪说的)；paradox(*n.* 自相矛盾的话)
osmotic [ɑːzˈmɑːtɪk]	*a.* 渗透的，渗透性的(of, relating to, caused by, or having the properties of osmosis) 例 *osmotic* pressure 渗透压(指溶液中的溶质促使水分子通过半透膜从一侧溶液扩散到另一侧溶液的力量)
ostentation [ˌɑːstenˈteɪʃn]	*n.* 夸示，炫耀(excessive display) 记 词根记忆：ostent(显现) + ation → 显现 → 炫耀 例 Structural *ostentation* and luxury were the order of the day.

□ oriented   □ originality   □ originate   □ originator   □ ornamentation □ orthodox
□ osmotic   □ ostentation

oust [aʊst]	*v.* 驱逐，剥夺（to remove from or dispossess of property or position by legal action, by force, or by the compulsion of necessity）；取代（to take the place of） 例 When evidence of financial wrongdoing by an elected official surfaces, it is the electorate who must decide whether the evidence warrants censuring him or *ousting* him from office. 派 ouster(*n.* 驱逐；罢黜)
outcome ['aʊtkʌm]	*n.* 结果（result, consequence） 记 来自词组 come out(真相；结果) 例 Critics of the proposals argue that the *outcomes* of public referenda would be biased.
outfit ['aʊtfɪt]	*v.* 配备，装备（to furnish） 例 In reality, early trading companies successfully purchased and *outfitted* ships, built and operated offices and warehouses.
outlaw ['aʊtlɔː]	*v.* 宣布…为非法（to make illegal）；*n.* 歹徒；罪犯（criminal） 例 For a local government to *outlaw* all strikes is a costly mistake.
outlay ['aʊtleɪ]	*n.* 支出，费用（expenditure, payment） 记 来自词组 lay out(消费；花钱) 例 *Outlays* for research and development increased 16.4 percent.
outlet ['aʊtlet]	*n.* 出口，通风口（exit, vent）；批发商店（a store through which a product is marketed） 记 联想记忆：out(外面) + let(让) → 让人出去的地方 → 出口 例 an *outlet* pipe 排水管 // *outlet* stores 代销店
outline ['aʊtlaɪn]	*n.* 轮廓（figure）；概述（summary）；*v.* 描画轮廓；概括（summarize） 例 This is an *outline* of a sign for an ice-cream store. // Three hypotheses were *outlined* in this scientific conference.
outlying ['aʊtlaɪɪŋ]	*a.* 远离城市的，边远的（remote from a center or main body） 记 联想记忆：out(出) + ly(看作 lie 位于) + ing → 位于外面的 → 边远的 例 Most *outlying* airfields are not equipped to handle commercial-airline traffic.
outmoded [ˌaʊt'moʊdɪd]	*a.* 过时了的，不再流行的（not being in style） 例 I wish we could get rid of that old and *outmoded* sofa.
outnumber [ˌaʊt'nʌmbər]	*v.* 在数量上超过（to exceed in number） 记 词根记忆：out(超过) + number(数量) → 在数量上超过 例 These stars vastly *outnumber* the other stars in a given galaxy.
outpatient ['aʊtpeɪʃnt]	*n.* 门诊病人（a patient who is admitted to a hospital or clinic for treatment that does not require an overnight stay） 记 和 inpatient(*n.* 住院病人)一起记 例 Public hospitals continued to provide services for *outpatients* and emergency services.

26

outpost [ˈaʊtpoʊst]	*n.* 前哨(站)(a detachment of troops stationed at a distance from a main force to guard against surprise attacks)
	记 词根记忆：out(外面的) + post(岗位) → 靠外的岗位 → 前哨
	例 In the Hudson's Bay Company, each far-flung trading *outpost* was managed by a salaried agent.
outrage [ˈaʊtreɪdʒ]	*v.* 激怒(to offend)；*n.* 愤怒(rage)
	记 词根记忆：out(过度) + rage(狂怒，狂暴) → 激怒
	例 Forrestal's appointment as Secretary of Defense was expected to *outrage* advocates of the Army air forces.
	派 outrageous(*a.* 无礼的，蛮横的)
outright [ˈaʊtraɪt]	*ad.* 直率地(flat-out)；全部地，彻底地(completely)
	记 来自词组 right out(明白地，坦率地)
	例 The Supreme Court ruled as long ago as 1880 that Blacks could not be excluded *outright* from jury service.
outsource [ˈaʊtsɔːrs]	*v.* 外包(to procure under contract with an outside supplier)
	记 联想记忆：out(外面的) + source(来源) → 资源来自外面 → 外包
	例 Among the parts of its business that Vernon does not plan to *outsource* are some that require standards of accuracy too high for most independent suppliers to provide at lower cost than Vernon can.
outstrip [ˌaʊtˈstrɪp]	*v.* 超过，胜出(to exceed)
	记 联想记忆：out(超过) + strip(条，带) → 最早超出终点线的人就胜出
	例 If the economy grows, the demand for motivated and educated people will far *outstrip* the supply.
oval [ˈoʊvl]	*a.* 卵形的，椭圆形的 (resembling an egg in shape, resembling an ellipse in shape)
	例 That planet's moon follows an *oval* orbit.
overall [ˌoʊvərˈɔːl]	*a.* 全部的(including everything)；整体上(regarded as a whole)；一般的 (general)
	例 As *overall* life expectancy continues to rise, the population of our country is growing increasingly older.
overcapitalize [ˌoʊvərˈkæpɪtəlaɪz]	*v.* 过分投资于(to capitalize beyond what the business or the profit-making prospects warrant)
	例 The practice of full-cost reimbursement encouraged capital investment and now the industry is *overcapitalized*.
	派 overcapitalization(*n.* 投资过高)
overcharge [ˌoʊvərˈtʃɑːrdʒ]	*v.* 过度充电；索价过高，收费过高(to charge too much)
	记 词根记忆：over(过度) + charge(收费) → 收费过高
	例 Many clients had been *overcharged*.
overextend [ˌoʊvərɪkˈstend]	*v.* 过度扩展(to extend or expand beyond a safe or reasonable point)；使冒过大风险
	记 词根记忆：over(过度的) + extend(扩展) → 过度扩展
	例 The speculative fever of the Roaring Twenties infected rich and poor alike; vast quantities of people were dangerously *overextended*.

overfish [ˌoʊvərˈfɪʃ]	v. 过度捕捞 (to fish to the detriment of (a fishing ground) or to the depletion of (a kind of organism)) 记 词根记忆：over(过度的) + fish(捕鱼) → 过度捕捞 例 There are no legal limits, as there are for cod and haddock, on the size of monkfish that can be caught, a circumstance that contributes to their depletion through *overfishing*.
overflow [ˌoʊvərˈfloʊ]	v. 溢出 (to fill a space and spread beyond its limits) 记 词根记忆：over(超过) + flow(流) → 流出 → 溢出 例 If the county continues to collect residential trash at current levels, landfills will soon be *overflowing*.
overlap [ˌoʊvərˈlæp]	v. 重叠 (to occupy the same area in part) 记 词根记忆：over(在…上) + lap(大腿) → 把一条腿放在另一条腿上 → 重叠 例 Each language occupies a distinct area of the brain in an adult learner, while language areas *overlap* in a young child.
overlay [ˌoʊvərˈleɪ]	v. 覆盖 (to cover) 例 These seas have a typical oceanic floor, except that the floor is *overlaid* by several kilometers of sediment.
overlie [ˌoʊvərˈlaɪ]	v. 躺(伏)在…上面 (to lie over or upon) 例 The blacksmith *overlay* wood with silver.
overlook [ˌoʊvərˈlʊk]	v. 忽略，忽视 (to neglect, to ignore) 例 They have *overlooked* the role that women's political activities played in the woman's rights movement.
overlord [ˈoʊvərlɔːrd]	n. 最高领主 (a lord over other lords) 记 词根记忆：over(超过) + lord(领主) → 领主上面的领主 → 最高领主 例 In the 18th century, Japan's feudal *overlords* found themselves under financial stress.
overpayment [ˌoʊvərˈpeɪmənt]	n. 多付的款额 (the overpaid fund) 例 The investigators were unable to determine the extent of possible earlier *overpayments*.
overrun [ˌoʊvəˈrʌn]	n. 泛滥，超出限度 (an exceeding of the costs estimated in a contract for development and manufacture of new equipment) 记 来自词组 run over(泛滥) 例 Overstocks may accumulate through production *overruns* or errors.
overstock [ˌoʊvərˈstɑːk]	v./n. 库存过剩 (to stock more than necessary or desirable) 例 The distributors' ordering more goods in the summer quarter left them *overstocked* for the fall quarter.
oversupply [ˌoʊvərsəˈplaɪ]	v. 过多供给 (to supply with an excess of)；n. 供给过多 (the quality of being so overabundant that prices fall) 记 分拆记忆：over(过多) + supply(供应) → 过多供给 例 An *oversupply* of computer chips has sent prices plunging. 同根词：supplier(n. 供应商；供应者)

26

overt

[oʊˈvɜːrt]

a. 公开的，非秘密的（open）

记 词根记忆：o(出) + vert(转) → 转出来 → 公开的

例 Economies of nonsocialist countries employ intentional price-fixing(价格限定), usually in an *overt* fashion.

overview

[ˈoʊvərvjuː]

n. 概观，概述（summary）

例 Methods widely used today include analysis of aerial images that yield a broad geological *overview*.

overwhelm

[ˌoʊvərˈwelm]

v. 淹没（to submerge）；压倒（to overcome by superior force or numbers）；(使)不知所措（to affect deeply in mind or emotion）

记 词根记忆：over(在…上) + whelm(淹没，压倒) → 淹没；压倒

例 People are *overwhelmed* by the increasing amount of information available on the computer. // The horrible scene of the film *overwhelmed* the audience.

派 overwhelming(*a.* 势不可挡的)

overwhelming

[ˌoʊvərˈwelmɪŋ]

a. 压倒性的（very great or very strong）；势不可挡的（so powerful that you cannot resist it or decide how to react）

记 词根记忆：over(胜过) + whelm(淹没，覆盖) + ing → 压倒性的

例 The *overwhelming* majority were quite satisfied with them.

派 overwhelmingly(*ad.* 压倒性地；势不可挡地)

同根词：overwhelm(*v.* 压倒；淹没)

ovulate

[ˈɑːvjuleɪt]

v. 排卵，产卵（to produce ova; discharge eggs from the ovary）

例 Some adult female mole rats neither *ovulate* nor breed.

oxidize

[ˈɑːksɪdaɪz]

v. 氧化，生锈（to unite with oxygen in burning or rusting）

记 词根记忆：oxid(氧化物) + ize → 氧化

例 He found that when the iron in ilmenites is highly *oxidized*, conditions in the magma were probably conducive to the formation of diamonds.

派 oxidizable(*a.* 可氧化的)

ozone

[ˈoʊzoʊn]

n. 臭氧

记 联想记忆：o(氧的化学符号) + zone(地带) → 氧气地带 → 臭氧

例 *ozone* layer 臭氧层

pacemaker

[ˈpeɪsmeɪkər]

n. 领跑者（a leader in a field）

记 分拆记忆：pace(速度) + maker(制造者) → 领跑者

例 Commuter diatoms have an internal *pacemaker* to keep time with the tide.

pact

[pækt]

n. 合同，条约（compact）

例 The warring countries signed a *pact* to end the war.

pad

[pæd]

n. 便笺本（tablet）；衬垫（a thin flat mat or cushion）；*v.* 填补（to expand or increase especially with needless, misleading, or fraudulent matter）

例 writing *pads* 便笺纸

pagination

[ˌpædʒɪˈneɪʃn]

n. 编页码，标注页码（the system by which pages are numbered）

记 词根记忆：pag(页) + ination → 标注页码

例 The technical term "*pagination*" is a process that leaves editors assemble the page images.

painstaking ['peɪnzteɪkɪŋ]	*a.* 辛勤的；费力的(taking pains) 记 词根记忆：pains(劳苦) + taking(接受) → 辛勤的 例 This intuition is not arbitrary or irrational, but is based on years of *painstaking* practice. 派 painstakingly(*ad.* 煞费苦心地)
palatable ['pælətəbl]	*a.* 美味的(tasty)；受欢迎的(agreeable to the mind) 记 来自 palate(*n.* 味觉) 例 His words might prove *palatable* to his audience. 派 palatability(*n.* 美味，口感)
paleoclimatologist [ˌpeɪliəuˌklaɪmə'tɒlədʒɪst]	*n.* 古气候学家(a scientist dealing with the climate of past ages) 例 During the last ice age, cooler weather led to lower·lake levels than *paleoclimatologists* had previously assumed. 同根词：paleontologist(*n.* 古生物学家)
paleolithic [ˌpeɪliə'lɪθɪk]	*a.* 旧石器时代的(of or relating to the earliest period of the Stone Age) 记 联想记忆：paleo(古) + lith(石头) + ic → 生产石制工具的时代 → 旧石器时代的 例 upper *Paleolithic* 旧石器时代晚期
paleontologist [ˌpeɪliɑːn'tɑːlədʒɪst]	*n.* 古生物学家(a specialist in paleontology) 记 来自 paleontology(*n.* 古生物学) 例 The first introduces the hypothesis proposed by the *paleontologist*.
paleozoologist [ˌpeɪliəuzəu'ɒlədʒɪst]	*n.* 古动物学家(people who are specialized in paleozoology) 记 词根记忆：paleo(古) + zoo(动物) + logist(学家) → 古动物学家 例 By analyzing the advanced olfactory apparatus of Pleistocene chordates, *paleozoologists* have discovered a link between the brain's regions of scent discrimination and its regions of long-term memory storage, a link that could prove invaluable in the treatment of amnesia victims.
pall [pɔːl]	*n.* 幕，遮盖物(covering) 例 a *pall* of dust 尘雾
pallid ['pælɪd]	*a.* 苍白的，没血色的(pale)；无生气的(lacking liveliness) 记 词根记忆：pall(=pale 苍白) + id → 苍白的，没血色的 例 a *pallid* countenance 脸色苍白
palm [pɑːm]	*n.* 棕榈(树/叶)；手掌 例 In Asia, where *palm* trees are non-native, the trees' flowers have traditionally been pollinated by hand.
paltry ['pɔːltri]	*a.* 无价值的，微不足道的(insignificant, trifling) 记 联想记忆：pal(看作 pale 苍白的) + try(努力) → 白努力 → 无价值的 例 Only *paltry* sums are available for excavating in archaeology.
pamphlet ['pæmflət]	*n.* 小册子(brochure) 记 来自拉丁文 pamphilus，是一首爱情名诗；pam(=pan 全部) + phil(爱) + us → 表达爱情(的小册子) → 小册子 例 A town's public health officials sent a *pamphlet* about mouth cancer to all town residents.

26

□ painstaking　□ palatable　　□ paleoclimatologist　□ paleolithic　　□ paleontologist　□ paleozoologist
□ pall　　　　□ pallid　　　□ palm　　　　　□ paltry　　　□ pamphlet

235

panacea [ˌpænəˈsiːə]	*n.* 灵丹妙药（cure-all） 记 词根记忆：pan（全部）+ acea（治疗）→ 全都能治疗的 → 灵丹妙药 例 In recent years proposed *panaceas* and new programs have proliferated at a feverish pace.
panel [ˈpænl]	*n.* 专门小组（a group of persons selected for some service） 例 A *panel* of experts discussed the epidemic on the news program.
pang [pæŋ]	*n.* 阵痛（a brief piercing spasm of pain）；极度悲痛（a sharp attack of mental anguish） 记 联想记忆：重击（bang）一下就造成了阵痛（pang）；pang 更常指精神、情感上的痛苦 例 In psychology, a psychopath（精神病患者）is someone who is apparently incapable of the *pangs* of conscience.
pant [pænt]	*v./n.* 喘，气喘，喘息（to breathe quickly; gasp） 记 注意：pants（*n.* 裤子） 例 These rats stay in burrows during the hot part of the day, thus avoiding loss of fluid through *panting* or sweating.
pantheon [ˈpænθiɑːn]	*n.* 万神殿（a circular temple in Rome, completed in 27 B.C. and dedicated to all the gods）；伟人祠（a public building commemorating and dedicated to the heroes and heroines of a nation） 记 词根记忆：pan（全部）+ the（神）+ on → 众神之地 → 万神殿 例 Nightingale's place in the national *pantheon* is largely due to the propagandistic efforts of contemporary newspaper reporters. 同根词：theology（*n.* 神学）
par [pɑːr]	*n.* 同等（equality） 记 和 per（*prep.* 每，每一）一起记 例 on a *par* 同等
paradigm [ˈpærədaɪm]	*n.* 范例，示范（pattern, example） 记 词根记忆：para（旁边）+ digm（显示）→ 显示给旁边看 → 示范 例 This episode may serve as a *paradigm* of industry's problems. 派 paradigmatic（*a.* 作为示范的，典范的）
paradox [ˈpærədɑːks]	*n.* 似非而是的说法（a statement that is seemingly opposed to common sense and yet is perhaps true）；自相矛盾的人（或事物） 记 词根记忆：para（类似）+ dox（观点）→ 与两边的观点都类似 → 自相矛盾的人（或事物） 例 "More haste, less speed" is a *paradox*. 派 paradoxical（*a.* 似非而是的） 同根词：orthodox（*a.* 正统的）；heterodox（*a.* 异端的）

parallel ['pærəlel]	*a.* 平行的(being an equal distance apart everywhere); 类似的(similar); *n.* 类似, 相似处(similarity) 记 词根记忆: para(旁) + allel(另一个) → 总在另一个旁边 → 平行的 例 They make *parallel* investments in internal and external projects. // The fight for civil rights in the United States had many strong *parallels* in both Mexican and Irish history. 同根词: parallelogram(*n.* 平行四边形)
paralysis [pə'ræləsɪs]	*n.* 瘫痪(loss or impairment of the ability to move a body part, usually as a result of damage to its nerve supply); 麻痹(loss of sensation over a region of the body) 记 来自 paralyse(*v.* 使麻痹) 例 Polio infection can cause *paralysis*. 派 paralytic(*a.* 瘫痪的; 麻痹的)
paramount ['pærəmaʊnt]	*a.* 最重要的, 决定性的(superior to all others) 记 词根记忆: para(超过) + mount(登上) → 登上并超过 → 最重要的, 决定性的 例 Cutting waste was a *paramount* goal in the senator's tax plan.
parasite ['pærəsaɪt]	*n.* 寄生虫(vermin); 食客(dependant) 记 词根记忆: para(旁边) + site(食物) → 在…旁边攫取食物 → 寄生虫 例 Cell-mediated immunity accounts for the destruction of intracellular *parasites*. 派 parasitic(*a.* 寄生的); parasitize(*v.* 寄生于)
parasitic [ˌpærə'sɪtɪk]	*a.* 寄生的(relating to or caused by parasites) 记 来自 parasite(*n.* 寄生虫) 例 *Parasitic* wasps use visual clues to calculate the size of a host egg.
parish ['pærɪʃ]	*n.* 教区(an administrative part of a diocese that has its own church in the Anglican, Roman Catholic, and some other churches); 教区全体居民(the members of such a parish; a religious community attending one church) 记 和 perish(*v.* 死亡)一起记 例 *parish* church 教区教堂
parity ['pærəti]	*n.* 同等, 相等(equality, equivalent) 记 词根记忆: par(相等) + ity → 相等 例 Our service needed to be improved to attain *parity* with the service provided by competing banks. 派 disparity(*n.* 不平等, 不相等)

26

237

Word List 27

parliament [ˈpɑːrləmənt]	*n.* 国会，议会(congress) 记 联想记忆: parl(说话) + ia + ment → 谈论政务的地方 → 国会，议会 例 The *parliament* passed all of the pending legislations. 派 parliamentary(*a.* 国会的) 同根词: parlour(*n.* 起居室); parley(*n.* 谈判); parlance(*n.* 说法)
parlor [ˈpɑːrlər]	*n.* 会客室(reception room); 店堂(a room equipped and furnished for a special function or business); (火车)餐车(dining car) 记 联想记忆: parl(讲话) + our(我们的) → 我们经常会客讲话的地方 → 会客室 例 ice cream *parlor* 冰淇淋屋
parole [pəˈroʊl]	*n.* 假释(a conditional release of a prisoner serving an indeterminate or unexpired sentence) 例 *Parole* violations have become significantly less frequent in recent years.
partial [ˈpɑːrʃl]	*a.* 部分的(sectional); 偏向的(biased) 记 词根记忆: part(部分) + ial → 部分的 例 I gave only a *partial* answer to the question. 派 partially(*ad.* 部分地; 偏向地) 同根词: impartial(*a.* 公平的，不偏不倚的)
participate [pɑːrˈtɪsɪpeɪt]	*v.* 分担(to possess some of the attributes of a person, thing, or quality); 参与(to take part); 分享(to have a part or share in sth.) 记 联想记忆: parti(看作 party 晚会) + cip(抓，拿) + ate(做) → 找人参加派对 → 参与 例 The structure of their jobs makes it difficult for these women to *participate* in exchange networks. 派 participation(*n.* 参与; 分享) 同根词: partner(*n.* 伙伴)

participation [pɑːrˌtɪsɪˈpeɪʃn]	*n.* 参加(the act of participating)；参与(the state of being related to a larger whole) 记 来自 participate(*v.* 参与；分享) 例 The cult of female domesticity was incompatible with women's *participation* in social activism. 同根词：partner(*n.* 合作伙伴)
participatory [pɑːrˈtɪsəpətɔːri]	*a.* 参与的(marked by, requiring, or involving participation, especially affording the opportunity for individual participation) 例 Civic education in the schools made little attempt to develop *participatory* political skills.
particle [ˈpɑːrtɪkl]	*n.* 极少量(a minute quantity)；微粒(atom) 记 联想记忆：part(部分) + icle → 物品的一部分 → 极少量 例 A meteor stream is composed of dust *particles*.
particular [pərˈtɪkjələr]	*n.* [*pl.*]详情，细节(detail)；*a.* 特殊的，特别的(special) 记 particular 和 particle(微粒)同词源，所以做名词用时可指细节 例 My boss stressed the important *particulars* of the project. // a *particular* historical period
particulate [pɑːrˈtɪkjələt]	*n.* 微粒，粒子(particle)；*a.* 微粒的(atomic) 例 *particulate* matter 颗粒物
partisan [ˈpɑːrtəzn]	*a.* 有(政治)偏见的(devoted to or biased in support of a party, group, or cause) 记 词根记忆：parti(=分开党) + san → 有分歧的 → 有(政治)偏见的 例 Her *partisan* speech angered the opposing party. 派 nonpartisan(*a.* 无党派的)
partridge [ˈpɑːrtrɪdʒ]	*n.* 鹧鸪；松鸡 例 The elimination of certain weeds from cereal crop fields has reduced the population of the small insects that live on those weeds and that form a major part of *partridge* chicks' diet.
passbook [ˈpæsbʊk]	*n.* 存折(bankbook) 例 They are abandoning traditional low-interest investment havens such as *passbook* accounts and life insurance policies.
passive [ˈpæsɪv]	*a.* 被动的，消极的(not active) 例 *passive* defence 消极防御 派 passivity(*n.* 被动性)
pastoral [ˈpæstərəl]	*a.* 乡村的，农村的(of or relating to the countryside)；*n.* 牧歌；田园诗(a literary work (as a poem or play) dealing with shepherds or rural life) 记 来自 pastor(*n.* 牧人) 例 *pastoral* community 乡村社区 派 pastoralist(*n.* 放牧者)
pasture [ˈpæstʃər]	*n.* 牧场，牧草(meadow, grassland) 记 联想记忆：pas(看作 pass 通过) + ture → 牛羊通过的地方 → 牧场 例 The farmer's *pasture* was enclosed by a wooden fence.

27

patch [pætʃ]	*v.* 缝补；修补(to repair, to mend)；*n.* 斑点(spot) 记 联想记忆：及时发觉(catch)漏洞，及时补上(patch) 例 The tailor *patched* my shirt with a matching piece of cloth. 派 patchy(*a.* 有斑或块的；不均匀的)
patent ['pætnt]	*n.* 专利权(证书)(capital asserts)；*v.* 取得…的专利(to obtain a patent on or for) 例 The new life-sustaining drug has not been *patented* yet.
paternalism [pə'tɜːrnəlɪzəm]	*n.* 家长式统治；家长主义(a policy or practice of treating or governing people in a fatherly manner especially by providing for their needs without giving them rights or responsibilities) 记 来自 paternal(*a.* 父亲的) 例 These men's *paternalism* toward African Americans was racist. 同根词：patriarchal(*a.* 家长的，族长的)
paternity [pə'tɜːrnəti]	*n.* 父权(the quality or state of being a father)；父系，父系后裔(origin or descent from a father) 记 词根记忆：pater(父亲) + nity → 父权；父系 例 Most European countries offer a variety of programs to assist working parents, including paid maternity and *paternity* leaves, financial allowances for families with children, and subsidized public nurseries and kindergartens. 同根词：paternal(*a.* 父亲的；父亲般的)
pathogenic ['pæθə'dʒenɪk]	*a.* 【医】病原的，致病的(causing or capable of causing disease) 记 词根记忆：path(病) + gen(产生) + ic → 能致病的 → 病原的 同根词：pathology(*n.* 病理学)
patriarchal [ˌpeɪtri'ɑːrkl]	*a.* 家长的，族长的(of, relating to, or being a patriarch or patriarchy) 记 词根记忆：patri(父亲) + arch(统治者) + al(…的) → 父亲统治 → 家长的 例 They felt their status as working women gave them a certain degree of independence from the *patriarchal* family. 同根词：patriarchy(*n.* 父权制；家长统治)
patriotic [ˌpeɪtri'ɑːtɪk]	*a.* 爱国的，有爱国心的(feeling expressing, or inspired by love for one's country) 例 The principal ingredients of a civic education were literacy and the inculcation of *patriotic* and moral virtues. 同根词：patriotism(*n.* 爱国主义，爱国心)
patriotism ['peɪtriətɪzəm]	*n.* 爱国主义，爱国心(love for or devotion to one's country) 例 The nation's three military academies have seen a dramatic rise in applications, fueled by a resurgence of *patriotism*, increasing tuition costs at private colleges, and improved recruiting by the academies. 同根词：patriotic(*a.* 爱国的)

□ patch □ patent □ paternalism □ paternity □ pathogenic □ patriarchal
□ patriotic □ patriotism

patrol [pə'troul]	*v./n.* 巡逻，巡查（to go the rounds） 记 和 petrol（*n.* 汽油）一起记 例 There is a large contingent of armed guards *patrolling* the country's borders.
patron ['peɪtrən]	*n.* 赞助者（benefactor）；顾客（customer） 例 In general, restaurant *patrons* who pay their bills in cash leave larger tips than do those who pay by credit card. 派 patronage（*n.* 赞助；惠顾）；patronize（*v.* 资助）
payroll ['peɪroul]	*n.* 薪金名单；工资总额（a list of employees receiving wages or salaries, with the amounts due to each; the total sum of money to be paid out to employees at a given time） 记 分拆记忆：pay（支付）+ roll（名单）→ 薪金名单 例 They tried to reduce their *payroll* expenses and save money.
peak [pi:k]	*n.* 顶点；*a.* 最高的（being at or reaching the maximum）；*v.* 到达最高点（to achieve a maximum of development, value or intensity） 记 peak 作为"山峰"一意大家都熟悉 例 *peak* profits 最大利润 // After increasing steadily for centuries, the total annual catch of all wild fish *peaked* in 1989.
peat [pi:t]	*n.* 泥煤（partially carbonized vegetable tissue formed by partial decomposition in water of various plants） 例 The Scottish Highlands were once the site of extensive forests, but these forests have mostly disappeared and been replaced by *peat* bogs. 派 peaty（*a.* 多泥煤的；泥煤似的）
peculiar [pɪ'kju:liər]	*a.* 独特的，特殊的（distinctive, characteristic） 例 The report described the *peculiar* economic features of the health-care industry.
pecuniary [pɪ'kju:nieri]	*a.* 金钱上的，金钱的（of/or relating to money） 记 词根记忆：pecuni（钱财）+ ary → 金钱的 例 *pecuniary* penalty 罚金
pedal ['pedl]	*n.* 踏板，脚蹬（a flat bar on a machine such as a bicycle, car, etc. that you push down with your foot to make parts of the machine move or work）；*v.* 骑脚踏车（to ride a bicycle） 记 词根记忆：ped（脚）+ al（东西）→ 脚蹬 例 A New York City ordinance of 1897 regulated the use of bicycles, requiring cyclists to keep feet on *pedals* and hands on handlebars at all times. 同根词：biped（*n.* 两足动物；*a.* 有两足的）
peddle ['pedl]	*v.* 兜售，叫卖（to sell or offer for sale from place to place） 记 词根记忆：ped（脚）+ dle → 行走在大街上叫卖 → 兜售 例 Someone on the street corner was *peddling* neckties and watches.
pedestrian [pə'destriən]	*n.* 行人（walker） 记 词根记忆：ped（脚）+ estrian → 用脚走的，徒步的 → 行人 例 *pedestrian* overpass 人行天桥

peel [piːl]	*v.* 削…的皮(to strip or cut away the skin, rind, or bark from); *n.* (水果等的)皮(the skin or rind of certain fruits and vegetables) 记 发音记忆: "皮儿" → 脱皮 例 *Peeled* potatoes in cans are more expensive than the less convenient fresh potatoes.
peer [pɪr]	*n.* 同等之人，同辈(one that is of equal standing with another); *v.* 凝视(to look narrowly or curiously) 例 Primary institutions comprising the support network include kinship *peer*, and neighborhood or community subgroups.
pelvis [ˈpelvɪs]	*n.* 骨盆(a basin-shaped structure of the vertebrate skeleton) 记 词根记忆: pell(容器) + vis → 骨盆 例 A wide, shallow *pelvis* is actually better suited to bipedal walking than is the rounder, bowl-like pelvis.
penalty [ˈpenəlti]	*n.* 处罚(punishment); 罚款(fine, forfeit) 记 来自 penal(*a.* 刑罚的，惩罚的) 例 Corporations are not subject to statutory *penalty* for failing to include women on their boards.
penetrate [ˈpenətreɪt]	*v.* 穿透，渗透(to pierce) 记 词根记忆: pen(全部) + etr(=enter 进入) + ate → 全部进入 → 穿透，渗透 例 The fumes *penetrated* the walls of the room.
peninsula [pəˈnɪnsələ]	*n.* 半岛(byland) 记 联想记忆: pen(几乎) + insula(小岛) → 几乎是个小岛 → 半岛 例 the Italian *peninsula*
pension [ˈpenʃn]	*n.* 养老金，退休金(retirement pay) 记 词根记忆: pens(挂，引申为钱) + ion → 养老金 例 They rely entirely on the government *pension* for their income.
per capita [pər ˈkæpɪtə]	*a.* 每人，照人数分配的(per unit of population; per person) 例 *Per capita* consumption of fish in Jurania was lower in 1989 than in 1980.
perceive [pərˈsiːv]	*v.* 察觉，发觉(to become aware of sth. through the senses) 记 联想记忆: per(全部) + ceive(拿住) → 察觉得早，才能全部拿住 → 察觉，发觉 注意: deceive(*v.* 欺骗，行骗) 例 I *perceived* a slight cinnamon taste in the coffee. 派 perception(*n.* 察觉，发觉) 同根词: conceive(*v.* 设计，想象)
perceptibly [pərˈseptəbli]	*ad.* 可察觉地，可辨地(sensibly, tangibly) 例 When the bottles are viewed side by side, this bottle is *perceptibly* taller than that one. 派 perceptive(*a.* 有感知的，有理解力的)

perception [pər'sepʃn]	*n.*感觉；洞察力（quick, acute, and intuitive cognition） 记 来自 percept(*v.* 感知，认识） 例 Evidence that pheromone responses may not involve conscious odor *perception* comes from the finding. 同根词：perceptive(*a.* 感知的)
perennial [pə'reniəl]	*a.*长期的（perpetual）；*n.*多年生植物（perennial plant） 记 词根记忆：per + enn(年) + ial → 一年到头的 → 长期的 例 *perennial* problem // The root systems of most flowering *perennials* always become too crowded. 派 perennially(*ad.* 长期地)
performance [pər'fɔːrməns]	*n.*性能（the manner in which a mechanism performs）；表演（the action of representing a character in a play）；成绩，绩效（sth. accomplished） 记 来自 perform(*v.* 执行；表演) 例 Such legislation would duplicate initiatives already being made by corporate boards to improve their own *performance*.
perfunctory [pər'fʌŋktəri]	*a.*草率的；敷衍的（lacking in care, interest or enthusiasm） 记 词根记忆：per(表面) + funct(做) + ory → 做表面功夫 → 敷衍的 例 Victorian criticism of works by women writers was *perfunctory*.
perimeter [pə'rɪmɪtər]	*n.*周长（the length of the outer edge of a closed geometric shape） 记 词根记忆：peri(周围) + meter(测量) → 周长 例 The *perimeter* of the rectangular garden is 360 feet.
periodic [ˌpɪri'ɑːdɪk]	*a.*周期的，定期的（occurring or recurring at regular intervals） 记 来自 period(*n.* 周期) 例 They still display *periodic* behavior, continuing to burrow on schedule for several weeks. 派 periodically(*ad.* 定期地；周期性地) 同根词：aperiodic(*a.* 不定期的；非周期性的)
periodical [ˌpɪri'ɑːdɪkl]	*a.*周期的，定期的（periodic）；期刊的（published in, characteristic of, or connected with a periodical）；*n.*期刊（a periodical publication） 例 The total of the expenditure for *periodicals* and newspapers was 25 percent less than the expenditure for books. 派 periodically(*ad.* 周期性地)
periphery [pə'rɪfəri]	*n.*外围（the outward bounds of something as distinguished from its internal regions or center） 记 词根记忆：peri(周围) + pher + y → 带到周围 → 外围 例 Most of the offices and classrooms were in the center of the college campus, and the dormitories were on the *periphery*. 派 peripheral(*a.* 外围的)

27

perishable

['perɪʃəbl]

a. 易腐败的 (likely to decay or go bad quickly); *n.* 易腐败的东西 (stuff subject to decay)

记 来自 perish (*v.* 腐烂)

例 Cooking is usually the final step in preparing food for consumption, whereas irradiation serves to ensure a longer shelf life for *perishable* foods.

派 perishability (*n.* 非持久性；易腐性)

同根词: perisher (*n.* 讨厌的人；死亡之物)

permanent

['pɜːrmənənt]

a. 永久的 (lasting)；固定的 (stable)

记 联想记忆: per (贯穿) + man (人类) + ent (…的) → 贯穿人类历史 → 永久的

例 The Issei (第一代移居北美的日本人) formed a *permanent*, family-based community.

派 permanently (*ad.* 永久地，固定地)

permeate

['pɜːrmieɪt]

v. 扩散 (to spread or diffuse through)；渗透 (to penetrate)

记 词根记忆: per (全部) + mea (通过) + te → 全通过 → 渗透

例 Neutrinos (微中子) are another form of radiation that *permeates* the universe.

permissive

[pər'mɪsɪv]

a. 许可的 (granting or inclined to grant permission；tolerant or lenient)；过分纵容的 (indulgent)

记 来自 permit (*v.* 许可，允许)

例 *permissive* terms 许可条款

派 permissively (*ad.* 许可地；自由地)

同根词: submissive (*a.* 顺从的)

permit

[pər'mɪt] *v.* 允许，许可 (to allow)

['pɜːrmɪt] *n.* 通行证，许可证 (a written warrant or license granted by one having authority)

记 词根记忆: per (全部) + mit (送，放出) → 全部放出 → 通行证

例 Personality development is hindered if a person is not *permitted* to be independent.

派 permission (*n.* 许可，允许)

pernicious

[pər'nɪʃəs]

a. 有害的 (highly injurious)；致命的 (deadly)

记 词根记忆: per (全部) + nic (毒) + ious → 有毒的 → 有害的；致命的

例 The sustained massive use of pesticides in farming has two side effects that are especially *pernicious*.

perpendicular

[ˌpɜːrpən'dɪkjələr]

a. 垂直的 (vertical, exactly upright)；*n.* 垂线 (a line at right angles to a line or plane)

记 词根记忆: per (自始至终) + pend (挂) + icular → 自始至终挂着 → 垂直的

例 A ladder 25 feet long is leaning against a wall that is *perpendicular* to level ground.

perpetrator	*n.* 作恶者(a person who does sth. considered outrageous); 犯罪者
[ˈpɜːrpətreɪtər]	(criminal)
	记 来自 perpetrate(*v.* 犯罪)
	例 The *perpetrators* are in effect told that they are not responsible for their actions.
	同根词: petrify(*v.* 石化, 僵化)
perpetuate	*v.* 延长…的存在, 使永记不忘(to cause to last indefinitely)
[pərˈpetʃueɪt]	记 词根记忆: per(自始至终) + pet(追求) + uate → 永远追求 → 永记不忘
	例 The myth is *perpetuated* by the compensation consulting industry.
perplex	*v.* 使(某人)困惑(to puzzle); (使)复杂化(to make intricate)
[pərˈpleks]	记 词根记忆: per(全部) + plex(重叠) → 全部重叠在一起 → 困惑
	例 The difficult math problem *perplexed* the students.
	派 perplexed(*a.* 困惑的)
persecute	*v.* 迫害(to oppress cruelly)
[ˈpɜːrsɪkjuːt]	记 词根记忆: per(始终) + secu(跟随) + te → 从头到尾跟随 → 迫害
	例 The two parties disprove the theory of the other, but unite in *persecuting* the dissenters.
persist	*v.* (in)坚持(to insist); 继续(to continue)
[pərˈsɪst]	记 词根记忆: per(始终) + sist(站立) → 始终站立 → 坚持; 继续
	例 He *persists* in riding that dreadful bicycle. // These effects may *persist* for three generations.
	派 persistence(*n.* 坚持不懈); persistent(*a.* 坚持不懈的)
personality	*n.* 个性, 品格(the quality or state of being a person); 名人(a person of importance, prominence, renown, or notoriety)
[ˌpɜːrsəˈnæləti]	记 来自 personal(*a.* 个人的, 私人的)
	例 It can assess more than 300 *personality* traits, including enthusiasm, imagination, and ambition.
	同根词: intrapersonal(*a.* 内心的)
personhood	*n.* 做人; 人格
[ˈpɜːrsənˌhʊd]	记 词根记忆: person(人) + hood → 人格
	例 In order to bolster her thesis, the historian adopted the anthropological perspective on *personhood*.
	同根词: personality(*n.* 个性; 品格)
personnel	*n.* 全体人员(a body of persons usually employed); 人事部门(a division of an organization concerned with personnel)
[ˌpɜːrsəˈnel]	记 词根记忆: person(人) + nel → 全体人员
	例 The company's *personnel* director surveyed employees about their satisfaction with the company's system.
perspective	*n.* (看待事物的)角度, 观点(point of view)
[pərˈspektɪv]	记 词根记忆: per(贯穿) + spect(看) + ive → 贯穿看, 透视法 → 角度, 观点
	例 The narrowness of this *perspective* ignores the pervasive recessions and joblessness.

27

□ perpetrator　　□ perpetuate　　□ perplex　　□ persecute　　□ persist　　□ personality
□ personhood　　□ personnel　　□ perspective

persuade [pərˈsweɪd]	*v.* 说服，劝说（to move by argument, entreaty, or expostulation to a belief, position, or course of action） 例 Major local efforts have been done to *persuade* the public to use public transportation for the past thirty years. 派 persuasion（*n.* 说服，说服力）
pertinent [ˈpɜːrtɪnənt]	*a.* 相关的（relevant） 记 词根记忆：per（始终）+ tin（拿住）+ ent → 始终拿住 → 相关的 例 *pertinent* evidence 相关证据
perturb [pərˈtɜːrb]	*v.* 打扰（to disturb）；【天】摄动（引起天体轨道变化） 记 词根记忆：per + turb（扰乱）→ 打扰 注意：disturb（*n.* 打扰） 例 Lisa was quite *perturbed* by Tom's strange behavior. // The dust particles' individual orbits are *perturbed* by planetary gravitational fields. 派 perturbation（*n.* 扰乱；摄动）
pervasive [pərˈveɪsɪv]	*a.* 普遍的，流行的（spreading throughout every part of） 记 来自 pervade（*v.* 遍及） 例 The ideology of eighteenth-century America was *pervasive* among farmers in early America.
perversion [pərˈvɜːrʒn]	*n.* 曲解，颠倒（the action of perverting） 记 词根记忆：per（始终）+ vers（转）+ ion → 始终转过去 → 颠倒 例 This movie is a *perversion* of the author's book. 同根词：reverse（*v.* 颠倒，倒退）
pesticide [ˈpestɪsaɪd]	*n.* 杀虫剂（an agent used to destroy pests） 记 词根记忆：pest（害虫）+ i + cide（杀）→ 杀害虫的东西 → 杀虫剂 例 chemical *pesticide* 化学杀虫剂
petition [pəˈtɪʃn]	*n.* 请愿（entreaty）；请愿书（a formal written request） 记 词根记忆：pet（寻求）+ ition → 寻求（帮助）→ 请愿 例 Do you want to sign a *petition* for statewide smoking restriction?
petroleum [pəˈtroʊliəm]	*n.* 石油（mineral oil occurring in many places in the upper strata of the earth which is prepared for use as gasoline naphtha, or other products by various refining processes） 记 词根记忆：petro（石）+ leum → 石油 例 The *petroleum* company has recently determined that it could cut its refining costs.
pharmaceutical [ˌfɑːrməˈsuːtɪkl]	*a.* 制药的（of the manufacture and sale of medicines） 记 来自 pharmacy（*n.* 药房；药剂学） 例 No industries other than the *pharmaceutical* industry have asked for an extension of the 20-year limit on patent protection. 同根词：pharmaceutics（*n.* 制药学）

246
□ persuade   □ pertinent   □ perturb   □ pervasive   ■ perversion   □ pesticide
□ petition   □ petroleum   □ pharmaceutical

音频

pharmacy [ˈfɑːrməsi]	*n.* 药房（drugstore）；药剂学 记 来自 pharma（*n.* 药，毒） 例 Our total sales have increased this year by 20 percent since we added a *pharmacy* section to our grocery store. 派 pharmaceutical（*a.* 药学的，药用的）；pharmacologist（*n.* 药理学家）
phase [feɪz]	*n.* 阶段（a distinguishable part in a course, development or cycle） 记 月亮的"月相"（新月，上弦，满月，下弦）也叫 phase 注意 phrase（*n.* 短语） 例 Pesticide sprayings were timed to coincide with various *phases* of the life cycles of the insects they destroyed.
phenomenon [fəˈnɑːmɪnən]	*n.* 现象（an observable fact or event）；奇迹（a rare or significant fact or event） 记 词根记忆：phen（=phan 出现）+ omenon → 现象 例 Two divergent views of a scientific *phenomenon* are reconciled. 派 phenomenal（*a.* 现象的；显著的）
philanthropic [ˌfɪlənˈθrɑːpɪk]	*a.* 慈善的，乐善好施的（benevolent） 记 词根记忆：phil（爱）+ anthrop（人）+ ic → 爱人的 → 慈善的 例 *Philanthropic* donations have provided some support for the hospitals.
philosophy [fəˈlɑːsəfi]	*n.* 哲学（search for knowledge and understanding of the nature and meaning of the universe and of human life）；哲理，见解（the most basic beliefs, concepts, and attitudes of an individual or group） 记 词根记忆：philo（爱）+ soph（智慧）+ y → 爱智慧 → 哲学 例 In most fields, the prevailing *philosophy* never stays in place very long.
photon [ˈfoʊtɑːn]	*n.* 光子，光量子（a quantum of electromagnetic radiation） 记 词根记忆：photo（照片；光）+ n → 光子 例 Virtually all astronomers rely on the detection of *photons* to know about objects outside the solar system. 同根词 photoperiod（*n.* 光周期）
photosynthesis [ˌfoʊtoʊˈsɪnθəsɪs]	*n.* 光合作用（process by which green plants convert carbon dioxide and water into food using the energy in sunlight） 记 词根记忆：photo（光）+ synthesis（综合）→ 光合作用 例 Symbiotic cells of algae carry out *photosynthesis*. 同根词 photics（*n.* 光学）

☐ pharmacy ☐ phase ☐ phenomenon ☐ philanthropic ☐ philosophy ☐ photon
☐ photosynthesis

physiological [ˌfɪziə'lɑːdʒɪkl]	*a.* 生理的(of, or concerning the bodily functions); 生理学上的(of, or concerning physiology) 记 来自 physiology(*n.* 生理学) 例 Taken in large quantities, these substances could have serious health effects, but they are present in quantities far too low to cause any *physiological* response in people who drink the water or bathe in it. 派 physiologically(*ad.* 生理学方面) 同根词: physiologist(*n.* 生理学家)
physiology [ˌfɪzi'ɑːlədʒi]	*n.* 生理学(a branch of biology that deals with the functions and activities of life or of living matter and of the physical and chemical phenomena involved); 生理机能(the organic processes and phenomena of an organism or any of its parts or of a particular bodily process) 记 词根记忆: physio(生理的) + logy(学科) → 生理学 例 Eusocial(完全群居的)insects' roles are defined by their behavior, body shape, and *physiology*. 派 physiological(*a.* 生理学的; 生理的)
pigment ['pɪgmənt]	*n.* 天然色素(a coloring matter in animals and plants especially in a cell or tissue); 干粉颜料(a powdered substance that is mixed with a liquid in which it is relatively insoluble and used especially to impart color to coating materials or to inks, plastics, and rubber) 例 natural *pigment* 天然色素
pinpoint ['pɪnpɔɪnt]	*n.* 针尖(the point of a pin); 极小之物(something that is extremely small or insignificant); *v.* 精确定位(to locate or aim with great precision or accuracy); 准确解释或确定(to fix, determine, or identify with precision) 记 联想记忆: pin(钉, 针) + point(点, 尖端) → 针尖 → 精确定位 例 The challenge in exploration is to *pinpoint* the position of buried minerals. // This kind of chemical could be used to *pinpoint* functions of other plant hormones.
pirate ['paɪrət]	*n.* 海盗; 盗版(one who commits or practices piracy); *v.* 盗版(to reproduce without authorization) 例 Stronger patent laws are needed to protect inventions from being *pirated*.
pivotal ['pɪvətl]	*a.* 中枢的(of, relating to, or constituting a pivot); 重要的(vitally important) 记 来自 pivot(*n.* 枢轴; 枢纽) 例 For global managers working with overseas clients, understanding cultural norms is at least as important as grasping the *pivotal* business issues.
placate ['pleɪkeɪt]	*v.* 安抚(to pacify) 记 词根记忆: plac(平静) + ate → 使平静 → 安抚 例 I *placated* the angry dog by throwing him some meat. 同根词: implacable(*a.* 难以平息的)

□ physiological □ physiology □ pigment □ pinpoint □ pirate □ pivotal
□ placate

plague [pleɪg]	*n.* 瘟疫(pestilence)；*v.* 使苦恼，烦扰(to disturb or annoy persistently) 记 词根记忆：plag(击，打) + ue → 能打倒人的 → 瘟疫 例 There was only one outbreak of *plague* in Florence in the 1100's. // Crime and violence *plagued* the nation's cities.
plaintiff ['pleɪntɪf]	*n.* 原告(a person who brings a legal action) 记 词根记忆：plaint(哀诉，抱怨) + iff → 哀诉的一方 → 原告 例 The judge is biased against women defendants or *plaintiffs* in cases that do not involve sex discrimination.
planetary ['plænəteri]	*a.* 行星的(of planet) 记 来自 planet(*n.* 行星) 例 The Copernican theory of *planetary* motion is inconsistent with the Ptolemaic account. 同根词：planetesimal(*a.* 小行星体的)
plankton ['plæŋktən]	*n.* 浮游生物(the passively floating or weakly swimming usually minute animal and plant life of a body of water) 记 联想记忆：plank(木板) + ton(很多) → 很多像木板似的生物漂浮在水面上 → 浮游生物 例 Nevertheless, some areas, though rich in these nitrogen compounds, have few *plankton*.
plantation [plæn'teɪʃn]	*n.* 栽植(a usually large group of plants and especially trees under cultivation) 记 来自 plant(*v.* 种植) 例 Newly freed workers enacted lien laws to hasten the downfall of the *plantation* economy. 同根词：plantlet(*n.* 小植物，苗木)
plateau [plæ'toʊ]	*n.* (上升后的)平台期(a level of attainment or achievement)；*v.* 达到平台期(to reach a level period, or condition of stability or maximum attainment) 记 词根记忆：plat(平) + eau → 平台期 例 When my sales hit a *plateau*, my boss gave me a pep talk(鼓舞士气的讲话). // Her fever *plateaued* at 103 degrees, and then began to fall.
platform ['plætfɔːrm]	*n.* 平台(a usually raised horizontal flat surface operating system) 记 词根记忆：plat(平的) + form(外形) → 平台 例 operating *platform* 操作平台
plausible ['plɔːzəbl]	*a.* 似是而非的，貌似有理的(superficially fair reasonable, or valuable but often specious) 记 联想记忆：plaus(鼓掌) + ible → 鼓掌的 → 看似有理，所以鼓掌 → 貌似有理的 例 Of the two *plausible* explanations for the decline in the population of sea otters, disease is the more likely one. 同根词：plaudit(*n.* 称赞)；applause(*n.* 鼓掌)
plead [pliːd]	*v.* 作为辩护或理由提出(to offer as a plea usually in defence) 例 The defendant *pled* no contest to criminal charges.

28

pledge [pledʒ]	*n./v.* 保证；许诺（to promise the performance of） 例 A $100 million investment in the search for extraterrestrial intelligence was *pledged* by the government.
plot [plɑːt]	*n.* 小块土地（a small land）；计划（plan）；情节（story） 例 experimental *plot* 实验田
plow/plough [plaʊ]	*n.* 犁（an implement used to cut, lift, and turn over soil especially in preparing a seedbed）；*v.* 费力穿过（to move through） 记 联想记忆：pl + ough（看作 tough 坚硬的）→ 在坚硬的土地上犁 → 犁；费力穿过 例 The ship *plowed* through the waves.
plume [pluːm]	*n.* （一）股，（一）团（尘、火、水等）（a cloud of sth. that rises and curves upwards in the air）；羽毛（a large feather）；（从火山或烟道喷出的）岩浆柱（any of several columns of molten rock rising from the earth's lower mantle） 例 The surface mark of an established *plume* is a hot spot—an isolated region of volcanoes and uplifted terrain located far from the edge of a surface plate.
plummet [ˈplʌmɪt]	*v.* （价格等）骤然下跌（to drop sharply and abruptly） 记 plummet 原意为"测深锤" 例 The value of the stock *plummeted*. 同根词：plumbing（*n.* 铅工业）
plunge [plʌndʒ]	*v.* 骤降（to descend suddenly）；跳进（to jump into） 例 The stock's value *plunged*. 派 plunging（*a.* 突进的）
plywood [ˈplaɪwʊd]	*n.* 胶合板（a structural material consisting of sheets of wood glued or cemented together with the grains of adjacent layers arranged at right angles or at a wide angle） 记 词根记忆：ply(重叠) + wood(木) → 重叠起来的木板 → 胶合板 例 Pressboard is an inexpensive new *plywood* substitute now often used in the construction of houses.
pneumonia [njuːˈmoʊniə]	*n.* 肺炎（serious illness with inflammation of one or both lungs, causing difficulty in breathing） 记 词根记忆：pneumon(肺) + ia(病) → 肺部的病 → 肺炎 例 A new study shows that toothbrushes can become contaminated with bacteria that cause *pneumonia*.
pneumonic [njuːˈmoʊnik]	*a.* 肺的（of, relating to, or affecting the lungs）；肺炎的（of, relating to, or affected with pneumonia） 例 In 1616–1619, *pneumonic* plague swept coastal New England, killing as many as nine out of ten.

poach [poutʃ]	*v.* 偷猎(to take game or hunt illegally)；水煮(to cook in simmering liquid) 例 Researchers have determined that, because of *poaching* and increased cultivation in their native habitats, there are fewer than 100 Arabian leopards left in the wild, and that these leopards are thus many times more rare than China's giant pandas. 派 poacher(*n.* 偷猎者)
poacher ['poutʃər]	*n.* 偷猎者(one who kills or takes wild animals illegally) 记 来自 poach(*v.* 偷猎) 例 The Wildlife Protection Committee plans to protect selected rhinoceroses (犀牛)from being killed by *poachers*.
polar ['poulər]	*a.* 地极的(of or relating to the South or North Pole) 例 *polar* regions 极地 派 polarize(*v.* 两极分化)
poll [poul]	*n.* 民意测验(survey of public opinion by putting questions to a representative selection of people) 例 Most of the respondents in a recent *poll* said they believed that the economy is likely to continue to improve.
pollen ['pɑ:lən]	*n.* 花粉(fine powder formed in flowers, which fertilizes other flowers when carried to them by the wind, insects, etc.) 例 Maize *pollen* is dispersed by the wind and frequently blows onto milkweed plants.
pollinate ['pɑ:ləneɪt]	*v.* 授粉，传粉(to make plants fertile with pollen) 记 词根记忆：pollin(花粉) + ate → 授粉 例 Their flowers are *pollinated* by birds. 派 pollination(*n.* 授粉)；pollinator(*n.* 传粉媒介，传粉昆虫)
pollutant [pə'lu:tənt]	*n.* 污染物(sth. that pollutes) 记 来自 pollute(*v.* 污染) 例 Nitrogen dioxide is a *pollutant* emitted by automobiles. 同根词：pollution(*n.* 污染)
polygraph ['pɑ:ligræf]	*n.* 测谎器(lie detector) 记 词根记忆：poly(多，众) + graph(写，记录) → 写得多的或从多方面记录的 → 测谎器 例 *polygraph* test 测谎
population [ˌpɑ:pju'leɪʃn]	*n.* 人口(the whole number of people or inhabitants in a country or region)；生物种群(the organisms inhabiting a particular locality) 记 词根记忆：popul(人，大众) + ation → 人口 例 Hunters alone are blamed for the decline in Greenrock National Forest's deer *population* over the past ten years. 同根词：popularity(*n.* 大众性；流行)
porcelain ['pɔ:rsəlɪn]	*n.* 瓷；瓷器(china) 记 发音记忆："跑四邻" → 卖瓷器需要跑四邻八方

28

porpoise
[ˈpɔːrpəs]

n. 海豚(dolphin)

例 Environmentalists advocate the use of acoustic alarms as a means of protecting the harbor *porpoise* population.

portfolio
[pɔːrtˈfouliou]

n. 文件夹(a hinged cover or flexible case for carrying loose papers, pictures, or pamphlets); 投资组合(如债券和股票)(the securities held by an investor)

例 Corporate officers and directors commonly buy and sell stocks in their own corporations for their own *portfolios*.

portrait
[ˈpɔːrtrət]

n. 肖像; 相片(picture, photo)

记 联想记忆: por + trait(特点, 特性) → 描绘某人的特点 → 肖像

例 Most *portrait* studios use more color film than black-and-white film.

portray
[pɔːrˈtreɪ]

v. 描写, 描绘(to describe in words)

记 联想记忆: por(看作 pour, 倒) + tray(碟) → 将颜料倒在碟子上 → 描写, 描绘

例 Not only does the GDP mask this erosion in the social structure, it can actually *portray* it as an economic gain.

派 portrayal(*n.* 描绘; 肖像)

posit
[ˈpɑːzɪt]

v. 断定, 认为(to assume or affirm the existence of)

记 联想记忆: 可以断定(posit), 确实(positive)是这样

例 They *posit* that biological distinctions between the sexes result in a necessary sexual division of labor.

positive
[ˈpɑːzətɪv]

a. 肯定的(sure); 积极的(active); 【数】正的

例 There are clear and *positive* signs that people are becoming more respectful of one another's differences. // *positive* integer 正整数

派 positively(*ad.* 断然地; 肯定地)

possess
[pəˈzes]

v. 具有, 拥有(to own)

例 The patrons who paid bills in cash did not *possess* credit cards.

派 possession(*n.* 拥有; 财产); possessed(*a.* 着迷的); possessiveness(*n.* 占有)

possibility
[ˌpɑːsəˈbɪləti]

n. 可能性(the condition or fact of being possible)

记 来自 possible(*a.*可能的; 合适的)

例 Early treatment of high cholesterol does not eliminate the *possibility* of a stroke later in life.

同根词: impossible(*a.* 不可能的)

postage
[ˈpoustɪdʒ]

n. 邮资, 邮费(the fee for postal service)

记 词根记忆: post(邮政) + age(费用) → 邮费, 邮资

例 The rarer something becomes, whether it is a baseball card or a musical recording or a *postage* stamp, the more avidly it is sought by collectors.

同根词: postal(*a.* 邮政的)

postal

['poustl]

a. 邮政的；邮局的(of or relating to the mails or the post office)

记 词根记忆：post(邮政) + al → 邮政的

例 *Postal* workers are representative of service workers in general.

同根词：postbox(*n.* 邮箱)；postcode(*n.* 邮政编码)

posterity

[pɑː'sterəti]

n. 子孙，后代(offspring)

记 词根记忆：post(后) + erity → 后面的人 → 后代

potent

['poʊtnt]

a. 效力强的，烈性的(chemically or medicinally effective)

记 词根记忆：pot(能力) + ent → 能力大的 → 效力强的，烈性的

例 The *potent* drug knocked John unconscious.

potential

[pə'tenʃl]

n. 潜能；可能性(existing in possibility)；a. 潜在的，有可能性的(capable of development into actuality)

记 词根记忆：potent(潜力的) + ial → 潜能

例 However, habitat loss has the *potential* to reduce genetic diversity.

派 potentially(*ad.* 可能地，潜在地)

potter

['pɑːtər]

n. 陶工(one that makes pottery)

例 The *potter* placed the wet clay in the oven.

派 pottery(*n.* 陶器；制陶术)

poultry

['poʊltri]

n. 家禽(domesticated birds kept for eggs or meat)

例 In 1989 Juranians consumed twice as much *poultry* as fish.

同根词：poulterer(*n.* 鸟贩；家禽贩)

practical

['præktɪkl]

a. 实际的(of, relating to, or manifested in practice or action)；实用性的(useful)

记 来自practice(*v.* 实践；练习)

例 They served a ceremonial as well as a *practical* function.

派 practically(*ad.* 实际地；事实上)

同根词：practicably(*ad.* 实用地；能用地)

practitioner

[præk'tɪʃənər]

n. 开业者(医生、律师等)(person who practices a profession, esp. medicine)

例 The document indicated that women activists were early *practitioners* of nonpartisan, issue-oriented politics.

pragmatic

[præg'mætɪk]

a. 实际的，注重实效的(practical)；实用主义的(relating to or being in accordance with philosophical pragmatism)

记 词根记忆：pragm(实际) + atic → 实际的，注重实效的

例 This *pragmatic* approach is buttressed by the government.

派 pragmatically(*ad.* 实际地，实用主义地)

同根词：pragmatism(*n.* 实用主义)；pragmatist(*n.* 实用主义者)

prairie

['preri]

n. 大草原(a tract of grassland)

记 联想记忆：pr + air(空气) + ie → 大草原上空气好

例 *prairie* dog 草原土拨鼠

prank

[præŋk]

n. 恶作剧，玩笑(a trick)

记 不要和plank(*n.* 厚木板)相混

例 Removing the boxes will reduce the number of *prank* calls without hampering people's ability to report a fire.

28

precaution [prɪˈkɔːʃn]	*n.* 预防，警惕(care taken in advance) 记 词根记忆：pre(预先) + caution(小心) → 事先小心 → 预防，警惕 例 Because sloth bears are smaller than brown and polar bears and are under greater threat from dangerous animals, they may have adopted the extra *precaution* of carrying their cubs.
precede [prɪˈsiːd]	*v.* 在…之前，早于(to be earlier than) 记 词根记忆：pre(前) + cede(走) → 走在前面 → 在…之前 例 Leibniz' notes are limited to early sections of Newton's book, sections that *precede* the ones in which Newton's calculus concepts and techniques are presented. 同根词：precedent(*n.* 先例；*a.* 在前的)
precedence [ˈpresɪdəns]	*n.* 优先，居先(the fact of preceding in time) 记 词根记忆：pre(前) + ced(走) + ence → 走在前面 → 优先 例 The water rights of the inhabitants of the Fort Berthold Indian Reservation would not take *precedence* over those of other citizens. 同根词：precedential(*a.* 有先例的)
preceding [prɪˈsiːdɪŋ]	*a.* 在前的(to surpass in rank, dignity, or importance) 记 来自precede(*v.* 领先，在…前面) 例 Present information contradicts the *preceding* paragraph. 同根词：precedent(*a.* 在前的；*n.* 先例)
precipitate	[prɪˈsɪpɪteɪt] *v.* 加速，促成(to bring about abruptly; hasten) [prɪˈsɪpɪtət] *a.* 鲁莽的(impetuous) 记 词根记忆：pre(预先) + cipit(落下) + ate → 先落下了 → 加速 例 However, since humans tended to migrate to areas as the climate in those areas began to warm, the extinctions might have been *precipitated* by the climatic warming rather than by human migration. 派 precipitation(*n.* 沉淀；沉淀物)
precipitation [prɪˌsɪpɪˈteɪʃn]	*n.* 沉淀(the quality or state of being precipitated)；沉淀物(sth. precipitated) 记 来自precipitate(*v.* 使…沉淀；促成) 例 The continental United States receives an average of 30 inches of *precipitation* a year. 同根词：precipitant(*n.* 沉淀剂)
precise [prɪˈsaɪs]	*a.* 准确的，精确的(exact)；严谨的(strict) 记 词根记忆：preci(价值，价格) + se → 定价一般都很精确 → 准确的，精确的 例 The witness gave a *precise* account of the murder. // *precise* statement 严谨的陈述 派 precision[*n.* 精确，精密(度)]
precursor [priːˈkɜːrsər]	*n.* 先驱；先兆；前身(forerunner, predecessor, a substance from which another substance is formed) 记 词根记忆：pre(前) + curs(跑) + or → 跑在前面的人 → 先驱 例 Lightning is a *precursor* of thunder.

□ precaution   □ precede   □ precedence   □ preceding   □ precipitate   □ precipitation
□ precise   □ precursor

predate [priˈdeit]	*v.* 居先，早于(antedate) 例 Some North American sites of human habitation *predate* any sites found in South America.
predation [priˈdeiʃn]	*n.* 捕食(行为、习性等)；掠夺行为(depredation) 例 In the snow goose's winter habitats, the goose faces no significant natural *predation*.
predator [ˈpredətər]	*n.* 食肉动物(animal that kills and eats other animals) 例 The seal tried to avoid *predators* by a deep dive. 派 predatory(*a.* 食肉的；掠夺的)
predatory [ˈpredətɔːri]	*a.* 掠夺的(of, relating to, or practicing plunder, pillage, or rapine)；食肉的(predaceous) 记 来自 predator(*n.* 掠夺者，捕食者) 例 The bones of Majungatholus atopus, a meat-eating dinosaur that is a distant relative of Tyrannosaurus rex and closely resembles South American *predatory* dinosaurs, have been discovered in Madagascar. 同根词：predation(*n.* 捕食；掠夺)
predecessor [ˈpredəsesər]	*n.* 前任者(a person who has previously occupied a position or office to which another has succeeded)；(被取代的)人或事物(precursor) 记 词根记忆：pre(先) + de + cess(走) + or → 走在前面的人 → 前任者 例 They are probably more concerned than their *predecessors* were about job security and economic benefits.
predicament [priˈdikəmənt]	*n.* 困境，窘境(plight) 例 I was in the *predicament* of competing against the best runner.
predicate [ˈpredikeit]	*v.* 使基于(found, base)；断言，肯定(affirm)；暗示(imply) 记 词根记忆：pre(预先) + dic(命令) + ate → 断言 例 These arguments are *predicated* on differences between the sexes. // He *predicated* the motive to be good. // His retraction *predicates* a change of attitude.

28

255

Word List 29

音频

predict [prɪˈdɪkt]	*v.* 预言，预测(to foretell)
	记 词根记忆：pre(前) + dict(说) → 说在前面的话 → 预言，预测
	例 We will be able to *predict* more precisely what items we should stock at any given time.
	派 predictive(*a.* 预言性的)
prediction [prɪˈdɪkʃn]	*n.* 预言(an act of predicting)；预报(forecast)
	记 来自 predict(*v.* 预言，预知)
	例 The value of the dollar declined several times in the year prior to the recent *prediction* of slower economic growth.
	同根词：predictive(*a.* 预言性的)
predisposition [ˌpriːdɪspəˈzɪʃn]	*n.* 倾向(tendency)；易患病的体质(susceptible)
	记 来自 predispose(*v.* 使倾向于)
	例 Tom has a *predisposition* to find fault.
predominant [prɪˈdɑːmɪnənt]	*a.* 有势力的(having superior strength; prevailing)；主要的(being most frequent or common)
	记 词根记忆：pre(前) + dominant(统治的) → 在前面统治的 → 有势力的
	例 In Greece, rhododendrons and oleander bloom only in springtime, when they are the *predominant* sources of nectar.
	派 predominantly(*ad.* 主要地；显著地)
	同根词：predominate(*v.* 支配；主宰)
predominantly [prɪˈdɑːmɪnəntli]	*ad.* 主要地(mainly)
	记 来自 predominant(*a.* 主要的)
	例 In the past, teachers, bank tellers and secretaries were *predominantly* men.
predominate [prɪˈdɑːmɪneɪt]	*v.* 统治，主导；占优势(to dominate)
	记 词根记忆：pre + domin(统治) + ate → 统治
	例 Individualist feminism came to *predominate* in English-speaking countries.
	同根词：predominance(*n.* 优势)

preeminent [prɪ'emɪnənt]	*a.* 卓越的，杰出的(outstanding) 🔑 词根记忆：pre(前) + eminent(著名的) → 在著名的人前面 → 卓越的，杰出的 📝 The *preeminent* author had received many awards. 📤 preeminence(*n.* 杰出，卓越)
preference ['prefrəns]	*n.* 偏爱，倾向(the act of preferring)；优先权(the act, fact, or principle of giving advantages to some over others) 🔑 来自prefer(*v.* 喜爱，喜欢) 📝 One example of social learning is the acquisition of *preferences* for novel foods. 同根词：preferential(*a.* 优先的；特惠的)
preferential [ˌprefə'renʃl]	*a.* 优先的(of, giving, receiving or showing preference) 📝 In most regions of the brain the cells not only adhere to one another but also adopt some *preferential* orientation.
prefigure [ˌpri:'fɪgjər]	*v.* 预示(to foreshow) 🔑 词根记忆：pre(提前) + figure(推测) → 预想 → 预示 📝 These events may *prefigure* a period of economic recession. 📤 prefiguration(*n.* 预兆，预示)
preflight [ˌpri:'flaɪt]	*a.* (飞机、人造卫星等)起飞前的(preparing for or preliminary to flight) 📝 The new guidelines for airlines were to standardize safety requirements governing *preflight* inspections.
pregnancy ['pregnənsi]	*n.* 怀孕(期)(state or period of being pregnant) 🔑 来自pregnant(*a.* 怀孕的)
preindustrial [ˌpri:ɪn'dʌstriəl]	*a.* 工业化前的(earlier than industrial)；未工业化的(not engaged in industry) 🔑 词根记忆：pre(前) + industrial(工业的) → 工业化前的 📝 They operated in a *preindustrial* world, grafting a system of capitalist international trade onto a premodern system of artisan and peasant production.
prejudice ['predʒudɪs]	*v./n.* 偏见，歧视(to bias) 🔑 词根记忆：pre(预先) + jud(判断) + ice → 先入为主的判断 → 偏见 📝 racial *prejudices* 种族歧视 📤 prejudicial(*a.* 有害的)；prejudiced(*a.* 有偏见的，歧视的) 同根词：judicious(*a.* 明智的)
preliminary [prɪ'lɪmɪneri]	*a.* 预备的；初步的，开始的(preparatory; coming before a more important action or event) 🔑 词根记忆：pre(前) + limin(门槛；限制) + ary → 入门前 → 初步的；预备的 📝 After some *preliminary* air drying or sun drying, they are laid in the wall in mud mortar.

29

premature [ˌpriːməˈtʃʊr]	*a.* 早产的(born early)；早熟的(happening before the proper, usual, or intended time) 记 词根记忆：pre(提前) + mature(成熟) → 早熟的 → 过早的 例 It is *premature* to talk about success at this stage.
premise [ˈpremɪs]	*n.* 前提，假设(presupposition) 记 词根记忆：pre(前) + mise(放) → 放在前面的东西 → 前提 例 The illogical proof was based on a faulty *premise*.
premium [ˈpriːmiəm]	*n.* 保险金(amount or instalment regularly paid for an insurance policy) 记 词根记忆：pr(e)(提前) + em(=empt 买) + ium → 提前交出的钱 → 保险金 例 Last year the annual *premium* on a certain hospitalization insurance policy was $408.
preoccupation [priˌɑːkjuˈpeɪʃn]	*n.* 先入之见(something that engages the interest or attention beforehand or preferentially)；*n.* 入神(extreme or excessive concern with something) 记 词根记忆：pre(先) + occupation(占据) → 预先占据 → 先入之见 例 The historian who writes the record of the past inevitably reflects the *preoccupations* of his own time.
prepay [ˌpriːˈpeɪ]	*v.* 预先支付(某费用)(to pay in advance) 例 A newly instituted program will allow parents to *prepay* their children's future college tuition at current rates.
preponderance [prɪˈpɑːndərəns]	*n.* (压倒性)优势；多数(majority) 记 联想记忆：pre(前面) + ponder(重量) + ance → 重量排名靠前 → 优势；多数 例 The enemy have a marked *preponderance* in the air.
prerequisite [ˌpriːˈrekwəzɪt]	*n.* 先决(必备)条件，前提(required as a condition for sth. to happen or exist) 记 词根记忆：pre(预先) + requisite(要求) → 预先要求 → 先决条件 例 A degree is an essential *prerequisite* for employment at this level.
prescribe [prɪˈskraɪb]	*v.* 开(药)，开处方(to write, give or order the use of, esp. medicine, remedy, etc.) 记 词根记忆：pre(预先) + scribe(写) → 预先写好 → 开处方 例 Physicians have the final say as to whether to *prescribe* a medication for a patient. 派 prescription(*n.* 处方)
prescription [prɪˈskrɪpʃn]	*n.* 药方(a written direction for a therapeutic or corrective agent)；指示(the action of laying down authoritative rules or directions)；惯例(convention) 记 来自 prescribe(*v.* 开处方) 例 A proposed law would allow general advertising of *prescription* medications. 同根词：prescriptive(*a.* 规定的，指定的)

258
□ premature □ premise □ premium □ preoccupation □ prepay □ preponderance
□ prerequisite □ prescribe □ prescription

presentation [ˌpriːzen'teɪʃn]	*n.* 报告；陈述 (something presented) 记 来自 present(*v.* 介绍) 例 At the stockholders meeting, investors heard a *presentation* on the numerous challenges the company faced.
preservation [ˌprezər'veɪʃn]	*n.* 保存，保留 (of or relating to protecting or maintaining) 记 来自 preserve(*v.* 保护，保存) 例 That is exactly why a more sensible *preservation* strategy would be to assist the farmers to modernize their farms to the extent needed to maintain viability.
preservative [pri'zɜːrvətɪv]	*a.* 防腐的 (having the power of preserving); *n.* 防腐剂 (an additive used to protect against decay) 记 词根记忆：pre(预先) + serv(保持) + ative(…的) → 预先用来保存的 → 防腐的 例 These wine makers have been able to duplicate the *preservative* effect produced by adding sulfites by means that do not involve adding any potentially allergenic substances to their wine.
preserve [pri'zɜːrv]	*v.* 保持，维持 (to protect, maintain); *n.* 野生动物保护区 (an area restricted for the protection and preservation of natural animals) 记 联想记忆：pre(前) + serve(服务) → 提前提供服务 → 维持 例 The local residents determined to *preserve* their religion and way of life. // A wildlife *preserve* is being planned for 3,000 rhinoceroses(犀牛). 派 preservative(*n.* 防腐剂)
preside [pri'zaɪd]	*v.* (over)担任主席，主持(会议等) (to act as chairman at a conference, meeting, etc.) 记 联想记忆：pre(前) + side(坐) → 坐在前面 → 担任主席 例 The council president *presided* over the meeting. 派 presidential(*a.* 总统的)
pressboard ['presbɔːd]	*n.* 压制板 (a strong highly glazed composition board resembling vulcanized fiber) 记 分拆记忆：press(压) + board(板) → 压出的板 → 压制板
prestige [pre'stiːʒ]	*n.* 威信，声望 (fame) 记 联想记忆：pres(看作 president 总统) + tige(看作 tiger 老虎) → 总统和老虎两者都是有威信、威望的 → 威信，威望 例 Inventions bring more *prestige* to universities than do books and articles. 派 prestigious(*a.* 有威信的，有影响力的)
prestigious [pre'stɪdʒəs]	*a.* 有名望的，有威信的 (having prestige; honored) 记 来自 prestige(*n.* 威信；魅力) 例 Kitchen is one of the most *prestigious* cooking-related magazines.
presume [pri'zuːm]	*v.* 假定，推测 (to assume) 例 The underlying economic forces of industrialism were *presumed* to be gender-blind. 派 presumably(*ad.* 据推测，大概)

29

□ presentation   □ preservation   □ preservative   □ preserve   □ preside   □ pressboard
□ prestige   □ prestigious   □ presume

presuppose

[ˌpriːsəˈpoʊz]

v. 以…为先决条件(to require as a condition)

记 词根记忆：pre(预先) + suppose(假定) → 预先假定 → 以…为先决条件

例 Effective prevention *presupposes* early diagnosis.

派 presupposition(n. 预想；先决条件)

pretax

[ˈpriːˈtæks]

a. (纳)税前的(before tax has been deducted)

记 词根记忆：pre(前) + tax(税) → 税前的

例 *pretax* income 税前收入

prevail

[prɪˈveɪl]

v. 战胜；盛行(to predominate)

记 联想记忆：pre(前) + vail(=val 力量) → 力量在别人之前 → 战胜

例 This activism and the views underlying it came to *prevail* in the United States labor movement.

派 prevailing(a. 流行的；一般的)

同根词：prevalence(n. 流行；普遍)

prevalence

[ˈprevələns]

n. 流行；普遍(the quality or state of being prevalent)

记 来自 prevalent(a. 流行的，普遍的)

例 They underestimated the *prevalence* of child labor among the working classes.

prevalent

[ˈprevələnt]

a. 流行的，普遍的(widespread)

记 联想记忆：pre(前) + val(力量) + ent → 有走在前面的力量 → 流行的

例 Hip-Hop is *prevalent* among teenagers these days.

派 prevalence(n. 盛行)

preventive

[prɪˈventɪv]

n. 预防药(sth. used to prevent disease)；预防法(sth. that prevents)；

a. 预防的，防止的(precautionary)

记 来自 prevent(v. 预防，阻止)

例 Employees at companies with on-site clinics seek *preventive* screening and are thus less likely to delay medical treatment.

previous

[ˈpriːviəs]

a. 前面的，在前的(earlier, coming before)

记 词根记忆：pre(前) + vi(路) + ous → 前面的路 → 前面的，在前的

例 *Previous* studies have indicated that eating chocolate increases the likelihood of getting heart disease.

prey

[preɪ]

n. 被掠食者(an animal taken by a predator as food)；v. (on)捕食(to seize and devour as prey)

记 注意：pray(v. 祈祷)

例 Some species of dolphins find their *prey* by echolocation. // Killer whales in the North Pacific usually *prey* on seals and sea lions.

priest

[priːst]

n. 牧师，神父(clergyman)

例 During the full moon, the *priest* chanted a special prayer.

primary

[ˈpraɪmeri]

a. 最初的(primitive)；基础的(fundamental)；首要的(principal)

记 词根记忆：prim(第一) + ary(…的) → 最初的

例 Sugar is the *primary* export of the country.

primate [ˈpraɪmeɪt]	*n.* 灵长类(动物)(any member of the most highly developed order of mammals that includes human beings apes and monkeys) 记 词根记忆: prim(第一) + ate → 人类最初祖先 → 灵长类 例 Humans are the most advanced of all the *primates*.
primer [ˈpraɪmər]	*n.* 识字课本(a small book for teaching children to read); 底漆, 首涂油, 打底剂(material used in priming a surface) 记 来自 prime(*n.* 初期; *a.* 主要的; 基本的) 例 A single layer of the new coating provides the aluminum skin of the airliner with less protection against corrosion than does a layer of *primer* of the usual thickness. 同根词: primitive(*n.* 原始人; *a.* 原始的)
primitive [ˈprɪmətɪv]	*a.* 原始的(original); 简单的(very simple, not complicated) 记 词根记忆: prim(第一) + itive → 最早的 → 原始的 例 Communications and transports of seventeenth century are too *primitive* to make comparisons with modern ones.
primordial [praɪˈmɔːrdiəl]	*a.* 原始的(first created or developed); 主要的(fundamental, primary) 记 词根记忆: prim(第一) + ord(顺序) + ial → 处于第一顺序的 → 主要的 例 *primordial* matter 原生物质
princely [ˈprɪnsli]	*a.* 高贵的(noble); 威严的(magnificent) 记 来自 prince(*n.* 王子) 例 The *princely* gentleman was polite, charming, and well liked.
principal [ˈprɪnsəpl]	*a.* 主要的(main, chief); *n.* 校长(headmaster) 例 In birds, the second finger is the *principal* strut of the wing, which consists primarily of feathers. // a school *principal* 学校校长 派 principally(*ad.* 主要地)
principle [ˈprɪnsəpl]	*n.* 原则(a rule or code of conduct); 原理(a comprehensive and fundamental law, doctrine, or assumption); 道义(a moral rule or a strong belief that influences your actions) 记 词根记忆: prin(第一) + cip(取) + le → 须第一位选取的 → 原则 例 It discusses an exception to a general *principle* outlined in the first paragraph. 派 principled(*a.* 有原则的, 有操守的) 同根词: principal(*a.* 最重要的)
priority [praɪˈɔːrəti]	*n.* 在先(be more important); 优先权(right to have or do sth. before others); 优先考虑的事(thing that is regarded as more important than others) 记 来自 prior(*a.* 在前的) 例 Airlines are assigning a higher *priority* to safe seating than to minimizing fuel costs.
pristine [ˈprɪstiːn]	*a.* 原始的(belonging to the earliest period or state); 未被破坏的(not spoiled, corrupted); 纯洁的(pure); 新鲜的(fresh and clean) 记 词根记忆: prist(=prim 最早的) + ine → 原始的 例 There are fewer salmon in degraded regions than in *pristine* ones.

29

privilege [ˈprɪvəlɪdʒ]	*n.* 特权；优惠 (a right granted as a peculiar favor) 例 Women in this community enjoyed unusual legal and economic *privileges*.
privy [ˈprɪvi]	*n.* 有利害关系的人 (a person having a legal interest of privity)；*a.* 私人的 (private, withdrawn)；不公开的，秘密参与的 (secret) 例 A watchdog group recently uncovered a trick that enables an interloper to rig an E-mail message so that this person will be *privy* to any comments that a recipient might add as the message is forwarded to others or sent back and forth. 派 privily(*ad.* 秘密地；暗中地)
probability [ˌprɑːbəˈbɪləti]	*n.* 概率；可能性 (the quality or state of being probable) 记 来自 probable(*a.* 可能的) 例 The *probability* is that a certain coin will turn up heads on any given toss.
probe [proʊb]	*v.* 探索 (to explore)；*n.* 探测器 (an instrument used for exploration) 记 词根记忆：prob(测试，证明) + e → 试着去证明 → 探索 例 Space *probes* indicate that the stars in the Milky Way galaxy are composed of several different types of gas.
procedure [prəˈsiːdʒər]	*n.* (议事)程序 (regular order or way of doing things, esp in business, law, politics, etc.)；步骤 (a series of steps) 例 Magnetic resonance imaging(MRI: 核磁共振成像)is a noninvasive diagnostic *procedure*.
proceed [proʊˈsiːd]	*v.* 继续进行 (to continue after a pause or interruption) 记 词根记忆：pro(向前) + ceed(前进) → 向前进 → 继续进行 例 Economic growth will *proceed* at a more moderate pace. 派 proceedings(*n.* 进行；会议记录)
proceeds [ˈproʊsiːdz]	*n.* 收益 (the total amount brought in) 例 Some of the *proceeds* from the new tax would go toward expanding the nonpolluting commuter rail system.
process	[ˈprɑːses] *n.* 过程，进行 (a series of actions or operations conducing to an end)；步骤 (steps) [prəˈses] *v.* 处理，加工 (to subject to a special process or treatment)；列队前进 (to move in a procession) 记 词根记忆：pro(前，向前) + cess(走) → 向前走 → 过程，进行 例 It allowed the foreman to control the production *process*. 派 procession(*n.* 队伍，行列) 同根词：recession(*n.* 衰退)
proclaim [prəˈkleɪm]	*v.* 宣告，声明 (to announce, to declare)；显示 (to show) 记 词根记忆：pro(在前) + claim(叫，喊) → 在前面喊 → 宣告 例 A sacred truce was *proclaimed* during the festival's month. // His manner *proclaimed* his genteel upbringing.

□ privilege   □ privy   □ probability   □ probe   □ procedure   □ proceed
□ proceeds   □ process   □ proclaim

procreative
[ˈprəukrɪeɪtɪv]

a. 生育的(producing or giving life to)

记 来自 procreate(*v.* 生育)

例 Women's *procreative* labor is currently undervalued by the society.

procure
[prəˈkjʊr]

v. 取得，获得(to acquire, to obtain)

记 联想记忆：pro(前) + cure(关心) → 关心在前 → 为了取得

例 My friend *procured* two concert tickets after waiting in line for hours.

派 procurement(*n.* 获得，接收)

prodigy
[ˈprɑːdədʒi]

n. 奇迹(an extraordinary, marvelous, or unusual accomplishment, deed, or event)；奇才(a highly talented child or youth)；奇观(sth. extraordinary or inexplicable)

例 A child *prodigy*, Clara Schumann developed into one of the greatest pianists of her time.

同根词：prodigious(*a.* 惊人的；异常的；奇妙的)

professional
[prəˈfeʃənl]

a. 专业的(characterized by or conforming to the technical or ethical standards of a profession)；职业的(of, relating to, or characteristic of a profession)；*n.* 专业人员(one that is professional)

记 来自 profession(*n.* 职业；专业)

例 Women began to study history as *professional* historians.

派 professionally(*ad.* 专业地；内行地)

同根词：professor(*n.* 教授)

proficient
[prəˈfɪʃnt]

a. 熟练的，精通的(skillful)

记 词根记忆：pro(在前) + fic(做的) + ient → 做在别人前面 → 熟练的

例 The linguist was *proficient* in five languages.

同根词：sufficient(*a.* 足够的)；deficient(*a.* 缺乏的)

profile
[ˈprəʊfaɪl]

n. 剖面(a side or sectional elevation)；轮廓(outline)；分布图(a set of data often in graphic form portraying the significant features of something)

记 词根记忆：pro(前面) + file(=fili 线条) → 前部的线条 → 轮廓

例 pollen *profile* 花粉剖面 // high *profile* 高姿态 // temperature *profile* 温度曲线图

profitability
[ˌprɑːfɪtəˈbɪləti]

n. 赢利能力，收益性(ability to afford profits)

记 来自 profit(*n.* 利润，利益；*v.* 获利，有益)

例 One study showed, for example, that acquiring firms were on average unable to maintain acquired firms' pre-merger levels of *profitability*.

同根词：profitable(*a.* 有利可图的；有益的)

profitable
[ˈprɑːfɪtəbl]

a. 有利可图的(offering profits)

记 来自 profit(*n.* 利益，利润；*v.* 获利)

例 Winter wheat and spring wheat are usually about equally *profitable*.

派 profitably(*ad.* 有利地，有益地)

同根词：nonprofit(*a.* 非赢利的)

29

profound [prə'faʊnd]	*a.* 深刻的，意义深远的(far-reaching) 记 词根记忆：pro + found(底部) → 探究到底部 → 深奥的 例 The fecundity effects may have the most *profound* impact on these plant species. 派 profundity(*n.* 深度，深刻)
prognosis [prɑːg'noʊsɪs]	*n.* 预后(对疾病的发作及结果的预言)(the prospect of recovery as anticipated from the usual course of disease) 记 词根记忆：pro(提前) + gnosis(知道) → 先知道 → 预后 例 A *prognosis* is made and evidence supporting it is discussed.
progression [prə'greʃn]	*n.* 进展(advance)；级数(a sequence of numbers in which each term is related to its predecessor by a uniform law) 例 geometric *progression* 几何级数，等比级数
progressive [prə'gresɪv]	*a.* 上进的(advancing)；【医】愈来愈严重的(increasing in severity) 记 来自 progress(*n.* 进步) 例 The ideal of "openness" has made Americans a *progressive* people. // The value of a treatment for a *progressive* disease may vary according to a patient's stage of disease. 派 progressively(*ad.* 逐渐地，逐步地)
prohibit [prə'hɪbɪt]	*v.* 禁止(to forbid by authority)；阻止(to prevent from doing sth.) 记 词根记忆：pro(提前) + hibit(拿住) → 提前拿住 → 禁止；阻止 例 Fishing regulations *prohibit* people from keeping any salmon they have caught in Lake Paqua. 派 prohibition(*n.* 禁止；禁令) 同根词：inhibit(*v.* 禁止)
project	['prɑːdʒekt] *n.* 工程；计划(scheme) [prə'dʒekt] *v.* 预计(to plan, figure, or estimate for the future) 记 词根记忆：pro(提前) + ject(扔) → 提前扔出来 → 预计 例 Aviation fuel is *projected* to decline in price over the next several years.
projection [prə'dʒekʃn]	*n.* 预测；规划(scheme) 记 词根记忆：pro(提前) + ject(扔) + ion → 提前扔出来 → 规划；预测 例 Weather forecasters make some use of computer *projections* to identify weather patterns.
prokaryote [prəʊ'kærɪəʊt]	*n.* 原核生物(any of the typically unicellular microorganisms that lack a distinct nucleus and membranebound organelles) 派 prokaryotic(*a.* 原核的)

proliferate [prə'lɪfəreɪt]	*v.* 激增(to increase profusely); 繁殖(to multiply) 记 词根记忆: pro(许多) + lifer(后代) + ate → 后代增加许多 → 繁殖 例 As new products *proliferate*, demand is divided among a growing number of stock-keeping units. 派 proliferation(*n.* 大量繁殖) 同根词: prolific(*a.* 多产的)
proliferation [prə,lɪfə'reɪʃn]	*n.* 增殖(growth by the rapid multiplication of parts); 扩散(a rapaid increase in number, especially in the numbe of deadly weapons) 记 来自 proliferate(*v.* 增殖) 例 The *proliferation* of Eurasian watermifoil in Frida Lake has led to reductions in the populations of some species of aquatic animals.
prolonged [prə'lɑːŋd]	*a.* 延长的(drawn out); 拖延的(tediously protracted); 持续很久的(continuing for a long time) 记 来自 prolong(*v.* 延长; 拖延) 例 *Prolonged* loss of sleep can lead to temporary impairment of judgment comparable to that induced by consuming several ounces of alcohol.
prominence ['prɑːmɪnəns]	*n.* 突出物(sth. prominent); 突出(the quality, state, or fact of being prominent or conspicuous) 记 来自 prominent(*a.* 显著的) 例 Since 1980, productivity improvements in manufacturing have moved the United States from a position of acute decline in manufacturing to one of world *prominence*. 同根词: eminent(*a.* 杰出的; 显著的)
prominent ['prɑːmɪnənt]	*a.* 显著的(noticeable); 杰出的(outstanding) 记 词根记忆: pro(向前) + minent(突出) → 凸出的 → 显著的 例 Alvin Toffler was one of the most *prominent* students in our college. 派 prominence(*n.* 突出, 显著)
promising ['prɑːmɪsɪŋ]	*a.* 有希望的, 有前途的(likely to succeed or to yield good results) 记 来自 promise(*v.* 给予希望) 例 The new theory has opened up *promising* possibilities for future research.

promote [prə'moʊt]	*v.* 提升(to give someone a higher position or rank); 促进(to help in the growth or development of) 记 词根记忆: pro(向前) + mot(动) + e → 向前动 → 促进 例 It helped to *promote* flexibility within their social system. 派 promotion(*n.* 提升; 促销) 同根词: demote(*v.* 使降级)
promotional [prə'moʊʃənl]	*a.* 促销的(of or relating to promotion); 增进的(of or relating to advancement) 记 来自promotion(*n.* 促进; 晋升; 推销) 例 Customers come to regard the *promotional* price as the fair price and the regular price as excessive. 同根词: promote(*v.* 促进; 促销)
prompt [prɑːmpt]	*v.* (to)促使, 推动(to serve as the inciting cause of); 提示(to cue); *a.* 敏捷的(performed readily or immediately) 记 词根记忆: pro(向前) + mpt → 使…向前 → 促使 例 The thermoreceptors(温度感应器)located within the skin's surface can *prompt* behavioral changes.
pronounced [prə'naʊnst]	*a.* 明显的, 显著的(evident, prominent) 记 来自pronounce(*v.* 宣称, 发音) 例 The division of labor is less *pronounced* among other vertebrates than among naked mole rats.
propagandistic [ˌprɑːpə'gændɪstik]	*a.* 宣传的(of or relating to or characterized by propaganda) 记 来自propagand(*v.* 宣传) 例 His place in the national pantheon is largely due to the *propagandistic* efforts of newspaper reporters.
propagate ['prɑːpəgeɪt]	*v.* 繁殖(to multiply); 宣传, 使普及(to spread, publicise) 记 联想记忆: pro + pag(砍, 切) + ate → 繁殖; 原意是把树的旁枝剪掉使主干成长, 引申为繁殖 例 The TV station *propagated* information about the bomb blast. 派 propagation(*n.* 繁殖)
propeller [prə'pelər]	*n.* 螺旋桨, 推进器(one that propels) 记 来自propel(*v.* 推进, 驱使) 例 The boat's powerful *propeller* created large waves.
property ['prɑːpərti]	*n.* 财产, 资产(assets); 性质(quality) 记 词根记忆: proper(本身所有的) + ty → 所有物 → 资产 例 *property* tax 财产税 // Sound quality is a very important *property* of a stereo system.
prophet ['prɑːfɪt]	*n.* 先知, 预言家(predictor) 记 联想记忆: 发音同"profit"(利益) → 人们对与自身利益有关的预言感兴趣 → 预言者 例 I asked the *prophet* for advice about my future.

propitious [prəˈpɪʃəs]	*a.* 适合的，有利于…的（favorable） 词 词根记忆：pro(向前) + pit(=pet 寻求) + ious → 所寻求的 → 适合的 例 It is not a *propitious* time to start a new business.
proponent [prəˈpounənt]	*n.* 拥护者，倡导者（advocate） 词 词根记忆：pro(向前) + pon(放) + ent → 处在前面的人 → 倡导者 注意：opponent(*n.* 对手，反对者) 例 The *proponents* of the proposed law rallied in the street.
proportion [prəˈpɔːrʃn]	*n.* 比例（ratio） 词 词根记忆：pro(相关) + portion(部分) → 与部分有关 → 比例 例 The *proportion* of nonsmokers in the United States population dropped slightly.
proportional [prəˈpɔːrʃənl]	*a.* (to)成比例的；均衡的（corresponding in size degree, or intensity） 例 The drugs' effectiveness against pain is *proportional* to their success in blocking this enzyme at the site of injury. 派 proportionally(*ad.* 按比例地)
proprietary [prəˈpraɪəteri]	*a.* 所有的，私人拥有的（of relating to, or characteristic of a proprietor） 词 词根记忆：propri(本身所有的) + etary → 所有的 例 *proprietary* rights 所有权
prorate [prəʊˈreɪt]	*v.* <美>按比例分配（to divide or distribute proportionately） 词 词根记忆：pro(赞成) + rate(比率) → 按比例分配 例 *prorate* dividends 按比例分红
prose [prouz]	*n.* 散文（written or spoken language that is not in verse form） 词 联想记忆：p + rose(玫瑰) → 散文如玫瑰花瓣，形散而神聚 例 Victorian women did write the first-rate *prose* and poetry. 派 prosaic(*a.* 散文的)
prosecute [ˈprɑːsɪkjuːt]	*v.* 对…提起公诉（to bring legal action against for redress or punishment of a crime or violation of law） 例 Few individuals are *prosecuted* for violating gun control laws. 派 prosecution(*n.* 起诉；经营)
prosecutor [ˈprɑːsɪkjuːtər]	*n.* 检察官 (a public official who charges sb. officially with a crime and prosecutes them in court); 起诉人，原告 (a person who institutes an official prosecution before a court) 词 联想记忆：pro(前) + secu(追随) + tor(人) → 追随你到法院门前的人 → 起诉人 例 Chief Public *Prosecutor* 首席检察官
prospect [ˈprɑːspekt]	*n.* 前景；期望（anticipation） 词 词根记忆：pro(向前) + spect(看) → 向前看 → 前景；期望 例 Undergraduates choose their major field primarily based on their perception of job *prospects* in that field. 派 prospecting(*n.* 勘探)

30

prospective [prə'spektɪv]	*n.* 预期，展望（anticipation）；*a.* 未来的；预期的（relating to or effective in the future） 记 词根记忆：pro（向前）+ spect（看）+ ive → 向前看的 → 未来的；预期的 例 The following appeared in a letter to *prospective* students from the admissions office at Plateau College. 派 prospectively（*ad.* 盼望中） 同根词：spectator（*n.* 观众，旁观者）
prosper ['prɑːspər]	*v.* 兴隆（to thrive）；成功（to succeed） 记 词根记忆：pro（在前）+ sper（希望）→ 希望在前 → 兴隆；成功 例 When people have a personal stake in something, they think about it, care about it, work to make it *prosper*. 派 prosperous（*a.* 繁荣富强的）
prosperity [prɑː'sperəti]	*n.* 成功（state of being successful）；繁荣（state of good fortune） 记 词根记忆：pro（很多）+ sper（希望）+ ity → 充满希望 → 成功 例 In general, urban migration has not provided economic *prosperity* or upward mobility for women in the lowest socioeconomic class, despite their intelligent and energetic utilization of the resources available to them. 同根词：prosperous（*a.* 繁荣的；兴旺的）
protégé ['proʊtəʒeɪ]	*n.*（女性为：protégée）被保护人；门徒（person whose welfare and career are looked after by an influential person, esp. over a long period） 记 法语词，一般两个 e 上都有点 注意：protect（*v.* 保护） 例 Bob became the famous painter's student and *protégé* when he was nineteen.
protein ['proʊtiːn]	*n.* 蛋白质（substance found in meat, eggs, fish, etc. that is an important body-building part of the diet of humans and animals） 记 词根记忆：prote（首要）+ in → 动植物体内最主要的 → 蛋白质 例 *Protein* synthesis begins when the gene encoding a protein is activated. 派 lipoprotein（*n.* 脂蛋白）
protestant ['prɑːtɪstənt]	*n.* 新教（徒）（a Christian, not of a Catholic or Eastern church）；新教（徒）的（of or relating to Protestants their churches, or their religion） 记 来自 protest（*v.* 反对） 例 The texts were infused with *Protestant* outlooks.
protocol ['proʊtəkɔːl]	*n.* 条约草案，协议（convention） 记 词根记忆：proto（=first 首先）+ col → 首先需要拟定的 → 条约草案 例 The *protocol's* regulations will be strictly followed.
proton ['proʊtɑːn]	*n.* 质子（elementary particle with a positive electric charge, which is present in the nuclei of all atoms） 记 词根记忆：proto（原始）+ n → 原始的东西 → 质子 例 Nucleus comprises neutron and *proton*.

prototype ['proʊtətaɪp]	*n.* 原型（archetype） 记 词根记忆：proto（原始）+ type（形状）→ 原始的形状 → 原型 例 The inventor constructed the *prototype* of the machine from scrap metal.
provenance ['prɑːvənəns]	*n.* 出处，起源（origin, derivation） 记 词根记忆：pro（在前）+ ven（来）+ ance → 以前来的东西 → 起源 例 The *provenance* of the artefact was unknown.
provided [prə'vaɪdɪd]	*conj.* 假如，倘若（on condition that） 记 词根记忆：pro（向前）+ vid（看）+ ed → 向前看的 → 预测的 → 假如 例 *Provided* this technology is effective, those fears are groundless. 同根词：provide（*v.* 预备；提供）
providing [prə'vaɪdɪŋ]	*conj.* 假如；以…为条件（on condition that） 记 来自 provide（*v.* 提供；给予） 例 *Providing* initial evidence that airports are a larger source of pollution than they were once believed to be, environmentalists in Chicago report this. 同根词：provision（*n.* 规定；条款）
provision [prə'vɪʒn]	*n.* 供应（the act or process of providing）；（法律等）条款（a legal rule） 记 来自 provide（*v.* 提供） 例 *Provision* of outpatient care has not been a major function of the private hospital.
provisional [prə'vɪʒənl]	*a.* 暂时的，临时的（temporary） 记 词根记忆：pro（前）+ vision（眼界）+ al → 眼前的 → 临时的 例 An arrest made by a Midville police officer is *provisional* until the officer has taken the suspect to the police station and the watch commander has officially approved the arrest. 派 provisionally（*ad.* 临时地，暂时地）
proviso [prə'vaɪzoʊ]	*n.* 限制性条款（an article or clause as in a contract that introduces a condition） 例 I agree to do the work with one *proviso* that I'm paid in advance.
provoke [prə'voʊk]	*v.* 产生，引起（to provide the needed stimulus for） 记 词根记忆：pro（在前）+ voke（呼喊）→ 在某人前面呼喊 → 引起 例 The issues they raised have *provoked* a broader debate.
proximity [prɑːk'sɪməti]	*n.* 接近（nearness） 记 词根记忆：proxim（近处）+ ity → 接近 例 Due to Bob's *proximity* to the microphone, his words were clearly recorded. 同根词：proximate（*a.* 最近的）
prudent ['pruːdnt]	*a.* 谨慎的（discreet）；精明的（sensible） 记 词根记忆：prud（小心）+ ent → 小心算计 → 谨慎的 例 Companies are making *prudent* preparations for a possible future development.

30

prudery [ˈpruːdəri]	*n.* 过分拘谨，故作正经（behaviour or attitude of a prude） 记 法语词，由 prude（*n.* 过分拘谨的人）而来 例 This is no time for *prudery*.
pseudonym [ˈsuːdənɪm]	*n.* 假名（a person's name that is not his or her real name）；笔名（pen name） 记 词根记忆：pseudo（=false 假，伪）+ nym（=name 名字）→ 假名；笔名 例 The author published his works under *pseudonym*.
psyche [ˈsaɪki]	*n.* 心智，精神（soul, mind） 记 词根记忆：psych（心理）+ e → 心智，精神；原指"普赛克"仙女，Psyche 是人类灵魂的象征，以长着蝴蝶翅膀的少女形象出现，和爱神丘比特相恋 例 After years of abuse, Mary's *psyche* was deeply scarred. 同根词：psychiatry（*n.* 精神病学）；psychopathic（*a.* 患精神病的）；psychotic（*a./n.* 精神病的/疯子）；psychic（*a.* 精神的）
psychological [ˌsaɪkəˈlɑːdʒɪkl]	*a.* 心理学的（of or relating to psychology）；心理的，精神的 记 词根记忆：psycho（心灵，精神）+ log（说）+ ical（…的）→ 心理的，精神的 例 Besides yielding such *psychological* rewards as relief from stress, deep relaxation, if practiced regularly, can strengthen the immune system and produce a host of other physiological benefits. 派 psychologically（*ad.* 心理上地；心理学上地）
psychopath [ˈsaɪkəpæθ]	*n.* 精神变态者（a person affected with antisocial personality disorder） 记 词根记忆：psycho（精神）+ path（病患者）→ 精神病患者 → 精神变态者 例 The *psychopath* was imprisoned in a private cell. 同根词：psychosis（*n.* 精神病，变态心理）
pugnacious [pʌɡˈneɪʃəs]	*a.* 好斗的（having a quarrelsome or combative nature） 记 词根记忆：pugn（打斗）+ acious（多…的）→ 好斗的 例 The Olympic Games helped to keep peace among the *pugnacious* states of the Greek world. 派 pugnacity（*n.* 好斗性）
pulp [pʌlp]	*n.* 浆状物（substance with a soft texture similar to these）；纸浆（soft mass of wood fibre, used for making paper） 记 和 bulb（*n.* 球形物；鳞茎）一起记 例 wood *pulp* 木质纸浆
punishable [ˈpʌnɪʃəbl]	*a.* 可罚的；该罚的（liable to or deserving punishment） 记 来自 punish（*v.* 惩罚） 例 Because of a law passed in 1933 making it a crime *punishable* by imprisonment for a United States citizen to hold gold in the form of bullion or coins, immigrants found that on arrival in the United States they had to surrender all of the gold they had brought with them. 同根词：punishment（*n.* 惩罚）
pup [pʌp]	*n.* 小狗（a young dog）；幼兽（one of the young of various animals）；*v.* 产患（to give birth to pups） 记 注意：pub（*n.* 小酒馆） 例 rat *pups* 幼鼠

purchase [ˈpɜːrtʃəs]	*v.* 购买(to constitute the means for buying); *n.* 购买(an act or instance of purchasing); 支点(阻止东西下滑)(a mechanical hold) 记 联想记忆: pur + chase(追逐) → 为了得到紧俏的商品而竞相追逐 → 购买 例 Homeowners aged 40 to 50 are more likely to *purchase* ice cream and are more likely to *purchase* it in larger amounts than are members of any other demographic group.
purchaser [ˈpɜːrtʃəsər]	*n.* 买方, 购买者(buyer) 记 来自 purchase(*v.* 购买) 例 They typically are instituted at the urging of the supplier rather than the *purchaser*. 同根词: purchasable(*a.* 可买的)
purification [ˌpjʊrɪfɪˈkeɪʃn]	*n.* 净化, 提纯(the act or an instance of purifying or of being purified) 记 来自 purify(*v.* 净化; 使…纯净) 例 water *purification* method 水质净化方法 同根词: purge(*v.* 使清净)
Puritan [ˈpjʊrɪtən]	*n.* 清教徒(a group of English Protestants in the 16th and 17th centuries who lived in a very strict and religious way); *a.* 清教徒的(of or relating to puritans) 记 词根记忆: pur(=pure 纯洁) + itan → 讲究道德纯洁 → 清教徒 例 The ideas and institutions developed by New England *Puritans* had powerful effects on North American culture. 派 Puritanism(*n.* 清教徒主义)
purport	[ˈpɜːrpɔːrt] *n.* 意图(intention) [pərˈpɔːrt] *v.* 声称(to claim) 记 注意: purpose(*n.* 目的) 例 The book *purports* to be an original work but is really a compilation. 派 purportedly(*ad.* 据称)
pursue [pərˈsuː]	*v.* 追求(to seek); 追击(to follow in order to capture, kill, or defeat); 继续(to proceed with) 记 词根记忆: pur(向前) + sue(求) → 向前追 → 追求 例 *pursue* pleasure 追求快乐 // Police were trying to *pursue* criminal copyright infringers. // The government decided to *pursue* its conservative economic policies. 派 pursuit(*n.* 追求; 研究)
purview [ˈpɜːrvjuː]	*n.* (工作、活动等的)范围(range of operation or activity; scope)
putty [ˈpʌti]	*n.* 油灰(a doughlike material typically made of whiting and linseed oil that is used especially to fasten glass in window frames and to fill crevices in woodwork); 易被摆布的人(one who is easily manipulated) 例 The plumber sealed the joint in the pipes with *putty*.

30

pyramid [ˈpɪrəmɪd]	*n.* 角锥 (solid figure of this shape with a base of three or more sides); 金字塔 (an ancient massive structure found especially in Egypt having typically a square ground plan, outside walls in the form of four triangles that meet in a point at the top) 例 The chambers inside the *pyramid* of the Pharaoh Menkaure (门卡乌拉法老王) were closed to visitors for cleaning.
quadrant [ˈkwɑːdrənt]	*n.* 象限 (被坐标轴分开的平面中的四个区域的任一个) (an instrument with an arc of 90 degrees marked off in degrees, for measuring angles) 记 词根记忆：quadr (四) + ant → 由四个部分组成的 → 象限 例 *quadrant* IV 第四象限 同根词：quadrilateral (*n.* 四边形)
quadruple [kwɑːˈdruːpl]	*v.* (使) 成四倍 (to become four times as great or as numerous) 记 词根记忆：quadru (四) + ple (加) → 加四次 → 成四倍 例 A certain culture of bacteria *quadruples* every hour.
quail [kweɪl]	*n.* 鹌鹑 例 Europeans have long known that eating *quail* sometimes makes the eater ill.
qualify [ˈkwɑːlɪfaɪ]	*v.* (使) 合格 (to meet the required standard); (使) 具有资格 (to certify) 记 词根记忆：qual (性质，特征) + ify (使…) → 使具有某种性质 → 具有资格 例 Farmers wished to *qualify* for support payments. 派 qualified (*a.* 有资格的；有限的); disqualify (*v.* 丧失资格)
qualitative [ˈkwɑːlɪtətɪv]	*a.* (性) 质的，质量的；定性的 (of, relating to, or involving quality or kind) 记 词根记忆：qual (性质，特征) + it + ative → 性质的 例 *qualitative* change 质变 // *qualitative* analysis 定性分析
quantitative [ˈkwɑːntəteɪtɪv]	*a.* (数) 量的，(定) 量的 (of, relating to, or involving the measurement of quantity or amount) 记 词根记忆：quant (量，数量) + it + ative → 量的 例 *quantitative* analyses 定量分析
quantum [ˈkwɑːntəm]	*n.* [*pl.* quanta] 量 (amount, quantity); 量子 (any of the very small increments or parcels into which many forms of energy are subdivided) 记 词根记忆：quant (量，数量) + um → 量 例 *quantum* chemistry 量子化学 同根词：quantity (*n.* 数量，总量); quantitative (*a.* 数量的)
quarantine [ˈkwɔːrəntiːn]	*n.* 隔离检疫期 (a restraint upon the activities or communication of persons or the transport of goods designed to prevent the spread of disease or pests) 例 It will be necessary to keep the dogs in *quarantine* for 30 days after importing them.
quarry [ˈkwɔːri]	*n.* 猎物 (prey); *v.* 挖掘 (to dig) 例 Snow geese are a popular *quarry* for hunters in the Arctic.

□ pyramid　　□ quadrant　　□ quadruple　　□ quail　　□ qualify　　□ qualitative
□ quantitative　　□ quantum　　□ quarantine　　□ quarry

quasar [ˈkweɪzɑːr]	n.【天】类星体（any of a class of celestial objects that resemble stars） 例 *Quasars* are so distant that their lights have taken billions of years to reach the Earth.
quest [kwest]	v./n. 寻找（search）；寻求（pursuit） 记 联想记忆：问题（question）丢了（ion）需要寻找（quest） 例 Contrary to the general impression, this *quest* for import relief has hurt more companies than it has helped.
questionnaire [ˌkwestʃəˈner]	n. 问卷，调查表（a set of questions for obtaining statistically useful or personal information from individuals） 例 survey *questionnaires* 调查问卷
quiescent [kwiˈesnt]	a. 静止的（marked by inactivity） 记 词根记忆：qui（=rest 安静的）+ escent（状态）→ 安静的状态 → 静止的 例 These pills will make the nerves electrically *quiescent*, thus no pain signals are sent to the brain.
quiz [kwiz]	n. 小测验（a short oral or written test） 记 联想记忆：他最终放弃（quit）了小测验（quiz） 例 Professor Wang gave a *quiz* to two classes.
quota [kwoʊtə]	n. 限额，配额（a proportional part or share） 记 词根记忆：quot（数目）+ a → 数目有限制 → 限额，配额 例 import *quota* 进口配额
quote [kwoʊt]	v. 引用，引述（to speak or write（a passage）from another usually with credit acknowledgment） 记 词根记忆：quot（引用）+ e → 引用，引述 例 The minister *quoted* the scriptures from the New Testament. 派 quotation（n. 引用语）

The important thing in life is to have a great aim, and the determination to attain it.

人生重要的事情就是确定一个伟大的目标，并决心实现它。

——德国诗人、戏剧家 歌德（Johan Goethe, German poet and dramatist）

30

☐ quasar ☐ quest ☐ questionnaire ☐ quiescent ☐ quiz ☐ quota
☐ quote

quotient ['kwouʃnt]	*n.* 【数】商（the number resulting from the division of one number by another） 例 If you divide 26 by 2, the *quotient* is 13.
raccoon [ræ'kuːn]	*n.* 浣熊 例 *Raccoons* are shy and active only at night.
racism ['reɪsɪzəm]	*n.* 种族歧视（racial prejudice or discrimination）；种族主义（a belief that race is the primary determinant of human traits and some races are superior to others） 记 词根记忆：rac(e)(种族) + ism(…主义) → 种族主义 同根词：racist(*n.* 种族主义者)
radiant ['reɪdiənt]	*a.* 辐射的；发光的（radiating rays or reflecting beams of light）；容光焕发的（marked by or expressive of love confidence, or happiness） 记 词根记忆：radi(光线，射线) + ant → 发光的 → 容光焕发的 例 a *radiant* smile 灿烂的笑容 同根词：radiation(*n.* 发光，传播)；radiator(*n.* 散热器)
radiate ['reɪdieɪt]	*v.* 放射，辐射（to send out in or as if in rays） 记 词根记忆：radi(光线) + ate → 发光，放热 → 放射，辐射 例 The national observatory has been observing x-rays *radiated* by compact stars for years. 派 radiation(*n.* 放射；放射物；放射线)
radical ['rædɪkl]	*a.* 激进的（extreme, drastic）；*n.* 激进分子（a person who is radical） 记 词根记忆：radic(根) + al → 根本不讲道理的 → 激进的 例 a *radical* feminist 激进的女权主义者 派 radically(*ad.* 彻底地；激进地)
radioactive ['reɪdiou'æktɪv]	*a.* 放射性的，有辐射能力的（of, caused by or exhibiting radioactivity） 记 词根记忆：radi(辐射；光线) + o + active(活跃的) → 发射光活跃的 → 放射性的 例 Calcium carbonate shells contain *radioactive* material.
radiocarbon [ˌreɪdiou'kɑːrbən]	*n.* 放射性碳 记 联想记忆：radio(无线的) + carbon(碳) → 不经过实体传播的碳 → 放射性碳 例 Using new *radiocarbon* dating techniques, it was determined that the charcoal from the Colorado site was at least 11,400 years old.

radius [ˈreɪdiəs]	*n.* 半径(a line segment extending from the center of a circle or sphere to the circumference or bounding surface) 记 注意：diameter(*n.* 直径)；circumference(*n.* 圆周) 例 The *radius* of the circle is 0.5 meter.
raffle [ˈræfl]	*n.* 抽奖(lottery) 记 联想记忆：raff(大量，一大堆) + le → 在一大堆里抽 → 抽奖 例 *raffle* tickets 抽彩券
ragtime [ˈrægtaɪm]	*n.* 拉格泰姆音乐(一种早期黑人爵士乐)(rhythm characterized by strong syncopation in the melody with a regularly accented accompaniment in stride-piano style)；*a.* 滑稽的(funny) 记 联想记忆：rag(破衣服) + time(时候) → 黑人穿破衣服的时候跳的爵士舞 例 Scott was a preeminent *ragtime* composer.
raid [reɪd]	*n./v.* 劫掠(foray)；突袭(a surprise attack) 例 The king began to *raid* and conquer the enemy territory. 派 raider(*n.* 袭击者)
railroad [ˈreɪlroʊd]	*n.* 铁路(a permanent road having a line of rails) 记 词根记忆：rail(铁轨) + road(路) → 铁路 例 The government should lower the *railroad* companies' property taxes.
rally [ˈræli]	*n.* (行情、价格等)跌后复升，反弹(rebound) 例 Economists predicted that there would be a *rally* in stocks and bonds.
ranch [ræntʃ]	*n.* 大农场(large farm, esp. in U.S. or Canada, where cattle are bred) 派 rancher(*n.* 农场主)
rangeland [ˈreɪndʒlænd]	*n.* 牧场(land used or suitable for range) 记 联想记忆：range(漫游) + land(土地) → 牛羊可以漫游的土地 → 牧场
ransom [ˈrænsəm]	*n.* 赎金(a consideration paid or demanded for the release of someone or something from captivity)；*v.* 救赎(to deliver from sin or its penalty) 记 联想记忆：ran(跑) + som(看作 sum 一笔钱) → 用一笔钱跑 → 赎金 注意：random(*a.* 随意的) 例 The hijackers demanded a *ransom* of a million pounds. // The prisoners should be *ransomed*.
ratification [ˌrætɪfɪˈkeɪʃn]	*n.* 正式批准(formal confirmation) 记 来自 ratify(*v.* 正式批准) 例 The role of Congress in the *ratification* of treaties with sovereign nations was eventually undermined.
rating [ˈreɪtɪŋ]	*n.* 等级；定额(a classification according to grade) 例 *Ratings* of productivity correlated highly with *ratings* of both accuracy and attendance. // Managers responded that productivity was the critical factor in assigning *ratings*.
ratio [ˈreɪʃioʊ]	*n.* 比例(proportion) 记 词根记忆：rat(计算) + io → 和计算有关的 → 比例 例 Statistics show that the *ratio* of women's earnings with that of men have been roughly static since 1960.

31

ration [ˈræʃn]	*n.* 定量配给(食物等)(fixed quantity, esp. an official allowance of food, etc. in times of shortage) 记 词根记忆：rat(计算) + ion → 计算着给 → 配给 例 a *rationing* mechanism 配给机制
rational [ˈræʃnəl]	*a.* 合理的，理性的 (having reason or understanding)；*n.* 有理数(an integer or a fraction) 记 词根记忆：ration(理性，定量) + al → 理性的，合理的 例 The majority of successful senior managers do not closely follow the classical *rational* model of first clarifying goals. 派 rationally(*ad.* 理性地) 同根词：rationalistic(*a.* 理性主义的；纯理论的)
rationale [ˌræʃəˈnæl]	*n.* 根本性的依据(an underlying reason, basis) 记 词根记忆：rat(计算) + ion + ale → 通过精密计算 → 根本性的依据 例 My professor disagreed with the *rationale* of my argument.
reactor [riˈæktər]	*n.* 起反应的人(one that reacts)；【原】反应堆(a device for the controlled release of nuclear energy) 记 词根记忆：react(反应) + or → 发生反应的东西 → 反应堆 例 nuclear *reactor* 核反应堆
readily [ˈredɪli]	*ad.* 乐意地(willingly)；容易地(easily) 例 Women accepted the more unattractive new industrial tasks more *readily* than did men. // Such foods are more *readily* available in China than in the U.S..
realm [relm]	*n.* 领域(domain)；国度(kingdom) 记 联想记忆：real(真正的) + m → 真正的好东西(如音乐，艺术)无国界 → 领域；国度 例 the *realm* of science 科学领域
rear [rɪr]	*v.* 抚养(to bring up)；*a.* 后面的(being at the back) 例 The identical twins were *reared* apart from each other. // *rear* wheel 后轮
reasoning [ˈriːzənɪŋ]	*n.* 推理，论证(argument)；*a.* 推理的(the use of reason) 记 来自 reason(*n.* 理由；理性；*v.* 说服；推论) 例 This confirms the alternative view that intuition is actually more effective than careful, methodical *reasoning*. 派 reasoningly(*ad.* 理性地；推论地) 同根词：reasonable(*a.* 合理的；公道的)
rebut [rɪˈbʌt]	*v.* 反驳(to refute) 记 词根记忆：re(反) + but(=butt 顶撞) → 反顶撞 → 反驳 例 The scientist *rebutted* the cigarette company's claims. 派 rebuttal(*n.* 反驳，反证)

recall [rɪ'kɔːl]	*v.* 回忆(to remember); *n.* 收回(a public call by a manufacturer for the return of a product that may be defective) 记 词根记忆: re(重新) + call(叫, 召集) → 重新叫一遍, 收集一遍 → 回收 例 Randomly generated passwords are difficult for employees to *recall*. // Although one link in the chain was weak, it's not sufficiently so to require the *recall* of the automobile.
receipt [rɪ'siːt]	*n.* 收据(a piece of paper as proof of receiving of goods or money); [*pl.*] 收入(sth. received) 记 词根记忆: re + ceipt(看作 cept 拿, 取) → 拿到的, 取到的 → 收入 例 gross *receipts* 总收入
reception [rɪ'sepʃn]	*n.* (无线电、电视等的)接收效果(the receiving of a radio or television broadcast) 例 For locations with poor television *reception*, cable televisions are recommended.
receptive [rɪ'septɪv]	*a.* (to)(愿意)接受的(inclined to receive) 记 词根记忆: re + cept(拿, 取) + ive → 愿意拿的 → 接受的 例 Jane was *receptive* to changes in her work schedule. 派 receptivity(*n.* 接受能力)
receptor [rɪ'septər]	*n.* 感(接)受器(receiver); 受体(sense organ) 记 词根记忆: re + cept(拿, 取) + or → 被拿的 → 受体, 主要用于生物学领域 例 The milk of many mammals contains substances that are known to stimulate certain *receptors* in the brain.
recession [rɪ'seʃn]	*n.* 衰退, 萧条(时期)(a period of reduced economic activity) 记 词根记忆: re(反) + cess(走) + ion → 反着走 → 衰退 例 It's impossible to decrease inflation without causing a *recession* and its concomitant increase in unemployment.
recipe ['resəpi]	*n.* 食谱(a set of instructions for making something from various ingredients) 记 联想记忆: re + cipe(抓) → 从饭里抓出的精华 → 食谱 例 There are a lot of delicious *recipes* in this cookbook.
recipient [rɪ'sɪpiənt]	*n.* 接受者(receiver); *a.* (愿意)接受的(receptive) 例 The *recipient* of the lottery's grand prize quit her job.
reciprocal [rɪ'sɪprəkl]	*a.* 相互的; 相应的(corresponding); *n.* 【数】倒数(either of a pair of numbers whose product is one); 互相起作用的事物(sth. in a reciprocal relationship to another) 记 联想记忆: 相互(reciprocal)乘积为 1 的一对数互为倒数 例 The services that are provided should be *reciprocal* to the amount of taxes that are paid.

31

reclaim
[rɪ'kleɪm]

v. 收回(to recover)；恢复(土地)(to restore to a previous natural state)

记 词根记忆：re(重新) + claim(要求) → 重新要求 → 收回

例 The manager *reclaimed* decision-making authority. // It'll be a costly project to *reclaim* surface coal mines.

派 reclamation(n. 改造)

recluse
['reklu:s]

n. 隐士 (a person who leads a secluded or solitary life)；a. 隐居的(marked by withdrawal from society)

记 词根记忆：re + cluse(关闭) → 重新把门关上 → 隐居的

例 Although the bite of the brown *recluse* spider is rarely fatal, it causes chronic flesh wounds and poses the greatest danger to infants and the elderly, who are particularly vulnerable to its poison.

派 reclusive(a. 隐居的)

recommend
[ˌrekə'mend]

v. 推荐；建议(to advise)

记 联想记忆：re + com(共同) + mend(修) → 这本书是大家一修再修的成果，强力推荐 → 推荐

例 We should *recommend* the use of such identification badges to all of our clients.

recommendation
[ˌrekəmen'deɪʃn]

n. 推荐(the act of recommending)；推荐信(sth. that recommends or expresses commendation)

记 来自 recommend(v. 推荐；介绍)

例 Such a *recommendation* could help us get the Windfall account by demonstrating to Windfall the rigorousness of our methods.

reconcile
['rekənsaɪl]

v. 调停，调解(to settle)；调和，使一致(to make consistent)；使协调，使和解(to restore to harmony or friendship)

记 联想记忆：re + concile(看作 council 委员会) → 召开委员会 → 调停，调解

例 Since the couple could not *reconcile* their differences, they decided to get a divorce. // Researchers are trying to *reconcile* the experimental result with their theory.

reconvene
[ˌri:kən'vi:n]

v. 再集会(to gather again)

记 词根记忆：re(重新) + convene(集会) → 再集会

例 Congress will *reconvene* in two weeks.

recoup
[rɪ'ku:p]

v. 补偿(to compensate)；恢复(to make good or make up for sth. lost)

例 The investor could not *recoup* the money she had spent on the stock.

recourse
['ri:kɔ:rs]

n. (to)求助；依靠(a turning to sb. or sth. for help or protection)

例 Police was his last *recourse*.

recover
[rɪ'kʌvər]

v. 恢复(to get back)

记 词根记忆：re(再，重新) + cover(遮盖) → 恢复

例 Most victims of infectious mononucleosis *recover* after a few weeks of listlessness, but an unlucky few may suffer for years.

派 recovery(n. 恢复，痊愈)

同根词：uncover(v. 发现，揭露)

recreation [ˌrekriˈeɪʃn]	*n.* 娱乐活动，消遣(refreshment) 记 来自 recreate(*v.* 娱乐) 例 The new residents do not need to travel into Lamberton regularly for shopping or *recreation*.
recreational [ˌrekriˈeɪʃənl]	*a.* 娱乐的(of, relating to, or characteristic of recreation) 记 来自 recreate(*v.* 娱乐) 例 Many Milville residents object to having to pay fees for *recreational* use of the park in the winter.
recruit [rɪˈkruːt]	*n.* 新成员(a newcomer to a field or activity); *v.* 招收(to engage, to hire) 记 联想记忆：re(重新) + cruit(=cres 成长) → 重新成长 → 新成员 例 We have had only marginal success in *recruiting* and training high-quality professional staff. 派 recruiter(*n.* 征兵人员)
rectangle [ˈrektæŋgl]	*n.* 长方形，矩形(a parallelogram all of whose angles are right angles) 记 词根记忆：rect(直) + angle(角) → 每个角均为直角的四边形 → 长方形 例 The three small *rectangles* have the same dimensions. 派 rectangular(*a.* 长方形的)
recur [rɪˈkɜːr]	*v.* 再发生(to happen again); 重新提起(to come up again for consideration) 记 词根记忆：re(重新) + cur(=run 跑) → 跑回来 → 再发生 例 A migraine afflicts one side of the head, and may *recur* as infrequently as once every other month, or as often as daily. 派 recurrent(*a.* 反复出现的; 再发生的)
redirect [ˌriːdəˈrekt]	*v.* 改寄(信件)(to send in a new direction); 改变方向(to change the course or direction of) 记 词根记忆：re(重新) + direct(指向) → 改变方向 例 The Chicago and Calumet Rivers, originally flowing into the St. Lawrence by way of Lake Michigan, have been *redirected* through the construction of canals so that the water now empties into the Mississippi by way of the Illinois River.
redress [rɪˈdres]	*v.* 改正(to correct); 调整(to set right) 记 联想记忆：re(重新) + dress(穿衣，整理) → 重新整理 → 改正 例 It is not likely that the competitive imbalance will be *redressed* during the foreseeable future.
reef [riːf]	*n.* 礁，暗礁(ridge of rock, shingle, sand, etc. at or near the surface of the sea) 例 coral *reef* 珊瑚礁
referendum [ˌrefəˈrendəm]	*n.* [*pl.* referenda]公民投票(referring of a political issue to a general vote by all the people of a country for a decision)
referral [rɪˈfɜːrəl]	*n.* 推荐，提及(the act, action, or an instance of referring) 例 Some business is difficult to obtain through *referrals* and word-of-mouth.

31

refine

[rɪˈfaɪn]

v. 精炼 (to free from impurities); 改善 (to improve)

记 词根记忆：re(重新) + fine(纯的，精美的) → 重新变纯 → 精炼

例 The oil needed to be *refined* before it could be used. // The company *refined* its hiring process.

派 refinement(*n.* 提炼；改进); refined(*a.* 精炼的)

refiner

[rɪˈfaɪnər]

n. 精炼机 (machines which make improvement by introducing subtleties or distinctions); 精制者，精炼者

记 来自 refine(*v.* 精炼；改善)

例 Heating-oil prices are expected to be higher this year than last because *refiners* are paying about $5 a barrel more for crude oil than they were last year.

refinery

[rɪˈfaɪnəri]

n. 精炼厂 (a building and equipment for refining or processing)

记 来自 refine(*v.* 精炼；改善)

例 The Tasberg *refinery* is more favorably situated than the Grenville *refinery* with respect to the major supply routes for raw petroleum.

同根词：refinement(*n.* 精制；提纯)

reflective

[rɪˈflektɪv]

a. 反射的，反照的 (capable of reflecting light, images, or sound waves); 深思熟虑的 (thoughtful)

记 词根记忆：re + flect(弯曲) + ive(形容词后缀) → 向后弯曲的 → 反射的

例 Antarctica receives more solar radiation than does any other place on Earth, yet the temperatures are so cold and the ice cap is so *reflective* that little of the polar ice melts during the summer.

派 reflectively(*ad.* 反应地；反照地)

reflex

[ˈriːfleks]

n. （对刺激的本能）反应 (an automatic and often inborn response to a stimulus); [~es]反应能力 (the power of acting or responding with adequate speed)

记 词根记忆：re(反) + flex(弯曲) → 反过来弯曲 → 反应

例 Fifteen-year-olds typically have much better eyesight, much better hand-eye coordination and much quicker *reflexes*.

派 reflexive(*a.* 自发的；反身的)

refraction

[rɪˈfrækʃn]

n. 折射 (bending of a ray of light)

记 来自 refract(*v.* 使折射)

例 The Chinese launched weather balloons near their theodolites to measure atmospheric temperature and pressure changes to better estimate *refraction* errors.

派 refractive(*a.* 折射的)

refrain

[rɪˈfreɪn]

v. 抑制，避免 (curb, restrain)

例 People must *refrain* from drinking if they will have to drive.

refuel

[ˌriːˈfjuːəl]

v. 补给燃料 (to provide with additional fuel); 重新得到燃料 (to take on additional fuel)

记 词根记忆：re(再) + fuel(燃料) → 重新得到燃料

例 The Skybus's fuel efficiency results in both lower fuel costs and reduced time spent *refueling*.

□ refine   □ refiner   □ refinery   □ reflective   □ reflex   □ refraction
□ refrain   □ refuel

refugee [ˌrefjuˈdʒiː]	n.难民（a person who has been forced to leave his or her country, home, etc. and seeks refuge, esp. from political or religious persecution） 记 词根记忆：re + fug(逃，离开) + ee → 逃离家园的人→ 难民 例 The recent immigrants didn't receive *refugee* benefits for their illegally entering the country.
refund [ˈriːfʌnd]	n.退款（to return money）；偿还（to give or put back） 记 词根记忆：re(重新) + fund(付钱) → 重新拿到所付的钱 → 退款 例 One government program would award low income families a *refund* of $1,000 for each child under age four.
refutation [ˌrefjuˈteɪʃn]	n.反驳，驳斥（the act or process of refuting） 例 sophistic *refutations* 似是而非的驳斥
refute [rɪˈfjuːt]	v.反驳，驳倒（to prove wrong by argument or evidence） 记 词根记忆：re + fute(打) → 反过来打 → 反驳 例 Clark *refutes* the extremes of the constructivists by both theoretical and empirical arguments. 派 refutation(n. 反驳); refutable(a. 可驳倒的)
regenerate [rɪˈdʒenəreɪt]	v.(使)再生，(使)恢复（to restore to original strength or properties） 记 词根记忆：re(重新) + generate(产生) → 重新产生 → (使)再生 例 Damaged nerves in the spinal cord do not *regenerate* themselves naturally. 派 regeneration(n. 再生); regenerator(n. 再发器)
regime [reɪˈʒiːm]	n.(气象等的)形态（a regular pattern of occurrence or action）；政权（polity） 例 climate *regime* 气候形态，气候建制
regiment [ˈredʒɪmənt]	n.军团（a military unit consisting usually of a number of battalions） 记 词根记忆：regi(=rigid 严格) + ment → 受严格控制的 → 军团 例 The soldier fought with the fifth *regiment*.
regionalization [ˌriːdʒənəlaɪˈzeɪʃən]	n.分成地区（dividing into regions）；按地区安排（arranging regionally） 记 来自region(n. 地区) 例 *regionalization* of commercial markets 贸易市场地区化
register [ˈredʒɪstər]	n.登记簿（a written record containing regular entries of items or details）； v.登记（to enroll one's name in a register） 例 Patients often *register* dissatisfaction with physicians who prescribe nothing for their ailments. 派 registration(n. 登记；注册)
regressive [rɪˈgresɪv]	a.(税率)递减的（decreasing in rate as the base increases） 记 词根记忆：re(后) + gress(走) + ive → 向后走 → 退步的 → 递减的 注意：progressive(a. 先进的) 例 Sales taxes tend to be *regressive*, affecting poor people more severely than wealthy people.

31

reign [reɪn]	*n.* 统治(时期)(sovereignty) 记 来自 rein(*v.* 统治)的变体 注意: regime(*n.* 政权) 例 The most ancient Egyptian temples were constructed in the *reign* of Ramses II.
reimburse [ˌriːɪm'bɜːrs]	*v.* 偿还(to repay) 记 词根记忆: re(重新) + im(进入) + burse(钱包) → 重新进入钱包 → 偿还 例 The insurance coverage(保险责任范围)does not *reimburse* subscribers for medical expenses incurred in a public hospital. 派 reimbursement(*n.* 偿还)

If you want to understand today, you have to search yesterday.

想要懂得今天，就必须研究昨天。

——美国女作家 赛珍珠(Pearl Buck, American female writer)

音频

Word List 32

reinforce [ˌriːɪnˈfɔːrs]	*v.* 加强 (to strengthen); 补充 (to strengthen by additional assistance, material) 记 词根记忆：re(再) + inforce(强化) → 加强 例 In birds, these hollow bones are *reinforced* more massively by internal struts.
reinvest [ˌriːɪnˈvest]	*v.* 再授给 (to invest in additional securities); 再投资 (to invest again or anew) 记 词根记忆：re(再) + invest(投资) → 再投资 例 The profits may be *reinvested* to increase economic growth through ecoefficiency.
reject [rɪˈdʒekt]	*v.* 拒绝，抵制 (to refuse) 记 词根记忆：re(反) + ject(扔) → 被扔回来 → 拒绝 例 Recently a court ruled that current law allows companies to *reject* a job applicant if working in the job would entail a 90 percent chance that the applicant would suffer a heart attack. 同根词：object(*v.* 反对; *n.* 目标)
rejection [rɪˈdʒekʃn]	*n.* 抛弃; 拒绝 (the action of rejecting); 被抛弃的东西 (sth. rejected) 记 来自 reject(*v.* 拒绝) 例 The first presents a goal that the argument rejects as ill-conceived; the second is evidence that is presented as grounds for that *rejection*. 同根词：ejection(*n.* 喷出; 排出物)
rekindle [ˌriːˈkɪndl]	*v.* 重新激起 (to cause sth. to light again) 记 词根记忆：re(重新) + kindle(点燃) → 重燃 → 重新激起 例 He is trying to *rekindle* pride in his compatriots.
relative [ˈrelətɪv]	*n.* 亲戚 (a person connected with another by blood or affinity); *a.* 相对的; 相关的 (not absolute or independent) 记 来自 relate(*v.* 相关，关系) 例 Once introduced into southern Europe, maize became popular with landowners because of its high yields *relative* to other cereal crops. 派 relatively(*ad.* 相对地) 同根词：relation(*n.* 关系)

relativity [ˌreləˈtɪvəti]	*n.* 相对论(Einstein's theory of the universe which shows that all motion is relative and treats time as a fourth dimension related to space) 例 general *relativity* 广义相对论
relay [rɪˈleɪ]	*v.* 中继转发，转播(to broadcast sth. by passing signals through a transmitting station) 例 Robot satellites *relay* important communications and identify weather patterns.
release [rɪˈliːs]	*v./n.* 排放(to send out)；发表(布)(to make available to the public)；解放，释放(to set free from restraint, confinement, or servitude) 记 词根记忆：re(一再) + lease(松弛，放松) → 解放，释放 例 The *release* of the iron compounds did not increase the supply of nitrogen compounds in the area.
relentless [rɪˈlentləs]	*a.* 无情的(unrelenting)；不断的(steady, persistent) 记 词根记忆：relent(变温和) + less → 不能变温和 → 无情的 例 *relentless* persecution 无情的迫害
reliable [rɪˈlaɪəbl]	*a.* 可靠的，可信赖的(dependable) 记 词根记忆：rel(y)(信赖) + iable(能…的) → 可靠的，可信赖的. 例 A more *reliable* study has indicated that eating chocolate does not increase the likelihood of getting heart disease. 派 reliability(*n.* 可靠性)；reliance(*n.* 信赖；信任)
reliance [rɪˈlaɪəns]	*n.* 信赖，信任(the state of being dependent on or having confidence in) 记 来自 rely(*v.* 信赖) 例 If these trends in fuel production and usage continue, Sidurian *reliance* on foreign sources for fuel should decline soon. 同根词：reliant(*a.* 信赖的)
relic [ˈrelɪk]	*n.* 文物(trace or feature surviving from a past age and serving to remind people of it) 例 The museum put the ancient *relics* on display.
relieve [rɪˈliːv]	*v.* 缓解；减轻(to lighten) 记 词根记忆：re + lieve(=lev 轻) → 使…轻 → 缓解；减轻 例 Solacium(a medicinal herb) can *relieve* tension and promote deep sleep. 派 relief(*n.* 轻松；缓解)；reliever(*n.* 救济者)
religious [rɪˈlɪdʒəs]	*a.* 宗教的(of religion)；虔诚的(of, relating to, or devoted to religious beliefs or observances) 例 It is almost universally agreed that political virtue must rest upon moral and *religious* precepts.
relinquish [rɪˈlɪŋkwɪʃ]	*v.* 放弃(to give up)；交出(to give over possession of) 记 词根记忆：re(重新) + linqu(=leave 离开) + ish → 再次离开 → 放弃 例 Max *relinquished* his ownership of a small piece of land needed by the city.

reluctant [rɪˈlʌktənt]	*a.* 不情愿的，勉强的(unwilling) 例 War industries during the Second World War were *reluctant* to hire women for factory work. 派 reluctance(*n.* 勉强)
remainder [rɪˈmeɪndər]	*n.* 【数】余数；剩余部分(a remaining group part, or trace) 记 来自 remain(*v.* 剩余)，指减法之后的余数 例 Please write the *remainder* as a fraction. // Mary did most of the work, and Susan finished the *remainder*.
remedy [ˈremədi]	*n.* 药(物)(a medicine)；*v.* 补救(relieve)；纠正(correct) 记 词根记忆：re + med(治疗) + y → 治疗 例 sovereign *remedy* 特效药 // We don't know how to *remedy* the serious problem. // *remedy* a mistake 纠正错误
reminiscent [ˌremɪˈnɪsnt]	*a.* 回忆的(marked by or given to reminiscence)；使人联想的(tending to remind) 记 联想记忆：把 remini 当作 remember + scent(香味) → 记起过去香味的 → 回忆的 例 Leon Forrest's work is more *reminiscent* of Henry Miller's obsessive narratives and Toni Morrison's mythic languages than James Joyce's internal explorations. 派 reminiscence(*n.* 回忆，怀旧)
remnant [ˈremnənt]	*n.* 残余物，残迹(a usually small part, member, or trace remaining) 例 More than twenty supernova *remnants* have been detected in X-ray studies.
renaissance [ˈrenəsɑːns]	*n.* 复兴，复活(rebirth, revival)；(the Renaissance) 文艺复兴(revival of art and literature in the 14th, 15th centuries based on classical forms) 记 词根记忆：re(重新) + naiss(=nas 出生) + ance → 新生 → 复兴 例 The *renaissance* of the feminist movement during the 1950's led to the Stasist school. (斯塔西学派是美国的一个学派，它反对走极端，主张东西部生活对妇女来说具有相似性)
renal [ˈriːnl]	*a.* 肾脏的，肾的(nephritic) 例 *renal* lithiasis 肾结石
render [ˈrendər]	*v.* 熔解(to melt down)；提供(to give)；使得(to make) 记 联想记忆：提供(render)后成为出借人(lender) 例 The paper can be *rendered* into paper pulp. // The Church *rendered* all sorts of educational and recreational activities. // Victorian prudery *rendered* all experience that was uniquely feminine unprintable. 派 rendition(*n.* 演唱，表演)
renegade [ˈrenɪɡeɪd]	*a.* 背弃的，离经叛道的(unconventional) 记 词根记忆：re + neg(否定) + ade → 遭到否定的 → 背弃的 例 Oberlin College in Ohio was a *renegade* institution at its 1833 founding for accepting both men and women as students.

32

renounce [rɪˈnaʊns]	*v.* 声明放弃(to abdicate); 拒绝承认(to refuse to follow, obey, or recognize any further) 记 词根记忆: re(反) + nounce(讲话, 通告) → 反过来宣布 → 拒绝承认 例 The King *renounced* his claim on the neighboring kingdom's land. // Eighteenth-century American peasants could not *renounce* the political objectives of the British Empire. 派 renunciation(*n.* 放弃) 同根词: denounce(*v.* 指责); enounce(*v.* 发音; 表达)
renovation [ˌrenəˈveɪʃn]	*n.* 整修(restoration), 革新(renewing) 记 来自 renovate(*v.* 修复, 革新) 例 The government provides one million dollars for the *renovation* of the famous large cathedral. // technical *renovation* 技术革新
renown [rɪˈnaʊn]	*n.* 名望, 声誉(fame) 记 词根记忆: re(反复) + nown(=nomen 名字) → 名字反复出现 → 名望 例 He won *renown* as a pianist. 派 renowned(*a.* 著名的)
rental [ˈrentl]	*n.* 租金(an amount paid or collected as rent), 租赁(an act of renting); *a.* 租赁的(of or relating to rent) 记 来自 rent(*v.* 租赁) 例 Although the daily rental fee for home use of films is generally the same as that for video games, the average *rental* period for a video game is longer than that for a film. 同根词: renter(*n.* 承租人; 房东)
reorganization [riːˌɔːrgənəˈzeɪʃn]	*n.* 改组; 整顿(the act or process of reorganizing) 记 词根记忆: re(再) + organiz(组织) + ation → 改组 例 After the *reorganization*, advertising sales increased. 同根词: organization(*n.* 组织)
repeal [rɪˈpiːl]	*v.* 【律】废除, 撤销(to annul by authoritative act) 记 词根记忆: re(反) + peal(驱动) → 反驱动 → 撤销 例 The city council *repealed* strict gun control laws. 同根词: appeal(*n./v.* 呼吁)
repertory [ˈrepərtɔːri]	*n.* 剧目, 作品(repertoire) 例 a pianist with a wide *repertory* 能演奏很多曲子的钢琴师
replacement [rɪˈpleɪsmənt]	*n.* 更换(the action or process of replacing), 代替者(one that replaces another especially in a job or function) 记 来自 replace(*v.* 取代, 替换) 例 They had great difficulty in finding a *replacement*. 同根词: replaceable(*a.* 可替换的)

replete [rɪˈpliːt]	*a.* 充满的 (full of) 记 词根记忆：re(重新) + plete(满) → 重新装满 → 充满的 例 The health-care economy is *replete* with unusual and even unique economic relationships. 派 repletion(*n.* 充满) 同根词：complete(*a.* 完全的)；deplete(*v.* 耗尽)
replicate [ˈreplɪkeɪt]	*v.* 复制，重复 (to duplicate, to repeat)；*n.* 复制品 (one of several identical experiments, procedures, or samples) 记 词根记忆：re(再) + plic(重复) + ate → 一再重复 → 复制 例 They did not attempt to *replicate* the original experiment.
repousse [rəˈpuːseɪ]	*n.* (冲压细工制成)凸纹面 (repousse decoration)；凸纹制作术 (repousse work)；*a.* 凸纹饰的；金属细工的 (shaped or ornamented with patterns in relief made by hammering or pressing on the reverse side—used especially of metal) 记 来自 repous(*v.* 冲压) 例 *Repousse* is a method of sculpture in which workers lay copper sheets over wooden molds and then, using a variety of exotic hammers, carefully pound the metal into shape.
representation [ˌreprɪzenˈteɪʃn]	*n.* 代表 (one that represents) 记 来自 represent(*v.* 代表；标志) 例 All of the animal figures in the Sepphoris mosaics are readily identifiable as *representations* of known species. 同根词：representative(*a.* 典型的；*n.* 代表)
representative [ˌreprɪˈzentətɪv]	*n.* 代表 (one that represents another or others delegate)；*a.* (of)有代表性的，典型的 (serving as a typical or characteristic example) 例 House of *Representatives* 众议院 // The students who didn't protest are more *representative* of the state's college students.
reproduce [ˌriːprəˈduːs]	*v.* 繁殖 (to have offspring or young)；复制 (to make a copy or equivalent of) 记 词根记忆：re(再) + produce(生产) → 不断生产 → 繁殖；复制 例 They can *reproduce* several times each year and produce large numbers of offspring. 派 reproducer(*n.* 复制程序；再生器) 同根词：productive(*a.* 多产的)
reproduction [ˌriːprəˈdʌkʃn]	*n.* 再生产 (the act or process of reproducing) 记 词根记忆：re(再)+production(生产) → 再生产 例 Paleontologist Stephen Jay Gould has argued that many biological traits are not the products of natural selection, favored because they enhance *reproduction* or survival, but are simply random by-products of other evolutionary developments.

32

reptile
['reptaɪl]

n. 爬行动物(any of a class of cold-blooded egg-laying animals including crocodiles, lizards snakes, turtles, etc. with relatively short legs or no legs at all)

记 词根记忆: rept(爬) + ile → 爬行动物

例 Although scales typically cover *reptiles*, the pterosaurs(翼龙)probably had hairy coats.

派 reptilian(*a.* 爬虫类的; 卑下的)

republican
[rɪ'pʌblɪkən]

n. 共和主义者(one that favors or supports a republican form of government); *a.* 共和国的(of, relating to, or having the characteristics of a republic)

记 词根记忆: republic(共和政体, 共和国) + an(表…的) → 共和国的

例 Introduction of the *republican* motherhood thesis dramatically changed historiography.

派 republicanism(*n.* 共和主义)

repudiate
[rɪ'pjuːdieɪt]

v. 拒绝(to decline); 拒付(to refuse to pay)

记 联想记忆: re(反) + pudi(感到羞耻) + ate → 反过来让对方羞耻 → 拒绝(别人)

例 The innocent man *repudiated* the charge of murder. // *repudiate* a debt 赖债

派 repudiation(*n.* 拒付)

rescind
[rɪ'sɪnd]

v. 废除(法律等)(to repeal)

记 词根记忆: re(反) + scind(=cut 砍) → 砍掉 → 废除

例 The outdated law was *rescinded* by the federal government.

resemble
[rɪ'zembl]

v. 类似于, 像(to be like or similar to)

记 词根记忆: re + semble(类似) → 类似于

例 The pterosaurs *resembled* both birds and bats in their overall structure and proportions.

派 resemblance(*n.* 相似; 相似处)

resent
[rɪ'zent]

v. 怨恨, 恼火(to feel or express ill will or annoyance at)

记 词根记忆: re(反) + sent(感情) → 反感 → 恼火

例 The hard-sell(强行推销)approach may make some consumers *resent* being told what to believe.

派 resentment(*n.* 怨恨, 愤恨); resentful(*a.* 愤慨的, 忿恨的)

同根词: sentiment(*n.* 情感)

reservation
[ˌrezər'veɪʃn]

n. 预订; 保存(an act of reserving sth.); 自然保护区(an area in which hunting is not permitted)

记 来自 reserve(*v.* 储存, 保存; 预订)

例 It failed to mention water rights to be enjoyed by the *reservation's* inhabitants.

同根词: preservation(*n.* 保存)

reserve [rɪˈzɜːrv]	*n.* 储备(sth. reserved or set aside for a particular purpose, use, or reason); *v.* 保留; 储备(to keep) 记 词根记忆: re + serve(服务, 保持) → 保持 → 储备; 保留 例 Federal *Reserve*(美国)联邦储备署 // The government intended to *reserve* water as well as land when establishing the reservation. 派 reservation(*n.* 保留)
reservoir [ˈrezərvwɑːr]	*n.* 水库; 蓄水池 an artificial lake or an apparatus where water is collected and kept in quantity for use) 记 来自 reserve(*v.* 保存, 储备) 例 The city council planned to build a *reservoir* along the river.
reside [rɪˈzaɪd]	*v.* 居住(to dwell); 存在(to present) 记 词根记忆: re + side(坐) → 坐落 → 存在 例 Some homeless people *reside* in group living quarters. 派 residence(*n.* 住处; 居住); residential(*a.* 居住的; 寄宿的)
residency [ˈrezɪdənsi]	*n.* 住宅, 住所 any address at which you dwell more than temporarily); 住院医生实习期(the period of time when a doctor working in a hospital receives special advanced training) 记 来自 resident(*n.* 居民) 例 The Immigration Service now has the discretionary power to keep families united even though not all their members meet the five-year *residency* requirement.
residential [ˌrezɪˈdenʃl]	*a.* 住宅的, 与居住有关的(of or relating to residence) 记 来自 resident(*n.* 居民) 例 Vehicle traffic in most *residential* areas of Arumville is heavier today than it was twenty years ago.
residual [rɪˈzɪdʒuəl]	*a.* 残余的, 剩余的(of, relating to, or constituting a residue) 记 联想记忆: re + sid(放置) + ual → 不能放回去的 → 残余的, 剩余的 例 This incineration generated a large quantity of *residual* ash. 同根词: residuum(*n.* 残留物; 残余)
residue [ˈrezɪduː]	*n.* 剩余物; 残余(remnant, remainder) 记 联想记忆: re + sid(放置) + ue → 不能放回去 → 残余 例 Ash *residue* from some types of trash can be used to condition garden soil.
resign [rɪˈzaɪn]	*v.* 辞职(to quit) 记 联想记忆: re(再次) + sign(签字) → 再次签字 → 辞职 例 Three of the present employees of the company were forced to *resign*. 派 resignation(*n.* 辞职)
resist [rɪˈzɪst]	*v.* 抵制, 抵抗(to oppose); 抗, 耐(to withstand the force of) 记 词根记忆: re(反) + sist(站) → 反过来站 → 抵抗 例 Managers under pressure to maximize cost-cutting will *resist* innovation. // *resist* heat 耐热 派 resistance(*n.* 抵制; 抵抗力); resistant(*a.* 抵抗的; 抗…的)

32

□ reserve   □ reservoir   □ reside   □ residency   □ residential   □ residual
□ residue   □ resign   □ resist

resistance
[rɪˈzɪstəns]

n. 抵抗（an act or instance of resisting）; 抵抗力; （电）阻力（the opposition offered by a body or substance to the passage through it of a steady electric current）

记 来自 resist（*v.* 阻止; 抵抗）

例 Scientists have made genetic modifications to cotton to increase its *resistance* to insect pests.

同根词: persistent（*a.* 固执的; 坚持的）

resolve
[rɪˈzɑːlv]

v. 解决（to deal with successfully）; 分解（to break up）; 决心（to determine）

记 词根记忆: re + solve（松开, 解开）→ 解决, 分解

例 Researchers *resolved* a particular scientific question concerning anole lizard（变色龙）species.

派 resolved（*a.* 下定决心的）; resolution（*n.* 正式决定; 分辨率）

resonance
[ˈrezənəns]

n. 共振（quality of being resonant）

例 magnetic *resonance* imaging 核磁共振成像

resort
[rɪˈzɔːrt]

v. （to）求助（to have recourse）; *n.* 度假胜地（popular holiday center）

记 联想记忆: 向上级打报告（report）求助（resort）

例 David *resorted* to jogging as a way to lose weight. // *resort* hotel 假日酒店

respective
[rɪˈspektɪv]

a. 分别的, 各自的（separate）

记 词根记忆: re（相反）+ spect（看）+ ive → 从相反的方向看 → 各自的

例 The tourists went back to their *respective* countries.

respiratory
[ˈrespərətɔːri]

a. 呼吸的（of respiration）

记 来自 respire（*v.* 呼吸）

例 Sulfur dioxide diminishes the *respiratory* system's ability to deal with all other pollutants.

同根词: expiration（*n.* 呼气; 终结）

respire
[rɪˈspaɪər]

v. 呼吸（to breathe）

记 和 inspire（*v.* 吸气）一起记

例 Although fruit can no longer grow once it is picked, it continues for some time to *respire*.

派 respiratory（*a.* 呼吸的）

resplendent
[rɪˈsplendənt]

a. 灿烂的; 辉煌的（splendid）

记 词根记忆: re + splend（发光）+ ent → 不断发光 → 辉煌的

例 *resplendent* achievement 辉煌成就

responsible
[rɪˈspɑːnsəbl]

a. （for）承担责任的（accountable）; 作为原因的（being the cause or explanation）

记 词根记忆: re + spons（约定）+ ible → 遵守约定 → 承担责任的

例 Manufacturers are *responsible* for ensuring that their products are safe. // An economist argued that the insurance was partly *responsible* for the high rate of bank failures.

派 responsibility（*n.* 责任, 职责）

□ resistance □ resolve □ resonance □ resort □ respective □ respiratory
□ respire □ resplendent □ responsible

responsive [rɪˈspɑːnsɪv]	*a.* (to) 有反应的(giving response)；反应迅速的, 敏感的(quick to respond or react appropriately or sympathetically, sensitive) 记 词根记忆：respons(反应) + ive → 有反应的 例 Lawmakers in the West were more *responsive* to women's concerns than lawmakers in the East were. 派 responsiveness(*n.* 反应)
restitution [ˌrestɪˈtuːʃn]	*n.* 归还(return)；赔偿(compensate) 记 词根记忆：re(重新) + stitut(放) + ion → 重新放回去 → 归还 例 The court ordered the *restitution* of assets to the company. // John sought *restitution* when David damaged his car. 同根词：institution(*n.* 创立, 建立); destitution(*n.* 贫穷)
restore [rɪˈstɔːr]	*v.* 恢复(to renew)；重建(to rebuild) 记 词根记忆：re(重新) + store(储存) → 身体重新储存能量 → 恢复 例 Investors could cut their losses by *restoring* their companies' productivity. // Some destroyed wild habitats have been *restored*. 派 restoration(*n.* 恢复；重建)
restrain [rɪˈstreɪn]	*v.* 抑制(to control)；限制；阻止(to prevent from doing) 记 联想记忆：re(重新) + strain(拉紧) → 重新拉紧 → 限制 例 A child-passenger protection law requires children under four years old to be *restrained* in a child safety seat. 派 restraint(*n.* 限制, 约束措施)
restrict [rɪˈstrɪkt]	*v.* 限制(to confine within bounds)；约束(to place under restrictions as to use or distribution) 记 联想记忆：re(一再) + strict(严格的) → 一再对其严格 → 约束 例 Other researchers *restrict* study participation to patients who have no ailments besides those being studied. 派 restrictive(*a.* 限制的；约束的); restriction(*n.* 限制) 同根词：constrict(*v.* 压缩；束紧)
restructure [ˌriːˈstrʌktʃər]	*v.* 调整, 重建(to change the makeup, organization, or pattern of)；更改结构(to restructure sth.) 记 词根记忆：re(重新) + structure(构造) → 重建 例 Our economy must be *restructured* as soon as possible.
resume [rɪˈzuːm]	*v.* (中断后)重新开始, 继续(to return to or begin again after interruption)；*n.* 简历(summary) 记 词根记忆：re(重新) + sume(拿起) → 重新拿起 → 重新开始 例 The research was *resumed* after its funding was reinstated.
resurgence [rɪˈsɜːrdʒəns]	*n.* 复苏, 复兴(revival) 记 词根记忆：re(重新) + surg(=surge 浪潮) + ence → 重起浪潮 → 复苏 例 Economists predicted that there would be a *resurgence* of inflation.

32

resuscitation
[rɪˌsʌsɪ'teɪʃn]

n. 复活 (the act of reviving a person and returning him to consciousness); 恢复 (recovery)

记 词根记忆：re(重新) + sus(下) + cit + at + ion(名词性后缀) → 重新从下面激活 → 恢复

例 To be successful, cardiopulmonary *resuscitation* should begin within one to four minutes after a cardiac arrest.

retail
['riːteɪl]

a. 零售的 (of, relating to, or engaged in the sale of commodities at retail); *v.* 零售 (to sell in small quantities directly to the ultimate consumer)

记 注意：wholesale(*n./v.* 批发)

例 *retail* price 零售价

派 retailer(*n.* 零售商人); retailing(*n.* 零售业)

retain
[rɪ'teɪn]

v. 保留，保持 (to preserve); 保存，留住 (to keep)

记 词根记忆：re(一再) + tain(拿) → 一再地拿 → 保留，保持

例 Business owners always attempt to *retain* control of their firms within their families. // The new legislation required that employers should *retain* all older workers.

retaliation
[rɪˌtæli'eɪʃn]

n. 报复 (revenge)

记 词根记忆：re(反) + tali(邪恶) + ation → 把邪恶还回去 → 报复

例 The released prisoner risked recapture or *retaliation* against his family.

I have nothing to offer but blood, toil, tears and sweat.
我能奉献的没有其他，只有热血、辛劳、眼泪与汗水。

——英国政治家 丘吉尔(Winston Churchill, British politician)

Word List 33

音频

retard [rɪˈtɑːrd]	*v.* 妨碍 (to impede)；减速 (to slow down) 📝 词根记忆：re + tard(迟缓) → 使迟缓 → 妨碍 📖 By sucking sap from the young twigs of the hemlock tree, the woolly adelgid *retards* tree growth, causing needles to change color from deep green to grayish green and to drop prematurely. 📕 retardation(*n.* 阻滞；延迟)
retarded [rɪˈtɑːrdɪd]	*a.* 智力迟钝的；发展迟缓的 (slow or limited in intellectual or emotional development or academic progress) 📝 来自 retard(*v.* 延迟；阻止) 📖 mentally *retarded* 智障，智力迟钝
retention [rɪˈtenʃn]	*n.* 保持，留住 (preserving, retaining) 📝 词根记忆：re(一再) + tent(拿住) + ion → 一再拿住 → 保持 📖 *Retention* of these territories became a sacred national cause.
reticent [ˈretɪsnt]	*a.* 缄默的 (inclined to be silent or uncommunicative) 📝 词根记忆：re(一再) + tic(=silent 安静) + ent → 一再安静 → 缄默的 📖 Investigators found the local witnesses were *reticent* and suspicious of strangers.
retrieve [rɪˈtriːv]	*v.* 取回 (to get and bring back)；恢复 (to regain)；检索 (to find again or extract stored information) 📝 词根记忆：re + trieve(=find 找到) → 重新找到 → 取回 📖 Jane *retrieved* the document from the computer's memory. // *retrieve* one's spirits 恢复精神 📕 retrieval(*n.* 取回)
revamp [ˌriːˈvæmp]	*v.* 改造 (to reconstruct)；修订，修改 (to revise) 📝 词根记忆：re(重新) + vamp(修补) → 修订 📖 The National Academy of Sciences(美国国家科学院) urged the nation to *revamp* computer security procedures.

reveal [rɪ'viːl]	*v.* （神）启示；揭露(to make（sth. secret or hidden）publicly or generally known)；显示(to open up to view) 记 联想记忆：re(反) + veal(看作 veil 面纱) → 除去面纱 → 揭露 例 Excavations in East Africa *reveal* a tenth-century change in architectural style to reflect North African patterns. 派 revealing(*a.* 透漏真情的；有启迪作用的)
revenue ['revənuː]	*n.* 收入(income)；税收(the total annual income of the State from taxes) 记 联想记忆：re(回) + ven(来) + ue → 回来的东西 → 收入 例 tax *revenue* 税收 同根词：revenant(*n.* 归来之人)
reverence ['revərəns]	*n.* 尊敬，崇敬(honor or respect felt or shown) 记 来自 revere(*v.* 尊崇，尊敬) 例 The pilgrims showed *reverence* to God by praying.
reversal [rɪ'vɜːrsl]	*n.* 逆转(an act or the process of reversing) 记 来自 reverse(*v.* 翻转) 例 New theories propose that catastrophic impacts of asteroids and comets may have caused *reversals* in the Earth's magnetic field. 同根词：reversely(*ad.* 相对地；反对地)
reverse [rɪ'vɜːrs]	*v.* 取消(to undo the effect of)；逆转(to change to the contrary)；*a.* 相反的(contrary) 记 词根记忆：re(回) + verse(转向) → 回转方向 → 相反的 例 Refraining from eating certain foods could help *reverse* blockage of coronary arteries（冠状动脉）. // The Ocean Wildlife Campaign urged States to undertake a number of remedies to *reverse* a decline in the shark population. // *reverse* fault 逆断层 派 reversal(*n.* 颠倒，逆转)；reversible(*a.* 可反转的，可逆的)
reversion [rɪ'vɜːrʒn]	*n.* 返回(原状，旧习惯)(an act of returning)；逆转(an act of turning the opposite way) 记 词根记忆：re(回) + vers(转) + ion → 转回去 → 返回 例 In spite of continuing national trends toward increased consumption of specialty foods, agronomists in the Midwest foresee a gradual *reversion* to the raising of agricultural staples: feed corn and hard red wheat. 同根词：inversion(*n.* 倒置)
revert [rɪ'vɜːrt]	*v.* (to)恢复原状(to come or go back, return) 记 词根记忆：re(回) + vert(转) → 重新转回去 → 恢复原状 例 Without endless watering, these fields will quickly *revert* to desert.
revise [rɪ'vaɪz]	*v.* 修订；修改(to correct) 记 词根记忆：re(重新) + vise(看) → 重新再看 → 修订，修改 例 Analysts *revised* their predictions. 派 revision(*n.* 修订；修订本)；revisionist(*a.* 修正主义的；*n.* 修正主义者)

revitalize [ˌriːˈvaɪtəlaɪz]	*v.* (使)新生，(使)得到复兴 (to give new life or vigor to, revive) 记 词根记忆：re(重新) + vital(有活力的) + ize → 重新充满活力 → 复活 例 The government made great efforts to *revitalize* this restored riverfront area. 同根词：vitality(*n.* 生命力；活力)；vital(*a.* 生死攸关的；生命的)
revive [rɪˈvaɪv]	*v.* (使)复苏 (to return to consciousness or life)；(使)恢复 (to bring back) 记 词根记忆：re(重新) + vive(生命) → 重新获得生命复苏 例 The lifeguard *revived* the drowning man. // The construction of an oil pipeline across the lake's bottom might *revive* pollution. 派 revival(*n.* 复苏；复兴)
revolution [ˌrevəˈluːʃn]	*n.* 革命 (overturn)；旋转 (revolving or rotating esp. of one planet round another) 记 词根记忆：re + volut(滚，卷) + ion → 不断向前席卷而来的 → 革命 例 The Industrial *Revolution* was marked by the use of new machines, new energy sources, and new basic materials. // This machine can make 300 *revolutions* per second. 派 revolutionary(*a.* 革命的)；revolutionize(*v.* 使变革)
revolutionary [ˌrevəˈluːʃəneri]	*a.* 革命的 (of, relating to, or constituting a revolution)；革命性的 (constituting or bringing about a major or fundamental change) 记 来自 revolution(*n.* 革命) 例 The American labor movement has never embraced *revolutionary* ideologies calling for the ultimate transformation of the economic order. 同根词：revolutionist(*n.* 革命家)
rewind [ˌriːˈwaɪnd]	*v.* 重绕；倒带 (to wind again) 记 词根记忆：re(重新) + wind(缠绕) → 重绕 例 It takes ten minutes to *rewind* the film.
rhetoric [ˈretərɪk]	*n.* 雄辩，辩才 (eloquence) 记 来自 Rhetor，古希腊的修辞学教师，演说家 例 Do you believe the empty *rhetoric* of politicians?
rheumatic [ruˈmætɪk]	*a.* 风湿病引起的 (affected with rheumatism) 例 *rheumatic* fever 风湿热 派 rheumatoid [*a.* (患)风湿病的]
rhinoceros [raɪˈnɑːsərəs]	*n.* (缩写 rhino)犀牛 (mammals of Africa and Asia that have one or two upright keratinous horns on the snout and thick gray to brown skin with little hair) 例 The Wildlife Protection Committee plans to protect selected *rhinoceroses*.
rib [rɪb]	*n.* 肋骨 (any of the paired curved bony or partly cartilaginous rods that stiffen the walls of the body of most vertebrates and protect the viscera)；【船】肋材 (curved part of the structure of sth. resembling a rib) 记 注意：肋骨、脉和伞骨形状比较类似，可以类推肋条，支撑物 例 One of the football player's *ribs* was cracked when he fell. // The canoe with small *ribs* was about twenty feet long and two feet wide.

33

ridge [rɪdʒ]	*n.* 山脊，岭（a range of hills or mountains） 记 联想记忆：桥梁（bridge）去掉 b 就是脊（ridge） 例 the South Atlantic *Ridge* 南大西洋海脊
ridicule [ˈrɪdɪkjuːl]	*n./v.* 嘲笑，嘲弄（to make fun of） 记 词根记忆：rid（笑）+ icule → 嘲笑 例 The children *ridiculed* John because of his poor clothing. 派 ridiculous（*a.* 荒唐的，可笑的） 同根词：deride（*v.* 嘲弄）
rigid [ˈrɪdʒɪd]	*a.* 严格的（strictly observed）；死板的（deficient in or devoid of flexibility） 记 词根记忆：rig（硬，刚）+ id → 强硬的 → 严格的 例 Eusocial insect societies have *rigid* caste systems. // My *rigid* boss refused to break the company's rules. 派 rigidly（*ad.* 坚硬地；严格地）
rigor [ˈrɪɡər]	*n.* （气候，条件等的）严酷（harshness）；严格（strictness）；严密（exactness） 记 词根记忆：rig（硬，刚）+ or → 严酷；严格 例 These soldiers are seasoned to the *rigors* of the climate. // the *rigor* of a scientific proof 科学实证的严密 派 rigorous（*a.* 严格的；严密的）；rigorously（*ad.* 严格地；严密地）
rigorous [ˈrɪɡərəs]	*a.* 严格的（manifesting, exercising, or favoring rigor） 记 来自 rigor（*n.* 严酷，严格） 例 Historians began to apply less *rigorous* scientific research criteria to the study of women's history. 派 rigorously（*ad.* 严厉地）
rim [rɪm]	*n.* 边（brink）；轮辋（the outer part of a wheel joined to the hub usually by spokes） 例 circular *rim* 轮辋
rinse [rɪns]	*v.* 冲洗（to clean by flushing with liquid） 记 联想记忆：rin（=rain 下雨）+ se → 雨水冲刷着地面冲洗 例 Tom *rinsed* his toothbrushes in the cold water.
ripple [ˈrɪpl]	*v.* （使）起波纹（to become lightly ruffled or covered with small waves）；传开（spread）；*n.* 波纹（dimple） 记 联想记忆：谜语（riddle）变 dd 为 pp → 波纹（ripple） 例 The rain *rippled* the surface of the lake. // The lake was covered with small *ripples*.
ritual [ˈrɪtʃuəl]	*n.* （宗教等的）仪式（ceremony）；*a.* 仪式的（ceremonial） 例 Many *rituals* rise from mythical beliefs. // In the Western Zhou Dynasty only emperors were allowed to perform the *ritual* worship of heaven.

rival [ˈraɪvl]	*n.* 竞争者（competor）; 可与匹敌的人（物）（peer）; *a.* 竞争的（competing）; *v.* 比得上（match） 记 联想记忆：对手（rival）隔河（river）相望，分外眼红 例 The boxer vowed to beat any *rival* who challenged him. // It promotes healthy competition between *rival* industries. // Anne's paintings *rival* the ones I see in art galleries. 派 rivalry（*n.* 竞争; 敌对）
rivalry [ˈraɪvlri]	*n.* 竞争，对抗（the state of being a rival） 记 来自 rival（*n.* 对手; 竞争） 例 Within the boundaries of artistic *rivalry* lies a sense of family: the shared genetic inheritance, or accident, that enables musicians to make music. 派 rivalrous（*a.* 敌对性的; 有竞争性的）
robust [roʊˈbʌst]	*a.* 健壮的（having or exhibiting strength） 记 联想记忆：中国的"乐百氏"（Robust）矿泉水就是这个单词 例 A large rise in the number of houses starting in the coming year should boost new construction dollars by several billion dollars, making the construction industry's economic health much more *robust* than it was five years ago.
rodent [ˈroʊdnt]	*n.* 啮齿类动物（any of an order of relatively small gnawing mammals that have in both jaws a single pair of incisors with a chisel-shaped edge） 记 词根记忆：rod(咬) + ent → 喜欢咬的动物 → 啮齿类动物 例 In some cities, recyclable trash is allowed to accumulate to attract *rodents*. 同根词：erode(*v.* 侵蚀); corrode(*v.* 腐蚀)
roost [ruːst]	*v.* 栖息（to perch） 例 A sparrow *roosted* in the small tree.
rotate [ˈroʊteɪt]	*v.* 旋转（to revolve）; 轮作（to cause to grow in rotation） 记 词根记忆：rot(旋转) + ate(使…) → 旋转 例 A circular rim is *rotating* 300 times per second. // *rotate* the crops 轮种庄稼 派 rotation(*n.* 旋转)
rotational [roʊˈteɪʃənl]	*a.* 转动的; 轮流的（of or pertaining to rotation） 记 来自 rotation(*n.* 旋转，回转) 例 Outside the nucleus the *rotational* velocity would decrease geometrically with distance from the center. 同根词：rotatable(*a.* 可旋转的; 可循环的)
roughly [ˈrʌfli]	*ad.* 大概（approximately）; 粗暴地（in a rough manner） 记 来自 rough(*a.* 粗暴的) 例 Total dollar sales for each of the company's divisions have remained *roughly* constant.

33

round [raʊnd]	*v.* 四舍五入 (to express as a round number); 完成 (to bring to completion); *a.* 圆的 (circular); *n.* 圆 (circle) 例 When the decimal is *rounded* to the nearest hundredth, 3.24 is the result.
royalty ['rɔɪəlti]	*n.* 皇室 (royal status or power); 版税, 专利税 (a payment to an author or composer for each copy of a work sold or to an inventor for each item sold under a patent) 记 来自 royal(*a.* 皇室的) 例 Faculty members should retain the *royalties* from books and articles they write. 同根词: royalist(*n.* 保皇主义者; *a.* 保皇的)
rudder ['rʌdər]	*n.* 船舵 (broad flat piece of wood or metal hinged vertically at the stern of a boat or ship, used for steering) 例 Mary turned the *rudder* sharply to avoid hitting the rock.
rudimentary [ˌruːdɪ'mentri]	*a.* 基础的, 初步的 (fundamental); 发育不全的 (very imperfectly developed) 记 词根记忆: rudi(无知的, 粗鲁的) + ment + ary → 无知状态 → 初步的 例 Technology for tabulating census information was *rudimentary* during the first half of the 19th century. 同根词: erudite(*a.* 深奥的)
rug [rʌg]	*n.* (小)地毯 (floor-mat); 毛毯 (a piece of thick heavy fabric used as a blanket or covering) 例 The floor is covered by a *rug*.
rugby ['rʌgbi]	*n.* 橄榄球 (a football game played with an oval ball which may be kicked or carried) 记 联想记忆: rug(地毯) + by → 在地毯一样的草坪上玩橄榄球 例 *rugby* team 橄榄球队
rugged ['rʌgɪd]	*a.* 高低不平的, 崎岖的 (jagged) 例 The Erie Canal(伊利运河)ran 363 miles across the *rugged* wilderness of upstate New York.
ruin ['ruːɪn]	*v.* (使)毁灭 (to devastate); (使)破产 (to bankrupt) 记 联想记忆: 大雨(rain)毁坏了(ruin)庄稼 → 毁灭 例 The bomb *ruined* the ancient city. // The recession *ruined* this investor financially. 派 ruinous(*a.* 破坏性的)
rumor ['ruːmər]	*n.* 传闻, 谣言 (talk an opinion widely disseminated with no discernible source) 记 联想记忆: rum(看作 run 跑) + or → 好事不出门, 坏事传千里 → 传闻 例 The *rumors* being spread about me are totally untrue.

runner [ˈrʌnər]	*n.* 蔓藤(an elongated horizontal root arising from the base of a plant); 推销员(one that smuggles or distributes illicit or contraband goods); 长跑者(racer) 记 联想记忆: run(跑) + ner → 会在墙上跑的植物 → 蔓藤 例 Some flowering plant species are able to reproduce themselves by means of shoots and *runners*.
rupture [ˈrʌptʃər]	*n.* 破裂, 断裂(cracking, break) 记 词根记忆: rupt(断) + ure → 断裂 例 *rupture* point 断裂点 同根词: erupt(*v.* 喷发); corrupt(*a.* 腐败的)
sacralization [ˌsækrəlaɪˈzeɪʃən]	*n.* 神化(the state of treating as sacred) 记 来自 sacralize(*v.* 使神圣化)
sacred [ˈseɪkrɪd]	*a.* 神圣的(holy) 记 词根记忆: sacr(神圣的) + ed → 神圣的 例 a *sacred* ceremony 神圣的仪式
sacrifice [ˈsækrɪfaɪs]	*n.* 牺牲(something offered in sacrifice); 放弃(giving up of sth., usually in return for sth. more important or valuable); *v.* (for, to) 牺牲(to suffer a loss, give up) 记 词根记忆: sacr(神圣的) + i + fice(做) → 牺牲是神圣的做法 例 It is unrealistic to expect individual nations to make the *sacrifices* necessary to conserve energy. // Slaves were willing to *sacrifice* their lives for freedom.
salable [ˈseɪləbl]	*a.* 可出售的, 卖得出的(marketable) 例 *salable* goods 畅销货
salient [ˈseɪliənt]	*a.* 显著的, 突出的(noticeable) 记 联想记忆: sal(跳) + ient → 跳起来 → 突出的 例 The event reported in newspapers is so *salient* in people's minds as their own personal experiences. 派 salience(*n.* 特点; 显著, 突出)
saline [ˈseɪliːn]	*a.* 含盐的, 咸的(salty) 记 词根记忆: sal(盐) + ine → 含盐的, 咸的 例 Mangroves normally dominate highly *saline* regions. 派 salinity(*n.* 盐分; 盐度)
salinity [səˈlɪnəti]	*n.* 盐度, 盐分(the relative proportion of salt) 记 词根记忆: sal(盐) + inity → 盐度, 盐分 例 The two layers have similar *salinity* levels, but the bottom layer is hotter than the top. 同根词: desalinize(*v.* 除去盐分; 淡化海水)

33

salvage [ˈsælvɪdʒ]	v. 抢救 (to rescue or save especially from wreckage or ruin) ；n. 抢救出的财物 记 词根记忆：salv (救) + age → 抢救 例 The divers *salvaged* chests of gold from the sunken ship. // The *salvage* from the old ship was placed in the national museum.
sample [ˈsæmpl]	n. 样品 (instance) ；标本 (specimen) ；v. 取样 (test) 记 联想记忆：简单的 (simple) 的样品 (sample) 例 writing *sample* 范文 // fossil *sample* 化石标本 // The sound is *sampled* too infrequently. 派 sampling (n. 取样)
samurai [ˈsæmuraɪ]	n. 武士 (warrior) ；[pl.] 武士阶层 (the military caste in feudal Japan) 记 来自日语，指推崇武士道的人 例 Years of peace made *samurai* reduced to idleness.
sanction [ˈsæŋkʃn]	n./v. 批准 (permission) ；制裁 (an economic or military coercive measure adopted usually by several nations in concert for forcing a nation violating international law to desist or yield to adjudication) 记 联想记忆：sanct (神圣) + ion → 神圣之物，原指教会的法令，引申为"批准" 例 The government *sanctioned* a special price increase. // The United Nations places *sanctions* on certain troubled countries.
sanctuary [ˈsæŋktʃueri]	n. 圣堂 (a consecrated place) ；避难所 (a place of refuge and protection) ；鸟兽禁猎区 (a refuge for wildlife where predators are controlled and hunting is illegal) 记 词根记忆：sanct (神圣) + uary (地方) → 圣堂，圣堂经常会成为避难所 例 Elephant *sanctuaries* were created on a widespread basis to guarantee elephants' sufficient natural vegetation.
sandbar [ˈsændbɑːr]	n. 沙洲 (a ridge of sand built up by currents especially in a river or in coastal waters) 例 The new airboat can travel at high speeds undeterred by *sandbars*.
sane [seɪn]	a. 健全的 (mentally sound, rational) ；明智的 (wise) 记 词根记忆：san (健全，健康) + e → 健全的 注意：insane (a. 疯狂的) 例 The defendant was judged to be *sane* and competent to stand trial. // a *sane* leader 英明的领导
sanitary [ˈsænəteri]	a. 卫生的 (free from dirt or substances that may cause disease, hygienic) ；公共卫生的 记 词根记忆：sanit (=san 健全，健康) + ary → 与健康有关的 → 卫生的 例 *sanitary* condition 公共卫生条件 同根词：sanitation (n. 公共卫生，卫生设施)
saturated [ˈsætʃəreɪtɪd]	a. 饱和的；浸透的 (made thoroughly wet) 记 来自 saturate (v. 浸透，充满) 例 The market for video recorders was *saturated*. // I came in from the rain and took off my *saturated* clothes.

scale [skeɪl]	*n.* 鳞片；规模 a relative level or degree）；等级 rank order） 例 Typically reptiles are covered with *scales*. // The *scale* of the playboy's spending is $500,000 a year. // There were differences in pay *scales* that cannot be explained by the human capital theory. 派 scaling（*n.* 缩放比例）
scandalize [ˈskændəlaɪz]	*v.* 使震惊 to shock）；诽谤 to speak falsely or maliciously of） 记 词根记忆：scandal（谣言，绯闻）+ ize → 诽谤 例 They were *scandalized* by his improper behavior. 同根词：scandalous（*a.* 可耻的；诽谤性的）
scapegoat [ˈskeɪpɡoʊt]	*n.* 替罪羊 one that bears the blame for others） 记 联想记忆：scape（看作 escape 逃跑）+ goat（羊）→ 替罪羊 例 The accused was used as a *scapegoat*.
scarce [skers]	*a.* 缺乏的 not plentiful or abundant）；稀有的 rare） 记 联想记忆：scar（伤疤）+ ce → 有伤疤，不完整的 → 缺乏的 例 Whenever fuel becomes *scarce*, it becomes expensive. 派 scarcity（*n.* 缺乏，不足）
scarcity [ˈskersəti]	*n.* 不足，缺乏 a state of being scarce） 记 来自 scarce（*a.* 缺乏的，不足的） 例 Either food *scarcity* or excessive hunting can threaten a population of animals. 同根词：scarceness（*n.* 稀少，缺乏）
scatter [ˈskætər]	*v.* 分散，散开 to disperse） 例 Billions of meteors are *scattered* across the galaxy.
scavenge [ˈskævɪndʒ]	*v.* 清除 to cleanse）；从废物中提取有用物质 to salvage from discarded or refuse material） 例 A jackal is a kind of animal that *scavenges* rotten meat. 派 scavenger（*n.* 清除剂）
scent [sent]	*n.* 气味 smell）；香味 fragrance） 记 联想记忆：开放的花朵送出（sent）沁人的香气（scent） 例 A chemical is added to natural gas to give it a *scent*.
scheme [skiːm]	*n.* 方案 a plan or program of action） 记 注意：schema（*n.* 图表，图解） 例 coding *scheme* 编码方案
scorn [skɔːrn]	*v./n.* 轻蔑 to despise）；嘲笑 to mock） 记 联想记忆：s + corn（玉米）→ 把别人当成玉米棒子 → 轻蔑 例 The disgruntled worker showed *scorn* towards his employer. // The team *scorned* the player who lost the game. 派 scornful（*a.* 轻蔑的；嘲笑的）

Word List 34

音频

scorpion [ˈskɔːrpiən]	*n.* 蝎子(any of an order of nocturnal arachnids that have an elongated body and a narrow segmented tail bearing a venomous stinger at the tip) 例 The *scorpion's* nerve cells are clustered in its head.
scour [ˈskauər]	*v.* 擦洗(to rub); 四处搜索(to move about quickly especially in search) 记 发音记忆: "四 call" → 一连四个电话(call) → 四处搜索 例 Investors of real estate regularly *scour* the country for areas to build new buildings.
scout [skaut]	*n.* 侦察员(或机、舰)(one sent to obtain information esp. a soldier, ship, or plane sent out in war to reconnoiter); *v.* 侦察; 寻找(to make a search) 记 联想记忆: sc + out(外面) → 在外面巡逻的人 → 侦察员 例 The *scout* surveyed the valley from the ridge. // Some bats are *scouting* outside the cave for new food and roosting sites now.
scramble [ˈskræmbl]	*v.* 攀登(to climb); (for)争夺(to struggle eagerly for possession of something) 例 He *scrambled* up a steep hillside. // *scramble* for power and wealth 争权夺利
scrap [skræp]	*n.* 碎屑, 废物(a small detached piece); *v.* 扔弃(discard); *a.* 零碎的(not complete) 例 metallic *scrap* 废金属 // Mary *scrapped* her broken radio. // *scrap* iron 铁屑
scrape [skreɪp]	*v./n.* 刮擦(to remove from a surface by usually repeated strokes of an edged instrument); 擦伤(to damage or injure the surface by contact with a rough surface) 记 词根记忆: scrap(切, 割) + e → 刮擦 例 I *scraped* my car when I drove into the bushes. // The child with a badly *scraped* elbow felt better after having a pain-killer.
scrawny [ˈskrɔːni]	*a.* 骨瘦如柴的(exceptionally thin and slight or meager in body or size) 例 A different variety of giant tortoise can be found on every island in the Galapagos, each with its own style of oversized dome and comically *scrawny* neck.

screen [skri:n]	*n.* 屏幕(a flat surface on which a picture or series of pictures is projected or reflected); *v.* 筛选；检查(to test or examine) 记 注意：screen 的动词意义都是由名词意思(屏幕，筛子)引申而来的，可以联系记忆 例 television *screen* 电视屏幕 // They *screened* applicants for risk of heart attack.
scribe [skraɪb]	*n.* 抄写员(a copier of manuscripts); *v.* 抄写(to write) 例 The manager asked the *scribe* to copy 30 pages of the document in a day.
scrub [skrʌb]	*v.* 擦洗(to clean with hard rubbing); *n.* 矮树(a stunted tree or shrub) 记 和 rub(*v.* 擦，摩擦)一起记 例 A *scrub* jay can remember when it cached a particular piece of food in a particular place. 派 scrubby(*a.* 矮小的；树丛繁盛的)
scrubber ['skrʌbər]	*n.* 刷子(one that scrubs); 净气器(an apparatus for removing impurities especially from gases) 例 Installing *scrubbers* in smokestacks can reduce harmful emissions.
scrupulous ['skru:pjələs]	*a.* 谨慎的(meticulous); 严格认真的(careful) 记 来自 scruple(*n./v.* 审慎) 例 She is *scrupulous* to a degree. // The newcomer works with *scrupulous* care. 派 unscrupulous(*a.* 肆无忌惮的)
scrutinize ['skru:tənaɪz]	*v.* 仔细观察, 审视(to examine closely) 记 词根记忆：scrutin(检查) + ize → 仔细观察 例 Analysts *scrutinized* unemployment patterns according to skill level, ethnicity, race, age, class, and gender. 派 scrutiny(*n.* 细察；监督)
scrutiny ['skru:təni]	*n.* 详细审查(examination); 监视(surveillance); 细看(a searching look) 记 来自 scrutinize(*v.* 仔细检查) 例 In corporate purchasing, competitive *scrutiny* is typically limited to suppliers of items that are directly related to end products.
scuba ['sku:bə]	*n.* 水肺；水中呼吸器(an apparatus used for breathing while swimming underwater) 记 联想记忆：s(看作 S 形状的) + cuba(音似：哭吧) → 潜水时丢了水中呼吸器只有哭吧 → 水中呼吸器 例 Archaeological remains are exposed to turbulence and are accessible to anyone in *scuba* gear.
sculpture ['skʌlptʃər]	*n.* 雕塑品(work produced by sculptor); 雕塑(术)(the action or art of processing plastic or hard materials into works of art); *v.* 雕刻(to carve, engrave) 例 This allegedly Roman *sculpture* was shown to be a forgery. // The art students all had to take a class in *sculpture*. // The potter *sculptured* the clay into an ashtray. 同根词：sculptor *n.* 雕刻(塑)家

34

scurrilous ['skɜːrələs]	*a.* 粗俗的；诽谤的（vulgar, foulmouthed） 记 词根记忆：scurril(下流) + ous → 下流的；和 scurry(*v.* 急奔)一起记 例 The magazine is constantly making *scurrilous* attacks on politicians.
seasonal ['siːzənl]	*a.* 季节的；周期性的（of, relating to, or varying in occurrence according to the season） 记 来自 season(*n.* 季节；时期；*v.* 给…调味) 例 The *seasonal* variation in group size can probably be explained by a *seasonal* variation in mortality among young voles. 派 seasonally(*ad.* 季节性地；周期性地) 同根词：seasonable(*a.* 适时的)
secluded [sɪ'kluːdɪd]	*a.* 隐居的（living in seclusion）；隐蔽的（screened or hidden from view） 记 来自 seclude(*v.* 隔离) 例 New houses built in *secluded* rural areas are relatively free of air pollutants. // a *secluded* life 隐居生活
secrete [sɪ'kriːt]	*v.* 藏匿（to hide）；【生】分泌（to form and give off） 记 词根记忆：se + crete(生长，增长) → 分泌 例 The human body *secretes* more pain-blocking hormones late at night than during the day. 派 secretion(*n.* 分泌；分泌物)
secretion [sɪ'kriːʃn]	*n.* 分泌（the process by which liquid substances are produced by parts of the body or plants）；分泌物（a product of secretion formed by an animal or plant） 记 来自 secrete(*v.* 分泌) 例 The two insect-repelling chemicals in the *secretions* of the millipedes are carcinogenic for humans but do not appear to be carcinogenic for capuchins.
secular ['sekjələr]	*a.* 世俗的，尘世的（worldly rather than spiritual） 记 联想记忆：sec(跟随) + ular → 跟随的；随大流的 → 世俗的 例 As an educator, a builder of institutions and organizations, and a major figure in the Black Church and *secular* feminist movements, Nannie Helen Burroughs was one of the best-known and most well-respected African Americans of the early twentieth century. 派 secularism(*n.* 世俗主义；现世主义)
secure [sə'kjʊr]	*v.* 获得（to obtain, to acquire）；*a.* 安全的（safe） 例 I *secured* the services of a good lawyer.
sedentary ['sednteri]	*a.* 久坐的；需长坐的（doing or requiring much sitting） 记 词根记忆：sed(坐) + ent + ary → 久坐的 例 Coronary patients who exercise most actively have half or less than half the chance of dying of a heart attack as those who are *sedentary*.

□ scurrilous   □ seasonal   □ secluded   □ secrete   □ secretion   □ secular
□ secure   □ sedentary

sediment ['sedɪmənt]	*n.* 【地】沉淀物(material deposited by water, wind or glaciers) 记 词根记忆：sedi(坐) + ment → 坐下去的东西 → 沉淀物 例 These *sediments* are composed of calcium carbonate shells of marine organisms. 派 sedimentary(*a.* 沉积的；沉淀性的); sedimentation(*n.* 沉积；沉淀)
sedimentary [ˌsedɪ'mentri]	*a.* 沉积的，沉淀性的(of, relating to, or containing sediment) 记 来自 sediment(*n.* 沉积) 例 The higher the ratio of oxygen 18 to oxygen 16 in a *sedimentary* specimen, the more land ice there was when the sediment was laid down. 同根词：sediment(*n.* 沉积，沉淀物)
seedling ['siːdlɪŋ]	*n.* 幼苗；树苗(sapling) 记 词根记忆：seed(种子) + ling(小) → 幼苗 例 *seedlings* of Douglas fir 花旗松的幼苗
seesaw ['siːˌsɔ]	*n.* 跷跷板(a pastime in which two children or groups of children ride on opposite ends of a plank balanced in the middle so that one end goes up as the other goes down) 记 联想记忆：see(看) + saw(see 的过去式，看) → 看了又看 → 上下或往复的移动 → 秋千
segment ['segmənt]	*n.* 线段(the finite part of a line between two points in the line)；部分，环节(fragment, part) 记 词根记忆：seg(=sect 部分) + ment → 线的一部分 → 线段 例 line *segment* 线段 // market *segment* 市场区隔
segregate ['segrɪgeɪt]	*v.* (from) 隔离(to isolate)；分开(to separate) 记 词根记忆：se(分开) + greg(团体) + ate → 和团体分开 → 隔离；分开 例 In many cities, blacks were *segregated* from whites. // The staff *segregated* the boys from the girls during gym class. 派 segregation(*n.* 隔离；分开)
segregation [ˌsegrɪ'geɪʃn]	*n.* 隔离，分离(the act or process of segregating) 记 来自 segregate(*v.* 使隔离) 例 Many young Americans are not able to imagine, even less to remember, what *segregation* was like. 派 segregationist(*n.* 种族隔离主义者) 同根词：segregator(*n.* 分离器)
seismic ['saɪzmɪk]	*a.* 地震的，有关地震的(of, subject to, or caused by an earthquake) 记 词根记忆：seism(地震) + ic → 地震的 例 *seismic* waves 地震波 派 seismologist(*n.* 地震学家)
select [sɪ'lekt]	*v.* 挑选，选择(to pick out) 记 词根记忆：se(分开) + lect(选) → 分开来选 → 挑选 例 The more a depositor has to deposit, the more careful he or she tends to be in *selecting* a bank. 派 selective(*a.* 选择性的)

34

□ sediment □ sedimentary □ seedling □ seesaw □ segment □ segregate
□ segregation □ seismic □ select

semicircle [ˈsemisɜːrkl]	*n.* 半圆(a half of a circle);半圆形体(an object or arrangement of objects in the form of a half circle) 词根记忆:semi(半) + circle(圆周,圆形) → 半圆形体 例 The rectangular region contains two circles and a *semicircle*.
semiconductor [ˌsemikənˈdʌktər]	*n.* 半导体(a substance whose electrical conductivity is between a conductor and an insulator) 词根记忆:semi(半) + conduct(传导) + or(物) → 半导体 例 Instead, *semiconductor* firms simply squeezed more patents out of existing research and development expenditures.
seminal [ˈsemɪnl]	*a.* 开创性的(creative, original);重要的(influential);种子的;精液的(of, relating to, or consisting of seed or semen) 词根记忆:semin(种子) + al → 种子破土而出 → 开创性的 例 the *seminal* existential novel 开创性存在主义小说 // a *seminal* book 有重大影响的书 同根词:disseminate(*v.* 播种)
seminar [ˈsemɪnɑːr]	*n.* 研讨会(a meeting for giving and discussing information) 联想记忆:semin(种子) + ar → 培养种子的地方,产生创意的地方 → 研讨会 注意:seminary(*n.* 神学院) 例 Many lawyers attended a *seminar* on tort reform.
senate [ˈsenət]	*n.* [S~] 参议院,上议院(an assembly or council usually possessing high deliberative and legislative functions) 词根记忆:sen(老) + ate(表人,职位) → 资格老的人组成的领导班子 → 上议院 例 The *Senate* has approved the immigration legislation. 派 senator(*n.* 参议员)
sensation [senˈseɪʃn]	*n.* 感觉(awareness);引起轰动的人或事(wonder) 词根记忆:sens(感觉) + ation → 感觉 例 the *sensation* of pain 疼痛感 // a worldwide *sensation* 举世轰动的事
sensational [senˈseɪʃənl]	*a.* 轰动的(of or relating to sensation or the senses);非常好的(exceedingly or unexpectedly excellent or great) 记 来自 sensation(*n.* 感觉;轰动) 例 Published during the late eighteenth century, Diderot's factual *Encyclopedia* and his friend Voltaire's fictional *Candide* were the cause of a scandal so *sensational* that both men prudently chose to embark on extended vacations in nearby Austria. 派 sensationalist(*n.* 感觉论者)
sensible [ˈsensəbl]	*a.* 明智的(wise) 例 A *sensible* preservation strategy would assist the farmers to modernize their farms.

sensitive ['sensətɪv]	*a.* (to)敏感的；易波动的 (highly responsive or susceptible) 记 词根记忆：sens(感觉) + itive → 感觉灵敏的 → 敏感的 例 Some insects are not *sensitive* to the pesticide. 派 sensitivity(*n.* 敏感；敏感度) 同根词：sensory(*a.* 感觉的；感官的)
sensitize ['sensətaɪz]	*v.* (使某人或某事物)敏感 (to make sensitive) 例 An allergy has *sensitized* my eyes to pollution in the air.
sentence ['sentəns]	*n.* 句子 (a string of words satisfying the grammatical rules of a language)；宣判，判决 (judgment)；*v.* 判决，宣判 (to impose a sentence on) 例 Some legislators advocate mandating a *sentence* of life in prison for anyone who, having twice served sentences for serious crimes, is subsequently convicted of a third serious crime. 派 sentential(*a.* 句子的；判决的)
sentient ['sentiənt]	*a.* 有感觉的，有知觉的 (aware) 记 词根记忆：sent(感觉) + ient → 有感觉的 例 Some people think that scientists ought not to test the safety of new drugs on *sentient* animals.
sentiment ['sentɪmənt]	*n.* 多愁善感 (a tender feeling or emotion)；思想感情 记 词根记忆：senti(感觉) + ment → 思想感情 例 There is considerable *sentiment* among voters in most areas of the state for restriction of smoking. 派 sentimental(*a.* 多愁善感的) 同根词：sensory(*a.* 感觉的)；resentment(*n.* 怨恨)
sentinel ['sentɪnl]	*n.* 哨兵 (sentry) 记 词根记忆：senti(感觉) + nel → 感觉者 → 哨兵 注意：sentry(*n.* 哨兵) 例 The *sentinel* was stationed on a hill.
separate	['seprət] *a.* 分开的 (detached)；单个的 (individual)；不同的 (distinct, dissimilar) ['sepəreɪt] *v.* (from)分开 (distinguish)；分类 (sort) 记 词根记忆：se(分开) + par(相等) + ate → (使)分成份 → 分开 例 Restaurants of the city can maintain *separate* dining areas where smoking is permitted. // Residents should *separate* recyclable bottles and cans from recyclable paper products. 派 separately(*ad.* 个别地；分离地)；separation(*n.* 分离)
sequence ['siːkwəns]	*n.* 顺序 (an order of succession)；序列 (an ordered set of quantities) 记 词根记忆：sequ(跟随) + ence → 跟随，连续 → 序列 例 New techniques for determining the molecular *sequence* of the RNA have produced evolutionary information. // arithmetic *sequence* 数列 派 sequential(*a.* 连续的；一连串的)

34

sequester
[sɪ'kwestər]

v. (使)隐退(to seclude; withdraw); 使隔离(to set apart)

记 注意不要和 sequestrate(*v.* 扣押)相混

例 As recently as 1950, tuberculosis was never curable unless patients were *sequestered* in sanitariums; today, the drug Isoniazid has made such treatment obsolete.

派 sequestered(*a.* 隐退的; 偏僻的)

session
['seʃn]

n. 会议(conference); 集会(a meeting devoted to a particular activity)

例 regular *session* 常规会议 // an all-night dancing *session* 通宵舞会

severe
[sɪ'vɪr]

a. 严重的(serious); 严厉的(austere); 严酷的(harsh)

记 联想记忆: 曾经(ever)严酷的(severe)日子, 一去不复返了

例 Most countries in the world have *severe* air pollution. // The angry parents gave the naughty child a *severe* punishment.

派 severely(*ad.* 严格地; 严重地); severity(*n.* 严重; 剧烈)

sewage
['suːɪdʒ]

n. 污物, 污水(refuse liquids or waste matter usually carried off by sewers)

记 词根记忆: sew(排水) + age → 排出的水 → 污水

例 *sewage* disposal 污水处理

shareholder
['ʃerhouldər]

n. 股票持有人; 股东(stockholder)

记 分拆记忆: share(分享; 股票) + holder(持有者) → 股票持有人

例 The individual *shareholder* will reap only a minute share of the gains.

派 shareholding(*n.* 股权)

shatter
['ʃætər]

v. 粉碎, 砸碎(to break into pieces); 破坏(to destroy; demolish)

记 与 scatter(*v.* 分散)一起记

例 The sea dashed the ship to *shatter* against the rock. // Heating could *shatter* the nutrition of food.

sheath
[ʃiːθ]

n. 鞘(a case for a blade (as of a knife)); 防护物(sheathing)

例 It is possible that many prehistoric microbes evolved without significant modification of their *sheaths*.

shed
[ʃed]

v. 脱落(即蜕皮)(discard); 流出, 散发(to give off or out)

例 Until they are fully grown, horseshoe crabs(马蹄蟹)*shed* their shells and grow new ones several times a year. // *shed* warmth and light 发光发热

sheer
[ʃɪr]

a. 薄的(thin); 纯粹的(pure)

例 *sheer* curtains 薄窗帘 // *sheer* brandy 纯正白兰地

shellfish
['ʃelfɪʃ]

n. 甲壳类动物(an aquatic invertebrate animal with a shell)

记 分拆记忆: shell(壳) + fish(鱼) → 甲壳类动物

例 As envisioned by researchers, commercial farming of lobsters will enable fisheries to sell the *shellfish* year-round.

shelter
['ʃeltər]

n. 躲避处(a protective structure); *v.* 庇护, 保护(protect)

例 food, clothing, *shelter* and transportation 衣食住行// The blue butterfly depended on the nests to *shelter* its offspring.

shield [ʃiːld]	*n.* 盾（a broad piece of defensive armor carried on the arm）; 保护物（protector）; *v.* (from)保护（protect）; 挡开（defend） 记 要牢记 shield 的原始意义"盾"，其他意义均可引申而来 例 If the protective *shield* is not in place, the machine will not operate. // The patents can *shield* patent-holding manufacturers from competitors. 派 windshield(*n.* 挡风玻璃)
shimmer ['ʃɪmər]	*n.* 微光，闪光（a light that shimmers）; *v.* 使闪烁，发闪烁的微光（to glimmer） 记 联想记忆：她站在夏天(summer)的夜空下看星星闪烁(shimmer)发光 例 The *shimmer* and sheen of both fabric and skin depend on the geometry of their internal structures—the exact arrangement of threads or protein fibres.
shortfall ['ʃɔːrtfɔːl]	*n.* 亏空（deficit）; 不足（shortage） 记 联想记忆：short(短) + fall(下落) → 因收入下降而短少 → 亏空 例 The new policy of tax cuts issued by the government resulted in a *shortfall* in Federal revenues. // There will be a *shortfall* in wheat supplies this year.
shrill [ʃrɪl]	*a.* (批评)尖锐的（sharp）; 刺耳的（piercing） 例 *shrill* criticism 尖锐的批评 // a *shrill* whistle 刺耳的汽笛声
shrink [ʃrɪŋk]	*v.* (使)收缩（to contract to less extent）; 减小（to dwindle） 记 联想记忆：童话里喝(drink)了巫婆的药水就能将身体收缩(shrink) 例 The number of students in our university has begun to *shrink*. 派 shrinkage(*n.* 收缩)
shroud [ʃraʊd]	*n.* 裹尸布（burial garment）; 覆盖物（cover） 记 联想记忆：sh(音似：尸) + roud(看作 round 围绕着) → 缠绕着尸体的 → 裹尸布 例 a *shroud* of dust 一层灰
shrub [ʃrʌb]	*n.* 灌木(丛)（a low and usually several-stemmed woody plant） 记 联想记忆：sh + rub(摩擦) → 灌木擦伤皮肤 → 灌木(丛) 例 John trimmed the *shrubs*.
shuttle ['ʃʌtl]	*n.* 航天飞机（spaceship）; 穿梭运输工具（aircraft, bus etc. that travels regularly between two places） 例 space *shuttle* 航天飞机 // The transit company expects commuters to ride the *shuttle* buses to the subway rather than drive there.
sibling ['sɪblɪŋ]	*n.* 兄弟或姊妹（one of two or more individuals having one common parent） 记 词根记忆：sib(同胞) + ling(小) → 兄弟或姊妹 例 *sibling* pair 孪生兄弟(姐妹)
sidestep ['saɪdstep]	*v.* 横跨一步躲避（to take a side step）; 回避（to avoid） 记 联想记忆：side(边) + step(步) → 向边上跨出一步 → 回避 例 The woman *sidestepped* the bicycle that was veering toward her. // The politician *sidestepped* the issue of tax evasion.

34

□ shield   □ shimmer   □ shortfall   □ shrill   □ shrink   □ shroud
□ shrub   □ shuttle   □ sibling   □ sidestep

siege [si:dʒ]	*n.* 包围，围攻（a military blockade of a city or fortified place to compel it to surrender） 记 发音记忆："吸脂" → 吸脂让您逃离脂肪的包围 例 *siege* warfare 包围战
signature ['sɪgnətʃər]	*n.* 签名，签字（person's name written by himself） 记 词根记忆：sign(记号) + ature → 加自己名字做记号 → 签名 例 A check's authenticity includes reminders to watch the endorsement, compare *signatures*, and view the watermark while holding the check to the light. 同根词：signify(*v.* 表示；意味）
significance [sɪg'nɪfɪkəns]	*n.* 意义；重要性（the quality of being important） 记 来自 significant(*a.* 有意义的；重大的） 例 A phenomenon is described and its scientific *significance* is discussed. 同根词：signify(*v.* 表示；有重要性）
significant [sɪg'nɪfɪkənt]	*a.* 相当数量的（considerable），意义重大的（having an important meaning） 记 词根记忆：sign(记号) + i + fic(做) + ant → 值得做记号的 → 意义重大的 例 Their removal may not have led to *significant* increases in populations of smaller predators. 派 significance(*n.* 意义）；significantly(*ad.* 显著地） 同根词：signature(*n.* 署名，签名）
signify ['sɪgnɪfaɪ]	*v.* 表示，意味着（to mean） 记 词根记忆：sign(信号) + ify → 用信号表示 例 Dark clouds *signify* that it will rain soon.
silkworm ['sɪlkwɜːrm]	*n.* 蚕，桑蚕（a moth whose larva spins a large amount of strong silk in constructing its cocoon） 记 分拆记忆：silk(蚕丝) + worm(虫) → 吐蚕丝的虫 → 蚕 例 The gypsy moth was imported into Massachusetts from Europe in 1869 by a French scientist attempting to develop a strong strain of silk-producing insects by crossing gypsy moths with adult *silkworms*.
similarity [ˌsɪmə'lærəti]	*n.* 相似点（the quality or state of being similar） 记 来自 similar(*a.* 相似的） 例 Almost like clones in their *similarity* to one another, members of the cheetah species are especially vulnerable to disease because of their homogeneity. 同根词：dissimilar(*a.* 不同的）

音频

simulate ['sɪmjuleɪt]	*v.* 模仿，假装（to imitate） 记 词根记忆：simul(类似) + ate → 使某物类似于某物模仿 例 Don't *simulate* the way I speak. // *simulate* death 装死 派 simulation(*n.* 假装；模仿); simulator(*n.* 模拟装置；假装者)
simultaneous [ˌsaɪml'teɪniəs]	*a.* 同时的，同步的（existing or occurring at the same time） 记 词根记忆：simult(相同) + aneous(…的) → 时间相同的 → 同时的 例 The survey explained the *simultaneous* increase in tobacco sales and decrease in the number of adults who smoke. 派 simultaneously(*ad.* 同时地)
sinew ['sɪnjuː]	*n.* 腱（tough cord of tissue joining a muscle to a bone）；肌肉（muscle） 例 The weightlifter's muscles and *sinews* were well defined.
single-entry ['sɪŋgl'entrɪ]	*a.* 单式的；单式记录的 例 *single-entry* ticket 单式门票（即被一次检票后立即失效）
singularly ['sɪŋgjələrli]	*ad.* 异常地（strangely）；特别地（exceptionally） 例 *singularly* wet weather 异常多雨的天气
sinus ['saɪnəs]	*n.* 穴；【解】窦（主要容纳静脉血的膨胀的通道或空腔）（cavity, hollow） 例 venous *sinus* 静脉窦 派 sinusitis(*n.* 窦炎)
sip [sɪp]	*v.* 啜饮，呷（to drink in small quantities） 记 联想记忆：高档酒店喝一小口(sip)酒也得给小费(tip) 例 Anne *sipped* at the coffee because it was hot.
skeleton ['skelɪtn]	*n.* 骨架，骨骼（framework of bones supporting an animal or a human body） 记 发音记忆："skin 里头" → 皮肤里头是骨骼 例 The structure of the *skeleton* of the creature resembled that of a reptile.
skeptic ['skeptɪk]	*n.* 怀疑者（an adherent or advocate of skepticism） 记 联想记忆：s + kept(保留) + ic → 持保留态度的人 → 怀疑者 例 The *skeptic* dismissed the president's plan as unworkable. 派 skeptical(*a.* 怀疑的); skepticism(*n.* 怀疑态度；怀疑论)

□ simulate   □ simultaneous   □ sinew   □ single-entry   □ singularly   □ sinus
□ sip   □ skeleton   □ skeptic

skeptical [ˈskeptɪkl]	*a.* 怀疑的(suspicious) 例 The tone of the passage was *skeptical* and questioning. 派 skepticism(*n.* 怀疑论); skeptics(*n.* 怀疑论者; 无神论者)
sketch [sketʃ]	*n.* 草图, 素描(draft); *v.* 画速写 例 field *sketch* 作业草图, 现场草图 派 sketchy(*a.* 粗略的)
skull [skʌl]	*n.* 头骨(the skeleton of the head) 记 联想记忆: 据说大脑壳(skull)的人掌握技能(skill)比较快 例 The *skulls*, pelvises(骨盆) and hind feet of pterosaurs(翼龙) are reptilian.
slam [slæm]	*v.* 猛烈撞击(to knock); 砰地关上(to shut noisily) 记 发音记忆: "死拉门" → 使劲关 → 砰地关上 例 The colossal object from space cut through the atmosphere and *slammed* into Earth.
slice [slaɪs]	*n.* 薄片, 切片(a thin flat piece cut from something); 部分(portion, share) 记 和 sly(*a.* 狡猾的)一起记 例 Mary put a *slice* of ham on her sandwich. // Taxes take a large *slice* of my income.
slick [slɪk]	*a.* 光滑的(slippery); 聪明的(clever) 例 The roads are *slick* with ice tonight. // Everyone laughed at John's *slick* response to Dave's insult.
slight [slaɪt]	*a.* 少量的(thin); 微不足道的(trivial) 记 联想记忆: s + light(轻的) → 轻微的 → 微不足道的 例 Products with *slight* manufacturing defects may hinder their sales. // The documentation of this epidemic was *slight*. 派 slightly(*ad.* 少量地)
slip [slɪp]	*n.* 纸片(a small piece of paper); 差错(error); *v.* 滑行(to slide); 下降(to decline) 记 注意: slipper(*n.* 拖鞋) 例 There were ten numbers written on a *slip* of blank paper. // Corporate profits *slipped* severely during the recession.
slope [sloʊp]	*n.* 斜坡(ramp); 【数】斜率(The rate at which an ordinate of a point of a line on a coordinate plane changes with respect to a change in the abscissa.) 例 continental *slope* 大陆坡
slot [slɑːt]	*n.* 狭缝(slit); 空位(vacancy) 记 联想记忆: s(音似: 丝) + lot(许多) → 许多丝状的狭缝 例 Anne placed a quarter into the *slot* of the vending machine. // takeoff and landing *slots*(飞机)起飞和降落所用的空位(即空闲跑道)

sloth [sloʊθ]	*n.* 树獭(any of various slow-moving arboreal edentate mammals[genera Bradypus and Choloepus]that inhabit tropical forests of South and Central America, hang from the branches back downward, and feed on leaves, shoots, and fruits); 懒惰(idleness) 记 联想记忆: slo(看作 slow 慢的) + th(看作 thing 事) → 做事慢吞吞的 → 懒惰 例 *Sloths* can hang from trees by their long rubbery limbs.
sluggish ['slʌgɪʃ]	*a.* 缓慢的(slow) 记 词根记忆: slugg(=slug 偷懒) + ish → 偷懒的 → 缓慢的 例 Analysts blamed *sluggish* retail sales of barbecue grills on bad weather.
slump [slʌmp]	*v./n.* 下降, 暴跌(to drop or slide down suddenly) 记 联想记忆: sl + ump(看作 jump 跳下) → 突然跳下 → 暴跌 例 The price of gold *slumped* for the second day in a row. // a *slump* in prices 价格暴跌
smear [smɪr]	*v.* 涂抹(to overspread with something adhesive); 弄脏(to dirty) 例 *smear* oil on machine parts // She *smeared* her finger with jam.
smelt [smelt]	*v.* 熔炼, 冶炼(to melt or fuse(as ore) often with an accompanying chemical change usually to separate the metal); 精炼(to refine) 记 联想记忆: s 细丝般冶炼 melt → 冶炼 例 Over the course of the eighteenth century, the average output of ironwork tripled as a result of several improvements in blowing machinery and because coal replaced charcoal as the fuel used in the *smelting* of iron ore. 派 smelter(*n.* 熔炉; 冶炼厂; 熔炼工)
smog [smɑːg]	*n.* 烟雾(fog) 记 缩合词: smoke + fog 例 Often visible as *smog*, ozone is formed in the atmosphere from hydrocarbons and nitrogen oxides.
smokestack ['smoʊkstæk]	*n.* 烟囱(chimney) 记 分拆记忆: smoke(烟) + stack(排烟道) → 烟囱 例 The easing of standards for *smokestack* emissions has led to an increase in air-pollution levels.
smuggler ['smʌglər]	*n.* 走私者(one who smuggles) 例 *Smugglers* had significantly more funds at their disposal when they organized as a group. 同根词: smuggling(*n.* 走私活动)
snap [snæp]	*n.* 揿扣(a catch or fastening that closes or locks with a click); *v.* 猛咬(seize something sharply with the mouth) 例 *snap* fastener 揿扣
sniper ['snaɪpər]	*n.* 狙击手(one who snipes) 记 联想记忆: snip(剪) + er → 像剪刀一样快的人 → 狙击手 例 The *sniper* snapped off six rapid shots.

35

snout [snaʊt]	*n.* (猪、象等的)口鼻部 (projecting nose and mouth of an animal, especially a pig) 记 联想记忆：s + nout(看作 nose 鼻子) → 口鼻部 例 *snout* beetle 象鼻虫
snuff [snʌf]	*v.* (用鼻子)吸 (to inhale through the nose noisily and forcibly)；*n.* 鼻烟 (powdered tobacco taken into the nose by sniffing) 例 *snuff* bottle 鼻烟壶
soar [sɔːr]	*v.* 高飞 (to sail or hover in the air)；猛增，剧增 (to rise or increase dramatically) 记 发音记忆："嗖"的一声 → 高飞 例 The plane *soared* high in the sky. // The region's standard of living has *soared* from 1965 on.
sodium ['soʊdiəm]	*n.* 【化】钠 (a silver-white soft waxy ductile element of the alkali metal group that occurs abundantly in nature in combined form and is very active chemically)
solar ['soʊlər]	*a.* 太阳的 (of, derived from, relating to, or caused by the sun)；(利用)太阳能的 (utilizing the sun's rays especially to produce heat or electricity) 记 词根记忆：sol(太阳) + ar → 太阳的 例 *solar* wind 太阳风 // *solar* energy 太阳能
solidarity [ˌsɑːlɪ'dærəti]	*n.* 团结，一致 (unity of a group or class) 记 词根记忆：solid(固定的) + arity → 固体状态 → 团结 例 ethnic *solidarity* 种族团结
solitary ['sɑːləteri]	*a.* 单独的 (alone)；【动】独居的 (living alone or in pairs only) 记 词根记忆：solit(单独) + ary → 单独的 例 Scientific research is not a *solitary* activity but relies on active cooperation among a group of colleagues. // The film depicted coyotes to be *solitary* and mournfully howling animals on the tops of distant hills.
solvency ['sɑːlvənsi]	*n.* 溶解力；偿付能力 (capability of meeting financial obligations) 记 词根记忆：solv(溶解，解决) + ency → 溶解力 例 *solvency* of petroleum spirit 汽油溶解能力 // financial *solvency* 财务清偿能力
songbird ['sɔːŋbɜːrd]	*n.* 鸣禽，鸣鸟 (a bird that utters a succession of musical tones)；女歌手 (a female singer) 记 分拆记忆：song(唱) + bird(鸟，鸟类) → 鸣禽；女歌手 例 They observed no significant effect on *songbird* nesting success.
sophisticated [sə'fɪstɪkeɪtɪd]	*a.* 老练的，精通的 (experienced)；(仪器)复杂的 (highly complicated) 记 来自 sophisticate(*n.* 老于世故的人) 例 The increase in access to literary classics will create a *sophisticated* reading audience. // This technique requires *sophisticated* computer programs.

□ snout □ snuff □ soar □ sodium □ solar □ solidarity
□ solitary □ solvency □ songbird □ sophisticated

sovereign [ˈsɑːvrən]	*n.* 君主(emperor)；元首(ruler with sovereign) 记 联想记忆：sove(看作 over 在…上) + reign(统治) → 高高在上的统治者 → 君主 例 the *sovereign* of the seas 海上的霸主 派 sovereignty [*n.* 君主；主权(国家)]
span [spæn]	*n.* 跨度(an extent, stretch, reach, or spread between two limits)；一段时间(a period of time) 记 注意：wingspan(*n.* 翼展) 例 life *span* 寿命 // time *span* 时间间隔
sparse [spɑːrs]	*a.* 稀少的，贫乏的(of few and scattered elements) 记 联想记忆：稀少的(sparse)火星(spark) 例 The population is very *sparse* in that remote, mountainous area.
spate [speɪt]	*n.* 大批，大量(a large number) 例 a *spate* of books 许多书
spatial [ˈspeɪʃl]	*a.* 空间的(relating to, occupying, or having the character of space) 记 来自 space(*n.* 空间) 例 Human beings can see the *spatial* relations among objects by processing information conveyed by light.
spawn [spɔːn]	*n.* 卵(eggs)；*v.* 大量产生；引起(bring forth, generate) 记 联想记忆：大虾(prawn)产卵(spawn) 例 The computer industry has *spawned* hundreds of new companies. // *spawn* revolt 激起叛乱
specialist [ˈspeʃəlɪst]	*n.* 专家(one who specializes in a particular occupation)；*a.* 专业的(professional) 记 来自 special(*a.* 专业的) 例 If each type of *specialist* evolved just once, similar *specialists* on different islands would be closely related. 同根词：specific(*a.* 特殊的；明确的)
specialization [ˌspeʃələˈzeɪʃn]	*n.* 特殊化(making or becoming specialized) 记 来自 special(*a.* 特殊的；专门的) 例 Both of these scenarios imply that *specialization* to each niche occurred only once. Alternatively, each specialist could have arisen independently on each of the islands. 同根词：specialist(*n.* 专家；*a.* 专业的)
specialize [ˈspeʃəlaɪz]	*v.* (in)专门从事(to concentrate one's efforts on a special activity, field, or practice) 记 来自 special(*a.* 特别的，特殊的) 例 The firm *specializes* in the analysis of handwriting. 派 specialization(*n.* 专门化；特殊化)；specialized(*a.* 专门的)

35

species [ˈspiːʃiːz]	*n.* 物种 (group of animals or plants within a genus differing only in minor details from the others, and able to breed with each other but not with other groups) 记 词根记忆：speci(种) + es → 物种 例 Some *species* become extinct because of accumulated gradual changes in their local environments.
specific [spəˈsɪfɪk]	*a.* 具体的 (explicit)；详细而精确的 (accurate)；特殊的 (special) 记 词根记忆：speci(种) + fic → 按种类说明 → 具体的 例 *specific* reasons 具体原因 // Complement(血清中的补体)will not work unless it is activated by a *specific* antibody. 派 specifically(*ad.* 明确地；清楚地)
specify [ˈspesɪfaɪ]	*v.* 详细说明 (to state explicitly or in detail) 记 词根记忆：speci(种) + fy(使…) → 使每一种都清楚 → 详细说明 例 The investigative report didn't *specify* how caffeine is lost in the manufacturing process. 派 specifically(*ad.* 特定地；明确地)；specification(*n.* 规格；说明)
specimen [ˈspesɪmən]	*n.* 样品；标本 (instance) 记 词根记忆：speci(种) + men → 种类 → 样品 例 a fossil *specimen* 化石标本
specious [ˈspiːʃəs]	*a.* 华而不实的；似是而非的 (having deceptive attraction or allure) 例 This is a *specious* argument.
spectacular [spekˈtækjələr]	*a.* 壮观的，壮丽的 (striking, sensational) 记 词根记忆：spect(看) + acular → 吸引人看的 → 壮观的 例 We saw a *spectacular* sunrise while we were camping.
spectator [ˈspekteɪtər]	*n.* 观众；旁观者 (one who looks on or watches) 记 词根记忆：spect(看) + ator → 观众；旁观者 例 The bleachers at the game were filled with *spectators*. // We mustn't stand by as a *spectator*.
specter [ˈspektər]	*n.* 幽灵 (ghost)；萦绕在心头的恐惧 (phantasm) 记 联想记忆：spect(看) + er → 引入注目的东西 → 幽灵 例 The princess saw a *specter* in the corridor. // John was haunted by the *specter* of his past sins.
spectrum [ˈspektrəm]	*n.* 范围 (scope)；光谱 (a continuum of color formed when a beam of white light is dispersed (as by passage through a prism) so that its component wavelengths are arranged in order) 记 词根记忆：spectr(光谱) + um → 光谱 例 Mary's *spectrum* of scientific knowledge ranged from anatomy to zoology. // The ultraviolet band of the *spectrum* emitted by the Sun is harmful to the human body. // X-ray *spectrum* X 射线谱 // electromagnetic *spectrum* 电磁波频谱

speculate [ˈspekjuleɪt]	*v.* 推测（to reflect, to think）; 做投机买卖（to assume a business risk） 记 词根记忆: specul(看) + ate → 用心看 → 推测 例 Marine biologists *speculated* that clicking sounds emitted by dolphins might have another function. // The banker *speculated* in mutual funds. 派 speculation(*n.* 推测; 投机买卖); speculative(*a.* 推测的)
speculation [ˌspekjuˈleɪʃn]	*n.* 思索; 推测（an act or instance of speculating）; 投机（a transaction involving such speculation） 记 来自speculate(*v.* 思索; 推测) 例 They have confirmed researchers' *speculation* that masses of hot rock are buoyant enough to rise to the upper part of Earth's mantle. 同根词: suspect(*v.* 怀疑; 猜想)
speculator [ˈspekjuleɪtər]	*n.* 投机者（someone who buys or sells in expectation of profiting from market fluctuations）; 思索者（someone who ponders） 记 来自speculate(*v.* 投机; 推测) 例 In 1929 relatively small declines in the market ruined many *speculators* who had bought on margin; they had to sell, and their selling pushed other investors to the brink. 同根词: speculative(*a.* 投机的; 推测的)
sphere [sfɪr]	*n.* 球（globe）; 领域（an area or range） 记 联想记忆: 地球是被大气(atmosphere)环绕着的球体(sphere) 例 armillary *sphere* 浑天仪 // material and spiritual *sphere* 物质领域和精神领域 同根词: hemisphere(*n.* 半球); atmosphere(*n.* 大气层); biosphere(*n.* 生物圈)
spherical [ˈsferɪkl]	*a.* 球的, 球状的（having the form of a sphere or of one of its segments） 记 来自sphere(*n.* 球体) 例 Cartographers have long struggled with the problem of how to draw the *spherical* Earth on a flat sheet of paper. 派 spherically(*ad.* 球地, 球状地) 同根词: sphericity(*n.* 球形; 球面)
spiced [spaɪst]	*a.* 加香料的, 加调料的（containing spice or spices） 例 The chef cooked the beef in a heavily *spiced* stew.
spin [spɪn]	*v.* 快速旋转（to revolve rapidly） 例 The machine was *spinning* faster and faster.
spinach [ˈspɪnɪtʃ]	*n.* 菠菜 例 Kale has more nutritional value than *spinach*.
spine [spaɪn]	*n.* 脊柱（spinal column, backbone）;（动植物身上的)刺（any of the sharp needle-like parts on some plants and animals） 记 词根记忆: spin(刺) + e → 刺 例 Many plant species have sharp *spines* on their stems to protect themselves from browsing mammals. 派 spinal(*a.* 脊柱的); spiny(*a.* 多刺的)

35

□ speculate   □ speculation   □ speculator   □ sphere   □ spherical   □ spiced
□ spin   □ spinach   □ spine

spiral ['spaɪrəl]	*a.* 螺旋形的(helical)；*v.* 盘旋上升(或下降)(to go and especially to rise or fall in a spiral course)；*n.* 螺旋(something having a spiral form) 记 来自 spire(*n.* 螺旋) 例 *spiral* galaxies 旋涡星系 // *spiraling* costs 螺旋式上升的费用 // The caterer cut the radishes into decorative *spirals*.
spiteful ['spaɪtfl]	*a.* 怀恨的，恶意的(malicious) 例 The *spiteful* girl told lies about her teachers.
splinter ['splɪntər]	*n.* 碎片(sliver) 例 Be careful! There are *splinters* of glass all over the floor.
split [splɪt]	*v.* 分裂，裂开(to divide into parts or portions) 记 发音记忆："死劈了它" → 劈开 → 分裂 例 In the late seventh century, in a dispute over whether the Prophet Muhammad's son-in-law, Ali, should carry on as the fourth caliph, Muhammad's successor, Islam *split* into two branches, the Sunnis and the Shiites.
splotchy ['splatʃɪ]	*a.* 有污点的，污渍斑斑的(spotty) 例 the *splotchy* surface 斑驳的表面
spoilage ['spɔɪlɪdʒ]	*n.* 损坏(the act or process of spoiling)；损坏物(sth. spoiled or wasted) 记 来自 spoil(*v.* 损坏) 例 The irradiation of food kills bacteria and thus retards *spoilage*. 同根词：spoilt(*a.* 宠坏的；损坏的)
sponsor ['spɑːnsər]	*v.* 赞助(to pay for a project or activity)；*n.* 赞助人(a person or an organization that pays for or plans and carries out a project or activity) 记 词根记忆：spons(允诺) + or → 答应给钱 → 赞助 例 government-*sponsored* 由政府赞助的 // The *sponsors* of the offensive program were arrested. 派 sponsorship(*n.* 资助，赞助)
sporadically [spə'rædɪkli]	*ad.* 偶发地(infrequently)；零星地 记 来自 sporadical(*a.* 零星的) 例 Lyme disease(莱姆关节炎)is not a common disease and occurs only *sporadically*. // The rebels fired *sporadically* towards police in their shelters.
spot [spɑːt]	*n.* 地点(a particular area or place)；斑点(an area marred or marked)；现场(the place of action) 例 After one year at the new *spot*, it is doing about the same volume of business as before. 派 spotter(*n.* 监视人；测位仪)
spouse [spaʊs]	*n.* 配偶，夫妻(husband or wife) 记 联想记忆：sp(看作 spend 度过) + ouse(看作 house 房子) → 在一间房子里共度人生 → 配偶，夫妻 例 My *spouse* and I have been married for four years.

spray
[spreɪ]

n. 喷雾(剂)(water flying in small drops or particles)；小花枝(a usually flowering branch or shoot)；*v.* 喷洒(to project spray or something resembling spray on or into)

记 联想记忆：sp + ray(光线) → 像光线一样散出 → 喷洒

例 nasal *spray* 鼻用喷雾剂 // A rare New Zealand species of mistletoe produces spectacular *sprays* of scarlet flowers. // Various pesticides have been *sprayed* in the past 25 years in efforts to control the spruce budworm.

Only those who have the patience to do simple things perfectly ever acquire the skill to do difficult things easily.

只有有耐心圆满完成简单工作的人，才能够轻而易举地完成困难的事。

——德国剧作家、诗人 席勒(Friedrich Schiller, German dramatist and poet)

35

Word List 36

音频

spring [sprɪŋ]	*n.* 泉 (a source of supply); 春天 (the season between winter and summer); *v.* 跳 (to leap or jump up suddenly); 出现 (to come into being) 记 联想记忆: sp + ring (铃声) → 泉水的叮咚声就好像是铃声 → 泉 例 His inventions typically *spring* to life from previous works.
sprinkler ['sprɪŋklər]	*n.* 洒水装置; 消防喷嘴 (a device for sprinkling water or as part of a fire-extinguishing system installed in a building) 记 来自 sprinkle (*v.* 洒, 喷洒) 例 The gardener set the *sprinkler* next to the tomato plants. // *Sprinklers* can be automatically triggered by the presence of a fire.
spruce [spruːs]	*n.* 云杉 例 *spruce* budworm 云杉蚜虫
spur [spɜːr]	*v.* 促进, 激励 (to stimulate); *n.* 刺激 (stimulus) 记 spur 的原意是马刺, 为使马匹快走 → 促进, 激励 例 Economic recovery of the country *spurred* its military and cultural expansion.
spurious ['spjʊriəs]	*a.* 假的 (false); 伪造的 (falsified, forged) 记 来自 spuria (*n.* 伪造的作品) 例 Presently, no objective test for whiplash exists, so it is true that *spurious* reports of whiplash injuries cannot be readily identified. 派 spuriously (*ad.* 伪造地; 虚假地)
squash [skwɑːʃ]	*n.* 南瓜 (pumpkin); *v.* 镇压 (to put down); 压扁 (to crush) 记 联想记忆: squ + ash (灰) → 挤成灰 → 压扁 例 The strong man *squashed* the tin can in his fist.
squeak [skwiːk]	*n.* 吱吱叫 (a sharp shrill cry or sound) 例 Dolphins lack vocal cords, but they do create sounds, producing a complicated system of whistles, *squeaks*, moans, trills, and clicks with sphincter muscles inside the blowhole. 派 squeaky (*a.* 吱吱响的)
squirrel ['skwɜːrəl]	*n.* 松鼠 (any of various small or medium-sized rodents); *v.* 贮藏 (to store up for future use) 记 联想记忆: 松鼠 (squirrel) 在广场 (square) 上跑来跑去 例 It was said a *squirrel* could jump from tree to tree without once touching the ground between New York State and Georgia.

□ spring　　　□ sprinkler　　　□ spruce　　　□ spur　　　□ spurious　　　□ squash
□ squeak　　　□ squirrel

stabilize
[ˈsteɪbəlaɪz]

v. 使稳定，使坚固(to make stable, steadfast, or firm)

记 词根记忆: sta(站) + bilize → 站稳了 → 使稳定

例 The yield of natural gas from Norway's Troll gas field is expected to increase annually until the year 2005 and then to *stabilize* at six billion cubic feet a day.

派 stabilization(n. 稳定，稳定化)

同根词: static(a. 静态的)

staggering
[ˈstæɡərɪŋ]

a. 令人惊愕的(astonishing, overwhelming)

记 来自 stagger(v. 不相信)

例 *staggering* disparity 令人惊愕的差异

stake
[steɪk]

n. 火刑柱(a post to which a person is bound for execution by burning); 股份(an interest or share in an undertaking or enterprise)

例 at *stake* 在危急之中 // A prominent investor held a large *stake* in our company.

stamina
[ˈstæmɪnə]

n. 耐力; 持久力(staying power, endurance)

记 发音记忆: "四袋米呢" → 吃了四袋米呢，一定有耐力

例 Sled dogs are notable for their *stamina*. // That young man lacks *stamina*.

stance
[stæns]

n. 态度，立场(intellectual attitude)

记 联想记忆: stan(站) + ce → 所站的位置 → 态度，立场

例 Sometimes the political *stance* of a third party will be more radical than that of either of the two major parties.

standardize
[ˈstændərdaɪz]

v. 使标准化(to bring into conformity with a standard); 用标准检验(to compare with a standard)

记 来自 standard(n. 标准)

例 The Federal Aviation Association issued new guidelines for airlines in order to *standardize* safety requirements governing preflight inspections.

派 standardization(n. 标准化)

staple
[ˈsteɪpl]

n. 主要产品，主要成分(the principal element); a. 主要的(principal, chief)

记 和 stable(a. 稳定的)一起记

例 When maize was introduced into southern Europe in the 19th century, it quickly became a dietary *staple*. // All of East and Southeast Asia is wholly dependent on rice to be its *staple* food.

startlingly
[ˈstɑːrtlɪŋlɪ]

ad. 令人吃惊地，惊人地(shockingly)

例 The *startlingly* high rate of geographical mobility in the 19th-century United States has puzzled historians.

static
[ˈstætɪk]

a. 不变的; 停滞的(stationary)

记 词根记忆: stat(站，立) + ic → 站立的 → 停滞的

例 The ratio of women's earnings with that of men has been roughly *static* since 1960.

36

□ stabilize   □ staggering   □ stake   □ stamina   □ stance   □ standardize
□ staple   □ startlingly   □ static
321

stationary ['steɪʃəneri]	*a.* 静止的(immobile) 记 词根记忆：station(位置) + ary → 固定在一个位置的 → 静止的 注意：stationery(*n.* 文具商；文具店) 例 Because of an accident, traffic was *stationary* for an hour.
stationery ['steɪʃəneri]	*n.* 文具；信纸(materials (as paper, pens, and ink) for writing or typing) 例 In market research surveys, few consumers identify Paper&Print as a book or *stationery* store but many recognize and value the broad range of magazines it carries. 同根词：stationer(*n.* 文具店；文具商)
statistic [stə'tɪstɪk]	*n.* 统计(estimate)；统计资料(数值)(a single term or datum in a collection of statistics) 记 联想记忆：stat(看作 state 国家) + istic → 一般都是由国家或国家部门做统计工作 → 统计 例 This *statistic* shows that the change in speed limit adversely affected the alertness of drivers. 派 statistical[*a.* 统计(学)的]；statistician(*n.* 统计员；统计学家)；statistics [*n.* 统计(学)]
statistical [stə'tɪstɪkl]	*a.* 统计的；统计学的(of, relating to, based on, or employing the principles of statistics) 记 和 statistic(*a.* 统计的，统计学的)一起记 例 There is a strong *statistical* link between volcanic eruptions and the severity of the rainy season in India. 派 statistically(*ad.* 统计地；统计学上)
stature ['stætʃər]	*n.* 身高(natural height) 记 词根记忆：stat(站) + ure(状态) → 站直后的状态 → 身高 例 Poor diet could affect *stature* negatively.
status ['stætəs]	*n.* 身份；地位(the position or rank in relation to others)；状况(the state or condition with respect to circumstances) 记 词根记忆：stat(站) + us → 从站的位置判断身份或地位 → 身份；地位 例 To the tailors, their *status* as guild members overlapped with their roles as heads of household. // social *status* 社会地位 // economic *status* 经济状况
status quo ante ['stætəs 'kwoʊ 'ænti]	<拉>原状(the state of affairs that existed previously) 记 和 ant(*n.* 蚂蚁)一起记 例 The United States, it was believed, had no *status quo ante*.
statute ['stætʃuːt]	*n.* 【律】法令，条例(law) 例 *statute* law 成文法 派 statutory(*a.* 法定的)
staunch [stɔːntʃ]	*a.* 坚定的；忠诚的(steadfast in loyalty or principle) 例 a *staunch* friend 忠诚的朋友 派 staunchly(*ad.* 坚定地；忠诚地)

□ stationary　　□ stationery　　□ statistic　　□ statistical　　□ stature　　□ status
□ status quo ante　□ statute　　□ staunch

stave [steɪv]	*n.* 狭板，木柱(staff) 记 和 starve(*v.* 饿死)一起记 例 *stave* churches 由木板建造的教堂
steep [stiːp]	*a.* 极高的(extremely or excessively high)；*v.* 沉浸(to make throughly wet)；充满(to fill with or subject to) 例 Producers rose prices at an unexpectedly *steep* rate in September. // The officers were *steeped* in the traditions of the separate services. 派 steeply(*ad.* 陡峭地)
steer [stɪr]	*n.* 肉用公牛(young, usu. castrated male animal of the ox family, raised for its meat)；*v.* 掌舵(to guide by mechanical means) 例 Cattle breeders have increasingly used crossbreeding so that their *steers* can acquire certain characteristics.
stem ·[stem]	*n.* 茎，干(the main trunk of a plant)；*v.* (from)起源于(to originate)；阻断(to stop or dam up) 例 brain *stem* 脑干 // Government revenues mainly *stem* from the various taxes. // The dam *stemmed* the river's flow.
steppe [step]	*n.* (尤指东南欧或西伯利亚地区)无树木的大草原(one of the vast usually level and treeless tracts in southeastern Europe or Asia) 记 联想记忆: step(步) + pe → 在大草原漫步一定很惬意 → 无树木的大草原 例 the Eurasian *steppes* 欧亚大草原
stereotype [ˈsteriətaɪp]	*n.* 铅版(a plate cast from a printing surface)；陈规(something conforming to a fixed or general pattern)；*v.* 使⋯一成不变(to repeat without variation) 例 break through the *stereotypes* 打破陈规 // Most Americans' knowledge of American Indian culture was *stereotyped*. 派 stereotyped(*a.* 固定不变的；刻板的)
sterile [ˈsterəl]	*a.* 不育的(failing to produce or incapable of producing offspring)；贫瘠的(barren)；无效果的(unproductive) 例 The *sterile* couple adopted two children. // *sterile* land 贫瘠的土地 // The economic reform of this country was *sterile*.
stew [stuː]	*n.* 炖菜(肉)(fish or meat usually with vegetables prepared by stewing)；*v.* 炖(to become cooked by stewing) 记 发音记忆: "死丢" → 拼命往锅里丢东西 → 炖 例 Meat of Iguanas(美洲大蜥蜴)is usually cooked in a heavily spiced *stew* by Latin Americans. // The cook *stewed* the ham hocks for a few hours.
stiffness [stɪfnəs]	*n.* 僵硬(rigidity)；顽固(stubbornness) 记 来自 stiff(*a.* 呆板的) 例 Unlike the body's inflammatory response to cuts and sprains in which widespread swelling and *stiffness* immobilize the injured area until it has healed, the body's more localized response to sunburn results in a distinct line dividing affected and unaffected areas of the skin.

36

stimulant [ˈstɪmjələnt]	*n.* 刺激物(stimulus); 兴奋剂(an agent, as a drug, that produces a temporary increase of the functional activity or efficiency of an organism or any of its parts) 记 词根记忆: stimul(刺激) + ant → 刺激物 例 An age of political excitement is usually a *stimulant* to literature. // Caffeine is the *stimulant* in coffee. 同根词: stimulus(*n.* 刺激; 刺激物)
stimulate [ˈstɪmjuleɪt]	*v.* 激励(to animate); 激发(to arouse) 记 词根记忆: stimul(刺激) + ate(使…) → 使受刺激 → 激发 例 Therefore, cannabinoids probably function to *stimulate* the appetite. 派 stimulus(*n.* 刺激); stimulant(*a.* 激励的)
stimuli [ˈstɪmjəlaɪ]	*n.* 刺激(incentive); 刺激物, 促进因素(sth. that rouses or incites to activity) 记 stimulus(*n.* 刺激; 刺激物)的复数 例 Rhesus monkeys respond with aggression to a wider range of *stimuli* than any other monkeys do. 同根词: stimulate(*v.* 刺激)
sting [stɪŋ]	*v.* 蜇, 叮(to prick painfully); *n.* 螫伤(a wound or pain caused by or as if by stinging) 记 发音记忆: "死叮" → 叮, 蜇 例 A hornet *stung* the boy who swatted at it. // A venomous *sting* of snakes is often fatal to humans.
stinger [ˈstɪŋər]	*n.* 刺(a sharp organ); 讽刺者(one that stings); 鸡尾酒(cocktail) 记 来自 sting(*v.* 刺痛; 刺) 例 The honeybee's *stinger* is heavily barbed. 同根词: stingy(*a.* 吝啬的; 有刺的)
stipend [ˈstaɪpend]	*n.* 薪水; 定期津贴(a fixed sum of money paid periodically for services or to defray expenses) 记 联想记忆: stip(点) + end(结束) → 在月末点结算 → 薪水 例 Those who lived on fixed *stipends* found it hard to make ends meet during the period of inflation.
stipulate [ˈstɪpjuleɪt]	*v.* 规定; 确定(to specify as a condition or requirement) 记 联想记忆: stip(点) + ulate → 点明了的事情 → 确定 例 The rich man *stipulated* that his estate was to be distributed equally to his three sons after his death.
stitch [stɪtʃ]	*n.* 缝针; 针脚(one in-and-out movement of a threaded needle in sewing, embroidering, or suturing) 例 Bill's gash required six *stitches*. // The *stitches* in the dress's hem match the color of the dress.

stock [stɑːk]	*n.* 股票(portion of this held by an investor); 库存(a store available); *v.* 储备(to put in stock) 例 *stock* price 股价 // buffer *stocks* 调节性库存 // The store *stocked* lots of new cleaning products. 派 stockbroker(*n.* 股票经纪人); stockholder(*n.* 股票持有人; 股东)
storefront ['stɔːrfrʌnt]	*n.* 店堂, 沿街铺面(the front side of a store or store building facing a street) 记 分拆记忆: store(商店) + front(前面) → 店堂 例 Those who come to church with a predisposition to religious belief will be happy in an auditorium or even a *storefront*.
strain [streɪn]	*n.* 血统(ancestry); 张力, 拉紧(an act of straining or the condition of being strained); 【生】品种(kind, sort); *v.* 拉紧(to draw tight) 例 Tom is of a noble *strain*. // Certain genetically modified *strains* of maize produce a powerful natural insecticide.
strait [streɪt]	*n.* 海峡(a comparatively narrow passageway connecting two large bodies of water) 例 the *Strait* of Gibraltar 直布罗陀海峡
strand [strænd]	*n.* (线等的)股, 缕(any of the threads, wires, etc. twisted together to form a rope or cable) 记 联想记忆: 只有一股绳(strand)是站(stand)不起来的 例 The ship is *stranded* at the beach. // Anne removed the *strands* of hair from the hairbrush.
strategic [strə'tiːdʒɪk]	*a.* 战略上的(of, relating to, or marked by strategy); 关键的, 重要的(necessary to or important) 记 来自 strategy(*n.* 战略, 策略) 例 Why firms adhere to or deviate from their *strategic* plans is poorly understood. 派 strategically(*ad.* 战略性地; 战略上) 同根词: strategist(*n.* 战略家; 军事家)
strategy ['strætədʒi]	*n.* 战略, 策略(art of planning and directing an operation in a war or campaign) 记 词根记忆: strat(层) + egy → 讲究层次和步骤 → 策略 例 Analysts assessed the effectiveness of this *strategy*. 派 strategic(*a.* 战略上的); strategist(*n.* 战略家)
stratosphere ['strætəsfɪr]	*n.* 平流层, 同温层(位于对流层之上中顶层之下的范围的大气)(the part of the earth's atmosphere which extends from the top of the troposphere to about 30 miles (50 kilometers) above the surface and in which temperature increases gradually to about 32°F (0°C) and clouds rarely form) 记 词根记忆: strato(=strat 层) + sphere(球) → 围绕在地球外的大气层 → 平流层 例 In the *stratosphere*, ozone layer shields the Earth from the most biologically harmful radiation emitted by the Sun.

36

stray [streɪ]	*v.* 偏离，迷路(to wander away)；*a.* 迷了路的(having strayed or escaped from a proper or intended place)；偶然发生的(occurring at random or sporadically) 記 发音记忆：死追 → 怎么追也追不上 → 迷路 例 Tourists often get lost and *stray* into dangerous areas. 派 strayer(*n.* 迷途者；流浪者)
strenuous ['strenjuəs]	*a.* 费力的(arduous) 記 词根记忆：stren(=strength 力量) + uous → 需要用力量的 → 费力的 例 Physical injuries sometimes result from entering a *strenuous* physical fitness program too quickly.
strife [straɪf]	*n.* 纷争，冲突(bitter and sometimes violent conflict) 記 词根记忆：strif(竞争) + e → 纷争 例 intestine *strife* 内讧
string [strɪŋ]	*v.* 用线串(to tie, hang, or fasten with string)；*n.* 弦(cord)；一串(a group of objects threaded on a string) 記 联想记忆：st + ring(铃) → 路上留下一串串清亮的铃声 → 一串 例 The jewelry maker *strung* beads to make a necklace. // guitar *strings* 吉他琴弦 // DNA *strings* 基因链
stringent ['strɪndʒənt]	*a.* 严格的(strict)；严厉的(rigid) 例 The Wildlife Protection Committee imposed more *stringent* penalties on poachers. 派 stringently(*ad.* 严格地，严厉地)
strip [strɪp]	*v.* 剥去(to remove surface matter from)；*n.* 狭长的一片(a long narrow piece) 記 联想记忆：s(音似：死) + trip(旅行) → 死亡剥夺了人在尘世的时间之旅 → 剥去 例 The only place where the wild form of emmer wheat has been found growing is a relatively narrow *strip* of southwest Asia. 派 stripy(*a.* 有条纹的)
strive [straɪv]	*v.* 努力，奋斗(to endeavor) 記 词根记忆：striv(竞争) + e → 不断迎接竞争 → 努力，奋斗 例 The directors of large firms will *strive* to reduce the costs of their products.
stroke [stroʊk]	*n.* 中风(sudden attack of illness in the brain that can cause loss of the power to move, speak clearly, etc.)；击(blow)，敲(钟)(act of striking, esp. of a bell)；一下完成的动作(a single unbroken movement) 例 Hypertension(高血压)can cause *strokes*. // at one *stroke* 一下子，突然
stroll [stroʊl]	*v./n.* 闲逛，散步(to go for a leisurely walk) 記 联想记忆：st + roll(摇摆，滚动) → 摇摇摆摆地去散步 → 闲逛 例 David *strolled* through the woods behind his house.
strut [strʌt]	*n.* 支柱，支撑(a structural piece designed to resist pressure) 例 In birds the second finger is the principal *strut* of the wing.

studious

[ˈstuːdiəs]

*a.*慎重的；有意的（deliberately or consciously planned）

例 *studious* criticism 慎重的批评 // The study(书房)was furnished with *studious* simplicity.

stumble

[ˈstʌmbl]

*v./n.*绊倒（to trip）

例 a *stumbling* block 绊脚石

stun

[stʌn]

v.(使)昏厥（daze），(使)震惊（astonish）

记 联想记忆：太阳(sun)里面多了一个 t，使人震惊(stun)

例 Dolphins used loud clicks to *stun* their prey at close range. // The president's assassination *stunned* the entire nation.

派 stunning(*a.* 足以使人晕厥的，极好的)

stunning

[ˈstʌnɪŋ]

*a.*极富魅力的（strikingly impressive in beauty or excellence）

记 来自 stun(*v.* 使震惊； *n.* 令人惊叹的事物)

例 Researchers in Germany have unearthed those wooden spears from what appears to be an ancient lakeshore hunting ground, *stunning* evidence that human ancestors systematically hunted big game much earlier than believed.

派 stunningly(*ad.* 绝妙地；令人震惊地)

同根词：stunner(*n.* 绝妙的东西；出色的人)

stunt

[stʌnt]

*n.*噱头（one performed or undertaken chiefly to gain attention or publicity）；*v.* 阻碍，妨碍（发育）（to hinder the normal growth, development, or progress of）

例 Smokers complained that their prospects for being hired and promoted are being *stunted* by their habit.

sturdy

[ˈstɜːrdi]

*a.*结实的；坚固的（firmly built or constituted）

记 和 study(*v.* 学习)一起记，身体强健(sturdy)才能学习(study)好

例 a worker's *sturdy* frame 工人强健的体格 // *sturdy* construction 坚固的结构

subgroup

[ˈsʌbgruːp]

*n.*小群；隶属的小组织（a subset of a mathematical group that is itself a group）

记 词根记忆：sub(副、次) + group(组织) → 隶属的小组织

例 It would help researchers to identify *subgroups* of patients with secondary conditions that might also be treatable.

subject

[ˈsʌbdʒekt]

a. (to)受制于…的（under the authority of sth./sb.） *n.*国民（citizen），主题（something represented or indicated in a work of art），科目（a department of knowledge）

记 词根记忆：sub(在下面) + ject(扔) → 被扔在下面 → 受制于

例 Any flying vertebrate is *subject* to aerodynamic constraints. // The queen is supported by her *subjects'* tax money.

派 subjective(*a.* 主观的；个人的)

36

sublanguage [ˈsʌbˌlæŋgwɪdʒ]	*n.* [计]子语言 记 词根记忆：sub(次；下级) + language(语言) → 子语言 例 Nobody knows exactly how many languages there are in the world, partly because of the difficulty of distinguishing between a language and the *sublanguages* or dialects within it, but those who have tried to count typically have found about five thousand.
submarine [ˌsʌbməˈriːn]	*n.* 潜艇(a naval vessel designed to operate underwater) 记 词根记忆：sub(下面) + marine(海洋) → 在海下面行进的 → 潜艇 例 nuclear *submarine* 核潜艇
submit [səbˈmɪt]	*v.* 提交(to present or propose to another for review consideration, or decision)；(to) 屈从(to yield) 记 词根记忆：sub(下面) + mit(送，发) → 从下往上送 → 提交 例 The article based on experiments was *submitted* for publication last year. // The peasants *submitted* themselves to the queen's rule. 派 submission(*n.* 屈服，服从)
subordinate [səˈbɔːrdɪnət]	*a.* (to)下级的(inferior)；*n.* 下级(a person who is subordinate) 记 词根记忆：sub(下面) + ordin(顺序) + ate → 顺序在下面的 → 下级的 例 The new recruit was *subordinate* to all of the officers. // The *supervisor* blamed one of his *subordinates* for the mistake.
subscribe [səbˈskraɪb]	*v.* (to)订阅(to receive a periodical or service regularly on order) 记 词根记忆：sub(下面) + scribe(写) → 写下订单 → 订阅 例 *subscribe* to a magazine 订阅杂志 派 subscriber(*n.* 订购者)；subscription(*n.* 捐助；订购)
subscription [səbˈskrɪpʃn]	*n.* 捐献(donation)；订阅(a payment for consecutive issues of a newspaper or magazine for a given period of time)；签署(the act of signing one's name) 记 来自 subscribe(*v.* 订阅) 例 Many of the magazine's long-time subscribers would continue their *subscriptions* even if the subscription price were increased. 同根词：transcribe(*v.* 抄写，誊写)
subsequent [ˈsʌbsɪkwənt]	*a.* 随后的，接续的(following in time, order, or place) 记 词根记忆：sub(下面) + sequ(跟随) + ent → 下面跟着的 → 随后的 例 The company plans to continue adding new departments and services in *subsequent* years. 派 subsequently(*ad.* 后来；随后)

subsidiary [səbˈsɪdieri]	*n.* 子公司 (a company wholly controlled by another); *a.* 附属的 (affiliated) 记 联想记忆: sub (在下面) + sid (坐) + iary → 坐在下面的公司 → 子公司 例 a *subsidiary* of a Chicago firm 一家芝加哥公司的子公司
subsidize [ˈsʌbsɪdaɪz]	*v.* 补助, 资助 (to furnish with a subsidy) 例 Government has proposed 2 million dollars to *subsidize* private medical schools. 派 subsidization (*n.* 补助, 资助)
subsidy [ˈsʌbsədi]	*n.* 津贴, 补助 (a grant or gift of money) 记 联想记忆: sub (下面) + sid (坐) + y → 坐在下面领补助 → 津贴, 补助 例 This company received a *subsidy* from a foreign government to build its plant abroad.
subsistence [səbˈsɪstəns]	*n.* 生存, 生计 (the minimum as of food and shelter necessary to support life) 记 来自 subsist (*v.* 生存) 例 Peasants living in the mountain areas were barely able to ensure their own *subsistence*. // *subsistence* farming 自给农业
substance [ˈsʌbstəns]	*n.* 实质 (essence); 物质 (material) 记 词根记忆: sub (下面) + stan (站) + ce → 站在下面的 → 实质 例 The teacher discussed the *substance* of the author's works. // An antigen is a *substance* foreign to the organism's body.
substantial [səbˈstænʃl]	*a.* 实际的 (real); 大量的 (ample) 记 来自 substance (*n.* 实质; 物质) 例 *substantial* increase 实际增长 // That small company made *substantial* investments in new plants, staff and equipment. 派 substantially (*ad.* 大量地)
substantiate [səbˈstænʃieɪt]	*v.* 证实, 证明 (to verify) 记 词根记忆: sub (下面) + stant (站) + iate → 可以立足的 → 证实 例 The researchers *substantiated* their figures with census data. 派 unsubstantiated (*a.* 未证实的, 无根据的)

substitute [ˈsʌbstɪtuːt]	*n.* (for)代替品 (a person or thing that takes the place or function of another)； *v.* (for)代替，替代 (to replace) 记 词根记忆：sub(下面) + stitute(建立) → 可以放在下面来用的 → 代替品 例 No acceptable *substitute* for this material exists. // Some governments *substituted* living allowances for their employees' paychecks. 派 substitution(*n.* 代替；替代)
substitution [ˌsʌbstɪˈtuːʃn]	*n.*代替 (replacement of one mathematical entity by another of equal value)；替代物 (one that is substituted for another) 记 来自 substitute(*v.* 替代) 例 Their *substitution* for more traditional fertilizers may accelerate soil structure deterioration and soil erosion. 同根词：institute(*v.* 制定，建立)
substrate [ˈsʌbstreɪt]	*n.*底土层，底土 (subsoil) 记 词根记忆：sub(下面) + strate(层) → 下面一层 → 底土层 例 a *substrate* of clay 粘土层
subtle [ˈsʌtl]	*a.*细微的 (delicate) 例 Coral reefs are sensitive to *subtle* changes in nutrient input to their waters. 派 subtly(*ad.* 敏锐地；精巧地)
subtract [səbˈtrækt]	*v.* (from)减，减去 (to deduct) 记 词根记忆：sub(下面) + tract(拉) → 拉到下面 → 减去 例 Tom *subtracted* the smaller number from the larger number. 派 subtraction(*n.* 减法)
subtraction [səbˈtrækʃn]	*n.*减法；减少 (an act, operation, or instance of subtracting) 记 来自 subtract(*v.* 减去，扣掉) 例 *subtraction* formula 减法公式 同根词：subtract(*v.* 减去，扣掉)
succession [səkˈseʃn]	*n.*连续 (sequence)；继位 (the right of a person or line to succeed)；【生】自然演替 (unidirectional change in the composition of an ecosystem as the available competing organisms and especially the plants respond to and modify the environment) 记 词根记忆：success(接替) + ion → 接替发生 → 连续 例 in *succession* 连续 // plant *succession* 植物的自然演替 同根词：successive(*a.* 连续的)；successor(*n.* 继任者；继承人)
sue [suː]	*v.*向…起诉，提起诉讼 (to seek justice or right from a person, etc., by legal process) 记 发音记忆："诉" → 起诉 例 In 1979, the parents of a three year old *sued* in New York for accidental-death damages and won an award of $750,000.

sufficiency [səˈfɪʃnsi]	*n.* 足量，充足(the quality or state of being sufficient) 记 来自 sufficient(*a.* 足够的，充分的) 例 Participation in the workplace and economic self-*sufficiency*, they believed, would make women socially useful and therefore deserving of equality with men.
sufficient [səˈfɪʃnt]	*a.* 足够的(enough to meet the needs) 记 来自 suffice(*v.* 使满足；有能力) 例 Some areas of ocean in the Southern Hemisphere do not contain *sufficient* nutrients to support large seaweed farms. 派 sufficiency(*n.* 足够，充足); sufficiently(*ad.* 充分地)
suffrage [ˈsʌfrɪdʒ]	*n.* 选举权，投票权(the right of voting) 记 词根记忆: suf + frage(表示拥护的喧闹声) → 投票权 例 It was stronger than their commitment to the *suffrage* struggle. 派 suffragist(*n.* 妇女政权论者)
sugarcane [ˈʃʊgərˌken]	*n.* 甘蔗(a stout tall perennial grass grows as a source of sugar) 记 词根记忆: sugar(糖) + cane(藤条，茎) → 糖条 → 甘蔗 例 Many small *sugarcane* growers joined together to form an association of sugarcane producers and began to buy supplies at low group rates.
sulfuric [sʌlˈfjʊrɪk]	*a.* 硫磺的；含多量硫磺的(of, relating to, or containing sulfur especially with a higher valence than sulfurous compounds) 记 来自 sulfur(*n.* 硫磺) 例 Acid rain and snow result from the chemical reactions between industrial emissions of sulfur dioxide and nitrogen oxides and atmospheric water vapor to produce highly corrosive *sulfuric* and nitric acids.
summit [ˈsʌmɪt]	*n.* 峰顶(peak)；最高级会议(a conference of highest-level officials) 例 The climbers placed their country's flag at the mountain's *summit*. // The president met with his advisors at a secret *summit*.
superb [suːˈpɜːrb]	*a.* 上乘的，极好的(splendid) 记 词根记忆: super(上等，超越) + b → 上乘的，极好的 例 The critic praised the *superb* movie highly.
superficial [ˌsuːpərˈfɪʃl]	*a.* 肤浅的(shallow)；粗略的(rough) 记 词根记忆: super(上面) + fic(做) + ial → 在上面做，表面上的 → 肤浅的 例 The study was either infrequent or *superficial*, or both. // a *superficial* reading 粗读 派 superficiality(*n.* 浅薄)
superior [suːˈpɪriər]	*a.* (to) 较好的(better)；*n.* 上级，长官(a person who is above another in rank, station, or office) 记 词根记忆: super(上面) + ior → 在人之上的人 → 上级 例 Our products are *superior* to that of our competitors. // The soldier saluted his *superior*. 派 superiority(*n.* 优越；优势)

37

superiority [suːpiri'ɔːrəti]	*n.* 优越(感)(the quality or state of being superior) 🔢 来自 superior(*a.* 优越的) 🔢 In contrast, the soft-sell approach involves the use of advertising claims that imply *superiority* more subtly. 同根词: superstratum(*n.* 上层)
supernova [ˌsuːpər'nouvə]	*n.* 【天】超新星(the explosion of a star in which the star may reach a maximum intrinsic luminosity one billion times that of the sun) 🔢 词根记忆: super(超) + nova(新星) → 超新星 🔢 *Supernovas* can produce clouds of high energy particles called cosmic rays.
supersede [ˌsuːpər'siːd]	*v.* 替代, 取代(to replace) 🔢 词根记忆: super(上面) + sede(坐) → 坐在别人的位置上 → 取代 🔢 The state law would *supersede* the local antismoking ordinances.
supersonic [ˌsuːpər'sɑːnɪk]	*a.* 超音速的(moving, capable of moving, or utilizing air currents moving at supersonic speed); *n.* 超声波(a supersonic wave or frequency) 🔢 词根记忆: super(超) + son(声音) + ic → 超音速的 🔢 A scramjet can attain high speeds by reducing airflow compression at the entrance of the engine and letting air pass through at *supersonic* speeds. 同根词: resonance(*n.* 反响, 共鸣)
supplement 	[ˈsʌplɪmənt] *v.* 补充, 增补(to add) [ˈsʌplɪmənt] *n.* 补充(物), 增补(物)(something that completes or makes an addition) 🔢 词根记忆: sup + ple(满) + ment → 使满 → 补充, 增补 🔢 The government proposed to *supplement* the income of those low-paid workers. // vitamin *supplements* 维生素添加剂
suppress [sə'pres]	*v.* 镇压(to subdue); 抑制, 阻止(to restrain or inhibit) 🔢 词根记忆: sup(在下面) + press(压) → 压下去 → 镇压 🔢 Police were ordered out to *suppress* the demonstrators. // Many malarial symptoms can be *suppressed* with anti-malarial medication. 🔢 suppressant(*n.* 抑制物); suppressed[*a.* 生长(发育)受阻的]
supreme [suː'priːm]	*a.* 最高的(highest in rank or authority); 极度的(highest in degree or quality) 🔢 词根记忆: supre(=super 超过) + me(我) → 超越我的 → 最高的 🔢 the *Supreme* Court 最高法院 // The very rich couple lived in *supreme* luxury.
surcharge [ˈsɜːrtʃɑːrdʒ]	*n.* 附加税; 额外费(an additional tax or cost) 🔢 词根记忆: sur(超过) + charge(收费) → 额外的收费 → 附加费 🔢 bunker *surcharge* 燃油附加税
surge [sɜːrdʒ]	*v./n.* 汹涌, 猛增(to rise suddenly and excessively) 🔢 联想记忆: s + urge(急迫的) → 水流湍急 → 汹涌 🔢 The huge wave *surged* over the beach. // The *surge* in new home sales may continue in the coming years.

332
□ superiority   □ supernova   □ supersede   □ supersonic   □ supplement   □ suppress
□ supreme   □ surcharge   □ surge

surgeon [ˈsɜːrdʒən]	*n.* 外科医师(a medical specialist who practices surgery) 记 联想记忆：surge(波动) + on → 做外科医师，情绪不能波动太大 → 外科医师 例 After 5 years hard study, Tom became a cardiac *surgeon*. 派 surgery(*n.* 手术)；surgical(*a.* 外科手术的)；surgically(*ad.* 使用外科手术地)
surpass [sərˈpæs]	*v.* 超越(to go beyond)；胜过(to exceed) 记 词根记忆：sur(上面) + pass(经过) → 从上面经过 → 超越 例 India may *surpass* China as the world's most populous nation by 2050. // The excellent runner *surpassed* all previous records.
surplus [ˈsɜːrplʌs]	*n.* 过剩，剩余〈物〉(remainder)；*a.* 剩余的(more than what is needed or used) 记 联想记忆：sur(下面) + plus(加，多余的) → 剩在下面的就是多余的 → 剩余的 例 The clothing factory donated its *surplus* to charity. // *Surplus* stocks of pepper have been reduced in the past three years.
survey	[sərˈveɪ] *v.* 调查(to investigate)；视察(to inspect) [ˈsɜːrveɪ] *n.* 调查(investigation) 例 marketing *survey* 市场调查 // The company will periodically *survey* its employees to determine the introduction of the new strategy. 派 surveyor(*n.* 测量员；检察员)
susceptible [səˈseptəbl]	*a.* (to)易受影响的(liable)；敏感的(responsive) 记 词根记忆：sus + cept(接受) + ible → 心里接受 → 易受影响的 例 Humans are genetically *susceptible* to some diseases. 派 susceptibility(*n.* 易感性)
suspect	[səˈspekt] *v.* 怀疑(to doubt)；推测(to speculate) [ˈsʌspekt] *n.* 嫌疑犯(a person suspected of a crime) 记 联想记忆：su + spect(看) → 偷偷看 → 怀疑 例 She *suspected* the police of having illegally taped her confidential conversations with her client. // The officer took the *suspect* to the police station.
suspicion [səˈspɪʃn]	*n.* 怀疑，猜疑(mistrust, doubt) 例 The action at once awakened *suspicion*. 同根词：suspicious(*a.* 猜疑的，可疑的)
sustain [səˈsteɪn]	*v.* 支持，维持(to keep up)；遭受(to suffer) 记 词根记忆：sus(下面) + tain → 在下面支撑住 → 支持 例 To compete in international markets, a nation's businesses must *sustain* investment in intangible and physical assets. 派 sustained(*a.* 持续不变的)
sustenance [ˈsʌstənəns]	*n.* 食物，养料(nourishment) 例 This article explained how reef communities acquire *sustenance* for survival.

37

swiftly [swɪftli]	*ad.* 很快地，即刻(quickly)
	记 来自 swift(*a.* 迅速的，快的)
	例 Passengers must exit airplanes *swiftly* after accidents, since gases released following accidents are toxic to humans.
symbiotic [ˌsɪmbaɪˈɑːtɪk]	*a.* 共生的，共栖的(living together in close union of two dissimilar organisms)
	记 词根记忆：sym(共同) + bio(生命) + tic → 享有共同的生命 → 共生的
	例 *symbiotic* relationship 共生关系
symmetry [ˈsɪmətri]	*n.* 对称；均衡(balanced proportions)
	记 词根记忆：sym(共同) + metr(测量) + y → 测量结果相同 → 对称；均衡
	例 geometrical *symmetries* 几何对称
	派 symmetrical(*a.* 匀称的；对称的)
sympathetic [ˌsɪmpəˈθetɪk]	*a.* 同情的(given to, marked by, or arising from sympathy, compassion or friendliness)；(to)赞同的(approving)
	记 词根记忆：sym(共同) + path(感情) + etic(…的) → 有共同感情的 → 赞同的
	例 a *sympathetic* person 富于同情心的人 // I was not *sympathetic* to what the author said in his book.
symptom [ˈsɪmptəm]	*n.* 征兆(trace)；(病)症状(something that indicates the presence of bodily disorder)
	记 词根记忆：sym(共同) + ptom(现象) → 共同的现象 → 症状
	例 Forests in this area didn't show visible *symptoms* of damage by acid rain. // This medication can relieve *symptoms* of colds.
synchronize [ˈsɪŋkrənaɪz]	*v.* 使同步(to make synchronous in operation)
	记 词根记忆：syn(同) + chron(=time 时间) + ize(使) → 使同时间 → 使同步
	例 Because of a similarity to dance, *synchronized* swimming—exhibition swimming in which the movements of one or more swimmers are synchronized with a musical accompaniment—is sometimes called water ballet, especially in theatrical situations.
	派 synchronization(*n.* 同步，同时性)
	同根词：synchrony(*n.* 同步)
syndrome [ˈsɪndroʊm]	*n.* 综合症状(a set of medical symptoms which represent a physical or mental disorder)
	记 词根记忆：syn(共同) + drome(跑) → (疾病)跑到一起 → 综合症状
	例 Anyone who works with his hands for long hours can get carpal tunnel *syndrome*.
	同根词：synthesize(*v.* 综合)

synthesis ['sɪnθəsɪs]	*n.* 综合；合成（integration, combination） 记 来自 synthesize(*v.* 综合；合成) 例 This project is a *synthesis* of hard work and patience. // The ribosome controls the rates of *synthesis* and degradation of RNA. 同根词：synthesize(*v.* 合成)；synthesizer(*n.* 音响合成器)；synthetic(*a.* 合成的；人造的)
synthesize ['sɪnθəsaɪz]	*v.* 综合；合成（to combine or produce by synthesis） 记 词根记忆：syn(共同) + thes(放) + ize → 放到一起 → 综合；合成 例 Although the enzyme has been *synthesized* in the laboratory, no large-scale production facilities exist as yet. 派 synthesizer(*n.* 合成器；合成者) 同根词：synthetic(*a.* 合成的；*n.* 合成物)
synthetic [sɪn'θetɪk]	*n.* 合成物（sth. resulting from synthesis rather than occurring naturally）；*a.* 合成的（relating to or involving synthesis） 记 词根记忆：syn(共同) + thet(放) + ic → 放到一起的 → 合成的 例 Farmers who switched from *synthetic* to organic farming last year have seen their crop yields decline. 派 synthetically(*ad.* 综合地；合成地) 同根词：antithetical(*a.* 对立的)
taboo [tæ'buː]	*a.* 讳忌的（banned on grounds of morality or taste）；*n.* 禁忌；禁止（prohibition） 记 发音记忆："特不" → 特别强调不准干的事 → 禁忌；禁止 例 *Taboo* topics from the 1930s are now discussed openly. // a *taboo* against sex before marriage 婚前禁止性行为
tactic ['tæktɪk]	*n.* 策略（a device for accomplishing an end）；战术（a method of employing forces in combat） 记 联想记忆：tact(接触) + ic → 短兵相接 → 策略；战术 例 Unions that have employed this *tactic* have achieved their goals. 派 tactical(*a.* 战术的)
tactile ['tæktl]	*a.* 触觉的（of or relating to the sense of touch） 记 词根记忆：tact(接触) + ile → 触觉的 例 *tactile* hair 触（觉）毛 同根词：contact(*n./v.* 联系)；tactometer(*n.* 触觉测量器)
takeover ['teɪkoʊvər]	*n.* 接管；收购（the action or an act of taking over） 记 来自词组 take over 接管 例 corporate *takeover* 公司收购
tangible ['tændʒəbl]	*a.* 可触摸的；切实的（substantially real） 记 词根记忆：tang(接触) + ible → 可触摸的 例 a *tangible* roughness 可触到的粗糙 // *tangible* benefits 切实利益 派 intangible(*a.* 无形的)；tangibility(*n.* 切实性)

37

tap [tæp]	*n.* 水龙头(faucet); *v.* 轻敲; 轻拍(to strike lightly especially with a slight sound) 例 Even though Saluda Natural Spring Water may seem expensive, drinking it instead of *tap* water is a wise investment in good health.
tariff ['tærɪf]	*n.* 关税(impost); 税率(a rate of duty to be paid on imports or exports) 例 reciprocal *tariff* 互惠税
taxable ['tæksəbl]	*a.* 应纳税的, 可征税的(subject to taxation) 记 来自 tax(*v.* 向…课税) 例 People who are not citizens of Levaska are not eligible to invest in the tax-free savings accounts, even if their income is *taxable* in Levaska. 派 taxability(*n.* 可课税性)
taxpayer ['tækspeɪər]	*n.* 纳税人(one that pays or is liable for a tax) 记 词根记忆: tax(税) + pay(付款) + er(人) → 付税的人 → 纳税人 例 *Taxpayers* do not differ from each other with respect to the rate of taxation that will cause them to evade taxes.
tectonics [tek'tɑːnɪks]	*n.* 构造学(a branch of geology concerned with the structure of the crust of a planet or moon); 地质构造(geological structural features as a whole) 记 词根记忆: tect(遮蔽) + on + ics → 被地球表面遮蔽的 → 地质构造 例 Plate *tectonics* cannot fully explain certain massive surface features.
teem [tiːm]	*v.* (with)充满, 到处都是(to abound) 记 和 team(*n.* 群, 队)一起记 例 The dry mountain *teems* with evidence of tropical marine life.
telecommunication [ˌtelikəˌmjuːnɪ'keɪʃn]	*n.* 远程通信(communication at a distance); 无线电通讯(technology that deals with telecommunication) 记 词根记忆: tele(远) + communication(交流) → 远程交流 → 远程通信 例 In recent years, networks of fiber-optic cable have been replacing electrical wire for transmitting *telecommunications* signals.
telephoto [ˌtelifoʊtoʊ]	*n.* 传真照片(a photograph taken with a camera having a telephoto lens); 摄远镜头(a telephoto lens); *a.* 用远距镜头照相的(being a camera lens system designed to give a large image of a distant object) 记 词根记忆: tele(远) + photo(照片) → 从远处传过来的照片 → 传真照片 例 Even without the aid of *telephoto* lenses, the visitor to Tanzania's Lake Manyara Park has an unequalled opportunity to photograph lions playing in trees..
temblor ['temblər]	*n.* <美>地震(earthquake) 记 和 tremble(*v.* 震动)一起记 例 Seismologists revealed that they detected strange electromagnetic signals hours before a *temblor*.
temperance ['tempərəns]	*n.* 节欲(restraint); 禁酒(abstinence from the use of alcoholic beverages) 记 词根记忆: temper(时间) + ance → 在一段时间内不许做 → 节欲; 禁酒 例 food *temperance* 节食 // the *temperance* movement 禁酒运动

temperate ['tempərət]	*a.* （气候）温和的(having a moderate climate which especially lacks extremes in temperature)；有节制的(keeping or held within limits) 记 词根记忆：temper(脾气) + ate → 好脾气的 → 温和的 例 *temperate* zone 温带 // He is *temperate* in eating.
temporary ['tempəreri]	*a.* 短暂的，暂时的(lasting for a limited time)；临时的(provisional) 记 词根记忆：tempor(时间) + ary → 时间很短 → 短暂的 例 The side-effect of this medicine is supposed to be *temporary*. // *temporary* worker 临时工 派 temporarily(*ad.* 短暂地；临时)
tempt [tempt]	*v.* 引诱，吸引(to lure) 记 本身为词根：尝试 例 Each rancher would be *tempted* to overuse common land. 派 temptation(*n.* 诱惑，引诱)
tenant ['tenənt]	*n.* 房客；佃户(dweller, occupant) 记 联想记忆：ten(十) + ant(蚂蚁) → 十只蚂蚁来住店 → 它们虽小也是房客 → 房客 例 This apartment building has fifty *tenants*. // *tenant* farmers 佃农
tenet ['tenɪt]	*n.* 信条，原则(a principle, belief, or doctrine) 记 联想记忆：ten(握住) + et → 握住的理念 → 信条 例 the basic *tenets* of Western democracy 西方民主的基本理念
tentative ['tentətɪv]	*a.* 试验(性)的，试探(性)的(not fully worked out or developed)；犹豫的(hesitant) 记 词根记忆：tent(伸) + ative → 伸出手的 → 试探(性)的 例 The company made a *tentative* proposal trying to cut the cost.
tenure ['tenjər]	*n.* 任期(term)；（土地）保有权(the act right, manner, or term of holding something, as a landed property, a position, or an office) 记 联想记忆：ten(拿住) + ure → 拿住职位 → 任期 例 life-long *tenure* 终身职务制 // land *tenure* 土地所有权
terminate ['tɜːrmɪneɪt]	*v.* (使)停止，终止(to come to an end, close)；解雇(to fire, to dismiss) 记 词根记忆：termin(界限，期限) + ate → 到了期限 → 停止 例 *terminating* decimal 有尽小数 // *terminate* workers 解雇工人
terminology [ˌtɜːrmə'nɑːlədʒi]	*n.* 术语(学)(the technical or special terms used in a business, art, science, or special subject) 记 词根记忆：term(术语) + in + ology → 术语(学) 例 medical *terminology* 医学术语
termite ['tɜːrmaɪt]	*n.* 【昆】白蚁 记 联想记忆：term(期间) + ite(看作 bite 咬) → 短时间内啃光木头的昆虫 → 白蚁 例 The fallen tree was infested with *termites*.

37

Word List 38

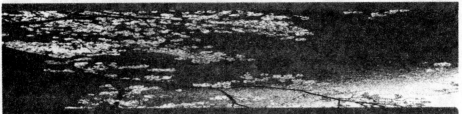

terrain [tə'reɪn]	*n.* 地势, 地形 (the physical features of a tract of land) 记 词根记忆: terr(地) + ain → 地势, 地形 例 Mongolia's *terrain* is suitable for grazing native herds. 派 terrestrial(*a.* 陆地的)
terrestrial [tə'restriəl]	*a.* 地球的 (of the earth); 陆地的 (relating to land) 记 词根记忆: terr(地) + estr + ial → 地球的; 陆地的 例 Some small *terrestrial* animals can achieve high speeds. 同根词: territorial(*a.* 领土的; 区域的)
territory ['terətɔːri]	*n.* 地区 (an area of land); 领土 (domain) 记 词根记忆: terr(地) + itory → 地区; 领土 例 Some explorers traveled in Native American *territory* in the early 19th century. // The empire regained its lost *territory*. 派 territorial(*a.* 领土的); territoriality(*n.* 领土权)
testify ['testɪfaɪ]	*v.* 作证 (to serve as evidence or proof); 证明 (to attest) 记 词根记忆: test(证据) + ify → 用证据来证明 → 作证; 证明 例 He *testified* that the car was being driven slowly at the time of the accident.
testimony ['testɪmoʊni]	*n.* 证词 (a solemn declaration usually made orally by a witness under oath in response to interrogation by a lawyer or authorized public official) 记 词根记忆: testi(=test 证据) + mony → 证词 例 John's *testimony* contradicted the defendant's testimony.
theme [θiːm]	*n.* 主题; 题目 (subject) 例 *theme* park 主题乐园 // Guilt and Punishment is the *theme* of the story.
theophylline [θɪə'fɪliːn]	*n.* 茶碱 (a colorless crystalline alkaloid, derived from tea leaves or made synthetically) 例 Caffeine and *theophylline* tend to have depressive rather than stimulatory effects on human behavior.

theoretical [ˌθiːəˈretɪkl]	*a.* 不切实际的（existing only in theory）；理论（上）的（relating to or having the character of theory） 🔑 来自 theory（*n.* 理论） 📖 *Theoretical* literature offers conflicting views on whether nonprofit hospitals are less financially efficient. 📌 theoretically（*ad.* 理论上） 同根词：theorist（*n.* 理论家）
therapeutic [ˌθerəˈpjuːtɪk]	*a.* 治病的（of the treatment of diseases） 🔑 词根记忆：therap（照看，治疗）+ eutic → 治病的 📖 Ancient Romans found it *therapeutic* to bathe in cold milk, crushed strawberries, or black caviar. 同根词：therapist（*n.* 临床医学家；治疗学家）
therapy [ˈθerəpi]	*n.* 治疗，疗法（treatment） 🔑 词根记忆：therap（照看，治疗）÷ y → 治疗方法 → 疗法 📖 physical *therapy* 物理疗法 📌 therapeutic（*a.* 治疗的）
thereafter [ˌðerˈæftər]	*ad.* 此后（after that） 🔑 分拆记忆：there（那）+ after（后来）→ 那之后 → 此后 📖 It rained until 8:30, and it snowed *thereafter*.
thermal [ˈθɜːrml]	*a.* 热的，热量的（of, relating to, or caused by heat） 🔑 词根记忆：therm（=thermo 热）+ al → 热的 📖 *thermal* gradient 热梯度（温度随距离的变化率）
thermostat [ˈθɜːrməstæt]	*n.* 恒温器，自动调温器（a similar device for actuating fire alarms or for controlling automatic sprinklers）；*v.* 为…配备恒温器；用恒温器控制（to provide with or control the temperature of by a thermostat） 🔑 词根记忆：thermo（热的）+ stat（站，立）→ 一直保持热着的东西 → 恒温器 📖 Although ice particles in the upper atmosphere benefit Earth, acting as a global *thermostat* and thus keeping Earth from either burning up or freezing over, they also accelerate the destruction of the ozone layer by reacting with chlorofluorocarbons. 📌 thermostatic（*a.* 恒温的；自动调节温度的）
threaten [ˈθretn]	*v.* 威胁（to utter threats against） 🔑 来自 threat（*n.* 威胁；凶兆） 📖 The ruffe is one of several nonnative species in the Great Lakes whose existence *threatens* the survival of lake whitefish populations there. 📌 threatened（*a.* 受到威胁的）
threshold [ˈθreʃhoʊld]	*n.* 门槛（sill），开端，起点（outset） 🔑 联想记忆：thres + hold（拥有）→ 从现有的出发 → 开端 📖 The year 2000 is the *threshold* of a new millennium.

38

thrive [θraɪv]	v. 兴旺 (to prosper); 茁壮生长 (to grow vigorously) 记 联想记忆: th + rive(看作 river 河流) → 许多大河都是文明的发源地 → 兴旺 例 Plankton(浮游生物) generally *thrive* in areas with sufficient nitrogen compounds.
throne [θroʊn]	n. 王位; 王权 (sovereignty) 记 联想记忆: thr(看作 the) + one → 唯我独尊 → 王权 例 The present queen took the *throne* when her father died.
tile [taɪl]	n. 瓦片; 瓷砖 (a flat or curved piece of fired clay, stone or concrete used especially for roofs, floors, or walls and often for ornamental work); v. 铺瓦(或瓷砖)于 (to install tile in) 记 联想记忆: 秘密文件(file)藏在瓦(tile)下 例 The entire building was covered with *tile*. // The worker *tiled* the kitchen floor in one day.
timber ['tɪmbər]	n. 木材, 木料 (wood suitable for building or for carpentry) 记 联想记忆: timb(看作 time 时间) + er → 树苗需要很长时间才能成材 例 cut *timber* 伐木 // Ancient settlers used mud and grass to build their homes, doing it without *timber* and nails.
tissue ['tɪʃuː]	n. 纸巾 (soft paper); 【生】组织(形态上相似的细胞和相关的细胞间物质的集合, 如: 肌肉组织) (an aggregate of cells, usually of a particular kind together with their intercellular substance that form one of the structural materials of a plant or an animal) 例 Animals acquire carotenoids(类胡萝卜素)in many ways and then store them in a variety of *tissues*.
toll [toʊl]	n. 过路(桥)费 (money paid for the use of a road, bridge, etc.); 伤亡人数, 损失 (loss or damage caused by sth.); v. (缓慢而有规律地)敲 (to sound with slow measured strokes) 记 发音记忆: "痛" → 受伤了, 所以痛 → 伤亡人数 例 Whenever bridge *tolls* are increased, the authority must pay a private contractor to adjust the automated toll-collecting machines. 派 toller(n. 敲钟人; 征收通行税的人)
tortoise ['tɔːrtəs]	n. 乌龟, 龟 (turtle) 例 Researchers hypothesize that granitic soil is the ideal construction material for the desert *tortoise*.
toxic ['tɑːksɪk]	a. 有毒的 (poisonous) 记 词根记忆: tox(毒) + ic → 有毒的 例 Among birds, social learning helps them avoid *toxic* substances. 派 nontoxic(a. 无毒的); toxicity(n. 毒性); toxication(n. 中毒) 同根词: detoxify(v. 解毒)
toxin ['tɑːksɪn]	n. 毒素, 毒质 (a poisonous substance) 例 Wood smoke contains dangerous *toxins* that cause changes in human cells.

□ thrive □ throne □ tile □ timber □ tissue □ toll
□ tortoise □ toxic □ toxin

tract [trækt]	*n.* 一片(土地)(an indefinite stretch of land); 【解】管道(a system of body parts or organs that act together to perform some functions) 例 The erosion of valuable topsoil will reduce the crop yield of a *tract* of land. // a vocal *tract* 声道
tragedy ['trædʒədi]	*n.* 惨事(misfortune); 灾难(calamity) 例 It was a *tragedy* that we lost the game in the last minute.
trait [treɪt]	*n.* 特征(characteristic); 特性(a distinguishing quality) 记 联想记忆: 要根据每位队员的特点(trait)进行训练(train) 例 Special genetic *traits* can easily be introduced into plant strains with the use of the new techniques. // personality *trait* 个性品质.
tranquilizer ['træŋkwəlaɪzər]	*n.* 镇定剂(one that tranquilizes) 记 来自 tranquilize(*v.* 使…镇定) 例 Probably some substance in the *tranquilizer* inhibits fertility. 同根词: tranquilization(*n.* 安静; 镇定)
transaction [træn'zækʃn]	*n.* 交易(an act, process, or instance of transacting); 事务(sth. transacted) 记 词根记忆: trans(穿过) + act(行为) + ion → 在两者之间发生的行为 → 交易 例 Increases in the volume of *transactions* in such firms are commonly believed to have necessitated this structural change. 派 transactional(*a.* 交易的; 事务的) 同根词: transcend(*v.* 超越; 胜过); transparent(*a.* 透明的)
transatlantic [ˌtrænzət'læntɪk]	*a.* 横渡大西洋的(轮船、航线等)(crossing or extending across the Atlantic) 记 词根记忆: trans(越过) + Atlantic(大西洋) → 横渡大西洋的 例 a solo *transatlantic* flight 个人横渡大西洋的飞行
transfer	[træns'fɜːr] *v.* 转移(to shift) ['trænsfɜːr] *n.* 调动(transfering or being transfered); 转让(conveyance of right, title, or interest in real or personal property from one person to another) 记 词根记忆: trans(改变) + fer(带来) → 带来改变 → 转移 例 The patient was *transferred* to another hospital. // *transfer* of jobs // land *transfer* 土地转让 派 transferable(*a.* 可转移的; 可传递的)
transform [træns'fɔːrm]	*v.* 使…变形(to change the outward form or appearance of); 改变(to change) 记 词根记忆: trans(改变) + form(形状) → 变形 例 The sculptor *transformed* the clay into the form of a bird. // The city *transformed* from a collection of suburban neighborhoods to a modern city. 派 transformation(*n.* 变化, 变革)

38

transit [ˈtrænzɪt]	*n.*运输，载运（transportation） 记 联想记忆：trans（改变）+ it → 改变它的地点 → 载运 例 *transit* company 运输公司 // mass *transit* 公共交通（工具） 同根词：transition（*n.* 转变；过渡）
transition [trænˈzɪʃn]	*n.*过渡，转变（a movement, development, or evolution from one form, stage, or style to another） 记 来自 transit（*v.* 通过；*n.* 转变） 例 They made a *transition* from old patterns of a association to new ones. 派 transitional（*a.* 变迁的；过渡期的） 同根词：transitive（*n.* 传递；*a.* 及物的）
transmission [trænsˈmɪʃn]	*n.*传递，传送（an act, process, or instance of transmitting） 记 来自 transmit（*v.* 发射；传导） 例 Recently two data *transmission* companies have each developed separate systems. 同根词：transmitter（*n.* 发射机；传达人）
transmit [trænsˈmɪt]	*v.*传送(信号)（to send out (a signal)）；传播（to spread） 记 词根记忆：trans（横过）+ mit（送）→ 送过去 → 传送 例 Some technologies can enable telecommunication signals to be *transmitted* without either wire or fiber-optic cable. // The mosquito *transmits* virus. 派 transmission（*n.* 传送；转播）；transmitter（*n.* 发射机）；transmittal（*n.* 传送，传输）
transnational [ˌtrænzˈnæʃnəl]	*a.*跨国的；超越国界的（extending or going beyond national boundaries） 记 词根记忆：trans（横过，越过）+ national（国家的）→ 超越国界的 例 *Transnational* cooperation involves projects too big for a single corporation to handle. 同根词：transfrontier（*a.* 在国境外的）
transplant [trænsˈplænt]	*v.*移栽（to lift and reset (a plant) in another soil or situation）；移植(器官)（to transfer (an organ or tissue) from one part or individual to another） 记 词根记忆：trans（改变）+ plant（种植）→ 改变种植地方 → 移植 例 Mary *transplanted* an elm tree into her backyard. // The surgeons *transplanted* the crash victim's liver into a dying patient.
transport [trænˈspɔːrt]	*v.*运输，运送（to transfer or convey from one place to another） 记 词根记忆：trans（改变）+ port（搬运）→ 搬运转移 → 运输 例 Tourists were *transported* by bus to the nearest museum. 派 transportation（*n.* 运送，运输）
transportation [ˌtrænspɔːrˈteɪʃn]	*n.*运输，运输系统（means of conveyance or travel from one place to another）；流放（banishment to a penal colony） 记 词根记忆：trans（转移）+ port（拿，运）+ ation → 从一个地方拿到另一个地方 → 运输 例 Buses provide the only means of public *transportation* in the city of Workney. 同根词：porter（*n.* 行李员；搬运工）

treasury [ˈtreʒəri]	*n.* [常 the T~] 财政部(a governmental department in charge of finances and especially the collection, management and expenditure of public revenues); 国库(a place in which public revenues are deposited, kept, and disbursed); 国库券(a government security (as a note or bill) issued by the Treasury) 记 来自 treasure(*n.* 财宝) 例 the *Treasury* Department 财政部 // *treasury* bill 短期国库券
treaty [ˈtriːti]	*n.* 协议, 条约(an agreement made by negotiation) 例 The two nations signed a *treaty* to protect each other from attack. 派 treatise(*n.* 论文)
tremendous [trəˈmendəs]	*a.* 惊人的; 巨大的(monstrous) 记 词根记忆: trem(颤抖) + endous → 让人发抖的 → 惊人的 例 A government is a *tremendous* burden to business.
trench [trentʃ]	*n.* 沟渠(ditch); 海沟(a long, narrow, and usually steep-sided depression in the ocean floor) 记 联想记忆: tr + ench(看作 bench 长凳) → 像长凳一样狭长的地区 → 沟渠 例 Workers dug *trenches* around the bases of the stone walls. // oceanic *trenches* 海沟
triangle [ˈtraɪæŋgl]	*n.* 三角, 三角形(a polygon having three sides) 记 词根记忆: tri(三) + angle(角) → 三角 例 right *triangles* 直角三角形 // equilateral *triangle* 等边三角形 派 triangular(*a.* 三角形的; 三人间的)
tribal [ˈtraɪbl]	*a.* 部落的, 宗族的(of, relating to, or characteristic of a tribe) 记 来自 tribe(*n.* 部落) 例 He became skilled in several *tribal* lingoes.
tribute [ˈtrɪbjuːt]	*n.* 礼物, 贡品(a gift showing respect, gratitude, or affection) 记 词根记忆: tribut(给予) + e → 给皇帝的东西 → 贡品 例 The British colonists collected *tributes* from the native population. 同根词: contribute(*v.* 捐献, 贡献); distribute(*v.* 分配, 分发)
trigger [ˈtrɪgər]	*n.* 扳机(the part of the action moved by the finger to fire a gun); *v.* 引发, 导致(to initiate or set off) 记 联想记忆: 扣动扳机(trigger)射杀了一只老虎(tiger) 例 You can't pull the *trigger* if the safety is locked. // Sometimes large budget deficits can *trigger* declines in currency value.
triple [ˈtrɪpl]	*v.* 三倍于(to become three times as great or as numerous); *n.* 三个一组(a combination, group, or series of three) 记 词根记忆: tri(三) + ple → 三倍于 例 Annual sales of mechanical pencils are expected to *triple* over the next five years. // *triple*-trailer truck 配有三个拖车的卡车
tri-state [ˈtraɪ ˈsteɪt]	*a.* 三州(间地区)的(of, relating to, or consisting of three adjoining states) 例 the *tri-state* region 三州的邻接地区

38

triumph [ˈtraɪʌmf]	*n.* 胜利，成功（a notable success）；欢欣（the joy or exultation of victory or success） 记 联想记忆：胜利（triumph）之后吹喇叭（trump） 例 return home in *triumph* 凯旋
trivial [ˈtrɪviəl]	*a.* 琐屑的，微不足道的（of little importance） 记 词根记忆：tri(三) + vial → 一分为三 → 琐屑的 例 It is simply too *trivial* to merit their attention. 派 triviality(*n.* 琐事)
tropical [ˈtrɑːpɪkl]	*a.* 热带的（of, relating to, occurring in, or suitable for use in the tropics） 例 Less than 50 percent of a certain *tropical* country's wildlands remain intact. 派 subtropical(*a.* 亚热带的)；neotropical(*a.* 新热带区的)
trout [traʊt]	*n.* 鳟鱼（any of various salmonid food and sport fishes that are mostly smaller than the typical salmons and are anadromous or restricted to cool clear freshwater） 例 For the next couple of years, steelhead *trout* returning from the sea to spawn were forced to find alternative streams.
truce [truːs]	*n.* 休战(协定)，停战(协定)（cease-fire） 记 联想记忆：休战协定（truce）确认了战败是真的（true） 例 The two rival states proclaimed a sacred *truce*.
trunk [trʌŋk]	*n.* 树干（the main stem of a tree apart from limbs and roots）；躯干（the human or animal body apart from the head and appendages）；主干（the central part of anything） 记 联想记忆：喝醉（drunk）了酒，倒在树干（trunk）上酣睡 例 The tree *trunks* will be used for lumber and the branches will be converted into wood chips to make fiberboard.
tuition [tuˈɪʃn]	*n.* 学费（the price of or payment for instruction） 记 词根记忆：tuit(监护，看管) + ion → 在学校的监护费用 → 学费 例 full *tuition* 全额学费
turbulence [ˈtɜːrbjələns]	*n.* 骚乱，动荡（the quality or state of being turbulent） 记 来自 turb(*v.* 搅动) 例 Small firms generate market *turbulence* that creates additional dimensions of competition. 同根词：disturb(*v.* 打扰；弄乱)；turbid(*a.* 混乱的；浑浊的)
turbulent [ˈtɜːrbjələnt]	*a.* 骚乱的，狂暴的（violently disturbed） 记 词根记忆：turb(搅动) + ulent → 搅得厉害 → 狂暴的 例 Its role in the explanation of *turbulent* friction has been significant. 派 turbulence(*n.* 动荡；震动)

344
□ triumph □ trivial □ tropical □ trout □ truce □ trunk
□ tuition □ turbulence □ turbulent

typhoid [ˈtaɪfɔɪd]	*n.* 伤寒（a disease of domestic animals resembling human typhus or typhoid）；*a.* 伤寒的，斑疹伤寒症的（of, relating to, or suggestive of typhus） 例 At an orientation meeting, the travelers were told that they would each need a visa, a landing card, and evidence of inoculation against *typhoid* fever.
ultimate [ˈʌltɪmət]	*a.* 最终的，结果的（final and conclusive, eventual） 记 词根记忆：ultim（最远，落后）+ ate → 最终的 例 Both economic factors and governmental policies strongly influence the *ultimate* success of any innovation. 派 ultimately（*ad.* 最后；根本） 同根词：ultimatum（*n.* 最后通谍）
ultrasound [ˈʌltrəsaʊnd]	*n.* 超声（波）（vibrations of the same physical nature as sound but with frequencies above the range of human hearing） 例 Physicians can use a Doppler *ultrasound* device to detect fetal heartbeats.
unaccompanied [ˌʌnəˈkʌmpənid]	*a.* 无伴奏的（being without instrumental accompaniment）；无伴随的（not companied） 记 词根记忆：un（无）+ accompan（陪伴）+ ied（…的）→ 无陪伴的 → 无伴随的 例 Euripides' Medea never appears in medieval manuscripts *unaccompanied* by ancient commentary. 同根词：accompanist（*n.* 伴奏者；伴随者）
unaffected [ˌʌnəˈfektɪd]	*a.* 自然的，不矫揉造作的（free from affectation; genuine） 记 词根记忆：un（不）+ affected（做作的）→ 不做作的 → 自然的 例 The designer has designed this exhibition hall in a simple and *unaffected* manner. 同根词：affection（*n.* 喜爱，感情；影响）
unanticipated [ˌʌnænˈtɪsɪpeɪtɪd]	*a.* 意料之外的，未预料到的（not anticipated） 记 词根记忆：un（非）+ anticipate（预料）+ d（…的）→ 非意料的 → 意料之外的 例 Because of the business community's uncertainty about the President's position on the deficit, an *unanticipated* rise in interest rates has occurred. 同根词：emancipate（*v.* 解放）
unavailable [ˌʌnəˈveɪləbl]	*a.* 难以获得的；不能利用的（not available or accessible or at hand） 记 词根记忆：un（不）+ avail（有用）+ able（能）→ 不能利用的 例 Community members may reside temporarily in one of the lower zones to manage the extraction of products *unavailable* in the homeland.
unbridled [ʌnˈbraɪdld]	*a.* 放纵的，无约束的（unrestrained） 记 词根记忆：un（放开）+ bridle（缰绳）+ d → 松开缰绳的 → 放纵的 例 His *unbridled* tongue has often got him into trouble.

38

345

unconfined [ˌʌnkənˈfaɪnd]	*a.* 未予限制的，自由的(free) 例 Community service sentences allow the criminals to remain *unconfined* while they perform specific jobs benefiting the public.
unconscious [ʌnˈkɑːnʃəs]	*a.* 不省人事的(having lost consciousness)；未发觉的，未意识到的(not knowing about sth.) 记 词根记忆：un(无) + conscious(意识的) → 未意识到的 例 The use of lie detectors is based on the assumption that lying produces emotional reactions in an individual that, in turn, create *unconscious* physiological responses. 派 unconsciously(*ad.* 不知不觉；无意识地) 同根词：consciousness(*n.* 义务；知觉)
unconstitutional [ˌʌnkɑːnstəˈtuːʃnl]	*a.* 违反宪法的(not according or consistent with the constitution of a body politic) 记 词根记忆：un(非) + constitution(宪法) + al(状态的) → 违反宪法的 例 In 1923, a minimum wage for women and children in the District of Columbia was declared *unconstitutional* by the Supreme Court.
underbelly [ˈʌndərbeli]	*n.* 下腹部(the underside of a body or mass)；薄弱部分(a corrupt or sordid part)；易受攻击的部位、区域等(a vulnerable area) 记 词根记忆：under(下面的) + belly(腹部) → 下腹部 例 The California newt's display of its red *underbelly* is a clear warning that predators ignore at their peril.
undercapitalize [ʌndərˈkæpɪtəlaɪz]	*v.* 投资不足(to have too little capital for efficient operation) 记 词根记忆：under(不足) + capitalize(使资本化) → 投资不足 例 The economic forces which may affect the new public offering of stock include sudden downturns in the market, hedging and other investor strategies for preventing losses, a loosening of the interest rates in Washington, and a fear that the company may still be *undercapitalized*.
undergo [ˌʌndərˈɡoʊ]	*v.* 经历，经受(to experience)；忍受(to endure) 记 联想记忆：under(底下) + go(走) → 从底下走 → 忍受 例 Viruses that have *undergone* no significant genetic change can also lead to epidemics. // Tom *underwent* great hardship during his childhood.
underlie [ˌʌndərˈlaɪ]	*v.* 位于…之下(to lie or be situated under)；成为…的基础或依据(to be at the basis of) 记 词根记忆：under(在…下) + lie(位于) → 位于…之下 例 Many facts *underlay* my argument.
underline [ˌʌndərˈlaɪn]	*n.* 下划线(to mark with a line underneath)；*v.* 强调，加强(to stress) 记 词根记忆：under(在…下) + line(划线) → 在…下面划线 → 强调 例 They *underline* women's physiological and psychological distinctiveness.

underlying [ˌʌndər'laɪɪŋ]	*a.* 在下面的 (lying beneath or below)；根本的，基础的 (basic, fundamental) 记 联想记忆：under(下) + lying(躺着的) → 在下面的，基础的 注意：underling (*n.* <常贬> 下属，手下) 例 The *underlying* economic forces of industrialism were presumed to be gender-blind.
undermine [ˌʌndər'maɪn]	*v.* 破坏，削弱 (to weaken) 记 词根记忆：under(在…下) + mine(挖) → 在下面挖 → 破坏 例 Low wages and repeated unemployment *undermine* the capacity for self-support of women.

When an end is lawful and obligatory, the indispensable means to it are also lawful and obligatory.

如果一个目的是正当而必须做的，则达到这个目的的必要手段也是正当而必须采取的。

——美国政治家 林肯(Abraham Lincoln, American statesman)

38

Word List 39

underscore [ˌʌndərˈskɔːr]	*v.* 强调(to emphasize, to stress) 记 词根记忆：under(在…下) + score(划线) → 在…之下划线 → 强调 例 The mayor *underscored* the need for more police officers.
undertake [ˌʌndərˈteɪk]	*v.* 采取(to attempt, to set about)；接受(to accept as responsibility) 例 The study urged states to *undertake* remedies to reverse a decline in the shark population. // Owners of farms will probably not *undertake* the expense of cutting down the trees. 派 undertaking(*n.* 事业)
underwrite [ˌʌndərˈraɪt]	*v.* 承诺支付(to agree to pay)；给…保险(to guarantee financial support of) 例 They are not granted governmental subsidies to assist in *underwriting* the cost of economic development.
underwriter [ˈʌndəraɪtər]	*n.* 保险公司, 保险业者(insurer)；担保人 (guarantor) 记 来自 underwrite(*v.* 给…保险) 例 Life insurance in England remained until the end of the seventeenth century a specialized contract between individual *underwriters* and their clients.
undesirable [ˌʌndɪˈzaɪərəbl]	*a.* 令人不悦的, 讨厌的(not desirable; unwanted) 记 词根记忆：un(不) + desirable(合意的) → 不合意的 → 令人不悦的 例 The second is presented by the argument as one likely consequence that is *undesirable*.
undeterred [ˌʌndɪˈtɜːrd]	*a.* 未受阻的(not deterred or discouraged) 例 The new airboat traveled at high speeds *undeterred* by sandbars.
undue [ˌʌnˈduː]	*a.* 过度的, 不适当的(excessive) 记 词根记忆：un(表否定) + due(适当的) → 不适当的 例 *undue* concern 过度关心
unearth [ʌnˈɜːrθ]	*v.* 出土(to dig up out of the earth) 记 词根记忆：un(打开) + earth(土地) → 从地下弄出来 → 发掘或挖出某物 例 Archaeologists *unearthed* some 4,500 year-old stone agricultural implements in the historical site.

unequalled [ʌnˈiːkwəld]	*a.* 无与伦比的(radically distinctive and without equal); 不等同的(not equalled) 🔢 词根记忆: un(否) + equalled(相同的) → 无与伦比的 📝 Even without the aid of telephoto lenses, the visitor to Tanzania's Lake Manyara Park has an *unequalled* opportunity to photograph lions playing in trees.
unequivocally [ˌʌnɪˈkwɪvəkəli]	*ad.* 不含糊地(unambiguously); 明确地(clearly) 📝 Microwave irradiations were considered *unequivocally* to produce "thermal effects".
uneven [ʌnˈiːvn]	*a.* 不规则的(not uniform); 不平坦的(rough); 不均匀的(unequal) 🔢 词根记忆: un(表否定) + even(平的, 一致的) → 不一致的 → 不规则的 📝 An ancient surface usually has *uneven* weathering. 📐 unevenly(*ad.* 不均衡地)
unfavorable [ʌnˈfeɪvərəbl]	*a.* 不宜的; 令人不快的(not pleasing); 不顺利的(not propitious) 🔢 词根记忆: un(不) + favorable(良好的, 讨人喜欢的) → 令人不快的 📝 In only one of these last eleven years was the weather *unfavorable* for growing citrus crops. 📐 unfavorably(*ad.* 不利地; 不适宜地) 同根词: favorite(*a.* 最喜爱的)
unification [ˌjuːnɪfɪˈkeɪʃn]	*n.* 统一; 联合(the act, process, or result of unifying) 🔢 来自 unify(*v.* 统一, 使成一体) 📝 national *unification* 民族统一 // economic *unification* 经济联合
uniform [ˈjuːnɪfɔːrm]	*n.* 制服(the dress of a distinctive design or fashion worn by members of a particular group and serving as a means of identification); *a.* 统一的(consonant); 相同的(same) 🔢 词根记忆: uni(单一) + form(形式) → 形式单一 → 统一的 📝 Some schools require all of its students to wear *uniforms* while at school. // Do you think all unprocessed cacao beans contain a *uniform* amount of caffeine? 📐 uniformity(*n.* 同样, 一致); uniformly(*ad.* 一律地)
unilateral [ˌjuːnɪˈlætrəl]	*a.* 单侧的; 单方面的(one sided; affecting only one side) 🔢 词根记忆: uni(单) + later(边) + al → 单边的 → 单侧的 📝 It becomes more difficult for Congress to exercise *unilateral* authority over Native American affairs. 📐 unilaterally(*ad.* 单方面地) 同根词: bilateral(*a.* 双边的)
uninitiated [ˌʌnɪˈnɪʃieɪtɪd]	*a.* 外行的, 缺乏丰富知识的(inexperienced) 🔢 联想记忆: un(表否定) + initiate(传授) + d → 不能传授知识的 → 缺乏丰富知识的 📝 the *uninitiated* reader 缺乏相应知识的读者

39

unionist [ˈjuːniənɪst]	*n.* 工会会员；联合主义者（an advocate or supporter of union or unionism） 记 来自 union（*n.* 联盟，协会） 例 It was not shared by most *unionists* until 1935. 同根词：unionism（*n.* 工会主义；联合主义）
unionization [ˌjuːniənaɪˈzeɪʃn]	*n.* 联合，组织工会（the action of organizing a labor union） 例 Politicians and administrators sometimes oppose *unionization* of clerical workers（行政人员）.
unique [juˈniːk]	*a.* 唯一的（sole）；独特的（distinctively characteristic） 记 词根记忆：uni（单一）+ que（…的）→ 唯一的；独特的 例 the *unique* human speech ability 人类独一无二的语言能力 // a *unique* opportunity 绝佳的机会 派 uniquely（*ad.* 独特地；唯一地）；uniqueness（*n.* 唯一性；独特性）
university [ˌjuːnɪˈvɜːrsəti]	*n.* 大学，高校 记 联想记忆：由宇宙 universe 引申为"知识" → 知识之地 → 大学 例 There is a common misconception that *university* hospitals are better than community or private hospitals. 同根词：universe（*n.* 宇宙；世界）
unleavened [ˌʌnˈlevnd]	*a.* 未经发酵的（(of bread) made without yeast or other raising agent） 例 Yeasts are capable of leavening bread, and for many centuries the ancient Egyptians made only *unleavened* bread.
unobtrusive [ˌʌnəbˈtruːsɪv]	*a.* 不显著的，不引人注目的（inconspicuous） 记 词根记忆：un（表否定）+ obtrusive（炫耀的）→ 不炫耀 → 不引人注目的 例 He is a quiet *unobtrusive* student, but always does well in examinations.
unparalleled [ʌnˈpærəleld]	*a.* 无比的，空前的（having no equal） 记 来自 parallel（*a.* 平行的） 例 Between the 8th and 11th centuries, the Byzantine Empire staged an almost *unparalleled* economic and cultural revival.
unprecedented [ʌnˈpresidentɪd]	*a.* 前所未有的，史无前例的（having no precedent） 记 来自 precedent（*n.* 先例） 例 The restaurant industry in the country has experienced *unprecedented* growth.
unpredictable [ˌʌnprɪˈdɪktəbl]	*a.* 不可预知的（unknown in advance） 记 词根记忆：un（无）+ predict（预言）+ able → 不可预知的 例 Unlike a chemical pesticide, a biocontrol agent may adapt in *unpredictable* ways. 派 unpredictably（*ad.* 无法预言地） 同根词：predict（*v.* 预言，预报）
unprocessed [ʌnˈproʊsest]	*a.* 未加工的（not be processed） 例 the *unprocessed* cacao beans 未加工的可可豆

unpromising [ʌn'prɑːmɪsɪŋ]	*a.* 无前途的，没有希望的（not promising） 记 词根记忆：un(无) + promising(有前途的) → 无前途的 例 Spanning more than 50 years, Friedrich Müller's career began in an *unpromising* apprenticeship as a Sanskrit scholar and culminated in virtually every honor that European governments and learned societies could bestow.
unravel [ʌn'rævl]	*v.* 解开，拆散（to resolve the complexity of） 记 词根记忆：un(打开，解开) + ravel(纠缠) → 解开纠缠 → 解开 例 The study of the fruit fly, a household nuisance but a time-honored experimental subject, has enabled scientists to begin to *unravel* the secrets of how embryos develop.
unrealistic [ˌʌnriːə'lɪstɪk]	*a.* 不切实际的，不实在的（not realistic） 记 词根记忆：un(非) + real(真实的) + istic(…的) → 不真实的 → 不切实际的 例 It would be *unrealistic* to suggest that illegal digging would stop if artifacts were sold on the open market.
unrefined [ˌʌnrɪ'faɪnd]	*a.* 未提炼的（the state of being not free from what is coarse, vulgar, or uncouth） 记 词根记忆：un(非) + refine(提炼) + d(…的) → 未提炼的 例 People who judge the quality of *unrefined* olive oils actually judge those oils by their acidity, which the judges can taste.
unreimbursed [ˌʌnriːɪm'bɜːrsd]	*a.* 未偿(付，赔)还（not paid） 记 来自 reimburse(*v.* 偿还，赔付) 例 United States hospitals have traditionally relied primarily on revenues to offset losses from *unreimbursed* care.
unscrupulous [ʌn'skruːpjələs]	*a.* 无道德原则的，不讲道德的（unprincipled） 记 词根记忆：un(表否定) + scrupulous(小心的) → 不讲道德的 例 an *unscrupulous* press 无道德的新闻
unsubstantiated [ˌʌnsəb'stænʃieɪtɪd]	*a.* 未经证实的，无事实根据的 记 词根记忆：un(表否定) + substantiate(证实) + d → 未证实的 例 Bailyn's fourth proposition is intriguing though *unsubstantiated*.
untainted [ʌn'teɪntɪd]	*a.* 无污点的 记 词根记忆：un(表否定) + taint(污点) + ed → 无污点的
untenable [ʌn'tenəbl]	*a.* 难以防守的；站不住脚的（not able to be defended） 记 词根记忆：un(不能) + ten(拿住) + able → 拿不住的 → 难以防守的 例 an *untenable* position 一个难于防守的阵地 // The researchers' conclusion is *untenable*.
unwarranted [ʌn'wɔːrəntɪd]	*a.* 无根据的（not justified） 记 词根记忆：un(不能) + warrant(保证) + ed → 未经保证的 → 无根据的 例 This conclusion is *unwarranted*.

39

unwieldy
[ʌn'wiːldi]

a. 麻烦的，难处理的 (not easily managed, handled or used)

记 词根记忆：un(不) + wieldy(支配的，控制的) → 不可控制的 → 麻烦的

例 Since many satellites are built by *unwieldy* international consortia, inefficiencies are inevitable.

updraft
['ʌpdræft]

n. 上升气流 (an upward movement of gas (as air))

记 词根记忆：up(向上) + draft(排水，排气) → 向上排气 → 上升气流

upheaval
[ʌp'hiːvl]

n. 大变动 (radical change)

记 来自 upheave(v. 举起，鼓起)

例 social *upheaval* 社会大变动

upholstered
[ʌp'houlstərd]

a. 装软垫的 (to be furnished with or as if with upholstery)

例 *upholstered* chairs 软椅

upstate
[ˌʌp'steɪt]

a. 在州北部的 (be in the northern sections of a state)

记 词根记忆：up(上) + state(州) → 地图上位于州上方的 → 州北部的

例 *upstate* New York 纽约州北部地区

upstream
[ˌʌp'striːm]

ad. 向上游；*a.* 位于上游的 (in the direction opposite to the flow of a stream)

例 The distribution of water allocations for irrigation is to prevent farms *upstream* from using water needed by farms downstream.

upsurge
['ʌpsɜːrdʒ]

n. 急剧上升 (a rapid rise)

记 词根记忆：up(向上) + surge(波动) → 向上波动 → 急剧上升

例 What accounts for this *upsurge* in unionization among clerical workers?

urbanization
[ˌɜːrbənə'zeɪʃn]

n. 都市化 (the quality or state of being urbanized or the process of becoming urbanized)

记 来自 urbanize(v. 使都市化)

例 The populations of these cantons shared similar views because *urbanization* furthered the diffusion of ideas among them.

urbanize
['ɜːrbənaɪz]

v. 使…都市化 (to cause to take on urban characteristics)

记 词根记忆：urban(都市) + ize(…化) → 使…都市化

例 The influx of new businesses *urbanized* the small town.

派 urbanization(*n.* 都市化)

urchin
['ɜːrtʃɪn]

n. 海胆 (any of numerous echinoderms that are usually enclosed in thin brittle globular tests covered with movable spines)

例 sea *urchin* 海胆

urine
['jʊrən]

n. 尿 (waste material that is secreted by the kidney in vertebrates, is rich in end products of protein metabolism together with salts and pigments, and forms a clear amber and usually slightly acid fluid in mammals but is semisolid in birds and reptiles)

记 词根记忆：ur(尿) + ine → 尿

同根词：urea(*n.* 尿素)

utensil
[juː'tensl]

n. 用具，器皿 (implement)

记 词根记忆：ut(用) + ensil → 用品 → 器皿

utilize [ˈjuːtəlaɪz]	*v.* 利用，使用(to make use of) 记 词根记忆：ut(用) + ilize → 利用 例 The system was originally *utilized* by the Chinese laborers who had preceded the Japanese. 派 utility(*n.* 功用；[常 *pl.*]公用事业)
vacant [ˈveɪkənt]	*a.* 空着的，未占用的(empty) 记 词根记忆：vac(空) + ant(…的) → 空着的 例 In any given day, one-fourth of all community beds are *vacant*. 派 vacancy(*n.* 空闲；空缺)
vaccinate [ˈvæksɪneɪt]	*v.* 接种疫苗(to administer a vaccine to usually by injection) 例 Many parents would be more inclined to have their children *vaccinated* against influenza if the vaccination did not require an injection.
vaccination [ˌvæksɪˈneɪʃn]	*n.* 接种疫苗(the act of vaccinating)；牛痘疤(the scar left by vaccinating) 记 词根记忆：vaccin(牛痘) + ation → 接种牛痘 → 接种疫苗 例 Many parents would be more inclined to have their children vaccinated against influenza if the *vaccination* did not require an injection.
vaccine [vækˈsiːn]	*n.* 牛痘苗，疫苗(a preparation of killed microorganisms, living attenuated organisms, or living fully virulent organisms that is administered to produce or artificially increase immunity to a particular disease) 记 词根记忆：vacc(牛) + ine → 牛痘苗 例 The new *vaccine* uses the same mechanism to ward off influenza as injectable vaccines do.
vacuum [ˈvækjuəm]	*n.* 真空(a space absolutely devoid of matter) 记 词根记忆：vacu(=vac 空) + um → 真空 例 Most astronomers believed that the space between the galaxies in our universe was a near perfect *vacuum*. // *vacuum* cleaners 真空吸尘器
vague [veɪg]	*a.* 模糊的，含糊的(obscure) 记 词根记忆：vag(游移) + ue → 游移不定的 → 模糊的 例 The confusing movie had a rather *vague* ending. 派 vaguely(*ad.* 含糊地，不明确地)
validity [vəˈlɪdəti]	*n.* 有效性；合法性(state of being legally acceptable)；正确性(state of being right) 记 来自 valid(*a.* 有效的，合法的) 例 The *validity* of a new scientific finding was questioned by most scientists.
vanish [ˈvænɪʃ]	*v.* 消失(to pass quickly from sight) 记 词根记忆：van(空) + ish → 消失 例 Of the five hundred million different species of living creatures that have appeared on Earth, nearly 99 percent have *vanished*. 同根词：vanity(*n.* 空虚；虚荣)

39

variable [ˈveriəbl]	*n.* 可变物 (something that is variable); 变量, 变数 (a quantity that may assume any one of a set of values) 记 词根记忆: vari(变化) + able → 可变的 → 变量 例 The key *variables* driving costs are size and type of order. 同根词: variation(变动); varied(各式各样的)
variation [ˌveriˈeɪʃn]	*n.* 变化; 变异 (the act or process of varying) 记 词根记忆: vari(改变) + ation(状态) → 变化 例 There is a considerable degree of *variation* in shade of color between weeds of different species. 同根词: variable(*a.* 易变的; *n.* 变量)
varsity [ˈvɑːrsəti]	*n.* 大学 (university); 大学代表队(尤指体育) (the principal squad representing a university, college, school, or club especially in a sport) 例 Their level of participation in extracurricular activities and *varsity* sports is unusually high.
vegetarian [ˌvedʒəˈteriən]	*n.* 素食者 (one who believes in or practices vegetarianism); *a.* 素食的 (consisting wholly of vegetables fruits, grains, nuts, and sometimes eggs or dairy products) 记 词根记忆: veget(植物) + arian → 只吃植物的人 → 素食者 例 *Vegetarians* refer to those whose diet consists of plant products only. // The diet of the ordinary Greek in classical times was largely *vegetarian*.
vegetation [ˌvedʒəˈteɪʃn]	*n.* 植被 (plant life or total plant cover (as of an area)) 记 词根记忆: veget(植物) + ation → 植物的集合 → 植被 例 The relationship between *vegetation* and climate is not direct. 同根词: vegetarian(*n.* 素食者)
vegetative [ˈvedʒɪteɪtɪv]	*a.* 植物的, 有关植物生长的 (relating to, composed of, or suggesting vegetation) 例 A plant's fecundity is high if it can reproduce quickly by means of *vegetative* growth.
vein [veɪn]	*n.* 纹理 (texture); 矿脉 (a regularly shaped and lengthy occurrence of an ore); 静脉 (a blood vessel that carries blood from the capillaries toward the heart) 例 A gold-quartz *vein* system originates in magmatic fluids.
velocity [vəˈlɑːsəti]	*n.* 速度 (speed); 速率 (rapidity) 记 词根记忆: veloc(速度) + ity → 速度 例 They are ejected by the comet at differing *velocities*.
velvet [ˈvelvɪt]	*a.* 天鹅绒的 (clad in velvet); *n.* 天鹅绒 (a clothing and upholstery fabric (as of silk, rayon, or wool) characterized by a short soft dense warp pile); 天鹅绒似的东西 例 On stage, the force of Carrick's personality and the vividness of his acting disguised the fact that he was, as his surviving *velvet* suit shows, a short man. 派 velvety(*a.* 天鹅绒般柔软的; 醇和的)

venom ['venəm]	*n.* 毒液(material that is poisonous); 痛恨(ill will malevolence) 记 词根记忆：ven(来) + om → 带来痛 → 痛恨 例 The yellow jacket (黄色胡蜂)carries a potent *venom* that can cause intense pain. 派 venomous(*a.* 有毒的)
venture ['ventʃər]	*v.* 冒险(to risk); *n.* (为盈利而投资其中的)企业(a business enterprise); 冒险事业(a risky undertaking) 记 发音记忆："玩车" → 玩车一族追求的就是冒险 → 冒险 例 joint *venture* 合资企业 // *venture* capitalist 风险资本家；风险投资商
verge [vɜːrdʒ]	*n.* 边缘(brink) 记 来自古法语 verge，"杆、棍" 例 His company is on the *verge* of bankruptcy.
verify ['verɪfaɪ]	*v.* 证明，证实(to confirm) 记 词根记忆：ver(真实的) + ify(使…) → 使…真实 → 证明，证实 例 Observations of animals' physiological behavior in the wild are not reliable unless *verified* by laboratory studies. 派 unverifiable(*a.* 无法证实的)
veritable ['verɪtəbl]	*a.* 确实的，真正的(not false, unreal, or imaginary, often used to stress the aptness of a metaphor) 记 词根记忆：veri(真实的) + table → 确实的 例 Such undertakings have been drowned by a *veritable* flood of public and private moneys.
versatile ['vɜːrsətl]	*a.* 多才多艺的(having many different kinds of skills); 多用途的(having many different uses) 记 词根记忆：vers(转) + at + ile(易于…的) → 容易转换角色的 → 多面手 → 多才多艺的 例 Camille Saint-Saens was among the most gifted and *versatile* musicians of his time. 派 versatility(*n.* 多功能性；多才多艺) 同根词：reverse(*v.* 颠倒; *a.* 相反的); diversify(*v.* 使多样化)
versatility [ˌvɜːrsə'tɪləti]	*n.* 多功能性(the quality or state of being versatile) 记 词根记忆：versa(转) + tility → 可以转动 → 多功能性 例 The computer software will not only meet the needs of that study, but also has the *versatility* of facilitating similar research endeavors. 同根词：versant(*a.* 精通的)
version ['vɜːrʒn]	*n.* 译本(a translation from another language); 版本(an account or description from a particular point of view especially as contrasted with another account) 记 联想记忆：vers(转) + ion → 转动之后产生的 → 译本 例 original *version* 原版 // film *version* 电影版

39

vertebrate [ˈvɜːrtɪbrət]	*n.* 脊椎动物（any of a subphylum（Vertebrata）of chordates possessing a spinal column that includes the mammals, birds, reptiles, amphibians, and fishes）; *a.* (鸟兽等)有脊柱的（having a spinal column） 记 词根记忆：verte(=vert 转) + brate → 可以灵活转动的 → 有脊柱的 派 invertebrate(*n.* 无脊椎动物; *a.* 无脊椎的)
vertical [ˈvɜːrtɪkl]	*a.* 垂直的（upright） 记 联想记忆：电影《垂直极限》的英文名 Vertical Limit 例 The *vertical* pressure gradients within the blood vessels are counteracted by similar pressure gradients in the surrounding water. 派 vertically(*ad.* 垂直地) 同根词：vertex(*n.* 顶点)
vertice [ˈvɜːrtɪs]	*n.* 顶点（summit） 例 intermediate *vertice* 中间顶点

If you would go up high, then use your own legs! Do not let yourselves carried aloft; do not seat yourselves on other people's backs and heads.

如果你想要走到高处，就要使用自己的两条腿！不要让别人把你抬到高处；不要坐在别人的背上和头上。

——德国哲学家 尼采(F. W. Nietzsche, German philosopher)

vessel [ˈvesl]	*n.* 船(ship)；容器(container)；导管(tube) 例 The cause of the wreck of the *vessel* is still unknown. // pottery *vessel* 陶容器 // blood *vessel* 血管
vestige [ˈvestɪdʒ]	*n.* 痕迹，残余(trace) 例 Most people have consciously rejected Confucianism, but *vestiges* of the old order remain.
veteran [ˈvetərən]	*n.* 老兵(an old soldier of long service, a former member of the armed forces) 记 发音记忆："为他人" → 本着为他人的思想，成为了光荣的老兵
viability [ˌvaɪəˈbɪləti]	*n.* 可行性(capability of working, functioning, or developing adequately)；生存能力(capability of living) 记 词根记忆：via(路) + bility → 有路可走的 → 可行性 例 It is a realistic possibility that casts the most serious doubt on the *viability* of the company's plan. // They help to ensure the continued economic *viability* of the world community.
viable [ˈvaɪəbl]	*a.* 可行的(feasible)；能活下去的(capable of living) 记 词根记忆：via(道路) + able + 有路可走 → 可行的 例 A food-product innovation can be technically feasible and still not be economically *viable*.
vicinity [vəˈsɪnəti]	*n.* 附近，接近(neighborhood) 记 词根记忆：vicin(邻近) + ity → 附近(地区) 例 The commission acknowledges that nothing can ensure the safety of people who live in the *vicinity* of a nuclear plant. 同根词：vicinage(*n.* 周围地区)
vicious [ˈvɪʃəs]	*a.* 邪恶的(evil)；恶性的(worsened by internal causes that reciprocally augment each other) 记 词根记忆：vic(e)(罪恶) + ious → 罪恶的 → 恶性的 例 When people evade income taxes by not declaring taxable income, a *vicious* cycle results.

victimize [ˈvɪktɪmaɪz]	*v.* 使受害，迫害；使牺牲(to cause someone to suffer unfairly) 记 来自 victim(*n.* 受害者) 例 The president of the block association tried to convince her neighbors that they should join forces to prevent crime in the neighborhood rather than continue to be *victimized*. 派 victimization(*n.* 牺牲；欺骗)
vigorous [ˈvɪɡərəs]	*a.* 精力旺盛的，健壮的(strong, healthy, and full of energy) 记 词根记忆：vig(活，活力) + or + ous → 活的，有活力的 → 精力旺盛的 例 Some species of Arctic birds are threatened by recent sharp increases in the population of snow geese, which breed in the Arctic and are displacing birds of less *vigorous* species. 派 vigorously(*ad.* 精力旺盛地；活泼地) 同根词：invigorate(*v.* 鼓舞)
vine [vaɪn]	*n.* 葡萄树；蔓生植物(any of various sprawling herbaceous plants (as a tomato or potato) that lack specialized adaptations for climbing) 例 insect-pollinated *vine* 由昆虫授粉的蔓生植物 派 vineyard(*n.* 葡萄园)
violate [ˈvaɪəleɪt]	*v.* 违反，违背(break, disregard) 记 发音记忆："why late" → 违反制度迟到了 → 违反，违背 例 Their activities *violate* the New York Consumer Protection Law. 派 violation(*n.* 违犯，违背)
virgin [ˈvɜːrdʒɪn]	*n.* 圣女；*a.* 处女的(characteristic of or befitting a virgin)；纯洁的(free of impurity or stain) 例 In June, 1981, six teenagers in the village of Medjugorje, Yugoslavia, claimed to have had visions of the *Virgin* Mary, who they say has continued to appear to them over the ensuing years. 派 virginity(*n.* 处女；纯洁)
virtue [ˈvɜːrtʃuː]	*n.* 美德(conformity to a standard of right)；优点(merit)；力量(potency) 例 *Virtue* was to be instilled not only by churches and schools, but by families, where the mother's role was crucial. 派 virtuous(*a.* 善良的；有道德的)
virtuoso [ˌvɜːrtʃuˈoʊsoʊ]	*n.* 演艺精湛的人(one who excels in the technique of an art) 记 联想记忆：virtuo(看作 virtue 美德) + so → 讲究美德的艺人一般都是演艺精湛的人
virtuous [ˈvɜːrtʃuəs]	*a.* 有道德的，品性好的(righteous, chaste) 记 来自 virtue(*n.* 美德) 例 To be completely *virtuous*, people had to be independent and free of the petty interests of the marketplace.
viscosity [vɪˈskɑːsəti]	*n.* 黏性，黏度(the quality or state of being viscous) 记 词根记忆：visc(黏) + osity(性质) → 黏性 例 The *viscosity* in the disk causes heating and radiation.

visual [ˈvɪʒuəl]	*a.* 看得见的(attained or maintained by sight)；视觉的(of, relating to, or used in vision) 记 词根记忆：vis(看) + ual → 看得见的 例 *visual* image 可见图像；目视图像 // *visual* arts 视觉艺术
vocal [ˈvoʊkl]	*a.* 声音的(of, relating to the voice)；歌唱的(relating to, composed or arranged for, or sung by the human voice) 记 词根记忆：voc(声音) + al → 声音的 例 *vocal* cords 声带 // *vocal* style 歌唱风格
volatile [ˈvɑːlətl]	*a.* 易变的，多变的(characterized by or subject to rapid change) 记 词根记忆：volat(飞) + ile → 飞来飞去的 → 多变的 例 *volatile* demand 多变的需求 同根词：volant(*a.*飞行的；敏捷的)；volary(*n.* 大型鸟舍)
volunteer [ˌvɑːlənˈtɪr]	*n.* 志愿者(a person who voluntarily undertakes or expresses a willingness to undertake a service)；*a.* 自愿的(being, consisting of, or engaged in by volunteers) 记 词根记忆：volunt(志愿) + eer(人) → 志愿者 例 We should disband our *volunteer* service and hire a commercial ambulance service. 同根词：benevolent(*a.* 善心的，好意的)；volition(*n.* 意志力)
voracious [vəˈreɪʃəs]	*a.* 狼吞虎咽的(devouring or craving food in great quantities)；贪婪的(excessively eager; insatiable) 记 词根记忆：vor(吃) + acious → 吃得多的 → 狼吞虎咽的 例 The survival of a rare New Zealand species of mistletoe is threatened both because its leaves are extremely tasty to a *voracious* opossum species and because its flowers are pollinated by two species of birds whose populations are in decline. 派 voraciously(*ad.* 狼吞虎咽地；贪得无厌地)
vortices [ˈvɔːrtɪsiːz]	*n.* 漩涡(vortex 的复数) 例 Sunspots, *vortices* of gas associated with strong electromagnetic activity are visible.
vulnerable [ˈvʌlnərəbl]	*a.* 易受攻击的(capable of being physically wounded; assailable) 记 词根记忆：vulner(伤) + able → 易受攻击的 例 The argument is most *vulnerable* to the objection. 派 vulnerably(*ad.* 脆弱地；易受伤害地)；vulnerability(*n.* 弱点；易损性)
wage [weɪdʒ]	*v.* 发动(战争)(to engage in or carry on)；*n.* 工资(a payment, usually of money for labor or services, usually according to contract and on an hourly, daily, or piecework basis) 记 wage 作为"工资"这一意思大家比较熟悉，可以理解为"为了工资而斗争" 例 Agricultural revenues in excess of the amount needed for subsistence were used by medieval kings to *wage* war.

wanton ['wɑːntən]	*a.* 无节制的，放纵的（being without check or limitation）；顽皮的（mischievous） 记 发音记忆："顽童" → 顽皮的 例 Customs inspectors are often treated not like government employees but *wanton* poachers by travelers.
warbler ['wɔːrblər]	*n.* (能叫出柔和颤音的)鸣禽 例 Blue-winged warblers are unlike most species of *warbler* in which it is very difficult to tell the male and female apart.
warrior ['wɔːriər]	*n.* 战士（a man engaged or experienced in warfare） 记 词根记忆：war(战争) + rior → 战斗的人 → 战士 例 terracotta *warriors* 秦始皇兵马俑
wary ['weri]	*a.* 谨慎的，慎重的（cautious） 例 The mail carrier was *wary* of dangerous dogs.
waterfront ['wɔːtərfrʌnt]	*n.* 海滨；滩（land, land with buildings fronting or abutting on a body of water） 记 词根记忆：water(水) + front(前沿) → 水的前沿 → 水边 → 海滨 例 With a new park, stadium, and entertainment complex along the Delaware River, Trenton, New Jersey, is but one of a large number of communities that are looking to use their *waterfronts* to improve the quality of urban life and attract new businesses.
welfare ['welfer]	*n.* 繁荣（the state of doing well especially in respect to good fortune, happiness, well-being, or prosperity）；福利（aid in the form of money or necessities for those in need） 记 联想记忆：well(看作 well 好的) + fare → 好的东西 → 福利 例 Public education was essential to the *welfare* of the Republic. // social *welfare* program 社会福利项目
well-being [ˌwel'biŋ]	*n.* 健康，幸福；福利（good health and prosperity） 例 The union protected the *well-being* of its members.
whim [wɪm]	*n.* 多变；怪念头（fancy） 记 是 whim-wham 的简写，表示多变(从 whim 跳到 wham） 例 It is not a license granted by government and revokable at *whim*. 同根词：whimsical(*a.* 古怪的，异想天开的)
whiplash ['wɪplæʃ]	*n.* 鞭绳（the lash of a whip）；鞭打（sth. resembling a blow from a whip） 记 分拆记忆：whip(鞭子) + lash(鞭子；抽打) → 鞭绳 例 It is true that spurious reports of *whiplash* injuries cannot be readily identified. 同根词：whippy(*a.* 像鞭子一样的)
whirl [wɜːrl]	*v.* 旋转，急转（to rotate, to move in a circle or similar curve especially with force or speed） 记 联想记忆：轮子(wheel)在不停地旋转(whirl） 例 In such a system, an accretion disk *whirls* about a neutron star rather than a white dwarf.

whisker ['wɪskər]	*n.* 腮须(the part of the beard growing on the sides of the face or on the chin); 胡须(mustache) 例 The pattern of *whisker* spots on the face of a male lion is a lifelong means of identification.
wholesale ['houlseɪl]	*n.* 批发(the sale of commodities in quantity usually for resale by a retail merchant) 记 词根记忆: whole(全部) + sale(卖) → 整个地卖 → 批发 派 wholesaler(*n.* 批发商)
wield [wi:ld]	*v.* 支配，掌握(to have at one's command or disposal) 记 和 yield(*v.* 生产; 屈服)一起记 例 The power that the skilled machinists *wielded* in the industry was intolerable to management.
wig [wɪg]	*n.* 假发(a manufactured covering of natural or synthetic hair for the head); *v.* 激动，发狂(to go crazy) 记 是 periwig 的简写。 注意: wag(*n.* 幽默的人)
wilderness ['wɪldərnəs]	*n.* 荒地(a tract or region uncultivated and uninhabited by human beings); 茫茫一片(a confusing multitude or mass) 记 词根记忆: wild(荒野) + er + ness → 荒地; 茫茫一片 例 Many people in Boravia are committed to preserving the country's *wilderness* areas. 同根词: wilder(*v.* 迷失)
withdraw [wɪð'drɔ:]	*v.* 收回(to take back, retract); 退出(to remove oneself from participation) 例 The land has been formally *withdrawn* from federal public lands. // The proposal would enable a prospective nominee to *withdraw* from competition.
withdrawal [wɪð'drɔ:əl]	*n.* 撤退(an operation by which a military force disengages from the enemy); 提款(removal from a place of deposit or investment); 取消(the act of taking back or away sth. that has been granted or possessed) 记 词根记忆: with(向后) + draw(拉) + al → 往后拉 → 撤退 例 *Withdrawals* from these accounts prior to age sixty-five would result in the investor's having to pay taxes on all the accumulated interest at the time of withdrawal. 同根词: withhold(*v.* 阻挡); withstand(*v.* 抵抗，反抗)
withstand [wɪð'stænd]	*v.* 经受住(to resist or endure successfully); 抵挡，反抗(to resist, to oppose) 例 In order to *withstand* tidal currents, juvenile horseshoe crabs frequently burrow in the sand. // Our army was strong enough to *withstand* the attack.
womb [wu:m]	*n.* 子宫; 孕育处(uterus (in women and other female mammals), the organ in which offspring is carried and nourished while it develops before birth) 记 联想记忆: wom(看作 women) + b(看作 box) → 女人的盒子 → 子宫 例 Babies emerge from the darkness of the *womb*.

40

woven [ˈwoʊvn]	*n.* 织物 (a woven fabric) 记 来自 weave (*v.* 编织) 例 Quantities of ***woven*** mantles, loincloths, blouses, and skirts were paid as tribute to local lords and to imperial tax stewards.
wrap [ræp]	*v.* 包, 裹 (to cover especially by winding or folding) 记 联想记忆: w + rap (说唱) → 说唱, 绕舌 → 绕 → 包, 裹 例 The figure shows the dimensions of a rectangular box that is completely ***wrapped*** with paper.
wreak [riːk]	*v.* 发泄 (to cause the infliction of vengeance); 引起 (to bring about, to cause) 记 联想记忆: 到处乱发脾气 (wreak) 是脆弱 (weak) 的表现 例 The thief ***wreaked*** his vengeance on Mary by destroying her house.
wreath [riːθ]	*n.* 花冠, 花环 (garland) 例 Victors in ancient Greek Olympic Games received cash prizes in addition to their laurel ***wreaths***.
wreck [rek]	*n.* 失事船只 (shipwreck); 残骸 (the broken remains of something wrecked or otherwise ruined) 例 The coast guard is conducting tests to see whether pigeons can be trained to help find survivors of ***wrecks*** at sea. 派 wreckage [*n.* (被毁物的) 残骸]
wrestle [ˈresl]	*v.* 摔跤; 搏斗 (to fight); 深思 (to engage in deep thought) 例 Scientists are ***wrestling*** with the study of a new kind of star.
y-axis [ˈwaɪˈæksɪs]	*n.* 坐标轴中的 Y 轴 例 Is this line parallel to the ***y-axis***?
yeast [jiːst]	*n.* 酵母 (a yellowish surface froth or sediment that occurs especially in saccharine liquids (as fruit juices) in which it promotes alcoholic fermentation, consists largely of cells of a fungus (as the saccharomyces, saccharomyces cerevisiae), and is used especially in the making of alcoholic liquors and as a leaven in baking) 记 发音记忆: "噎死他", 酵母在嗓子里膨胀, 当然会把人噎死啦 例 ***Yeast*** is used to leaven bread.
yen [jen]	*n.* 日元 (Japanese money) 例 The United States attempts to deal with the fall of the dollar against the ***yen***.
yield [jiːld]	*n.* 产量 (the amount or quantity produced or returned); *v.* 产生 (bear, produce); 屈从 (to give way to pressure) 例 The ***yield*** of natural gas from Norway's Troll gas field is expected to increase annually until the year 2005. // They discuss how such two methods have ***yielded*** contradictory data.

□ woven □ wrap □ wreak □ wreath □ wreck □ wrestle
□ y-axis □ yeast □ yen □ yield

附录一 GMAT 阅读中的态度词

adulatory 奉承的

ambivalence 矛盾，矛盾心理

ambivalent 模棱两可的

amusement 感兴趣，愉快

skeptical amusement 不确定的兴趣

annoyance 烦恼

appreciation 感激

apprehensive 理解的

advocacy 支持

fervent advocacy 狂热的支持

anger 愤怒

indignant anger 出离愤怒

astonishment 惊讶，诧异

perplexed astonishment 复杂的诧异

acceptance 接受

qualified acceptance 有保留的接受

tentative acceptance 谨慎的接受

admiration 赞美，赞扬

qualified admiration 有保留的赞扬

approbation 认可，同意

qualified approbation 有保留的认可

apprehension 理解

slight apprehension 浅层次的理解

approval 同意

uncertain approval 不确定的同意

approving 同意的，满意的

warmly approving 强烈的赞同

analytical 善于分析的

annoyed 生气的

bitter 痛苦的，苦涩的

cautious 谨慎的

concern 关注，关心

wary concern 谨慎的关心

concerned 关心的

condescending 屈尊的；谦逊的

contemptuous 轻蔑的

critical 批评的

criticism 批评

pointed criticism 尖锐的批评

studious criticism 慎重的批评

cynical 愤世嫉俗的

defensive 自卫的

deferential 尊重的；恭顺的

denial 否定，拒绝

limited denial 有保留的否定

denunciatory 公开指责的

disappointed 失望的

bitterly disappointed 苦涩的失望

disapproval 不同意

impatient disapproval 不耐心的否定

disapproving 不同意的

disbelief 不相信，不信任

complete disbelief 完全的不信任

disdainful 轻蔑的

harshly disdainful 苛刻的蔑视

disenchanted 清醒的

disinterested 不感兴趣的

dismay 沮丧；惊慌

agitated dismay 不安的沮丧

dismissal 拒绝

careful dismissal 谨慎的拒绝

distrustful 不信任的

endorsement 认可

whole hearted endorsement 完全赞同

enthusiastic 热心的

envious 嫉妒的，羡慕的

frustrated 失意的

hesitance 犹豫不决

idealistic 理想主义的

indifference 漠然，不关心

absolute indifference 绝对的漠然

complete indifference 完全的漠然

indifferent 不关心的

interest 兴趣

mild interest 适度的兴趣

interested 感兴趣的

naive 天真的

neutrality 中立

scrupulous neutrality 谨慎的中立

pragmatic 实际的

prejudiced 带偏见的

realistic 现实的

regard 关注

respectful regard 带有尊敬的关注

regret 后悔

relief 安慰

resigned 听之任之的

respect 尊敬

unqualified respect 绝对的尊敬

respectful 尊敬的

scornful 蔑视的

shocked 震惊的

profoundly shocked 极度的震惊

skepticism 怀疑

guarded skepticism 谨慎的怀疑

hostile skepticism 敌意的怀疑

implied skepticism 暗自怀疑

mild skepticism 略带怀疑

polite skepticism 礼貌的怀疑

spiteful 怀恨的

supportive 支持的

sympathetic 同情的，赞同的

mildly sympathetic 适度的同情

sympathy 同情

uncertain 不确定的

understanding 理解的

unpatriotic 不爱国的

unsympathetic 不同情的，反感的

附录二　GMAT 阅读词汇分类

经济类

aggregate demand 累积总需求

backward integration
　　反向合并(指企业介入原供应商的生产活动)

bargaining chips(blue-chip)
　　讨价还价的筹码；蓝色筹码股票，即热门
　　股票

cash nexus 金钱关系；现金交易关系

chartered trading company 特许贸易公司

common year 平年(365天)

comparable worth
　　可比价值(即同工同酬，是针对性别平等提出来
　　的)

compound interest 复利

concern 公司，企业；商号

cost 成本

cost-accounting 成本会计

decrease by 减少了⋯

decrease to 减少到⋯

depreciation 折旧

discount 打折

dividend 红利，奖金，额外利息

down payment 直接付款；预付款，定金

downsizing 裁员

dumping ground 倾销市场

economic gain 经济增长；经济成果

economic rationality 经济理性

economic utility 经济效用

end product 成品；最终产品；最后结果

exchange rates 汇率

financial resource 资金来源；财政或财力资源

fiscal restraint 财政紧缩

GDP per capita 人均国内生产总值

global expansion 全球扩张

guild membership 行会成员

highest bidder 最高价竞买人

human capital 人力资本，技能资本

increase by 增加了⋯

increase to 增加到⋯

in-kind 以货代款

intangible assets 无形资本

intercalary year(leap year) 闰年(366天)

interest rate 利率

Internal Revenue Service 美国国税局

investment vehicle
　　投资工具，投资媒体(即投资的任何方法)

labor costs 劳动力成本

labor rates 工资率

land tenure 土地所有制

legal property rights 法定财产权

list price 标价

margin 利润

mark down 降价

mark up 涨价

multinational corporation 多国或跨国公司

nominal GDP
　　名义国民生产总值(根据当前市场价格计算的
　　一国利用其要素所生产的全部最终产品和服
　　务的价值)

original price 原价

patent-granting 专利授予

per capita 每人

physical assets 实物资产

principal 本金

production facility 生产设备，工业企业

productive value 生产价值

profit margin 利润率

purchasing power 购买力

purchasing price 买价，收购价格

ratio 比率

rational expectations theory 理性预期理论

real GDP

实际国内生产总值(实际GDP是考虑通货膨胀因素并加以扣除的GDP)

retail price 零售价

rotating credit associations 互贷组织

sale price 售价

service industry 服务业

simple interest 单利

supplier relations 供给关系

target market 目标市场

tax incentive 税收鼓励

the Small Business Administration(SBA)

小型企业管理局，小企业主利益保护局

tie to 依靠，依赖

trading post 商栈，交易站

trust land 托管地

venture capital 风险资本

write off 注销，勾销

现代科技类

alkaline 碱性的，碱的

analog recording 模拟录音(相对于数码录音digital recording而言)

argon 【化】氩(18号元素)

arsenic 砷；砒霜；砷的；含砷的

asphalt 沥青

atom 原子

baryonic 重子的

cannabinoid

大麻的化学成分(可指任何一种，如四氢大麻醇、大麻醇等)

carton 纸板箱

charge 【物】电荷

chlorofluorocarbon

氟氯化碳(一种能够破坏臭氧层的物质，主要用于冰箱、空调等的制冷)

draftsman 【测】绘图员；起草者；立案者

dust particle 尘粒，微尘

electric charge 电核

electromagnetic radiation 电磁辐射

electron 电子

ethylene 【化】乙烯，次乙基

evaporative cooling 蒸发冷却

ferrous metal 黑色金属，即铁类金属

formaldehyde 【化】甲醛

gamma ray 伽马射线

helium 【化】氦

high-energy particle 高能粒子

hydrocarbon 【化】烃，碳氢化合物

ilmenite 【矿】钛铁矿

inertia theory 惯性定律

ion 【物】离子

isotope 【化】同位素

Kelvin 【物】绝对温标

methane 甲烷，沼气

molecule 分子

morphogenetic 形态基因的

morphological 形态(学)的；【语】词法的，形态的

muon 介子

neutrino 微中子

neutron star 中子星

neutron 中子

nucleons 核子

particle 粒子

phosphate fertilizer 磷肥

phosphate 磷酸盐，磷酸酯

phosphodiesterase 磷酸二酯酶

photon 【物】光子；【医】见光度

plutonium 【化】钚

potassium【化】钾

protein synthesis 蛋白质合成

protons 质子

quantizing error 量化误差

radiometric 公制辐射仪的

ramjet 冲压式喷气发动机

sampling error 抽样误差

scramjet 超音速燃烧冲压喷气发动机

sulphate【化】硫酸盐；用硫酸处理

The Montreal Protocol

蒙特利尔议定书(一项恢复地球日益恶化的平流臭氧层的具有里程碑意义的国际协定)

white lead 铅粉；白铅矿

自然科学类

accretion disks

吸积盘(是由绕行一个强重力源，而轨道越来越紧密的物质所组成)

big bang 宇宙大爆炸

cataclysmic variable

激变变星(一种爆发性的恒星，或称为CV型变星，指新星、超新星、耀星和其它正在爆发的恒星)

coral reef 珊瑚礁

fault【地】断层

galactic nebula 银河星云

galactic nucleus 星系核

gas clouds 气体云

Geminid 双子星座

globular cluster 球状星团

halo【气】(日月周围的)晕轮

high tide 满潮，高潮时间，顶点

low tide 低潮，低潮时间

meridian

【天】子午线，经线；顶点；子午线的；最高点的

meteor shower 流星雨

meteor stream 流星群

obsidian 黑曜石

orbital energy 轨道能量，轨函能量

parallax【物】【天】视差；【天】周年(日)视差

photoperiod 光周期

planetary gravitational field 行星引力场

Pleistocene【地】更新世(的)

protogalaxy 原星系

pulsar【天】脉冲星

quasar 恒星状球体，类星体

radio galaxy 射电星系

rock plates 岩石板块

rock salt 石盐，岩盐

sierra【地】锯齿山脊；呈齿状起伏的山脉

solar system 太阳系

solar-day 太阳日

spiral galaxies 旋涡星系，螺旋星系

stratosphere【天】平流层

subsurface geology 地下地质学

the Milky Way 银河

tidal cycle 潮汐周期

white dwarf star 白矮星

生物类

adenosine 腺苷；腺苷酸

aerobic【微】有氧代谢的

aflatoxin【生】黄曲霉毒素

amino acid【生】氨基酸

anaerobe【微】厌氧微生物

anaerobic【微】厌氧的

anaerobic metabolism 无氧代谢

biocontrol agents 真菌与细菌性微生物制剂

cell elongation 细胞延长

cell nucleus 细胞核

cytoplasm【生】细胞质

endorphin【生化】内腓肽

eukaryote 真核细胞

eukaryotic【生】真核细胞的；真核生物的

histidine【生化】组氨酸

intracellular 细胞内部的

lactic acid 乳酸

leucine【生化】白氨酸，亮氨酸

lipoprotein 脂蛋白

macrophage【生】巨噬细胞

messenger RNA 信使核糖核酸

molecular biology 分子生物学

nucleotide【生化】核苷酸

organelle【生】细胞器官

ovarian follicle 卵泡

peptide【生化】肽，缩氨酸

pheromone 费洛蒙；信息素

plasma cell 浆细胞；用以合成抗体

polymorph【生】多态动物(植物)；【化】多晶形物

prokaryotic cell 原核细胞

protoplasm 原生质，原浆；细胞质

ribosome【生化】核糖体

tryptophan【生化】色氨酸

tyrosine【生化】酪氨酸

动植物类

archaeopteryx 始祖鸟

barnacle【无脊椎】藤壶；茗荷介

bipedal 两足动物；两足动物的；二足的

boll weevil
棉籽象鼻虫(一种破坏棉花的害虫，又称棉铃象甲)

bollworm 一种蛾的幼虫；螟蛉虫

bowerbird 园丁鸟

broccoli 硬花球花椰菜，花茎甘蓝

budworm 蚜虫

cheetah 猎豹

citrus
柑橘属果树；柑橘类的植物；柑橘属植物的

cornstalk 玉米杆

coyote 一种产于北美大草原的小狼

cranberry 蔓越橘

diatom 硅藻

ecological niche 生态龛位

gecko【脊椎】壁虎

guillemot 海鸠；海雀

haddock【鱼】黑线鳕

lepidopter 鳞翅类昆虫

lepidoptera 鳞翅目

macaque【脊椎】猕猴，恒河猴；短尾猿

mammoth 长毛象；猛犸象

marine invertebrates 海洋无脊椎动物

mastodon 乳齿象

milkweed 乳草属植物

monkfish 扁鲨；安康鱼

myrmecophagous【动】食蚁的

opossum 负鼠

osprey【鸟】鹗(一种鱼鹰，腹部羽毛为白色)

periwinkle 小长春花；玉黍螺

phalarope 矶鹬之类；瓣蹼鹬

photosynthesis 光合作用

plant succession 植物演替；植生继续

pollen grain 花粉粒

pollen profile 花粉剖面

pterosaur 翼龙

reindeer【脊椎】【畜牧】驯鹿

sandpiper 鹬

succession【农】轮栽；【生】演替

tyrannosaurus 暴龙

ungulate 有蹄类动物；有蹄的；像蹄子的

医学类

adrenal cortex 肾上腺皮质

adrenal 肾上腺的，肾上腺附近的

amoxicillin 阿莫西林；羟氨苄青霉素

angioplasty 血管成形术

bone marrow 骨髓

brain stem 脑干

bubonic 腹股沟腺炎的

carcinogen【医】致癌物，诱癌物

cardiopulmonary 心肺的

cardiovascular【医】心血管的

caries[拉]【医】龋　骨疡

carotenoid【生化】类胡萝卜素

cartilage 软骨

cholesterol【生化】胆固醇

clavicle【解】锁骨

coronary artery 冠状动脉

dengue【医】登革热

encephalitis 脑炎

follicle【解】小囊，滤泡，卵泡

genetic coding 基因密码

hemoglobin【生化】血红蛋白

hemolytic【生理】【免疫】溶血的

hypertherm【医】人工发热器

hypothalamus【生】下丘脑

ibuprofen【药】布洛芬(镇痛药)

indomethacin【药】消炎痛

inoculation【医】接种；接木

insulin 胰岛素

internal pacemaker 生物钟

keratitis【眼】角膜炎

leukemia【内科】【肿瘤】白血病

licorice

　　欧亚甘草；甘草汁；甘草糖(等于liquorice)

Lyme 莱姆关节炎(伴有疼痛、发热与皮肤红斑)

lymph【医】淋巴，淋巴液；(淋巴液似的)浆，苗

lymphocyte【解】淋巴细胞

lysis【医】(病的)渐退；消散；【生化】细胞溶解

melatonin 褪黑激素

mesothelioma【肿瘤】间皮瘤

migraine【医】周期性偏头痛

neuron 神经元，神经细胞

neurotransmitter【生理】神经递质

novocaine 奴佛卜因(一种麻醉药)

osteoarthritis【外科】骨关节炎

pellagra【皮】糙皮病；玉蜀黍疹

pelvic【解】骨盆的

phagocytosis【医】吞噬(细胞)，噬菌作用

pituitary【解】脑垂体的；粘液的

pituitary gland 脑下垂体

poliomyelitis 小儿麻痹症

prostaglandin【生化】前列腺素

prostate【解】前列腺；前列腺的

prosthetic hand 假手

rheumatoid 风湿病的，类风湿病的

rhinovirus 鼻病毒

saffron 藏红花

schistosomiasis【医】血吸虫病，裂体吸虫病

serotonin 血清素

sinusitis【医】窦炎(sinus窦)

spinal cord 脊髓

strep throat【医】脓毒性咽喉炎

thyroid gland 甲状腺

gold-quartz 金丝水晶

coleslaw 酸卷心菜丝

附录三　GMAT 常考短语及词组

aerial image 空间象；虚象

air envelope 大气层

all the more 更加

an encounter action 遭遇战

antitrust law 反托拉斯法

assembly line 装配线

as-yet-unexploited 尚未开发利用的

at best 至多

at issue 在争论中，不和的；待裁决的

at odds 争执，不一致

at one stroke 一笔，一举

at stake 存亡攸关，危若累卵

average out 达到平均数，最终得到平衡

bargain on doing sth. 商定做某事

be at a disadvantage 处于不利地位

be leery of 小心、警惕地对待…

bind to 订约，约定

black hole【天】黑洞

blind spot【物】盲点，【无】静区

Board of Education 学校董事会

bona fide [拉]真诚地(的)，真实地(的)

bona fides [拉]诚意，善意

buffer stock 调节性库存储备

business world 工商界

by-product 副产品

call for 要求

call off 放弃

capitalize on the opponent's mistake
　　利用对手的错误

capitalize on 利用

cash in on 靠…赚钱，趁机利用

center on 集中于

clerical supplies 文具供应

clerical work 行政工作

cling to 坚持，墨守；依靠，依恋

closed-circuit television 闭路电视

collective consciousness 集体意识

common law 习惯法；不成文法

competitive edge 竞争力优势

compound interest
　　复利(即以本和利为基础的利率)

consumer goods 生活消费品

Customs Service 海关总署

daylight saving time 夏时制

delve into 深入探究，钻研

digital audiotape 数字音带

dote on 溺爱，宠爱

draw in 收(网)，引诱；天近黄昏；紧缩开支

draw on 戴上(手套)；吸收，利用；向…支取

draw to 使接近，吸引到…方面来

earthquake focus 震源

ecological systems 生态系统

episodic memory 事件记忆

fall into a rut 陷入陈规，落入俗套

fall under 受到(影响等)，被归入

field sketch 作业草图，现场草图

fly by
　　(一架或几架飞机)在低空飞过指定地点，飞
　　越；宇宙飞船飞近天体

fool around 闲荡，干蠢事(或无用，琐碎的事)

free market 自由竞争的市场

gain on 逼近，超过，侵蚀

general management 综合管理

get by 通过；勉强混过

get through
　　到达；办完，花光；通过；打通(电话)

give rise to 引起，发生

give way to 让位于…

government intervention 政府干预

government service 公职

hand on 传递下去

head start 领先

hierarchical management 分线管理

hit show 风行一时的演出

housing start 楼房破土动工

Humpty-Dumpty 矮胖的人

ice age 冰河时代，冰川期

ice sheet 大冰原，冰盾

import relief 进口援助(设置壁垒以保护民族工业)

in concert 一致；共同

in full bloom 全盛时期

in kind 以货代款，以实物(援助等)

in light of 按照，根据

in sb.'s favor 对某人有利；得某人欢心

in so far as 在…的限度内，在…的范围内

indentured servant 契约佣工

internal variable 内变量

Jim Crow 黑人(贬义)

labor contractor 包工头

laissez-faire capitalism 自由资本主义

lay off 解雇；(临时)解雇期；关闭；停止活动

lecture series 专题讲稿丛集

line of work 职业，行业

list price 标价，订价

live show 现场表演

lock into 受困于

look to 指望

make allowances 留出余地，体谅

make(both)ends meet

　　使收支相抵，量入为出；靠微薄收入为生

mark down 降价

mark up 涨价

maternity leave 产假

military service 兵役

mirror image 镜像，映像

more often than not 经常，时常(=often)

more than ever 尤其

on a par 同等

on behalf of 代表…

on one's word of honor 以某人的人格担保

on pain of death (违者)以死论处

open market 露天市场

other than 除了

oyabun-kobun 亲子关系

part company 指双方持有不同或相反的观点

pass up 放弃；错过；拒绝机会

penny-pinching 吝啬的

play off

　　(尤指为渔利而)使相斗；使出丑；把…假装

pride of place 首要的地位，傲慢

prime-time ratings 黄金时间收视率

prior to 在…之前

processed food 腌制食品

public policy 国家政策

pull away 脱身，离开；脱出

purchasing price 买价

push up 增加，提高

put away 把…收起来，放好；储存

rain down 大量降下

reading list 参考书目，阅读书目

recruiting agent 征兵员

resort to 求助，凭借；诉诸

retirement age 退休年龄

roller coaster 云霄飞车，翻滚过山车

rule of thumb

　　单凭经验的方法，比较简单但有效的方法

set up as 当上了…，干…的工作

sewage disposal 污水处理

shock wave 冲击波

shut off 关掉(煤气等)；切断

side effect 副作用

simple interest 单利

slash-and-burn 游垦，火耕，山田烧垦方式

sluggish economy 经济萧条

small-lot production 小批量生产

social learning 社交学习

speculative fever 投机热

speed velocity 速度

status quo ante [拉]原状，以前的状态

status quo [拉]现状

stumbling block 障碍物，绊脚石

subject to 使服从；使遭受

take issue with 与…争论

take over 接收，接管，接任

take precedence over 优先于…；地位在…之上

team up 合作，协作

technical merit 技术水平

technological determinism 技术决定论

teem with 充满

tough-minded 实际的，坚强的

trade in...for 以…对换；购买

trade off
　　交替换位；通过交换抛掉弊病、某事的不利
　　之处

transatlantic migrate 横越大西洋的移民

transnational cooperation 跨国公司

turn down 拒绝，摒斥；把(音量)调低

upscale clientele 高层次的顾客

Vichy government 二战时期法国维希政权

virgin soil 未开垦的土地

wade through 涉(水，泥泞等)；很吃力地通过…

Wall Street 华尔街(美国金融业集中之地)

willy-nilly 不管愿意不愿意；不容分辩的

word-of-mouth 口头的，口述的

附录四　GMAT 数学词汇

A. 算术

1. 整数
billion 十亿
composite number 合数
consecutive even integer 连续偶数
consecutive integer 连续的整数
consecutive odd integer 连续奇数
divisor 除数，约数
even 偶数
integer 整数
multiple 倍数
negative whole number 负整数
odd 奇数
positive whole number 正整数
prime factor 质因子，质因数
prime number 质数，素数
quotient 商
real number 实数
remainder 余数
whole number 整数

2. 分数
least common denominator 最小公分母
least common multiple 最小公倍数
algebraic fraction 分式
common denominator 公分母
common divisor 公约数
common factor 公因子
common multiple 公倍数
complex fraction 繁分数
denominator 分母
division sign 除号，斜线分数号
divisor 因子，除数
equivalent fractions 等值分数

evenly even integer 能再平分的偶数
fraction 分数
greatest common divisor 最大公约数
improper fraction 假分数
mixed number 带分数
numerator 分子
percentage 百分数
proper fraction 真分数
reciprocal/inverse 倒数
simple fraction 简分数
vulgar fraction/common fraction 普通分数

3. 小数
3-digit number 三位数
decimal fraction 纯小数
decimal point 小数点
decimal 小数
infinite decimal 无穷小数
mixed decimal 混合小数
recurring decimal 循环小数
tenths unit 十分位

4. 实数
absolute value 绝对值
constant 常数
decimal system 十进制
digit 位
infinitesimal 无穷小
infinity 无穷大
irrational(number) 无理数
natural number 自然数
negative number 负数
nonnegative 非负的
nonzero number 非零数
nonzero 非零的

numerical 数字的，数值的

positive number 正数

rational 有理数

tens digit 十位数

tens 十位

tenths 十分位

units digit 个位数

units 个位

5. 比例

common ratio 公比

direct proportion 正比

inverse proportion 反比

percent 百分比

proportion 比例

ratio 比率

the extremes of a proportion 比例外项

the means of a proportion 比例内项

6. 幂和根

base/power 底数/指数

cardinal 基数

common logarithm 常用对数

cube root 立方根

exponent 指数，幂

logarithm 对数

natural logarithm 自然对数

power 幂，乘方

product 乘积

radical sign/root sign 根号

root sign 根号

root 根

square root 平方根

7. 集合

empty set 空集

equivalence relation 等价关系

equivalency 等价；相等（等于equivalence）

intersection 交集

interval 区间

ordinal 序数

proper subset 真子集

set 集合

solution set 解集

subset 子集

union 合集，并集

8. 描述统计学

apiece 每个，每件，每人

arithmetic mean 算术平均数

average value 平均值

average 平均数

cumulative graph 累积图

dispersion 差量，离差

distribution (频数或频率)分布

equidistant 等距的

evenly spaced 等间隔的

frequency distribution 频数分布

frequency 频率

geometric mean 几何平均数

least possible value 最小可能值

maximum 最大值

median 中数

minimum 最小值

mode 众数(在一系列数中出现最多的数)

normal distribution 正态分布

probability 概率；或然率

random 随机的

range 值域(一系列数中最大值减最小值)

standard deviation 标准方差

variance 方差

weighted average 加权平均值

9. 计算方法

approximate 近似

approximation 近似值

arithmetic 算术

assign 赋值

calculate to three decimal places

计算结果保留三位小数

cancellation 相消，相约

clear an equation of fractions
　　将分式方程整式化

combination 组合

factorial notation 阶乘

permutations 排列

10. **数学运算**

add/plus 加

aliquant 除不尽的

aliquot 除得尽的

amount to 合计

cross multiply 交叉相乘

decimal arithmetic 十进制运算

decrease by 减少了

decrease to 减少到

decrease 减少

deduct 减去

difference 差

divide 除

divided evenly 被整除

dividend 被除数

divisible 可被整除的

division ①除；②部分

factorial 阶乘

factorization 因式分解

increase by 增加了

increase to 增加到

increase 增加

minuend 被减数

minus 减，负；负数

multiplicand 被乘数

multiplication 乘法

multiplier 乘数

multiply/times 乘

subtract/minus 减

sum 和

total ①总数(用在加法中，相当于+)；②总计(用于减法中，相当于-)

11. **度量单位**

centigrade 摄氏

centimeter 厘米，公分

cubic meter 立方米

dime 一角，一角硬币

dozen 一打，十二个

Fahrenheit 华氏

foot 英尺

gross 十二打，罗；总额

inch 英寸

meter 米

micron 微米

mileage 英里数

milliliter 毫升

nickel 五美分硬币

pint 品脱

quart 夸脱

score 二十

square measure 平方单位制

yard 码

B. 代数式、方程及不等式

a unique solution 唯一解

algebraic expression 代数式

algebraic term 代数项

alternant 交替函数，交替行列式

arithmetic progression 等差数列

be equivalent to another equation
　　与另一方程同等

binomial 二项式

coefficient 系数

common difference 等差数列的公差

complementary function 余函数

constant term 常数项

domain 定义域

equation·of the first degree 一次方程

equation 方程式，等式

equivalent equation 同解方程，等价方程

expression 表达式

factor 因子；系数

factorable quadratic equation

    可因式分解的二次方程

function 函数

geometric progression 等比数列

incomplete quadratic equation 不完全二次方程

inequality 不等式

inverse function 反函数

linear equation 线性方程

linear 一次的，线性的

literal coefficient 字母系数

minor 子行列式，子式

monomial 单项式

numerical coefficient 数字系数

original equation 原方程

polynomial 多项式

quadratic 二次方程

quantic 齐次多项式，多元齐次多项式

quartic equation 四次方程

sequence 数列

similar terms 同类项

simultaneous equations 联立方程组

solution (方程的)解

term 项

trigonometric function 三角函数

trinomial 三项式

variable 变量

C. 几何

1. 直线和垂线

a line segment 线段

a right angle 直角

bisect 平分

bisector 平分线

collinear 共线的，在同一条直线的

endpoint 端点

line graph 线图

midpoint 中点

parallel lines 平行线

perpendicular bisector 垂直平分线

perpendicular lines 垂直线

perpendicular 垂线

segment 线段

transversal 截线

vertical 垂直线；垂直的

2. 相交线和角

a straight line 直线

acute angle 锐角

adjacent angle 邻角

alternate angle 内错角

angle bisector 角平分线

angle 角

central angle 圆心角

complementary angle 余角

corresponding angle 同位角

diagonal 对角线

exterior angle 外角

exterior angles on the same side of the trans-

    versal 同旁外角

included angle 夹角

interior angle 内角

intersect 相交

obtuse angle 钝角

remote interior angle 不相邻内角

round angle 周角

straight angle 平角

supplementary angle 补角

vertex angle 顶角

vertical angle 对顶角

3. 四边形和多边形

adjacent vertices 相邻顶点

concave polygon 凹多边形

convex polygon 凸多边形

decagon 十边形

equilateral 等边形

heptagon 七边形

hexagon 六边形

multilateral 多边的

nonagon 九边形

octagon 八边形

parallelogram 平行四边形

pentagon 五边形

perimeter 周长

polygon 多边形

quadrilateral 四边形

rectangle 长方形

rectangular 矩形的；成直角的

regular polygon 正多边形

rhombus 菱形

side 边长

square 正方形

trapezoid 梯形

4. 三角形

acute triangle 锐角三角形

altitude (三角形的)高

arm 直角三角形的股

base 底

common base triangles 同底三角形

congruent 全等的

equilateral triangle 等边三角形

hypotenuse 斜边

included side 夹边

inscribed triangle 内接三角形

isosceles triangle 等腰三角形

leg 直角边

median of a triangle 三角形的中线

oblique 斜三角形

opposite 直角三角形中的对边

Pythagorean theorem
毕达哥拉斯定理，勾股定理

right triangle 直角三角形

scalene triangle 不等边三角形

triangle inequality 三角不等式

triangle 三角形

triangular 三角形的

trigonometry 三角学

vertex 顶点

5. 圆

arc 弧

center of a circle 圆心

chord 弦

circle 圆形

circular 圆形的

circumference 圆周长

circumscribe 外切，外接

circumscribed 外接的，外切的

concentric circles 同心圆

curvature 曲率

diameter 直径

inscribe 内切，内接

oblateness 椭圆形

point of tangency 切点

radian 弧度(弧长/半径)

radius 半径

segment of a circle 弧形

semicircle 半圆

semicircular 半圆的

surface area 表面积

tangency 相切

tangent 正切

6. 立体几何

altitude 高

bar graph 柱状图

circle graph 饼图，扇面图，圆形图

cone 圆锥

cross section 横截面

cube 立方体

cylinder 圆柱体

cylindrical 圆柱体的

depth 深度

dimension 维数

edge 边

length 长

pie chart 饼图

plane 平面

pyramid 角锥

quadrihedron 三角锥，四面体

rectangular solid 长方体

regular prism 正棱柱

regular pyramid 正棱锥

regular solid/regular polyhedron 正多面体

right circular cylinder 直圆柱体

scalene cylinder 不等边的斜柱体

solid geometry 立体几何

sphere 球体

spherical 球形的，球面的

volume 体积

width 宽

7.坐标几何

abscissa 横坐标

clockwise 顺时针方向

coordinate plane 坐标平面

coordinate system 坐标系

coordinate 坐标

counterclockwise 逆时针方向

hyperbola 双曲线

intercept 截距

minor axis 椭圆的短轴

no solution 无解

number line 数轴

ordinate 纵坐标

origin 原点

parabola 抛物线

quadrant 象限

rectangular coordinate 直角坐标系

slope 斜率

symmetric 对称的

x-axis X轴

D. 公式

0! =1! =1 零的阶乘=1的阶乘=1

多边形内角和= $(n-2) \times 180°$

$S_\triangle = 1/2$底 × 高

$S_{梯} = ($上底+下底$) \times h/2$

圆周长=$2\pi r$ (r=radius半径)

$S_{圆} = \pi r^2$

弧长= $(X°/360°) \times$ 圆周长

$S_{立方体} = 6a^2$

$S_{圆柱} = 2\pi r\, (r+h)$

$S_{矩形} = lw$

$S_{平行四边形} = bh$

$S_{菱形}$=products of two diagonals/2

$V_{长} =$长 × 宽 × 高

$V_{圆柱} = \pi r^2 h$

$V_{圆锥} = 1/3\pi r^2 h$

$V_{立方体} = a^3$

$V_{球体} = \dfrac{4}{3}\pi r^3$

等差数列的通项公式 $a_n = a_1 + (n-1)d$ (d为常数)

等差求和 $S_n = \dfrac{n(a_1+a_n)}{2} = na_1 + \dfrac{n(n-1)}{2}d$

等比数列的通项公式 $a_n = a_1 q^{n-1}$

等比求和 $S_n = \dfrac{a_1(1-q^n)}{(1-q)}\,(q \neq 1)$

$\qquad\quad S_n = na_1\,(q=1)$

排列 $P_n^m = \dfrac{n!}{(n-m)!} = n(n-1)(n-2)...(n-m+1)$

组合 $C_n^m = \dfrac{n!}{m!(n-m)!} = \dfrac{n(n-1)(n-2)...(n-m+1)}{1\times2\times3...m}$

折扣 Discount=Cost × rate of discount

利息= principle(本金) × interest rate(利率) × time

二次方程求根公式 $X=\dfrac{1}{2a}(-b\pm\sqrt{b^2-4ac})$

(x,y)和(a,b)两点间的距离=

$$\sqrt{(x-a)^2+(y-b)^2}$$

E. 句型

The ratio of A to B is ... A比B(A/B)

A is a divisor of B A是B的除数(约数)(B/A)

A divided by B A/B

A divided into B B/A

Twice as many A as B A是B的两倍

A is 20% more than B (A-B)/B=20%

A is 20% less than B (B-A)/B=20%

no less than 大于等于

no more than 小于等于

is equal to 等于

round to 四舍五入

to the nearest 四舍五入

is parallel to 平行

is perpendicular to 垂直

closest approximation 最相近似的

F. 实际应用

car pool 拼车；汽车的合伙使用

simple interest 单利

compound interest 复利

compound annual interest 年复利

down payment 首付款，预付定金

define 定义

graph 图

graph theory 图论

inference 推理，推论

interest 利息

margin 利润，赚头

markup 涨价

markdown 降价

tie 打平

附录

《词以类记：GMAT词汇》
张红岩 编著

◎ 全面收录GMAT最新核心词汇，提高备考效率

◎ 按学科和意群分类，细分至最小同义词区间，符合记忆规律

◎ 结合全球顶级商学院学习经历，提炼MBA核心应用词汇表

◎ 精心设计自测练习，提高记忆效果

定价：35元　开本：32开　页码：416页

《GMAT逻辑推理：分类思维训练及试题解析》
陈向东 编著

◎ 归纳总结GMAT逻辑推理解题分析思路

◎ 梳理GMAT逻辑推理出题原则及解题步骤

◎ 分类讲解GMAT逻辑推理重点难点试题

◎ 提供15套考前模拟冲刺试题及精准译文

定价：59元　开本：16开　页码：532页

《GMAT语法改错精解》
刘振民 编著

◎ 深入讲解GMAT句子改错题目特点

◎ 全面介绍GMAT句子改错解题方法

◎ 分类剖析典型题目，补充必需语法知识

◎ 科学设置仿真试题，模拟真实考场情境

定价：40元　开本：16开　页码：332页

《GMAT数学高分快速突破》
陈向东 编著

◎ 详尽梳理归纳GMAT数学考点

◎ 分项强化GMAT数学题目思维训练

◎ 全面总结GMAT数学术语、解题技巧

◎ 科学设置与考试难度相当的仿真模考题

定价：40元　开本：16开　页码：300页

《GMAT官方指南（综合）》（第13版）

GMAC（美国管理专业研究生入学考试委员会）编著

◎ GMAC（GMAT考试的命题机构）中国大陆唯一授权

◎ GMAT考试必备辅导书

◎ 900道全真试题，涵盖GMAT考试所有题型，并配有全面的答案解析

◎ 针对GMAT数学部分，进行综合性数学复习

◎ 全新的语法复习涵盖GMAT语文部分所有概念

◎ 真实作文题目、回答范例及评分信息

定价：228元　开本：16开　页码：840页

《GMAT官方指南（语文）》

GMAC（美国管理专业研究生入学考试委员会）编著

◎ GMAC（GMAT考试的命题机构）中国大陆唯一授权

◎ GMAT考试（语文）部分必备权威辅导书

◎ 300道全真试题，涵盖GMAT考试语文部分所有题型，并配有全面的答案解析

◎ 题目按难易程度排列，节省考生时间

◎ 全新的语法复习涵盖GMAT语文部分所有考点

◎ 原汁原味的作文题目、回答范例及评分信息

定价：99元　开本：16开　页码：336页

《GMAT官方指南（数学）》

GMAC（美国管理专业研究生入学考试委员会）编著

◎ GMAC（GMAT考试的命题机构）中国大陆唯一授权

◎ 300道全真试题，涵盖GMAT考试数学部分所有题型，并配有全面的答案解析

◎ GMAT考试（数学）部分必备权威辅导书

◎ 题目按难易程度排列，节省考生时间

定价：99元　开本：16开　页码：216页